Shakespeare's Tragedies
notes

D0964383

Summaries and Critical Commentaries about the
Tragedies of William Shakespeare, including:
Titus Andronicus • *Romeo and Juliet*
Julius Caesar • *Hamlet* • *Othello*
King Lear • *Macbeth* • *Timon of Athens*
Antony and Cleopatra • *Coriolanus*

INCORPORATED
LINCOLN, NEBRASKA 68501

Editor

Gary Carey, M.A.
University of Colorado

Consulting Editor

James L. Roberts, Ph.D.
Department of English
University of Nebraska

ISBN 0-8220-0088-1

Titus Andronicus Notes © Copyright 1983; *Romeo and Juliet* Notes ©
Copyright 1979; *Julius Caesar* Notes © Copyright 1980; *Hamlet* Notes ©
Copyright 1971; *Othello* Notes © Copyright 1980; *King Lear* Notes ©
Copyright 1968; *Macbeth* Notes © Copyright 1979; *Timon of Athens* Notes
© Copyright 1981; *Antony and Cleopatra* Notes © Copyright 1981;
Coriolanus Notes © Copyright 1981 by Cliffs Notes, Inc.
All Rights Reserved. Printed in U.S.A.

1999 Printing.

ACKNOWLEDGMENT

Authors of the following Notes on Shakespeare's tragedies are: *Titus
Andronicus,* Evelyn McLellan, Ph.D.; *Romeo and Juliet,* G. K. Carey,
M.A.; *Julius Caesar,* James E. Vickers, M.A.; *Hamlet,* James K. Lowers,
Ph.D.; *Othello,* Gary Carey, M.A.; *King Lear,* James K. Lowers, Ph.D.;
Macbeth, Denis Calandra, Ph.D.; *Timon of Athens,* James E. Vickers,
M.A.; *Antony and Cleopatra,* James F. Bellman, Jr., M.A., and Kathryn
Bellman, M.A., J.D.; *Coriolanus,* James E. Vickers, M.A.

Cliffs Notes, Inc.   Lincoln, Nebraska

CONTENTS

CONTENTS

shakespeare's life and background

Many books have assembled facts, reasonable suppositions, traditions, and speculations concerning the life and career of William Shakespeare. Taken as a whole, these materials give a rather comprehensive picture of England's foremost dramatic poet. Tradition and sober supposition are not necessarily false because they lack proved bases for their existence. It is important, however, that persons interested in Shakespeare should distinguish between *facts* and *beliefs* about his life.

From one point of view, modern scholars are fortunate to know as much as they do about a man of middle-class origin who left a small country town and embarked on a professional career in sixteenth-century London. From another point of view, they know surprisingly little about the writer who has continued to influence the English language and its drama and poetry for more than three hundred years. Sparse and scattered as these facts of his life are, they are sufficient to prove that a man from Stratford by the name of William Shakespeare wrote the major portion of the thirty-seven plays which scholars ascribe to him. The concise review which follows will concern itself with some of these records.

No one knows the exact date of William Shakespeare's birth. His baptism occurred on Wednesday, April 26, 1564. His father was John Shakespeare, tanner, glover, dealer in grain, and town official of Stratford; his mother, Mary, was the daughter of Robert Arden, a prosperous gentleman-farmer. The Shakespeares lived on Henley Street.

Under a bond dated November 28, 1582, William Shakespeare and Anne Hathaway entered into a marriage contract. The baptism of their eldest child, Susanna, took place in Stratford in May 1583. One year and nine months later, their twins, Hamnet and Judith, were christened in the same church. The parents named them for two of the poet's friends, Hamnet and Judith Sadler.

Early in 1596, William Shakespeare, in his father's name, applied to the College of Heralds for a coat of arms. Although positive proof is lacking, there is reason to believe that the Heralds granted this request, for in 1599, Shakespeare again made application for the right to quarter his coat of arms with that of his mother.

Entitled to her father's coat of arms, Mary had lost this privilege when she married John Shakespeare before he held the official status of gentleman.

In May 1597, Shakespeare purchased New Place, the outstanding residential property in Stratford at that time. Since John Shakespeare had suffered financial reverses prior to this date, William must have achieved success for himself.

Court records show that in 1601–02, William Shakespeare began rooming in the household of Christopher Mountjoy in London. Subsequent disputes over the wedding settlement and agreement between Mountjoy and his son-in-law, Stephen Belott, led to a series of legal actions, and in 1612, the court scribe recorded Shakespeare's deposition of testimony relating to the case.

In July 1605, William Shakespeare paid four hundred and forty pounds for the lease of a large portion of the tithes on certain real estate in and near Stratford. This was an arrangement whereby Shakespeare purchased half the annual tithes, or taxes, on certain agricultural products from parcels of land in and near Stratford. In addition to receiving approximately ten percent income on his investment, he almost doubled his capital. This was possibly the most important and successful investment of his lifetime, and it paid a steady income for many years.

Shakespeare is next mentioned when John Combe, a resident of Stratford, died on July 12, 1614. To his friend, Combe bequeathed the sum of five pounds. These records and similar ones are important, not because of their economic significance but because they prove the existence of a William Shakespeare in Stratford and in London during this period.

On March 25, 1616, William Shakespeare revised his last will and testament. He died on April 23 of the same year. His body lies within the chancel and before the altar of the Stratford church. A rather wry inscription is carved upon his tombstone:

> Good Friend, For Jesus' sake, forbear
> To dig the dust enclosed here;
> Blest be the man that spares these stones,
> And curst be he who moves my bones.

The last direct descendant of William Shakespeare was his granddaughter, Elizabeth Hall, who died in 1670.

These are the most outstanding facts about Shakespeare the man, as apart from those about the dramatist and poet. Such pieces of information, scattered from 1564 through 1616, declare the existence of such a person, not as a writer or actor, but as a private citizen. It is illogical to think that anyone would or could have fabricated these details for the purpose of deceiving later generations.

In similar fashion, the evidence establishing William Shakespeare as the foremost playwright of his day is positive and persuasive. Robert Greene's *Groatsworth of Wit*, in which he attacked Shakespeare, a mere actor, for presuming to write plays in competition with Greene and his fellow playwrights, was entered in the Stationers' Register on September 20, 1592. In 1594, Shakespeare acted before Queen Elizabeth, and in 1594 and 1595, his name appeared as one of the shareholders of the Lord Chamberlain's Company. Francis Meres, in his *Palladis Tamia* (1598), called Shakespeare "mellifluous and hony-tongued" and compared his comedies and tragedies with those of Plautus and Seneca in excellence.

Shakespeare's name appears as one of the owners of the Globe in 1599. On May 19, 1603, he and his fellow actors received a patent from James I designating them as the King's Men and making them Grooms of the Chamber. Late in 1608 or early in 1609, Shakespeare and his colleagues purchased the Blackfriars Theatre and began using it as their winter location when weather made production at the Globe inconvenient.

Other specific allusions to Shakespeare, to his acting and his writing, occur in numerous places. Put together, they form irrefutable testimony that William Shakespeare of Stratford and London was the leader among Elizabethan playwrights.

One of the most impressive of all proofs of Shakespeare's authorship of his plays is the First Folio of 1623, with the dedicatory verse which appeared in it. John Heminge and Henry Condell, members of Shakespeare's own company, stated that they collected and issued the plays as a memorial to their fellow actor. Many contemporary poets contributed eulogies to Shakespeare; one of the best known of these poems is by Ben Jonson, a fellow actor and, later, a friendly rival. Jonson also criticized Shakespeare's dramatic work in *Timber: or, Discoveries* (1641).

Certainly there are many things about Shakespeare's genius and career which the most diligent scholars do not know and cannot explain, but the facts which do exist are sufficient to establish Shakespeare's identity as a man and his authorship of the thirty-seven plays which reputable critics acknowledge to be his. Someone obviously wrote these dramatic masterpieces, and Shakespeare remains the only candidate worthy of serious consideration.

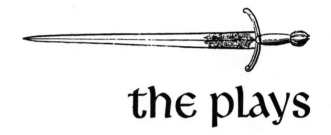

the plays

1591-92

titus
andronicus

TITUS ANDRONICUS

LIST OF CHARACTERS

Titus Andronicus

A popular Roman general who proves that he is not a wise statesman. Starting from a dramatic high point when he is proclaimed the new Emperor of Rome, he manages to alienate Saturninus, the emperor whom he selects to replace him, in addition to the high-ranking Goth captives and, at one time or another, his entire family. After feigning madness long enough to gain a reputation for it, he descends to the level of a psychopathic killer. Other than mastering revenge, however, Titus learns nothing; therefore, he cannot be classified as a tragic hero.

Marcus Andronicus

The brother of Titus Andronicus; a Roman tribune. He represents statesmanship in contrast to his brother's warlike ways. Although he cannot save Titus or most of his nephews and his niece Lavinia, he does manage to help teach Titus' only surviving son, Lucius, and grandson, young Lucius, enough of wisdom and justice to leave the impression that Rome will improve under their leadership.

Saturninus

Son of the late Emperor of Rome and Titus' personal choice to replace himself as the new emperor. Like Titus, he displays no ability to learn about statesmanship, wisdom, or justice. Arrogant and demanding in the opening scene, he remains so up to the moment of his death at Titus' bloody revenge banquet.

Tamora

The captive Queen of the Goths, she is Saturninus' rash choice for a bride only seconds after Lavinia is dragged away from his proposal. Tamora cavorts with Aaron, enjoys the high spirits of her sons when they want to rape Lavinia, and provides consistently bad advice to her new husband. She dies by Titus' sword.

Aaron

A Moor attached to the party of captured Goths. Tamora, Queen of the Goths, is his mistress. A black Moor, like Othello, he is also a prototype of Iago. Evil, evil, evil—how he loves it. The mover of bloody action for most of the play, he is ultimately responsible for most of the thirteen dead bodies and for Lavinia's mutilation. Only the black son who is born to Tamora moves him to any recognizably "normal" actions. While fleeing to save the baby's life, he is captured by Lucius, who condemns him to a barbarously cruel death. Aaron regrets only that he has run out of time to enjoy more evil deeds.

Bassianus

The brother of Saturninus, he is a generally murky character. After a garbled opposition to his brother's plot to win the post of emperor by force, he drops his own cause to support Titus. Just as quickly, he swings back to Saturninus at Titus' request. When Saturinus wants to marry Lavinia, Bassianus is granted his demand to marry Lavinia. When he briefly reappears as a happy bridegroom, he allows himself to be tricked into quarreling with Tamora. Demetrius, while supposedly defending his mother's honor, kills Bassianus with one quick knife thrust.

Lavinia

Apparently, Titus' only daughter. After her husband, Bassianus, is killed, she is raped and mutilated by Chiron and Demetrius. Once she is finally able to communicate what happened, however, she initiates the downfall of Saturninus. She is eventually killed by her father in order to free her from her pain and shame.

Lucius

The only son of Titus Andronicus who survives. At the end of the play, he becomes the new Emperor of Rome.

Quintus and Martius

Two more sons of Titus Andronicus. They are duped by Aaron and trapped in the pit that holds Bassianus' body. Saturninus orders them executed for that murder.

Mutius

Another son of Titus Andronicus. He is killed by Titus in the opening scene of the play.

Young Lucius

The young son of Lucius, grandson of Titus. Like his father, he not only survives, but he learns something during the course of the play.

Alarbus

The oldest son of Tamora. He is sacrificed to appease the souls of the slain Andronicus brothers.

Demetrius and Chiron

Two sons of Tamora; they rape and mutilate Lavinia. Titus' revenge is to kill them, bake them in a meat pie, and serve them to their mother. That leaves the black bastard by Aaron as Tamora's only surviving son.

Publius

The son of Marcus Andronicus. He serves no significant role in the action.

Sempronius, Caius, and Valentine

Andronicus kinsmen who, like Publius, serve only minor background functions.

Aemilius

A noble Roman who steps in after the slaughter at the banquet scene to declare that Lucius is to be the new Emperor of Rome.

SUMMARIES AND COMMENTARIES

ACT I

Summary

This act consists of only one scene—the open area near the Capitol in Rome. Gathering to the sounds of drums and trumpets, the Tribunes and the Senators gather on a higher level in preparation for the proclamation of Rome's new emperor. The conflict for this post is set when Saturninus, the eldest son of the previous Emperor of Rome, gathers his followers on one side of the stage and his brother, Bassianus, enters with his followers on the opposite side.

Saturninus appeals to both the "noble patricians" and his "countrymen" to take up arms and fight for his right to be emperor. Bassianus calls on the people to fight also, but for the right of election.

Marcus Andronicus, the brother of Titus, enters with the crown in hand. He informs both princes that their ambitions have already been overruled by a special vote, which resulted in the unanimous choice of Titus Andronicus as their next emperor. Enumerating Titus' credentials, Marcus provides a brief history. Titus and his surviving sons have just returned from a ten-year campaign against the militantly strong Goth nation. Today's arrival marks the fifth time that Titus has returned victorious from long and bloody wars, faced with the sad task of burying more of his gallant sons.

Marcus then successfully appeals to the two princes to publicly withdraw their appeals and to dismiss their followers in honor of their government and Titus' heroic reputation. They both call off the proposed civil war and then withdraw to join the Senators and Tribunes.

With the triumphant entry of Titus and his entourage, the remaining major characters are brought into the action. Titus greets the crowd; he pleads for both honor and rewards for his four remaining sons, survivors of twenty-five.

As Titus prepares to inter the coffin in the Andronicus tomb, which is conveniently located within view of the Capitol, Lucius interrupts to demand a Goth prisoner as expiation for his brothers. When Titus selects Alarbus for the sacrifice, Tamora appeals to Titus' understanding of parental love and the nature of war. Titus responds that Tamora must understand that the sacrifice of her son is necessary for his deceased sons' souls to rest in the shadowy world of death. Demetrius advises his mother that she cannot save Alarbus but that she can begin a plan for revenge.

Lavinia arrives to welcome home her father and her remaining brothers and to mourn the dead. Titus expresses pleasure for her virtuous existence.

Marcus then steps forward to welcome them home and to inform Titus that he, Titus, has been elected Emperor of Rome. Titus immediately responds that he is too old, and he says further that in order to save everyone the trouble of electing a successor in a short time, he would like an honorable retirement instead. Saturninus demands the empty post, and in anger, Bassianus vows to back Titus. Titus, surprisingly however, selects Saturninus. Marcus then leads the acclamation to accept him.

As proof of his gratitude, Saturninus honors the Andronicus family by requesting Lavinia as his bride and empress. But Bassianus demands that *his* betrothal to Lavinia be honored; the Andronicus sons back Bassianus and kidnap Lavinia. Titus kills his son Mutius when he tries to stop his father from preventing Lavinia's escape, and Titus denounces all his children for their treasonous behavior.

Saturninus also denounces the family and chooses Tamora as his bride. Only Titus is not invited to join the wedding party. Fuming at the slight, he confronts his brother and his sons as they return to bury Mutius. Marcus has to convince Titus to allow Mutius in the family tomb.

Saturninus and Bassianus again enter from different doors, this time with their separate wedding parties. Saturninus threatens to punish his brother for the "rape" of Lavinia. Bassianus reiterates his right to marry his betrothed and then pleads Titus' case. Titus retorts that he does not want representation from the very man who caused his family's dishonor.

Tamora publicly entreats Saturninus to forgive Titus, then she privately cautions him against confronting the old soldier when so many of his supporters are gathered. She promises that she will find a way to "massacre them all" without risking insurrection. Tamora vows revenge against those who forced her to beg in vain for the life of Alarbus.

Tamora then fraudulently orchestrates reluctant reconciliation among all of the protesting parties. Saturninus voices forgiveness, invites Lavinia and her wedding party to join his own, and accepts Titus' invitation to join a hunting party the following day.

Commentary

Act I presents a series of conflicts without focus. Without a sharp conflict, no plot exists; without focus, no drama exists. This problem, plus some weak characterization and a lot of poor verse, causes many critics to squirm about accepting *Titus Andronicus* as a play written by William Shakespeare.

Although these weaknesses must be acknowledged, they should not obliterate the innate talent of a young playwright who displays some dramatic strengths among the obvious weaknesses.

Conflicts in this act include Saturninus versus Bassianus, Saturninus versus Titus Andronicus, Tamora versus the Andronicus family, honor versus dishonor, and mercy versus revenge. Where is the focus? Undoubtedly, during a performance of this play, the focus of the audience would dwell on Titus' stabbing of his son because the sudden violence and blood would be shocking and memorable. If the actress cast as Tamora plays her part well, she will probably carry the act because she can work with the horror surrounding Alarbus' cruel death, and, in addition, she manipulates everyone into a fake reconciliation at the end of the act. Thus, she can be motivated by hate throughout most of the rest of the act.

In contrast, Saturninus and Titus vacillate throughout this act. They oppose each other, swear loyalty to each other, and then repeat the cycle. Marcus seems to be in a position of focus, but he loses it when he participates in the kidnapping of Lavinia.

Obviously, Titus is supposed to be the protagonist, and he will draw attention because of that. But the audience will see a strong man who cannot define honor, yet a man who storms into action— motivated by quickly changing interpretations of it. We know he fights. We suspect that he does not know what he wants, nor does he think deeply. With those handicaps, he cannot initiate action as a good protagonist should.

Saturninus serves as a good example of a character who acts without discernible motivation. At the play's opening, he calls on his followers and the populace to "defend the justice of my cause with arms" rather than "wrong mine age with this indignity." Yet, the cause of persuasion is sufficient to sway him to "commit myself, my person, and the cause." As soon as Titus refuses the offer to become emperor, Saturninus demands, "Patricians, draw your swords, and sheathe them not / Till Saturninus be Rome's Emperor." Within moments after Titus orchestrates his election as emperor, Saturninus promises to reward the Andronicus family and, for a start, selects Lavinia as his empress. When he is thwarted in that effort because his brother claims *his* right to Lavinia, Saturninus turns against Bassianus and the entire Andronicus family. With as much thought as he has given to all of his other actions, Saturninus suddenly chooses Tamora, the captive Queen of the Goths, as his bride and the new Empress of Rome. Although he has not yet even been formally introduced to the woman, he accepts her advice on the proper handling of the Andronicus matter.

Thus, Act I ends on an improbable note. At this stage, we might well conclude that the central conflict will be between Titus and Saturninus, but we would be wrong. We might also believe that a classic revenge tragedy is developing because so many characters mention *revenge*, but we would again be proven wrong by the actual development of the play.

ACT II

Summary

No change of scene or time occurs between the end of Act I and Aaron's soliloquy at the beginning of this act. With the wedding party just begun, Aaron is already reveling in lascivious fantasies about his affair with Tamora and his improved status as the lover of the Empress of Rome.

Tamora's two remaining sons, Chiron and Demetrius, interrupt Aaron's lusty reverie with their own warring lusts. They propose a duel to decide who is to win the right to seduce Lavinia. Aaron chastises them for carrying on this quarrel, especially when the emperor will certainly hear of it and their mother will be dishonored. He further warns them that Bassianus is a prince who has the power to punish them for their very thoughts.

When asked how he proposes to have Lavinia, Demetrius responds that any woman, no matter the rank of her husband, can be seduced. Aaron takes a moment to smirk about cuckolding someone with the rank of Saturninus. But immediately after this aside,

Aaron begins counseling the boys to be reconciled so that they may *both* enjoy Lavinia. He insists that Lavinia is too virtuous to be seduced, but he entices them with the thought of a lustful rape at the reconciliation hunt. Aaron further insists that they involve their mother's talent for treachery in the rape. Chiron and Demetrius, thrilled at the prospect, exit with their new mentor. ´

Marking the first change of scene, Titus enters to announce "The hunt is up." He cautions his sons to treat the emperor well, primarily because his, Titus', troubled sleep has left him with a vague foreboding.

The hunting party gathers amidst bawdy jokes about newly-weds and bragging about hunting prowess. Demetrius encapsulates the general tone with a thinly disguised threat to ravish Lavinia.

Setting the scene for the approaching multiple perfidies, Aaron enters to bury a bag of gold and hint at his carefully designed plot. Tamora approaches Aaron with lusty hints about what they could enjoy in this isolated spot. Aaron makes it clear that he wants nothing but revenge this morning.

With the approach of Bassianus and Lavinia, Aaron begins the plot anew with instructions to Tamora to start a quarrel. He exits to fetch her sons for a staged duel of honor. When pricked by Tamora, Bassianus and Lavinia both cast slurs about Tamora's affair with Aaron. When Demetrius enters, Tamora concocts a tale about a threat from Bassianus and Lavinia to tie her up and leave her to die of fright beside the viper-filled pit, embellishing the tale by reporting the truthful slur about her adulterous conduct, then demanding that Demetrius revenge the threat on his mother's life. No duel ensues; Demetrius merely stabs Bassianus, then Chiron finishes him off. When Lavinia challenges them to kill her too, Tamora wants to comply; Demetrius stops her, however, with the thought that revenge should include the loss of Lavinia's virtue. Tamora approves the plan but cautions the boys to kill Lavinia when they're through with their fun.

Lavinia pleads with Tamora to intervene, but Tamora reminds her that no one listened to *her* when she pleaded for Alarbus. Death would be preferable, declares Lavinia, and she asks that Tamora kill her. Tamora refuses to interfere with her sons' fun; the boys then throw Bassianus' body into the prepared pit and drag Lavinia away.

Tamora waves them off, reminding them one more time to kill Lavinia when they're through.

Tamora declares satisfaction with Lavinia's plight but vows not to be happy until all the Andronicus family are dead. She wanders off to find Aaron. She misses him, however, because he enters with Quintus and Martius, luring them on with the promise of a panther in the now-familiar pit. Both of Titus' sons complain about their foggy sight and wits, apparently in reference to being drugged. Martius falls into the pit, which is covered over with briars. Quintus notices fresh blood on the briars, so he asks Martius if he has been hurt. Only in the heart, replies Martius, by the sight of Bassianus' body. Aaron slips away, and Quintus is almost paralyzed by a vague fear. Demanding to know how Martius can identify Bassianus in such a dark pit, Quintus is told that Bassianus is wearing a ring that illuminates the hole. Quintus tries to help Martius out of the pit and vows to either accomplish his goal or join Martius. True to his word, Quintus falls in.

Saturninus enters just in time to catch sight of Quintus falling. Mistaking the fall for a leap, he goes over to investigate. At Saturninus' demand for identification, Martius replies that these two unhappy sons of Titus have discovered the body of Bassianus.

At first disbelieving, Saturninus is nudged by the timely entrance of Tamora to read a letter that contains a plot to murder Bassianus. Following the tip in the letter that a reward of gold will be waiting at the elder tree, Saturinus discovers the bag of gold that Aaron had planted there earlier. Tamora implicates Titus by reporting that he handed her the letter. True to form, Saturninus jumps to the conclusion that Quintus and Martius are guilty. He orders that they be tortured and executed without trial. Titus' pleas for bond and a trial go unheeded.

As the emperor's party leaves with the prisoners, Tamora soothes Titus with the promise that she'll see to the safety of his sons. Titus urges Lucius to leave quietly with him.

Thus, no one is left at the scene when Chiron and Demetrius return with the ravished and mutilated Lavinia. After a few coarse remarks about their independent decision to leave Lavinia alive without hands or tongue to identify them, they leave her. Marcus discovers her and laments the loss of her sweet hands and tongue. He tenderly leads her away.

Commentary

At the opening of Act II, Aaron swings the focus onto himself and never relinquishes it again. Aaron's plot not only causes him to function as the protagonist; it structures a focus for this entire act. Therefore, at this point, the play tightens up after a meandering, confusing first act.

The conflict here clearly pits Aaron against the Andronicus family. Aaron's allies, Tamora and her sons, take action under her direction. In the only major departure from this turn of events, Chiron and Demetrius commit a fatal error when they ignore their mother's order to kill Lavinia. (One should note that although Tamora utters the order in this act, Aaron first instructed them to do this in Act I.) In this particular act, also note that Saturninus, Titus, Lavinia, Bassianus, Martius, and Quintus act only in response to Aaron's manipulation.

However, characterization is again weak. Aaron and Tamora speak often of a revenge motive, but they certainly do not move in classic fashion. What has Bassianus done to motivate revenge? His murder might be triggered because of his occasional vague mutterings against the emperor, but this motivation is never strongly developed. Tamora is certainly supplied with a motive for revenge against the Andronicus family because they sacrificed Alarbus, but she has no right to defend her *virtue*. When she falls in with Demetrius' argument against allowing Lavinia to die virtuous, Tamora knows very well that she is guilty of adultery with Aaron and that the slurs by Bassianus and Lavinia do not justify revenge.

Saturninus' character is developing a consistency for rash action, but that hardly translates into an understandable motivation. He is still unaccountably influenced by the Goths in his court, and, indeed, he never seems to have a trusted Roman adviser nearby.

Titus is a mere puppet in this act. He never initiates a strong action, nor does he seem to have any internal motivation other than subservience to Saturninus.

Motivation for Chiron and Demetrius' rape of Lavinia is clear and their misdirected "revenge" is understandable. As for the sons of Titus, Martius and Quintus behave like sheep, and Lucius does not contribute a thing.

That leaves Aaron with the only strong motivation, and it is not revenge. He simply loves evil. He loves to plot, to manipulate, to kill

or at least cause death. He detests every character thus far introduced and will never change his attitude about any of them.
Although Aaron mentions ambition at the opening of this act, he is
not really ambitious for anything but the opportunity to indulge in
evil. However, his expressed willingness to betray trust is later
upheld. This duplicity is evident in his contempt for both Tamora
and Saturninus when he declares his intent "to mount aloft with thy
imperial mistress, / And mount her pitch whom thou in triumph
long / Hast prisoner held, fett'red in amorous chains." Aaron is identified as a contra-Machiavel character, which the Elizabethans dis-
tilled from Machiavelli's *The Prince*.

Contempt for virtue and honor is upheld as a prevailing theme
during this act and will hold as a primary motivation for several
characters as the play develops.

ACT III

Summary

Before this act is over, all the harm that Rome inflicts on the
family of Titus Andronicus will have been done. As the act opens,
however, Titus is frantically pleading with the authorities who are
leading Martius and Quintus to their execution. Titus, a general who
marshaled a grand procession at the beginning of the play, now
debases himself by lying prone in the street in a feeble attempt to
stop the execution march. Just as Tamora's pleas for Alarbus had
been useless, so now are the pleas of Titus for his two doomed sons.

Lucius enters and tells Titus that he is alone, lamenting to the
stones that make up the road. He also informs his father that he,
Lucius, has been banished because of a vain attempt to rescue his
brothers. Titus responds that Rome is "a wilderness of tigers" that
are preying on his family and that Lucius is fortunate to be banished.

At this juncture, Marcus leads Lavinia to Titus and Lucius.
Whereas Lucius is speechless before the horror of Lavinia's mutilation, Titus is sturdy and has a lot to say. He expresses a grief that
"disdaineth bounds," again curses Rome for what it has done to his
family, and in a moment of foreshadowing, offers to cut off both his
hands. Titus summarizes the wrongs perpetrated by the Romans
that he had fought for: the execution of his two sons, the murder

of Bassianus, the mutilation of Lavinia, and now, the banishment of Lucius.

Lavinia is crying, perhaps, Marcus speculates, because she knows that her two brothers are innocent of the murder of her husband. Titus begs to know what they can do to make Lavinia feel better: cut off their hands, bite off their tongues, plot revenge? Lucius tells Titus to stop crying because Lavinia's sorrow increases with his. He then tenderly wipes away his sister's tears.

At this juncture, when horror and grief seem to have peaked for the Andronicus family, Aaron appears with a fiendish plan. He tells Lucius, Titus, and Marcus that if any one of them will sever a hand for him to deliver to Saturninus, then Martius and Quintus will be returned alive. Each of the Andronicus family offers to sacrifice his hand, and they finally concoct a team plan in which Marcus is to fetch the axe, Lucius is to wield it, and Titus is to contribute his hand. When Marcus and Lucius exit, however, Titus quickly convinces Aaron to chop off the hand. Aaron quickly complies, after promising in an aside to deceive Titus within the half hour.

Titus sends his hand with Aaron in a spirit of hopefulness and service. He requests that Saturninus bury the faithful hand and return Titus' two sons. Titus regards the hand as a small price to pay for the lives of Martius and Quintus. Aaron promises Titus that his two sons shall soon be with him, and then he reveals in an aside that he means their *heads*.

Titus and Lavinia pose together, displaying their gore and horrible mutilations, while Titus expresses the immensity of his sorrow. Marcus calls for "reason to govern thy lament." Just as Titus finishes expressing the absence of reason in all that has befallen the Andronicus family, a messenger enters carrying the heads of Martius and Quintus, as well as the hand of Titus.

The messenger, a traditional bearer of bad news, reports that the sacrifice of the hand was mocked and that he feels more sorrow at delivering this message and viewing these events than at the death of his own father.

This message sparks the first show of anger in the ever-reasonable Marcus. He urges the unnaturally quiet Titus to now express his overwhelming grief. Titus laughs, saying that all of his tears have been used up, and he declares that sorrow would only interfere with revenge. Urging his remaining family to vow revenge before the severed heads, Titus organizes a grisly parade with the remains of his family. He commands Marcus to carry one head, as he picks up another; he orders Lavinia to pick up his own severed hand with her teeth, and he sends Lucius off to raise an army of Goths. Lucius watches the pathetic parade exit, and then he vows to revenge the woes of the Andronicus family.

The final scene of the act is set at a banquet for those of the Andronicus family who remain in Rome. Here, Lucius' son, young Lucius, is introduced. Titus recites the family's woes for the morose group. Marcus reprimands his brother for suggesting that Lavinia commit suicide if she cannot stop crying. Titus cannot see the harm since she has no hands to enable her to commit such an act. He recites the sadness that he believes his daughter to be feeling, and he vows to learn to understand her so that she can communicate. Young Lucius suggests that his grandfather change the subject and try to amuse Lavinia; then he breaks down and cries.

Suddenly, Marcus violently strikes his plate with a knife. When Titus asks why, Marcus replies that he has killed a fly. Titus, outraged at the murder, commands Marcus to leave. He insists that the fly had a family, was happy and innocent, and deserved to live. But when Marcus compares the black fly to the black Moor, Titus closes the scene by joining in the violence upon the fly and then leading off Lavinia and Lucius for a story hour.

Commentary

Tension again eases at the opening of this act because Shakespeare presents no clear conflict. Titus and Lucius are reacting against both mute authority and offstage action.

Thus, when Aaron enters with his plot to trick Titus into severing his hand, he again swings the play's focus onto himself. After Aaron exits, this act sinks into meandering melodrama during which the Andronicus family is not even able to identify a definite focus for their planned revenge.

Both Titus and Lucius are vague about their quest for revenge. Titus seems to hear the two heads of his sons speaking, threatening no peace for their father "till all these mischiefs be returned again / Even in their throats that hath committed them." But Titus names no names and describes no plans. Lucius is more explicit when he vows to "make proud Saturnine and his Empress / Beg at the gates like

Tarquin and his queen," but almost immediately he defuses this specificity by pledging to raise an army of Goths "to be revenged on Rome and Saturnine." Thus, we are left with the impression that the Andronicus family is pitted against all of Rome, but that impression, like so many in the vague use of the revenge theme, would be an incorrect one.

Characterization remains weak or nonexistent for most of the characters unless one supplies undue emphasis for the weeping capacity of the Andronicus family or the capacity for rage in Marcus. Lucius begins displaying leadership strength, but he does not actually do anything with it in this act.

The exception to characterization is, again, Aaron. He succinctly identifies his motivation when he declares, "Let fools do good, and fair men call for grace, / Aaron will have his soul black like his face."

When Titus writhes within the vision of the complete breakdown of nature, he irresistibly invites comparison with Lear's rage at the opening of Act III, Scene 2. But the difference in the quality of language illustrates why so many critics are reluctant to accept the two plays as being written by the same playwright. Lear challenges nature with "Blow, winds, and crack your cheeks. Rage. Blow." In contrast, Titus passively describes his grief in hyperbole: "If the winds rage, doth not the sea wax mad, / Threatening the welkin with his big-swoll'n face?" And whereas Lear parallels the raging storm to "the tempest in my mind," Titus disintegrates to the distasteful: "For why my bowels cannot hide her woes, / But like a drunkard must I vomit them."

The macabre, melodramatic scenes in Act III have aroused much ridicule. But a comparison to the popularity of modern horror movies should temper that contempt. Is there not something "modern" about displaying gory heads and hands, about severing a limb with a gush of blood, about over-dramatizing death and mutilation? Perhaps comparing all this excess with our own bloody box-office movies can tap some understanding for the popularity of this play in its own day.

ACT IV

Summary

In a setting not clearly defined in the script, Act IV opens with a frightened young Lucius fleeing from his apparently mad, as well as mutilated, Aunt Lavinia. When the boy appeals to Titus and Marcus for help, they assure him that Lavinia means him no harm and urge him to guess what it is that she wants.

The boy reports that he had thrown down his books in his haste to escape but realizes now that his aunt loves him too much to harm him. Meanwhile, Lavinia is frantically working with Lucius' books, turning them over with the stumps of her arms. All three of them then try to guess why Lavinia is throwing the books into the air, and then, in the first breakthrough of communication, they realize that she is repeatedly throwing Ovid's *Metamorphoses*.

Titus reads the book at the page she has turned to and informs everyone that she has located the tale of Philomel, which, he then deduces, identifies rape as the "root of thine annoy." Expanding on this myth, Titus realizes that the rape took place in the woods during that fatal hunt.

Searching now for the name of the rapist, Marcus is inspired to use his staff, guided by his feet and mouth, to write his name in the sand. He then hands the staff to Lavinia, who uses her mouth and stumps to write the word "Stuprum" (rape) and the names of Chiron and Demetrius.

Marcus now joins the other Andronicus members in composing a litany of revenge, requesting Titus and young Lucius to join with him to swear that they will kill the "traitorous Goths" or die in the attempt.

Young Lucius readily learns the stance of revenge, and he cooperates with Titus' plan to carry weapons as gifts to Tamora's sons. Marcus asks the heavens to support this action of Titus and vows to do so himself as a welcome balm for the emotional scars that Titus has suffered.

In Scene 2, young Lucius meets Aaron, Chiron, and Demetrius, again at an unidentified location, to present the gift of weapons. A model of courtesy and deportment during his presentation, young Lucius lets the audience know in asides that he well knows that he is dealing with villains.

Later, Demetrius discovers a message wrapped around the weapons. He recognizes it as a verse from Horace, but only Aaron understands that the Latin inscription translates into a recognition of the boys' guilt. He decides, however, in an aside, not to inform Tamora or the boys yet. During a brief exchange, Tamora's sons gloat over what they believe to be a successful humiliation of the Andronicus family and wish for somewhere between a thousand and twenty thousand Roman women to enjoy as they enjoyed Lavinia. They all agree that Tamora would approve. Then the boys announce that they want to go off to pray for their mother, who is in labor.

At that moment, the emperor's trumpets sound, announcing the birth of a son. The nurse arrives with the baby, who is obviously Aaron's son since it is black. Tamora has sent instructions to have the baby killed. Chiron and Demetrius are shocked and angered at what Aaron has done to their mother. The boys realize that either the baby must die or their mother is ruined. Demetrius volunteers to kill the baby, but Aaron protects his infant son. He warns Tamora's sons that he will kill them if they threaten the baby's life; he instructs the nurse to inform Tamora that he will keep the son, and he makes it clear that the child is more precious to him than Tamora is.

Chiron, Demetrius, and the nurse all berate Aaron for planning to abandon Tamora and her family. Aaron curses them as cowards, making fun of their flushed pale skin while his black son exudes only calmness and smiles. Then Aaron reminds the boys that this baby is their brother.

Believing now that only Aaron can save them, the three frightened people turn to him for advice. As always, Aaron quickly concocts a plot. After learning from the nurse how many witnesses there were to the birth, he kills her. He explains to the shocked boys that he will leave no witnesses. Aaron instructs them to go and persuade another Moor and his wife, who have a pale newborn, to give up their son in return for their promise that the baby will be raised as the emperor's son. The boys leave with instructions to bury the nurse, substitute the other baby, and then send the other witnesses of the birth to Aaron to be killed. Demetrius thanks Aaron for taking such good care of his mother. Aaron delivers his son to the safety of the Goths, who are to raise him as a military leader.

Scene 3 opens with Titus leading a group who bear arrows with messages at their tips. Titus instructs some to shoot the arrows into the air while Publius and Sempronius attempt to dig to the center of the earth in order to leave a message with Pluto. He identifies his motivation as the sorrows inflicted on him by Rome, and he assumes the guilt for aiding Saturninus to the throne.

Marcus and his son Publius cluck their tongues over Titus' madness, for they realize the need to carefully watch him day and night. Marcus also urges his kinsmen to revenge the loss of Titus' mind by joining the Goths in war against Rome.

Titus returns for a progress report on the trip to Hades. Publius reports that Pluto is ready to aid in revenge but that "Justice" is unavailable. Titus is outraged by the delay and swears to hunt down "Justice" to perform her duty. He then lines up his archers to shoot their messages to all of the gods in a trajectory that will cause all the arrows to fall into the emperor's court.

A clown enters with a basket and two pigeons. Titus calls for the messages from heaven that the birds will be carrying. The clown protests that he knows nothing of any messages from heaven and is only carrying the pigeons to the emperor's court in order to settle a dispute. Titus convinces the poor clown to deliver a message to the emperor.

Scene 4 features Saturninus and Tamora. Saturninus is carrying the arrows that were shot in the previous scene and is raving about the attacks by Titus. The old general's madness serves as no excuse to the enraged emperor. Saturninus regards the appeals to the gods as libelous against Rome's machinery of justice and vows that if he lives, he'll order Titus executed.

Tamora soothes her husband's distemper but reveals in an aside that she is gloating both for her victory over the Andronicus family and for her escape from condemnation over a black baby's birth.

The hapless clown enters with Titus' letter. After reading the letter, Saturninus orders that the clown be hanged. He then orders that Titus be dragged in for execution, thinking that this will stop a subtle plot for Titus to become emperor. But Titus is saved when Aemilius dashes in with the news that Lucius has arrived with an army of Goths. Saturninus panics because Lucius is even more favored as an emperor than is Titus. Saturninus is afraid that the citizens will revolt in order to advance Lucius to the throne.

Tamora reassures her husband by promising to enchant Titus in order to lure Lucius to his death. She sends him off to regain his good spirits, and he sends her off to initiate her plot.

Commentary

Act IV is largely a shambles because it is a repeat of the play's original problem with a lack of focus. Consider the action covered in this act: It includes the first communication by Lavinia; messages from Titus to Tamora's sons and lover that convey their guilts; vows and acts of revenge by Lucius, young Lucius, Marcus, Saturninus, Tamora, and Titus; and, of course, Aaron's plot to save his son. Groups move on and off stage to change the hodgepodge of scenes, always with some spoken reason but with dramatically flimsy motivation.

In spite of all the activity, only three major advances in the action are achieved: Lavinia identifies her attackers, Lucius arrives with the Goth army, and Tamora initiates the arrangements for the final, fatal banquet. Aaron's baby and Titus' madness occupy a lot of time without contributing much to the plot. Most of the characters bemoan what is happening, but none of them grow in character nor contribute much to the action.

As usual, character development is difficult to discover. Although Titus is described as incompetent, his conduct will soon surface as a disguise. Young Lucius changes the most because he learns the fundamentals of revenge. Aaron maintains his evil motivation, especially in his barbaric murder to cover up for the birth of his son.

ACT V

Summary

Lucius opens Act V with a peroration to the Goth troops, urging them to avenge Rome's recent victory over them. An unnamed Goth wants Tamora's death to be a part of the revenge. Another unnamed Goth enters with Aaron and his son in tow. He narrates the scene of discovery wherein Aaron had been trying to quiet the crying baby. Since Aaron chose to soothe his son with recriminations for being "tawny" instead of "coal-black," everyone realizes that the mother was fair.

Lucius quickly surmises that the mother is Tamora and stirs up the Goths with that news. In a rage because of Aaron's part in the cruel ruin of the Andronicuses, Lucius wants to hang the infant where Aaron and the rest can observe its death throes. He orders Aaron to climb a ladder and hang the child.

Aaron suggests, instead, that Lucius save the child and bear it to Tamora in exchange for some vague, wondrous result. As an alternative, he can only conjure a curse. Lucius urges him to develop the plot; Aaron promises to reveal all the villainies if only the child is allowed to live. Aaron demands a vow from Lucius to protect the baby. Lucius asks what he can possibly swear by which Aaron would believe in. Aaron says it does not matter what he believes in because he knows Lucius to be a religious and honorable man.

Having extracted the vow, Aaron reveals that the baby is his and Tamora's, that Tamora's sons killed Bassianus, and that Tamora's sons shared the rape and mutilation of Lavinia.

While Lucius raves at the villains, Aaron rather proudly admits to being their tutor but claims that their potential was inherited from their mother. Aaron presses on with his revelations of his involvement in the various treacheries. He shocks his listeners with the recall of his delight at the incident wherein he tricked Titus into sacrificing his hand in exchange for the heads of his two executed sons, embellishing his story with laughter until his tears run as fast as Titus' tears of sorrow; he recalls also being rewarded by Tamora's "twenty kisses" for such a successful attack on the old man.

When asked if he's sorry for anything that he has done, Aaron replies, "Ay, that I had not done a thousand more." He then recites a list of other cruelties that he has enjoyed in his lifetime and expands his desire to 10,000 other uninflicted cruelties.

Lucius decides that hanging is too easy a death for such a cruel man. When Aaron fantasizes about the pleasurable eternity of being a devil to torment them all in hell, Lucius orders him gagged.

Aemilius then enters to invite Lucius and the Goth princes to a parley at Titus' home. Saturninus offers any hostages whom they might demand to feel assured of their safety. Lucius waves away the hostage offer with a request that Saturninus substitute pledges to Titus and Marcus, whereupon they all march off the stage.

That clears the stage for Tamora and her two sons to change the scene to Titus' house. They enter in disguise. Tamora decides that she will identify herself as Revenge when she knocks on Titus' door. At first, Titus refuses entrance to the trio on the grounds that they will interfere with his concentrated melancholy. But when Tamora hints that knowing who she is will change his mind, Titus declares that he is not mad and knows very well that she is Tamora. She declares, however, that she is Revenge, the enemy of Tamora, so she can help torment all those who have been cruel to him. Titus deceives her by pretending to believe the story, and he identifies her sons as Rape and Murder. He challenges her, therefore, to murder them and to bring back the heads of all other murderers so that he can pledge obedience to her. Tamora counters by claiming that her two attendants are actually her *ministers*, called Rape and Murder because they wreak vengeance on those guilty of the two crimes. After marveling at the resemblance of Rape and Murder to Tamora's two sons, Titus pretends to welcome them.

During a brief time when Titus absents himself from the scene, Tamora reveals her plot to her sons. She believes that Titus is both crazy and convinced of her identity as Revenge. This seems to present the possibility that she can invite Lucius and the Goth princes to a banquet so that she can split the alliance.

Titus returns to welcome them, and he makes a few more comments about their resemblance to Tamora and her sons; then he expresses the idle wish that they could also have a black devil Moor to carry out evil schemes. When asked for orders, Titus tells them to go out and find people who look just like themselves because these people must be murdered for their crimes.

Tamora praises the plan but asks if it wouldn't be better to wait until Lucius attended a banquet, during which she would present the emperor and his family for revenge. Immediately, Titus calls in Marcus and instructs him to deliver the invitation. Tamora then proposes to leave with her two ministers, but Titus persuades her to leave them if she does not want the invitation to Lucius to be canceled. The deceivers are deceived by their belief in Titus' madness, so they agree to the plan.

Titus then summons Publius, Caius, and Valentine. When Publius identifies Chiron and Demetrius, Titus corrects him by saying they are Rape and Murder and must, therefore, be bound and, if necessary, gagged. Chiron protests, but both are gagged and are unable to plead when Titus returns with a knife. Lavinia appears with a basin. Titus presents Lavinia to her tormentors, summarizes their crimes, and then details what is about to happen to them. He will cut their throats, Lavinia will catch their blood in the basin, then he will cut them up, grind their bones, bake their heads in a meat pie, and serve them to their mother at the banquet. Thus, he cuts their throats and catches the blood, and then they all leave, carrying the boys into the kitchen.

Lucius then enters with Marcus, Aaron and his baby, and the Goths. He tells Marcus that he is content to be there if Titus thinks it's right, but he wants Aaron safely held for testimony against Tamora since he does not trust the emperor.

Trumpets announce Saturninus' arrival with his attendants. Verbal sparring between Lucius and Saturninus is quieted by Marcus, who calls for them to sit down to a peaceful banquet.

But Titus has other plans. After beginning to serve the banquet, he continues the flow of blood by killing Lavinia—to release her from her suffering, he tells the shocked guests. When Saturninus is informed of the guilt of Chiron and Demetrius, he orders them to be brought to him, but he is informed by Titus that they were served at the dinner and already "daintily fed upon" by their mother. Saturninus then stabs Titus, and Lucius stabs Saturninus.

Marcus immediately initiates arbitration by begging the Romans to listen to the truth that Lucius will share. Lucius then recites the wrongs inflicted upon the Andronicus family. Marcus picks up the story by displaying the son of Aaron and Tamora, then calls upon the Romans to decide whether the remainder of the Andronicus family should kill themselves. Aemilius calls for a vote to designate Lucius as the new emperor. An acclamation vote accomplishes that.

Marcus summons Aaron to his punishment, then joins Lucius in a reverent farewell to Titus. Young Lucius is also pushed forward to kiss his grandfather a final time. At this juncture, Aaron is presented for judgment. Lucius calls for Aaron to be buried chest-deep and starved to death, portraying an end during which Aaron will be begging for sustenance. Aaron vows that he will not say a word; furthermore, he repents only any good deed that he *might* have performed by *mistake*. Lucius then issues orders for the disposal of the bodies, and the play ends with the mass exit of the survivors.

Commentary

Act V's bloody climax probably saves the performance. After

the restlessness of Acts III and IV, the audience experiences a series of tense, shocking scenes.

The action climaxes in a blood bath in the name of revenge. However, Titus behaves like a pathological killer with his pig-sticking approach to killing Chiron and Demetrius in order to serve them in a cannibalistic pie at the banquet, not to mention summarily murdering his own daughter. The structural weakness of the plot then disintegrates into a morass of verbal maneuvering to put a rightful ruler in place, a situation soothing to Elizabethans but unappreciated today.

The weakness has been present since the beginning of the play; the two opposing forces that must be in conflict in order to create a plot are never clearly identified. In Act V, some of the conflicts are the Andronicus family versus Saturninus, the Andronicus family versus Tamora and sons, the Goths versus Tamora, the Goths versus the Romans, and Titus versus Nature (madness).

Aaron is still pitted against the world at large but more as character motivation than plot action. He remains the strongest character to the very end, surely stealing the final scene from Lucius by manipulating his sentence to a horrible death into another show of strength. And, of course, he manages to save his son's life in spite of all the people who were determined to kill the infant.

Shakespeare provides Aaron with a total physical domination during Act V, Scene 1. While Lucius appears to dominate Aaron through capture and the planned executions of father and son, Aaron is perched on a ladder (thus physically dominating the stage) and is provided with shocking, single-action dialogue (thus verbally dominating the scene). One must conclude that Shakespeare favored this character from beginning to end and probably should have written the play about him instead of Titus.

One other point of interest about Act V is the injection of the Morality Interlude. Since the disguises of Tamora and her sons were totally ineffective and the appearance of Revenge had little to do with advancing the plot, the scene is probably there as a result of the playwright's shrewd ability to give everybody in the audience something that they wanted to see. And the important thing to remember after all the negative comments about *Titus Andronicus* is that it was probably a popular play.

1595

ROMEO
AND JULIET

ROMEO AND JULIET

LIST OF CHARACTERS

Escalus, Prince of Verona

He is the symbol of law and order and justice in Verona. He threatens Capulet and Montague with death if Verona's peace is ever again disturbed; unfortunately, he tempers his threat. The fact that the prince must intervene is especially significant to this play because it serves to lift the action out of the realm of a domestic tragedy—that is, the feud has reached the stage where the issue is of public import.

Paris

A kinsman of the prince. He is handsome and courteous, and he hopes to marry Juliet. He duels with Romeo in the Capulet tomb, mistakenly believing that Romeo has come to desecrate the bodies of Juliet and Tybalt.

Montague

As the father of Romeo, he is worried about his son's disturbed emotional state. After Romeo's death, Montague promises Capulet to honor Juliet with a golden statue.

Capulet

Juliet's father is onstage much more than Montague. He is very likeable in the ball scene as he reminisces with an old kinsman while watching the young people dance, and later when he is defending Romeo and upbraiding Tybalt. But his moods can undergo immediate change, as when he feels crossed by Juliet.

Juliet

To many critics, the play, for all purposes, is hers—a thirteen-year-old girl, discovering love, being loved, then abruptly being, according to her Nurse, as good as widowed; throughout, there is an interplay of her happy, romantic youth and the responsibility of her new womanhood. It should be noted that she has far more control of her emotions than Romeo; never does she dissolve in hysterics.

The Nurse

Shakespeare created one of his immortal comic figures in Juliet's Nurse. Life is for living; to love means to make love—her philosophy is that basic. She is a realist, a woman who compromises easily and is a coarse talker, fond of joking, anecdotes, sentimentalizing, and intrigue. She has reared Juliet and seems at times more fond of her than is Juliet's own mother.

Mercutio

He is a satirist whose devastating wit remains with him to the end. He is a cynic but attractive; the bitter tang of his sophistication is a refreshing accompaniment to Romeo's dark Petrarchan misery. For Mercutio, love is often fraudulent. His tongue is, as his name suggests, mercurial. His Queen Mab speech is a fantasy of impromptu invention; his bawdy exchanges with Juliet's Nurse have become memorable. Some critics say Shakespeare killed off Mercutio because he began to emerge as a vitally interesting character, one so well developed that his continued presence might have diminished the importance of Romeo and even Juliet.

Benvolio

He is Romeo's companion who attempts to soften Mercutio's jests and to bring Romeo out of his gloom. It is he who explains to the prince the circumstances of Tybalt's death; thereafter, he vanishes from the plot.

Tybalt

He is hot tempered and quick to anger. He immediately swears revenge when he discovers Romeo at the Capulets' ball. Mercutio describes him as shallow and affected, though he does admit that he is a fierce and skilled fencer. Tybalt is killed by Romeo.

Friar Laurence

Trying only to bring peace to Verona, he agrees to help Romeo and Juliet, but he quickly finds himself more and more entangled in new complications. Unfortunately, his well-laid plans depend on chance. The Friar is a good man and, as the prince recognizes in the final scene, a man of good intentions.

Friar John

A Franciscan, he is sent to Mantua by Friar Laurence to deliver a letter to Romeo, explaining the Friar's plan for the lovers.

Romeo

As the son of Montague, he is well spoken of in Verona. We first see him as a Petrarchan lover: He is amusing, and he uses language in an artificial and witty manner; he is consciously "love sick." Love for Juliet transforms him: His declarations of love are lyric and vivid, and he is defiant and passionate. His love for her is desperate and impulsive; his death also. He dies triumphant, believing that he has defied fate and has rejoined Juliet.

Lady Montague

She abhors the violence of the opening quarrel and is much relieved to learn that Romeo was not involved. Later, we learn that she has died, grieving for her son. Hers is yet another life sacrificed to the old, bitter feud.

Lady Capulet

The rather young wife of Capulet, she has a nasty temper. After she learns that her nephew Tybalt has been killed, she demands that the prince execute Romeo. The prince wisely punishes him, however, according to the circumstances and not according to Lady Capulet's desire for revenge. Ultimately, she is humbled when she is brought in to see her daughter dead, with Romeo's dagger in her breast.

Balthasar

Servant to Romeo.

Samson and Gregory

Servants to Capulet.

Peter

Servant to Juliet's Nurse.

The Apothecary

A shabby shopkeeper whose poverty forces him to (illegally) sell poison to Romeo.

SUMMARIES AND COMMENTARIES

PROLOGUE

This opening speech serves as an introduction, or program, to the play but seems unnecessary to most modern audiences. It is usually delivered by a single narrator (usually one of the other characters in the play) but was intended to be spoken by a chorus of voices. In form, this Prologue resembles a Shakespearean sonnet with fourteen lines and a rhyming couplet at the end.

The Prologue directs our attention to the important part that fate plays in the lives of the two young lovers, who are to some extent the victims of their parents' strife. Thus their love is described as being "death-mark'd." The "loins of these two foes"—that is, of the two families concerned—are "fatal" for the offspring of them. Fate hovers over all, as in a Greek tragedy. The end is prefigured in the beginning with tragic inevitability.

The point of this Prologue is to make it clear that the fate of the two young lovers is not their fault; instead, it is their misfortune, for which they are not entirely responsible.

ACT I

Summary

In a public square of Verona, two Capulet serving men, Sampson and Gregory, encounter two Montague serving men, Abram and another. Sampson insults Abram and then attacks him, just as Benvolio (Montague's nephew) and Tybalt (Capulet's nephew) enter from opposing directions. Benvolio attempts to stop the fight between the serving men, but Tybalt engages him in combat. Numerous citizens enter to take sides in the fray, and presently they are joined by the heads of the two opposed houses, Capulet and Montague, each accompanied by his wife. The prince then enters, with attendants, and stops the fight. He dismisses the two factions, threatening to execute Capulet and Montague if the peace of Verona is broken by another brawl.

Benvolio, Montague, and Montague's wife, remaining onstage after the general exit, discuss Romeo's secretive and melancholy behavior; the Montagues then leave the stage as Romeo comes on. His dialogue with Benvolio reveals that he is hopelessly in love. Benvolio suggests that he can learn to forget the girl by comparing her beauty with that of other girls. Romeo resolutely denies the possibility.

The County Paris, a young nobleman of Verona, asks Capulet for Juliet's hand in marriage. Capulet, after arguing halfheartedly that his daughter is too young to marry, says that he will give his consent to the match if Paris can succeed in gaining Juliet's consent. He then invites Paris to a feast (festival) to be held that night at his house and sends his servant off with a list containing the names of additional guests.

As it happens, Capulet's servant is illiterate and cannot read the list of guests. (It contains, among others, the names of Rosaline, Tybalt, and Mercutio.) Hence when the servant meets Romeo and Benvolio on the street, he asks Romeo to read the list for him. Romeo does so, and thus he and Benvolio learn of the Capulet feast. They decide to attend. Benvolio hopes that Romeo will see a beautiful girl who will make him forget about Rosaline; Romeo simply hopes that he will see Rosaline.

In the brief Scene 3, Capulet's wife informs Juliet that it is time for her to think of marriage, specifically with Paris. There will be an opportunity for Juliet to see him at the feast that night. Juliet replies dutifully that she will be guided by her parents' choice. The Nurse reminisces garrulously and bawdily about Juliet's childhood.

Romeo, Benvolio, and another friend, Mercutio, wind their way

to Capulet's house with "five or six other maskers." There they plan
to enter without announcing themselves and stay long enough for a
single dance. Romeo is still mourning his unrequited love and is in
no mood for dancing. Mercutio, quick-witted and expressive, delivers a delightful and imaginative speech on Queen Mab, who brings
strange dreams to mankind. The scene closes with Romeo's presentiment of coming troubles, with a foreboding of something "hanging
in the stars."

The maskers remain onstage from Scene 4, but the scene of the
action changes from outside to inside the house as they "march
about the stage" and four Capulet serving men "come forth." The
maskers then stand aside during a short dialogue by the serving
men, which gives an amusing impression of the domestic confusion
attendant upon a large entertainment. Capulet and the other guests
enter, and Capulet welcomes the maskers. There is dancing. Capulet converses with an older member of the family, probably his
uncle; they cannot agree on whether it is twenty-five or thirty years
since they themselves last went to a masked ball, such as their
guests are now doing.

Romeo sees Juliet, is struck by her beauty, and falls in love with
her immediately. Tybalt recognizes Romeo by his voice and sends
for his rapier, ready to attack him. However, Capulet is well-dis-
posed toward Romeo, and, in a show of anger, Tybalt does so with
difficulty and leaves the feast. Romeo and Juliet converse wittily,
and he kisses her. The Nurse calls her away and then, upon being
questioned by Romeo, informs him that Juliet is a Capulet. The
maskers decide to leave the feast. As they are going out, Juliet sends
the Nurse to find out Romeo's name. Thus she learns that he
is a Montague.

Commentary

Scene 1 opens with two servants who indulge in some crude and
lively repartee. Then suddenly the stage flares into violence. We
hear the clash of swords and see the flash of variously colored
Renaissance costumes. It is a magnetic piece of theater that immediately captures the attention of the audience. The participants in the
quarrel are not important characters, but the brawl is immediate
proof that the houses of Montague and Capulet are such enemies
that the hostility extends even to the servants.

The characters of Capulet and Montague are delineated in a few strokes. They are old but still ready to enter into a fight. Benvolio's character as a peacemaker is shown in his first words, "Part, fools!" Tybalt's hot temper and unreasonable nature are displayed when he attacks Benvolio, who is trying to reason with him. The feud between the families is no mere quarrel; this is an ancient, bitter hatred that has affected the entire city and has become a public issue.

The second half of the scene concerns Romeo. The battle is over, the hero did not take part in it, nor was he on hand to help settle it. Romeo enters most unheroically, mooning about unrequited love. He is romantic and imaginative, and he has a bit of the poseur about him. He is a Petrarchan lover—that is, he is in love with the idea of being in love, luxuriating in his melancholy. He has been stirred by the poetry of love, not by passion, and we are given this view of him as a measure and as a contrast for the later Romeo, the Romeo in love with Juliet.

In Scene 1, we learn that a certain lady (later identified as Rosaline) has denied Romeo her love, and we hear Romeo describe himself as dead, though alive (230). Concerning Romeo's "love" for Rosaline, note that his unrequited love has many Petrarchan ingredients. He speaks in couplets and fashionable oxymorons. He worships an aloof, chaste woman; she is, in fact, such an abstraction that she is not, strictly speaking, a character in the play. To Romeo, Rosaline is a tormenting sickness. Benvolio, too, is of the Petrarchan school; notice that he speaks of love in terms of pain, infection, and poison. Soon we shall see that these two attitudes toward love— the "proper" attitude of Paris later, and the "poetic," Petrarchan approach of Romeo here—are far removed from the deep love Romeo will soon feel for Juliet.

Later in the play, two families and fate will deny Juliet to Romeo, but he will no longer be the suffering, listless lover. He will be thoroughly defiant. The power of Romeo's love for Juliet is one of the strongest forces in this play and will seem all the more enthusiastic and convincing because of the contrast with this opening scene. Romeo is not in love with Rosaline, yet he thinks he is. He affects all the attitudes, strikes all the poses he thinks are appropriate, and says all the proper phrases, but his love lacks sincerity. Once Romeo sees Juliet, the attitudes he had toward Rosaline are hollow and pale compared with his new, passionate feelings.

Two other matters that should be noted in Scene 1 are the foreshadowing and the emphasis on the age-youth theme. Concerning the foreshadowing, be aware that the prince is prophetic when he says, "If ever you disturb our streets again / Your lives shall pay the forfeit of the peace" (103–104). Of course, neither old Montague nor old Capulet pay with their lives, but they do pay with the extension of their lives—with a son and a daughter. The lives of their children will be the price for continuing their hatred. The feud is a very old feud between very old men. Capulet, for example, is scoffed at by his wife when he calls for his sword. She jeers that a crutch would be more appropriate. And Montague's wife cries, "Thou shalt not stir a foot to seek a foe" (87). But the old men are not yet tamed and the old, festering hatred between them will be in contrast with the newly discovered love between their children, the young lovers.

In the short Scene 2, two sets of conversations should be considered: that between Capulet and Paris, and that between Romeo and Benvolio. In the former, we find the age-youth theme. Walking beside young Paris, Capulet talks of his old age and of his daughter's youth. Juliet is obviously very dear to her father; he says that "the earth hath swallow'd all [his] hopes but she" (15). In Scene 1, we saw the love and concern of the Montagues for Romeo; now we see how precious Juliet is to Capulet. He describes his daughter as being not ripe enough to be a bride; earlier, Montague described Romeo as being like a bud. The youth of the children and the extreme affection of the parents for them juxtapose the grudge between the old fathers, which will eventually destroy the young lovers.

In this scene, Capulet seems capable of discussing peace; theoretically, he says, it shouldn't be too difficult to maintain. As he enters, we discern that he has been discussing the matter with Paris. But Capulet has a volatile disposition, as we already noted about the first scene. We should recall how quickly he roared for his sword, ready to charge into the street brawl; in fact, Capulet has a far more dramatic (in a sense, more "youthful") temperament than young Paris.

Paris is pleasant and respectful of his elders, and it is interesting to listen to how he and Capulet speak of love and compare it with Romeo and Benvolio's discussion of love. Paris conducts his courtship with proper protocol, in accordance with long-established conventions; he consults Capulet and asks for permission to court Juliet. These are certain formalities and he observes them. Romeo, in contrast, will very soon break all the rules in his courtship of Juliet, for even as Scene 2 closes, he has decided to attend the Capulets' ball—uninvited.

The role of fate, mentioned in the Prologue, is already beginning to affect the destinies of Romeo and Juliet; for example, the encounter with the illiterate servant seems unlikely. It can only be fate that arranges for Romeo to be able to disguise himself, trespass into Capulet territory, and discover Juliet.

Just as we heard about Romeo before he appeared onstage, through his parents' anxious concern, so are we introduced to Juliet in a similar way in Scene 3. In the last scene, Capulet spoke of his daughter's being "a stranger in the world" (8). The emphasis was on her youth. She is thirteen years old, and marriage for her is already being discussed. Now we are introduced to Juliet herself, and again the emphasis is on her youth. The Nurse clucks lovingly over her, fussing and using such diminutives as "ladybird" and "lamb." (Some critics maintain that the word "ladybird" also meant "loose woman" or "strumpet," thus provoking the nurse to say "God forbid" in the next sentence.)

As she enters in Scene 3, Juliet's first speech reveals politeness and obedience. She does indeed seem like a lamb, but later in the play, she, like Romeo, will change. She will no longer be a docile young girl. Love will transform her. And already we have a hint of her later rebelliousness. Juliet appears obedient, but Shakespeare shows us that Juliet does not quite obey all of her mother's requests. She is not particularly excited about the marriage that her parents are arranging for her (this procedure, it should be said, was long-established; Juliet's parents are not ogres to suggest such a match), but were she truly obedient, she would accept the proposition. The answer she gives her mother has a certain bite to it: She says that she will consider Paris "if looking liking move" (97).

The idea of love and marriage is new to Juliet; she has never been in love. We realize therefore that when she marries Romeo, she will bring him not only a virgin body but also a virgin love. And it will be a love quite different from the Nurse's idea of love or, for that matter, her own mother's idea of love. Lady Capulet, for example, was no doubt married according to her parents' wishes; the idea of a "love marriage" was rarely considered. In fact, her speeches in Scene 3 tell us a great deal about her. She is still a young woman, probably less than thirty years old, and married to an old man. It is not surprising that she favors the handsome Paris for her daughter. Both she and the Nurse obviously consider Paris most attractive.

Not being a "lady," the Nurse is free to say exactly what she thinks in her own, undisciplined way. To her, Paris is one of the most handsome and sexy men she's ever laid eyes on. If she were Juliet, she'd jump at the chance to marry Paris and bed down with him. And that's the Nurse—one of the bawdiest, richest creations of Shakespeare. She's frank and earthy; love and sex are part and parcel of one another. Love means happy nights and happy days; it is not a word, it is an act. Already she's shown us how natural she is. Saying whatever comes to mind, she's spoken of how Juliet might have "suck'd wisdom from [her] teat" (68); of weaning Juliet with wormwood; of how someday Juliet will enjoy tumbling under a man; and of Juliet's future pregnancy. Her vulgarity, however, is never offensive. She doesn't babble to shock; she merely babbles. She's as freely candid as Lady Capulet is artificial. Her familiarity and her ignorant talkativeness run throughout the play as a balance and contrast to the tragedy.

Scene 4 completes the exposition—the weaving together of several threads of plot, which will later form a web so tangled and complex that tragedy is bound to result: the bitter feud between the two families; Romeo's romantic state of mind; Paris' proposal to marry Juliet; Romeo's accidental chance to attend Capulets' feast; and Juliet's youth and protected life. And now suspense grows as Romeo and his friends are actually on their way to the house of the enemy.

Here we watch Mercutio verbally attacking Romeo's continuing pose as a "lover." It is necessary that once more, before Romeo falls in love with Juliet, we see him as a Petrarchan lover, and not as a genuine lover. It is delightful to watch Mercutio nimbly parry Romeo's dreamy, woe-is-me posturing. Benvolio, as usual, nurses Romeo's moods, but Mercutio ridicules his friend's Petrarchan suffering. Note that Romeo still seems to be unenthusiastic about the ball; remember that he had to be coaxed into going. He knows that Rosaline will be there, but he has no wish to dance with her. Crushed because she refuses to love him, he asks only to stand in the shadows of the merriment and watch his ladylove from afar. Yet he laces his plea so carefully with wit that it is obvious that his senses are not completely addled by "love." It is humorously apropos that Romeo and his friends are on their way to a masked ball because Romeo wears his unrequited love very much like a mask, one with a fixed expression of pain and sorrow.

Mercutio's Queen Mab speech is a ploy to humor Romeo into joining into the spirit of the adventure. In contrast with Mercutio's earlier, rapier-sharp wit, this speech is exquisite. In fact, some critics think it too beautiful, too contrived, but it is still Mercutio speaking, imaginatively cynical beneath the poetics. The speech concerns fancy—the fabric of Romeo's "love" for Rosaline—then undercuts itself with coarseness. There is a constant, clever interplay between fantasy and fact. The term "fairies' midwife" is a kernel of the speech. "Fairy" suggests something lovely, ethereal, and gossamer-like; "midwife" suggests birthing and blood, life and death. Actually Queen Mab herself is most unfairylike. She may be borne in a carriage made of spider webs and grasshopper wings, but her mission is often one of mischief, exposing the dreams of a parson to be materialistic and those of a soldier to be of murder, not valiance. Mercutio is trying to reveal to Romeo how full of fancy his "love" for Rosaline is. Love and dreams are mires: Mercutio laughs at them; he is trying to be midwife to revelation.

Although it is not excitement that Romeo feels as he agrees to continue on toward the ball, it is also not wholly the weight of his melancholy for Rosaline. Much fun has been made about dreams and fancies, and much of what Mercutio has joked about we can agree with, but Romeo speaks now of another kind of fancy— unexplainable presentiment. Fate is brought before us again. The idea of doom momentarily stains the playful mood of the scene. Some consequence "hanging in the stars" (107) recalls the reference to the "star-cross'd" lovers in the Prologue; the mention of "untimely death" sharply preludes the instantaneous love in the following scene.

Scene 5 brings the two lovers together and has them fall in love and realize their perilous situation as children of two rival houses. Romeo's fanciful dreaming of love is suddenly turned to serious and sincere feeling toward Juliet; his words now express real emotion instead of a desire to display his wit and cleverness in imagined sensations. Juliet also seems older than when we first met her; her dignity and self-possession are increasing.

We note first that this ball is a very special event and that Capulet is thoroughly enjoying it. He speaks of the last masked ball he attended as a masker, and the age-youth theme reappears. He emphasizes that he is an old man; his youth and his days of flirting behind a mask are "gone, 'tis gone" (26). He and a kinsman sit and quibble over whether twenty-five or thirty years have passed since their last masked ball. In short, his character is humanized in this scene. He is a happy host, pleased to see the young people dancing, satisfied to sit by and reminisce. And when Tybalt threatens to duel with Romeo, Capulet, as head of the house, refuses to allow it. In fact, he is far more angry with Tybalt's bad manners that threaten to ruin the party than he is with Romeo's intrusion. He confesses to harboring no special hate for Romeo; Verona speaks well of him, and Capulet is doing his best to obey the prince's command to keep the peace.

Interestingly, Tybalt is lusting to duel with Romeo because a Montague has dared invade the Capulet house; he thinks Romeo has come to "scorn." This is dramatic irony; we know what has been happening to Romeo during the dancing scene; Tybalt does not. If he knew, he would certainly not be content to curb his temper and merely mutter an ominous warning.

Romeo's moments with Juliet seem especially quiet and private after they follow Capulet's angry words with Tybalt. The contrast between anger and love is striking. In the midst of the noisy, crowded ballroom, Romeo and Juliet are aware of only one another. Of Juliet, Romeo says that she is like a jewel, like a snowy dove; his imagery reflects her purity, her preciousness. Of their love, Romeo speaks in holy terms—of pilgrims, saints, palmers, devotions, and shrines. This attitude is antithetical to the grief, the gall, and the pain of his "love" for Rosaline. Romeo's first speech to Juliet and her speech to him form a sonnet, a literary form far more appropriate to love than Romeo's previous, punning couplets. Juliet says that she won't return Romeo's kiss, but she does return poetry to him. The love is clearly reciprocal. It is a delicate, rather playful meeting, but it is touched with a bit of irony: Both Juliet and Romeo were reluctant to attend the ball but consented—Romeo to see Rosaline, Juliet to see Paris. And they discovered one another.

Their love is so instant that they neglect to ask one another's name, yet once they have discovered one another's identity, they are not flippant or ignorant of the seriousness of being from rival families. Romeo says, "Is she a Capulet? / O dear account! my life is my foe's debt" ("I owe my new interest in life to my enemy") (119-20). Juliet's comment is "Prodigious birth of love it is to me / That I must love a loathed enemy" (142-43). Both feel a heavy foreboding about the consequences of their love.

PROLOGUE

Like Act I, Act II opens with a Prologue meant to be recited by a chorus of voices but is usually spoken by a single narrator in today's productions, when it is not omitted. This Prologue adds little to the action of the play and impedes rather than speeds the flow. For this and other reasons, this Prologue is frequently regarded as an insertion from the pen of a different writer, but it is unprofitable to haggle over this. The Prologue merely points out in a condensed way what has already taken place: Romeo has replaced an infatuation with a true love; his love is returned, despite the fact that both lovers realize the perils of their attachment to one another. Romeo cannot have free access to Juliet since their families are antagonistic to each other; for the same reason, she cannot without difficulty arrange to meet him; nevertheless, "passion lends them power, time means, to meet"—and the dangers overcome make their meetings extremely sweet.

ACT II

Summary

Romeo, on his way home from the feast, leaps over the wall of Capulet's orchard, hoping to see Juliet once more. Benvolio and Mercutio are unaware that he has already forgotten Rosaline, and Mercutio playfully calls him by summoning the power of Rosaline's beauty. But Romeo remains in hiding, and Benvolio, knowing Romeo's love of solitude, persuades Mercutio to give up and come away with him.

Romeo remains onstage from the previous scene, in the orchard beneath Juliet's chamber window. Presently, Juliet appears in the window. Thinking herself alone, she reveals, in a soliloquy, her love for Romeo. He then speaks to her and reveals his love for her. They agree to marry. Twice the Nurse calls Juliet from inside the house, and twice Juliet leaves the window only to return almost immediately. Day is breaking as the lovers finally say farewell.

Friar Laurence, Romeo's friend and confessor, is up early and is gathering herbs. He discourses on their opposed potentialities as medicine and poison, comparing these to the opposed potentialities of man for good and evil. Romeo greets him, tells him of the love that has sprung up between himself and Juliet, and asks the Friar to marry them. After gently chiding Romeo for having forgotten Rosaline so quickly, the Friar agrees to marry him to Juliet in the hope that the marriage will bring an end to the feud between the houses of Montague and Capulet.

Benvolio and Mercutio, in a public square, reveal that Tybalt has sent Romeo a challenge to a duel. Mercutio comments satirically on Romeo's love of Rosaline and on Tybalt's affected preoccupation with the finer points of fencing etiquette. Romeo joins them, and he and Mercutio engage in a wit-combat consisting of a long series of linked puns and quibbles. The Nurse then appears, with her servant Peter, in search of Romeo. Mercutio, after exasperating her with his mockery, goes off with Benvolio. Romeo tips the Nurse and commissions her to tell Juliet that he will marry her that afternoon at the Friar's cell. Later he will send a rope ladder to the Nurse so that he can climb to Juliet's chamber window at night.

Juliet impatiently waits in the orchard for the Nurse's return. Three hours have seemed endless to her. The Nurse deliberately teases her with a recital of her woes, which serves to aggravate Juliet, who is eager to hear what she has to say. Juliet manages with difficulty to keep her temper until the Nurse finally gives her the message: Juliet is to go to the Friar's cell, where she will be married to Romeo.

While Romeo and the Friar are waiting for Juliet to arrive, Friar Laurence again warns against too hasty an act; Romeo agrees, but in his joy he challenges even death itself to destroy his present happiness. The lovers then meet, and the Friar leads them away to perform the marriage ceremony.

Commentary

The purpose of Scene 1 is twofold: to show that Benvolio and Mercutio understandably believe that Romeo is still playing the love game, and to isolate the lovers from family and friends. As before, Benvolio is sympathetic to Romeo's moods, but Mercutio is still the jester, mocking Romeo's Petrarchan sighs and rhymes. But this time his taunts are even more sharply barbed. Since Romeo will not respond to wit, Mercutio tries ribaldry. He calls to Romeo in the name of Rosaline's "scarlet lip" and "quivering thigh" and the pleasures "that there adjacent lie" (18–20). He playfully profanes the chastity that has caused Romeo to suffer his so-called living death.

Ironically, Romeo is very much in love, but not with Rosaline, and since we know this complication, Mercutio's jests are not as amusing as they once were. The complications of Romeo's situation are far more serious now than his former problem with Rosaline's chastity. In fact, this new love discovered by Romeo and Juliet only moments before seems even more pure and sincere when compared to Mercutio's scoffing taunts of sensuality.

Scene 2 is one of the lyric and romantic peaks of the play; it emphasizes the haste and the rashness of the courtship and it gives a hint of possible tragedy to follow. Romeo is strengthening; his wordy, artificial expressions of sentiment have given place to genuine feeling. He is also learning to think of another's feelings as well as his own. Like Romeo, Juliet is also changing. Earlier she had no idea of the power of love; from now on, her own strong feelings will guide her. And the fact that Romeo overhears Juliet expressing her love for him makes it possible to proceed without delay in their plans. If he had not discovered her true feelings, a long courtship might have taken place, which would have had entirely different consequences from their hasty, secret courtship and marriage.

The "light" imagery in this particular scene is profuse, and in addition to its being used in very fine, lyric poetry, it serves another function: It illuminates what is happening between Romeo and Juliet. The image that Romeo first used to describe Juliet, that of teaching "the torches to burn bright" (I. v. 46), is reintroduced here and richly embroidered. Juliet, on her balcony above Romeo, is said to be like the sun, the source of love and of warmth. Romeo compares her eyes to twinkling stars; he says that if they were set in the heavens, night would seem to be day. He speaks fancifully of the sun killing the moon, yet this is, metaphorically, what is taking place: Juliet (the sun) is outshining and replacing Rosaline (the moon). When Romeo claimed to be infatuated with Rosaline, he compared her to

Diana, the mythical, virgin goddess of the moon. Rosaline's chastity was as absolute as Diana's; her love was cold, like the moon. Juliet's love is warm, like the sun; it has rekindled life into Romeo. Their love, he says, is light, "which the dark night hath so discovered" (106). When Romeo "loved" Rosaline, his mood was dark, like the night; he even tried to create an artificial night by shutting himself up in a darkened room, yet neither that "night" nor its "moon goddess" (Rosaline) brought him happiness. Now, in a reversal, in the dark of an actual night, he has discovered Juliet and love—the sun and its light.

Besides emphasizing Juliet's "light," Romeo also speaks of her sacredness, recalling the holy motif of their first conversation together. She is his "bright angel"; she is like a "winged messenger of heaven," a "dear saint," and he vows to be "new baptiz'd" for her.

The romantic mood of Scene 2 is enhanced by the lovers' flashes of fear at their dangerous situation. Romeo fears that this may be like a dream (Mercutio was contemptuous of dreams in the preceding scene), and Juliet fears for Romeo's life; she knows that their love is "too rash, too unadvised, too sudden" (118). She also uses "light" imagery as she describes their love as being "like the lightning." But despite all their anxieties, the two yield to love, and we witness their betrothal, their exchange of vows.

The introduction of the Friar, in Scene 3, is a contrast to the mood of the scene just finished. The balcony scene expressed the feelings of youth and passion; Scene 3 contains an atmosphere of age, caution, and considered affection. Romeo is still eager; he is impatient for his plans to be carried out, but the Friar is thorough and philosophical.

The subject of the medicinal use of plants should be recalled when Shakespeare later introduces drugs into the plot line—first, the potion that Juliet takes to produce a trance that approximates death, to escape a marriage with Paris; and later, the poison (from the apothecary) that Romeo takes when he believes that Juliet is really dead. But, apart from the dramatic purpose of the Friar's discourse on herbs, it reveals him as of a philosophical and thoughtful turn of mind. His cautionary advice to Romeo shows that he is understanding and broadminded, even as he jokingly reproves Romeo for his fickleness.

Perhaps, though, the major reason why we admire the Friar is that he is practical enough to foresee that a marriage between a Montague and a Capulet could put an end to the feud that disturbs the peace of the city. But the hope of resolution is precarious: His talk of medicinal herbs being both good and evil reminds us of the tragedy that has been promised to be a part of this young, perfect love—that out of the lovers' deaths, the two feuding families will be reunited.

Scene 4 serves several purposes. First, it creates suspense by mentioning the challenge which Tybalt has sent to Romeo. It intensifies our impression of Tybalt's hasty temper and of Mercutio's antagonism toward him. And Mercutio's attitude toward Tybalt is an important matter to consider. But the seriousness of the scene is lightened by another kind of dueling, two duels in fact—duels of wit: one between Mercutio and Romeo, the other between Mercutio and the Nurse. In Romeo's case, he is clearly no longer the melancholy, lovesick Petrarchan. His happiness in real love expresses itself in a brilliant play of wit, which camouflages his deeper feelings. He exchanges quip for quip; Mercutio thrusts and Romeo delivers a quick return. Mercutio is delighted that his friend Romeo has recovered from his black mood. He has no use for lovelorn gloom and is quick to insult Romeo's former "drivelling" with a salty, sexual entendre, an exchange that is one of the bawdiest in the play. The taunt is strong, and, understandably, Benvolio, the peacemaker, attempts to quiet the duel.

But Mercutio is feeling playful and readily takes on another opponent, Juliet's Nurse. Puffing and calling for her fan, she sails on stage, rigged with mock importance. She is attended, like a grand lady, by a servant. Mercutio pricks at her absurd, malapropped pomposity, but the Nurse is able to fend him off. His bawdiness does not embarrass her, but his harassing is bothersome. Actually, were she not on an errand for Juliet and not "attended," one feels sure that she could match Mercutio vulgarism for vulgarism. And as soon as Mercutio leaves, the Nurse resorts to her familiar coarseness, lambasting Mercutio for his sauciness. It is good comedy, most appropriate in an inverse way, to accompany the news of the approaching marriage; the private, serious passion of Romeo and Juliet has very often been paralleled by colorful, sexual joking.

Thus an atmosphere of happy anticipation for the coming marriage is presented to us. The arrangements for the marriage in the afternoon and for the consummation that night are complete. The speed of the courtship is underscored: Juliet and Romeo have known each other for only a few hours yet already the lovers are about to be married.

In Scene 3, we saw how impatient Romeo was to be married; he insisted that Friar Laurence marry him and Juliet today. Now, in Scene 5, we observe Juliet's impatience, and, as in Scene 3, she, like Romeo, is frustrated with a longwinded but trusted elder. But whereas Friar Laurence was attempting to understand and counsel Romeo's impetuousness, Juliet's Nurse is far from being serious. So we have another amusing interlude: the lithe and beautiful young Juliet pleading about her love and the buxom, bawdy old Nurse complaining of her aches and pains.

The Nurse does like to tease, but she is not a malicious busybody. She knows how fast Juliet's heart beats, she measures the young girl's breathless impatience, and she leisurely plays with her anxious, impatient curiosity. And, after all, the Nurse is tired. She has a headache and is out of breath. It is a hot July day, Renaissance clothes are hot and heavy, and the Nurse is a big woman. (When Mercutio saw her coming down the street, he likened her to a sail.) Her complaints are perfectly believable; they are natural excuses for her to indulge and exaggerate. Thus they set off Juliet's impatience, plus increasing our own anticipation.

At last when she does give Romeo's news to Juliet, the Nurse is as succinct as she is usually rambling. She knows that Juliet is becoming vexed, so she ends the game and gives Romeo's message to Juliet. However, completely in character, she ends the scene with an extra moan of complaint and also with an extra dash of ribald humor: She must bear the responsibility for arranging for both the marriage and its consummation, but she notes that soon Juliet will also be bearing a burden, the child of this marriage.

In Scene 6, the prelude to the wedding is very short, yet Shakespeare did not include it as merely a quiet, beautiful tableau of young love. This element is present, of course, but Romeo and Juliet's love for one another is only one part of this scene; there is another element here. We have been reminded of the possibility of catastrophe hovering above this union. Shakespeare is particularly careful to guide our imagination in this scene, and we are never to forget the tragedy that attends this "star-cross'd" love.

The Friar is deeply disturbed; he is performing the ceremony in good faith, hoping to bring the feud to an end, but he seems to have a presentiment. Whenever he speaks of happiness, he also speaks of sorrow; he talks of "violent delights" and "violent ends." Romeo and Juliet are quiet as they meet one another, but the words of Friar Laurence recall the lovers' violent and impetuous passion for one another. They are young, and this passion is part of their youth. At the other emotional pole of Shakespeare's theme is age—the old and wise Friar. He counsels moderation, but youth is not, by nature, moderate. Time, for them, means *now*. Neither Romeo nor Juliet is to be put off by family, the holy father, or by fate. Not even "love-devouring Death" is able to shake Romeo's conviction that he and Juliet share a special, precious love.

When he sees Juliet approaching, Romeo uses a variation of the figure of speech he used when he first saw her. At the ball, he described her in terms of shining light; now he speaks of her "light" (airy) step. There have been shadows of doom in Friar Laurence's caution, but at this moment neither of the lovers is fully aware of the extent of the "darkness" that is companion to their "light."

ACT III

Summary

Mercutio and Benvolio, in a public square, are accosted by Tybalt in search of Romeo. Mercutio and Tybalt are on the point of fighting when Romeo appears. Tybalt insults Romeo in order to provoke him to fight, but Romeo, who is now secretly married to Tybalt's cousin, returns a soft answer. Mercutio is incensed at Tybalt's having insulted Romeo with impunity. He attacks Tybalt, and they fight. Romeo and Benvolio attempt to stop the fight, and when Romeo comes between the two swordsmen, Tybalt, under Romeo's arm, gives Mercutio a fatal wound. Mercutio is helped into a nearby house by Benvolio, who presently returns to inform Romeo that Mercutio is dead. In a moment Tybalt also returns, and Romeo, resolved on revenge, attacks him. They fight, and Tybalt is killed. By this time the citizens are up in arms. The citizens enter, followed shortly by the prince, and by Montague, Capulet, and their wives. Benvolio gives the prince a long account of the fighting, and the prince exiles Romeo under penalty of death.

Juliet is impatiently waiting for night to fall. The Nurse arrives with the rope ladder and news of Tybalt's death, which Juliet at first mistakenly supposes to be news of Romeo's death. Juliet's grief is somewhat lessened when she learns the truth, but Romeo's banishment is almost as distracting to her as his death would be. The Nurse tells her that Romeo is hidden at the Friar's cell, whereupon Juliet orders the Nurse to take a ring to Romeo as a token and to bid him come to her that night for a last farewell.

Romeo, at the Friar's cell, despairingly discusses his situation with the Friar, who attempts to console him. However, Romeo will not be consoled and throws himself on the floor in an extravagant display of grief. The Nurse then arrives, bringing news of Juliet, but this, adding fuel to Romeo's grief, only results in an unsuccessful attempt at suicide. The Friar scolds Romeo and points out that the situation could be much worse, and then he proposes a plan. Romeo will visit Juliet that night as has been agreed upon, leaving the city before daybreak and proceeding to Mantua, where he will stay until it is safe to return to Verona. Romeo agrees.

Paris is discussing with Capulet and Lady Capulet his projected marriage to Juliet. They protest that Tybalt's death has made it impossible to think of marriage. However, as Paris is about to leave, Capulet, firmly confident that Juliet will be ruled by his wishes in the matter, suddenly takes it upon himself to offer her hand in marriage and enthusiastically sets the date for Thursday. (Since it is now Monday, he considers Wednesday to be too soon.) Paris is delighted and takes his leave.

Romeo and Juliet are in her chamber and are about to take leave of each other on the first morning of their married life. Juliet argues that it is still night, that the bird they hear is the nightingale, not the lark, whose song means the coming of the day. But when Romeo, at first insisting that it is time for him to be on his way to Mantua, finally agrees with her, Juliet drops the pretense and urges him to leave the city before he is found and put to death.

The Nurse enters, warning them that Lady Capulet is coming to see Juliet. Romeo climbs down the rope ladder, and the lovers take a last farewell. Juliet feels remorseful, commenting, "O, think'st thou we shall ever meet again?"

She is astonished by her mother's early visit to her room, and she explains her own woebegone appearance, fresh from her parting with Romeo, as being due to her grief for her cousin Tybalt. Lady Capulet, believing that she wishes to avenge her cousin's death, proposes to arrange that Romeo be poisoned. Then she tells her some news that she hopes will cheer Juliet and take her mind from her troubles: Capulet's well-intended plans for her early marriage to Paris.

Capulet then joins them, teasing Juliet for her tearful demeanor. He is astounded to hear that she will not agree to his plans. When she persists in her refusal, Capulet loses his temper, upbraids Juliet vigorously, and threatens to turn her out of the house and disinherit her if she persists in refusing to marry Paris. He stalks off angrily. Juliet turns to her mother for comfort, but Lady Capulet will not speak to her and also leaves. Juliet then turns to the Nurse, who suggests that she marry Paris after all; in her opinion, Paris now seems much superior to Romeo. The Nurse goes off, leaving Juliet alone. Disillusioned in the Nurse, as well as in her mother and father, Juliet resolves to seek aid from the Friar.

Commentary

Up to this moment, perhaps there might have been a solution: If the marriage of Romeo and Juliet had been made public before he and Tybalt encountered one another, the two families might well have been glad to lay aside their age-long feud. But in that case, the drama would be incomplete; it would be a short comedy instead of a full-length tragedy, and it has been building up to tragedy: Juliet, Romeo, and the Friar have all had forebodings of difficulties to come.

Now the antipathy between Mercutio and Tybalt mounts; the fierce resentment of Tybalt against Romeo erupts. All of Benvolio's efforts for peace are in vain; his efforts to restrain Mercutio are brushed aside. A strong, new conflict takes place in Romeo, a conflict between his newly acquired feeling of benevolence toward his wife's family and between his natural resentment at Tybalt's insults. His forbearance toward Tybalt is completely understandable under the circumstances, but when Mercutio is killed, Romeo's sense of honor and loyalty leaves him no alternative: He must avenge his friend's death. His necessity for avenging Mercutio's death must overcome his wish to spare Juliet sorrow.

Before his death, Mercutio's sparkling brilliance comes to a climax; even as he dies, he jokes and puns about his wound. Also, his regret is not so much for his hurt as for the ignominy of having received it at the hands of the man he despised—"A dog, a rat, a mouse, a cat, to scratch a man to death! a braggart, a rogue, a villain, that fights by the book of arithmetic!" (103–105). He has only a brief reproach for Romeo's mistaken interference, "Why the devil came you between us? I was hurt under your arm." But his thrice-called curse, "A plague o' both your houses!" is only too soon to be carried out.

Scene 2 opens very much like Scene 5 of Act II. Then, Juliet was in the garden, impatient for the Nurse's return so that she might learn what news there was from Romeo. Now she is in the orchard, impatiently waiting for Romeo himself. Earlier we could smile at her impatience and delight in her youthful anguish. Now we cannot. She is still impatient and eager, but she is ignorant of what we have just witnessed. We know that her cousin Tybalt has been killed and that her husband, Romeo, has been banished. Her youthful impatience is made both pitiful and tragic by the dramatic irony. The imagery of her speeches colors the scene's poignancy. Earlier, when Juliet waited for the Nurse's news of Romeo, Juliet spoke of time and the sun's beams "driving back shadows over low'ring hills" (II. v. 6). Romeo's love was able to do this for her. Juliet was "light" to him and he to her. Now she waits for night and for the consummation of her marriage. She pleads for "cloudy night immediately" (4). And, figuratively, the bad news she is soon to receive is indeed dark, like a cloudy night about to blacken the bright joy of her marriage day. She calls for the night, "thou sober-suited matron," but it is not the darkness of night that is to come to her; it is the dark news of death: Tybalt is dead and Romeo is soon to be separated from her. She speaks of Romeo's dying and being cut into "little stars," but she has no idea that her marriage has already suffered a mortal blow.

The Nurse adds to the suspense of Scene 2 by again being herself, distraught and asking for a drink. We understand that the woman is old and confused and upset, and so our sympathy deepens for Juliet as she tries to fathom the fragments of the Nurse's ravings. The news, when it is complete, overwhelms Juliet. Her reaction is particularly important; first, Shakespeare shows us the child-woman in Juliet. For a long moment, she denounces Romeo. It is impulsive, typical of her youth; then she changes. She is also a woman and realizes the depth of her love for Romeo. This is the reaction of an adult, just as was Romeo's slaying of Tybalt. In that situation, he had a duty as a man: According to his code, he had to avenge Mercutio's death. He could not shirk this duty, even to spare Juliet great sorrow. Now we see Juliet realizing what her duty is— as a wife, and especially as a new wife. Her decision shows gallant courage. It is clear that the love of these two young people is stronger than any other bond, even that of family.

"Banishment" is repeated again and again in Scene 2; the horror of this punishment resounds. It will be a kind of "living death" for the lovers. This was a term that Romeo bandied about in Act I, claiming that because of Rosaline's attitude, he was dead, though alive. Then, however, he was lamenting over Rosaline's self-imposed chastity. Now that he is truly in love, it is uncertain whether or not Juliet will not also be forever a virgin. She herself says that "death, not Romeo," will "take [her] maidenhead" (137).

Scene 3 is a complement to the preceding scene. Earlier we watched how Juliet received the news of Romeo's banishment; now we see Romeo reacting to the news. In both cases, Romeo and Juliet each has an older confidant with them. In this scene, the Friar is contrasted with the Nurse; whereas she was incoherent as she rushed to Juliet, the Friar is calm and philosophical. His words are heavy with philosophy and his figures of speech are weighted with irony. In his first speech with Romeo, he observes that Romeo is "wedded to calamity." Immediately we are reminded that when we last viewed the Friar's cell, it was shortly before the wedding. Romeo's very recent wedding is evoked to intensify our sympathy for his predicament.

The difference between the age of the Friar and the youth of Romeo is most clearly evident in their individual reactions to Romeo's banishment. The Friar brings the sentence as "tidings," as a "gentler judgment," and as "dear mercy." He counsels Romeo to be patient, saying that the world extends beyond Verona's walls. Romeo retorts that death is more bearable than banishment; he raves melodramatically. But, as we have seen before, Romeo is very emotional and very rash. He fell out of "love" with Rosaline and fell in love with Juliet in a moment, wooed her, and demanded of the Friar that they be married immediately. The speed of their courtship was reckless. Romeo is young and it is the voice of youth speaking as he chastises the Friar; the holy father is old and has never been in this extreme, agonizing predicament: deeply in love, just married, just killed an in-law, and now banished. The Friar's whole life has been one of quiet work and meditation. Romeo's life with Juliet has been intense, and now, it is seemingly destroyed before it truly has begun. There is very little that the old man can answer and very little that is effective. Luckily, the Friar's frustration is saved by the Nurse's knocking at the door.

As she was with Juliet, the Nurse is again rather longwinded and babbling, describing Juliet's wailing and Romeo's wailing, but she is stern with Romeo. Like the Friar, she tells him that "death's the end of all." Compared to death, banishment is mild. She upbraids him for his woman-like weeping. Romeo's hysteria subsides only when Juliet's ring is produced. He leaves, excusing himself because of a "joy past joy." He refers to his love for Juliet much as he did just before their marriage (II. vi. 3-4), when he described the joy "that one short minute gives me in her sight." But if seeing Juliet means a joy past (exceeding) joy, it is soon to be, literally, a past joy.

Scene 4 increases the sense of haste and precipitance, and it is another indication of how fate intervenes in the course of these "star-cross'd lovers." Capulet, of course, has no suspicion that Juliet will object to his authority. After all, she has always been an obedient daughter. He cannot possibly know what we do—that as he discusses Juliet's coming marriage, she has been married this very day and is, at this very moment, upstairs consummating that marriage. His surprising decision to marry Juliet in three days makes this irony even more dramatic. Certainly his decision seems to be a whim because in Act I, Scene 2, he urged Paris to wait until Juliet was older. He advised the young man to woo her first, to get her heart: "My will to her consent is but a part" (17)—that is, her own consent must be gained before Capulet himself takes part in the matter. He even advised Paris to attend the feast so that he might compare Juliet with others before making up his mind. In the present scene, he has assumed the part of the all-powerful father: Juliet is to do as he wishes and without delay. We have no clue as to why Capulet changes his mind. It is simply another example of fate at work.

In Scene 5, there is an exquisite tension in Juliet's speeches as she realizes that Romeo must leave her: The child in her, satisfied and happy, begs Romeo to stay, but the woman in her, fearing for Romeo's safety, begs him to leave. She refuses to recognize the signs of morning, the song of the lark and the early rays of light, and she grows fearful as Romeo speaks of death and dying. "Night's candles," he says, "are burnt out" (9); the length of their night together has also burnt out. The lovers realize the tragic parallel. It is dawn, a time of division, separating day from the night. In this time of division, Romeo must also be divided from Juliet. His speeches are portentous, particularly with light-dark imagery. Traditionally, day and light suggest freshness, beginnings, and hope, but this is not true here. They promise separation, isolation, and misery. "More light and light," he says twice, stressing that "more dark and dark our woes" (36). And Juliet divines that the future forebodes evil for them; she says that she sees Romeo laid out "as one dead in the bottom of a tomb" (56). It is an accurate omen; that is exactly what will happen. When next they meet, it will be in a tomb and Romeo will be dead. Even the Nurse's lines in this scene contribute to the irony of the light-dark motif. "The day is broke," she says. Very shortly it will be further shattered by the Capulets' announcement that Juliet must marry Paris.

The quiet, anxious farewell between the young lovers is in stark contrast with the remainder of the scene, which is loud and furious as old age demands that youth obey. Both of the Capulets are vehement in their denunciation of their daughter, particularly in view of their previous consideration of her extreme youth and her own inclinations. They are baffled and furious at her willful refusal to marry Paris, but we are not. We know that Juliet is no longer just a daughter; she is a wife. She is no longer a young maiden; she is a young woman.

That Capulet has a temper is no surprise. We saw him eager to join the street fighting in Act I, and, in a later scene, we saw him angrily upbraid Tybalt. Now he lashes out at his daughter, who only a few hours before he described as being "the hopeful lady of my earth." He calls her "green-sickness carrion," "young baggage," a "disobedient wretch," a "wretched puling fool," and a "whining mammet," and he threatens to disown her if she does not obey his commands. Both Romeo and Juliet have been threatened with exile—in his case, from his country; in hers, from her home.

As for Lady Capulet, she shows unexpected fierceness. She mocked her husband earlier when he shouted for his sword, and talking with Juliet earlier, she seemed the essence of cold correctness. Now she proposes to have Romeo poisoned and declares that she'd like to see "the fool [Juliet] married to her grave." Again, there is heavy irony, for Juliet herself had earlier said, "I'll to my wedding bed; / And death, not Romeo, take my maidenhead!" (III. ii. 136–37).

But these are only some of many ironies in Scene 5. The entire conversation between Juliet and her mother is built on dramatic irony and double meanings. As examples, note these speeches of Juliet:

"Yet let me weep for such a feeling loss" (75)—Lady Capulet believes that Juliet is grieving over the loss of Tybalt, while Juliet is thinking of her separation from Romeo.

"And yet no man like he [Romeo] doth grieve my heart" (84)—by his absence.

"Would none but I might venge my cousin's death" (87)—in which case Romeo would go unpunished.

"Madam, if you could find out but a man / To bear a poison, I would temper it / That Romeo should, upon receipt thereof, / Soon sleep in quiet" (97–100)—which Lady Capulet understands as meaning sleep in death.

"Indeed I shall never be satisfied / With Romeo, till I behold him—dead—Is my poor heart, so for a kinsman vex'd" (94–96)—Juliet longs to see Romeo, to behold him; she also desires to behold him "dead"; in Elizabethan vernacular, a man "died" when he experienced a sexual orgasm. Her marriage has just been consummated; she longs for the time when she can join with Romeo (to behold him and to hold him, as she did less than an hour before) and have their marriage consummated once more. "Dead" is used very artfully here, for her phrase continues: "dead . . . for a kinsman" (not merely for a cousin, but for a husband).

Some critics have agreed with Juliet's condemnation of the Nurse in Scene 5 and have also labeled her "amoral," "unsympathetic," and "lacking in feeling." The Nurse, however, is no villain. The Capulets' wrath has been fierce; the father has turned on even the Nurse. She knows her place, and she has lived long enough to know that if one is wise, one does not defy authority (Capulet, in this case). Juliet does, however; she defies fortune and death and her family. To her, the Nurse has no integrity; she has betrayed truth and also Juliet. But the Nurse, like the Friar, is only trying to bring peace to the household. Obviously Shakespeare is saying that it is far easier for age to compromise than it is for youth to do so.

ACT IV

Summary

Paris visits the Friar's cell to tell him of Capulet's plans for his marriage to Juliet on Thursday. In his dismay at this news, the Friar offers various reasons for delay, but Paris explains that he believes that it is Capulet's concern for Juliet's grief over Tybalt that has moved him to hasten the marriage plans.

At this point, Juliet arrives and shows great self-control when she encounters Paris. She carries on a short, cleverly worded sort of banter, skillfully putting aside his compliments. The Friar dismisses the young man, and Juliet drops her mask of self-possession. Like Romeo, she believes that death is the only solution. But the Friar, who is an expert in the use of herbs and drugs, holds out hope for a remedy. Juliet is to take a certain drug on Wednesday night, the evening before the proposed wedding day. It will render her unconscious, and to all outward appearance, she will seem dead for forty-two hours. Then her body will be laid in the family vault of the Capulets by her mourning relatives. In the meantime, the Friar will let Romeo know of his plan. Juliet unhesitatingly consents and departs with the Friar's vial.

In the Capulet house, Juliet's parents, the Nurse, and the servants are in the midst of domestic preparations for the wedding feast. Juliet returns from her visit to the Friar, begs her father's pardon, and declares that henceforth she will always be ruled by his wishes. Capulet is so pleased at her apparent change of heart that he advances the day of the wedding from Thursday to Wednesday. Thus, Juliet will be married the very next day. Lady Capulet protests at this haste; there will not be enough time to prepare Juliet or to arrange for the guests. But Capulet, delighted at the prospect, proposes to stay up all night in order to make preparations and to tell Paris the good news.

It is Tuesday night, and the Nurse is helping Juliet choose clothes for the wedding. Juliet, keeping even the Nurse out of her confidence, begs to be left to her prayers. Lady Capulet enters, but Juliet urges her to leave and take the Nurse with her.

Alone, she fears that the drug may not take effect; in that case, she will use the dagger with which she contemplated suicide in the Friar's cell. Then she has a sudden fear that the Friar has given her a poison so that his part in the plot will never be discovered. Her imagination begins to make her envision what horrors are before her in case she awakens in the tomb before Romeo arrives to release her. She may be stifled with the foul air or by the atmosphere of the vault. She seems to see the ghost of Tybalt, searching for his slayer (Romeo), and with a cry, Juliet drinks the liquid.

It is three o'clock, very early Wednesday morning. While Juliet lies unconscious, the rest of the household is busily overseeing the cooking of the wedding feast. Capulet, hearing music, knows that Paris is approaching, and he sends the Nurse to awaken Juliet.

The Nurse comes to wake Juliet and finds her lying senseless on the bed. She is unable to awaken her and presently realizes that Juliet is apparently dead. She calls for help. Lady Capulet comes in, followed first by Capulet, and then by Paris and the Friar. They all indulge in lamentation until the Friar stops their grief by pointing out that Juliet is in heaven and that Divine Will must be accepted. Capulet orders that the wedding preparations be converted to funeral preparations. They go off, leaving the Nurse.

At this point, the musicians come in. After speaking to them briefly, the Nurse goes out. The Nurse's servant, Peter, now comes in, and there is a brief comic scene between Peter and the three musicians.

Commentary

Time-wise, Scene 1 of Act IV is positioned about midway in the drama. It occurs on Tuesday, two days since Juliet met Romeo and two days before Juliet's father has promised her to Paris. The scene acts as a sort of fulcrum, placing Juliet between Romeo and Paris, and also between life and death. Today Juliet will decide to accept the Friar's potion. We have known Juliet for two days (the ball on Sunday; her wedding day on Monday), and in two days she will be dead (Wednesday, she will be discovered "dead"; Thursday night, she will commit suicide).

Juliet's meeting with Friar Laurence is very much like the scene between Romeo and the Friar. Both he and Juliet, in their desperation, turn from their real fathers and their families to their father-confessor. Romeo fled to Friar Laurence for refuge and for advice; likewise, Juliet comes to him as a refuge from her family's callousness and from what she believes is her Nurse's betrayal.

Note Juliet's self-control here; her strength of character seems to grow with every scene. Certainly she was not expecting to find Paris with the Friar, but she manages to hide her despair from him. Paris is confident and courteous, a gentleman. He addresses Juliet with the familiar "thou" and is genuinely concerned over her grief; he is obviously very fond of her. Juliet, however, addresses him as "sir," and uses the formal "you" while she is talking with him. She detests the idea of marrying him, but she is polite toward him and somewhat ironical, though only we and Friar Laurence understand her double meanings. She confuses Paris when she says of her face, "it is not mine own" (36), but we understand: Her face, like herself, belongs to Romeo.

After the strained, careful exchange by both Juliet and the Friar with Paris, the mood changes. Alone with the Friar, Juliet's tears prelude two long catalogues of Gothic descriptions of death. They are part of the trappings of tragedy, and they exercise our imagination. Now we understand further how Shakespeare has incorporated past scenes and past imagery into this present agony. The Friar, for instance, does not offer his solution to Juliet's problem from sudden impulse or inspiration. When we first saw him, he was carrying a basket for herbs. Yet, until now, this fact has been relatively unimportant, merely the hobby of an old friar. But we recall what he said then: He spoke of "baleful weeds and precious-juiced flowers" (II. iii. 8). One kind of plants that he gathers is evil, one good. What he proposes for Juliet is also compounded of opposites. He will give her the appearance of death so that she may regain life and love. Also earlier, he spoke of the earth "that's nature's mother is her tomb" (II. iii. 9). He will suggest a tomb for Juliet, hoping in effect to make it, figuratively, a womb for her rebirth. "Virtue," he said, "turns vice, being misapplied" (II. iii. 21). He hoped to end the feud by secretly marrying Romeo and Juliet; now he hopes to reunite Juliet with Romeo by giving her the potion. Friar Laurence's intentions are good; he is on the side of love and of peace, yet his goodness, his "virtue," will result in "vice," in the ultimate death of both of the lovers.

In addition to Friar Laurence's earlier speeches, remember that in Act III, Scene 5, Juliet's mother blurted out, "I would the fool were married to her grave" (141). Her hasty wish will soon become true; not only will she see Juliet "dead" of poison, but shortly thereafter she will see her daughter twice dead, finally of a self-inflicted stabbing. Indeed, the subject of death permeates the second half of Scene 1. Juliet says that she would, rather than marry Paris, leap

> From off the battlements of yonder tower,
> Or walk in thievish ways; or bid me lurk
> Where serpents are; chain me with roaring bears,
> Or shut me nightly in a charnel-house,
> O'er-cover'd quite with dead men's rattling bones,
> With reeky shanks and yellow chapless skulls;
> Or bid me go into a new-made grave
> And hide me with a dead man in his shroud,—
>
> (78–85)

Her last two lines are frighteningly prophetic; in a few hours she will be laid out in a "new-made grave" (her own), and she will be near "a dead man in his shroud" (Tybalt). And her earlier prophecy of death being her bridegroom will, in a sense, be enacted. These horrors of the tomb are to be feigned but, tragically, will soon be true.

Dramatic irony abounds in Scene 2. The Capulets are readying for the wedding while Juliet readies herself for her "death." Capulet's character here is consistent—impulsive, hospitable, and hot-tempered, but he is quick to forget his resentment when he has his own way. As for Juliet, she shows remarkable powers of duplicity, but one must remember that it is no longer so difficult for her to appear joyful: Her secret affairs seem to be reaching a solution. Listen to Juliet's speech concerning Paris, for example: "I met the youthful lord at Laurence's cell; / And gave him what becomed love I might, / Not stepping o'er the bounds of modesty" (25–27). To her parents, this seems a simple statement of an encounter between the two; Juliet herself, knowing that she is married to Romeo, means that all her love is Romeo's and that she gave none to the Count.

Juliet's feigned joy is infectious; it would seem that Capulet advances Juliet's wedding day precisely because his daughter seems so happy. And thus fate appears again: Juliet will be "buried alive" twenty-four hours before the Friar's scheduled time.

In Scene 3, Juliet ostensibly asks to be alone so that she may say her prayers, but she says none. Instead, she utters a long nightmarish soliloquy, revealing her fears and uncertainty. It is a set piece, full of verbal extravagance and rhetoric, but it can be justified because it is another of Shakespeare's ingredients for tragedy. Also, it illustrates Juliet's sense of responsibility for what she is doing. The play, after all, has been largely deterministic, but now Juliet is attempting alone to defy fate, which has caused Romeo's banishment, and also her parents, who are forcing her to be hastily married to Paris.

There is irony when Juliet tells the Nurse that she hopes for "the heavens to smile upon [her] state" (4). So far, the heavens (fate) have not been kind; from the beginning she sensed the doom that has shadowed her love for Romeo. She was distressed when she first learned Romeo's name ("My only love, sprung from my only hate!"). In the balcony scene, she cautioned Romeo that Jove laughs at lovers' perjuries; even then the idea of fate toying with their love disturbed her, and, as the play has progressed, her recognition of the role of fate has been increasingly noted.

It is not a "brave" soliloquy that Juliet utters in Scene 3. She does not pray, asking forgiveness from God, and then heroically empty the vial. She is frightened; her youthful imagination conjures up fearsome, Gothic images: her own body cold as death; the possibility of being truly poisoned; suffocating to death; the festering corpse of Tybalt; loathsome smells and hideous, ghostly screams. For a moment, she almost calls the Nurse back. But Juliet no longer needs her Nurse. She is Romeo's wife, and he is the only person she can trust, for, looking at the vial of potion, she questions even the Friar's credibility.

She is hysterical as she swallows the poison. Tybalt's ghost has threatened Romeo, and she panics to hurry to her husband's side. In Scene 1 of this act, she left Friar Laurence's cell crying "Love give me strength!" It is love, love for Romeo, that gives her the strength to finally take the drug.

In contrast to the grotesque images of death and of Juliet's apparent condition of "death," Scene 4 is dominated by life. The humor and the bustling here strengthen the tension of the scenes preceding and following. As Juliet's body grows cold, as her breath slows, and as her blood settles, life quickens in the Capulet house while preparations are made for the wedding. The tempo is brisk. The element of haste, which has run throughout the lovers' courtship and Capulet's decision to marry his daughter to Paris, generates this scene. "Come, stir, stir, stir!" says Capulet, and later, "Make haste, make haste! . . . Make haste! . . . Make haste, I say" (3-27).

The comedy of the short preceding scene continues into Scene 5. The Nurse is still her lusty self (1-11), teasing Juliet, calling her "lamb" and "slug-abed," bawdily suggesting that Juliet will soon be spending quite enough time in bed once she's wedded to Paris. The irony is sharp: Within moments, she will discover Juliet "wedded" and "bedded" with death, and a few moments later, the image will be doubled by Lord Capulet's "death is my son-in-law"; we recall Lady Capulet's angry wish that her daughter might be "married to her grave." Her father once referred to her as carrion when she refused to marry Paris; now the "hopeful lady of [his] earth" seemingly is carrion, about to be reclaimed by the earth that "hath swallowed all my hopes but she." He cries out that he cannot speak; dramatically, this is very effective. When he cursed Tybalt and later when he denounced Juliet, he surged with anger. Death has stilled his usual bombast. Instead of endless lamentation, he says simply, "Death lies on her like untimely frost / Upon the sweetest flower of all the field" (28-29). It is the most beautiful line in the entire scene.

Friar Laurence's consolation is typically that of a friar, or a priest, or a minister: Juliet is not dead; she lives in heaven. He has a difficult part to play, but he does so smoothly and successfully. It must be kept in mind that his purpose is good; he hopes to unite the two warring houses by marrying their children. Perhaps more than anyone else, he sees the error of hate, of haste, and horrendous coincidence; hence, his portentous warning.

ACT V

Summary

Romeo, in Mantua, has just had an ominous dream (which he misinterprets). His servant Balthasar arrives from Verona with the news that Juliet is dead. Romeo, controlling his grief, resolves to return to Verona. He sends Balthasar to hire some horses, then knocks at the door of an apothecary's shop, whom he asks to sell him poison. At first the apothecary refuses to do so since it is against the law to traffic in poison. However, the apothecary is poor and Romeo offers the large sum of forty ducats; thus the apothecary's scruples are overcome, and he gives Romeo the poison.

Friar John, whom Friar Laurence sent to Mantua with a letter to Romeo explaining that Juliet is not really dead, returns to Friar Laurence with the news that he was quarantined in Verona because of the suspicion of plague, and he was therefore unable to deliver the letter. The Friar then hastens toward the Capulet burial vault since Juliet is due to awaken shortly.

The final scene of the play takes place at the Capulets' tomb in the churchyard. Paris is mourning the death of his bride and strews flowers as a memorial to her. His page warns him that someone is coming, and he hides to watch.

Romeo and Balthasar arrive with tools to open the tomb. Romeo pretends that he wants to look one last time upon Juliet and take a ring from her finger. He sends Balthasar with a letter to his father, threatening the servant with violence if he spies upon him. The servant promises to leave, but suspicious of his master's wild looks, he hides to see what will happen.

Paris, seeing Romeo opening the tomb, challenges him, thinking that he is going to desecrate the bodies of his enemies. Paris is killed, and as he dies, he begs Romeo to lay him in the tomb beside Juliet. Romeo, recognizing him and remembering that he was Juliet's suitor, is filled with pity and grants his last request. Then Romeo sees Juliet's body and is overcome by her beauty even in death. In a brief, manly, and beautiful passage, he promises Juliet to remain beside her forever, then without hesitation he drinks the poison, kisses her, and falls by her side.

A moment too late, the Friar comes in. He approaches the tomb, sees the bloody swords at the entrance, and enters to find the bodies of Paris and Romeo. Juliet awakens with a clear mind and memory. She realizes where she is and hopefully asks the Friar, "Where is my Romeo?"

The Friar, desperate, urges her to come with him. There is no time to break the news gently—"thy husband in thy bosom there lies dead; / And Paris too" (155–56). Juliet refuses to leave, and the Friar flees; her last friend has left her. She sees the vial of poison in Romeo's hand and attempts to drink from it, but it is empty. As she hears the sounds of the watchmen approaching, she snatches Romeo's dagger and stabs herself, falling dead beside him.

The prince enters, followed by the Montagues and Capulets. There are numerous questions, during which Montague tells of his wife's sudden death because of her grief over Romeo's banishment. The prince orders the tomb to be sealed up until the matter can be cleared.

Friar Laurence courageously tells his story, accusing himself but telling his reasons for his course of action. He offers his life in expiation. The prince is reasonable: "We still have known thee for a holy man." Balthasar and the page tell their stories, throwing further light upon the night's events. The prince, reading Romeo's letter to his father, finds that it substantiates the Friar's story. Turning upon Montague and the Capulets, he blames their hate and his own leniency in dealing with it. Capulet and Montague make their peace, and each promises to honor the other's loss with a golden statue. The prince closes the play with a mournful couplet: "For never was a story of more woe / Than this of Juliet and her Romeo."

Commentary

Scene 1 begins with another of many ironies in the play. Romeo is in exile, yet he is not sad. He is happy. We do not expect to see him happy in Mantua, yet he is—because he has dreamed of Juliet. Even dreams, he says (describing his dream of Juliet as "love's shadows"), can be "rich in joy." But the shadows of his "love's shadows" are dark, and he fails to perceive this. He dreamed of death, of his own death, yet because Juliet restored him to life with a kiss, the dream does not trouble him. It seems like a good omen. (Something of this sort was exactly what Friar Laurence has planned, only in reverse: Juliet would be awakened by Romeo.) The dream's deadly significance is exposed when Balthasar dashes in and tells Romeo of Juliet's death. Mercutio's earlier remark (I. iv. 51) that "dreamers often lie" is recalled; that is, they lie to themselves. Dreams, Mercutio said, are "begot of nothing but vain fantasy . . . more inconstant than the wind" (I. iv. 98–100). But this idea is not really news to us: When this scene opened, Romeo's mentioning a dream about death had an immediate chilling effect. Our mood darkened; Romeo's joy seemed incongruous. We have just witnessed Juliet's "death"; we heard Friar Laurence's description of how she would appear; we heard Capulet describe her settled blood, her stiff joints, and her coldness; and we listened to the long wailings of the Capulets over Juliet's body. The dramatic effect of Romeo's joy at his dream about death and our antithetical reaction is carefully constructed.

In Scene 1, note that the news of Juliet's death is broken gently. Balthasar says that "her body sleeps." His kindness echoes Friar Laurence's consolation for the Capulets; he consoled them that Juliet lives in heaven; Balthasar says that Juliet lives with the angels. But neither heaven nor the angels consoles Romeo. He shakes his fist at them. In yet his strongest utterance, he cries, "Then I defy you, stars!" (24); we recall how many times before "stars" have been a part of Romeo and Juliet's love. Before Romeo attended the Capulets' ball, he had a strange feeling of some "consequence, yet hanging in the stars"; he described Juliet's eyes as she stood on the balcony as "two of the fairest stars in all the heaven"; and the stars that shined during the consummation of their wedding Romeo called "night's candles." Juliet spoke of Romeo as being cut into tiny, shining stars, yet she and Romeo misread the signs. The stars seemed too often to enhance their love.

Romeo now realizes that he was duped, just as he was by his recent dream of Juliet. He defies the stars and so he defies fate. He defies whatever force in the stars has tried to separate him from Juliet. Remember that he does not know that Juliet's death was, supposedly, suicide. He only knows that she is dead—struck down, most probably by fate. He defied the Capulets and also the Montagues by marrying Juliet secretly; he would be married to her despite the feud between the families. Fate, seemingly, brought them together, and now it has capriciously separated Juliet from him, not merely by exile but by death. It is too great a punishment. He will not be separated from her; he will challenge fate and the stars that seek to separate them. He will join Juliet in death.

Note the change in Romeo after his "I defy you, stars!" He is instantly more worldly and cynical. His defiance has made him bitter and even more impulsive. Balthasar's "Sir, have patience" is futile advice, identical to Friar Laurence's earlier "wisely and slow; they stumble that run fast" (II. iii. 94). Haste and impulsiveness have propelled this tragedy forward: Consider, for example, the impulsive, hasty courtship of the lovers and old Capulet's equally hasty and impulsive arrangement of Juliet's match with Paris.

The swift pace of Scene 1 is heightened by Romeo's macabre description of the apothecary and his shop. The thin body, the heavy brows, and the tattered clothes sound like a grim description of the figure of death. Even the shop, hung with hides and stuffed animals, sounds repulsively like a kind of vault. Add to this grisly picture the fact that the apothecary sells death—poison—to Romeo, and the Gothic horror is complete.

Speaking to the vial, Romeo addresses it as a cordial, ending the scene with a reversal (a reversal began the scene: a dream of love proved to be an omen of death; Juliet revived Romeo from death). This "cordial" (a liquor used to revive) will unite him with Juliet in death. A dream of death began the scene; a dram of death ends it.

Fate, coincidence, and the stars—they have all dealt the lovers yet another blow. Now we realize why Friar Laurence's plans went astray. The reason is at last made clear why Romeo failed to receive Friar Laurence's message. The destinies of the lovers depended on the element of chance; fate denied it to them. Plague was proclaimed and Friar John was quarantined. Friar John's "speed to Mantua . . . was stay'd" (V. ii. 12). The ironies compound. After Romeo's impetuousness, Juliet's haste, old Capulet's speed, and now Romeo's haste to return to Verona, Friar John's "speed" was arrested because of plague (death). Friar Laurence's statement, "Unhappy fortune!" epitomizes the situation. He has woven himself into this web of secrecy. Now he must try to rescue the situation and also Juliet. He must rescue her "living corse" in a "dead man's tomb" (V. ii. 30). Until now the Friar has usually been philosophical, full of good advice and clever intrigue, but now he is at a loss. His deceptions and the role of fate in this tragedy are beginning to overwhelm him.

Appropriately, the final scene is set at night. Romeo and Juliet first met during the night, at the Capulets' ball, the balcony scene was set in the darkness of night, and the consummation of the marriage was during the night. In each of these scenes, the lovers used the background of night, many times, as part of a simile, or another figure of speech, to describe either the moment or their love for one another. Particularly they used the night in conjunction with the contrasting image of light. Romeo first described Juliet as "a rich jewel set in an Ethiope's ear" (I. v. 48), and Juliet described Romeo in terms of stars: " . . . and, when he shall die, / Take him and cut him out in little stars, / And he will make the face of heaven so fine / That all the world will be in love with night" (III. ii. 21–24).

Figuratively, Romeo and Juliet are about to be reunited in this scene: They themselves will be light in darkness, life in death. In Mantua, Romeo vowed to defy fate, and, with Juliet, "I will lie with thee tonight" (V. i. 34). He will reclaim her as his wife even if it must be in death. Together they will lie; the emphasis is on reunion, and, figuratively, there is the connotation of sexual reunion. He will lie physically beside her; he will "die" beside her, as he did the night their marriage was consummated. Note the images of death: Sexually, a man "dies" within a woman; Romeo describes the tomb as being a "womb of death," a "detestable maw," and he dies after drinking poison from a round-lipped cup. The sexual symbols of death he uses to accompany his death are circular, those of a woman. Juliet dies by plunging Romeo's dagger into herself; the image is clearly phallic. Symbolically, they have eternally re-con-summated their marriage.

The sexual symbols surrounding the lovers began early in the play. Already several references have been mentioned alluding to Juliet's "marrying" death or the grave, and, here, Paris speaks of Juliet's tomb as being her bridal bed. In addition, Romeo speaks of the macabre idea of death as bridegroom and lover: "Death is amorous, / And that the lean abhorred monster keeps / Thee here in dark to be his paramour?" (103–105).

The "bride" receives two visitors tonight: the intended bride-groom and also her husband. So thus the confrontation; the situation is very similar to two rivals battling for a lady. They fight in near darkness and battle blindly. Romeo does not know whom he fights, and Paris does not know that he battles Juliet's husband.

Paris asks Romeo, "Can vengeance be pursued further than death?" (55) He speaks of one thing, but if we reflect we realize that, in a sense, Paris' question has other implications. Romeo is reveng-ing himself against fate. Fate would separate him from Juliet, first through banishment, then by death. But if Romeo kills himself, then he rejoins himself with Juliet, and after they are thus reunited, they will be victorious and Romeo will have truly avenged himself. He will have shaken "the yoke of inauspicious stars" (111), the yoke of submission to fate. Fate, however, is wily. Note that Romeo moans that Juliet's beauty appears to be still living; he sees the crimson in her cheeks. This is a clue for us; Juliet is returning to consciousness. When her family discovered her body, her joints were stiff and her blood was "settled." "Life and these lips," Lord Capulet said, "have long been separated" (IV. v. 27). Now Romeo kisses these lips and is pained that they seem so alive. Juliet is about to revive, and if he were not so hasty and impetuous, he and Juliet would be together again—and alive, not dead. The irony of fate is keen. "Sour misfortune," Friar Laurence says on discovering the bodies of Paris and Romeo. But the Friar is, in fact, saved by fate. His letter to Romeo could not save the lovers, but Romeo's letter to his father is able to save the Friar, who, after all, was only trying to bring peace to Verona. Fate again. And it is even fate, or coincidence, again that lights the setting for the discovery of the three deaths. When Romeo first saw Juliet, by chance, he said, "She doth teach the torches to burn bright." Now she is, in a sense, still responsible for making the torches burn bright. Both Paris and Romeo have brought torches for their rendezvous with Juliet, and pointing to the tomb, Paris' boy says to the watchmen, "This is the place; there, where the torch doth burn" (171).

So the tragedy ends, and Old Capulet and Old Montague are reconciled. But the price of peace has been high. No one but the audience fully understands how much was sacrificed. Not just a son and not just a daughter. A bright light, for a brief while, flashed in the midst of a dark, hateful feud. The love of Romeo and Juliet did indeed prove to be, as Juliet said on her balcony, "Too like the lightning, which doth cease to be / Ere one can say 'It lightens'" (II. ii. 119–20). The brief light of Romeo and Juliet's love is dark now; the dark feud has been lightened.

Friar Laurence's attempts to bring peace were thwarted by fate and coincidence; death was the result, but peace was born from that death. The contradictions and paradoxes were sounded by the Friar himself when he spoke of virtue being vice, suggesting that good and evil were but different sides of the same coin. These contradictions, plus the injustice of the lovers being sacrificed for their parents' peace, and the simple, tragic fact that this promise of love was so suddenly aborted—all these are part of this tale of woe. But it is finally not the woe that has made the names of Romeo and Juliet synonymous with love; it is the ecstasy of their young love.

1599

JULIUS CAESAR

JULIUS CAESAR

LIST OF CHARACTERS

Flavius and Marullus

Tribunes who desire to protect the plebians from Caesar's tyranny; they break up a crowd of commoners waiting to witness Caesar's triumph and are "put to silence" during the Feast of Lupercal for removing ornaments from Caesar's statues. (Flavius the tribune and Flavius the soldier, briefly mentioned in Act IV, Scene 3, are not the same.)

Julius Caesar

The emperor of Rome; he is imperious, easily flattered, superstitious, and ambitious to become king of the Roman state. He is assassinated midway through the play; later, his spirit appears to Brutus at Sardis and also at Philippi.

Casca

He appears first as a lackey to Caesar and later as a shrewd, cynical poseur who affects an outwardly boorish appearance in order to obscure his true intents. He joins the conspiracy on the night before the assassination, and he is the first conspirator to stab Caesar.

Calpurnia

The wife of Julius Caesar; she urges him to stay at home on the day of the assassination because of the many unnatural events that have occurred during the previous night and because she has had nightmares about his murder.

Marcus Antonius (Mark Antony)

He appears first as a confidant and a devoted follower of Caesar, and he offers Caesar a crown during the Feast of Lupercal. He has a reputation for sensuous living, but he is a very shrewd contriver and a skilled orator, able to dupe Brutus by appealing to his noble idealism and able to excite the crowd to rebellion during his oration over the body of Caesar. He is one of the triumvirs, and he and Octavius defeat Brutus and Cassius at Philippi.

A Soothsayer

He warns Caesar during the celebration of the Feast of Lupercal to "beware the Ides of March." He again warns Caesar as Caesar enters the Senate House.

Marcus Brutus

A praetor—that is, a judicial magistrate of Rome; he is widely admired for his noble nature. He joins the conspiracy because he genuinely fears that Caesar will become a tyrant, but his idealism causes him to make several poor judgments and impedes his ability to fathom those less scrupulous than himself, most notably Cassius and Antony. He defeats Octavius' forces in the first battle at Philippi, but he loses the second battle and commits suicide rather than be taken prisoner.

Cassius

The brother-in-law of Brutus and an acute judge of human nature; he organizes the conspiracy against Caesar and recruits Brutus by passionate argument and by deviously placed forged letters. He argues that Antony should be assassinated along with Caesar, that Antony should not speak at Caesar's funeral, and that he and Brutus should not fight at Philippi, but he eventually defers to Brutus in each instance. He is defeated by Antony at the first battle of Philippi, and he commits suicide when he mistakenly believes that Brutus has been defeated.

Cicero

A senator and a famous orator of Rome. He is calm and philosophical when he meets the excited Casca during the night of portentous tumult preceding the day of the assassination. The triumvirs have him put to death.

Cinna

The conspirator who urges Cassius to bring "noble" Brutus into the conspiracy; he assists by placing some of Cassius' forged letters where Brutus will discover them.

Lucius

Brutus' young servant; Brutus treats him with understanding, gentleness, and tolerance.

Decius Brutus

The conspirator who persuades Caesar to attend the Senate on the day of the Ides of March by fabricating a flattering interpretation of Calpurnia's portentous dream and by telling Caesar that the Senate intends to crown him king.

Metellus Cimber

The conspirator who attracts Caesar's attention by requesting that his brother's banishment be repealed, allowing the assassins to surround Caesar and thereby giving Casca the opportunity to stab him from behind.

Trebonius

The first of the conspirators to second Brutus' argument that Antony be spared; he lures Antony out of the Senate House so that the other conspirators can kill Caesar without having to fear Antony's intervention. Consequently, he is the only conspirator who does not actually stab Caesar.

Portia

The wife of Brutus and the daughter of Marcus Cato. She argues that those familial relationships make her strong enough to conceal Brutus' secrets, but on the morning of the assassination, she is extremely agitated by the fear that she will reveal what Brutus has told her. She commits suicide when she realizes that her husband's fortunes are doomed.

Caius Ligarius

The final member of the conspiracy during the early morning of the Ides of March; at first, he feigns illness, but later he says that Brutus has cured his sickness and that he will do anything Brutus desires of him.

Publius

An elderly senator who arrives with the conspirators to escort Caesar to the Capitol. He is stunned as he witnesses the assassination. Brutus sends him out to tell the citizens that no one else will be harmed.

Artemidorus

He gives Caesar a letter as the emperor enters the Capitol; in the letter, he lists the conspirators by name and indicates that they intend to kill him, but Caesar does not read the letter.

Popilius Lena

The senator who wishes Cassius well in his "enterprise" as Caesar enters the Senate House. This comment intensifies the dramatic tension in the moments immediately prior to the assassination by causing Cassius and Brutus to fear briefly that they have been betrayed.

Cinna, a Poet

On his way to attend Caesar's funeral, he is caught up in the riot caused by Antony's funeral oration. The mob at first confuses him with Cinna the conspirator, but even after they discover their error, they kill him anyway "for his bad verses."

Octavius Caesar

The adopted son and heir of Julius Caesar; he is one of the triumvirs who rule following the death of Caesar. He and Antony lead the army that defeats Cassius and Brutus at Philippi.

M. Aemilius Lepidus

He joins Antony and Octavius to form the Second Triumvirate

to rule the Roman Empire following the assassination of Caesar. He is weak, and Antony uses him essentially to run errands.

Lucilius

The officer who impersonates Brutus at the second battle at Philippi, he is captured by Antony's soldiers. Antony admires his loyalty to Brutus and thus he protects him, hoping that Lucilius will choose to serve him as loyally as he did Brutus.

Pindarus

At Philippi, he erroneously tells his master Cassius that the scout Titinius has been captured by the enemy when the scout has actually been greeted by the victorious forces of Brutus. Thinking that all is lost, Cassius decides to die; he has Pindarus kill him with the sword that he used to help slay Caesar.

Titinius

An officer in the army commanded by Cassius and Brutus; he guards the tent at Sardis during the argument between the two generals, and he is a scout at Philippi for Cassius. After Cassius commits suicide when he mistakenly believes Titinius to have been taken prisoner by the enemy, Titinius kills himself in emulation of Cassius.

Messala

A soldier serving under Brutus and Cassius; he gives information concerning the proscription of the triumvirs, and he reports Portia's death to Brutus at Sardis. At Philippi, he hears Cassius confess that he believes in portents. Later, he discovers Cassius' body.

Varro and Claudius

Servants of Brutus, they spend the night in his tent at Sardis. Neither of them observes the ghost of Caesar that appears to Brutus.

Young Cato

The son of Marcus Cato, the brother of Portia, the brother-in-law of Brutus, and a soldier in the army commanded by Brutus and

Cassius. He dies during the second battle at Philippi while trying to inspire the army by loudly proclaiming that he is the son of Marcus Cato and that he is still fighting.

Clitus and Dardanius

Servants of Brutus; they refuse their master's request at Philippi to kill him.

Volumnius

A friend of Brutus and a soldier under his command at Philippi. He refuses to hold a sword for Brutus to impale himself on.

Strato

The loyal servant who holds Brutus' sword so that he may commit suicide. Later, he becomes a servant to Octavius.

SUMMARIES AND COMMENTARIES

ACT I

Summary

On a street in ancient Rome, Flavius and Marullus, two tribunes of Rome, accost a group of workmen and ask them to name their trades and to explain their absence from work. The First Commoner answers straightforwardly, but the Second Commoner answers with a spirited string of puns that he is a cobbler and that he and his fellow workmen have gathered to see Caesar and to rejoice in his triumph over Pompey. Marullus accuses the workmen of forgetting that they are desecrating the great Pompey, whose triumphs they once cheered so enthusiastically. He upbraids them for wanting to honor the man who is celebrating a victory in battle over Pompey's sons, and he commands them to return to their homes to ask forgiveness of the gods for their offensive ingratitude. Flavius orders them to assemble all the commoners they can and take them to the banks of the Tiber and fill it with their tears of remorse for the dishonor they have shown Pompey.

Flavius then tells Marullus to assist him in removing the ceremonial decorations that have been placed on public statues in honor of Caesar's triumph. Marullus questions the propriety of doing so on the day during which the Feast of Lupercal is being celebrated, but Flavius says that they must remove the ornaments to prevent Caesar from becoming a godlike tyrant.

Caesar, having entered Rome in triumph, calls to his wife, Calpurnia, and orders her to stand where Mark Antony, about to run in the traditional foot race of the Lupercal, can touch her as he passes. Caesar shares the belief that if a childless woman is touched by one of the holy runners, she will lose her sterility. A soothsayer calls from the crowd warning Caesar to "Beware the Ides of March," but Caesar pays no attention and departs with his attendants, leaving Brutus and Cassius behind.

Cassius begins to probe Brutus about his feelings toward Caesar and the prospect of Caesar's becoming a dictator in Rome. Brutus has clearly been disturbed for some time. Cassius reminds Brutus that Caesar is merely a mortal like them, with ordinary human weaknesses, and he says that he would rather die than see such a man become his master. He reminds Brutus of Brutus' noble ancestry and of the expectations of his fellow Romans that he will serve his country as his ancestors did. Brutus is obviously moved, but he is unsure of what to do.

Several times during their conversation, Cassius and Brutus hear shouts and the sounds of trumpets. Caesar reenters with his attendants and, in passing, remarks to Mark Antony that he feels suspicious of Cassius, who "has a lean and hungry look; / He thinks too much. Such men are dangerous."

As Caesar exits, Brutus and Cassius stop Casca and converse with him. He tells them that Mark Antony offered the crown to Caesar three times, but Caesar rejected it each time and then fell down in an epileptic seizure. The three men agree to think further about the matter, and when Casca and Brutus have gone, Cassius in a brief soliloquy indicates his plans to secure Brutus firmly for the conspiracy that he is planning against Caesar.

That evening, Cicero and Casca meet on a street in Rome. There has been a terrible storm, and Casca describes to Cicero the unnatural phenomena that have occurred: An owl hooted in the marketplace at noon, the sheeted dead rose out of their graves, and so on. Cicero then departs, and Cassius enters. He interprets the supernatural happenings as divine warnings that Caesar threatens to destroy the republic. He urges Casca to work with him in opposing Caesar. When Cinna, another conspirator, joins them, Cassius urges him to throw a message through Brutus' window and to take other steps that will induce Brutus to participate in the plot. The three conspirators, now firmly united in an attempt to unseat Caesar, agree to meet with others of their party—Decius Brutus, Trebonius, and Metellus Cimber—at "Pompey's Porch." They are confidant that they will soon win Brutus to their cause.

Commentary

Scene 1 is important for several reasons. Most important, it establishes the central theme that will dominate the play until the assassination of Caesar; there is a republican nobility of Rome who want to retain senate rule, and the conflict of the play will concern their defiance of a popular dictatorship and its supporters. Thus the play begins during a tense political situation, but for the present, the situation is stable. Caesar is popular. This is demonstrated by the enthusiasm with which the commoners participate in his triumph; but certain nobles within the political establishment are discontented to the extent that they are willing to risk their offices and even their personal safety to protest and to attempt to control the power exercised by Caesar. As tribunes, Marullus and Flavius have the duty to protect the rights of the commoners of Rome, but obviously the commoners see nothing to fear in Caesar and, in fact, willingly and approvingly participate in his triumph even though he is being honored for defeating other Romans rather than foreigners. As a consequence, the tribunes are convinced that they must turn the commoners against the ambitions of Caesar.

The conflict between the tribunes and the commoners is further accented by the manner in which the tribunes and the commoners address each other. The tribunes are from a higher social order, and they refer to the commoners as "creatures," "knaves," "blocks," and "stones," among other insulting terms. The Second Commoner, who cannot openly insult a socially superior official, defends himself against the tribunes' derisive onslaught by resorting to verbal wit to confound the officials and to amuse himself and his friends.

A second major theme in the first scene concerns the fickleness of the common people. They have as much enthusiasm for the man who defeated Pompey and who has more recently defeated

Pompey's sons as they once had for the great Pompey himself, and they are easily persuaded by authority and by appeals to their emotions. Their submission to Flavius and Marullus' demands establishes a precedent for Antony's manipulation of them during Caesar's funeral oration, a manipulation that determines the action for the concluding acts of the play.

The first scene of the play ended with Flavius and Marullus striving to prevent Caesar from becoming a godlike tyrant; Scene 2 begins with Caesar uttering imperial-like commands and receiving the submissive attentions of Casca and Antony. This is Shakespeare's initial purpose for the scene.

Next, and more important, Shakespeare concentrates on delineating three of the principal characters of the play: Caesar, Brutus, and Cassius. The basic characteristics of Caesar appear in a few bold strokes; the characters of Brutus and Cassius are developed more slowly and more thoroughly. In the first twenty-four lines of Scene 2, for example, Shakespeare very economically exposes Caesar to be a vain, superstitious dictator who sees himself as the center of the world; he represents a genuine threat to those who wish to retain republican government and political freedom. Caesar's authority and eminence are stressed in Casca's command for all present to remain silent while Caesar speaks to Calpurnia, and in Antony's response, "When Caesar says 'Do this,' it is performed." It is noteworthy that Brutus is the only person in this brief section who speaks naturally and straightforwardly to Caesar, and the fact that Brutus is the person to repeat the soothsayer's warning to Caesar is one of the first of many ironies that pervade the play.

In Scene 2, Shakespeare also establishes Caesar's vain and superstitious nature. Caesar hopes that Calpurnia may be cured of her sterility by superstition, yet at the same time he shuns the soothsayer's warning, as he will ignore other ominous signs, because his extreme vanity leads him to believe that he is absolutely secure from attack by mere humans. He later reveals to Antony that Cassius is a dangerous man, and by then the audience knows what Cassius is planning for Caesar. Thematically, his firm belief that he is immune to any threat from Cassius will cause him to participate in his own slaughter by successively ignoring the soothsayer, the scheming Cassius, numerous portents, his wife's warnings, along with those of his priests, and Artemidorus' letter. However, Caesar exposes a flaw in his elevated opinion of himself when he reveals his partial deafness. This man who considers himself imperially godlike has physical infirmities; Cassius has already revealed other weaknesses of Caesar, and, of course, the audience at all times knows what will happen to him. Shakespeare's emphasis on Caesar's less admirable traits, then, emphasizes the dangers that Caesar poses to Roman liberty and lends credence to the conspiracy that is forming against him (a credence further substantiated by Flavius' and Marullus' being "put to silence" for opposing him). Yet if only Caesar's admirable qualities were drawn, of which he had many, the audience would not sympathize with Brutus and Cassius.

Caesar, however, is not imperceptive. He correctly evaluates Cassius as a danger to those in power, an evaluation made more ironic and dramatic because only moments earlier Cassius correctly analyzed Caesar's desire to be a godlike tyrant, and Caesar shows himself to be exactly that by having Flavius and Marullus "put to silence."

Antony's brief appearance in Scene 2 does little more than introduce him as an important person in Caesar's government. He is a trusted confidant and friend of Caesar, he respects and recognizes Caesar as head of state, and he is "gamesome," a facet of his character that will contribute to Brutus' fatal misjudgment of him.

Brutus and Cassius are revealed far more thoroughly in this scene than either Caesar or Antony. Very briefly, Brutus is an introspective Stoic who is fond of literature and music, considerate to people from all stations of Roman life, possessed of a congenial home life, and respected for his nobility and his integrity.

Cassius is a man with keen insight, jealous of Caesar, and resentful of the authority that the dictator has usurped. Cassius is also capable of using any available means to reach his desired ends, and he is more concerned with practical matters than with ethics or morality, but he is also able to form an enduring friendship for Brutus in spite of essential differences in their personalities and opinions.

When Cassius first confronts Brutus after Caesar and his entourage have departed to attend the games, Brutus has already seriously considered the matter of Caesar's tyranny, which is one reason why he chooses not to be a part of the worshipful party accompanying Caesar to the festivities. At this time, however,

Brutus has considered the matter only privately; he has told neither his friends nor his wife what he has been pondering, and he specifically tells Cassius that he has been thinking about "Conceptions only proper to myself." The intensity of his introspection becomes evident at the offstage crowd's first flourishes and shouts, when he responds, "I do fear the people / Choose Caesar for their king." His involuntary reaction gives Cassius an opportunity to question him directly and to allow Brutus to state openly his opposition to Caesar's being crowned king.

As he continues to reveal himself and his values more thoroughly, Brutus soon exhibits a deep and sincere commitment to personal honor and nobility. After Cassius extracts from him a clear statement that he does not wish Caesar to be king, Brutus apprehensively asks Cassius to express himself with more clarity. But when Cassius states bluntly that assassination may be the only solution, Brutus wants to hear no more for the present; he wants to consider the question further in private before he commits himself, and for the remainder of the play he will continue to contemplate his participation in the assassination in terms of honor and nobility. His idealism causes him to view with disfavor the intrigues and the manipulations common to the political man; his decisions throughout the play repeatedly point to his political naiveté. Nevertheless, Brutus is sufficiently perceptive and intelligent to recognize Cassius' indirect approach, and he abruptly asks him, "Into what dangers would you lead me," even before he unintentionally reveals his fear of crowning Caesar. Brutus is consistently a slow, deliberate thinker when faced with moral choices, but he has an equally consistent tendency to make quick decisions on important matters involving the conspiracy, both before and after the assassination.

Unlike Brutus, Cassius has no problem separating his feelings toward Caesar the man from his feelings toward Caesar the tyrant, nor does he have any qualms about including others in a private issue, especially the nobility whom he now sees as being subservient to Caesar. But Cassius is more than a man obsessed with a personal hatred for a political superior. He honestly equates personal freedom with personal honor, and he faithfully fulfills his promises to Brutus and the conspiracy; moreover, in the course of events, he changes from being a shrewd, passionate manipulator of Brutus and others and becomes a compassionate, resigned victim of his and

Brutus' failure to plan more carefully and to act more decisively and ruthlessly. In his dialogue with Brutus in this scene, he attacks Caesar on a personal level, which has the effect of accenting his envy and jealousy of Caesar, and he realizes that Caesar hates him in return ("Caesar doth bear me hard"). Nevertheless, Cassius' determination to oppose Caesar is neither entirely envious nor cowardly, and in the last two lines of Scene 2, he realizes that he will either ultimately defeat Caesar or be utterly defeated himself.

To eliminate Caesar, Cassius must have allies, and in order to accumulate allies, he desperately needs the noble and respected Brutus. He values Brutus' dedication to honor, and he is aware that the leading nobles of Rome recognize this quality as well, as Casca and Cinna explicitly attest to in the next scene. To win Brutus over, then, Cassius resorts to all of his powers of persuasion, and in his concluding soliloquy as he stands alone, he lays plans for deceiving Brutus with forged letters, supposedly written by Roman nobles, that will praise Brutus' character and declare a deep fear for Caesar's political ambitions.

One of the key dramatic purposes of this scene, obviously, is to verify Cassius' keen insight into human nature. This is borne out by Cassius' analysis of the vain and tyrannical Caesar, who immediately displays those very features. Cassius is also successful in summing up Caesar's character to Brutus and in assessing and manipulating Casca.

Cassius first demonstrates his sharp insight by the approach he takes to persuade Brutus to conspire against Caesar. He is devious with Brutus from the very beginning of their long conversation. By encouraging the lingering Brutus to attend the games, and by noting his recent lack of friendliness, Cassius elicits Brutus' acknowledgment that he has been engrossed in private thoughts, and Cassius immediately reacts by claiming he has held back some ideas of his own because he feared Brutus was no longer a friend. He then launches into a very complimentary account of the respect that the leading nobles of Rome have for Brutus' merit and nobility. Cassius is aware that Brutus highly values his reputation for honor and nobility; by suggesting that others are very much aware of those admirable traits, Cassius is cleverly courting Brutus' favor. When Brutus shows some apprehension by asking what danger Cassius would lead him into, Cassius expresses the great respect which the public has for Brutus. Cassius also claims himself to be a valid judge because he is a serious, straightforward, modest, and observant man. The offstage flourishes and shouts cause Brutus to broach the subject of Caesar's ambition to be king and to reveal that he also has been concerned with that ambition.

Cassius now senses that he has captured Brutus' attention. Brutus asks Cassius to speak clearly what he has in mind; he will ignore the danger it may entail since "I love / The name of honour more than I fear death." The tone of Brutus' remark indicates that Cassius now has Brutus partly persuaded, but after briefly expressing his love of freedom, Cassius ignores the concept of honor and dwells instead upon Caesar's physical weaknesses.

Since Caesar is not essentially different physically, Cassius argues, why should he and Brutus treat him as the god he desires to be and allow themselves to be ruled by him? He refers to Caesar as the "immortal Caesar," but by emphasizing Caesar's weaknesses, he undercuts his first remark purposely. Caesar, Cassius believes, "is now become a god," and he comments on Caesar's desire to rule with godlike authority. However, he does not blame Caesar for the power he has accumulated, although he does resent it on a very personal level; he blames the weak-willed nobility of Rome. Now, the only way that Caesar can increase his power is to increase his authority over those already under his rule by becoming even more tyrannical, and Cassius has no question about what it will take to remedy the situation. The nobility of Rome have created Caesar; since they cannot rely on such fanciful notions as divine intervention, they must destroy him themselves.

One further matter in Scene 2 has an important thematic bearing on the play. Caesar returns from the ceremonies very angry after Antony had offered him a crown to test the crowd's willingness to accept him as their king. When Caesar rejected it the first time, the crowd, instead of demanding that he accept it, cheered him for refusing it. Yet he and Antony continued their plan to crown him until Caesar's emotions overcame him and he collapsed in an epileptic seizure. Casca never states explicitly that the crowd's reaction is what angers Caesar, but all evidence points to it. Caesar refused the crown as a dramatic gesture only, refusing it less emphatically each time his confidant Antony offered it. When he realized that he would not be symbolically crowned by popular acclaim, he became physically overwrought and collapsed; ironically, the people applauded as though they were observing a theatrical performance (which, in a sense, they were).

With Cassius' final words foreseeing the possibility of "worse days" still echoing in the minds of the audience, Scene 3 opens with thunder and lightning in the background as Casca, who was so self-controlled and cynical in the previous scene, enters a darkened street in Rome and reveals to Cicero that he has witnessed an unusual number of unnatural, ominous events earlier in the night. Casca believes that the gods are intent on destroying Rome for some unknown reason. Cicero, however, believes that such things as Casca describes were only natural; men let themselves be guided by their superstitions and they interpret events to mean whatever they desire. Although the audience might more likely agree with Cicero's rational interpretation, it ironically proves to be incorrect. Shakespeare knows that his audience is aware that Caesar will be killed, and, in addition, he has shown that Caesar himself is superstitious. He prefers dramatic consistency to logical consistency, using the stormy night and the numerous portents of ill omen to build the dramatic tension that is developing on several fronts: The conspiracy must be kept secret to succeed; the possibility exists that Caesar can thwart the plot by interpreting the signs as being intended for him and staying away from the Capitol; Brutus struggles with himself to decide what he should do; Cassius compares the tumult to Caesar's rule; the audience equates it as a danger to Caesar; and the "hundred ghastly women" in Casca's account are representative of the Roman citizens who will eventually be decisive in the events following the assassination.

The portents of this particular night, the night during which the plans for the assassination are being finalized, would unquestionably cause the conspirators to have second thoughts about their venture, and, logically, Casca would probably not join an enterprise that could conceivably be the object of so much divine wrath. But again Shakespeare is willing to risk logic to heighten the dramatic tension that accompanies the danger threatening the superstitious Caesar. In addition, he intentionally confuses chronological time to provide more dramatic impact to the opening of the scene. A month has passed since Scene 2; this is made clear in the following scene, set in Brutus' orchard, which occurs on the same night as this scene.

Basically in Scene 3, Cassius is consistent with the characterization of him which Shakespeare has created. He assesses very
quickly what is frightening Casca, and he professes to believe that
the gods are sending the unnatural portents of nature as warnings
against the unnatural political state of Rome so that he may take
advantage of Casca's superstitious nature. He uses many of the tech-
niques to persuade Casca to join him that he used earlier on Brutus;
with Brutus, he manipulated his honor and nobility, and with Casca,
Cassius uses his fright and superstition. He emphasized to Brutus
his real worth; he interprets for Casca the "true" meaning of the portents. He lets each man first refer to Caesar as a person to be feared,
then he tells each of them that the nobility of Rome are responsible
for Caesar's possessing excessive power. In Scene 2, Cassius revealed the psychology and the approach he would use and, thus,
note here that when Casca offers to join a group seeking redress,
Cassius reveals that he has already formed such a group, and later in
the scene, when Cinna shows a desire to discuss the strange occur-
rences of the night, Cassius quickly shifts the discussion back to the
business of the conspiracy. The reason for this is clear: He has won
Casca and has no further need for duplicity concerning portents.
Throughout the scene, he remains obsessed by his hatred for Caesar
and equally obsessed by a way and a means to assassinate him.

Casca reveals that the next day, the Senate intends to crown
Caesar king of all the Roman dominions "save here in Italy." In a
sense, this removes a prime reason for the conspiracy since the
republican nobles of Rome will not have to endure a king directly.
However, Caesar's attitude toward himself and his position as head
of the Roman government, Antony's and Casca's treatment of him in
Act I, Scene 2, and Caesar's action against Marullus and Flavius
emphasize that he is a potential threat to personal liberty.

ACT II

Summary

Brutus is in his orchard. It is night, and he calls impatiently for
his servant, Lucius, and sends him to light a candle in his study.
When Lucius has gone, Brutus speaks one of the most important
and controversial soliloquies in the play. He says that he has "no personal cause to spurn at" Caesar except "for the general," meaning

that there are general reasons for the public good. Thus far, Caesar has seemingly been as virtuous as any other man, but Brutus fears that after he is "augmented" (crowned), his character will change, for it is in the nature of things that power produces tyranny. He therefore decides to agree to Caesar's assassination: to "think him as a serpent's egg, / Which, hatched, would as his kind, grow mischievous, / And kill him in the shell."

Lucius reenters and gives Brutus a letter which has been thrown into his window. The various conspirators—Cassius, Casca, Decius, Cinna, Metellus Cimber, and Trebonius—now arrive. Cassius proposes that they all seal their compact with an oath, but Brutus objects on the ground that honorable men acting in a just cause need no such bond. When Cassius raises the question of inviting Cicero into the conspiracy, Brutus persuades the conspirators to exclude Cicero from the conspiracy. Cassius then argues that Mark Antony should be killed along with Caesar; Brutus opposes this too as being too bloody a course, and he urges that they be "sacrificers, but not butchers." It is the spirit of Caesar, he asserts, to which they stand opposed, and "in the spirit of men there is no blood."

When the conspirators have departed, Brutus notices that his servant, Lucius, has fallen asleep. At this moment, Portia, his wife, enters, disturbed and concerned by her husband's strange behavior. She demands to know what is troubling him. She asserts her strength and reminds Brutus that because she is Cato's daughter, her quality of mind raises her above ordinary women; she asks to share his burden with him. Deeply impressed by her speech, Brutus promises to tell her what has been troubling him.

Portia leaves, and Lucius is awakened and ushers in Caius Ligarius, who has been sick, but who now declares that to follow Brutus in his noble endeavor, "I here discard my sickness." They set forth together.

Scene 2 is set in Caesar's house during a night of thunder and lightning, and Caesar is commenting on the tumultuous weather and upon his wife Calpurnia's having dreamed of his being murdered. He sends a servant to instruct his "augurers" to perform a sacrifice. Calpurnia enters and implores Caesar not to leave home today. She describes the unnatural phenomena that have brought her to believe in the validity of omens. Caesar replies that no one can alter the plans of the gods and that he will go out. When Calpurnia contends that the heavens proclaim the deaths of princes, not beggars, Caesar contends that the fear of death is senseless since men cannot avoid its inevitability.

The servant returns with information that the priests suggest that Caesar stay at home today since they could not find a heart in the sacrificed beast. Caesar rejects their interpretation, but Calpurnia does finally persuade him to stay at home and have Antony tell the senators that he is sick. Decius then enters, and Caesar decides to send the message by him; Decius asks what reason he is to give to the senators for Caesar's failure to attend today's session, and Caesar says to tell them simply that he "will not come. / That is enough to satisfy the Senate." Privately, however, he admits to Decius that it is because of Calpurnia's dream, in which many "smiling Romans" dipped their hands in blood flowing from a statue of him. Decius, resorting to the flattery to which he knows Caesar is susceptible, reinterprets the dream and says that Calpurnia's dream is symbolic of Caesar's blood reviving Rome; the smiling Romans are seeking distinctive vitality from the great Caesar. When Decius suggests that the Senate will ridicule Caesar for being governed by his wife's dreams, Caesar expresses shame for having been swayed by Calpurnia's foolish fears. He declares that he will go to the Capitol.

Publius and the remaining conspirators, all except Cassius, enter, and Brutus reminds Caesar that it is after eight o'clock. Caesar heartily welcomes Antony, commenting on his habit of partying late into the night. Caesar then prepares to leave and requests that Trebonius "be near me" today to conduct some business. Trebonius consents and in an aside states that he will be closer than Caesar's "best friends" would like for him to be. Caesar says that they should all have some wine and then go to the Capitol together like friends. In a brief aside, Brutus grieves when he realizes that all of Caesar's apparent friends are not true friends.

Artemidorus enters a street near the Capitol reading from a paper that warns Caesar of danger and that names each of the conspirators. He intends to give the letter to Caesar, and he reasons that Caesar may survive if the Fates do not ally themselves with the conspirators.

Portia and Lucius enter the street in front of Brutus' house, and Portia is extremely excited. She suggests that Brutus has told her of his plans (in fact, he has not had an opportunity), and she repeatedly gives Lucius incomplete instructions concerning an errand to the Capitol. She struggles to maintain self-control, and she reacts violently to imagined noises that seem to her to emanate from the Capitol.

A soothsayer enters and says that he is on his way to see Caesar enter the Senate House. Portia inquires if he knows of any plans to harm Caesar, and he answers only that he fears what may happen to Caesar. Then he leaves to seek a place from which he can speak to Caesar. Portia sends Lucius to give her greetings to Brutus and to tell him that she is in good spirits, then to report back immediately to her.

Commentary

In Scene 1, the disturbances in the stormy night sky parallel the internal discord of Brutus. Alone after Lucius leaves, Brutus begins his contemplation of what to do about Caesar with the declaration, "It must be by his death," indicating that he has made up his mind. As his soliloquy proceeds, however, he proves to be far less certain than he would perhaps like to be. His lack of a particular personal grievance against Caesar, combined with Caesar's generally benevolent rule, makes it difficult for him to accept the necessity of assassination, but (perhaps because of what Cassius has said) he fears that the nobles of Rome may give Caesar so much potential power for evil that he will no longer be able to resist the temptation to suppress the rights of Roman citizens, especially the rights of the nobility. For a month now, since Cassius first approached him, Brutus has pondered the danger that Caesar represents to Rome, but he has not reached a conclusion, and he is aware that he must try, at least, to justify the assassination to, besides himself, the public. Thus his reasoning is based wholly, as he admits to himself, on the conjecture that it is human nature to abuse power. As he decides to join the conspiracy, we have the feeling that he does so with a divided heart. One moment he says that Caesar is not a tyrant, and a few minutes later, he promises to correct an unbearable situation by assassinating Caesar. His inconsistency results from his inability to resolve to his own satisfaction the moral propriety of murdering Caesar. He uses "a little kingdom" in rebellion as a metaphor for his mind in conflict with itself, and that metaphor will continue and will be an apt description until the end of the play, when he will claim to have more glory in defeat than Antony and Octavius will have in victory. He is able to suppress his internal conflict momentarily, but he never succeeds in resolving it fully and permanently. However, once he has participated in the assassination, he never expresses remorse for his decision, nor does he express regret for his act.

In Shakespeare's portrait of Brutus, he creates both a public man of affairs in the Roman government and a private man, compassionate for his fellow beings and fond of his wife and home life. His tragedy comes about because the qualities that make him a good man and a good husband are the very qualities that condemn him to failure when he is pitted against Antony, whose decisions are always pragmatic, expedient, and untainted by moral considerations. Brutus' relationships with Lucius and Portia delineate the private man. He envies the peace of mind that allows his servant to relax and to sleep so easily, for he realizes that it is his concern for the world that keeps him from sharing that serenity. Likewise, Brutus' episode with Portia at the conclusion of Scene 1 gives the audience further insight into him as a private man. He cannot put off her questions with simplistic falsehoods; she knows him too well. She is also aware of the value which Brutus associates with honor, and she appeals to his sense of honor while demonstrating her own—by displaying the scars of the self-inflicted wound in her thigh (a symbol of her loyalty to Brutus)—in an effort to learn what has changed him so much that it threatens the well-being of their marriage. Brutus' withdrawal has already begun to disrupt his pleasant home life; shortly, the assassination will destroy the private Brutus, in addition to the public Brutus, as well as the republic that he hopes to protect.

Clearly, Cassius' passionate argument in Act I, Scene 2, and his anonymous notes have influenced Brutus. Upon entering the orchard, Cassius repeated a proven method of approach by referring again to Brutus' "honour," which had been noted by "every noble Roman." Brutus, however, should be aware that the letters can be traced directly to Cassius; in Act I, Scene 2, Cassius asks Brutus, "Can you see your face?" and offers to be the mirror in which he can see his hidden value. In the letter, he urges Brutus to "awake and see thyself!" Cassius also told Brutus, "I had as lief not be as live to be / In awe of such a thing as I myself," and he blames the Roman nobles for allowing Rome to be ruled by one man; in the anonymous letter, he asks, "Shall Rome stand under one man's awe?" Cassius reminds Brutus of his ancestor who drove the Tarquins from Rome; the letter repeats the reference. Unlike Cassius, Brutus cannot look "quite through the deeds of men."

Scene 1 progresses, Brutus' frustration mounts; he clearly cannot resolve his attitude toward the conspiracy. When Lucius informs him that Cassius and some other men are awaiting entry, Brutus comments on the shame associated with the necessity of hiding the "monstrous visage" of conspiracy in "smiles and affability." Nevertheless, after joining the group, he objects to the conspirators' taking an oath of secrecy because they, the "secret Romans," are united by the justice of their cause. In bidding them adieu, he ironically tells them to do the very thing he had minutes before abhorred—that is, to put on false visages by looking "fresh and merrily" and by comporting themselves "as Roman actors do." He overrules Cassius' suggestion that Antony be killed by asking that they "be sacrificers, but not butchers," and by wishing "O that he could . . . come by Caesar's spirit / And not dismember Caesar!" Brutus will continue this ritual theme by having the assassins symbolically bathe in Caesar's blood, but Antony will directly counter this concept of the assassination in Act III, Scene 2, and in Act V, Scene 1; he will treat Caesar's death as foul, as a murder perpetrated by envy in order to incite the citizens of Rome to revolt against the conspirators. Ironically, the spirit of Caesar, even after his death, will remain a potent force in the play, quieted only by Brutus' suicide.

Note that after deciding to join the conspiracy, Brutus becomes somewhat dictatorial. He vetoes the inclusion of Cicero into the group, he limits the objective of the plot (only Caesar is to be killed—not Antony), and he sets the tone for the enterprise by placing the entire undertaking within the context of a religious ceremony.

Concerning the decision not to include Cicero in the plot, Metellus' reasons for wanting to include Cicero are essentially the same as those given by Cassius, Casca, and Cinna for wanting to include Brutus—that is, Cicero will contribute respectability. Brutus' rejection of Cicero is, we gather, personal; seemingly he wants to be the most (and only) highly respected member of the group.

When Metellus suggests that Caius Ligarius be included, Brutus reveals that he has already asked him to be, even before he himself formally joined. Cassius concedes to Brutus' objection to assassinating Antony mainly because he does not want to create discord within the conspiracy now that it is formed, nor does he want to antagonize Brutus. Cassius' first concession to Brutus, leaving Cicero out of the conspiracy, does no apparent harm, but his following series of concessions will contribute directly to the downfall of the republican fortunes.

At the opening of Scene 2, the thunder and lightning remind us of the evil portents, and they prepare us for Caesar's assassination. Caesar himself adds to the ominous signs by referring to Calpurnia's dream and by having his priests sacrifice a beast and "read" its entrails. The dramatic tension is now focused on Caesar and his reaction to the measures that will protect him from the evil signs.

Shakespeare focuses in this scene first on Caesar's vanity and superstition and then on Caesar's sense of inviolability, which is most evident when he says that by facing things he removes their danger. This statement gives a double twist of irony: The audience is aware of the conspiracy, and it also knows that the assassination attempt will succeed. Caesar is both rational and fatalistic when he tells Calpurnia that it is absurd for men to fear inevitable death, but he quickly switches back to a suspicious mysticism when he asks for the results of the sacrifice. Yet he rejects the warning sent by the priests. He attempts to steel his courage by referring to his lack of fear and by boasting that he is more terrible than imagined danger; this is again a suggestion that the plotters may have good reason to fear his growing power and ambition. Caesar steadfastly refuses to accept the possibility that the portents are warnings to him, but when Calpurnia suggests that he can use her fear as an excuse for remaining at home, note that he condescends to her pleadings. He agrees to send a message by their friend Antony. However, his pride will not allow him to humiliate himself to Decius, with whom he has a more formal relationship, and in doing so he becomes an easy prey for the devious Decius, who claims that the conquering warrior should not be driven by fear to lie to elderly senators. Decius appeals to Caesar's vanity and hints that the senators will ridicule Caesar's excuse with laughter. When Caesar then confides that Calpurnia's dream is the true reason why he will not go, Decius interprets the dream in an excessively flattering manner. Decius appeals to Caesar's ambition to be king by feigning deep friendship for Caesar and concern for Caesar's future career. Whereas Cassius lured Brutus into participating in the murder plot by devious means and by appealing to his sense of nobility, and Antony will dupe Brutus into his downfall with outright falsehoods and appeals to his nobility and sense of fair play, Decius dupes Caesar into becoming a victim by falsehoods and by appeals to his vanity. Shakespeare further compares and contrasts Caesar and Brutus by presenting each in scenes of public and private life. Later we shall see Brutus doomed as a public man because he chooses to follow noble and idealistic principles in an environment that recognizes them only to take advantage of them; Caesar is doomed as a public man because he is too confident that he is impervious to harm from mere men.

Mark Antony plays a very small role at the end of Scene 2, but his appearance serves to place him in the chain of events leading up to and following the assassination. Calpurnia's earlier suggestion that Caesar have Antony deliver the false message indicates that he is a close political ally who can be trusted, and Antony's line, "So to noble Caesar," reinforces his respect for Caesar as a man and as a leader. Shakespeare strikes two other themes again at the conclusion of the scene, both of which enhance past and future action and heighten the dramatic tension. Caesar tells Caius Ligarius that he has never been so much an enemy as the sickness "which hath made you lean"; here, the audience should recall that other lean man, Cassius, whom Caesar professes not to fear but who has constructed a conspiracy whose members at this very moment stand in Caesar's presence, waiting to accompany him to his death.

To keep the conspirators' plans on schedule, Brutus reminds Caesar that it is time to go to the Capitol, and Caesar responds with courteous thanks and then suggests that all present drink a toast of friendship. Trebonius speaks a cynical aside, but, in his aside, Brutus grieves that his role requires that he wear a false face. One should compare this remark with his lines in the previous scene, lines 224–28. Brutus continues to experience the inner struggle that has characterized him from the beginning and that will characterize him to the end. He is a moral man about to commit an act that he cannot satisfactorily correlate with his strong sense of morality.

The very brief Scene 3 creates suspense by revealing that word of the conspiracy has leaked out. Artemidorus has very up-to-date information because Brutus joined the conspiracy only moments before three o'clock A.M., less than six hours ago, and Ligarius joined even later. Yet both men are mentioned. The letter constitutes another possible warning to Caesar; it invokes "immortal" Caesar and urges him not to be overconfident, a repetition of Calpurnia's warning.

Artemidorus also represents another side of Roman public opinion toward Caesar. The conspirators have spoken at length of Caesar's potential for evil, Antony has subordinated himself to a powerful superior, Calpurnia has appealed to a vain husband, but Artemidorus is the first person to display admiration for a virtuous Caesar and to view the conspirators as envious usurpers. In addition, Brutus' private deliberations and Cassius' revelations in his soliloquy in Act I, Scene 2, have implied that there is sufficient reason for us to consider that right is not totally on the side of the conspirators. Note also that Brutus' presence in the conspiracy does not cause Artemidorus to think it a noble undertaking.

Although Caesar does not appear in Scene 4, the knowledge that he is nearing the Capitol increases our suspense, and Portia's frenzied activity and anticipation serve to increase that suspense even further. From the time he left his home in the company of Caius Ligarus until this moment, Brutus has not had an occasion to tell Portia his plans. However, Shakespeare is obviously not interested in logical development; he is far more concerned with thematic development and in the creation of dramatic tension. For a moment, Portia fears that the soothsayer is privy to her husband's "enterprise," and although her tension does ease somewhat, the audience knows that Artemidorus is waiting to warn Caesar, that the soothsayer is on his way to warn Caesar again, that today is the Ides of March, and that the plans of the conspirators are now known by some nonparticipants. The primary dramatic concern at the moment involves whether or not Caesar will learn of the conspiracy in time to take defensive action.

Portia prays, "O Brutus, / The heavens speed thee in thine enterprise!" She has not tried to stop him; she is anxious primarily to learn if he has succeeded or failed. She wants to keep her secret thoughts from Lucius, but she never questions the morality of the assassination.

ACT III

Summary

Outside the Capitol, Caesar appears with Antony, Lepidus, and all of the conspirators. He sees the soothsayer and reminds the man that "The Ides of March are come." The soothsayer answers, "Aye, Caesar, but not gone." Artemidorus calls to Caesar, urging him to read the paper containing his warning, but Caesar refuses to read it. Caesar then enters the Capitol, and Popilius Lena whispers to Cassius, "I wish your enterprise to-day may thrive." The rest enter the Capitol, and Trebonius deliberately and discreetly takes Mark Antony offstage so that he will not interfere with the assassination. At this point, Metellus Cimber pleads with Caesar that his brother's banishment be repealed; Caesar refuses, and Brutus, Casca, and the others join in the plea. Their pleadings rise in intensity, and suddenly, from behind, Casca stabs Caesar; as the others also stab Caesar, he falls and dies, saying "Et tu, Bruté!"

While the conspirators attempt to quiet the onlookers, Trebonius enters with the news that Mark Antony has fled home. Then the conspirators all stoop, bathe their hands in Caesar's blood, and brandish their weapons aloft, preparing to walk "waving our red weapons o'er our heads" out into the marketplace, crying "Peace, freedom, and liberty!"

A servant now enters bearing Mark Antony's request that he be permitted to come to them and "be resolved / How Caesar hath deserved to lie in death." Brutus grants the plea and Antony enters. Antony gives a farewell address to the dead body of Caesar; then he pretends a reconciliation with the conspirators, shakes the hand of each of them, and requests permission to make a speech at Caesar's funeral. This Brutus grants him in spite of Cassius' objections.

When the conspirators have departed, Antony begs pardon of Caesar's dead body for his having been "meek and gentle with these butchers." He predicts that "Caesar's spirit, ranging for revenge," will bring civil war and chaos to all of Italy. A servant enters then and says that Octavius Caesar is seven leagues from Rome and that he is coming. Antony tells the young man that he is going into the marketplace to "try, / In my oration, how the people take / The cruel issue of these bloody men." He wants the servant to witness his oration to the people so that he can relate to Octavius how they were affected. The two men exit, carrying the body of Caesar.

Brutus and Cassius enter the Forum, which is thronged with citizens demanding satisfaction. They divide the crowd—Cassius leading off a portion to hear his argument, and Brutus presenting reasons to those remaining behind at the Forum. After he mounts the rostrum, Brutus asks the citizens to contain their emotions until he has finished, to bear in mind that he is honorable, and to use their reason in order to judge him. Brutus says that he loved Caesar more than any man present, that when he killed Caesar, he did not love him less; he "loved Rome more." He asks them what they would prefer to be—slaves, governed by a living Caesar, or free men, freed by Caesar's death? He grieves for Caesar, his dead friend, and he celebrates Caesar's successes and honors his valor, but he says that he was compelled to kill him because of Caesar's tyrannical ambition. He feels that his actions could only offend the ignorant or the unpatriotic, and he asks if anyone is offended. The citizens all respond that they are not offended, and Brutus refers them to documents placed in the Capitol that explain why Caesar's death was necessary. He then brings the crowd's attention to Antony, entering with Caesar's body, and he assures them that Antony was not a part of the conspiracy. He concludes his oration by promising to slay himself when his own death will benefit his country. The crowd emotionally cries out that he should be given honors and made dictator and king. Brutus calms them and instructs them to hear Antony; then he exits to acclamations that they will obey him, that Caesar was a tyrant, and that they will listen attentively to Antony.

Antony begins his oration with the now-famous "Friends, Romans, countrymen, lend me your ears; / I come to bury Caesar, not to praise him." He indicates that, like Brutus, he will deliver a reasoned oration. He refers to Brutus' accusation that Caesar was ambitious, and he acknowledges that he speaks with "honourable" Brutus' permission, but he questions if Caesar's well-known generosity in sharing the spoils of victory with the public and his compassion for the poor are consistent with condemnations of ambition. He also points to Caesar's refusal of the crown three times at the Feast of Lupercal: Is this the act of a man dangerously ambitious? The crowd considers Antony's words, the wrong done Caesar, Caesar's now questionable "ambition," and Antony's sorrow and nobility.

Antony resumes speaking and laments that none of the citizens seems to feel humble enough to honor the mighty Caesar. He professes that he would prefer to wrong Caesar, himself, and even his audience rather than wrong "such honourable men" as Brutus and Cassius by stirring the citizens to riot. He then displays a piece of parchment that he says is Caesar's will, and he claims that the common people would profoundly mourn and search for mementos of their benefactor, Caesar, if they were to hear the contents of the will, but that he does not intend to read the will (he knows, of course, that the crowd will demand that he read it, which they instantly do). Then Antony continues, telling them that Caesar's generosity to them would anger them too much if he were to read the will. They continue to demand that he read it, and he expresses a fear that perhaps he has already said too much; he may have wronged "the honourable men / Whose daggers have stabb'd Caesar." The citizens then denounce the conspirators as murderers, and they demand that Antony read Caesar's will. Antony pretends submission and steps down among them to stand beside the body of Caesar. He lifts Caesar's cloak, points to the wounds in it that were slashed by the knives of the conspirators, and refers to Brutus as Caesar's very dear friend and "angel," whose stab "was the most unkindest cut of all."

Commending the citizens for being moved to tears by the sight of the torn and bloody cloak, he removes it to expose the body itself. The crowd's reaction is, first, one of pity; then they become angry and disperse, uttering cries for revenge. Under the pretense of not wanting to stir them to riot and mutiny, Antony calls them back and suggests that the "honourable" men (the assassins) will no doubt provide acceptable reasons for the assassination. Speaking with supreme irony, he confesses to lacking Brutus' oratorical power, being himself only a "plain blunt man." But, he continues, if he had Brutus' ability to persuade, he would move the very "stones of Rome to rise and mutiny."

Now that the suggestion has been uttered, the mob rushes off wildly to search for the conspirators. One more time Antony calls them back to remind them that they have forgotten Caesar's will. He says that Caesar left seventy-five drachmas to every male Roman citizen, and the crowd praises Caesar's nobility. Caesar also left them his woodlands, walks, and orchards on the Forum side of the Tiber, and Antony inquires when they can expect another ruler like

Caesar. Shouting "Never," they leave to cremate Caesar's body with due reverence, to burn the houses of the assassins, and to wreak general destruction. Antony is content; he muses, "Mischief, thou art afoot, / Take thou what course thou wilt!"

A servant enters then and informs Antony that Octavius has arrived and is with Lepidus at Caesar's house. Antony is pleased and decides to visit him immediately to plan to take advantage of the chaos he has created. The servant reports that Brutus and Cassius have fled Rome, and Antony suspects that they have heard of his rousing the people to madness.

Cinna the poet is on his way to attend Caesar's funeral when he is accosted by a group of riotous citizens who demand to know who he is and where he is going. He tells them that his name is Cinna and his destination is Caesar's funeral. They mistake him, however, for the conspirator Cinna and move to assault him. He pleads that he is Cinna the poet and not Cinna the conspirator, but they reply that they will kill him anyway because of "his bad verses." With Cinna captive, the crowd exits, declaring their intent to burn the houses belonging to Brutus, Cassius, Decius, Casca, and Ligarius.

Commentary

During the opening lines of Scene 1, tension builds rapidly. The soothsayer offers Caesar a verbal warning, and Artemidorus offers him a written warning, but Decius and Cassius intercede to distract him. The suspense peaks when Popilius Lena wishes Cassius success in his enterprise. All this occurs in the first twenty-four lines of the scene. Trebonius escorts Antony from the chamber, and the conspirators are free to stalk and kill Caesar unopposed.

Obviously, the climax of the play occurs in this scene. All the previous action has led to the assassination of Caesar; all the following action results directly from the assassination. However, literary commentators often disagree about the specific location of the climax. Some believe that the action of the play shifts with the actual murder; some believe it occurs when Antony reenters the Capitol, planning revenge; still others believe that it occurs when Brutus agrees to allow Antony to speak at Caesar's funeral. In any event, however, Caesar's death is the major event in the play.

So far the play has not been characterized by extensive physical movement, but the action leading up to the assassination is deliberate and dramatic. The conspirators group together, then disperse a bit to supplicate Caesar on the pretense of gaining a repeal for Publius Cimber, but in reality they wish to gain better access to his person. When Caesar once more displays his imperial arrogance and puts off reading Artemidorus' letter with a great show of sham humility, Metellus and Cassius almost parody his vain manner in their exaggerated abasement as they kneel before him. Even Brutus, although he keeps his appeal on a more reasonable level, kisses Caesar's hand and kneels. The conspirators' subservient entreaties lead Caesar to make his most exaggerated statements regarding his concept of his superiority to the men who now literally surround him. In his own opinion, he is not an ordinary man, and thus he will not be moved by "couchings," "lowly courtesies," "low-crooked court'sies," "base spaniel-fawning," or "prayers." He boasts to being the most resolute of living men, as "constant as the North Star." Then, as Cinna and Decius prepare to add their requests, crouched in feigned servility, Caesar rises to his most imperious extremity and compares himself to the Olympian gods; he points to the futility of the noble Brutus' humble entreaty. With extremely dramatic irony, Casca fatally strikes this "god" from behind.

Immediately following the assassination, the conspirators try to calm the frightened spectators by proclaiming that they, the conspirators, have acted in order to end tyranny, to restore freedom, and to punish Caesar for his ambition. From this point on, Brutus' position as the recognized leader of the conspiracy (and the single man with whom Antony must deal) becomes increasingly evident. He becomes the leader because of the respect that the other conspirators have shown him, because he actively took charge the night before, and because he has been, as it were, the guiding voice of the conspiracy.

Cassius shows a gentleness and a concern for his fellow man not seen before when he moves to protect Publius against possible false incrimination. For the remainder of the play, he will remain a shrewd thinker and an expedient soldier and planner, but he will continue to yield to Brutus. However, he will do so because he is motivated by a deepening friendship and by a sense of despair rather than by a desire to manipulate and deceive.

Mark Antony assumes a role of major importance in the play with the message he sends to Brutus. His servant kneels and then prostrates himself before Brutus in what Antony will reveal in Act V, Scene 1, to be a parody of the conspirators' exaggerated and false servility before Caesar even as they prepared to strike him dead. Cassius knew earlier that the most promising approach to take with Brutus was to appeal to his sense of honor and nobility, and now Antony sends word that while he honored and loved Caesar, he also feared him, a statement clearly designed to prompt Brutus to consider Antony a kindred spirit who has weighed Caesar's positive qualities against his potential for evil. Antony asks Brutus to promise two things: first, a safe passage for him to visit the Capitol, and second, an explanation of why Caesar was assassinated. Antony knows, as the audience knows, that Brutus will keep his word, but to insure that his request will be more palatable to Brutus, Antony insinuates that he desires to join the conspirators in establishing a new government.

Brutus welcomes Antony's offer and promises both a safe passage and a satisfactory explanation. Confident that Brutus will not revoke a personal pledge, Antony is now free to try to attain his real objective: an opportunity to speak at Caesar's funeral. Consequently, his statements are influenced by a genuine sorrow for the death of his friend and patron, Caesar, by the knowledge that Brutus is vulnerable to requests couched in terms of nobility and honor, and by the knowledge that he must not make his desire to speak to the people too obvious.

Concentrating solely on convincing Brutus that he offers no threat to him, Antony salutes the body of Caesar, knowing that it will be manifestly hypocritical not to do so; he refers to the conspirators as "gentlemen," further implying that he has no covert motive in appearing before them, and he states his willingness to be slain in the presence of his dead friend, knowing also that Brutus is too honorable to deny his promise of safety for Antony. Having elicited from Brutus additional assurances that he will be safe and that he will be given explanations, Antony shakes hands with each conspirator and raises a subject which he knows that each of the men must be concerned about. Because of Antony's well-known friendship with Caesar, his overt friendliness with the conspirators must, of necessity, now appear to be either calculated duplicity or cowardice, and he puns on his delicate situation and the bloody surroundings when he says that he "now stands on slippery grounds."

Cassius, not wholly believing Antony's display of "noble" sentiments, makes a straightforward request that Antony make his intentions absolutely clear, but Antony refuses to be dictated to by
Cassius' demands when he knows that Brutus is the real authority
present. Thus he appeals to Brutus' sense of nobility again by claiming that the sight of Caesar's corpse has overcome his reason and by
repeating that all he desires is an explanation. When Brutus promises that their reasons will satisfy Antony if he were Caesar's very
own son, Antony senses that the time is right for him to make a decisive act. He asks, as though it were an insignificant request, if he
may speak at Caesar's funeral. He plays his role to perfection, and
he secures Brutus' agreement, contingent upon Antony's speaking
second and promising not to blame the conspirators.

Brutus then asks them all to remain calm, and he rebukes
Metellus' suggestion that the conspirators remain defensively clus-
tered. He naively but firmly believes that the others are guided by
the same idealistic principles that he follows, and that reason exerts
a stronger influence upon men than emotion. As a result, his confidence that he has acted honorably leads him to believe that the populace will accept without question his reasons for the assassination
as being valid. When he gives Antony permission to speak, he sees
no overt danger because he believes that the crowd will interpret
the conspirators' permission for Antony to speak as further proof
that they can be trusted. Furthermore, Brutus believes that Antony
will keep his word, and he believes that by speaking first himself,
before Antony, he will be able to calm the crowd completely with
convincing reasons.

Brutus, almost from the first, has attempted to view Caesar's
assassination as a ritual, one in which he carved Caesar "as a dish fit
for the gods," and he tells Antony that he will provide him with justi-
fying reasons "or else were this a savage spectacle." Antony perceives the murder precisely as a "savage spectacle" of cold-blooded
murder. He sees another view of Brutus' ritualistic conception; to
Antony, Caesar was a noble deer slaughtered by hounds and bloody
hunters. Brutus wished to "come by Caesar's spirit" without killing
the man himself, but he could not do that, so he tried the next best
thing and tried to reduce the murder to symbol and ritual in order to
fit his idealistic view of the world. Ironically, he released Caesar's
"spirit," and this "spirit" becomes a significant and dramatic force in

the second half of the play. Caesar's "spirit" is now embodied within Antony, who will ruthlessly seek to revenge Caesar's death, ironically, by forcefully imposing another dictatorial order. Accordingly, Antony now unhesitatingly agrees to Brutus' stipulation that he not speak ill of the conspirators. And in his oration he will mockingly keep his word—that is, for a time, he will keep his word before openly reneging on his promise. He thoroughly dupes Brutus, who is clearly not the man to rule Rome in these turbulent and unscrupulous times.

Antony, who knows that Brutus is not a cunning man, has directed his attention to him rather than to Cassius, who clearly knows that Antony is a "shrewd contriver" who will make trouble if he is allowed to live. Before Antony arrives back at the Capitol, Brutus declares that Antony will be a friend, but Cassius emphatically repeats his fear of Antony. On two occasions, Cassius tries to appeal to Antony's ambition by offering him a voice in forming a new government, but on both occasions Brutus returns the discussion to the subject of merely providing Antony with a satisfying explanation, thereby relieving Antony from having to answer Cassius specifically. When Brutus agrees to let Antony speak at Caesar's funeral, Cassius tells Brutus, "You do not know what you do!" His appeals are in vain, and Antony reveals in his soliloquy what he intends to do with the opportunity which Brutus has given him. The downfall of the conspirators has begun.

Antony plays his role with dexterity but also with considerable effort; in his soliloquy, he releases his pent-up emotion in a torrent of invective, expressing his deep hatred, his desire for revenge, and his intent to create political chaos throughout Italy. He refers to the assassins as "these butchers," not as the "gentlemen" he mockingly called them earlier. He will not be satisfied with simple revenge on the murderers; only with the creation of "domestic fury and fierce civil strife" will he be satisfied, and Antony is willing to use all of the Roman world as a tool to gain power.

Chronologically, Scene 2, at the Forum, immediately follows the scene in the Capitol, and it is as powerful as any scene in the works of Shakespeare, or, for that matter, in all of dramatic literature. Antony's oration is a masterpiece of irony and crowd manipulation; he is able to persuade a crowd who is worshipful of Brutus and hostile toward Caesar to rebel against Brutus and revere Caesar. It is a

masterful scene, basically constructed around the differences between Antony and Brutus: Brutus defends the assassination, and
Antony attacks it; Brutus relies on reason, and Antony relies on the
demagogue's appeal to emotions; Brutus fails to establish order, and
Antony successfully creates a riotous mob and political chaos.

Brutus asks the crowd to be patient and not to interrupt him
until the end of his speech. He wants to inform them, not to
harangue or excite them; he believes that they will rationally and
logically conclude that Caesar's death was necessary to preserve the
republic. He mistakenly believes that everyone respects reason as
much as he, and that reason is the most powerful tool at the command of the orator. He speaks wholly in prose, in carefully balanced
and parallel statements; for example, he says, "Hear me for my
cause, and be silent, that you may hear. Believe me for mine honour,
and have respect for mine honour, that you may believe." In referring to his close friendship for Caesar, he maintains that a living
Caesar would have meant that all other Romans would have been
slaves. He willingly admits that Caesar possessed many virtues, but
he is convinced that Caesar's single, major flaw—his excessive
ambition—outweighed all his virtues. Assassination was the only
way to curb Caesar's ambition.

Brutus then refers them to documents that he has filed in the
Capitol, and the crowd calls for him to be crowned king. Here, especially, Brutus' lack of insight into human nature is obvious. He fails
to realize that the crowd has reacted not with reason but with excessive emotion to his words, to his speech which he specifically constructed to appeal to their sense of reason. He does not see the irony
in their responding to his discourse on the evils of tyranny by asking
him to become the new tyrant. And when Antony enters with Caesar's body, Brutus should realize that the people at the Forum are not
capable of accepting the responsibilities of self-rule, that they are
subject to being swayed by anyone who appeals to their emotions.

Antony, in contrast, knows that the crowd is incapable of acting
reasonably, and he relies specifically on that very inability as he
manipulates their emotions, concentrating increasingly on their
mounting passion. Note that when he first begins to speak, the
crowd is clamoring so loudly in appreciation of Brutus that he
cannot make himself heard. Acknowledging that he speaks with
Brutus' permission, he quickly focuses on Brutus' prime reason

for killing Caesar, but he qualifies Brutus' claim of excessive ambition with the innocuous-sounding phrase, "if it were so." Then he directly attacks the argument that Caesar was ambitious by referring to Caesar's generosity in sharing the spoils of war with the citizens of Rome and by pointing out that Caesar always showed compassion for the poor. Antony knows that this crowd is emotional, and his statement that "ambition should be made of sterner stuff" is a direct effort to implant in the minds of the individuals a tie to a Caesar who was not ashamed to display his emotions.

He next recalls for them Caesar's rejecting the crown at Lupercal three times, proving that he was not excessively ambitious. Yet one should remember that Antony himself was a central figure in that episode; he is aware of the duplicity that Caesar was utilizing when he only acted as if he did not want the crown. Although Antony accuses the crowd of having lost its reason in its refusal to mourn Caesar, he is intentionally leading them away from a rational consideration of the explanation which Brutus has given them. His distortions of facts and his emotional display of grief over Caesar's body succeed in gaining their sympathetic attention. The crowd begins to ponder the possibility that Caesar may have been wronged.

Antony then utilizes a variety of oratorical devices to bring the crowd to act as he desires—that is, he pretends to turn them away from "mutiny and rage" while methodically leading them to riot. After having shown that the assassins committed a deed that should be considered dishonorable, he says he would rather wrong himself, and them, and even Caesar rather than wrong the "honourable" conspirators. He brings each individual into personal participation by informing them that each of them stands to profit from Caesar's legacies now that he is dead. His direct appeal to greed brings about the response he has worked and hoped for, and the crowd abandons its relatively calm laments and praise to clamor furiously to hear the contents of the will.

From the moment that they first shout for the will, Antony even more deliberately manipulates their emotions; he brings them repeatedly to the point of angry outbreak by mentioning "the honourable men / Whose daggers have stabb'd Caesar," and he claims that if he had Brutus' power to persuade, he would bring them "to rise and mutiny." Finally, he has the crowd totally under his control, and he treats them with even more sarcasm and contempt in his determination to call every emotion possible into play before he releases them.

When he is finished, they will be no longer a crowd; they will have become a mob, enraged to riot. Thus he mentions the will again and again, yet he asks at line 161, "You will compel me, then, to read the will?"; he implies that he is at their mercy when in reality they are totally in his control. In line 173 and several lines following, he lowers the death of Caesar from high-minded political assassination to foul, envious murder, thereby again involving the individuals as citizens wrongly deprived of their beloved leader by cowardly traitors. Yet all the while that Antony brings the crowd to its highly emotional state, note that he does not ignore Brutus' reasons; he very carefully refutes them with half-truths, pathetic appeals, and open falsehoods. As a climax, Antony reads the will and releases the mob to seek out the conspirators and to destroy whatever order remains in Rome.

As the mob runs off, Antony says in an aside, "Now let it work. Mischief, thou art afoot, / Take thou then what course thou wilt." Antony, however, will not let things stand to chance. He will meet with Octavius to plan how to take advantage of the turmoil he has deliberately instigated to create the "domestic fury and fierce civil strife" he referred to in his soliloquy ending Act III, Scene 1.

Scene 3 dramatically demonstrates the effects of Antony's turning the shallow-thinking, emotional crowd into an angry, hysterical mob bent on mass destruction to satisfy its fury. The scene confirms his success in having created civil strife so terrible that his prediction in Scene 1 of this act, lines 265–68, has come true:

> Blood and destruction shall be so in use
> And dreadful objects so familiar
> That mothers shall but smile when they behold
> Their infants quartered with the hands of
>   war.

The completely irrational mob will not be deterred from its lust for blood by learning that Cinna the poet is innocent of any complicity in Caesar's murder, but its actions are consistent with what has just occurred because of Antony's brilliant oratorical pyrotechnics. Although these are essentially the same people that appeared in the opening scene as individually distinguishable commoners, Shakespeare has carefully shown that they have become a murderous mob. They submitted to Flavius and Marullus in Act I, Scene 1, without resistance; Antony and Caesar duped them in Act I, Scene 2; and their transformation from individuals to a mob was the central concern of Act II, Scene 2, in which Brutus unintentionally and Antony with the most deliberate intent aroused their emotions and turned them into this disordered chaotic rabble.

Scene 3 also continues some other important themes of the play. For example, Cinna's revelation of his dream and his strange presentiments recall the numerous portents that preceded Caesar's death, and they carry a foreshadowing of further violence and personal tragedy. Brutus and the conspirators intended to remove a tyrant, but instead they gave Antony an opportunity to turn a republican government into an unruly mob.

ACT IV

Summary

After they have formed the Second Triumvirate, Antony, Octavius, and Lepidus meet in Rome to decide which Romans shall live and which shall die. Lepidus agrees to the death of his brother, and Antony agrees to the death of a nephew. Antony then sends Lepidus to get Caesar's will so that they can reduce some of the bequests. After he exits, Antony tells Octavius that Lepidus may be fit to run errands but that he is not fit to rule one-third of the world; after they are through using him, they will assume the power he temporarily enjoys. Octavius does not want to argue with Antony, but he recognizes Lepidus to be a proven, brave soldier. Antony answers that his horse also has those qualities; therefore, Lepidus will be trained and used. Antony and Octavius then agree that they must make immediate plans to combat the army being organized by Brutus and Cassius.

Outside of his tent at a camp near Sardis, Brutus greets Titinius and Pindarus, who bring him word that Cassius is approaching. Brutus complains that Cassius has offended him, and he looks forward to hearing Cassius' explanation. Pindarus, Cassius' servant, is certain that the explanation will satisfy Brutus. Lucilius says that Cassius has received him with proper protocol, but he qualifies his statement, adding that Cassius' greeting was not with his accustomed affection. Brutus says that Lucilius has just described a cooling friendship, and he suggests that Cassius may fail them when put to the test. Cassius arrives then with most of his army and immediately accuses Brutus of having wronged him. Brutus responds that he would not wrong a friend and suggests that they converse inside his tent so that "both our armies" will not see them quarreling. The two men then order their subordinates to lead off the armies, to guard their privacy, and they all exit.

As soon as the two men are within the tent, Cassius accuses Brutus of having wronged him by condemning Lucius Pella for taking bribes from the Sardians in spite of Cassius' letters in his defense. Brutus replies that Cassius should not have written defending such a cause, and he charges him with having an "itching palm"—that is, Cassius has been selling offices. Brutus reminds Cassius that it was for the sake of justice that they killed Caesar, and he says strongly that he would "rather be a dog and bay the moon" than be a Roman who would sell his honor for money. The quarrel grows in intensity as Cassius threatens Brutus, but Brutus ignores his threats. He reminds Cassius of his failure to send sums of gold that Brutus had requested for his troops. Cassius denies this and laments that his friend no longer loves him; he invites Brutus to kill him. Finally the two men are reconciled, and they grasp one another's hands in renewed friendship.

Brutus and Cassius drink together as Titinius and Messala join them. From the conversation that follows, we learn that Octavius Caesar and Mark Antony are marching with their armies toward Philippi and that they "have put to death an hundred senators," including Cicero. Messala also reports the death of Portia, but Brutus stoically gives no indication that he already knows of her suicide. He proposes that they march toward Philippi to meet the enemy at once. Cassius disagrees, maintaining that it would be better to wait for the enemy to come to them. This strategy would weary the enemy forces while their own men remain fresh. Brutus persists, however, and Cassius at last gives in to him.

When his guests have departed, Brutus tells his servant, Lucius, to call some of his men to sleep with him in his tent. Varro and Claudius enter and offer to stand watch while Brutus sleeps, but he urges them to lie down and sleep as well. Brutus then asks Lucius to play some music. Lucius sings briefly, then falls asleep. Brutus resumes reading a book he has begun, but he is suddenly interrupted by the entry of Caesar's ghost. Brutus asks the ghost if it is "some god, some angel, or some devil," and it says that it is "thy evil spirit." It has appeared only to say that they will meet again at Philippi. The ghost then disappears, whereupon Brutus calls to Lucius, Varro, and Claudius, all of whom he accuses of crying out in their sleep. They all swear that they have seen nothing and that they have heard nothing.

Commentary

The previous scene showed how the mindless mob was driven to violence in the streets. In contrast, Act IV, Scene 1 is quiet as Antony craftily prepares his next strategy; here we see how the new triumvirs are using their violently gained power, how they plan to maintain power, and we can compare these triumvirs with the conspirators—especially by comparing Antony and Brutus.

Brutus and his colleagues tried to keep their plot contained; they decided against slaying Antony to enhance their own safety, and they made no basic plans for the period following the assassination. Conversely, the triumvirs intend to seize power by force and to eliminate everyone who even might be an enemy. Lepidus' consenting to his brother's death and Antony's agreeing to have his nephew killed signify the extent to which these men are willing to ignore ethical and moral considerations in their concentration on political practicality and expedience.

After sending Lepidus to get Caesar's will, Antony refers to him as a "slight" man of little merit and outlines his plan to use Lepidus only so long as he is an asset; then he plans to usurp his power and turn him out. He readily agrees with Octavius that Lepidus is a "tried and valiant soldier," but in his ambition to increase his rule from one-third to one-half of the territory controlled by Rome, Antony does not intend to let his admiration for Lepidus' positive qualities interfere with his taking advantage of Lepidus' weaknesses. Remember that Antony used the mob to serve his own ends— that is, he showed no consideration for them as fellow human beings. Now he intends to deny them all that he can of Caesar's legacy. They have served his purpose and can be dealt with differently now, and he is ready to use Lepidus in a like manner.

Octavius, however, is a part of the Roman political establishment; he is a man of independent ideas and volition, and he does not hesitate to disagree with Antony, although he avoids divisive argument. Yet in his own way, he is just as ruthless as Antony, and he observes carefully all those who "act" friendly to the triumvirs. Both men are exceedingly wary and power hungry. The scene ends with their drawing up plans to meet the armies of Cassius and Brutus. That impending conflict will dominate the remainder of the play.

Scene 1 ended with Antony and Octavius planning a military campaign; now Scene 2 focuses on a sharp division that has developed between Brutus and Cassius, the men who are the objects of the triumvirs' plans. From this point until the end of the play, Brutus and Cassius are the only conspirators who figure in the action (Antony briefly mentions Casca in Act V, Scene 1), and their declining fortunes are matched in counterpoint by the rising fortunes of Antony and Octavius. The opening martial sounds and commands set the scene clearly in a military camp, and Brutus, who has fundamentally failed in the political arena, will face his next test on the battlefield.

Brutus and Cassius have had a very serious argument, and their conflict has endured long enough to threaten their friendship and the morale of their armies. Hearing Lucilius' report of Cassius' overly formal, cool greeting, Brutus reacts as the Stoic that he is, philosophically discoursing on the decline of friendship. Conjecturing on the larger significance of Cassius' "enforced ceremony," Brutus predicts that he will fail to be a gallant soldier, and he suggests that he may even have become docile. When Cassius enters, however, he is anything but calm, and he accuses Brutus of affecting a calm demeanor to hide unjust and unfair actions. The men agree to discuss their differences in private, and they exit to continue their argument.

Scene 3, in Brutus' tent, consists of three rather distinct divisions: the argument and reconciliation that lasts until the entry of the poet at line 124; the discussion leading to the decision to move the armies to Philippi, which ends when Cassius, Titinius, and Messala leave the tent at line 238; and Brutus' confrontation with the ghost of Caesar at the conclusion of the scene.

Brutus' interior conflict of conscience continues unabated during his long argument with Cassius, but he remains firmly committed to the course of action he has undertaken. Cassius has raised money to support their armies using methods not compatible with

Brutus' sense of honesty. Brutus is disturbed because he fears that the conspiracy has become corrupt, perhaps even more corrupt than the tyrant they hoped to replace. For the first time, Brutus implies that one of the reasons for the assassination was Caesar's dishonesty: "Did not great Julius bleed for justice sake? / . . . But for supporting robbers"? He condemns Cassius for filling important positions with the highest bidders rather than filling the positions with the most capable and noble men available.

The basic personality differences between Cassius and Brutus that have been developed in the previous scenes of the play constitute the essential reasons for their argument. Brutus is noble and moral, and he strives to remain true to his principles in a situation that calls for more unscrupulous resources if he and Cassius hope to succeed. Cassius, on the other hand, realizes that his very life is dependent upon the success of his enterprise. He has stated many times that he will commit suicide before he will submit to tyranny, and he is willing to place survival first. He does not hesitate to gather money to finance his and Brutus' armies by plunder, crippling taxation, bribes, and selling commissions. He would argue that the times are too desperate for them to adhere to strict moral and ethical standards in all instances.

The two men's lack of mutual understanding and the personal level of their argument are perhaps most evident in their disagreement over Cassius' claim to being the "abler" soldier. Cassius intends to imply that he has had more experience in military service and is therefore better able to manage affairs than Brutus, a praetor. Brutus interprets Cassius' remark as meaning that a better soldier in battle, by definition, implies a better leader in general. Thus, their fundamental differences of personality and principles lead them finally to argue about very petty things, especially considering the seriousness of what they have ultimately at stake.

In Scene 3, note that despite Brutus' basic nobility, Shakespeare reveals that Brutus is often unable to think matters through to their logical conclusions. He apparently does not realize that by accepting what he considers ill-gotten funds, he unavoidably becomes a participant in the methods used to obtain them. As a consequence, he does not always see beyond the immediate effects of his actions. Brutus' "flaw" is idealistic naiveté. Earlier, he should have realized that Antony would have to die along with Caesar if the goals of the conspiracy were to be realized; he failed to comprehend that Antony was a "shrewd contriver," a man not to be trusted to keep his word when provided with a political forum. Now he fails to realize that he will play into Antony's and Octavius' hands if he moves his republican armies to Philippi. His very admirable commitments to moral and ethical behavior and his belief that other men are guided by like principles doom him in his struggle for survival against forces guided by those who are pragmatic and expedient. Cassius, more attuned to the real world he inhabits, is doomed because of his alliance with Brutus.

In the long argument opening Scene 3, Shakespeare shows us Brutus the private man acting under the influence of an anger caused by the frustration of being forced to compromise his principles and intensified by his having learned of Portia's suicide. He shows us Brutus the public man responding with proper Stoic fortitude when Messala reveals Portia's death to him. Shakespeare further compares Brutus the public man to Antony. Brutus and the conspirators chose to limit their violence to Caesar alone in an effort to keep their enterprise on as idealistic a level as possible; Antony and his colleagues have murdered scores of senators in their efforts to raise money from confiscated estates and to eliminate all potential enemies to their rule. After Cassius, Titinius, and Messala leave his tent, Brutus is able to relax briefly in the company of music, literature, and his servant, Lucius. He even becomes sentimental over Lucius, telling the boy, "If I do live, / I will be good to thee." Portia is dead, the triumvirs have him at bay, and thus Brutus laments his lost tranquillity while observing the young, innocent, loyal boy. At this moment, the tragedy of Brutus' situation is most poignant. The man so well qualified to lead a satisfying, noble private life has chosen to engage in a public life in which his greatest virtues are also his greatest handicaps.

The appearance of Caesar's ghost brings to the fore the irony of Brutus' desire to "come by Caesar's spirit, / And not dismember Caesar" (II. i. 169–70). The conspirators have killed the corporeal Caesar, but in so doing, they have freed a "spirit" of evil and destruction far more terrible than the living dictator.

ACT V

Summary

On·the plain of Philippi, Octavius and Antony with their forces await Brutus, Cassius, and their forces. A messenger arrives and warns them that the enemy is approaching. Antony orders Octavius to take the left side of the field, but Octavius insists upon taking the right and Antony taking the left.

Brutus, Cassius, and their followers enter, and the opposing generals confront one another in parley. The two sides immediately hurl insults at one another. Antony accuses Brutus of hypocrisy in the assassination, and he derides the conspirators for the cowardly way that they killed Caesar. Cassius accuses Antony of using deceit in his meeting with the conspirators following the assassination, and he reminds Brutus that they would not have to endure Antony's offensive language now had he died alongside Caesar. Octavius suggests that they cease talking and begin fighting, and he boasts that he will not sheath his sword until he has either revenged Caesar or has been killed himself by traitors. Brutus denies being a traitor. Cassius calls Octavius a "peevish schoolboy" and Antony a "masker and a reveller." Antony responds that Cassius is "Old Cassius still," and Octavius challenges Brutus and Cassius to fight now or whenever they muster the courage. Octavius, Antony, and their armies exit.

During the early course of the battle at Philippi, Brutus sends Messala with a message, urging Cassius to engage the enemy forces at once. Brutus believes that the forces under Octavius, which are positioned before him, are currently unspirited and vulnerable to attack.

On another part of the field, Cassius sees his men retreating; Brutus' forces, having driven back those of Octavius, are foraging about the battlefield for spoils, leaving Antony's army free to encircle Cassius' troops. Thus he sends Titinius to ride toward the soldiers he sees in the distance and determine who they are, and he asks Pindarus to mount the hill and watch Titinius. When Pindarus reports that he saw Titinius alight from his horse among soldiers who were shouting with joy, Cassius mistakenly concludes that Titinius has been taken prisoner by the enemy. He asks Pindarus to keep his oath of obedience and to stab him. Pindarus does so, and

Cassius dies, saying "Caesar, thou art revenged, / Even with the sword that killed thee."

Titinius was not captured at all but hailed by some of Brutus' troops when he arrived on horseback. He now enters with Messala, hoping to comfort Cassius with the news that Octavius' men have been overthrown by Brutus. They find Cassius' dead body. While Messala goes to report his tragic discovery to Brutus, Titinius kills himself with Cassius' sword.

Brutus comes onstage with Messala, Young Cato, Strato, Volumnius, and Lucilius and finds the bodies of Titinius and Cassius. To both of them, he pays a sad farewell, calling Cassius "the last of all the Romans." The men leave then for another encounter with the enemy.

On the battlefield, in the midst of fighting, Brutus enters with Young Cato, Lucilius, and others. He urges them all to stand upright and brave. He exits, and Young Cato shouts his name and his loyalty to Rome (some texts give lines 7 and 8 in Scene 4 to Lucilius). He is killed, and Lucilius is captured by Antony's soldiers, who think that he is Brutus. He is then left under guard as one of the soldiers runs to bring Antony to the prisoner whom he believes to be Brutus. When Antony arrives and asks for Brutus, Lucilius tells him that Brutus is alive and will never be taken prisoner. Antony sets guard over the loyal Lucilius, and he sends his soldiers to search for Brutus and to report to him later at Octavius' tent.

Brutus, Dardanius, Clitus, Strato, and Volumnius enter. They are tired from battle, and Brutus whispers a request first to Clitus and then to Dardanius; he wants one of the men to kill him. They both refuse him. He tells Volumnius that Caesar's ghost appeared to him again; he knows that it is time for him to die. Volumnius disagrees, but Brutus argues that the enemy has them cornered, and he asks Volumnius to hold his sword while he runs onto it. Volumnius refuses, believing it an improper act for a friend to perform. An alarm signals the approach of the enemy, and Clitus warns Brutus to flee. Brutus wishes his comrades farewell, including Strato, who has awakened from a quick nap; he repeats that it is time for him to die. Offstage shouts prompt him to send his soldiers onward, and he and Strato remain alone. Strato agrees to hold Brutus' sword; they shake hands, and Brutus runs onto the sword, killing himself.

Amid alarms signaling the rout of Brutus' army, Octavius,

Antony, Messala, Lucilius, and others enter and come upon Strato and Brutus' body. Octavius offers to take into his service all who have followed Brutus, and Antony delivers a brief and now-famous oration over the body of Brutus, beginning "This was the noblest Roman of them all." Antony believes that all the other conspirators attacked Caesar because of personal envy; Brutus alone did it because he believed that it would be for the general good of Rome. Octavius promises an appropriate funeral for Brutus, and he gives orders to stop the battle. Finally, he calls on his colleagues to join him in celebrating their victory.

Commentary

The last scene of Act IV ended with the republicans preparing to move to Philippi; Act V begins with Antony and Octavius witnessing their arrival. The contrast between the leaders of the opposing armies is pronounced. Antony and Octavius are fully confident of victory; Brutus and Cassius, in contrast, are haunted with doubt and uncertainty. Note that even from the beginning of the generals' parley, Brutus asks, in effect, for conciliation, for he declares, "Good words are better than bad strokes, Octavius"; but neither Octavius nor Antony shows any inclination to negotiate a peace. Antony verbally attacks Brutus and the other conspirators, calling the assassination a cruel murder, compared to the ritual that Brutus hoped people would consider it; thus he places Brutus in a position where he must defend a single assassination to men who have murdered hundreds. In comparing Antony's "honeyed" words to the sounds of the Hybla bees, Cassius obliquely refers to Antony's deceptive performance following the assassination; he accuses Antony of stealing the "buzzing" of the bees, and Brutus cleverly continues the metaphor. But Antony is no mere "bee," nor is he now merely an orator and actor. Now he is the commander of a mighty army, and Brutus is at bay, although he is still technically on the offensive. Antony seizes on the metaphor sardonically when he confidently implies that he has the "sting" of the Hybla bees. In a direct contrast to Brutus' opening words, Octavius ends the parley with a blunt challenge for Brutus and Cassius to attack whenever they dare.

When Cassius refers to Octavius as a "peevish schoolboy" and to Antony as a "masker and a reveller," Antony responds with "Old Cassius still"; he refers to Cassius' well-known cynicism and caustic wit. Cassius is a shrewd judge of human nature, and he is well aware that Antony is not simply a lover of theatrical plays and a partygoer but rather a dangerous enemy, one capable of astute planning and skillful execution. But Cassius has changed, and he exposes the degree to which he has changed in his conversation with Messala. Earlier, he was a calculating manipulator of Brutus; then he became dependent upon Brutus' membership in the conspiracy, which limited his ability to utilize his insight. Later, he developed a close friendship with Brutus, to whom he deferred for the sake of that friendship. Now he is both sentimental and despondent; he believes the coincidence of his birthday and the battle may signify an end to the cycle of his life. He is also fearful of risking everything on the outcome of one battle; he is afraid that he and Brutus will be defeated, and, more important, he has doubts that the philosophy that he has followed all of his adult life is valid. Eagles were the symbols of the Roman legions, and the departure of the eagles that have accompanied his army from Sardis has been replaced by "ravens [and] crows"; they cause him to suspect that the gods are telling him symbolically that he and his army are prey to the birds that have traditionally signified death. In Act II, Scene 1, he informed the other conspirators that Caesar was "superstitious . . . of late"; now it is Cassius who has grown superstitious. But he tells Messala that he has not given way to complete despair, and he repeats his resolve to face all dangers bravely, yet he and Brutus will conduct their parting conversation in the context of its possibly being their last.

Brutus also prepares for the eventuality of defeat. His Stoic philosophy requires that he show a fortitude that specifically forbids suicide. He resolves to choose personal honor over philosophical consistency and will commit suicide before he will allow Antony and Octavius to drag his body through Rome. Brutus' sense of despair and his fatalism are further emphasized by his desire to end the war one way or another and by his resigned acceptance of the fate of which they will learn soon enough.

Antony and Octavius also have their differences. As Scene 1 opens, Octavius is arguing with Antony, and later he contradicts Antony's order that he lead his army on the left side of the battlefield. Octavius insists on making his own decisions when he feels competent to do so; he challenges the far more experienced Antony. After the death of Caesar, Antony would probably be regarded as the greatest general of his age; yet Shakespeare has Octavius cross him in order to bring out the rivalry between the two men and also to characterize the character of Octavius as a headstrong boy. Antony, a more mature soldier, does not protest because there is no time; besides, it is important that the two men have no division between them, now of all times.

As a political man, Brutus erred in allowing Antony to live and in allowing him to speak at Caesar's funeral. As a general, he has insisted on facing Antony and Octavius at Philippi; now, despite Cassius' objection, he will risk all on one battle—that is, the battle that will provide the material for the rest of the play.

In Scene 2, the battle has begun, and Brutus' hopes for victory are at their highest. He takes their combined fate into his own hands and acts on his own intuition. He does not consider sufficiently what may happen to Cassius if their armies do not act simultaneously, and when he attacks prematurely, he leaves Cassius' flank exposed to encirclement by Antony. The next scene reveals the tragic consequences of the action begun in this scene.

In Scene 3, Brutus' premature attack and its aftermath expose Cassius to attack. Brutus' soldiers clearly do not share their commander's repugnance of gaining wealth by "vile means," and following their rout of Octavius' army, they fall to looting; they thereby leave Cassius vulnerable to attack by Antony, who takes advantage of this opportunity. Rather than having the battle simulated onstage, however, Shakespeare has Pindarus report the action occurring on the surrounding battlefield to Cassius and to the audience, and it is Pindarus' unintentionally mistaken report which sets the action for the remainder of the scene.

In the first scene of this act, Cassius showed the extent to which he had changed, and the dramatic structure of the play has been one factor in emphasizing this change. In the first half of the play, his pragmatism, his envy, and his dislike of Caesar were in clear contrast to Brutus' idealism and his moral dilemma concerning the attack on Caesar. Now the second half of the play highlights the contrasts between Brutus and Cassius. In the first half, Cassius is a conspirator tainted by dubious motives; in the second half, he is a genuine friend to Brutus and a defender of republican principles. But in Scene 3, Cassius commits a fatal error. It is ironic that the man who has consistently demonstrated such clear foresight suffers from weak eyesight and that he commits suicide because of a false report by the man he chooses to observe for him. It is also ironic that the great respect that his associates have for him becomes evident only after his death: Pindarus disappears after Cassius dies, and Titinius commits suicide in order to follow his friend and commander. Brutus calls Cassius "the last of all the Romans." Cassius has fought bravely in battle; he has even slain his retreating standard bearer in order to keep his army in the field. His act of suicide is consistent with his often repeated desire either to live as a free man or to die. Brutus acknowledges his friendship for Cassius, but in this instance, he is entirely practical in removing Cassius' body for later burial; this will avoid a depressing ceremony, and he already possesses a demoralized army once they all become aware that Cassius is dead.

The spirit of Caesar enters into the action when Cassius commits suicide with the sword he used to kill Caesar. When he utters the words "Caesar, thou art revenged," Cassius, in effect, revenges the murder of Caesar by murdering himself. But Caesar's spirit is still abroad, a fact that Brutus understands when he views Cassius' body and exclaims, "O Julius Caesar, thou art mighty yet!"

The first battle at Philippi ended indecisively. Brutus defeated Octavius and routed his army; Antony defeated Cassius, and a messenger's mistake caused Cassius to commit suicide. In Scene 4, Young Cato, Brutus, and Lucilius try to spur their army to continue fighting bravely, but Brutus sets the tone for their lack of real hope of victory in his opening statement, "Yet, countrymen, O yet hold up your heads!" Young Cato dies, uttering his hatred of tyranny, ironically demonstrating that Brutus' increasingly tragic effort to remove tyranny in the person of Caesar is swiftly leading to the establishment of a far more ruthless tyranny under the Triumvirate. Young Cato's death and Lucilius' capture are proof that the defeat of the republican armies is at hand. They are now retreating in disarray, and Antony is so confident of victory that he trusts the outcome of the battle to his soldiers; he himself retires to Octavius' tent to await news of final victory.

Significantly, Shakespeare emphasizes Lucilius' loyalty here; the young man impersonates Brutus in an effort to give Brutus time to regroup or to flee. This absolute faith that Brutus will always conduct himself honorably continues the theme of Brutus' nobility and sets it in the context of an admiring friend's observation of the whole of Brutus' life. Antony realizes the value of having loyal followers, and, planning for his and Octavius' future government, he orders that Lucilius be protected; he realizes that Lucilius is "a prize no less in worth [than Brutus]."

The alarms being sounded as Scene 5 begins add a sense of urgency to the already desperate situation for Brutus and his army, and Brutus' first speech removes any doubt that he and his friends have lost. "Come," he says, "poor remains of friends, rest on this rock." Like Cassius in the previous scene, Brutus now believes that the cycle of his life is complete. The only question remaining concerns whether he will surrender and subject himself to the will of his enemies, or whether he must kill himself. Clitus, Dardanius, and Volumnius refuse to kill him because of their respect for his nobility and their friendship for him, and Brutus, it must be admitted, takes some satisfaction in their refusal. Yet he prepares to die, believing that he has won a moral victory. Brutus reconciles his defeat in the belief that "in all my life / I found no man but he was true to me." He is not, of course, precisely correct. Cassius used him before becoming a genuine friend, and Mark Antony was thoroughly dishonest with him when he promised that he wanted to be a friend and, later, when he promised that he would not blame Brutus and the conspirators for killing Caesar. Antony was especially dishonest with Brutus because he knew that Brutus was genuinely honorable and noble, that he prided himself on his noble integrity, and that he would fulfill his promises. Antony took advantage of Brutus' admirable but wholly naive qualities. However, Brutus believes that he will be honored more in defeat than Antony; Brutus will be honored in defeat because he knows that he has steadfastly maintained his honor, his nobility, and his dignity. He has struggled mentally both before and after the assassination in an effort to justify his actions according to his personal code. He has never expressed regret for having killed Caesar, and he does not question his action in his final moments.

Shakespeare consistently strives to end his plays with a resolution of the main action. He knows that his audience is aware that Antony and Octavius will eventually become enemies, that Antony will succumb to the charms of Cleopatra and the sensuous life of Egypt, and that Octavius will become Augustus, for whom the age has been named; however, at the end of *Julius Caesar*, they have defeated their enemies, and they strive to heal the political wounds of Rome so that they can restore order and rule a reunited dominion. Octavius offers to take the defeated supporters into the new political establishment, and Antony praises the nobility of Brutus, the leader of their defeated opponents. Antony is not being inconsistent with what he said to Brutus in the first scene of this act; he meant what he said then because he was speaking face to face with an assassin and a political and military enemy. Likewise, he means what he says here because he recognizes that Brutus was, in fact, a noble and idealistic man. Antony can now acknowledge with no irony nor sarcasm, but still with self-serving intent, that Brutus was an "honourable man."

Brutus wished that he could still the spirit of Caesar without killing Caesar the man. The death of Caesar motivated Antony both to seek revenge and to take advantage of a volatile political situation. Brutus reveals in the final scene that the ghost of Caesar has visited him again at Philippi, and his final words are "Caesar, now be still; / I killed not thee with half so good a will." The spirit of Caesar, as it became manifest in Antony, is now finally still; and as Antony and Octavius prepare to celebrate their victory, they make no mention of having revenged Caesar nor of having fought to venerate his person and his rule. The old order has passed away; their concerns are wholly on establishing a new order.

1601-02

hamlet

HAMLET

LIST OF CHARACTERS

Hamlet, Prince of Denmark

Son of the dead King Hamlet and nephew to the present ruler of Denmark; he has returned to Elsinore because of his father's death.

Claudius, King of Denmark

Hamlet's uncle who succeeded his brother to the throne and married his brother's wife.

Gertrude

Queen of Denmark and mother of Hamlet.

Polonius

Elderly Lord Chamberlain and thus chief counselor to Claudius.

Horatio

Commoner who is a fellow student and loyal friend of Hamlet.

Laertes

Polonius' son, a student at the University of Paris who, like Hamlet, has returned to Elsinore because of King Hamlet's death.

Ophelia

Obedient daughter of Polonius and sister of Laertes; the young court lady who Gertrude hoped would be Hamlet's bride.

Rosencrantz and Guildenstern

One-time schoolfellows and friends of Hamlet.

Fortinbras

Prince of Norway, a valiant young man who, like Hamlet, has lost a father.

Osric

Affected courtier who plays a minor role as the king's messenger and as umpire of the fencing match between Hamlet and Laertes.

Voltimand and Cornelius

Danish courtiers who are sent as ambassadors to the Court of Norway.

Marcellus and Bernardo

Danish officers on guard at the castle of Elsinore.

Francisco

Danish soldier on guard duty at the castle of Elsinore.

Reynaldo

Young man whom Polonius instructs and sends to Paris to observe and report on Laertes' conduct.

The Gravediggers

Two humorous fellows who dig Ophelia's grave, the first of whom is engaged by Hamlet in a grimly humorous conversation.

SUMMARIES AND COMMENTARIES

ACT I

Summary

The setting is the royal castle at Elsinore. On a platform before the castle, Francisco, a soldier on guard duty, challenges Bernardo, an officer, who appears to relieve Francisco at midnight. Francisco expresses his thanks, for it is "bitter cold" and he is "sick at heart." Horatio and Marcellus, who are to join Bernardo in the watch, arrive and identify themselves as loyal Danes. "What, has this thing appear'd tonight?" asks Marcellus, and it is revealed that a strange, frightening apparition was seen during the watch on a previous occasion. Horatio, who has not seen it, has assured Marcellus that it is a hallucination but, at the officer's entreaty, has agreed to join in the watch.

As Bernardo is telling Horatio how the specter had appeared one hour after midnight, the Ghost itself enters. It is "like the King that's dead"—that is, it appears in the "fair and warlike form" of the late King Hamlet of Denmark. Marcellus urges Horatio to question it, but when Horatio charges the Ghost in heaven's name to speak, the apparition stalks away. The pale and trembling Horatio admits that it is "something more than fantasy."

In the ensuing discussion, one learns that the Ghost has appeared twice before in the same armor King Hamlet wore when he fought the ambitious old Fortinbras, King of Norway, and when he defeated the Poles. Further, in accordance with the solemn agreement made by the two contestants, King Hamlet won Norwegian territory when he defeated and slew his adversary. Now the dead king's son and namesake, young Fortinbras, has raised a force of men willing to fight only for subsistence and is determined to take back the lands his father lost. Thus the military preparations and the nightly watch at Elsinore are explained. Bernardo suggests that the Ghost's appearance may be a portent relating to the martial threat, and Horatio recalls the terrifying omens which preceded the assassination of Julius Caesar.

Again the Ghost appears, and again Horatio courageously challenges it to speak. But at the crow of a cock, it moves from one place to another and then departs. All agree that Hamlet, son of the king whose spirit they may have seen, must be told.

In a room of state at Elsinore, King Claudius and Queen Gertrude enter, accompanied by Lord Chamberlain Polonius, his son Laertes, and various members of the Court and attendants. The king addresses all present. First, he speaks of mourning the death of his "dear brother," King Hamlet, and explains that "discretion" prohibits excessive grief. He has married his brother's widow and has done so with the concurrence of the members of his council. Next, he speaks about young Fortinbras, who demands the surrender of those lands lost by his father to King Hamlet. Claudius informs the

Court that he is sending Cornelius and Voltimand with a letter to the bedridden King of Norway, requesting him to restrain his nephew.

Having concluded official business, Claudius listens to the suit of Laertes, who requests "leave and favour" to return to France after having returned to Denmark to attend the coronation ceremonies. The king first determines that Laertes has his father's permission and then graciously gives his own.

Claudius now turns to young Hamlet and asks why he still grieves. Queen Gertrude joins the king in urging her son to accept his father's death philosophically and to recognize that his own bereavement is not unique. After Hamlet assures his mother that he has not assumed a pose for effect, Claudius develops Gertrude's argument: It is "sweet and commendable" for Hamlet to show love for a dead father through immediate grief, but sustained grief is unmanly and evidence of "impious stubbornness." The queen urges her son to remain at Elsinore. When Hamlet replies that he will strive to obey her, the king commends him. As Claudius and the queen prepare to leave, the king announces that a celebration, replete with drink and the thunder of cannon, will be held in honor of Hamlet's "gentle and unforc'd accord" (I. ii. 123). All but the prince leave the room.

Alone, Hamlet expresses his innermost thoughts. Were it not against God's law, he would commit suicide, for his world has become "weary, stale, flat, and unprofitable." But it is not just the death of a beloved father and king which has reduced him to this state of despair; it is the fact that his mother has married a man much inferior to King Hamlet, a man who was her brother-in-law, and has done so less than two months after her husband's death.

Horatio, in the company of Marcellus and Bernardo, enters. When he greets Hamlet, the young prince, lost in his thoughts, makes a perfunctory reply. But promptly he recognizes Horatio and warmly returns the greeting. Horatio explains that he has returned from Wittenberg to attend the funeral of Hamlet's father. The prince then asks Horatio not to mock him, remarking that his friend must have returned to attend the queen's marriage to Claudius. Horatio concedes that little time elapsed between the funeral and the marriage.

Fervently, Hamlet expresses his regret that the marriage has taken place. Then, when he tells Horatio that he thinks he sees his father, Horatio is startled. "Oh, where, my lord?" he asks. Hamlet explains that he evoked imaginatively the image of the dead king. This provides Horatio the opportunity to report what he and the guards saw the night before—"A figure like your father, / Arm'd at all points exactly" (I. ii. 199–200). Hamlet questions his friend closely and concludes that, come what may, he will accost the apparition. Both Horatio and Marcellus swear to honor Hamlet's injunction of silence regarding whatever may happen. Alone once more, the prince expresses his conviction that the Ghost, appareled like his father, is an omen that "All is not well."

In a room at Polonius' house, Laertes is saying farewell to Ophelia, his sister. Assuming the prerogatives of a brother, he has words of advice for her. She is not to take seriously Hamlet's attentions and, above all, must be wary to protect her virtue. Ophelia goodnaturedly accepts this advice but urges her brother to practice what he preaches.

Polonius enters, telling his son not to delay and then offering him fatherly advice on how to conduct himself. Laertes departs, and Polonius turns to his daughter to find out what her brother has been saying to her. When Ophelia replies that it related to Hamlet, who has "of late made many tenders / Of his affection" for her, the elderly father remarks that he has heard that the prince has been attentive to her. He scoffs at the very thought that Hamlet's intentions are serious and honorable, and he warns her to conduct herself so as not to make him appear a fool. He knows how young men importune young ladies and for what purpose. Ophelia is to avoid the prince's company. "I shall obey," replies this dutiful daughter of the Lord Chamberlain.

Near midnight, Horatio and Marcellus again appear on the platform before the castle. As pre-arranged, Hamlet is now with them. When cannon fire and the sound of trumpets are heard, the prince explains that the king and members of his court are participating in a revel during which the wine flows freely and "the swagg'ring upspring reels"—that is, all are participating in boisterous dancing. Hamlet tells Horatio that such drunken revelry has earned for the Danes a reputation for drunkenness. This leads him to reflect aloud on how one particular fault may lead to "general censure."

"Look, my lord, it comes!" exclaims Horatio. The Ghost has made its appearance. Whether it comes from heaven or hell, Hamlet declares that he will address it and call it "Hamlet, King, father." He implores the Ghost to answer him, but instead it beckons to the prince. Horatio urges Hamlet not to follow the Ghost, warning him that it may lead him to his death. Both Marcellus and Horatio forcibly try to hold back the prince, but he will not be restrained. He threatens to make a ghost of the one who tries to stop him and orders both to stand apart. Convinced that Hamlet is in a state of desperation, the two decide to follow the prince and the Ghost.

The Ghost tells Hamlet that it is the spirit of his father, doomed for a time to walk on earth during the nights and to endure purgatorial fires during daytime in expiation for sins committed during life. The Ghost calls upon him to prove his love for his father: "Revenge his foul and most unnatural murder." Hamlet is told that although King Hamlet's death was attributed to the sting of a serpent, it was Claudius, "that incestuous, that adulterate beast," who murdered his brother. The prince receives this startling news as if it were confirmation of his suspicions. The Ghost then fills in the details. The lustful Claudius, who won the affections of Queen Gertrude, poured poison into the ear of the sleeping King Hamlet, sending him to his death without sacraments and extreme unction, thus depriving him at once "Of life, of crown, and queen." No longer must Denmark be ruled by the incestuous murderer; Hamlet is called upon to kill his uncle. But the Ghost adds a word of caution: The son is not to contaminate himself by seeking to punish his mother; he is to leave her punishment to heaven and to her own conscience. "Hamlet, remember me," the Ghost intones as it departs. The prince solemnly vows to wipe away all else from his memory except that which the Ghost has told him.

It is a highly excited Hamlet who answers the calls of Horatio and Marcellus. His replies to their questions are evasive. When he calls upon the two to take an oath of secrecy regarding what they have seen this night, the voice of the Ghost is heard repeatedly from below the platform: "Swear." Hamlet moves wildly about the platform, now addressing the Ghost, now calling upon his friends to place their hands upon his sword and take the oath. In a more restrained mood, the prince enlarges the conditions of the oath. If he chooses to pretend to be mentally deranged, they are not to give the slightest indication that they know the reason for his behavior. Again the Ghost's voice is heard: "Swear." When the oath is taken,

Hamlet, now subdued, thanks his friends and then expresses his heartfelt desolation.

Commentary

First to be noted in Scene 1 is the skill with which Shakespeare evokes a mood appropriate to this tragedy. The members of the guard appear in the bitter cold of a northern winter night. Francisco welcomes relief, although his has been a "quiet guard." His feeling of sickness at heart suggests that neither the hour nor the weather explains his uneasiness.

"Long live the king!" exclaims Bernardo, voicing the password when he is challenged by Francisco. "What king?" one asks; and as details relating to Denmark are provided, it seems to be evident that the changing of the guard is symbolic, "a re-enactment of those dynastic changes which frame the play," as one critic says. Support for such a conclusion is found in Horatio's words when he first addresses the Ghost as one "that usurp'st this time of night" (46).

What of the Ghost, "this thing . . . this dreaded sight," as Marcellus calls it, which fills Horatio with "fear and wonder"? Some knowledge of Elizabethan and Jacobean ghost-lore is needed. Shakespeare may or may not have believed in ghosts; the characters in this play do, and so did most of his contemporaries, including James I. The prevailing theories were that a ghost may be (1) a hallucination, (2) a spirit returned to perform some deed left undone in life, (3) a specter seen as a portent, (4) a spirit returned from the grave or from purgatory by divine permission, or (5) a devil disguised as a dead person. In the course of the play each of these theories is put to test. Immediately the first is rejected, but much later in the play it will arise again. The educated, skeptical Horatio proves to his own satisfaction that this particular ghost is a real one, not an illusion. Appearing in "warlike form" and as the image of the late King Hamlet, the second may be applicable or, more probably, the third, since Denmark expects an attack led by the young Norwegian Prince Fortinbras. Horatio dwells upon this latter possibility when he speaks of the portents seen just before Julius Caesar was slain in the Roman Forum.

But Horatio and members of the guard particularly fear that the Ghost is diabolical. Horatio properly is called upon to question it because he is a scholar (42), trained in Latin and knowledgeable in arcane things. Among the mortals in this scene, only he is qualified to exorcise an evil spirit. As dawn, heralded by the cock's crow, begins to break and light begins to replace darkness, the Ghost "started like a guilty thing" (148). Marcellus is reminded that, according to a tradition accepted by many, the "bird of dawning singeth all night long" during the Christmas season and then "no spirit can walk abroad" (158 ff.). Indeed this apparition may be a thing of evil.

Significantly, *The Tragedy of Hamlet* is given a Christian setting from the start. Not only is reference made in Scene 1 to "our Saviour's birth" in Marcellus' speech, but also Horatio uses the proper Christian formula in challenging the Ghost: "By heaven I charge thee, speak!" (49)—and his words, according to Marcellus, offend the Ghost, which stalks away. The possibility still remains, however, that it is a spirit divinely sanctioned to return in order to carry out some mission.

One does not yet meet young Fortinbras in Scene 1, but what is learned about him is sufficiently interesting. He is a young man "of unproved mettle," one who has recently lost a royal father and who is not content to brood over his loss. Swiftly he has raised a force of "landless resolutes"—a gang of adventurers—and is determined to regain the territory which his father lost in combat.

In Scene 2, Claudius emerges as the antagonist; he is heard first and calls for first attention. It should be obvious that here is no weak individual but one who is adroit and determined. He is fully aware that his marriage to Gertrude is incestuous according to canon law, which is based on the dictum that man and wife become one flesh. He knows further that the marriage, even were it lawful, took place with undue haste. Typically, royal periods of mourning last for a full year; this marriage took place less than two months after the death of Claudius' brother. But this new ruler has taken care to obtain the approval of his Court. How he was able to do so in the face of canon law is revealed by his carefully chosen words in the first twenty-five lines of his opening speech, concluding with "So much for him." Notice the skillfully balanced phrases, the careful parallelisms, the antitheses which he employs as he rationalizes his act. Discretion (reason) is set against grief and nature; Gertrude is referred to first as "sometime sister," then as queen, and finally as "imperial jointress" of Denmark. The effect is to convince his audience that he has been motivated by a high sense of public duty.

When he turns to state affairs, Claudius is no less confident, and one must concede that he exhibits decisiveness and capability as a ruler. Although Denmark fears an invasion led by young Fortinbras, the Court and the people in general may rest assured that their king has taken proper action. Claudius appears to show tact for all concerned when he ascertains that Polonius will not oppose his son's departure. King Claudius' public image is a favorable one.

Nor does it appear to diminish when he turns to Hamlet. But again the careful reader will note that, in addressing the prince as "my cousin [kinsman] Hamlet, and my son," Claudius adroitly makes clear the fact that he is in full command and that Hamlet is subject to his pleasure. Once more it is an appeal to reason that seems to color the king's words as he reproves his nephew for undue grief and urges him to embrace forgetfulness. On strict philosophical and religious grounds, his argument is impeccable. All humanity must bow to the inevitable and learn to accept it, for life in general must go on. From this point of view, continued and debilitating sorrow is indeed "a fault to heaven, / A fault against the dead, a fault to nature" (I. ii. 101–102).

In Scene 2, when Claudius accuses Hamlet of "impious stubbornness" (94), of possessing "A heart unfortified" and "a mind impatient" and "An understanding simple and unschool'd" (96–97), he is saying, in so many words, that the prince lacks the qualities required to rule a kingdom. Thus the king may well intend to strengthen the belief of the Danish counselors that it was best for Claudius to succeed his brother. Certainly the king's words have a declamatory quality which suggests that he knows that Gertrude and the members of the Court also hear his words.

Claudius' call for a celebration with festive drink is, in effect, an order that Hamlet especially, and all others, forget the past and accept the new order. Some commentators (Samuel Johnson, for example) have argued that the king's intemperance, suggested here, is strongly impressed in the play. If this be true, Claudius' appetite for strong drink, according to Renaissance moral philosophy, points to his rejection of reason, which is equated with virtue. But admittedly the evidence to support such a conclusion is rather slight at this stage of the action.

Nothing that Queen Gertrude says or does in this scene informs against her except the fact that she is obviously undisturbed by her new status as wife to Claudius. Her concern for her son seems to be that of a genuinely concerned mother. If Claudius' words tend to arouse suspicions as to his true motives, not so Gertrude's. Her plea, "Let not thy mother lose her prayers, Hamlet" (118), has the ring of sincerity. It is not until one hears the prince speak in soliloquy that Gertrude takes her place, as it were, among the unsympathetic characters. Far more serious than the haste of the marriage to Claudius is the fact that it is incestuous: Her marriage to her brother-in-law was a gross violation of the law of the Church. Hamlet's indictment of his mother may provide the key to her character-weakness manifested by sensual passion: "Must I remember? Why, she would hang on him / As if increase of appetite had grown / By what it fed on" (I. ii. 143–45).

Present also in Scene 2 is Laertes, who speaks just less than seven lines. He appears as the well-bred son of the Lord Chamberlain, observing the amenities appropriate to his station and the occasion. More significant is one's reaction to his father, Polonius, chief counselor to the king, although he speaks just four lines. Just as there is a contrived element apparent in Claudius' first speech, so there is an artificiality in that of Polonius. The adjective, it has been said, can be the enemy of the noun. Polonius loves adjectives. Note the pattern of his discourse: " . . . slow leave . . . laboursome petition . . . hard consent" (58–60). This hardly suggests naturalness or spontaneity.

But the play belongs to Hamlet. Almost everything other characters do or say is relevant primarily to him. His tragedy is already in progress when he first appears. In this way he provides a contrast to the usual tragic hero of Renaissance drama, including Shakespeare's own Othello and Macbeth. Hamlet does not move from a state of well-being or happiness to adversity and suffering. Nor is his state of unhappiness attributed to the death of a beloved and honored father; rather, it is the marriage of his mother to his uncle, who now is King of Denmark. This is implicit in his first words in Scene 2, an aside. When Claudius refers to him as cousin and son, the prince remarks bitterly: "A little more than kin, and less than kind" (65). He is saying that the uncle-father relationship is monstrous in the literal sense, that is, contrary to the law of nature.

Hamlet's next words are addressed to Claudius and heard by others. They include a quibble. Do the clouds of grief still hang on him? No, he is "too much i' th' sun" (67). Clearly, this young prince and university student has a gift for irony, one which presupposes intellectuality and involves a kind of grim humor. At the literal level, he is saying that he is sunburned; at the metaphorical level, he is saying that, having lost first a father and then a mother, he is unsheltered. It is quite possible, as some have suggested, that Hamlet also puns upon the word sun, since the sun was often used as a symbol of kingship and the word, of course, is a homonym of son. Obviously Hamlet deeply resents Claudius' referring to him as his son. It should be added that those who see *Hamlet* primarily as an ambition play find here their first evidence that the tragic hero is motivated by a strong desire to dethrone Claudius and to rule Denmark.

Much critical attention has been directed to Hamlet's emphatic use of the word *seems* when his mother asks him, "Why seems it [his father's death] so particular with thee?" (75), and to his use of the expression "*shows* of grief . . . that a man might *play*." His own feeling "passeth show." It has been argued that here Shakespeare develops the theme of appearance versus reality and that he intends to stress Hamlet's dedication to truth in contrast to appearances which serve others, notably Claudius. Certainly he is presented as a discordant figure in this assembly, and his "inky cloak" and suit of "solemn black" provide a telling criticism of Claudius and Gertrude. Others may act a part, making use of "windy suspiration of forc'd breath" (sighing) and "fruitful river in the eye" (weeping); Hamlet is incapable of such posturing.

As has been stated above, the overwhelming cause of Hamlet's grief is revealed in his soliloquy: the incestuous union of his mother and his uncle. Since the doctrine involved here is not a current one, and indeed was not universal when Shakespeare wrote *Hamlet*, some explication is desirable. That marriage between a man and his dead brother's wife not only took place but also was sometimes legally authorized before and after Shakespeare wrote the play is undeniable. But according to the canonical law which informs Shakespeare's play, such a marriage is strictly forbidden. That law is based upon the sacramental view of a mystical bond formed in marriage which creates a relationship between man and wife as close as that which exists between blood relations. From the religious point of view, which cannot be ignored if one is to do justice to Shakespeare's intentions, the marriage of Claudius and Gertrude is, to use the official language of the period, "incestuous and unlawful and altogether null and void." To be sure, one wonders why the subjects of the king and queen voiced no protest or expressed no feeling of shock. But for the poet-dramatist's purpose, it is enough that the young, idealistic Christian prince should believe that the honor of the Danish royal family has been stained. It may be added that, traditionally, incest was considered to be an offense against the whole of society. If that view is applicable in Shakespeare's play, then Hamlet has a public duty to oppose Claudius, and the issue is not merely a personal, or domestic, one.

So great is Hamlet's grief that, were it not for the religious injunction against suicide, that ultimate act of despair and thus a mortal sin, he would take his own life: "O, that this too too solid flesh would melt." Since the Second Quarto has *sallied* for *solid*, some editors and critics are convinced that Hamlet actually speaks of his "sullied" flesh, a reading that certainly illuminates the prince's attitude toward the marriage. Here, then, is the crushing discovery of great evil by a young idealist. Little wonder that his world has become "stale, flat, and unprofitable." The metaphor Hamlet uses is fitting: His world has become an "unweeded garden." Elsewhere in Shakespeare's plays, notably in *Richard II*, garden and weed imagery is used for the development of theme. The properly tended garden represents an orderly world; weeds represent disease or corruption which destroys order.

Consistent with this outlook, Hamlet identifies his dead father with Hyperion in comparison to Claudius, who is likened to a satyr. Hyperion, or Apollo, was the god of light, and light traditionally has been equated with order and virtue. A satyr is something of a goatish caricature of a human being, and has attained the secondary meaning of "lecherous man." For Hamlet, lust, not love, determines the relationship between Claudius and Gertrude. According to the moral philosophy of the Renaissance, lust was viewed as evidence of general degradation, involving bestiality and the rejection of God-given reason. The prince now sees his mother as incapable of love, for he refers to her earlier regard for King Hamlet in terms of physical appetite: "Why, she would hang on him / As if increase of appetite had grown / By what it fed on" (143–45). Most devastating is his indictment, "O, most wicked speed, to post / With such dexterity to incestuous sheets!" (156–57).

In this soliloquy, Hamlet first demonstrates his considerable ability to move from particulars to generalization. If a mother and wife who appeared so loving can so degrade herself, then all women, all daughters of Eve, are immoral: "Frailty, thy name is woman!" (146). It will be, perhaps, to test his own conclusion that Hamlet will turn to Ophelia—so some competent critics have reasoned.

Facing this tormenting situation, Hamlet says that he "must hold [his] tongue" (159)—that is, he can do nothing. But perhaps some indication that he is called upon to act has been provided. Claudius, he declares, is no more like his royal brother than Hamlet himself is to Hercules (152–53). The prince's disparagement of his own prowess may suggest that, heretofore uncalled upon to prove himself, he soon will face a task which, in its way, will be as challenging as any of the labors of Hercules.

"I am glad to see you well," says Hamlet perfunctorily when Horatio greets him, interrupting his thoughts. But then he is all graciousness and warmth when he recognizes his friend and fellow-student. Some have seen all this either as a sudden change in mood (which is an early indication of emotional instability caused by excessive grief) or merely as an effort on Hamlet's part to control himself. But it may be more reasonable to conclude that, for the first of many times in this play, Shakespeare provides a glimpse of Hamlet's normal self—the Hamlet before his tragedy began, as it were.

The mention of the funeral provokes Hamlet's grimly witty replies. Surely Horatio has returned to attend the wedding of Hamlet's mother for which "The funeral bak'd-meats / Did coldly furnish forth the marriage tables" (180–81). However high-spirited, these words reveal that his mood has changed back to that of profound melancholy. Quite naturally he evokes mentally the image of his father, and quite naturally Horatio is startled. The transition to Horatio's report of what he and the guard have seen is thus skillfully achieved. Before proceeding, however, one should not ignore Hamlet's tribute to his father. In the soliloquy, the late king was identified with a Greek god; here in Scene 2, Hamlet does not depend upon the language of the scholar and, if anything, pays greater homage: "He was a man, take him for all in all, I shall not look upon his like again" (187–88). A *man*, a *human* being, not "a beast, that wants discourse of reason." In both *King Lear* and *Macbeth*, two of the four great Shakespearean tragedies, which include *Hamlet*, the dramatist uses the word *man* in this sense. The implications with reference to Claudius, who now rules Denmark and calls himself Hamlet's father, are evident.

It is an excited prince who cross-examines Horatio, Marcellus, and Bernardo: "Where was this? . . . Did you not speak to it? . . . Arm'd, say you? . . . Stay'd it long?" There follows the expression of determination to "watch to-night" and his insistence that they tell no one else what they have seen. Perhaps there is significance in Hamlet's question, "Then saw you not his [not *its*] face?" (228). At this point, the question may indicate that the prince is sure that the Ghost is "honest," not a "goblin damn'd"; later he will not be so sure. To be noted also is the fact that Horatio reports that the Ghost appeared "more / In sorrow" than in anger, a statement that is contrary to his earlier observation.

The words that Hamlet speaks alone at the end of Scene 2 suggest, first, that he now considers the possibility of the apparition's being an omen of evil; and, second, that he suspects some "foul play."

In Scene 3, we meet Polonius and his family at home and learn much about each member, particularly the son and the father. Moreover, a new story element is introduced—Hamlet's apparent love for Ophelia.

How does Laertes appear? On the debit side, he seems to be the devoted brother quite rightly concerned with protecting his young sister; he also seems to be the dutiful son who accords his father proper respect. But in the total of fifty-three lines of blank verse that constitute Laertes' lecture on sisterly conduct, the note of artificiality and lack of spontaneity come through strongly. This is the contrived style of the young courtier, with a succession of metaphors, studied parallelisms, and antitheses. Taken together with Polonius' advice to his son and his words to his daughter, Laertes' lines suggest a limitation as regards the family's concept of honor.

Polonius' lines in Scene 3 are even more revealing. His advice to Laertes (59–80) comprises one of the very well-known passages in the play. Although some early commentators took the Lord Chamberlain's words to be "golden" and as evidence of profound wisdom, the consensus is that the elderly Lord Chamberlain is merely parroting copybook maxims familiar to any Elizabethan schoolboy. His lines reveal a vain and limited character. As one informed critic has pointed out, most of what Polonius tells his son relates to etiquette, not ethics. This father is coaching his son on how to "act," how to "seem," how to "show" himself publicly. Yet his final precept is ethical, not practical, worldly counsel: "This above all: to thine own self be true, / And it must follow, as the night the day, / Thou canst not then be false to any man" (77–79). Climaxing his rather long speech, this change of tone can only be taken ironically.

If all this seems to be unduly harsh at this early stage of the action, consider his questions and remarks to Ophelia, who dutifully reports that Hamlet has "made many tenders / Of affection" but has done so "In honourable fashion." Polonius flatly rejects the possibility of sincere affection; he is convinced that "the holy vows of heaven" are no more than snares to entrap the innocent and unwary. He seems to take positive delight in his own off-color interpretation of Hamlet's recent interest in his daughter. Most damaging is his admonition, "Tender yourself more dearly, / Or—not to crack the wind of the poor phrase, / Running it thus—you'll tender me a fool" (107–109). Vanity and suspicion come through strongly in this passage. Polonius appears to be much more concerned about his public image than about the welfare of his daughter. And his emphasis is also upon how one should play a role, how one should act, show, seem.

One other significant point is made clear in Scene 3, one relating to the status of Hamlet. He is not a *private* individual but a *public* one; what he does has public, not merely personal, import. This Laertes says:

> His greatness weigh'd, his will is not his own;
> For he himself is subject to his birth.
> He may not, as unvalued persons do,
> Carve for himself, for on his choice depends
> The sanity and health of the whole state.
>
> (17–21)

This is the first passage that has been cited to support the argument that Hamlet unmistakably has the duty to avenge his father's death and to do so without procrastination.

In Scene 4, setting and mood are provided economically in broken lines of blank verse and informal diction. It is very close to midnight, the hour when the spirit appeared on the previous occasion.

Hamlet's "dram of evil" speech (19-38) is of special interest and possibly of major importance. Inspired as it is by his reaction to the sound of drunken revelry coming from the court where Claudius fulfills his pledge to celebrate what he called Hamlet's "gentle and unforc'd accord" (I. ii. 123-28), the prince again demonstrates his ability to move from particulars to generalization. Propensity for excessive drink, encouraged now by the king himself, leads other nations to use the "swinish phrase" *drunkards* when speaking of the Danes; in the same way, a fault in an individual may override his virtues and lead to his downfall.

Many commentators argue, understandably, that the subject of Hamlet's discourse is specifically the reputation of Claudius, who now rules Denmark but who, according to Hamlet, is no more like his predecessor than is Hyperion to a satyr. The king's taking "his rouse" may also serve to illustrate the deterioration of Elsinore since the death of King Hamlet. Moreover, his speech may be intended to illustrate the prince's propensity for thought; those who accept the Romantic view of a Hamlet rendered incapable of positive action by this very propensity find no reason for looking for more in the "dram of evil" speech. However, a sufficient number of distinguished Shakespeareans consider Hamlet to be a superior individual who, nevertheless, becomes a slave of passion. To them, these lines incorporate an exploration of the problem of good and evil (the problem basic to tragedy) and may well provide the key to the Hamlet mystery. Their views deserve notice.

When one hears Hamlet speak of the "o'ergrowth of some complexion," "the stamp of one defect," corruption from a "particular fault" leading to the corruption of an individual "as pure as grace" in other ways, the inclination is to believe that Shakespeare is underscoring a significant theme. Hamlet provides three possible answers to the problem of evil—three reasons why there may be present "some vicious mole of nature" which may lead to general censure and downfall. The first one is inherited defect ("As, in their birth"), which obviously does not involve human responsibility, the individual being a victim of fate ("fortune's star"). If that were the answer in *Hamlet*, then the play cannot be classified as Renaissance high tragedy, but rather as one based on, or consistent with, the Medieval theory, according to which individual choice and responsibility have no place.

The second answer involves the "o'ergrowth of some complexion" that often breaks "down the pales and forts of reason." Here human responsibility is evident. Some knowledge of Renaissance moral theory relating to the "complexions" is required if one is to understand Hamlet's words. At the simplest literal level, the term *complexion* may be defined as "natural quality." But for Shakespeare's generation, it had a more specific meaning. It referred to a person's temperament resulting from the supposed combination of four bodily fluids called "humours." The complexions were sanguine, melancholic, choleric, and phlegmatic. Proper balance of the humours in the body made possible the healthy individual; an excess or deficiency of one humour led to a psychological or physical imbalance. According to this theory, so widely accepted in the Elizabethan and Jacobean ages, the intellectual was especially susceptible to melancholy, often in its extreme form, which was called melancholy adust. This passion of excessive grief negated the powers of reason and thus the ability to act positively. Those who see Hamlet as the victim of excessive grief that causes him to delay or to act only on impulse find here support for this theory. That the prince himself should provide doctrinal support, it is argued, is not surprising: His intellectual superiority is well established in the play and, in the course of the action, he emerges as the best critic of himself on more than one occasion.

The third answer is that relating to "some habit that too much o'er-leavens [mixes with] / The form of plausive [pleasing] manners." Excessive drink obviously is one such habit, and it is the one that Hamlet must have in mind in view of the carousal that motivates his speech. Such a habit, like the "o'ergrowth of some complexion," may lead an individual, however virtuous he may appear to be in other respects, to reject reason, the quality that distinguishes him from the beast. It will be recalled that Hamlet uses bestial imagery in referring to the drunken revelry, speaking of how the "kettle-drum and trumpet thus bray out" (11) and of the "swinish phrase" used to describe those prone to excessive drinking. Obviously, the charge of bestiality could be applicable only to Claudius. But Hamlet himself is deeply concerned with public reputation and certainly with the honor of his family. One need not fear that he will be guilty of indulging a bad habit leading to the rejection of reason. If any of the answers to the problem of evil that he advances turn out to be applicable to him, it must be either adverse fate or uncontrolled passion.

"Angels and ministers of grace defend us!" exclaims Hamlet as he sees the apparition for the first time, voicing the orthodox Christian formula to be used on such a terrifying occasion. Consistent with contemporary ideas relating to ghosts, he knows that it may be "a spirit of health" (one divinely allowed to return to accomplish a rightful mission) or a "goblin damn'd" (an evil spirit, a devil, or even the Devil himself) appearing in the form and dress of King Hamlet and intent on leading the prince to destruction—perhaps to draw him into madness, as Horatio warns (69-78). But, in the stress of powerful emotion, Hamlet makes a positive identification of the Ghost as "King, father; royal Dane" (45). He assumes that the spirit has come from the grave where the body of King Hamlet, in "the very armour he had on / When he th' ambitious Norway combated" (I. i. 60-62), had been buried.

Despite argument and attempts to restrain him physically, the prince obeys the summons of the Ghost. What if his life be threatened? Having listened to him voice his innermost thoughts, one knows that he does not value life in a world where traditional virtues no longer flourish.

In Scene 5, one of the prime concerns of the Ghost is that, as a mortal, it was denied the opportunity to be shriven (receive absolution for sins prior to death) and thus must endure spiritual purgation before it can be admitted to heaven. But what of the "foul crimes" admitted to have been committed by King Hamlet, the man whom his son so much reveres? Obviously he was not perfect; no mortal is, according to church doctrine, because humanity remains tainted as the result of original sin. The Ghost is only too aware of mortal imperfections; it has a conscience practically Calvinistic in its strictness.

Hamlet will later have doubts about the nature of the Ghost, although they will be dispelled. But some Shakespearean commentators have remained dubious that Hamlet's doubts have been dispelled, and their view should not be ignored. It has been pointed out that a repentant spirit from purgatory would not appear as an armed warrior even if its mortal body had been so accoutered for burial. But since the Ghost's mission is to call upon Hamlet to attack Claudius, who now rules an armed Denmark, its martial costume is held to be the proper one. One may add that it is most effective theatrically.

Nevertheless, a degree of uncertainty remains. When the Ghost warns Hamlet against failure to execute revenge, it employs a simile that is rather strained, especially for a Christian spirit from purgatory, not from the pagan underworld or Elysium: "And duller shouldst thou be than the fat weed / That rots itself in ease on Lethe wharf, / Wouldst thou not stir in this" (32–34). Lethe, it will be recalled, is the Greek mythological river of Hades whose waters, when drunk, caused forgetfulness of the past. To be sure, much Renaissance poetry is filled with a mixture of pagan and Christian elements. Yet one recalls that the Ghost "started like a guilty thing" when the cock crew at daybreak (I. ii. 148). Is this the reaction of a Christian spirit? But it must be conceded that in the present scene the Ghost's behavior never suggests guilt. To Hamlet it says, "But soft! methinks I scent the morning's air. / Brief let me be" (58–59). In the earlier scene, dawn began to break before the Ghost, unable to speak its words to the proper person, was aware that its allotted time was up. When Horatio reported what he had seen, he said only that "it shrunk in haste" away (I. ii. 219). His earlier words were natural enough under the circumstances; they emphasized his uncertainty and fright.

The climax of the Ghost's recital in Scene 5 is reached after just twenty-two lines: "If thou didst ever thy dear father love— / . . . / Revenge his foul and most unnatural murder" (23, 25).

The two major issues basic to Hamlet's tragedy are now joined: the murder of a king and father, and the marriage of Claudius and Gertrude. The slaying of a king especially is foul and unnatural because he is God's minister on earth, so loyal Elizabethans and Jacobeans fervently believed. The Ghost denounces Claudius as "that incestuous, that adulterate beast" (41) and speaks of Gertrude as that "seeming-virtuous queen" (46). Hamlet is implored not to let "the royal bed of Denmark be / A couch for luxury [sensuality] and damned incest" (82–83). The adultery and incest, which concern the Ghost quite as much as does the murder by means of "leperous distilment," may simply refer to the marriage.

Whether or not Gertrude was unfaithful prior to the death of King Hamlet remains a disputed point. But one thing is clear: Prince Hamlet is not alone in his revulsion, unless this Ghost is indeed "goblin damn'd," intent upon leading the young prince to destruction—or unless one takes the unusual and radical view that Hamlet, separated from his companions on the platform, is the victim of a hallucination and that the Ghost is actually voicing Hamlet's own thoughts. If this is indeed "an honest Ghost," its concern for the purity of "the royal bed of Denmark," as well as the Crown, suggests that Hamlet is being called upon to execute public justice, not private revenge. Yet this spirit remains curiously tender in its attitude toward Gertrude: "Taint not thy mind, nor let thy soul contrive / Against thy mother aught. Leave her to heaven" (85–86). The question of the nature of the Ghost and the propriety of its injunction have not yet been answered definitively.

In a state of great excitement, Hamlet declares himself ready to sweep to revenge. He does so even before the identification of the murderer is made and the details of the crime are provided (29–31), although it is reasonable to conclude that he could suspect no one but Claudius. The figurative language that he uses to emphasize his determination deserves attention. He will sweep to his revenge "with wings as swift / As meditation or the thoughts of love" (29–30). The simile is appropriate for a young university scholar and a lover, and Hamlet has been established as both. But does prompt execution of an action involve meditation? In the present circumstances, does it not call for unquestioned, dutiful acceptance of the execution of blood-revenge, an eye for an eye, a tooth for a tooth? Blood-revenge is based on the barbarous *lex talionis*, the primitive law of the blood feud, whereby the nearest of kin is bound to avenge the victim by slaying his murderer. Is Shakespeare, then, restricted by his source or sources, including the original thirteenth-century version by Saxo Grammaticus? Or has he intentionally complicated Hamlet's problem in his play for which he provided a Christian framework?

The Ghost's injunction, "remember me," spoken just before its exit, becomes for Hamlet an obsession. From the cellarage, the Ghost repeats the command to "Swear" after Horatio and Marcellus rejoin the distracted prince. Emotionally, most audiences and readers accept the Ghost as "a spirit of health," just as Hamlet does in Scene 5. But, if only in afterthought, it remains a puzzling, disturbing thing. It may be relevant, in this connection, that the cellarage (which term gives this scene its usual name) was the cavernous area under the Elizabethan stage which was popularly called "hell."

"Come on; you hear this fellow in the cellarage," says Hamlet to

Horatio and Marcellus (151). A few critics wonder if the two friends did hear the Ghost, although Horatio immediately replies, "Propose the oath, my lord." Although he comes close to revealing the Ghost's testimony to his friends, Hamlet does not do so. Both Horatio and Marcellus prove their loyalty to him by taking the solemn oath not to reveal what they have *seen*.

Much has been written about Hamlet's decision to feign madness, "To put an antic disposition on." Some commentators are content to observe that the hero's pose of madness is basic to the original story of Hamlet and must have been included in the pre-Shakespearean *Ur-Hamlet*, and to conclude that audiences expected the hero to feign madness. But such an answer does not suffice for those who refuse to believe that the poet-dramatist permitted himself to be rigidly bound by his source or that he pandered to popular taste in this play, one of his great tragedies. The sources of *Othello* and *King Lear* are known and available; his use of those sources establishes his essential independence and originality. Perhaps Hamlet's own words and behavior, after he was joined by his friends, suggested to him the adoption of the antic disposition; clearly he knew that the shock of discovery made impossible normal behavior: "The time is out of joint; —O cursed spite, / That ever I was born to set it right" (189–90).

For Goethe, who envisioned Hamlet as a delicate soul unequal to the performance of the great task laid upon him, these two lines proved the "key to Hamlet's whole procedure" (*Wilhelm Meister*, 1778). Later critics, most of whom do not accept the Romantic interpretation of the prince's character, nevertheless agree that these are indeed key lines. The Ghost warns Hamlet not to taint his mind by seeking to punish Gertrude. Can he, however, kill his uncle-king without his mind becoming tainted?

ACT II

Summary

At his home, Polonius instructs Reynaldo to journey to Paris and to give Laertes money and messages. Reynaldo is also given detailed instructions on how to find out if Laertes is conducting himself. Reynaldo is to seek out other Danes in Paris, ones who are sure to know Laertes, and to obtain all the gossip relating to him.

Ophelia enters in a state of fright. She tells Polonius that Hamlet has come to her, his clothes in disarray, his face devoid of color, the very picture of despair. Her father promptly diagnoses Hamlet's condition: The prince suffers from love-madness brought on by Ophelia's refusal to accept his attention in accordance with her father's instructions. Polonius now believes that he should not have been so strict in this affair. He will inform the king what he has just learned.

In the castle, the king, accompanied by his queen, welcomes Rosencrantz and Guildenstern, who have obeyed his summons to Court. Claudius speaks of Hamlet's strange behavior and asks these two friends of the prince to see if they can find out the reason. The queen adds her entreaty that they do so. Showing their respect for royal authority, both agree to do their utmost to learn the cause of Hamlet's affliction. The king and queen express their gratitude, and the two young men leave.

Polonius enters and announces the return of Cornelius and Voltimand, who were sent as ambassadors to Norway. When Claudius thanks him as "the father of good news," the Lord Chamberlain takes the opportunity to inform the king that he has found the "very cause of Hamlet's lunacy." Claudius urges him to speak of that, but Polonius suggests that the king first receive his ambassadors.

Voltimand is the one who makes the report to Claudius. The elderly and ailing King of Norway has restrained his nephew Fortinbras. Instead of moving against Denmark, the latter agrees to lead his troops against the Poles. The Norwegian ruler asks that Fortinbras be given permission to pass through Danish territory. Claudius expresses his pleasure in hearing the report and states that he will reply to the request after giving it full consideration.

Polonius now holds forth in an elaborate, wordy manner. Hamlet, he declares, is infatuated with Ophelia, in proof whereof the Lord Chamberlain reads a love letter written by the prince partly in overwrought, highly artificial prose, partly in rhymed lines which never approach poetry. He then provides details relating to Hamlet and Ophelia and concludes that he has indeed found the source and cause of the prince's affliction. After all, has he ever been found in error when the king has asked him to express his firm opinion? Both Claudius and Gertrude agree that love-madness may indeed explain Hamlet's behavior, but the cautious king wants additional proof.

Polonius is ready with a plan. He will let Ophelia meet the prince; the king and Polonius will conceal themselves and observe the encounter. At the Lord Chamberlain's request, the royal couple and their attendants leave just after Hamlet enters, reading a book, thus giving Polonius a chance to find out what he can from the young prince.

In his answers to Polonius' questions, Hamlet convinces Polonius that he is indeed the victim of unrequited love. Actually his own questions and his responses comprise scathing ridicule of Polonius. Furthermore, he tacitly warns the Lord Chamberlain that Ophelia's virtue is in jeopardy, and he expresses his own wish for death. Still convinced that he has diagnosed Hamlet's condition accurately, Polonius nevertheless is impressed by what he calls "method" (basic sense) in the prince's discourse.

When Polonius leaves, Rosencrantz and Guildenstern enter. Hamlet greets them cordially as his "excellent good friends." Yet in the verbal exchange that follows, he becomes increasingly sardonic and suspicious of the motives of these two. Finally he succeeds in making them admit that they had been instructed by the king and queen to seek him out and to observe him carefully. The prince then tells them what to report to their majesties: He has lost his mirth and foregone most normal activities because the universe, which he believed to be wondrous, now appears to him to be foul; and man, the so-called paragon of the animals, no longer delights him—nor does woman either. The two then remark that in his present mood, the prince will not enjoy the performance of the actors who have just arrived in Elsinore. But Hamlet immediately shows his interest, especially in "He that plays the king."

Learning that these are "the tragedians of the city" whose performances have previously pleased him, Hamlet asks why they are traveling. He is told that an acting company of children have engaged in an attack upon the "common plays" and that theatrical performances by the adult companies have been suspended, popular fancy having turned to the child actors. The prince then tells Rosencrantz and Guildenstern that they, like the actors, are welcome; but he adds that Claudius and Gertrude are deceived about his madness.

Polonius returns to announce the arrival of the players. Hamlet promptly resumes the antic pose, baiting the elderly Lord Chamberlain but hardly repressing his verbosity. Then, when four or five players enter, he greets them warmly and shows a keen interest in and knowledge of the theater.

At Hamlet's request, the First Player recites a set speech from a play based on Aeneas' tale to Dido as told in Virgil's *Aeneid*, one that Hamlet describes as excellent but lacking popular appeal. The speech, which is in epic style, tells of the slaying of King Priam by Pyhrrus, son of Achilles.

After requesting Polonius to see to it that the players are well housed, Hamlet speaks in private to the First Player. It is arranged that on the next day the acting company will present a play called *The Murder of Gonzago*, the script of which will include some twelve to sixteen lines provided by the prince.

Alone, Hamlet again voices his innermost thoughts. First, he expresses wonder that a player could so realistically portray grief over the death of a character in dramatic fiction. He himself has genuine cause for passion, yet what has he done? Bitterly he denounces himself for failing to act positively against Claudius; he accuses himself of lethargy, cowardice, even villainy. Suddenly the prince interrupts himself and acknowledges that he has been indulging in futile railing. He then reveals his intentions in having the players enact *The Murder of Gonzago* before the king and the assembled Court. During the performance, he will keep his eyes fast on Claudius, who, if guilty, will surely flinch and thus inadvertently prove that the Ghost spoke true words. However convinced he had been that it was an "honest" spirit when he listened to its words, Hamlet now is not sure; perhaps it is the Devil who has used his power "to assume a pleasing shape" in order to lead the prince to damnation.

Commentary

The late T. S. Eliot found nothing relevant in Scene 1 as far as the instructions to Reynaldo are concerned. Others have argued that it is included only to convey the sense of stagnation in Elsinore, for much time has elapsed since Laertes' departure and Hamlet's encounter with the Ghost. Surely there is much more to be said in justification of the scene.

Earlier the statement was made that this is Hamlet's play and that almost everything any other character says or does relates in some way to him. Polonius is the leading courtier at Elsinore and chief adviser of King Claudius. Already certain limitations in his character have been revealed—the artificiality of his discourse, an inclination toward cynicism and suspicion of other people's motives, and a self-confidence amounting to vanity. This portrait of the Lord Chamberlain, whose major concern earlier was that Ophelia's behavior might tender him a fool, is now no less concerned that Laertes' conduct in Paris does not make him look bad. In his worldliness and cynicism, he is absolutely sure that he knows how young men behave when away from parental control—drinking, fencing, quarreling, and wenching. Reynaldo, Polonius says, is to let Laertes "ply his music" (73)—that is, keep a close eye on him and let him reveal his secrets. Not only is Polonius ready to believe the worst about his son, but also he seems to be incapable of honesty in his methods. His outlook and conduct suggest the kind of world in which Hamlet is now living. Indirection—espionage—becomes an elaborate game very soon in this play; this episode prepares the way for it.

The second episode in Scene 1 is concerned with Ophelia's report to her father. From her description of Hamlet, his clothes in disarray, "Pale as his shirt, his knees knocking each other," it is obvious that he has adopted the antic disposition. But when Ophelia says that he appeared " . . . with a look so piteous in purport / As if he had been loosed out of hell / To speak of horrors" (82–84), one inevitably recalls the Ghost's revelations. This and other details relating to Hamlet's distress suggest that more is involved here than assumed madness.

Hamlet has chosen to appear before Ophelia, who refused to accept his letters or to let him talk to her, as the courtly lover suffering from amatory ague. It is inconceivable that Hamlet would indulge in such posturing even if Ophelia's rejection of his attentions were a crushing blow. Perhaps, as some critics believe, those "tenders of affection" of which Ophelia spoke earlier may have been made by Hamlet in order to test the validity of his own generalization: "Frailty, thy name is woman!" (I. ii. 146). It will be recalled that in the same soliloquy he had declared that all "uses of this world" had become for him "weary, stale, flat, and unprofitable." This hardly suggests that he was in the mood for love. But this is not to deny that Hamlet was attracted to Ophelia. The essential point is this: If one is to do justice to Hamlet's status as a tragic hero who rejects "seeming," it must not be assumed that he now appears as a sentimental poseur. Adopting the antic disposition is something else again. In this world of Elsinore, where Polonius is established as the wisest counselor, the prince must meet indirection with indirection. Claudius must not learn what Hamlet intends; let his Lord Chamberlain report that his nephew suffers only from love-madness.

Polonius' reaction is, of course, predictable. With complete self-confidence, he declares that Hamlet suffers from "the very ecstasy of love." To be sure, it may be argued that his decision to report to Claudius what he has learned is a proper one under the circumstances, and that he really believes the well-being not only of Hamlet but also of Queen Gertrude to be involved. But when one recalls his prime concern with his own reputation rather than with the welfare of his daughter, the inclination is to see him as being anxious chiefly to prove how wise he is.

On the surface, Claudius appears gracious, genuinely solicitous about his nephew's well-being, and competent as a ruler in his attention to state affairs. No one should underestimate his capabilities, and these include positive action. Threats against the Crown coming from abroad can be and are met; Cornelius and Voltimand report that Fortinbras will not invade Denmark. But the threat to Claudius implicit in Hamlet's behavior remains. The intensity of the king's concern is evident especially when the confident Polonius assures him in Scene 2 that he has "found / The very cause of Hamlet's lunacy." He exclaims, "O, speak of that; that I do long to hear" (50). Gertrude is sufficiently concerned; but it is Claudius, not she, who speaks of Hamlet's madness. Only at Polonius' urging does the king agree to see his ambassadors before exploring that subject. It will be noted that the queen is not convinced that her son suffers from love-madness: "I doubt it is no other but the main, / His father's death and our o'er hasty marriage" (56–57).

When Claudius tells Rosencrantz and Guildenstern in Scene 2 about Hamlet's "transformation," he says that neither "th' exterior nor the inward man / Resembles that it was" (6–7). Recalling the unctuousness in Claudius' first speech in this play, one may find evidence of Machiavellianism here. Claudius is quite aware of how appearances may deceive, how it is possible to seem, to act a part.

If this generalization on the basis of one brief passage seems to be unwarranted, consider how readily Claudius approves of Polonius' underhanded methods and remains undisturbed by the unsavory terms in which the Lord Chamberlain speaks of them. Polonius refers to hunting the "trail of policy" (47) and says that he will "loose" Ophelia to Hamlet (162). The prince, apparently, is the prey of hunters, and poor Ophelia is to be cast in the role of a hound. The king's use of the word *sift* ["Well, we shall sift him" (58)] is good Elizabethan English, but its connotation here is as unsavory as are the phrases used by the Lord Chamberlain.

In their interview with the king and queen in Scene 2, Rosencrantz and Guildenstern present themselves as dutiful subjects of the Crown, willing to serve when called upon. Although their supposed concern for Hamlet's well-being is not expressed until the end of this episode, they also appear to be loyal friends of the prince. Yet the very way in which their concern is expressed arouses some suspicions: "Heaven make our presence and our practices / Pleasant and helpful to him" (38-39). Perhaps the use of the word *practices* suggests that they are not acting unselfishly and honestly, that they fit very well into this atmosphere of suspicion and underhandedness. Moreover, certain echoes in their words and in the words addressed to them may be revealing. "*Both* your Majesties" might have commanded rather than requested, says Rosencrantz (26-29); "we *both* obey," chimes in Guildenstern. The latter goes on to say that they "give up ourselves, in the full bent / To lay our services freely at your feet, / To be commanded" (30-32). This is indeed a strained way of saying that they will honor Claudius' request. "Thanks, Rosencrantz and gentle Guildenstern," says the king; "Thanks, Guildenstern and gentle Rosencrantz," echoes the queen. As one early critic remarked, the parallelism suggests their nullity; it is as if neither is more than half a person.

The return of Cornelius and Voltimand with their report about Fortinbras will have special import much later in the play, but it has some significance here in Scene 2. Among other things, it provides a clear indication of how much time has elapsed since Hamlet saw and listened to the Ghost. Also, here is the third reference to the young Norwegian prince who, like Hamlet, has lost a father and who, unlike Hamlet, has promptly taken positive action to avenge his father's death. But Fortinbras, one now learns, has mastered passion; he will obey his royal uncle, rejecting the idea of revenge, and will expend his energy in an attack upon Poland. Fortinbras, it would seem, is emerging as a foil to Hamlet, Prince of Denmark.

Matters relating to foreign relations having been settled, Polonius is ready to demonstrate his sagacity in solving the mystery of Hamlet's behavior. Now he emerges as an utter fool—and as a marvelous comic creation—pompous, smug, and frivolous. The Lord Chamberlain's repetitions, parallelisms, play on words—all delivered with supreme confidence in his own ability—result in a full-length picture, perhaps a caricature, of a zany. However exaggerated it may be, Shakespeare prepared his audience for it. Most amusing is the fact that Polonius is his own best critic, as when, after a verbal exercise involving the words *day, night,* and *time,* he concludes, "Therefore, since brevity is the soul of wit, / And tediousness the limbs and outward flourishes, / I will be brief" (90–92). And later, despite the queen's admonition that he provide "more matter, with less art," he indulges in another such exercise involving the words *true* and *pity,* and then concludes: "A foolish figure!" (98).

Such broad comedy is welcome as a relief from tragic seriousness; nevertheless, it is functional in relation to the major action. In Hamlet's world, Polonius is accepted as the wise, if not wisest, counselor; and Polonius plays that role with all the artifice peculiar to his limited character. Respect for age had an important place in ideal Renaissance philosophy, but it did not follow that an individual who had reached, or was close to, dotage would be permitted to remain in a public position. It must be assumed that earlier, and with strict reference to ordinary affairs, Polonius had proved satisfactory; if this were not so, surely the competent Claudius would not depend upon him to such an extent.

Hamlet's love letter, which Polonius reads, is a curious composition, what with its stilted prose and bad verse. For once, one must agree with Polonius, who immediately sets himself up as a critic of style: "'beautified' is a vile phrase" (111). It suggests the use of make-up, the "plast'ring art," to use the term Hamlet will employ later. In the first mad scene, Ophelia will enter, asking, "Where is the beauteous majesty of Denmark?" (IV. v. 21). Her use of another oblique form of the word *beauty* has the same connotation in context as *beautified* does here.

It is generally agreed that the love letter is part of Hamlet's pretense of madness on the grounds that, unless it were contrived, the scholarly Hamlet could never have written it. Certainly it is consistent with the portrait of a lovesick Hamlet, as described by Ophelia, and what has been said with reference to that is applicable here. It seems reasonable to conclude that Hamlet knew that the letter would fall into the hands of the foolish Polonius. Nevertheless, the first two lines of verse may have some special significance: "Doubt thou the stars are fire, / Doubt that the sun doth move" (116–17). Doubts relating to the stars and sun in the universe arose in the late Renaissance and represented a challenge to the traditional view of the universe. Some find here evidence that Hamlet, after his crushing discovery of great evil, has lost his faith in traditional values, which include the belief that woman can be both fair and true. Finally, certain Romantics insist that Hamlet suffers primarily because his love for Ophelia has not been requited. Such emphasis on the love theme, however, seriously reduces the element of conflict involving Hamlet and Claudius, and removes the play itself from the realm of high tragedy.

The king and queen depart with their attendants as soon as they see Hamlet coming. The queen's words, "But look where sadly the poor wretch comes reading" (168), provide useful stage directions, but they do more. They suggest, as do certain other passages in the play, that Gertrude's love and concern for her son are genuine. The Ghost, commanding Hamlet to "Leave her to heaven," had called her "a weak vessel"—and so she is, for she willingly became a partner in an incestuous marriage. But her ready response to the attentions of Claudius seems to be the extent of her guilt.

Enter Hamlet, reading. This is the prince who had vowed to "sweep to [his] revenge" without delay, wiping away "all trivial fond records, / All saws of books" (I. v. 31, 99–100). Perhaps through such reading and through contemplation, he has gained emotional control. In this episode in Scene 2, his antic disposition, manifested in his satirical baiting of Polonius, actually reveals a rational mind. His replies and questions addressed to the Lord Chamberlain call for rather close attention.

Does Hamlet recognize Polonius? Yes. Polonius is a fishmonger (174), an appellation that the Lord Chamberlain immediately denies. Yet here is Polonius on another fishing expedition using his "bait of falsehood" and, by indirections, seeking to find directions out. Moreover, *fishmonger* was a cant Elizabethan term for *bawd*— not an inappropriate word, however vulgar, for a man who has just declared that he would "loose" his daughter on Hamlet. The prince may already be aware of the real fisherman, King Claudius, on whose behalf Polonius is acting.

That Hamlet uses a metaphor relating to lust is suggested by his remark "Then I would you were so honest" (176) since the term *honesty* frequently was used as the opposite of *frailty*, or sexual immorality. In so many words, then, Hamlet is denouncing Polonius as being more immoral than a procurer. Apparently the disillusioned idealist, the prince seems to be obsessed with the subject of honesty. Among those in authoritative positions, he finds no honesty. Even innocent daughters may be corrupted; even the ostensibly healthful rays of the sun may lead to the breeding of maggots in a dead dog, "being a good kissing carrion" (181–82). He does not finish the statement; instead, he suddenly asks Polonius, "Have you a daughter?" Then he provides riddling advice: "Let her not walk i' th' sun. Conception is a blessing, but not as your daughter may conceive" (185–87).

Page after page has been filled with explication of this brief passage with its plays on the words *sun* and *conception*. Among the interpretations widely accepted is that these lines emphasize Hamlet's awareness of rottenness in the Court and his conviction that Claudius, the new ruler, is the source of that rottenness which threatens to contaminate or destroy all at Elsinore. There remains the possibility that, since Hamlet seems to know that Polonius will "loose" his daughter upon him, Ophelia has become an obsession for Hamlet. The difficulty with this conclusion is that it is exactly the one reached by Polonius. One point is indisputable. Hamlet is overwhelmingly successful in convincing the Lord Chamberlain that he is "far gone," suffering "much extremity for love" (190–92).

That Hamlet the scholar has been preoccupied with the problem of morality is indicated by his reference in Scene 2 to "the satirical slave," whose remarks on senility he paraphrases (198–202). The reference is to Juvenal, second-century Roman moral satirist; it follows, then, that the larger subject of Hamlet's discourse in this episode is the prevalence of evil. The prince's melancholy, never far below the surface, is evident. Once more, death seems to him to be preferable to life. "Will you walk out of the air, my lord?" asks Polonius. "Into my grave?" Hamlet counters (210).

In warmth, Hamlet's greeting of Rosencrantz and Guildenstern as his "excellent good friends" matches the greeting that he accorded Horatio. It at once gives an insight into the normal mood of Hamlet before his tragedy began and reveals his yearning for honest comradeship. Add to this the fact that again he demonstrates his capacity for a quick change of mood. At first his remarks are spontaneous, good-natured ones, but not long after the subject of Fortune is introduced, they become serious and revealing—specifically when Rosencrantz remarks that he has no news to report "but that the world's grown honest" (241). Rejecting this conclusion, Hamlet, ostensibly changing the subject, speaks of Denmark and the world itself as a prison. From this emerges the theme of ambition. Now Hamlet is fully aware of what these two supposed friends are up to. Characteristically, he asks them in the name of friendship to be honest with him; just as characteristically, they seek to evade a direct answer but are practically forced to admit that the king and queen have sent for them.

There follows one of the several especially memorable passages in the play, one in which the prince is revealed as the disillusioned idealist (306–19). Here is a young intellectual who once embraced the Renaissance view of an ordered and moral universe in which man, endowed with reason, was the noblest creature, far above the bestial and near to the angelic. According to this concept, inherited from the Middle Ages, man occupies a place on a hierarchical scale midway between the beast and the angel: The first represents absence or rejection of reason; the second, pure reason that is equated with virtue. But Hamlet has learned that humanity has a terrifying capacity to reject reason, to descend to the bestial level: Subjects may murder kings, brother may kill brother; wives and mothers may hasten to incestuous sheets; boyhood friends may permit themselves to be used as spies, rejecting the sacred principles of friendship. Philosophy offers poor consolation under such conditions. For Hamlet, the world has become "a sterile promontory" and man no more than the "quintessence of dust."

Hamlet's speech (304 ff.), which includes the famous apostrophe to man, is more than a purple patch; it has significance in terms of the plot. Hamlet finds it desirable to explain his emotional state to Rosencrantz and Guildenstern, and he does so without revealing its cause. Rosencrantz laughs and makes a facetious remark relating to women, and this provides an easy transition to the next episode in this long scene.

Ultimately the actors will serve the prince in his first positive move against Claudius—reason enough for the announcement of their arrival and for the talk relating to them. But there are other points to be noticed here. "He that plays the king shall be welcome" (332). This is Hamlet's immediate response to the news; it is clearly a reference to Claudius, whom the prince holds to be no more than a Player-King, however skillful in acting the part. But is there possible relevance in the rivalry between the Children's Company and the adult companies (343 ff.)? Of course this is a topical allusion to the so-called "war of the theaters"—the rise of the companies of child actors which became serious rivals to the adult companies, including Shakespeare's, at the turn of the century. Having learned the details of this "late innovation," as Rosencrantz calls it, Hamlet moves from the particular to the general. His uncle, an object of ridicule when King Hamlet ruled Denmark, is now revered by the populace. The new popularity of both child actor and uncle-king, whom Hamlet sees as a shadow rather than the substance of royalty, illustrates the fickleness of public taste.

Just before the players appear in Scene 2, Polonius enters, confident that only he can inform Hamlet of their arrival. Again he is the target of Hamlet's biting satire. Most of the prince's remarks the Lord Chamberlain either does not hear or, at least, understand. Just as he had set himself up as an authority on word choice, so now he presents himself as one on drama (414–21). His catalogue of types of Elizabethan drama, pure and hybrid, provides wonderful comedy, all the more amusing because Polonius remains deadly serious. It also reveals Shakespeare's own familiarity with Elizabethan drama, the classical tragedies of Plautus, the tragedies of Seneca, and (to some extent) dramatic theory. With reference to Polonius, the implication is plain. As his advice to Laertes indicated, he is an educated individual; unfortunately, knowledge does not always lead to wisdom. In Polonius' case, vanity and age have taken their toll. If his methods were not so contemptible, perhaps he would deserve sympathy.

"O Jephthah, judge of Israel, what a treasure hadst thou!" exclaims Hamlet (422), having adopted the antic pose to the bewilderment of the Lord Chamberlain. But to paraphrase Polonius' words (207–208), there is method in his "madness." Jephthah sacrificed a beloved daughter, however unwillingly; in a sense, Polonius is sacrificing his daughter.

Hamlet then greets the players, once more demonstrating a

rapid change in mood. His warmth and genuine pleasure are apparent. Here, then, is another glimpse of Hamlet's mood prior to his discovery of appalling evil. This Wittenberg student, devoted to his studies, nevertheless enjoyed the theater just as he treasured companionship. His witty, good-natured remarks to the bearded player and to the youth who had played women's roles suggest a Hamlet anything but a dreamer. When he recalls the *Aeneas and Dido* play as one devoid of crowd-pleasing sallets (spicy improprieties) and affectation, the prince anticipates the point he will make later in his advice to the players (III. ii. 1–16). He endorses restraint and modesty as opposed to excess.

A grateful Hamlet pays tribute to the acting profession and directs Polonius to see that the players are "well us'd." Having made the arrangements for the performance of *The Murder of Gonzago* with the insertion of lines to be provided by him, Hamlet is left alone; again he soliloquizes at length. The prince now emerges as his own severest critic, denouncing himself as "a dull and muddy-mettled [irresolute] rascal," a dreamer "unpregnant of [unstirred by] my cause." But, rather curiously, it is the actor's description of Hecuba's grief, the histrionic display of sorrow for the death of Priam, that Hamlet most wanted to hear and that leads him to inveigh against himself, insisting that he has greater "motive and the cue for passion" (587). Passionate expression of grief is not positive action; indeed, it inhibits action. One wonders why the prince did not dwell upon Pyrrhus' act of vengeance, which seems to have unmistakable applicability to Hamlet.

Pyrrhus, enraged by the violent death of his father, Achilles, is determined to execute vengeance on King Priam, father of Achilles' slayer. Pyrrhus did delay, but only momentarily:

> for, lo! his sword,
> Which was declining on the milky head
> Of reverend Priam, seem'd i' th' air to stick,
> So, as a painted tyrant, Pyrrhus stood
> And, like a neutral to his will and matter,
> Did nothing.
>
> (499–504)

Hamlet unmistakably sees himself as "a neutral to his will and matter." In the lines spoken by the player, Pyrrhus promptly emerges as the perfect revenger, the very prototype of the king-killer:

> And never did the Cyclops' hammers fall
> On Mars his armour forg'd for proof eterne
> With less remorse than Pyrrhus' bleeding sword
> Now falls on Priam.
>
> (511–14)

A whole school of critics, beginning with the Romantics, have taken Hamlet's self-criticism as the essential truth: He is the inveterate dreamer; he cannot bring himself to act positively until it is too late to prevent his own downfall. But is one to assume that Hamlet, scholar and son of a father idolized for his superior virtues, would identify himself with the blood-smeared Pyrrhus who made "malicious sport / In mincing with his sword [Priam's] limbs" (536–37)? If the Greek warrior is held to be the model of the dutiful son avenging his father's death, little wonder that Hamlet said after hearing the Ghost's accusation and injunction, "O cursed spite, / That ever I was born to set it right" (I. v. 189–90). Yet so intense are his feelings at this point that Hamlet denounces himself as a coward, apparently for not having acted as promptly as Pyrrhus did. And he reaches the climax of passion as he denounces Claudius and cries out for vengeance: "Bloody, bawdy villain! / Remorseless, treacherous, lecherous, kindless [unnatural] villain! / O, vengeance!" (608–10). But Hamlet masters his fury; he is aware that he has permitted passion, not reason, to dominate him. It is now that he reveals his plan to "catch the conscience of the King"—unmistakably to establish Claudius' guilt.

Little wonder that *The Tragedy of Hamlet* has been referred to sometimes as "The Mystery of Hamlet." In the last scene of Act I, Hamlet vowed to sweep to his revenge; weeks have passed and he has not made even an attempt. Many have argued that the wary Claudius, well protected by his palace guard, has not given the prince a chance to attack him. But there is another complication. After rejoining Marcellus and Horatio, Hamlet declared, "It is an honest ghost, that let me tell you" (I. v. 138). Now, at the end of Act II, he has genuine doubts regarding the nature of the Ghost and feels compelled to confirm its testimony. As in the discovery scene, he may speak of heaven, but the thought of hell persists in his mind

(See I. v. 92–93 and II. ii. 613). So far, only when he was in a state of great excitement marked by "wild and whirling words" has Hamlet had no doubts about the Ghost. Although he becomes quite excited emotionally at the climax of his soliloquy, he controls himself and immediately plans to verify the Ghost's accusation. The conclusion to be drawn is that when Hamlet is in control of his passion, he recognizes, as Horatio did, that the Ghost may represent evil: "The spirit that I have seen / May be the devil; and the devil hath power / T' assume a pleasing shape" (627–29). A sufficient number of honored Shakespearean critics agree that this is a real fear, not an excuse for inaction. But the Gonzago play seems to be designed primarily to force Claudius to reveal his guilt rather than to establish the Ghost's honesty. Does it follow, then, that Hamlet is intent upon making clear to all that he will execute public justice, not carry out barbaric blood-revenge?

Some critics insist that this entire episode serves first of all to emphasize Hamlet's inability to act positively. Does not the prince refer to his "weakness" and his "melancholy" (630)? And was it not the lines dealing with Hecuba's grief which he was most anxious to hear? Certain distinguished Shakespeareans find Hamlet to be a victim of passion—the passion of excessive grief, which was known as melancholy adust. Whether or not one agrees that Hamlet delays fatally because he is the victim of the destructive passion of melancholy, the subject deserves attention. Certainly it would be a mistake to ignore the many textual references, direct and indirect, to melancholy. For the immediate purpose, it must suffice to state that when Hamlet speaks in Scene 2 of the world as a prison (249–53), when he declares that he has "foregone all custom of exercise" and that for him the earth seems to be "a sterile promontory" and the air "a foul and pestilent congregation of vapours" (305–15), when he tells Rosencrantz and Guildenstern that he is "but mad north-north-west," and that he knows "a hawk from a handsaw" when "the wind is southerly" (396–97), the ideas and words derive from prevailing Renaissance theories on melancholy. According to the theorists, the melancholy individual was prone to dwelling at inordinate length upon his difficulties, real or imagined; but, so far from remaining lethargic, he often would become hysterical and would act impulsively. It must be admitted that much of this could be considered applicable to Hamlet. But, of course, one's sympathies remain with him. He indeed has "great cause"—the moral "falling off" of a mother; the death of a beloved father and king; the survival and elevation to kingship of a man who, however adroit, is manifestly inferior to the late King Hamlet. Moreover, consistent with his honesty with himself and his superior intelligence, the prince anticipates, as it were, any and all his critics in his recognition that passion threatens to engulf him and to make it impossible for him to be "express [exact] and admirable in action" and "noble in reason."

It is a completely controlled, rational Hamlet who speaks the lines at the very end of this long, complex Scene 2: "I'll have grounds / More relative than this. The play's the thing / Wherein I'll catch the conscience of the King" (632–34). Some stage Hamlets—the late John Barrymore, for example—rendered these lines as hysterical rant; those who grasped the character and situation accurately—Sir John Gielgud, for example—spoke them with vigor and determination, devoid of all rant.

ACT III

Summary

Rosencrantz and Guildenstern report to the king and queen that Hamlet admits feeling "distracted" but will not tell them the cause and keeps himself aloof "with a crafty madness." In reply to Gertrude's question, they report that Hamlet received them graciously and seemed pleased to hear of the players' arrival. Polonius adds that the prince wants the king and queen to witness the performance of a play. Claudius expresses his pleasure at hearing that Hamlet shows such an interest and agrees to attend the performance. He then instructs Rosencrantz and Guildenstern to encourage Hamlet's new interest. The two depart.

At the king's request, Gertrude leaves. Now Polonius' plan to have Ophelia meet Hamlet while the king and the Lord Chamberlain secretly observe and listen can be put into effect. Polonius instructs his daughter: Ophelia is to appear to be reading a book of devotions so that the prince will not suspect her purpose. In an aside, Claudius reveals the extent to which Polonius' words lash his conscience. Counselor and king withdraw just before Hamlet enters.

For the third time in the play, Hamlet soliloquizes. He now ponders the question of "To be, or not to be" when one is faced with great difficulties and tribulations. At the sight of Ophelia, he is aroused from contemplation. Assuming that she is indeed reading a book of devotions, he urges her to pray for him.

When Ophelia says that she has certain gifts that she has received from him and now wishes to return, he declares that he has given her nothing. To her bewilderment, he proceeds to question her honesty and denies that he ever loved her, whatever he may have said in the past. All men, Hamlet declares, are "arrant knaves"; none should be believed. Therefore, he concludes, she should seek haven in a nunnery. Quite abruptly the prince asks Ophelia where her father is. She replies that he is at home. Again he returns to the general subject of love, declaring that should she ever marry, she will "not escape calumny." And again he gives her bitter advice: "Get thee to a nunnery, go." Left to herself, Ophelia expresses her profound sorrow at witnessing what she is convinced is the overthrow of a noble mind which had been the very pattern of virtue and accomplishment.

Promptly, the king and Polonius join Ophelia. Claudius now is convinced that love is not the cause of Hamlet's affliction; rather, it is "something in his soul / O'er which his melancholy sits on brood" (172–73). No less convinced that Hamlet's behavior constitutes a great threat to him, the king tells Polonius that he has suddenly decided to have Hamlet conducted to England, whose ruler owes tribute to Denmark. Polonius is still convinced that the prince suffers from love-madness, but he endorses Claudius' decision. He then tells his daughter that she need not say anything since the king and he heard all. The Lord Chamberlain urges that one more attempt be made to ferret out Hamlet's secret: let the queen talk with her son severely on the subject of his melancholy while Polonius listens from a place of concealment; then, if Hamlet's secret is not exposed, let Claudius send the prince to England or confine him elsewhere. "It shall be so," says the king. "Madness in great ones must not unwatch'd go" (195–96).

Hamlet instructs the players how to deliver the lines of *The Murder of Gonzago* and discusses the art of acting in general, urging them to avoid unnatural extremes in the imitation of an action. Polonius enters with Rosencrantz and Guildenstern; he announces that the king and the queen are ready to "hear" the play.

While members of the Court assemble, Hamlet praises Horatio for his steady temperament and then gives him the details relating to *The Murder of Gonzago*. He asks Horatio to keep close watch on the king, just as he himself will do, and to note the king's reaction to one speech in particular. If Claudius does not reveal guilt at that point, the prince continues, both have seen "a damned ghost," not the honest spirit of the late King Hamlet. The faithful Horatio assures the prince that he will follow the instructions carefully.

The Court group enters the hall. Claudius greets his nephew and receives a baffling reply. There follows a brief exchange between Hamlet and Polonius. When his mother invites him to sit beside her, Hamlet declines, lying down at Ophelia's feet.

The play itself is preceded by a dumb-show, or pantomime, depicting a king and queen deeply in love with each other. When the king falls asleep on a bed of flowers, the queen departs. A man enters, removes the king's crown and kisses it, pours poison into the king's ear, and leaves. The queen returns, finds her husband dead, and gives expression of grief. The murderer returns and, after the king's body has been carried away, woos the queen. At first she resists his attentions, but soon accepts his love.

In answer to Ophelia's question, Hamlet assures her that the actor who enters to speak the lines of the prologue will "tell all"— that is, explain the significance of the action. When the four lines of the prologue are recited, Ophelia remarks that it is brief. "As woman's love," Hamlet replies. The performance of the play then commences.

The action in *The Murder of Gonzago* is the same as that depicted in the dumb-show up to the point where the murderer, identified as one Lucianus, nephew to the king, pours the poison in the king's ear. The queen is emphatic in her declaration never to remarry should she become a widow. In the words of the player-king, spoken as he is about to "beguile / The tedious day with sleep . . . 'Tis deeply sworn."

The brief interlude gives Hamlet the opportunity to ask Gertrude how she likes the play. "The lady protests too much," she replies. Claudius then asks Hamlet if he is familiar with the dramatic story and if it is in any way an offense. The prince replies: "No, no, they do but jest, poison in jest. No offence i' th' world." Again in reply to a question by Claudius, he explains that the play is called "The Mouse-trap." The prince's words to Ophelia especially reveal his state of excitement. He calls upon the actor playing the role of the murderer to stop grimacing and begin to speak his lines. All along he has been, as Ophelia says, "a good chorus." When the murderer pours the poison into the player-king's ear, he assures the audience that this is the dramatization of an actual murder and that they will see how the murderer "gets the love of Gonzago's wife."

Alarmed, Claudius rises. Polonius calls for an end of the play. The king cries out: "Give me some light. Away!" All but Hamlet and Horatio leave the hall. It is a triumphant prince who, after reciting a bit of doggerel and indulging in ironic banter with Horatio, declares that he will "take the ghost's word for a thousand pound." Horatio agrees that the king reacted like a guilty man.

Rosencrantz and Guildenstern return to inform Hamlet that the king is greatly disturbed and that the queen wishes to speak with her son privately. In his state of high excitement, the prince takes special pleasure in confusing the two. Aware that they tend to believe that personal ambition explains his behavior, Hamlet explains that he lacks "advancement." Especially his ironic remarks reveal his contempt for so-called friends who will not be forthright with him and presume to think that they can "pluck out the heart of [his] mystery." Polonius enters with the same message for Hamlet: The queen wishes to speak with him. Again the prince adopts the antic style, voicing absurd irrelevancies before he informs the Lord Chamberlain that he will honor his mother's request. He is then left to himself.

Now Hamlet's words, spoken in soliloquy, reveal a bloodthirsty mood. But he counsels himself not to inflict physical harm upon his mother, to whose chamber he will now go: "Let me be cruel, not unnatural," he says.

The king informs Rosencrantz and Guildenstern that since it is unsafe to let Hamlet's "madness range," they are commissioned to conduct the prince to England as soon as possible. Guildenstern and Rosencrantz express their dedication to the service of the king and their conviction that the welfare of the State depends upon his health and safety. They assure the king that they will waste no time in carrying out his instructions.

Polonius enters and reports that Hamlet is going to his mother's chamber and that he himself will hide behind the arras (wall hanging of tapestry) to hear what is said. Claudius thanks him, and the Lord Chamberlain departs.

Alone, a conscience-stricken Claudius reveals his thoughts. He identifies himself with Cain, the first murderer and the first fratricide, and asks himself whether or not, in view of the magnitude of his crime, he can hope for divine mercy. He answers his own question: Christian mercy is denied to no one who is truly penitent. But he knows full well that penance is more than the expression of regret; restitution, to the extent possible, is necessary. Since he will not give up either the crown or his dead brother's wife, the efficacy of prayer is denied him. In despair and torment he cries out: "Help, angels! Make assay!" (69). And he expresses the fervent hope that "All may be well" (72) as he kneels in an attempt to pray.

Hamlet enters with drawn sword but restrains himself from slaying Claudius because his father was killed before he could be shriven of his sins, venial and/or mortal. Hamlet is determined that Claudius die in a state of sin: Hell, not heaven or even purgatory, must be his destination. The prince leaves for his mother's chamber. The king rises, aware that his words "fly up" but that his "thoughts remain below."

Polonius, good as his word, has preceded Hamlet to the queen's chamber and now instructs her to be firm with her son. He hides behind the arras just before the prince enters.

Gertrude begins firmly to reprove her son, but his replies and his insistence that she sit down and listen to him so frighten her that she calls out for help. From behind the arras, Polonius echoes her cry. Promptly Hamlet draws his rapier, runs it through the arras, and kills the Lord Chamberlain. "Is it the King?" he asks his distraught mother. But Gertrude can only exclaim upon the monstrosity of the deed. Fiercely Hamlet replies, "Almost as bad, good mother, / As kill a king, and marry with his brother" (28–29). Only then does he lift up the arras and reveal the dead Polonius, whom he describes as a fool.

The prince then begins to castigate Gertrude. He shows her contrasting portraits, one of King Hamlet, whom he lauds, the other of Claudius, whom he execrates. How, he asks, could she have given herself to Claudius? Hamlet, in effect, answers his own question, accusing his mother of lustfulness. The tormented Gertrude implores him to speak no more.

Suddenly the Ghost appears—but only to Hamlet, who is sure that it comes to reprove him for his delay. Solemnly the Ghost says that it comes "to whet [Hamlet's] almost blunted purpose" (111). But immediately it expresses concern for Gertrude, who is convinced that her son has lost his mind. At its behest, Hamlet speaks gently to his mother but becomes highly excited in his effort to convince her of the presence of King Hamlet's spirit. The Ghost departs.

When Gertrude expresses her conviction that her son is the victim of a hallucination, Hamlet replies that it is not madness that he has spoken and implores her to acknowledge her guilt, confessing herself to heaven. At least, he says, let her assume a virtue, or take the first step toward virtue by avoiding further cohabitation with Claudius. Now in a calmer mood, the prince points to the body of Polonius and voices his regret for the death of the Lord Chamberlain. He bids his mother goodnight and adds that he must be cruel only to be kind. But when she asks what she must do, his reply is bitterly ironic: let her return in wantonness to Claudius; let her report that he is "mad in craft." Is that not the duty of a loving queen? Gertrude vows that she will not breathe a word of what her son has said to her.

Hamlet tells his mother that he is being sent to England, accompanied by his two schoolfellows whom he completely distrusts. Convinced that they function as agents for his destruction, he will turn the tables on them. In this mood of violent determination, the prince callously states that he will remove Polonius' body: "I'll lug the guts into the neighbour room." Again he bids Gertrude goodnight.

Commentary

It is an increasingly fearful Claudius who appears in Scene 1 of Act III, although he remains in control of himself. As the conflict between him and Hamlet intensifies, he demonstrates his decisiveness, his capacity for immediate action. His control is especially manifest in his care to keep up the appearance of being unselfishly concerned about his nephew's well-being and in his apparent graciousness with which he agrees promptly to honor Hamlet's request that he and the queen witness the performance of the play. But the intensity of his concern makes it clear that he recognizes Hamlet's so-called "turbulent . . . lunacy" as a dangerous threat to himself.

Claudius' aside (50–54) explicitly reveals the mind of a man

tormented by guilt. In his aside, Claudius applies the words to himself: "How smart a lash that speech doth give my conscience!" He
compares his "painted word"—what he says publicly—to the "harlot's cheek, beautied with plast'ring art" (51–53). Since Hamlet also
will dwell upon the "plast'ring art" and upon the subject of illicit
sex, the king's words suggest that the prince is not suffering just
from sexual nausea caused by his mother's incestuous marriage.
Illicit sex or lust, here represented by the harlot, symbolizes pervading evil and man's descent to the bestial level. "O heavy burden!" the
king concludes. He has emerged as a human being, however sinful.
Shakespeare has provided Claudius' private confession of guilt, but
one is not told here what is the crime or crimes.

Needless to say, Claudius remains the powerful adversary. He is
Machiavellian not only in his ability to dissemble and his use of
underhanded methods but also in his capacity for prompt action.
Rosencrantz and Guildenstern are directed to renew their efforts
and Polonius will be given another chance to verify his judgment.
But the king stands ready to send Hamlet away—not back to Wittenberg, but to England, where he can be taken care of in one way or
another. "Madness in great ones must not unwatch'd go" (196). This
line deserves repetition. It reveals at once the king's increasing fear
and his care to express himself so that the listener (Polonius here)
assumes that only the welfare of the prince and the State are
involved. Moreover, this line serves to remind members of the audience (and readers) that Hamlet is no ordinary individual. In a hierarchical society, he is one of the "great ones," which means that all that
affects him has public, not merely private, import.

Both Polonius and Gertrude remain in character. The Lord
Chamberlain is the author of what Claudius chooses to call "lawful
espials"; it is he who coaches his daughter on how to play her ignoble part; it is he who remains vainly confident that only he is qualified to counsel the king. If Polonius acknowledges blame for using
underhanded methods (46–49), he seems to do so only in vanity,
welcoming this chance to display himself as a man of wisdom.

As before, Gertrude shows proper motherly concern for an
ailing son. In this connection, it will be noted that she is the one who
asks if Rosencrantz and Guildenstern have tried to interest Hamlet
in some amusement or other (14–15). But also as before, the queen
accepts uncritically whatever Claudius says and willingly accedes

to his wishes. She is the dutiful wife, to be sure—but in a marriage that is incestuous.

The "To be, or not to be" soliloquy (56–89) in Scene 1 is surely one of the great dramatic monologues in world literature; it is as well known as any passage in the Shakespearean canon and a favorite selection for memorization. The prince's meditation transcends the personal. Much of what he says is applicable to all humanity, especially when he provides a generalized list of human miseries:

> For who would bear the whips and scorns of time,
> The oppressor's wrong, the proud man's
>   contumely,
> The pangs of dispriz'd love, the law's delay,
> The insolence of office, and the spurns
> That patient merit of the unworthy takes . . .
>
> (70–74)

The entire speech has been called the "central soliloquy" in the play, coming as it does at the midpoint of the entire action. It poses many critical problems. In view of the often widely disparate interpretations of this soliloquy, it would be naive to ignore the difficulties of interpretation.

In the first place, the soliloquy comes as something of a surprise after the conclusion of Act II, which exhibited Hamlet rational and determined, intent upon carrying out a positive action that, he was sure, would resolve all doubts relating to Claudius. Now he seems to have reverted to the mood of the first soliloquy (I. ii. 129–59)—the mood of the prince who would welcome death, crushed as he was primarily by his mother's marriage to her brother-in-law. There are lines that may support any one of the major interpretations of the play. The Romantics, who see Hamlet as the dreamer, find support when the prince says:

> And thus the native hue of resolution
> Is sicklied o'er with the pale cast of thought,
> And enterprises of great pith and moment
> With this regard their currents turn awry,
> And lose the name of action.
>
> (84–88)

Those who are convinced that the tragic hero procrastinates because he is suffering from excessive grief find in the soliloquy one of those violent oscillations of mood typical of the extreme melancholic individual, although the subsequent episode involving Ophelia provides a better example. And then there are those who find in this soliloquy evidence of Hamlet's moral scrupulousness which makes it impossible for him to abandon the resources of God-given reason and sweep to his revenge in the manner of Pyrrhus. In his restraint they find an intellectual skepticism and honesty with himself that are commendable. For all three groups of theorists, Hamlet's eloquent speech elucidates his expression of despair at the end of Act I, Scene 5: "The time is out of joint; —O cursed spite, / That ever I was born to set it right."

"To be, or not to be: that is the question." So Hamlet begins his contemplations. In view of his words shortly thereafter, the assumption usually is made that he is asking whether one should choose to live or to die. But immediately after posing the question, the prince defines two possible courses, neither one of which involves death and certainly not suicide. First, he asks if passive acceptance of "outrageous fortune" is not the nobler course to follow. Stoic philosophy, particularly the Roman Stoicism of Seneca, inculcated such forbearance. According to the dedicated Stoic, pagan and Christian, the final aim of moral action is to destroy passion since no action can be virtuous unless it proceeds from a healthy and upright will.

The second course involves positive action—taking "arms against a sea of troubles, / And by opposing end them." If, as is widely held, Hamlet has a public obligation to remove the rottenness in Denmark, Shakespeare here may have had in mind the contrasting philosophical arguments of Cicero, which vied with those of Seneca in popularity among educated Elizabethans. In his orations, Cicero ridiculed Stoicism, arguing that cloistered virtue is a form of cowardice. On the basis of all this, it follows that Hamlet indeed faces a moral dilemma.

The young prince next considers a third possible solution to his problem—suicide. Unlike the Greek and certain Roman Stoics, Seneca argued against self-slaughter. One is puzzled because Hamlet expresses thoughts that are completely at variance with those he voiced earlier, and for that matter with what he has experienced. In the first soliloquy, he showed himself to be restrained by his knowledge that "the Everlasting had . . . fix'd / His canon 'gainst self-slaughter" (I. ii. 131–32). But the Christian argument finds no place in this later soliloquy. Hamlet states, in effect, that oblivion may be preferable—but only if death brings oblivion:

> To die; to sleep;—
> To sleep? Perchance to dream! Ay, there's the
> rub [obstacle in a game of bowls];
> For in that sleep of death what dreams may come,
> When we have shuffl'd off this mortal coil,
> Must give us pause.
>
> (64–68)

The reason for this fear of death (if that is what it is) is made more explicit in three memorable lines: "But that the dread of something after death, / The undiscover'd country from whose bourn / No traveller returns, puzzles the will" (78–80). How are these lines to be interpreted? Does Hamlet not reject the possibility that the Ghost was the spirit of his father? Earlier in the play, he spoke of his soul as immortal (I. v. 66–67). Why now should it be that the thought of death "puzzles the will"? The Ghost described its condition of afterlife not as an "undiscover'd country" but as the Catholic purgatory necessary for the soul's purification before translation to heaven. Has Hamlet now embraced the Elizabethan Protestant belief, stated and amplified in sermon and devotional literature that, once separated from the body, the soul cannot return to this world? The eminent Swiss reformer Henry Bullinger (1504–75), many of whose works were translated into English, wrote on this very subject in words that anticipate those of Shakespeare found in this soliloquy. Souls "go a journey, chancing into unknown countries . . . from whence they cannot return." Perhaps the dramatist has simply made poetic use of what had become a popular tradition by the time he wrote *Hamlet*. There may be another explanation; Shakespeare may have had in mind the difference between the return from the grave of an individual like Lazarus in flesh and blood, in contrast to the return of the spirit, or soul. But one thing is clear. Hamlet has not departed from Christianity; there is no evidence that he doubts the existence of heaven and hell, both of which prompt him to his revenge, or so he has said.

All this does not exhaust the complexities in this soliloquy. Hamlet concludes with these lines:

> Thus conscience does make cowards of us all
> And thus the native hue of resolution
> Is sicklied o'er with the pale cast of thought,
> And enterprises of great pith and moment
> With this regard their currents turn awry,
> And lose the name of action.
>
> (83–88)

Do these lines point unmistakably to a Hamlet who falters after the discovery of great evil and who has difficulty deciding what action can be taken without violating one's own moral code?

Consider the first aphoristic line. In general usage, conscience means ethical sense or scrupulousness; its function is to determine the moral quality of action, enjoining what is good. Prompt action without concern for morality is not desirable.

The word *conscience*, however, also meant "consequences" in Shakespeare's time. That meaning is applicable here since Hamlet has been speaking of suicide as an escape from life's burdens. Understandably, some critics insist that fear of death, even if that death be the result of suicide or not, goes far toward explaining his procrastination. But would one prefer a Hamlet who did not pause to reflect upon the morality involved in "enterprises of great pith and moment"? It has been held that Hamlet's comment "Thus conscience does make cowards of us all" is the central utterance in the play, for it reveals the civilized and Christian Hamlet incapable of revenge.

The prince has been restrained by doubts relating to the nature of the Ghost that would have him execute prompt revenge on Claudius but have him leave Gertrude "to heaven." That is indisputable. But there are two other possible reasons for Hamlet's delay. The players have just arrived at Elsinore, and only now does Hamlet have an opportunity to force Claudius into a position where the guilt acknowledged in his private thoughts may be exposed publicly. There is also the possibility that he is held back by his awareness of his intense personal hatred of his uncle-king. Schooled in idealistic philosophy and religious thought, he may believe that his motive for action is not a pure one, that the personal element contaminates that of public justice. If any or all of this be true, then the soliloquy is not to be interpreted as just another manifestation of morbid introspection peculiar to a philosophical dreamer or to an individual suffering from the passion of excessive grief.

The episode that follows provides a shocking change of mood and shows a Hamlet cruel in his treatment of Ophelia.

Shakespeare prepared his audience for this episode which relates back to the one in Act II, Scene 2, where Hamlet baited Polonius with riddling words: "Let her [your daughter] not walk i' th' sun. Conception is a blessing, but not as your daughter may conceive. Friend, look to't" (185–87). Polonius has not looked to it; in the king's service, he has "loosed" Ophelia upon Hamlet. As in the earlier episode, the prince introduces the theme of honesty—an obsession with him, be it with reference to his own manifestations of grief ("Seems, madam! Nay, it is; I know not 'seems.'"), the nature of the Ghost, the behavior of onetime friends, or the moral character of women. In view of all this, it is difficult to avoid the conclusion that Hamlet, like members of the audience, is fully aware of what is happening: Ophelia is being used just as Rosencrantz and Guildenstern were used; the king and Polonius are spying on him even now. Hamlet, it would appear, is only too aware that Ophelia represents "innocent love" corrupted—coming to him not of her own volition but as a spy seeking by indirections to find directions out. And the ultimate source of the corruption is King Claudius, who rules in a world where women prove "frail" and few men can be believed.

Hamlet's mood is exactly that which dominated him when, after eulogizing man, he said to Rosencrantz and Guildenstern, "Man delights not me, —no, nor woman neither, though by your smiling you seem to say so" (II. ii. 321–22). No individual can escape contamination in the world as Hamlet now finds it. Not without logic, then, the disillusioned prince declares that he had never given Ophelia tokens of love and that he was never honest with her: "You should not have believ'd me, for virtue cannot / so innoculate our old stock but we shall relish it. / I loved you not" (118–20). In other words, since the Fall of Adam and Eve, all are sinners; none can escape corruption. Hamlet accuses himself of pride, vengefulness, selfish ambition—indeed, of more offenses than he is able to think of: "We are arrant knaves all; believe none of us." These words are heard by Ophelia and overheard by Claudius and Polonius, but Hamlet really speaks to and for Everyman.

What then can Ophelia do? Hamlet tells her, "Go thy ways to a nunnery" (131–32). That he is fully aware that Ophelia has been and remains chaste, that she is the hapless victim of a father incapable of honest methods, is implicit in Hamlet's admonition:

> If thou dost marry, I'll give thee this plague for
> thy dowry: be thou as chaste as ice, as pure as
> snow, thou shalt not escape calumny. Get thee to a
> nunnery, go.
>
> (139–42)

Surely these lines would have little significance if Ophelia were unchaste and if Hamlet were not aware of how she had been "loosed" upon him.

There is a second level of meaning here, one that is consistent with Hamlet's bitter statement that time has proven feminine beauty and honesty to be incompatible (111–16). In the present scene, he says that women make monsters of the men they marry (143–44); and, like the harlots of whom the conscience-stricken Claudius spoke in his aside, their cheeks are "beautied with plast'ring art" and they seek to excuse their wantonness as ignorance (148–52). After this devastating pronouncement, Hamlet repeats the injunction, "To a nunnery, go." In the slang of the militantly Protestant Elizabethan England, the term *nunnery* also meant "brothel." No member of Shakespeare's sixteenth- and seventeenth-century audience was likely to miss this scurrilous second level of meaning.

That the ultimate source of Hamlet's cynicism is his mother's marriage to her brother-in-law is evident when he says, "Those that are married already (all but one) shall live" (155–56). This includes an unmistakable reference to Claudius and probably a threat. Left to herself, Ophelia speaks lines which at once reveal the genuineness of her lost love and provide a full-length portrait of Hamlet before his tragedy began. It is the picture of the completely accomplished Renaissance man:

> O, what a noble mind is here o'erthrown!
> The courtier's, soldier's, scholar's, eye, tongue,
>   sword;
> The expectancy and rose of the fair state,
> The glass of fashion and the mould of form,
> The observ'd of all observers, quite, quite down!
>
> (158–62)

She is convinced that Hamlet is insane. He is not, however emotionally disturbed he may be. Nevertheless, it is possible that she expresses a basic truth—or so some respected critics believe. Perhaps Hamlet's suffering has resulted in such extreme disillusionment and melancholy that a once noble mind has been overthrown in the sense that he has become passion's slave. Certainly this interpretation is not to be ignored.

Emerging with Polonius from the hiding place, Claudius rejects the theory that his nephew suffers from love-madness, but, like his Lord Chamberlain, he is aware of an apparent method in the prince's alleged madness. In a state of uncertainty, he will allow Polonius another chance to force Hamlet into revealing the cause of his strange behavior. But if that proves futile, the king will have Hamlet sent to England. It is to be noted that Claudius continues to present the public image of a man who is unselfishly concerned and especially of one dedicated to the welfare of the State. This is implicit in his final line, which also includes an involuntary tribute to Hamlet's status: "Madness in great ones must not unwatch'd go."

In Scene 2, Hamlet's advice to the players, which takes up some fifty lines, seems on the surface to be interesting primarily not for what it contributes to *The Tragedy of Hamlet* but for what one learns about Shakespeare, the professional actor and playwright concerned that actors do justice to his script. Scholars have pointed out that a rival company of actors was noted for splitting the ears of the groundlings, those less affluent members of the audience who stood in the pit of the theater, pandering to those who confused bombast with eloquence and realism. That there is a personal element here seems likely, especially when Hamlet says, "And let those that play your clowns speak no more than is set down for them" (42–44), counsel hardly applicable to actors performing *The Murder of Gonzago*.

This episode also provides a desirable release of tension after the disturbing nunnery scene. And again it provides evidence of Hamlet's breadth of character and normal interests. He is shown to have been a young man who enjoyed the theater and as one whose critical judgment has been highly developed. If nothing else, this tends to refute the theory that the prince was the complete introvert unduly given to introspection, just as it adds somewhat to his intellectual stature.

Hamlet's chief concern in this episode is that *The Murder of Gonzago* be so performed that it will be a convincing imitation of life itself and, in this sense, will hold "the mirror up to nature." Only then can he be sure that it will provide the test of Claudius' conscience. If an unskillful player oversteps "the modesty of nature," presenting a "whirlwind of passion" that "out-herods Herod" (a character in the mystery plays notorious for bombast), the performance cannot possibly impress the courtly audience as worthy of serious consideration.

But there is more here. At another level, Hamlet is providing a commentary on humanity in general and making a plea for the use of God-given reason and a concern for truth as opposed to appearance. In a word, let man vindicate his supposed status as a "wondrous work" and the "paragon of animals." When the prince speaks of holding the mirror up to nature, one inevitably recalls Ophelia's encomium of a Hamlet who had been the "glass of fashion and the mould of form" (III. i. 161). Moreover, this episode looks forward to Hamlet's praise of Horatio as one who is not passion's slave.

Hamlet's praise of Horatio in Scene 2 (59–79) has been accepted by a great many commentators as the passage that establishes Horatio as the norm character in relation to the tragic hero—that is, as the individual in the play who possesses the very qualities that Hamlet should have if he is to avoid tragic downfall. The young man whom the prince so much admires is depicted as the true Stoic, one who accepts "Fortune's buffets" (strokes of ill fortune) with equanimity because he maintains proper balance between "blood and judgement" (74)—that is, between emotion and reason—and thus is not "passion's slave." One can understand why many believe this passage provides a key to the interpretation of *The Tragedy of Hamlet.* To be sure, the commoner Horatio, admirable as he is, has never been put to a test comparable in magnitude to that which Hamlet faces: Tragic heroes must be tested and the test must be a great one.

Hamlet requests Horatio to watch the king closely to see if Claudius' "occulted [hidden] guilt / Do not itself unkennel in one speech" (85–86). It is of some interest to know that the prince now has *his* spy. At Elsinore, where "seeming" and the use of indirections are commonplace, he will fight fire with fire, as it were. Ophelia has been "loosed" upon him; now he will have Horatio help in "unkenneling" Claudius' secret. His words reveal at least a premonition of the king's guilt; but then, since they are expressed in a conditional clause and since Hamlet goes on to consider the possibility that his "imaginations are as foul / As Vulcan's stithy" (88–89), the element of doubt relating to the nature of the Ghost is stressed once more. The question that disturbs some commentators remains: Is it an assumption of the play that the establishment of Claudius' guilt proves that Hamlet saw and listened to an "honest" ghost, not to an evil spirit, perhaps the Devil himself, who used a truth to make possible Hamlet's death and damnation?

As all prepare to see the play, Hamlet's state of high excitement comes through. "I must be idle," he says to Horatio (95), and this is a cue that he will adopt the antic pose again. This pose gives him the opportunity to make remarks to the king, to Polonius, and to Ophelia that may be interpreted as evidence of mental instability and, at the same time, serve to perplex a vitally concerned listener like Claudius. It may even be argued that at this moment shortly before the Mouse-trap is sprung, Hamlet is close to the breaking point. His reply to the king's apparently gracious concern for how Hamlet "fares" is calculated to strengthen the ambition theory first advanced by Rosencrantz and Guildenstern: "Excellent, i' faith, —of the chameleon's dish. I eat / the air, promise-cramm'd. You cannot feed capons / so" (98–100). No one should underestimate Claudius' intelligence; he is fully aware of the play upon the word *air* (heir) and of Hamlet's tacit reference to the fact that his uncle, not Hamlet himself, succeeded the late king. One satirical barb suffices for the time being. Hamlet next turns to Polonius, giving the Lord Chamberlain an opportunity to boast about his talent as an actor, indeed as one who once created the role of Julius Caesar in a university production. It will be recalled that Polonius has taken pride in skillful acting almost from the first, thus his directions first to Reynaldo and then to Ophelia, both of whom he coached on how to act their respective parts. One other point can be made in this connection. When Hamlet is told that Caesar was killed by Brutus, he replies: "It was a brute part of him to kill so capital a calf there" (110–12). For the prince to refer to Polonius as a calf is consistent with his calling him a "fishmonger" and "that great baby . . . not yet out of his swathing-clouts"; that is, it is another expression of contempt for this foolish old counselor. But not long hereafter, Polonius, engaged in another spying expedition, will be slain; and it will be Hamlet himself who will play the brute part. Shakespeare provides a bit of dramatic presaging here.

For his purpose, Hamlet must find a place where he can closely watch Claudius. But in his reply to Gertrude's invitation that he sit next to her, he is able to contribute to Polonius' theory; that is, he is mad for the love of Ophelia. The bawdy remarks he makes to that young lady carry forward the theme of honesty in women. "You are merry, my lord," says Ophelia. Hamlet's reply reveals his state of tension and his disillusionment. "O God, your only jig-maker" (132) may be paraphrased as "life is a farce." His lines which follow are packed with bitterness, and his ironic reference to the length of man's memory may be an indictment not only of Gertrude but also of himself: "remember me," the Ghost had intoned repeatedly. Hamlet, who had then declared that he would sweep to his revenge without delay, is reminded in this episode that four months have elapsed since his father's death.

Especially in pre-Shakespearean drama, the dumb-show was used to indicate action that was not presented in the play proper or to symbolize what was to be presented. The dumb-show here poses certain problems. It is certainly not one of those "inexplicable dumb-shows" Hamlet had criticized earlier (13). It includes most of the circumstances of the murder as told by the Ghost, although it includes nothing suggesting that Gertrude was unfaithful to King Hamlet when he was alive or that she was involved in the murder. Why did Shakespeare include this dumb-show? Why is not Claudius startled and aroused by it? These have been abiding questions among Shakespearean critics.

Since the play-within-a-play is written advisedly in an artificial style in contrast to the play proper, Shakespeare may have added the dumb-show to intensify the contrasting elements—so a few critics have believed. But, although Ophelia suggests that it may impart the argument (150), such was not the practice among English drama-tists. Then why should Shakespeare depart radically from the usual practice if he wished only to provide contrast? This has led to other conjectures. One is that Hamlet, who has arranged for the entire production, includes the dumb-show so that he will have a double opportunity of catching the conscience of the king. Another is that Hamlet did not anticipate the dumb-show and is annoyed at its pre-sentation. A third is that Claudius pays no attention to the prelimi-nary stage business, occupying himself, perhaps, in low-voiced talk with Gertrude. Thus he asks a bit later, "Have you heard the argument? Is there no offence in't?" (242–43). And, since all this is in the realm of conjecture, one may argue that Claudius, no ordinary villain, exercised supreme control during the dumb-show, a control he could not sustain when, in the play itself, Lucianus pours poison into the ear of the sleeping player-king. Whatever the answer may be, one thing is indisputable. Shakespeare achieves a dramatic master stroke, a moment of supreme excitement, when the king rises in fright and cries out: "Give me some light. Away!" (280). The Mouse-trap has been sprung; Hamlet has caught the conscience of the king.

The prince's reaction is not one of horror but of elation—understandably because, despite his expression of doubt, he now has absolute proof of Claudius' guilt. Perhaps he is relieved especially because he can act as one executing public justice, not just as a son carrying out blood revenge in accordance with an old, barbaric code. The difficulty, however, is that nowhere in the play does Hamlet explicitly question the propriety of revenge. One is reminded that some critics believe that Shakespeare was unable to surmount the basic difficulties of transmuting the earlier *Hamlet* material when he provided an unmistakably Christian framework for his dramatic version. The Ghost spoke truly: Claudius is guilty of fratricide and regicide. But is Hamlet to emerge as minister (one righteously carrying out God's vengeance upon a heinous sinner) or as scourge (one whose sinful act of taking vengeance into his own hands God permits for His own purpose, but who ultimately will face God's punishment). Again, it should be noted, Hamlet's prime concern has been to establish Claudius' guilt, not the "honesty" of the Ghost. All this deserves notice if one is to do justice to *The Tragedy of Hamlet* and to understand why it has been subject to apparently endless discussion. But this is not to deny that readers and audiences have not the slightest doubt that Hamlet, Prince of Denmark, should slay Claudius and remove the source of all rottenness in the State.

Exactly which lines Hamlet composed for insertion into *The Murder of Gonzago* is not known. But there are lines spoken by the player-king that seem to have direct applicability to Hamlet and his problem, certainly not to Claudius. Consider lines 197–207, begin ning "But what we do determine oft we break." Hamlet's announced purpose to move swiftly to revenge his father's murder was of "violent birth," and especially in his second soliloquy (II. ii. 576 ff.), he had questioned, in effect, whether or not his purpose lacked "validity" (strength) since Claudius survived and even seemed to flourish. The player-king's words on passion (204–207) may be a kind of indictment of Hamlet; some who see the prince as the slave of extreme melancholy particularly think so.

Hamlet's mood of excitement and elation is sustained in the first part of his dialogue with Rosencrantz and Guildenstern, one of whom informs him that the king is "In his retirement marvellous distemper'd" (312). "With drink, sir?" asks Hamlet, and one is reminded of his "dram of evil" speech, voiced when he waited for the appearance of the Ghost (I. iv. 13 ff.). In this current display of the antic disposition, his discourse, wild though it sounds to the king's spies, shows method and basic rationality. Especially this comes through when, after stating that he will obey his mother's request, he asks, "Have you any further trade with us?"—advisedly using the plural form of the pronoun and thus presenting himself to them not as a former schoolfellow and as a friend but as the Prince of Denmark (347). His use of irony is quite bitter and penetrating when he assures Rosencrantz and Guildenstern "by these pickers and stealers" that he still loves them. In an earlier scene, when they first sought him out, Hamlet had spoken of handshaking as the "appurtenance of welcome" employed as a matter of fashion and ceremony (II. ii. 388–89); his reference here in Scene 2 to hands and fingers as "pickers and stealers" is far more devastating. Apparently Hamlet enjoys misleading these two. "Sir, I lack advancement," he says to Rosencrantz; and then he concludes with a reference to a proverb that is indeed musty: "While the grass grows . . . " (358). But it is quite possible that the prince is again being ironical; he may well be expressing a strong desire to get on with the act of revenge.

When one of the players reenters with a recorder (an old type of flute), Hamlet, deadly serious, finds an even more devastating way of showing his contempt for Guildenstern. His longer speech at this point has wider application. Guildenstern states that he lacks the skill to play a recorder; yet he is presumptuous enough to think that he can "play" upon Hamlet, as the latter makes abundantly clear:

'Sblood,
do you think that I am easier to be play'd on than a

pipe? Call me what instrument you will, though
you can fret me, you cannot play upon me.

(385–88)"

In his praise of his true friend Horatio, Hamlet had lauded those
who "are not a pipe for Fortune's finger / To sound what stop she
please" (75–76). Now, having forced Claudius to reveal his guilt, perhaps Hamlet is announcing his right to be numbered as one of those.
But surely, in terms of the entire play, there is more here. The late
Aldous Huxley wrote provocatively that Hamlet, an idealist dedicated to truth, alone knew that man could be a whole orchestra, not
just a simple pipe to be played on. If that reading is correct, then
Hamlet, with his gift for universalizing, speaks for man who, were
he to realize his potential, indeed is the paragon of animals, like
unto the angels. Only the pragmatic, earth-bound and self-seeking,
be they high-placed or not, reject their heritage and imitate humanity so abominably in the theater of life.

Polonius, that easy target for Hamlet's barbs, enters. Once more
he is the bearer of stale news, and once more this old counselor renders himself ridiculous. He does, however, get an answer from the
prince; Hamlet will come to his mother by and by. And then, just
before all but Hamlet leave, the latter says, somewhat ambiguously,
"'By and by' is easily said" (404). It is possible that he is showing
again his awareness of having found occasion to delay.

So far in Scene 2, Hamlet has manifested first the mood of the
decisive, composed intellectual in his advice to the players; next, the
mood of the generous-minded and idealistic friend in his warm
praise of Horatio; then the mood of satirical gaiety in his words to
the king, Polonius, and Ophelia; and last, the mood of contempt and
aloofness in his words to Rosencrantz and Guildenstern. Now,
speaking in soliloquy at the end of this climactic scene, he provides a
prime example of a shocking shift in emotion. This is not the Hamlet
who exclaimed, "O cursed spite, / That ever I was born to set it
right!"—the Hamlet who recoiled at the thought of being called upon
to execute vengeance. Rather it is the Hamlet who, immediately
after hearing the Ghost's story, inveighed against Gertrude ("O most
pernicious woman!") and Claudius ("O villain, villain, smiling,
damned villain!"). It is the Hamlet who, in his second soliloquy, after
having denounced himself as "a rogue and peasant slave," cried
out, "Bloody, bawdy villain! / Remorseless, treacherous, lecherous,

kindless villain! / O, vengeance!" (II. ii. 608–10). If anything, his words here are even more greatly overwrought, what with the reference to yawning churchyards (open graves), hell's contagion, and (the very language of a Black Mass) drinking hot blood. These are words one would expect to hear not from the gifted hero of a high tragedy but rather from the protagonist in a melodramatic revenge play; they are not those of a tragic hero intent upon executing public justice but of an individual determined to carry out blood revenge come what may. Yet Shakespeare has provided motivation, and Hamlet's emotional stress is understandable. At the same time, it would seem that the dramatist exhibits in this passage a hero who is far from being able to accept "Fortune's buffets and rewards . . . with equal thanks"; in terms of the high standard of personal control that he found exemplified in Horatio, Hamlet is enslaved by passion.

But, characteristically, Hamlet checks himself: "Soft! now to my mother. / O heart, lose not thy nature" (410–11). Nor does one find here another excuse for delay, for Rosencrantz and Guildenstern had reported that the king was inaccessible. That his mother's sin remains a great part of his tragedy is re-emphasized. Hamlet prays that he will not follow the example of the matricidal Nero. He will "be cruel, not unnatural"; he will "speak daggers to her, but use none" (411–14).

In Scene 3, Claudius' soliloquy provides a second and far more detailed self-acknowledgment of guilt. As was said with reference to the first soliloquy (III. i. 50–54), villain though he is, Claudius (like Macbeth and in contrast to such a dedicated sinner as Richard III) possesses a conscience, one that hardly makes him cowardly but rather makes him an erring human being, not an inhuman monster. Claudius clearly is not a born villain; nor, however much he has sought to conceal his real self from others, does he seek to avoid moral and religious truth. He is orthodox and well schooled in Christian doctrine, fully aware that, so long as he holds on to what he has gained through acts of mortal sin, he cannot purge his soul of guilt. In his anguish he is indeed a "limed soul." At this particular moment in the action, it is possible to feel some pity for this tormented man despite his appalling crimes.

The Hamlet whose thoughts are revealed when he comes upon Claudius kneeling in an attempt to pray has startled and offended one commentator after another over the years, so vindictive does he seem to be. In an attempt to explain Hamlet's words, which, some insist, make any humane person recoil, that ever-present means for resolving doubts has been used again: Tradition—the original Hamlet story and the pattern established by typical Elizabethan and Jacobean revenge plays—asserts itself. It is undeniable that personal hatred, not just the concern for executing justice, motivates the prince in this speech. He would see his adversary eternally damned, not just deprived of mortality. But if it is possible to find sympathy for Claudius the tormented sinner, it is possible to understand Hamlet's inability to shake off the personal wrath against the man who killed his father and whored his mother.

Among the Romantics, all this is held to be another and, in this instance, crucial example of Hamlet's vacillation. It is argued that, so far from Hamlet's expressing a terrible resolve to kill Claudius in a state of sin, he is indulging in self-deception, grasping at another excuse for delay. Romantics (and other critics, for that matter) long since have found here the turning-point in the play. Indeed, had Hamlet slain Claudius in this scene, all other violent deaths, especially that of the tragic hero, would not have occurred. In reply, one may point out the obvious: The play would end prematurely and it would not be *The Tragedy of Hamlet* but rather a very unsatisfactory melodrama that ends abruptly after tantalizing the audience by introducing profound questions and complexities of character. More telling is this question: Who would like to have a Hamlet who, in a bloodthirsty mood, swept to his revenge, slaughtering the kneeling king? Despite all that one has learned about him up to this point in the action, Hamlet could not win sympathy; such a bloody act would lead to the conclusion that indeed a noble mind had been overthrown.

A last point may be made. Ironically, Hamlet is restrained by the belief that Claudius is making a "good" confession and thus escaping damnation. Thanks to the convention of the soliloquy, one is aware that he is unable to do so.

It is upon Scene 4, in particular, that the neo-Freudians depend for support of their explanation of Hamlet's conduct since here the tragic hero does manifest an overwhelming concern about Gertrude's sexual life. They find in this scene a Hamlet moved not by idealism and the Renaissance concept of family honor but by consuming jealousy due to his unconscious, incestuous love for his mother. For them, Hamlet's hatred of Claudius results from the fact that Claudius—rather than Hamlet himself—killed the king. In contrast to the neo-Freudians, the orthodox Shakespeareans, who never forget that Shakespeare was a man of the Renaissance, find in this scene a Hamlet who is a moral idealist and who neither exaggerates Gertrude's guilt nor indulges in self-righteousness.

It is quite possible that the neo-Freudian interpretation of Hamlet was popularized by the Laurence Olivier motion picture version of the play, which dates from the late 1940s. There, Gertrude and her son were depicted sitting upon a bed, the satin coverlet of which was arranged in voluptuous folds, when the two engaged in emotionally charged discourse. A closet, be it that of the queen or of Ophelia (mentioned earlier in the play), was a private sitting room, sometimes a sewing room but never a bedroom. In this scene, it is the private chamber to which Gertrude, with lady attendants on occasion, could retire.

In his counsel to Gertrude, Polonius urges her to let Hamlet know that "his pranks have been too broad to bear with" (2). It is probable that he refers specifically to the prince's remarks about a second marriage made in the course of the Mouse-trap play. When the Lord Chamberlain goes on to say, "I'll silence me e'en here" (4), Shakespeare achieves dramatic irony, probably well appreciated by his audience since the basic story elements were almost as well known as those of *Romeo and Juliet*.

Up to this scene, the extent of Gertrude's guilt has not been made clear. Now it may be concluded that she knew nothing about the murder of King Hamlet. She is appalled when Hamlet draws his rapier and drives the blade through the arras, killing Polonius. But her horror and surprise are just as great when Hamlet picks up her words and goes on to excoriate her: "A bloody deed! Almost as bad, good mother, / As kill a king, and marry his brother" (28–29). To paraphrase the Ghost's words when it first spoke to Hamlet, Gertrude is the weak vessel, deficient in moral insight and therefore susceptible to the importunings of Claudius. This estimate of her character finds support especially when her son, directing her to look upon the portraits of King Hamlet and Claudius, asks, "Ha! have you eyes?" (67). Only with reluctance can she move just a step toward moral awareness and self-criticism: "O, speak to me no more / These words like daggers enter in mine ears. / No more, sweet

Hamlet!" (94–96). Although she assures the prince that she will not breathe a word of what has been said (197–99), she does not promise to avoid further intimacy with Claudius. When the Ghost appears to Hamlet, Gertrude exclaims, "Alas, he's mad!" (105). Under the circumstances, her reaction is a natural one; but may not this serve to relieve her of the tormenting belief that Hamlet spoke truly to her, however cruelly? Her conduct in subsequent scenes tends to support such a conclusion.

The range of emotions that Hamlet exhibits in Scene 4 is great indeed. After concluding the "shenting" of Gertrude with a caustic indictment of "the bloat king," he practically gloats over the prospect of outdoing in craft Rosencrantz and Guildenstern, the willing servants of Claudius. He will thrust them as he would "adders fang'd"; they will "marshal [him] to knavery": "For 'tis the sport to have the engineer / Hoist with his own petar" (206–207). Here speaks a Hamlet who is far from being "A man that Fortune's buffets and rewards" takes "with equal thanks," but rather one who is prepared to "drink hot blood." However aware one is that Hamlet has "great cause," one should not ignore the fact that he is far from the ideal of which he declared Horatio to be the exemplar (III. ii. 68).

Many of the prince's lines seem to be as cruel as those he addressed to Ophelia in the nunnery scene, although the motivation is sounder since he has sprung the Mouse-trap and is addressing a mother notoriously lax in conduct. From the start, his tone is harsh enough to make Gertrude fear for her life. (There is no textual evidence that he threatens her with physical violence; the traditional stage directions indicate that he draws his sword only when he hears Polonius cry out from behind the arras.) "How now! A rat?" he asks—and one is forcibly reminded of the Mouse-trap set for Claudius. Once discovering that he has killed the elderly Lord Chamberlain, his remarks are callous and perfunctory: "Thou wretched, rash, intruding fool, farewell! / I took thee for thy better. Take thy fortune. / Thou find'st to be too busy is some danger" (31–33). Turning to Gertrude, Hamlet says coldly, "Leave wringing of your hands."

At the end of Scene 4, Hamlet's mood is determined not only by thoughts of the marriage bed but also by the "knavery" of Rosencrantz and Guildenstern. He speaks even more unfeelingly: "I'll lug the guts into the neighbour room" (212). Then he indulges himself in irony at the expense of the once-voluble Polonius, that "foolish prating knave." To be sure, one is aware that, in a sense, Polonius silenced himself—that is, he was an engineer hoisted by "his own petar," paying a steep price for his underhanded methods and over-confidence. But to assume that Hamlet has executed public justice simply will not do, as the prince's own words, to be noted below, make clear.

Little wonder that *Hamlet* has been called the most problematic play ever written and that the tragic hero's world has been described as one that is predominantly interrogative in mood. The discussion above does not exhaust the questions posed in Scene 4. In the pre-ceding scene, Hamlet had been restrained from killing his uncle-king only by vindictiveness, a determination not only to take the life of his adversary but also to insure Claudius' damnation. Now, acting impulsively, he strikes with his sword, convinced that its blade will reach the king. How could he explain the violent death? Would the testimony of the commoner Horatio be sufficient to clear his treas-ured reputation for honor? More important, would a subdued, rational Hamlet be satisfied that his motive for revenge was not tainted by a personal hatred outweighing public duty? These are questions which have been raised and which should not be ignored. So intense is Hamlet's detestation of Claudius that, in this scene, his invectives match those he used in the first and second soliloquies; but here they are amplified. Claudius is not only "A king of shreds and patches" (102); he is the "bloat king," a "paddock [toad]," a "bat," and a "gib [tom-cat]." The bestial images are used to represent extreme, loathsome sensuality.

All this is developed most effectively when Hamlet calls upon Gertrude to look at the pictures, the "counterfeit presentment of two brothers" (53–65). His words relate back to two important, earlier passages in the play, his first soliloquy and his advice to the players. In the soliloquy, the prince provided the initial contrast between his father and Claudius, deploring the sensuality of his mother that led to the incestuous marriage:

> So excellent a king; that was, to this,
> Hyperion to a satyr . . .
>
> . . . .
>
> My father's brother, but no more like my father
> Than I to Hercules.
>
> (I. ii. 139–40, 52–53)

In his advice to the players, Hamlet urged them not to overstep "the modesty of nature" but rather to hold "the mirror up to nature," showing "virtue her own feature, scorn her own image" (III. ii. 18 ff.). To Hamlet, Claudius, whose portrait contrasts so unfavorably with that of the dead ruler, imitates humanity abominably. Now King Hamlet is identified with four gods of the classical Pantheon:

> See, what a grace was seated on his brow:
> Hyperion's curls, the front of Jove himself,
> An eye like Mars, to threaten or command,
> A station like the herald Mercury
> New-lighted on a heaven-kissing hill.
>
> (55–59)

"This was your husband," he continues, and then he directs her attention to the picture of Claudius: "Here is your husband, like a mildew'd ear, / Blasting his wholesome brother." When the prince goes on to compare Claudius to a "moor" upon whom Gertrude now "battens" (gorges herself), he is strongly emphasizing appetite as opposed to reason.

Hamlet had ended his first soliloquy with a lament: "But break my heart, for I must hold my tongue" (I. ii. 159). The antic disposition did give him opportunities to express his heartfelt thoughts covertly, but never directly, to his mother and only rarely to his uncle-king. Having sprung the Mouse-trap and proved to his own satisfaction that Claudius, once an object of derision (II. ii. 380–83) but now the powerful ruler of Denmark, is guilty of regicide and usurpation, he need not suffer in silence. Claudius now is fully aware that Hamlet has ferreted out his secret; in the dramatization of *The Murder of Gonzago*, he saw a portrait of himself. It is now Gertrude's turn to see her true image. That Hamlet believed Claudius (whose inaccessibility had been reported to him) was hiding in Gertrude's chamber just might be the immediate reason for his outburst; so a few have reasoned. But even if that were true, it does not follow that the prince is motivated by an overpowering Oedipal urge to slay Claudius.

All this, however, is not to deny that Hamlet dwells upon the theme of lechery with an emphasis, and in such detail, that some find him to be fascinated by the very thing that nauseates him. The hasty marriage of Claudius and Gertrude was an incestuous one according to the Christian doctrine that informs this play, a fact that is worth repeating. Hamlet is the son of a father whom he revered not only as godlike but as a *man*, with all the far-reaching implications of that monosyllabic term (see I. ii. 188–89). Above all, Gertrude's frailty is a stain upon the cherished honor of the royal family. But for Hamlet, with his propensity for universalizing, it transcends the family level, staining all humanity. "Man delights not me," the prince had said to Rosencrantz and Guildenstern, "no, nor woman neither, though by your smiling you seem to say so" (II. ii. 321–22). Related to all this is the established fact that in the mature Shakespeare (as elsewhere in much of the serious literature of the period), illicit sex was a symbol of pervading evil. Hamlet's apparent obsession with the sensual, amounting to what has been called sexual nausea, is no more an indication of abnormality than is King Lear's ironic defense of adultery. Consider the prince's reply to Gertrude when she asks why he berates her:

> Such an act
> That blurs the grace and blush of modesty,
> Calls virtue hypocrite, takes off the rose
> From the fair forehead of an innocent love
> And sets a blister there, makes marriage vows
> As false as dicers' oaths.
>
> (40–45)

"Sets a blister," as here used, means "brands as a harlot." One immediately recalls the nunnery scene. For the Lord Chamberlain's daughter had been "loosed" upon Hamlet, and to him she was not "honest"; in a sense, she was being prostituted by an unprincipled father in the service of the satyr-like Claudius. Yet he surely knew that Ophelia was a hapless victim. The source of the corruption was the king, who had won over Gertrude as a partner in an unholy union. And that was an act that the idealistic Christian Prince finds to be so monstrous that it admits to generalization with reference to humanity and especially to man's brave claim to being the paragon of animals.

Hamlet indeed has spoken daggers in his "shenting" of Gertrude. But when the Ghost appears and not only rebukes him for procrastination but also urges him to "step between [Gertrude] and her fighting soul" (113), Hamlet seems to be aware that he has violated the Ghost's earlier admonition—tainting his mind by striving against his mother instead of leaving her to heaven. Not without compassion, he now implores her not to interpret his words as evidence of madness and thus an excuse for her to ignore her guilt. Rather, let her confess herself to heaven, or at the very least avoid compounding her sin by going to Claudius' bed (144–70).

In this calmer mood, the prince now can express repentance for the slaying of Polonius and declare that he will not shirk from reporting the deed honestly. Yet his words are of special interest: ". . . but Heaven hath pleas'd it so, / To punish me with this and this with me, / That I must be their scourge and minister" (173–75). A scourge, it will be recalled, is a wicked person who adds to his evil deeds even while functioning as the instrument of God's vengeance; ultimately he will fall and will endure eternal damnation. A minister is the virtuous instrument of God's justice. Is it possible for anyone to be both scourge and minister? Among many theories advanced by Shakespearean critics, this question is as important as any other one. It is quite possible that the poet-dramatist intends to show that the tragic hero himself is still in doubt regarding the morality of the task that remains to be performed. One recalls Hamlet's words of despair uttered at the end of Act I, where he first encountered the Ghost, listened to its story, and received the injunction to avenge the death of King Hamlet: "The time is out of joint; — O cursed spite, / That ever I was born to set it right!" (I. v. 189–90). It may be argued that Hamlet's words in both the earlier and the present scene serve to illuminate the dilemma he has faced practically from the start: Is it possible to accept as a moral duty the execution of revenge upon Claudius without tainting his own mind? Should he be the Pyrrhus-type revenger, the man of blood and passion, prompt in action, undeterred by the processes of thought? In a moment of passion, he acted without the slightest delay, with the result that the underhanded, foolish, but certainly not arch-criminal Polonius was killed—the act of a scourge, not of a noble mind called upon to function as God's minister. His passion inflamed again when he makes his reply to Gertrude's question "What shall I do?" (180), Hamlet then expresses his determination to outdo Rosencrantz and Guildenstern in knavery. So great are the difficulties of conduct in his world where Claudius is king and Polonius was accepted as the wisest counselor, a world of vice and hypocrisy, that the prince cannot avoid being the pawn of Fortune. This, at least, is the protagonist who, for many students of the play, emerges at the end of Act III.

Finally, the Ghost in Scene 4 demands attention, especially because this time only Hamlet sees it. First, why does it make its last appearance at this particular place and only to one of the two persons present? A widely accepted theory is that it does so because Hamlet is doing something that he should not do—speaking daggers to the woman who should be left to heaven. Such an action, so the argument goes, would be proper for the spirit of the Hyperion-like King Hamlet; moreover, it would be the action of a benevolent spirit, an "honest" ghost. But it also has been argued that since Gertrude does not see or hear the Ghost and therefore believes her son to be mad, the Ghost's appearance only to Hamlet serves to defeat her intention to repent. If this reading is valid, then the Ghost may be malignant. When the prince first sees it, he exclaims, "Save me, and hover o'er me with your wings, / You heavenly guards!" (103–104). This is a variation of the orthodox Christian formula to be used when one sees a ghost; it is similar to what Hamlet voiced on the platform at Elsinore (I. iv. 39). One may reasonably ask why he should use this formula if he really is convinced that this is "a spirit of health," not a "goblin damn'd." Still another conjecture is that Gertrude cannot see the Ghost because she is a grievous sinner.

An indisputable reason for the Ghost's appearance, acknowledged by Hamlet and confirmed by the Ghost itself, is to reprove the prince for delaying the revenge. Just possibly its appearance may be due to Hamlet's failure to take advantage of the opportunity when Claudius knelt in an attempt to pray. However, one may well ask: Would a benevolent spirit have approved of action under such circumstances?

Other commentators point out another disturbing possibility. May not Hamlet, in a state of great passion, actually be experiencing a hallucination, the reflection of his own state of mind? Although this theory is not generally accepted, it cannot be dismissed summarily as just another flight into the stratosphere of impressionistic criticism. The startled prince addresses the Ghost in these words: "Do you not come your tardy son to chide, / That, laps'd in time and passion, lets go by / Th' important acting of your dread command?" (106–108). These words of self-accusation, so it has been argued, are motivated by Hamlet's failure to kill Claudius when he had his chance shortly after springing the Mouse-trap. Further, Hamlet repeats in essence just what he said about himself earlier, notably when he denounced himself as being "A dull and muddy-mettled rascal . . . unpregnant of [his] cause" (II. ii. 594–95) and referred to his "weakness" and his "melancholy" (II. ii. 630), and also in his third soliloquy when he spoke of the "native hue of resolution" being "sicklied o'er with the pale cast of thought" (III. i. 84–85). Consistent with this argument is the Ghost's reply: "Do not forget! This visitation / Is but to whet thy almost blunted purpose" (110–11).

There remains only to repeat that the usual interpretation is that this is the Ghost of Hamlet's father, that Hamlet is right in believing that it has come to spur him to positive action, that its concern for Gertrude is no more than consistent with its original admonition that she should be left to heaven, and that one death—that of Claudius—will satisfy it.

ACT IV

Summary

Claudius expresses concern for the emotionally disturbed Gertrude and asks where her son is. First dismissing Rosencrantz and Guildenstern, the queen replies that Hamlet, "Mad as the seas and winds, when both contend / Which is the mightier," has killed Polonius, the "unseen good old man." The king deplores the violent deed, aware that he would have been the victim had he been behind the arras. Charging himself with being derelict for not restraining Hamlet earlier, he wonders how he will be able to explain Polonius' death to his subjects. Gertrude informs him that the prince, lamenting his action, is removing the body of the Lord Chamberlain.

The king states that Hamlet must be sent away at once, and he calls for Guildenstern. When the latter enters with Rosencrantz, the two are told what has happened and instructed to seek out Hamlet, talk with him as if nothing had occurred, and bring Polonius' body to the chapel. They depart. Claudius then informs Gertrude that they must turn to their wisest friends and tell them what they "mean to do / And what's untimely done" (IV. i. 39–40). Perhaps then they will not be held accountable for the death of Polonius.

Hamlet, adopting the same ironic and riddling style of discourse that he used earlier, refuses to tell Rosencrantz and Guildenstern where he placed the body of Polonius, but he agrees to go with them to see the king.

Addressing a small group of courtiers, Claudius states that he has sent for Hamlet, who must not be confined, despite his dangerous lunacy, because the "distracted multitude," lacking true judgment, love him. The decision to exile Hamlet must be represented as the verdict of the wisest counselors. Rosencrantz enters and reports that Hamlet will not reveal what he has done with Polonius' body. In response to the king's command, he calls to Guildenstern to bring in the prince.

Questioned by the king, Hamlet replies with witty, yet cynical, evasion. Finally, he states that Polonius' body may be found if one goes "up the stairs into the lobby" (IV iii. 37–39). When told that he must be sent to England, Hamlet continues to bait the king, bidding him "Farewell, dear mother," and then, perhaps unnecessarily, explaining the propriety of such a designation.

After Hamlet has left, Claudius orders Rosencrantz and Guildenstern to see to it that the prince is aboard ship by nightfall. Left to himself, he then voices his thoughts, which are addressed to the English ruler: Hamlet is to be put to death as soon as he arrives in England; only then can Claudius find repose.

Fortinbras leads his army across a plain in Denmark. He leaves a captain to greet Claudius and get his approval for the march through Danish territory. Hamlet, escorted by Rosencrantz and Guildenstern, appears and questions the captain. He learns that the Norwegian soldiers are about to fight with the Poles over "a little patch of ground" that is practically worthless. Requesting his escort to move ahead, the prince pauses to reflect upon the implications of what he has just learned. He sees in Fortinbras' determined move against the Poles another reproach of himself. True greatness, he concludes, means to act decisively when honor is the issue. Yet he, whose father has been murdered and whose mother has been morally corrupted, has let time lapse without executing revenge upon Claudius. From now on, his "thoughts [will] be bloody, or be nothing worth" (IV. iv. 66).

A court gentleman informs Gertrude that Ophelia seems to be out of her mind and in her pitiable state has become troublesome. Gertrude flatly states that she will not see her. When the gentleman tells how Ophelia speaks constantly of her father and behaves in a most erratic manner, Horatio points out that her wild discourse may arouse suspicion. Gertrude then agrees to see her.

Ophelia enters, asks for "the beauteous majesty of Denmark," talks incoherently, and sings verses of ballads, one obviously relating thematically to the death of her elderly father, the other two relating to the seduction of an innocent maiden. Claudius, who has joined the group, addresses her graciously but receives no rational reply. He is convinced that her father's death has driven her mad. When she leaves, he orders that she be closely watched. He then turns to Gertrude, summarizing the troubles in Elsinore: Polonius slain; Hamlet no longer in the kingdom; the body of the Lord Chamberlain hastily and secretly buried; the king's subjects suspicious and increasingly restless; Laertes, returned in secret from France, being incited by unwholesome rumors. Claudius is in a state of torment.

Loud noises are heard, and the king calls for his Switzers (mercenary soldiers) to guard the door, just as a messenger enters to report that Laertes and a mob who hail him as Claudius' successor have overcome officers of the guard and are about to break in. That is exactly what happens. But Laertes orders his followers to take up a position outside the room and then addresses the king and queen, demanding that they "give" him his father. Gertrude urges him to calm down, but it is the politic Claudius who succeeds in reasoning with the distraught Laertes.

Ophelia returns, again singing snatches of a ballad, the words of which relate to the sad death of a man with "beard as white as snow," and again talking incoherently. In fantasy, she distributes various flowers to those who watch and listen to her. Laertes is beside himself with grief for his "kind sister, sweet Ophelia." When Ophelia leaves, Claudius succeeds in getting Laertes' attention. He promises to join Laertes in punishing the guilty in the matter of Polonius' death.

Horatio is told by his attendant that some sailors wish to give him certain letters. Aware that he knows of no one except Hamlet who might have written to him, he immediately instructs the attendant to let the sailors enter. From the letter, Horatio learns that the ship bearing Hamlet to England was attacked by pirates. During the engagement, Hamlet boarded the pirate ship and was made captive.

He has been well treated and brought back to Denmark in return for his promise to do them a good turn. Horatio is to deliver the other letters to the king and then come to Hamlet without delay, for he has much to tell his friend. Horatio promises to reward the sailors when they have guided him to the prince.

The king has told Laertes that Hamlet killed Polonius and sought to kill him, Claudius. When Laertes asks why the king did not apprehend the prince and have him punished for such capital offences, Claudius explains that he did not do so for two reasons: First, the queen dotes upon her son, and, devoted as he is to her, he restrained himself; second, he could not expect support from the public, who reveres Hamlet. He assures Laertes that he has never considered letting the prince escape punishment, about which Laertes will hear more.

At this point, a messenger enters with letters from Hamlet, one for the king and one for the queen. From his letter, Claudius learns that the prince has returned to Denmark. Immediately the king proceeds to engage Laertes in a plot to kill Hamlet. The king tells him how Hamlet's sense of rivalry was aroused by the report of Laertes' skill in fencing. Laertes, he says, can prove that he loved his father by taking advantage of this situation as a means of avenging Polonius' death without risking injury to himself. When Laertes declares that nothing could restrain him from acting against Hamlet, Claudius tells him that he will arrange a fencing match between the two and that Laertes will use a foil with an unblunted point. Laertes then can kill Hamlet before the eyes of the spectators without appearing to intend any harm to his adversary. Laertes not only agrees but plans to go beyond this: He will dip the point of his rapier in deadly poison. Claudius adds a second means of insuring Hamlet's death. He will have prepared, and available, a cup of poisoned wine for Hamlet to drink if Laertes somehow fails to draw blood in the duel.

Gertrude enters, lamenting. She informs Laertes that his sister is drowned. Both he and Claudius learn that while Ophelia was weaving fantastic garlands and hanging them on the limbs of a willow tree, a limb broke and she fell into the stream. For a brief time she had floated, then she sank to her death. Laertes strives to control his grief but cannot do so. Nor can he speak the fiery words he had intended to address to Claudius. When he leaves, Claudius tells Gertrude that now he must begin once more the task of calming Laertes' rage.

Commentary

In Scene 1, Gertrude's explanation of what happened with Hamlet has been subject to contrasting interpretations. To most readers, it seems evident that she honestly believes her son to be mad because she speaks of his grief as evidence of his basic purity (24–27) and because Claudius' lines point to his awareness of her genuine love and concern for her son. Others see Gertrude as making good her promise not to reveal Hamlet's secret, but as having accepted eagerly the belief that he is mentally unbalanced as a "flattering unction to [her] soul," to use the prince's own words (III. iv. 145). By this latter group, much is made of the fact that her regard for Claudius seems to be undisturbed by Hamlet's accusations and invectives.

Claudius' words and actions in Scene 1 pose no such problem of interpretation. In the course of the action so far in this play, his concern for his own security has been linked to Hamlet. The behavior of Hamlet now has become an obsession with him. "Ah, my good lord, what I have seen tonight!" exclaims Gertrude, and Claudius promptly asks, "How does Hamlet?" And, at the end of the scene, he says, "My soul is full of discord and dismay." But, appropriately, fear does not incapacitate Claudius; with Machiavellian skill, he expresses his conviction that Hamlet is now a threat not only to the Crown but also to all subjects; and he blames himself for permitting his "love" for the prince to interfere with duty. The intensity of the conflict is perhaps best indicated by the king's use of a military figure of speech when he tells Gertrude how they must report the death of Polonius.

Finally, it now seems possible that Hamlet's slaying of Polonius has worked to the advantage of his adversary. Only select members of the Court witnessed Hamlet's antic behavior and heard his antic discourse. The prince, who, as Ophelia's encomium made clear, was the "expectancy and rose of the fair state" (III. i. 160), can now be removed from Denmark without causing subjects to ask troublesome questions.

Why Hamlet chooses to provoke the king and his spies by hiding Polonius' body is a bit of a puzzle. Many find here a perverseness unworthy of a tragic hero; others find further evidence of the prince's morbid preoccupation with death, first manifested in his soliloquy at the end of Act I, Scene 2, and developed in the "To be, or not to be" soliloquy in Act III, Scene 1.

The prince's utter contempt for Rosencrantz and Guildenstern finds expression once more in Scene 2. Speaking to the former, he has a devastating term to explain Rosencrantz' motive for abjectly serving Claudius: This former schoolfellow is a sponge that "soaks up the King's countenance [reference to the coin of the realm], his rewards, his authorities" (16–17); like other servile individuals, the king keeps him "as an ape doth nuts, in the corner of his jaw; first mouth'd, to be last swallowed" (19–20). Having listened to the sanctimonious platitudes about the sanctity of kingship (II. ii. 26–29), one is hardly surprised that Guildenstern should express shock when he hears Hamlet refer to the king as a "thing" (31).

Hamlet seems to take great satisfaction in capitalizing upon his pretended madness; but, if anything, his wit is grimmer than ever. Again he seems to be completely morbid in his preoccupation with death. Questioned about Polonius' body, he develops the "worm's meat" theme, inherited by the Renaissance from the Middle Ages, with telling effect upon Claudius. However high-spirited Hamlet may seem, however callous in his attitude toward the dead Polonius, this is the same Hamlet who, after his moving eulogy of mankind as "the beauty of the world," asked, "And yet, to me, what is this quintessence of dust?"—and then went on to declare that man did not please him (II. ii. 315 ff.). It is the same Hamlet who was at least half in love with death when he gave voice to his thoughts in the "To be, or not to be" soliloquy (III. i. 56 ff.). In a word, it is Hamlet the disillusioned idealist who has discovered how bestial man may become. So now in Scene 2, he gets a perverse pleasure out of telling Claudius that

> A certain convocation of politic [politically
> minded] worms are e'en at him [Polonius]. Your
> worm is your only emperor for diet. We fat all
> creatures else to fat us, and we fat ourselves for
> maggots. Your fat king and your lean beggar is
> but variable service, two dishes, but to one table;
> that's the end.
>
> (21–26)

In the development of the "worm's meat" theme during the Middle Ages, the aim was to inculcate the religious lesson that heaven should be recognized as man's destination and ultimate home, and that he should not be misled by whatever temporal life has to offer. But there is no consolation of religion implicit in Hamlet's grim remarks; the whole emphasis is upon man's insignificance. However nihilistic all this may seem, the prince remains the accomplished moral satirist. For example, he achieves a metaphysical conceit and a political pun when he informs the king that "A man may fish with the worm that hath eat of a / king, and eat of the fish that hath fed of that worm" (28–30) and goes on to explain that all this means "Nothing but to show you how a king may go a progress through the guts of a beggar" (32–33). It would be desirable to keep this episode in mind when one comes to the graveyard scene in the last act.

Finally, Hamlet caustically bids farewell to the king, calling him his mother and going on to explain, "Father and mother is man and wife, man and wife is one flesh [as they are called in Scriptures], and so, my mother" (53–55). One is reminded that the cause of Hamlet's tragedy is two-fold. Never does he forget his father's death; but the incestuous marriage continues to torment him.

In Scene 4, Hamlet soliloquizes at length for the last time. Some critics have described this soliloquy as Hamlet's most decisive one in that it puts an end to doubt and vacillation. This may be true, but as much as any passage in the play, it poses problems and raises questions. Once more Hamlet's words often echo what he has said earlier, and they have the curious effect of refuting certain theories confidently advanced by some critics.

"How all occasions do inform against me, / And spur my dull revenge" Hamlet begins. What are the "occasions" to which he may be making reference? If he is referring to decisive action in general, the primary example has been provided by Claudius, when he authorized the "lawful espials" of Polonius and of Rosencrantz and Guildenstern, and certainly when he arranged for Hamlet's departure to England, where he would be put to death. They may well include the example of the king-slayer Pyrrhus, who delayed only momentarily, as was made clear in the lines recited by the First Player during the recital of a part of *Aeneas and Dido*, which the prince wished to hear. Both are indeed "Examples gross as earth" (46): the first, devoid of all honor and motivated by criminal ambition and fear; the other, the barbarous execution of personal blood-revenge. The present example, as Hamlet's own words indicate, is no less gross. Surely, no one would wish to see the prince follow such patterns of action.

Hamlet's comparison of himself to Fortinbras in Scene 4 has been widely recognized as thematic, and there are some commentators who insist that the young Norwegian prince is the most important foil to Hamlet in this play. Like the Prince of Denmark, he has lost a royal father and is intent on executing prompt revenge, for which purpose he has raised his army of "landless resolutes" (I. i. 95 ff.). He had planned to invade Denmark, but thanks to Claudius' diplomatic efforts, the ruler of Norway was persuaded to forego revenge and to expend his martial energy in an attack on Poland (II. ii. 65 ff.). It has been argued that Fortinbras, unlike Hamlet, has mastered passion, embraced the dictates of reason, yet does not lapse into inactivity. From this point of view, he does provide a contrast to Hamlet. The difficulty, however, lies in the immediate reason given for Fortinbras' decision to engage the Polish forces. Does Hamlet mean that it is "divine ambition" that makes the Norwegian prince dare "fortune, death, and danger," knowing that some twenty thousand men probably will be slaughtered—all for the possession of a worthless patch of ground, all for what he deems to be an honorable cause? Surely this cannot be the case, as Hamlet's next lines, properly understood, indicate:

> Rightly to be great
> Is not to stir without great argument
> But greatly to find quarrel in a straw
> When honour's at the stake.
>
> (53–56)

The difficulty of interpretation lies in the phrase "Is not to stir." Perhaps a comma after *Is*, indicating that the "not" belongs with the linking verb rather than with the infinitive, would help; otherwise, it appears that the perceptive, intellectual young Hamlet suddenly embraces a very superficial view of honor. The only possible example that Fortinbras provides Hamlet, then, relates to his prompt action, undeterred by thoughts of consequences. Hamlet's own reason for acting—his "quarrel" (argument)—is not in "a straw," nor is the enterprise of vindicating family honor and punishing a fratricide and usurper an "eggshell."

But what of the most impressively philosophical lines in this soliloquy?

> What is a man,
> If his chief good and market of his time
> Be but to sleep and feed? A beast, no more.
> Sure, He that made us with such large discourse,
> Looking before and after, gave us not
> That capability and god-like reason
> To lust in us unus'd.
>
> (33–39)

These lines relate back to Hamlet's "What a piece of work is a man" speech (II. ii. 315–19) and amplify what he said then: Man is endowed with reason and must put this divine gift to use through positive action. Hamlet goes on to accuse himself of either "Bestial oblivion" (which may be discounted immediately) or "Of thinking too precisely on th' event," arguing that "thought which, quarter'd hath but one part wisdom / And ever three parts coward" (40–43). This is the passage upon which the Romantics, including Goethe and Coleridge, especially depend to justify their concept of Hamlet as the ineffectual dreamer, convinced, it would seem, that his lacerating self-criticism is valid here and elsewhere in the play, rather than providing evidence of his difficulty in subduing passion or of his understandable sense of frustration in view of the obstacles that have prevented him from sweeping to his revenge. It may be argued that "thinking too precisely on th' event" would mean to reject effective reason and that it is better to have only one-fourth wisdom than to try to solve momentous questions with none at all. If all this be true, then one may conclude that Shakespeare is particularly interested in working toward a precise definition of the moral issue that his tragic hero faces.

And what is to be made of the following lines spoken by Hamlet after he has accused himself of cowardice?

> I do not know
> Why yet I live to say, "This thing's to do,"
> Sith I have cause and will and strength and means
> To do't.
>
> (43–46)

This is exactly the temper of the Hamlet who soliloquized "O, wha a rogue and peasant slave am I!" and of the Hamlet of the "To be, o. not to be" soliloquy. In the brief time that has elapsed since he sprang the Mouse-trap, Hamlet has had one real opportunity to kil Claudius, but he does know why he failed to do so. Understandably, some commentators suggest that this soliloquy has been misplaced; but it is more logical to conclude that the prince has been emotionally aroused by just what he says—one more "occasion" reminding him that after many months, the murderer-usurper survives and rules Denmark with Gertrude as his "imperial jointress."

"O, from this time forth, / My thoughts be bloody, or be nothing worth!" the prince concludes. His thoughts were sufficiently bloody when he spoke the lines of his second soliloquy and certainly when he came upon the kneeling Claudius shortly after he had sprung the Mouse-trap and caught the conscience of the king. Perhaps Fortinbras' single-minded pursuit of his goal has provided Hamlet with an example, however gross, that will make it possible for him to act positively and promptly if an opportunity presents itself. So full of self-reproach is he now that apparently the end will justify whatever means he can find. In part, such a conclusion is supported by the fact that Scene 4 leads to the final, larger movement in the play, one in which the tragic hero no longer will have the need to express his doubts and his perplexities.

The irony in Scene 5 is quite striking. Ophelia has spoken of Hamlet's mind as being "o'erthrown" (III. i. 158), but it is she who is now mad. Some have raised the question of whether her madness, so distressing since she has been no more than the dutiful daughter of a vain and foolish father, is necessary to the plot. One critic, for example, argues that Laertes has motive enough to act as he does without his sister's madness, which he calls a "dramatic luxury." Furthermore, if one is convinced that Hamlet should have left Claudius, as well as Gertrude, to heaven (in which case the Ghost is an evil spirit intent on leading Hamlet to his destruction), Ophelia's madness and subsequent death result from "the frightening process of a course that never should have been initiated." The consensus is that Ophelia's madness and death have a logical place in the entire action because they coincide with and illustrate one result of disorder in the State—the rottenness that has been spreading through the body politic.

The second tragic love song sung by Ophelia, beginning with "Tomorrow is Saint Valentine's day" and concluding with "An thou hadst not come to my bed," has intrigued many commentators. Those who read the play primarily as a romantic love tragedy involving Hamlet and Ophelia recall that Ophelia has already spoken of having "suck'd the honey of his music vows" (III. i. 164) and are convinced that Hamlet has had his way with Ophelia and then rejected her. For some of these romantics, this is the primary cause of her mental collapse, the death of her father being the secondary cause. They have at least the virtue of consistency when they come to the next scene, where Ophelia's death by drowning is reported: The young lady, it seems, drowned herself because, to her disgrace, she was carrying Hamlet's child! Like Polonius, when he first learned that the prince was paying attention to his daughter, this group of interpreters believe that Hamlet did not have honorable intentions. This is obviously the *reductio ad absurdum* of impressionism.

What is the justification for having Ophelia sing a song, the theme of which is the seduction and abandonment of an innocent maiden? It will be recalled that the suspicious Polonius had instructed his daughter not to be so naive as to think that the prince would marry her—not to be misled by Hamlet's importuning her in what she reported as "honourable fashion"; he ordered her to spend no more time in Hamlet's company (I. iii. 126 ff.). Thereafter she sought him out only when directed to do so by Polonius, who ignored the prince's warning that "Conception is a blessing, but not as [his] daughter may conceive" (II. ii. 185–87), an indication that Hamlet was fully aware that Ophelia had reported to her father how he had appeared to her when he first adopted the antic disposition. The ambiguity in Hamlet's later injunction, "Get thee to a nunnery, go" (III. i. 142), made clear (as has been pointed out) that he was aware of her personal innocence and, at the same time, knew that she had been "loosed" upon him. Earlier, in his third long soliloquy, he spoke bitterly of the "pangs of dispriz'd love" (III. i. 72), and in the shenting scene, he told Gertrude that her marriage to Claudius was

> Such an act
> That blurs the grace and blush of modesty,
> Calls virtue hypocrite, takes off the rose

> From the fair forehead of an innocent love
> And sets a blister there.
>
> (III. iv. 40–44)

In the commentary, the implications of this speech and especially its application to the unfortunate Ophelia were emphasized. Further, it has been pointed out that illicit sex in Shakespeare's later dramas is repeatedly used as a symbol of pervading evil. All this adds up to one conclusion: Ophelia's song is intended to underscore the destructive force of evil in the kingdom. And the source of the infection is Claudius, murderer and usurper, who has won over the weak Gertrude to an incestuous marriage, encouraged the underhanded activities of his old Lord Chamberlain, and now has arranged for the murder of Hamlet. Ophelia is the latest victim; little wonder, then, that she should sing of "dispriz'd love." Nor is this conclusion inconsistent with the claim that Hamlet's harsh words to her in the nunnery scene planted the image of illicit sex in her mind.

Ophelia's distribution of the flowers is of some interest in terms of symbolism. To her brother she gives rosemary, which was used at both weddings and funerals as a symbol of remembrance. It may be her impending death, not just that of Polonius, that is symbolized here; if so, her words indeed comprise "A document [piece of instruction] in madness," as Laertes says (178). Pansies, which she also gives to Laertes, symbolize thoughts and therefore are no less appropriate. Apparently the fennel, representing flattery, is given to the king, and the columbines, symbolizing thanklessness, to the queen. To Gertrude also are given the rue and daisy; the first ("herb of grace") symbolizes sorrow, and the second may represent a warning to women who are too easily persuaded to love. Neither Gertrude nor Claudius is given violets, which stand for faithfulness—but perhaps Ophelia's words explaining why she cannot distribute the violets are addressed to Horatio.

In this scene, it is Laertes who emerges as a foil to Hamlet. He has been stirred by "great argument," to use the phrase from the prince's last soliloquy. Like Hamlet, he has lost a beloved father, one who was slain. When the Ghost concluded its account of King Hamlet's murder, it had called upon Hamlet to prove that he had "nature" (natural feelings) in him by avenging his father's death (I. v. 81). There is no question regarding such nature in Laertes, who is not to be restrained in his determination to prove that he is his father's son. Laertes is "stirred" to vindicate the honor of his family. After the news of his father's death reached him in Paris, he left for Elsinore; now he has burst into the room and threatens the king. Laertes, it would seem, is the model avenger for a tragedy of blood. He will act first and act promptly, undeterred by questions of public duty, morality, or consequences:

> I dare damnation. To this point I stand,
> That both the worlds I give to negligence,
> Let come what comes; only I'll be reveng'd
> Most thoroughly for my father.
>
> (133–36)

There is little danger of conscience making a coward of Laertes or of his thinking too precisely on the event. In his own way, he is as single-minded as Fortinbras, who is determined to fight over "a little patch of ground," whatever the cost in human lives may be.

When Laertes first sees Ophelia, now deranged, the dramatic poignancy of the meeting is not to be denied. Yet his speech (154–63) beginning "O heat, dry up my brains!" is sufficiently overwrought and artificial in style to suggest that the player describing the grief of Hecuba might well have recited it. Perhaps all this may seem to be too harsh a criticism of a youth who loved and was loyal to the members of his family, one who was especially concerned that his father had been denied proper burial and honors appropriate for a Lord Chamberlain (see lines 212–17). But the point is that, although he too may serve as a foil to Hamlet, he is anything but a norm character. If there has been an excess evident in the prince's lines, it has been present only when he soliloquizes.

Before leaving the discussion of Laertes in Scene 5, one should call attention to the fact that he was able to raise a rebellion of sorts. It is reasonable to ask why Hamlet, whose popularity was established by the testimony of Ophelia (III. i. 159 ff.) and that of Claudius (IV. iii. 4), did not secure public support in a revolt against the king. Some have believed that he could have done so, succeeded in deposing Claudius, and even had the usurper brought to trial for regicide. All this, of course, would have entailed a drastic revision of the original story elements. Moreover, in Shakespeare's play, evidence of political discontent, of disorder in the body politic, has been presented only subsequent to the death of Polonius.

Close attention to the lines spoken by Claudius in Scene 5 makes clear how intense the conflict in this play has become. "O Gertrude, Gertrude," says the guilt-ridden king, "When sorrows come, they come not single spies, / But in battalions" (77–79). Of course he is striving to sustain the public image of a virtuous ruler and concerned kinsman of a prince who, in his madness, has disrupted an orderly realm. Actually Claudius is an increasingly fearful individual. But he remains a strong adversary; there is no danger that he will collapse or suddenly abandon the conflict. He is still the adroit Machiavellian, gifted in dissembling and prompt in action. In this role, Claudius achieves supreme irony when he speaks sententiously of "poor Ophelia" (85–87) and when he urges Gertrude not to restrain the enraged Laertes, mouthing orthodox Renaissance political doctrine: "Let him go, Gertrude; do not fear our person. / There's such divinity doth hedge a king / That treason can but peep to what it would" (121–23). This is the public image of a ruler which the competent Claudius has presented, although one may agree with Hamlet that he is actually "a king of shreds and patches." No one is likely to underestimate his skill when he succeeds in quelling Laertes' wrath, assuring the Lord Chamberlain's son that, if he (Claudius) is found to be to blame in any degree, he will forfeit both kingdom and life (203–209), and promising that Laertes will be given complete satisfaction: "And where the offence is let the great axe fall" (218). When one comes to the final scene, the resolution of this tragedy, these words will be recognized as ironic; but immediately they reveal the king not only saving himself from the immediate threat posed by Laertes' revolt but also capitalizing upon that very turn of events. If Hamlet is put to death in accordance with Claudius' instructions, the members of the Court and, one may assume, the public at large, convinced by Claudius that he has become a homicidal maniac, will not be "Thick and unwholesome in their thoughts and whispers," to use the king's own words (82).

There remains something to be said about Gertrude in Scene 5. Once more she exhibits passive compliance in her relationship with Claudius, but there is more to be said about her. Although she sincerely believes that her son is mentally ill, she too suffers from the "unquiet mind" of the mortal sinner.

In Scene 6, the sailors, it is sufficiently clear, are some of the pirates who detained Hamlet and then returned him to Denmark.

The return of Hamlet is a plain indication that the resolution of the entire action is not far off.

Repeatedly, Claudius has been described as Machiavellian in his villainy. But it also has been pointed out that, unlike the usual Machiavellian villain of the Elizabethan stage, he suffers the pangs of conscience and is not the heartless diabolist who scoffs at religion and gloats over his own wickedness. As one definitely learns in Scene 7, he is genuinely fond of Gertrude; and this capacity for love is another characteristic that differentiates him from the completely dedicated Machiavellian. In other respects—cunning, capacity for cruelty, sagacity however misdirected, adeptness at improvision—Claudius, especially in this scene, can take his place at the side of Richard III, Iago, Edmund, and other stage villains who in many ways, if not all, are Machiavellian types.

In winning over Laertes, the last and most formidable agent he uses against Hamlet, Claudius succeeds in presenting himself as a ruler who has failed to act for a reason that tends to reflect favorably upon his character. Although he acknowledges the fact that his nephew is popular, he is astute enough not to mention that, as he had said in an earlier scene, the prince is "lov'd by the distracted multitude." It is also characteristic of him that he should formulate a plan that if executed properly will not involve much risk: "And for his death no wind of blame shall breathe, / But even his mother shall uncharge the practice / And call it accident" (67-69). This, of course, is the practical, the politic way in which "Diseases desperate grown" are relieved in a world where "seeming" and "acting" are a way of life. To use Polonius' words spoken to Reynaldo, it is the way employed by those of "wisdom and of reach" (II. i. 64). There is, then, a certain logic, even inevitability, in the choice of poison for the purpose of killing Hamlet: It was poison that Claudius used to gain his crown and wife; poison began the whole process of this villainy.

Claudius' Machiavellianism is evident not only in his prompt approval of Laertes' plan to use a foil tipped with poison but also in planning to have the poisoned drink ready should Laertes fail. To some extent, it is also evident in his report that the Norman horseman had the highest praise for Laertes' skill in swordsmanship and that Hamlet became envious when he heard Laertes praised. And so when, having learned that Hamlet has returned to Denmark alone and "naked" (unarmed), Claudius asks Laertes: "Can you advise me?" (54). Perhaps Claudius knows very well that modesty is not a notable trait in Polonius' son, and certainly he knows that flattery can be an effective device.

Laertes remains the "perfect" revenger, one not to be deterred by anything, just as in Act IV, Scene 5, when he burst into the room and confronted Claudius. But now there is a great falling off in his character. Whatever his limitations may have been heretofore, he invited great sympathy. His cause was great: a father slain and denied a decent funeral, his sister driven mad. It is not just that he is easily won over by Claudius; to decide on that basis that he is quite naive is to underestimate the formidability of Hamlet's adversary. Rather it is that he is the one who, even prior to listening to Claudius' plan, intended to use a rapier with a poisoned tip. One can only conclude that he is his father's son and cannot be wholly above-board. But the issue now is one of life and death. Admittedly, Laertes recovers one's sympathy after he learns of Ophelia's death, especially because, in contrast to the ranting style he used when he saw and heard his demented sister in Act IV, Scene 5, he now speaks moving words and is impressively restrained (186–92). Nevertheless, it is this report of Ophelia's death that seals the pact between Laertes and Claudius.

Unlike Hamlet, neither Claudius nor Laertes can be charged with dullness or delay; both intend to act promptly and decisively. In a sense, these two provide another "occasion" which Hamlet might well see as one that informs against him. And, although Laertes has shown himself to be voluble enough, from the moment of his return to Denmark he has been acting positively, motivated by the single intention of avenging his father's death. Conscience will not make him a coward; he stands ready to cut Hamlet's throat in the church.

When Claudius asks Laertes if his father was dear to him (108), one recalls the Ghost's words to Hamlet, "If thou didst ever thy dear father love—" and its command that Hamlet prove his love: "Revenge his foul and most unnatural murder" (I. v. 23–25). Audience and reader alike are forcibly reminded that the prince has delayed; months have elapsed, yet Claudius survives as King of Denmark. Among those who go far toward accepting Hamlet's self-indictment for not sweeping to his revenge (the victim of excessive grief), this entire episode is called upon to support their interpretation. It would seem more reasonable to conclude that throughout Scene 7, in which he does not appear, Hamlet emerges as the admirable tragic hero despite delays and alleged rationalizations for them. Claudius acknowledges him to be "Most generous and free from all contriving" (136). It follows that, although procrastination made possible what has been called the "increase in the area of destruction," the prince himself is the sacrificial victim of his superior morality: His very virtues work to his disadvantage in the corrupt world in which he finds himself. Laertes surely could use considerable "thinking . . . precisely on th' event," the propensity for which Hamlet felt might be the cause of his failure to carry out the Ghost's injunction (IV. iv. 41). And when Laertes declares his willingness to cut Hamlet's throat in the church, he obviously could use some of Hamlet's moral scrupulousness. But even here, it may be pointed out (if only to demonstrate the difficulties which this play poses) that when Laertes makes his wild statement, one is reminded of Hamlet's refusal to kill Claudius as the latter knelt for prayer. One also recalls that the prince was motivated not by religious compunction but by a determination to obtain "perfect" revenge. Yet, in the balance, the Prince of Denmark emerges as admirable. He could no more seek to avenge his father's death in the way adopted by Laertes than he could emulate Fortinbras in leading troops to slaughter for the sake of a worthless patch of ground, despite his generalization regarding what constitutes true greatness when honor is the issue. Although his slaying of Polonius was the result of an impulsive action, he had lamented the fact that he should have been called upon to be either minister or scourge.

"One woe doth tread upon another's heel, / So fast they follow," says the distraught Gertrude (164), and Ophelia's sad death by drowning is revealed. One recalls Claudius' words of despair when he witnessed her madness: "O Gertrude, Gertrude, / When sorrows come, they come not single spies, / But in battalions" (IV. v. 77–79). The rottenness in the state of Denmark, present from the beginning of this play, has spread. The tragic course of events has been gaining increasing momentum and has reached this crucial point at the end of Act IV. Gertrude's highly lyrical and touching description of Ophelia's death is a set-piece. That it is appropriate to the queen has been questioned; but the Gertrude who has emerged as genuinely devoted to her son surely is capable of sincere grief for the death of

Ophelia. More relevant is the fact that, from Gertrude's report, it is clear that Ophelia's death was accidental, not suicide, a fact that poses a minor problem in view of the disputation in the next scene regarding her burial.

ACT V

Summary

Two gravediggers discuss the recent inquest of the death of Ophelia, held to determine whether or not she was a suicide and, concomitantly, whether or not she merits a Christian burial. The First Gravedigger is convinced that she will be accorded that privilege only because she is a gentlewoman. In the grimly comic dialogue which follows, the two identify themselves with Adam, the "first gentleman" and the first delver, and then with the gallows-maker, who builds a frame that outlives its tenants.

While the Second Gravedigger goes to fetch a pot of liquor, Hamlet and Horatio enter, pausing to listen to the First Gravedigger as he sings snatches of a ballad and digs in the earth. When he tosses up a skull and dashes it to the ground, the prince is impelled to muse upon death as the great leveler of all people. He then questions the First Gravedigger, who answers him in chop-logic, a particular kind of dialectical speech in which the practitioner insists upon confining himself to a special meaning of a given word or phrase. In reply to a question, the gravedigger states that he has followed his calling since the day when King Hamlet defeated old King Fortinbras of Norway, on which day young Hamlet ("he that was mad, and sent into England") was born—thirty years ago, so he says.

Hamlet questions him further. The gravedigger identifies the skull as that of Yorick, the king's jester, who died twenty-three years ago. Hamlet picks it up and tells Horatio that Yorick was his childhood favorite. Now once more he dwells upon death, which brings not only a court jester to this state but also the vain court lady and even great conquerors like Alexander the Great and Caesar, whose dust may now fill a bunghole or a chink in a wall.

As Ophelia's funeral procession enters, the members of which include the king, the queen, and Laertes, Hamlet and Horatio step back, unobserved. Laertes complains to the Priest about the limited rites accorded his dead sister. The surly Priest insists that Ophelia is being accorded obsequies which she really does not deserve in view of the doubtful circumstances of her death.

When Ophelia's body is lowered into the grave, the queen strews the coffin with flowers and speaks touchingly of her defeated hope that Ophelia would have become Hamlet's wife. Laertes, no longer able to restrain himself, cries out in grief and then leaps into the grave, asking that he be buried with his sister. At this point in the action, Hamlet steps forth and demands to know why Laertes should so emphasize his sorrow. Announcing himself as "Hamlet, the Dane," he too leaps into the grave. Laertes seizes him by the throat, and the two grapple until they are separated by attendants and then climb out of the grave.

Horatio attempts to calm the prince, but the latter is not to be silenced. He declares that he loved Ophelia far more than Laertes could have loved her, bitterly criticizes Laertes for indulging in bombast, and then insists that he has always held him in high esteem. Gertrude again expresses her belief that her son is mad. After Hamlet leaves, Claudius speaks to Laertes, reminding him that he has not long to wait for vengeance.

Hamlet now has the time and the opportunity to tell Horatio all that he experienced since he embarked with Rosencrantz and Guildenstern for England. During the first night at sea, he roused himself, sought out the quarters occupied by the king's agents, and took the sealed packet containing Claudius' instructions to the English king. Thus he discovered that Claudius had ordered that he be beheaded. Immediately Hamlet devised new instructions in the official style requesting that Claudius' servants who brought the communication to the King of England be put to death. The prince folded these instructions and placed them in the packet, which he sealed, making use of his father's signet. Then he replaced the packet. On the next day, the sea-fight with the pirates took place, as Hamlet informed Horatio in his letter. Only Hamlet was taken captive; the others proceeded on the voyage to England.

Horatio is appalled to learn the extent of Claudius' villainy, and Hamlet points out that he righteously could slay the man who has killed his royal father, whored his mother, and prevented him from succeeding to the throne. Horatio points out that Claudius will soon learn what has happened to Rosencrantz and Guildenstern, but Hamlet replies that the interim, short though it will be, belongs to him.

Osric, an emissary from the king, enters. Hamlet promptly recognizes him as the affected, overly polite courtier in the service of Claudius. Sardonically, the prince adopts the same stilted style employed by this "water-fly" and, with a straight face, asks questions and makes comments intended to make Osric exhaust himself in artificial expression. But at last the message is conveyed: Hamlet is challenged to a friendly duel with Laertes, the match to take place before the king and queen and their attendants. Osric informs the prince that Claudius is confident that he will excel Laertes in swordsmanship. Hamlet declares that he will win for the king's sake if he can. Osric departs, leaving Hamlet and Horatio to remark on how ridiculous he is. Another emissary, this time a lord, arrives to ask when Hamlet will be ready for the match. The prince replies that he awaits the king's pleasure. He is told that both king and queen are now coming to witness the contest.

When the two are alone, Horatio warns Hamlet that he will lose the wager, but Hamlet replies that he does not think so, explaining that he has been in continual practice from the time Laertes left for France. Yet he concedes that he is heartsick—and then dismisses the thought as unmanly. Horatio urges him to postpone the match if he has any misgivings and offers to report that the prince is indisposed. But Hamlet is resolute; he expresses his willingness to accept whatever is in store for him.

The king, the queen, Laertes, Osric, and various attendants with foils and gauntlets enter. Next to Claudius' chair is a table on which are flagons of wine. Before taking his seat, the king puts Laertes' hand into that of Hamlet. Hamlet asks Laertes' pardon for having wronged him, stating that he had not intended any real harm but, sorely distracted, behaved as if he were out of his wits. Laertes replies stiffly that he bears no grudge against Hamlet as far as his personal feelings are concerned but that he cannot accept the apology until experts in the matter of honor have proved to him that his reputation remains undamaged. Graciously, Hamlet accepts these conditions, asks that the foils be produced, and assures Laertes that he will serve as foil in the sense that Laertes will perform brilliantly in the duel. Laertes is sure that the prince is mocking him, despite Hamlet's denial.

At Claudius' command, Osric brings the foils. While Laertes carefully chooses his, the king asks Hamlet if he knows about the wager. The prince replies that Claudius is wagering on the weaker side, but the king assures him that he knows better, although the odds favor Laertes. Hamlet takes his foil, asking only whether or not it is the same length as the others. Before the contest starts, the king orders that if Hamlet achieves the first or second hit, ordnance will be fired in his honor and the king himself will drink "to Hamlet's better breath." Moreover, he will place a precious pearl in the cup, which will belong to the duelist when he drinks to his own success. After the sound of kettledrums, trumpets, and the blast of cannons, Claudius drinks to Hamlet's health. The match begins.

Hamlet gets the first hit, and Claudius calls for the cup of wine, urging the prince to drink and get the pearl he has won. But Hamlet wishes to continue the contest before drinking. Again he scores a hit, which is acknowledged by Laertes. During the short interval, Claudius remarks to Gertrude that their son will win. Gertrude expresses some doubt, remarking that Hamlet is out of condition. To the consternation of Claudius, she picks up the poisoned cup of wine that her husband has prepared for the prince and drinks from it. She then offers it to Hamlet, who again refuses to drink. She offers to wipe his face. This brief interlude provides Laertes with the opportunity to reassure Claudius, but the king is no longer confident that Laertes will be able to score a hit upon Hamlet. Laertes himself, as his aside indicates, is struck at least momentarily with a sense of guilt.

The match is resumed. Laertes does wound Hamlet, and in the scuffle between the two, the rapiers are exchanged. After they are parted, Hamlet is able to wound Laertes. At that very moment the queen collapses. Horatio expresses his concern for the bleeding Hamlet, as Osric does for the bleeding Laertes. The Lord Chamberlain's son, aware that he is close to death, acknowledges that he is "justly kill'd with [his] own treachery" (ii. 318). When Hamlet cries out in concern for the queen, Claudius replies that she has fainted at the sight of blood. But Gertrude survives just long enough to tell what has happened: "The drink, the drink! I am poison'd" (ii. 321).

Hamlet calls for the doors to be locked and demands that the treachery be exposed to the assembled members of the Court. Laertes then speaks up. He states that not only he, but also Hamlet, is near death and that the prince now holds the "treacherous instrument" in his hand. Further, he declares that Gertrude has been poisoned and that the author of all this destruction is Claudius: "—the King, the King's to blame" (ii. 331). Hamlet lunges at Claudius, exclaiming, "Then, venom, to thy work" (ii. 333). The king survives only long enough to hear himself denounced by his nephew as the "incestuous, murderous, damn'd Dane" (ii. 336). Before dying, the contrite Laertes expresses his conviction that Claudius "is justly serv'd." He asks Hamlet's pardon, assuring the prince that "Mine and my father's death come not upon thee, / Nor thine on me!"

Hamlet voices his wish that divine justice will absolve Laertes of any guilt and adds that he will follow Laertes in death. Turning to his dead mother, he bids the "wretched queen" farewell. He then implores Horatio to report all that happened fully and accurately so that there will be no misunderstandings after his death. But the faithful Horatio is ready to join Hamlet in death and is restrained only by the prince's insistence that he survive to clear Hamlet's "wounded name."

The sounds of marching soldiers and a cannon shot are heard. Osric announces that young Fortinbras, fresh from conquest in Poland, has fired a salute in honor of the newly arrived English ambassadors. Hamlet lives just long enough to prophesy and to approve the election of Fortinbras as King of Denmark. Horatio speaks moving words of sorrow and tribute as Hamlet dies.

Fortinbras and the English ambassadors enter. The Norwegian prince, used to bloodshed in battle, is shocked at the spectacle of death. The ambassadors, gazing on the "dismal" sight, are aware that the news which they were to bring to Claudius has arrived too late: They were to inform him that Rosencrantz and Guildenstern had been executed in accordance with his instructions. Horatio then speaks lines that go far toward summarizing the whole tragedy, the violent acts of which include adultery, murder, accidental deaths, deaths cunningly planned, and deaths that resulted from plans that went awry.

Fortinbras orders four captains to see to it that Hamlet is accorded full honors, including "soldiers' music and the rites of war."

Commentary

In the first act, Claudius, addressing the assembled Court, had spoken of "mirth in funeral" and "delight and dole" (I. ii. 12–13). His words well express the theme of the first part of Act V, Scene 1. The gravediggers are identified as "two clowns"; that is, they are lowly (and often rustic) characters who will provide broad comedy in the midst of tragic action. It should be apparent that the comic element in this scene has comparable relevancy. Moreover, the First Gravedigger, so far as his gift for paradox is concerned, has at his level and, in his way, a certain affinity with Hamlet himself when the prince chooses to exercise his sardonic wit. However brief his appearance may be in this play, the First Gravedigger is a memorable figure.

More often than not, incongruity is basic to comedy. For these two lowly gravediggers to discuss with such intensity a profound theological and legal question, and especially to hear the first one endeavor to introduce into his argument technical Latinisms and to organize his argument in strict accordance with the rules of Aristotelian logic, with its careful definition of a key term—all this is wonderful comedy of words. Inevitably, the malapropism finds a place. Instead of *se defendendo* (in self-defense), the First Gravedigger says *se offendendo*, and he renders the Latin *ergo* (therefore) as *argal*. In what amounts to a burlesque of the scholastic method of disputation, he defines the "three branches" of an act, with a resulting redundancy that is hilarious. The two are no less amusing when the transition is made to Adam, the first delver and the progenitor of the human race—proof that the gravediggers, like gardeners and ditchdiggers, are descendents of the first human being, who was a gentleman (Could Adam delve without arms?). Shakespeare and all members of his audience were familiar with the traditional doggerel: "When Adam delved and Eve span, / Who was then the gentleman?" The underlying note of social protest gives way to grim humor when the First Gravedigger proposes his riddle—indeed, the ultimate riddle: "What is he that builds stronger than either the mason, the shipwright, or the carpenter?" (46–47). His fellow gravedigger is praised for the case he makes in favor of the gallows-maker (that specialist among carpenters), but he proves to be too obtuse to hit the obvious answers.

Few can miss the underlying seriousness in much of this buffoonery. If nothing else, it serves to emphasize the Christian framework of *Hamlet* and to remind one that Hamlet himself is a

Christian Prince who has been called upon to execute revenge. Ophelia's guilt, if any, depends upon whether or not her drowning was a voluntary act. If it was voluntary, obviously she was guilty of self-murder. Other lives have been taken in the course of the action, including that of Polonius; others soon will be lost—and not just the life of Hamlet's adversary. The prince has been, and will be, involved in most of these deaths. What, if any, is the extent of his guilt? In all instances does he, and will he, function as the righteous minister of God's justice or as a scourge? These are proper questions, although neither takes into consideration the special difficulties posed by the corruption prevalent in Denmark and the element of chance.

The gravediggers' dialogue, with its emphasis largely on death, also serves as a prologue to the "worm's meat" or "Dance of Death" theme developed in this same scene by Hamlet. Perhaps there is even relevancy in the song which the First Gravedigger sings, a conventional Tudor one in which youth and age are contrasted. Admittedly, it may do no more than show some feeling on the part of the singer, despite Hamlet's question, "Has this fellow no feeling of his business that he sings at grave-making?" (73-74). But youth and age are not the only subjects of the song; love and renunciation are also contrasted. Time is the destroyer of youth, inevitably; but it can also destroy love. And this too looks forward to the subject of Hamlet's morbid remarks.

When Hamlet sees the First Gravedigger toss up the skulls, he exclaims: "How the knave jowls it to the ground, as if it were Cain's jawbone, that did the first murder!" (84-85). Since Cain's crime was fratricide, the special import of this exclamation is evident. One recalls Claudius' words, spoken in soliloquy, after the Mouse-trap had been sprung: "O, my offence is rank, it smells to heaven; / It hath the primal eldest curse upon't, / A brother's murder" (III. iii. 36-38). Carried along by his satirical imagination and universalizing tendencies, Hamlet meditates on the ironical fact that overreaching politicians, lawyers with all their tricks, self-seeking courtiers, vain court ladies, even those held to be exemplars of greatness in this world ultimately are no more than the "quintessence of dust."

Among the examples of earthly vanity that Hamlet adduces, the following is the culminating one: "Now get you to my lady's chamber, / and tell her, let her paint an inch thick, to this / favour she must come. Make her laugh at that" (212-14). It is quite possible that more than human vanity is involved here. In two significant, earlier passages, comparable references to woman's efforts at beautification were used to exemplify hypocrisy or dishonesty in general. The first was included in the king's aside after he heard Polonius instruct Ophelia on how to conduct herself once she was "loosed" upon Hamlet: "The harlot's cheek, beautified with plast'ring art, / Is not more ugly to the thing that helps it / Than is my deed to my most painted word" (III. i. 51-53). The second reference was part of Hamlet's bitter indictment of Ophelia in the nunnery scene: "I have heard of your paintings too, well enough. / God has given you one face, and you make yourself / another" (III. i. 148-50). The conclusion to be drawn, then, is that Hamlet's discourse is not just another example of morbid preoccupation with death, amounting to what some insist is a death wish; nor is it a premonition of his own impending death. Rather, it underscores once more, and this late in the play, the extent of his disillusionment. Were he to sweep to his revenge and survive to rule Denmark, Hamlet's outlook on life could never be the optimistic one that once made it possible for him to embrace the idealistic Renaissance view of man as the paragon of animals, like unto the angels.

All this provides a transition to the puzzling remarks that the First Gravedigger makes to Hamlet. From his words, one learns that he began his career on the very day Hamlet was born (160-61) and has served for thirty years (177). A thirty-year-old Hamlet, undergraduate at Wittenberg? One who apparently was not considered as eligible to succeed his father because of his youth? This has been and remains a crux. It has been argued that the Hamlet whom one meets in Act V has experienced so much that he is no longer the youth who, overwhelmed not only by the sudden death of a beloved father but more especially by the hasty and incestuous marriage of his mother, wishes for death. Such an impressionistic theory would be consistent with much that has been written about Hamlet's development of the "worm's meat" theme in this play. But there have been other conjectures about Hamlet's age as reported by the First Gravedigger. It has been pointed out correctly that Shakespeare was not always careful about exact details, either those relating to chronology or those relating to topography. Further, the Elizabethans not infrequently made use of round numbers, the

implication here being that the gravedigger means that he had followed his vocation for somewhat more than twenty years. Finally,
there are those who believe that in this passage Shakespeare inadvertently included a detail peculiar to an earlier version of the
Hamlet story. One other theory may well be added to these: Hamlet
suddenly emerges as a man of thirty years, thanks to a careless tran-
scriber or printer. Most Shakespeareans refuse to trouble themselves greatly over this detail, convinced that the poet-dramatist
intended his tragic hero to be the gifted son of King Hamlet put to
the test not in his adult maturity but at his inception to manhood. The student may well look to the end of the play and read
Fortinbras' encomium. The Norwegian prince's words could hardly
refer to an individual who had been a promising young man for a
decade or more.

The discussion of Ophelia's burial in Scene 1, in which the Priest
and Laertes take part, calls for some commentary. The Priest's insistence that "Her death was doubtful" (250) is at variance with Gertrude's report of accidental death in the preceding scene. One learns
that Ophelia is to be buried in sanctified ground only because "great
command o'ersways the order" (251), an indication that the king
himself interceded after the coroner's verdict. It is established, however, that the pathetic Ophelia died chaste and therefore is allowed
"virgin rites" (255). Not without interest also is the fact that once
more she is associated with flowers. "Lay her i' th' earth," Laertes
exclaims in anguish, "And from her fair and unpolluted flesh / May
violets spring!" (261–62). Gertrude, who appears most sympathetic
in this scene, scatters flowers on the coffin and says, "Sweets to the
sweet; farewell!" (266). When Ophelia first appeared in this play, she
was associated with flowers and specifically with the violet, a
symbol of faithfulness, but also a flower that is "sweet, not lasting";
she was associated also with other "infants of the spring" (I. iii. 7–8,
39–40). Much later in the play, a demented Ophelia distributed flowers among the members of the Court group, but these did not
include violets, for they had withered when her father died (IV. vi.
179–85). All this adds up to a sufficiently obvious conclusion:
Ophelia metaphorically is the flower destroyed by "Contagious
blastments," to use Laertes' words (I. iii. 42), in a Denmark ruled by a
usurper and regicide who lives in incestuous union with his queen.

It may come as something of a surprise to find the queen saying, as she scatters flowers on Ophelia's coffin, "I hop'd thou shouldst have been my Hamlet's wife. / I thought thy bride-bed to have deck'd, sweet maid, / And not t' have strew'd thy grave" (267–69). One recalls that both Laertes (I. iii. 14–21) and Polonius (I. iv. 123–30) rejected the idea that Hamlet might marry Ophelia, the former arguing that the prince would have to have a political marriage, the latter, typically refusing to believe that Hamlet could have honorable intentions. The queen's words make all the more pathetic the death of Ophelia and show how destructive the force of evil has been up to this point, late in the play. Those who read into *Hamlet* romantic love as the primary element make much of Gertrude's words, just as they do Hamlet's declaration that he loved Ophelia more than forty thousand times as much as brother could love sister (292–93). But when one stays with the text, he knows that love between Hamlet and Ophelia has been excluded from the very first; Hamlet can speak of it only when she is dead. The prince returned to Elsinore only when he learned of his father's death. Both Laertes and Polonius spoke of the recent attentions Hamlet paid to Ophelia. There are two possibilities: First, he did love her deeply prior to his mother's marriage to Claudius, which took place less than two months after his father's funeral, and then was repulsed by the conviction that she had deserted him; second, he had turned to her originally to test the validity of his own generalization voiced in his first soliloquy: "Frailty, thy name is woman!" If the latter be true, then one may well conclude that his declaration of boundless love for Ophelia is to be interpreted as an expression of his shock at, and genuine sorrow for, the death of Ophelia, whose only possible offense was that she was obedient to a father who was a rash, intruding fool.

Overlapping the problem of interpretation here in Scene 1 and adding to the complexity are the performances of Laertes and Hamlet. As the funeral procession arrives, the prince speaks of Laertes to Horatio: "That is Laertes, a very noble youth" (247), an inadvertently ironic remark in view of what has been revealed about Laertes. One hardly equates nobility with the kind of underhanded scheming revealed in the last scene of Act IV. Is it possible that Hamlet's gracious tribute is intended as a hint for evaluating Laertes' words and actions that soon follow and, to some extent, make understandable Hamlet's reaction?

To be sure, Laertes invites great sympathy, just as he did when he and his sister said their farewells early in the play. But, it has been argued, his advice to Ophelia in that early scene was notable for its affected style; it was anything but natural and spontaneous. Consider also the Laertes whose rebellion had, in Claudius' words, looked so "giant-like" and who was willing to "dare damnation" even if he had to slit an adversary's throat in the church (IV. v. 121, 133; vii. 127). Now, in the present scene, his rhetorical outburst, followed by his leap into the grave, is so excessive that he appears to be overacting the role of the grief-stricken brother, his expression of grief exceeding that of Hecuba, as described in the player's lines from *Aeneas and Dido*. If this be true, then Hamlet's violent reaction is completely understandable, and especially so when one recalls how he had urged the players to avoid overacting and rant and "to hold . . . the mirror up to nature" (III. ii. 22–38). The prince's own words provide the soundest criticism of Laertes' performance:

> What is he whose grief
> Bears such an emphasis, whose phrase of sorrow
> Conjures the wand'ring stars and makes them
> stand
> Like wonder-wounded hearers?

> (277–80)

After the two are separated, he speaks the lines that are completely devastating, beginning, "Woo 't weep? Woo 't fight? Woo 't fast? / Woo 't tear thyself? / Woo 't drink up eisel [vinegar]? Eat a crocodile?" and concluding, "Nay, an thou'lt mouth, I'll rant as well as thou" (298–307). "Woo 't" was a form used only by illiterates and therefore is intended to be insulting, as are all the elements of competitive hyperbole that follow. If Hamlet has spoken "wild and whirling words" in a state of high excitement, as when he first encountered the Ghost, if he could voice the bitterest words of self-criticism, as he has done in soliloquy on two notable occasions, he is incapable of "mouthing," of "rant." It simply will not do to say, as the neo-Freudians do, that Hamlet's lines are a manifestation of overemphasis resulting from a bad conscience.

"This is I, Hamlet, the Dane!" the prince exclaims when he moves out from his place of retirement where he has been observing what takes place (280–81). In these words he takes on his father's title. Is he now a prince who, after indulging himself in meditations, or permitting himself to be engulfed in excessive grief, now speaks with an absolute authority that indicates that he will no longer procrastinate? So some have argued, reasoning that his experience on the voyage to England and the shock of learning that Ophelia is dead have effected this change in his character. Certainly Hamlet no longer is willing to tolerate "seeming" and "acting," any more than he was willing to tolerate the actions of Rosencrantz and Guildenstern, the king's agents. When Laertes grasps him by the throat, he speaks words that are at once decisive and controlled:

> I prithee, take thy fingers from my throat.
> Sir, though I am not splentive [hot-tempered] and
>   rash,
> Yet have I something in me dangerous,
> Which let thy wiseness fear. Away thy hand!
>
> (283–86)

Yet there remain perplexing questions. "What is the reason that you use me thus?" he asks (312). Can Hamlet possibly have forgotten that he has slain Laertes' father? May he not have suspected at least some connection between Polonius' death and that of Ophelia? One readily may discount Gertrude's statement that Hamlet's words and actions comprise evidence of his madness, following which "His silence will sit drooping" (307–11); but Hamlet's last two lines at least suggest that he may have put on the antic disposition for the last time: "Let Hercules himself do what he may, / The cat will mew and dog will have his day" (314–15).

In Scene 2, as he begins to fill in the details of what happened to him since he left Denmark, Hamlet concedes that "there was a kind of fighting" in his heart (4). But clearly his inner turmoil has been manifested from the time of his first appearance in this play. Now one is to hear no more expression of self-reproach or doubts that he will act positively against Claudius. What is impressive is his decisiveness. Thanks to what he calls "rashness" and "indiscretion," he is able to formulate a plan and to execute it without delay. As Samuel Johnson observed, Hamlet has found man's wisdom, or reason, to have its limitations: Fortune, accident, chance—call it what one will—can determine the course of events, as his own experience aboard the ship proves. He was able to find in the dark the commission for his own death; by chance, he had in his possession his father's signet for sealing the forged document. No less by chance, the pirates proved "kind" and, for sufficient compensation, returned him to Denmark.

"So Guildenstern and Rosencrantz go to't," says Horatio laconically (56). Some commentators read disapproval into his words. Certainly the deaths of these two servants of the king have led to much discussion. In Belleforest's non-dramatic version of *Hamlet*, both knew the contents of the commission; in Shakespeare's play, there is no evidence that Rosencrantz and Guildenstern knew that they were conducting the prince to his death. As George Steevens, late eighteenth-century editor and critic of Shakespeare, remarked, "It is not [the critic's] office to interpret the plays of Shakespeare according to the novels on which they were founded—novels which the poet sometimes followed, but often materially deserted." If there is justification for Hamlet's action, then, it must be found in the text of the play. Was it a vindictive Hamlet who wrote that the two should be executed, no "shriving time allow'd" (47)? If so, he can hardly be said to have acted as one executing public justice rather than personal revenge. And it follows that, if indeed a divinity guided him at this time when, by his own testimony, he did not pause for thought, he functioned as God's scourge, not His minister.

But most commentators do not believe that Shakespeare intended so to denigrate the character of his tragic hero. If he makes Hamlet human enough to get grim satisfaction out of the fact that Rosencrantz and Guildenstern are not to be allowed time to purge their souls of sin, the essential point made by Hamlet is that there be no delay in the execution of the two and therefore no chance that the forgery would be discovered. More convincing is Horatio's reaction when Hamlet explains why "They are not near [his] conscience" (58–62). He insists that they loved their employment. One recalls that earlier he denounced them to their faces as sponges "that soak up the King's countenance" (IV. ii. 16 ff.)—that is, they stood ready to do the king's every wish for the sake of personal reward. These two have been presented as servile half-men from the start. Rosencrantz and Guildenstern were surrogates of Claudius, Hamlet's mighty opposite. And of him, Horatio says, "Why, what a king is this!"

Yet it must be admitted that after itemizing Claudius' major crimes, the prince does not receive an answer to his question, one that is basic to his status as a moral symbol in the play: "—is't not perfect conscience, / To quit him with this arm? And is't not to be damn'd, / To let this canker of our nature come / In further evil?" (67–70). A. C. Bradley, among a few other critics, sees here a Hamlet who is still in doubt, still troubled by his conscience; and this view should not be ignored if only because it illustrates once more the difficulties of interpretation. One may argue that there is no need for Horatio to answer Hamlet's question since he has already expressed deep shock at the latest evidence of Claudius' villainy. So, for many critics, the Hamlet in Scene 2 has resolved all doubts; there is no longer "a kind of fighting" in his heart.

Of some significance is Hamlet's summary of Claudius' major offenses: "He that hath kill'd my king and whor'd my mother, / Popp'd in between th' election and my hopes, / Thrown out his angle for my proper life" (64–66). First, there is no evidence of a fixation on an incestuous mother here, perhaps to the chagrin of the neo-Freudians. Second, although Hamlet has made reference to having an ambition to rule Denmark, he has done so primarily to mislead Claudius (see II. ii. 259 ff.; III. ii. 97–99). Heretofore, the protagonist's ambition to rule Denmark has not been emphasized. Now he accuses his uncle of frustrating that ambition. Coming this late, however, the effect is not to transmute the play into an ambition tragedy. Claudius, however formidable as the antagonist to Hamlet, has been identified as a man notoriously inferior to the late king (see I. iv. 8–12; II. ii. 380–85). If Hamlet will perform a public duty in slaying Claudius, would it not be his duty also to prove himself to be his father's son by accepting the responsibilities of kingship? In experience, the young prince has grown in stature since he spoke the lines of his first soliloquy and referred to both Claudius and himself in these words: "My father's brother, but no more like my father / Than I to Hercules" (I. ii. 152–53). He knows that he remains a mortal, but he knows also that he would not be "a king of shreds and patches."

When Horatio reminds Hamlet that Claudius is sure to learn soon what has happened to Rosencrantz and Guildenstern, Hamlet's reply (73–74) shows him to be controlled and confident. Now he expresses regret that he had so "forgot" himself as to offend Laertes, stating that he sees the image of his own cause in that of Ophelia's brother. Probably no more is intended than that Hamlet makes reference to the fact that both have endured great losses, for Hamlet's cause transcends the personal or domestic, involving as it does the welfare of the State. The prince's determination to win back the goodwill of Laertes makes understandable his prompt agreement to participate in the fencing match.

Osric, a young courtier, brings to Hamlet the message from Claudius relating to the duel. A few lines would have sufficed for this purpose, but Shakespeare chose to present a full-length portrait of the fashionable, affected courtier, a familiar object of satire during the Renaissance. Hamlet identifies him as a "water-fly"—that is, an insect darting about the surface of water without any apparent purpose or reason—a busy trifler. Such lines as Hamlet's "Put your bonnet to his right use; 'tis for the head" (96) tell the reader how excessively formal Osric's gestures are. The courtier's style of dis-course, burlesqued by the prince, is marked by an overuse of Lat-inisms and elaborate metaphors. The attention that the poet-dramatist pays to Osric may be justified, at least to some extent, on the grounds that he serves to illustrate artificiality and pretense, which characterize the Court, the leader of which is Clau-dius. But since both qualities have been well established already, some may conclude that the portrait of Osric is no more than a tour de force which the dramatist enjoyed creating.

"You will lose this wager, my lord," says Horatio after Osric has left (219). But Hamlet reassures his friend, saying that while Laertes was in France, he (Hamlet) has "been in continual practice." One should not split hairs in the realm of critical commentary; neverthe-less, some critics are reminded that the prince himself had said that he had "forgone all custom of exercise" (II. ii. 308). Later in the present scene, Gertrude will remark that her son is out of condition. Yet there is no question of Hamlet's skill as a swordsman. Ophelia's encomium described Hamlet as the ideal prince and courtier—the accomplished Renaissance man, "The courtier's, soldier's, scholar's, eye, tongue, sword" (III. i. 159).

Despite his confidence that he will "win at the odds," Hamlet concedes that he is heartsick (222–23). How could he be otherwise in view of all that has happened, and especially in view of the fact that although Hamlet has been involved in violence, Claudius, the source of all rottenness, survives, ruling Denmark with Gertrude, the "imperial jointress"?

When Horatio urges him to consider withdrawing from the match, Hamlet makes reply in words weighty with import:

> . . . we defy augury. There's a
> special providence in the fall of a sparrow. If it be
> now, 'tis not to come; if it be not to come, it will
> be now; if it be not now, yet it will come; the readi-
> ness is all.
>
> (230-34)

What the prince says here is consistent with what he said earlier in Scene 2 when he declared that "There's a divinity that shapes our ends" (10). And if he is still heartsick, this passage provides additional evidence that no longer is there "a kind of fighting" in his heart—the kind that, early in the play, made him lament the fact that he was called upon to act violently because the "time is out of joint" (I. v. 189-90), and later expend his energy in denunciation of his "mighty opposite" and accuse himself of inexcusable delay. Hamlet now seems to have resolved all doubts as to whether he functions as minister or as scourge. Finally, he no longer fears death or what may await him after death. When he says, "There's a special providence in the fall of a sparrow" (230-31), he is, of course, paraphrasing verses from the Bible—Matthew 10:28-31; Luke 12:4-7.

The "readiness is all." This dictum suggests that Hamlet has mastered passion. Inevitably it calls to one's mind his praise of Horatio as a man who is not passion's slave. Of him, the prince said, "for thou hast been / As one, in suffering all, that suffers nothing, / A man that Fortune's buffets and rewards / Hath ta'en with equal thanks" (III. ii. 70-73). Some students will remember that in *King Lear*, Edgar, striving once more to win over his blind and oppressed father, the Earl of Gloucester, from despair, said, "What, in ill thoughts again? Men must endure / Their going hence even as their coming hither; / Ripeness is all" (V. ii. 9-11). Gloucester, like Hamlet, would have welcomed death, although, unlike Hamlet, he was not restrained by conscience. He had lost faith in a supreme power or powers concerned with man's destiny. Thanks to the good offices of his son Edgar, he finally learns to accept Fortune's buffets with patience. In a word, he embraces Stoicism. Hamlet, who now knows that "readiness is all," has also embraced Stoicism. Curiously, at least one well-known Shakespearean editor and critic argues that

Hamlet cannot become a Stoic as Gloucester did because Gloucester's world is pagan, not Christian as Hamlet's world is. Surely it is rather late to ignore the fact that Stoicism in its practical application to life had long since been Christianized in Western thought. Indeed there is a biblical echo in Edgar's words quoted above (cf. Job 14:12).

In his apology to Laertes, Hamlet is the soul of graciousness and sincerity. One remembers how he told Horatio how much he regretted his behavior in the graveyard (75–78). Nevertheless, there are certain disturbing elements in this episode preliminary to the fencing match. He tells Laertes that "madness" has been his enemy, yet again and again, from the time he told Horatio and members of the guard that he planned to adopt an "antic disposition," evidence has been presented to show that however extravagant his words and even his actions may have been on occasion, he was anything but demented. The conclusion to be made is that he refers here to that "kind of fighting" in his heart that led to emotional extremes. Certainly he has not "purpos'd evil"; but some critics find it strange that Hamlet makes no specific reference either to Polonius or to Ophelia. He merely asks Laertes to believe "That I have shot mine arrow o'er the house / And hurt my brother" (254–55). Ironically, if Gertrude spoke truly when she said that she had hoped that Ophelia would have become Hamlet's wife (V. i. 267), Laertes might have become the prince's brother. "I'll be your foil," says Hamlet in the spirit of good fellowship (266), quibbling upon the word, which may mean "rapier" or "something which, by contrast, enhances a jewel." But, as things turn out, *Laertes* is the foil—in a far different sense.

No one is likely to underestimate the king as he appears during these preliminaries. From his first appearance in this play, he has demonstrated his skill at dissembling, presenting himself as the living embodiment of affability. It is he who places Laertes' hand in that of Hamlet; all hear him express absolute confidence in and support of his nephew. With an apparent abundance of goodwill, he promises Hamlet a princely reward. At his orders, martial music is sounded, and he drinks to Hamlet's success. Claudius is no ordinary villain; he is an accomplished one, the mighty opposite of the tragic hero. If Laertes were to wound Hamlet and survive unscathed, he alone would be aware of Claudius' fear and hatred of Hamlet.

Queen Gertrude is heard from only after the match has begun and Hamlet has scored the first hit with his blunted foil. No one should misinterpret her remark "He's fat, and scant of breath" (298), made just before she offers to wipe Hamlet's brow and prepares to drink to his success. Yet a few have managed to do just that, concluding that the prince is corpulent. (A favorite theory, among this group, is that Richard Burbage, who created the role of Hamlet in the Elizabethan theater, had put on a bit too much weight in middle age.) But, as King James I is reported to have said, no melancholy man was ever fat. The context should tell even a modern critic that Gertrude is referring to the fact that Hamlet is perspiring, perhaps excessively—an indication, as she believes, that he is out of condition.

The action that follows is as exciting as any to be found in drama. Laertes is allowed to express twinges of conscience just before he wounds Hamlet; and, when he himself is fatally wounded, he has the good grace to acknowledge that his own treachery is responsible for his impending death. Moreover, just after the queen cries out that she has been poisoned, he survives to place the blame upon Claudius. Demands of the plot at this point of its resolution, in part, explain Laertes' free confession and accusation. But it is not inappropriate that Laertes, who shortly before had declared that he stood aloof from Hamlet "in terms of honor" (258–60) and then faced the prince armed with an unblunted and poisoned rapier, should be allowed to retrieve himself through full confession. Claudius must, and does, remain the villain of the piece.

"The point envenom'd too!" exclaims Hamlet at the moment of complete discovery, aware that he will soon join his mother and Laertes in death. One recalls that venom—poison—used by Claudius was the source of the rottenness in Denmark. It has spread throughout Elsinore and beyond. Polonius, Ophelia, and Rosencrantz and Guildenstern are among its victims.

At long last, Hamlet slays Claudius. The prince survives not only to philosophize briefly on "this fell sergeant, Death," who is so "strict in his arrest" (347–48), but also, more important, to implore Horatio to report him and his cause aright—to clear his "wounded name." Certainly he does not want subjects of the Crown to believe that his slaying of Claudius was the latest and most shocking action of a Hamlet who, in the words of the First Gravedigger, was mad. Even less does he want to be remembered as the Pyrrhus-type of king-killer. Hamlet's concept of honor, implicit from the beginning, is something far above that held by Laertes and Polonius. He wishes to be remembered as the worthy son of the superior King Hamlet, as minister called upon to execute public justice, *not* as scourge. The moving words of Horatio, who knew him best, provide the best epitaph: "Now cracks a noble heart. Good-night, sweet prince, / And flights of angels sing thee to thy rest" (370–71). For Hamlet was the "sweet prince"; and, in the Renaissance, the epithet *sweet* (like the adjective *gentle*) had special force, emphasizing superiority when applied to a person.

Fortinbras, who arrives near the very end of the play, also provides an epitaph:

> Let four captains
> Bear Hamlet, like a soldier, to the stage
> For he was likely, had he been put on,
> To have prov'd most royally.
>
> (406–409)

It is quite significant that Hamlet, who did not survive to rule Denmark (and in that sense had not "been put on"), is accorded a soldier's funeral. One is reminded again that the issue in the conflict between Hamlet and Claudius was a public one involving the health of the State.

In his dying words, Hamlet casts his vote for Fortinbras as the new ruler of Denmark. Fortinbras, one recalls, has been presented as one of the foils to Hamlet. Pointing out that the warlike Norwegian prince, first determined to avenge his father's death, come what may, had listened to his royal uncle's reasoned argument and had turned his energies to a conquest of the Poles, some critics are sure that his ascension to the throne is especially fitting. According to their argument, Hamlet has paid the price for his inability to master passion before it was too late for him to avoid catastrophe (which in Renaissance high tragedy is always the death of the protagonist). Others, conceding that Hamlet failed in that he did not survive to prove himself his father's son as ruler of Denmark, insist that the very condition that made inevitable his failure, especially his unwillingness to act without much thought, is the measure of his greatness. For them, the prince emerges finally as the sacrificial victim, one whose death is inevitable but makes possible the purging of great evil and the restoration of a moral universe.

1604

othello

OTHELLO

LIST OF CHARACTERS

Othello

A Moorish general serving the city-state of Venice. He is a seasoned warrior, an honest man, and a new husband. His flaw is that he allows his ensign's diabolical nature to corrupt him and make him believe that his young wife, Desdemona, is unfaithful. It is only after Othello kills her that he learns that he has been duped. In deep anguish, he executes himself for his crime.

Iago

Othello's ensign, who hoped to be promoted to the position of lieutenant. The position went to Michael Cassio, and Iago vows revenge. He manages to destroy Othello, Desdemona, his own wife (Emilia), and even his Venetian patron, Roderigo. He has often been said to be Shakespeare's most consummate villain.

Desdemona

The daughter of the Venetian Senator Brabantio and the wife of the Venetian General Othello. Against her father's wishes, she marries a foreigner, a Moor—a man of another color and of another race. Her love for Othello is so deep, however, that as she is dying, she attempts to protect him from his crime.

Cassio

Othello's Florentine lieutenant is young and handsome. He is courteous to the ladies and, in order to seem a good soldier and friend to Iago, he drinks too much, wounds Montano, Governor of Cyprus, and is dismissed from his post by Othello. By sheer luck, he manages to escape being killed in a murder plot contrived by Iago. At the end of the play, it is Cassio who is appointed Governor of Cyprus.

Emilia

Iago's wife is outspoken, a bit bawdy, and has a certain cynicism about men—due mainly to years of living with Iago. Despite this, however, even she does not suspect her husband of his labyrinthine web of evil machinations. In one sense, one can say that she is an agent in the death of Desdemona. She has an opportunity to explain to Othello that his wife did not give a sentimentally prized handkerchief to young Cassio, but she remains silent. After Iago stabs Emilia and as she is dying, she finally manages to convince Othello that his wife was faithful.

Roderigo

A Venetian who is deeply enamored with Desdemona. Iago convinces him that if Roderigo will pay him sufficiently, he will arrange, eventually, for Roderigo to have Desdemona.

The Duke of Venice

He appoints Othello to lead the Venetian forces against the Turks and, because of his admiration for the Moor, tries to placate Brabantio's anger against his daughter and her new husband.

Brabantio

He is a senator of Venice; he is also Desdemona's father and is outraged and heartbroken when he learns of her marriage to the Moor, Othello.

Gratiano

Brabantio's brother, who, together with a kinsman, Lodovico, discovers Cassio lying wounded after he has been attacked by Roderigo.

Montano

Governor of Cyprus; a friend and loyal supporter of Othello.

Clown

Othello's servant; he teases the Cyprian musicians about their instruments, and he serves as a messenger between Cassio and Desdemona.

Bianca

Cassio's jealous mistress; he gives her Desdemona's handkerchief, not realizing whose handkerchief it really is.

Lodovico

Kinsman to Brabantio; he and Gratiano discover Cassio lying wounded after he has been attacked by Roderigo.

SUMMARIES AND COMMENTARIES

ACT I

Summary

The play opens late at night on a street in Venice. Iago, an ensign in the Venetian navy, and Roderigo, a wealthy Venetian gentleman, are discussing the recent elopement of Desdemona, a woman Roderigo hoped to marry. Roderigo protests indignantly that he paid Iago good money to keep him informed about Desdemona's romantic attachments and, we infer, to try to kindle a love match between the two. Iago failed, and Desdemona eloped with Iago's general; the fact that Iago did not inform Roderigo immediately seems to prove to Roderigo that Iago's loyalty is really with Othello. In defense, Iago declares that he has no special loyalty toward his general. In fact, he has every reason to hate the man; after all, Othello recently made Cassio, instead of Iago, his new lieutenant. Iago then tells Roderigo that his is a difficult role; to the public, he must seem to be a dutiful servant to Othello, but, in fact, he is seeking his own "peculiar [private] end" (60).

Meanwhile, Iago and Roderigo have reached Desdemona's father's house and decide to wake up her father, Brabantio, and tell him that his daughter has eloped with Othello. Brabantio is understandably furious and demands vengeance, and while Iago slips away on business of his own, Brabantio sets off with Roderigo and a search party to find his missing daughter and Othello.

Shortly afterward, on another street, Iago has just joined Othello when Cassio delivers a message from the Duke of Venice that summons Othello immediately to a military council. Then, as

Brabantio and Roderigo enter, accompanied by armed officers, the scene nearly erupts into violence. Brabantio accuses Othello of having bewitched Desdemona and demands that he be thrown at once into prison. With dignity, Othello manages to pacify the others and persuades Brabantio to take his complaint before the duke.

Later the same night, the duke and his senators, in council, are discussing discrepancies in the several reports about the threatening Turkish fleet. Othello, Brabantio, Iago, Roderigo, and others enter and interrupt this attempt to solve a national crisis. Presenting to them his own personal crisis, Brabantio declares that nothing but witchcraft could have induced his daughter to marry Othello; Othello denies the charge, and the duke sends attendants to fetch Desdemona, Iago accompanying them at Othello's request. Desdemona is called to speak for herself; in the meanwhile, Othello tells them all how he met and courted his new wife and how he fascinated her with accounts of his travels and adventures. Desdemona arrives and gently resolves the dispute by acknowledging split loyalties to her father and to her new husband but making it clear that she now belongs to Othello. Brabantio bitterly rejects his daughter and also the duke's attempts to console him. The duke returns his attention to the Turks and directs Othello to leave for Cyprus. Desdemona will join Othello later in Cyprus under Iago's protection. As the others leave, Iago and Roderigo are once again alone. Despite Roderigo's threats of suicide, Iago revitalizes his patron's hopes and fools him into thinking that he may still win Desdemona. Left alone, Iago admits to himself that money and amusement are his real reasons for befriending Roderigo. Then he begins to plan the deception of Othello which will afford him revenge for his many grievances against the Moor.

Commentary

The play begins with two people conversing, establishing theatrical time, place, and situation. This is an often-used theatrical convention, giving us background information and creating curiosity about the main character before he appears onstage. Yet the conversation here is not merely idle chatter. This is a quarrel of sorts and, as such, serves several functions. Its tone easily catches our interest, and, second, it reveals Iago's wily nature; he must make amends to Roderigo for failing to arouse Desdemona's interest in him. After all,

Iago intends to keep a hand in this wealthy nobleman's pocketbook, which, Roderigo says, belongs to Iago, "as if the strings were thine" (3). Iago apologizes profusely for failing Roderigo. Never did he dream that such an elopement might occur: "If ever I did dream of such a matter," he says, "Abhor me" (5–6).

Exactly how long Iago has been capitalizing upon the gullibility of Roderigo, this Venetian dandy, we do not know, but it is clear that Iago has no respect for the man's intelligence. The guile he openly uses in Scene 1 to stay in Roderigo's good stead is not even particularly crafty; blatantly, for example, he tells Roderigo, "I am not what I am" (65). Besides this statement being a capsule condemnation of Iago, it serves to point out that Roderigo trusts this man. Thus Roderigo gains a measure of our pity; he is a weak figure, probably victimized by everybody, not only in this matter of deceit.

Far more important, however, than catching our interest and establishing Iago's basic character, Scene 1 sets forth the key elements of the tragedy's conflict—that is, it reveals Iago's deep resentment toward Othello. Iago believed that he would be promoted to the rank of Othello's first lieutenant. He was not. Instead, Othello chose a man whose military ineptitude is an insult to Iago's proven superiority on the battlefield. Iago points out to Roderigo that Cassio, the newly appointed lieutenant, is not a true soldier. He is not even a Venetian. Cassio is a Florentine, a damning epithet condemning the city's reputation as being a collection of financiers and bookkeepers. What knowledge Cassio has of the battlefield he gained from textbooks; in other words, he is a student, not a practitioner of battle. Even a spinster, Iago says, knows more of the "division of a battle" (23) than this "bookish theoric" (24). We are inclined to believe Iago even though we have known him for only a short time. True, he has said, "I am not what I am" (65), but here he states his case concisely and without undue exaggeration. He does seem to be a superior, professional soldier who has had to step aside for a promotion that he feels he deserves. In fact, his candidacy for the position was supported by "three great ones of the city" (8). Iago apparently knows his worth. He has risen through the ranks and has proven his bravery and skill "at Rhodes, at Cyprus, and on other grounds / Christen'd and heathen" (29–30). He rose through the ranks by sheer ability, hoping for a position next highest to a general and was denied it. He rankles at being Othello's "ancient"—that is, his ensign. Furthermore, there is nothing Iago can do about the situation: "there's no remedy" (35). He realizes that "preferment goes by letter and affection" (36) and not by "old gradation" (37) (the traditional order of society). But he will continue to appear to "serve" Othello so that eventually he can "serve [his] turn upon him" (42).

Shakespeare makes a strong case for Iago's anger toward Othello and for his motive for revenge. Here we have a clear-cut picture of a man who is professionally wounded; his self-esteem has been insulted, and we must, of necessity, realize how deeply he has been offended if we are to understand the full extent of his revenge upon Othello.

Iago, however, is not bent on mere revenge. It would not be an exaggeration to say that revenge consumes him, and in Scene 1 he reveals himself to Roderigo and to us as a super-egotist, a self-seeking, malicious individual who will use every device in order to attain his "peculiar end" (60).

Iago's first act of revenge is quickly initiated: He will alert and incense Desdemona's father. He tells Roderigo to "call up her father, / Rouse him. Make after him, poison his delight" (67–68) and make such a noise that it will seem as though "fire / [has been] spied" (76–77). Roderigo obeys, but Iago is still not satisfied, and he must add his strong voice to Roderigo's, crying out loudly four times that "thieves" have plundered Brabantio's home. When Brabantio appears at the window, Iago continues to use the robbery metaphor: "You're robbed," he says, and "have lost half your soul" (85, 87).

Here Iago spews forth particularly coarse insults on his general. He calls Othello "an old black ram" (88), referring to the fact that Othello is a Moor, a dark-skinned man; Iago shouts out into the quiet night that this "ram" is "tupping" (88) (copulating with) Brabantio's "white ewe" (89) (Desdemona). He even conjures up another picture of visual horror for the sleepy old gentleman: If Brabantio doesn't rouse the Venetian citizens and rescue Desdemona, "the devil" (91) (another reference to the Moor's soot-colored skin) will make Brabantio a grandfather. The focus here is clearly on Othello's being a demoniac animal—a lust-driven ram raping the pure, white Desdemona. The language is crude and obscene, but one might note here that earlier the seemingly mild-natured Roderigo also made a tasteless reference to Othello as "the thick-lips" (66).

Yet while Iago calls Othello names, he has not yet called him by name; he has referred to him only with damning epithets. Brabantio is still half-asleep, and he has not fully grasped the situation. He is more annoyed that Roderigo has awakened him than he is about the possibility that his house may have been "robbed." Iago's offensive, figurative language has not riled him. We learn that he has warned Roderigo "not to haunt about my doors" (96); "my daughter is not for thee" (98). Thus another dimension of this situation presents itself. Roderigo is not just a rich, lovesick suitor who is paying Iago good wages to further his case with the senator's daughter. Roderigo has been rejected by Brabantio as a candidate for Desdemona's hand—a fact which offers an interesting parallel: Iago has been denied his chance to become Othello's lieutenant, and Roderigo has been denied his chance to become a recognized suitor of Desdemona. Rejection and revenge, then, are doubly potent ingredients in this tragedy.

Iago is quick to realize that the timid Roderigo will never sufficiently raise the ire of Desdemona's father and, for this reason, he interrupts his patron and heaps even more insults on Othello. Yet— and this fact is important—Iago has still not named Othello as being the culprit, as being the man who kidnapped Desdemona and eloped with her. This neglect on Iago's part—his failing to identify Othello—is dramatically important. Because Brabantio seems dense and uncomprehending, Iago can continue to curse Othello's socalled villainous nature and, thereby, reveal to us the depths of his own corruptness.

For example, Iago shouts out that Desdemona, at this moment, is being mounted by a "Barbary horse" (112). Brabantio's nephews, he says, will neigh, and, likewise, Brabantio's cousins will be "gennets" (113) (black Spanish horses). Still, however, he has not identified Othello by name; nor does he stress that it is Venice's General Othello who has absconded with Brabantio's daughter; Iago's emphasis is on Desdemona's sexual violation and the fact that at this very moment she and the Moor "are [now] making the beast with two backs" (117), a bawdy Elizabethan euphemism for sexual intercourse.

Iago's brazen assertions and Roderigo's timorous apologies for awakening Brabantio are finally effective. Brabantio comprehends what Iago and Roderigo are saying and that they have not been over-indulging in "distemp'ring draughts" (99) of liquor. Coincidentally, Brabantio was having a dream that foretold of just such a calamity. Dreams and omens of this sort are common in literature of this time and create the sense that fate somehow has a hand in the tragic events about to follow. Brabantio calls for "light," as well as for the light of insight to help him understand fully what has happened and how to deal with it. Then, as Brabantio moves into action, calling for more lights and arousing members of his household, Iago steals away, but not before explaining his reasons for doing so: It must not be public knowledge that Iago himself is an enemy of Othello; if Iago's machinations are to be successful, he must outwardly "show out a flag and sign of love, / Which is indeed but sign" (157-58). Thus he will manage to stay in Othello's good graces. For this reason, he must go and rejoin his general.

In addition to this speech reminding us of Iago's dangerous, diabolical treachery, it also serves to inform us about Othello's significance to Venice. Othello is a superior public figure, one who will soon be summoned to end the Cyprian wars, and a man upon whom the Venetian state depends for its safety. This fact is contained in Iago's comment that "another of his fathom they have none / To lead their business" (153-54). Othello is a man of high position, as well as one of high honor and one who is, therefore, worthy of being considered a tragic hero.

The subsequent action, in which the distraught and almost incredulous father appears, concludes Scene 1 in an exciting, sustaining manner. Brabantio is pathetic in his nightgown, standing distraught in the light of his servants' torches, realizing that his daughter is indeed gone. His sentences are unfinished, half-thoughts of disbelief. He appeals to fathers everywhere not to trust their daughters' words, only "what you see them act" (172). In his despair, he turns to Roderigo (Desdemona's suitor whom he earlier scorned) for confirmation that perhaps Othello used magic charms to win Desdemona. He is furious with himself for not having allowed Roderigo to court Desdemona. Suddenly Roderigo is ironically elevated to Brabantio's "lieutenant"; Brabantio tells him to "lead on" (181) and to alert every house. Thus Roderigo and Brabantio's search party sets out for The Sagittary, an inn where Iago said that Othello and Desdemona can be found.

The first words we hear from Iago in Scene 2 are lies. Posing as the trustworthy, honest soldier, the "loyal ancient" to his general, Iago says that when he inadvertently witnessed Roderigo's rousing

Brabantio, he would "nine or ten times . . . have yerk'd [stabbed] him [Roderigo] under the ribs" (4–5); he did not do so only because of his "little godliness" (9), because of his lack of "iniquity" (3), he says, and because he had not the "very stuff o' th' conscience / To do no contriv'd murder" (2–3). Iago is a practiced, pathological liar, attributing to Roderigo the "scurvy and provoking terms / Against [Othello's] honor" (7–8) that he himself proclaimed. Hypocritically, he sighs that it was "full hard [to] forbear him [Roderigo]" (10). This deceitful tone will characterize Iago throughout the play. Just as he earlier pretended great loyalty to Roderigo to continue to fatten his purse, here he pretends full loyalty to Othello, as he will throughout the play. In addition, he feigns over-concern that Brabantio's powerful position in Venice will bring Othello great grief and may dissolve Othello's marriage to Desdemona. Iago is a very versatile villain and wears many masks, in contrast to the commanding integrity of Othello.

Othello answers Iago in just five words: "'Tis better as it is" he says, meaning that it is good that Iago was not rash in handling Roderigo, for Othello does not fear Brabantio's temper. Our first view of Othello, then, is of a calm man who is in complete control of himself. He does not panic when he hears secondhand information about Roderigo's alleged animosity; nor does he seem to be the "lascivious Moor" (127) that Iago described in the previous scene. Here we will see proof that Othello is a public officer of great importance. "Let him [Brabantio] do his spite," Othello says. "My services . . . shall out-tongue his complaints" (117–19). Although Othello dislikes boasting, he cites the fact that he is no commoner: "I fetch my life and being / From men of royal siege" (21–22)—that is, he may be black, but he is of royal descent among the Moors, who earlier in history fought their way to the conquest of Spain and made a valiant effort to conquer all of western Europe. And of prime importance in this matter between himself and Brabantio is the fact that he loves "the gentle Desdemona" (25). He speaks with simple and intense feeling for her. He loved his bachelor freedom, but he loved Desdemona more; otherwise, he would not have "confined" his "unhoused free condition" (26), not even for all "the sea's worth" (28).

As he continues to await Desdemona's father in Scene 2, Othello still exhibits neither guilt nor fear. Even when Iago cautions that he sees torches approaching and urges Othello to go within, Othello refuses to hide. He has no apprehension concerning Desdemona's father, nor will he avoid confronting Brabantio's armed party. He is a man confident and prepared: "My parts, my title, and my perfect soul / Shall manifest me rightly" (31–32). Othello commands our respect and admiration.

Iago's brief acknowledgment of the Moor's character, his swearing softly "by Janus" (33), is almost a throwaway line, one that might go unnoticed, but he could not have selected a more proper or ironical God to swear by, for Janus was the two-faced god of the Romans.

Surprisingly, the party that approaches Othello is not Brabantio's; it is from the duke of Venice and is led by Cassio, Othello's new Florentine lieutenant, who says that the duke requires Othello's appearance "haste-post-haste" (37). There is a Turkish threat to the island of Cyprus, an island that is crucial to the defense of Venice. Once more Othello's impeccable and highly regarded reputation is indicated; three search parties have been sent out to find him. It is he who has been singled out, "hotly called for" (44) by the duke to stop the Turkish uprising and protect Venice.

Furtively, while Othello is gone, Iago tries to whisper to Cassio some news about Othello's elopement, but Othello returns before Iago can begin his gossip. At this point, Brabantio, Roderigo, and their party enter. Swords are drawn, but Othello calmly attempts to reason with Brabantio. He appeals to Brabantio's dignity, that the senator's "years" (60) are more able at commanding than are his "weapons" (61). The grief-stricken father, however, does not listen to Othello's eloquent words of wisdom, and he soundly denounces his unwanted son-in-law. The facts of the elopement are so incredible to him that he is sure that the Moor has used some sort of "foul charms" (73) or even drugs to win Desdemona: "thou hast enchanted her" (63). The marriage seems to be monstrous—in the sense that it represents a deviation from that which is natural. How else, Brabantio asks, would Desdemona, so carefully reared, have brought such scandal upon herself and her father by shunning "the wealthy curled darlings of our nation" (68) and running to the Moor's "sooty bosom" (70).

Othello continues to remain cool and self-confident when Brabantio orders him arrested and punished. He displays himself as the admirably self-possessed master of the situation. He is willing to answer all of Brabantio's charges, but a prison cell hardly seems the logical place to answer his father-in-law, for the Duke of Venice himself has just now summoned him. Grumbling, Brabantio realizes that he must cease his threats for the present, but he consoles himself with the hope that the duke and the other senators will surely "feel this wrong as 'twere their own" (97).

Scene 3 opens with a rather lengthy conference concerning how Venice must deal with its Turkish enemy. Assembled in the Venetian Council Chamber is the governing body of the state, headed by the duke. All are pondering the conflicting, dangerous news that has been sent to them from Cyprus and from which they find no clear statement as to the size of the Turkish fleet nor its exact destination. None, however, underestimates the very real danger involved; each is sure that the enemy intends to move against the Venetians by attacking Cyprus, despite the fact that a newly arrived sailor reports that one Signior Angelo, who is not identified here nor heard of again, insists that the Turks are headed for Rhodes and not for Cyprus. One senator argues that in view of the importance of Cyprus, an island that the enemy covets, the apparent move toward Rhodes must be an obvious ruse to catch the Cyprians off guard. The duke agrees. Then a messenger from Montano, Governor of Cyprus, enters: The fleet approaching Rhodes has joined with a reinforcing fleet; now the entire fleet sails toward Cyprus.

At this point, Brabantio, Othello, Iago, Roderigo, and some officers enter the chamber. The fact that the duke addresses the Moor immediately, not even noticing Senator Brabantio, is another indication of the extent to which Venice places its hopes on "valiant Othello" (48)—more evidence, that is, of Othello's high status as the hero of the play, the man who has been singled out to conquer "the general enemy Ottoman" (49).

Because Brabantio, an aristocratic senator, is so overwrought, matters of state are shelved momentarily as he makes his startling charges and appeals for help. In fact, his grief is so copious that at first the duke and the others believe that Desdemona must be dead. Continuing, Brabantio characterizes Desdemona as being the victim of "spells and medicine" (61). Otherwise, how could "nature so prepost'rously . . . err" (62)? Only by using witchcraft could his daughter's heart have been "stol'n" (60) by a black man. The duke attempts to quiet Brabantio with the assurance that the culprit will be dealt with in accordance with the "bloody book of law" (67). When the aggrieved father points to Othello as the man against whom these charges are brought, the members of the council all react with unanimous consternation.

Othello's defense is the first of many of his major speeches in this play, and there is much to be noted and remembered in this speech, for it helps us to understand why such a noble and stable individual would reject reason and willingly, as it were, become a victim of love's passion and elope with the senator's daughter. With simple dignity, apologizing for his "rudeness" (lack of polish), the Moor addresses his "unvarnish'd tale" (90) to the group, conceding that he indeed has married Brabantio's daughter, but he denies that he did so by means of witchcraft. He presents to the duke and the others a portrait of himself as a man who has spent almost all of his life in the field as a successful, active soldier. Humbly, he submits he knows nothing of witchcraft and little of the world, for that matter, save that which pertains to warfare.

Brabantio's impassioned speech that follows Othello's quiet statements of fact is ineffectual. It is grounded in racial prejudice and supported only by such shabby phrases as "in spite of nature" (96) and "against all rules of nature" (101). It is clearly Brabantio, not Desdemona, who finds Othello something "fear'd to look on" (98) in contrast to the fair-skinned Venetian men.

Quite reasonably, the duke points out that Brabantio must substantiate his charges. But Othello, wanting to put an immediate end to this ridiculous accusation, asks that Desdemona herself be brought forth to speak, adding that if he is found to be guilty by her testimony, he will not protest any sentence imposed upon him.

While the duke awaits Desdemona, Othello delivers his second memorable soliloquy. In it, he reveals that in the past Brabantio himself has shown high regard for Othello; "her father lov'd me," says Othello, and "oft invited me [to his house]" (128), where he urged the Moor to tell him stories of his adventurous, exciting life, filled with "disastrous chances" (134), "moving accidents by flood and field" (135), and "hair-breadth scapes" (136). Here, Othello recalls stories about his being captured and enslaved, about cannibals and about certain "Anthropophagi," men whose heads grew "beneath their shoulders" (145). (Lest one should dwell too long on the matter of these "Anthropophagi," it should be stated that Greek romances, popular in Shakespeare's time, often included accounts of such fabulous barbarians. Othello was not indulging in self-aggrandizement to impress Desdemona or her father.)

The picture we have here of Othello, then, is of a spellbinding raconteur, regaling Brabantio and his daughter with tales of romantic daring. Little wonder that Desdemona would have been enthralled by this exotic man of action and thereby neglect the "wealthy curled darlings" (68) of Venice. Desdemona "lov'd me for the dangers I had pass'd," Othello says. "This only is the witchcraft I have us'd" (167, 69).

The duke's response to Othello's frankness is warmly humorous; he's convinced that "this tale would win my daughter too" (171), and he counsels Brabantio to "take up this mangled matter at the best" (173)—that is, to make the best he can of this situation.

Considering that the play is set approximately in the late sixteenth century, Desdemona's defense of her actions is remarkably forthright, spirited, and courageous. Clearly, she was aware of the great risk involved when she married a man of another race and, moreover, one so completely different from her Venetian suitors. Her ten brief lines are models of concise rationale. Hers, she says, was and is a "divided duty" (181): She remains bound to her noble father for her "life and education" (182); he remains her "lord of duty" (184), and she will always honor him as such. Now, however, she has a husband, and she must recognize her duties to him, just as her mother did to Brabantio.

Brabantio is crushed; he is a defeated man who realizes that the Moor did neither steal nor bewitch his daughter. But he will never understand how his "jewel" (195) renounced all of his paternal guidance and secretly married a man of a different race and nation.

The duke then informs Othello of the Turks' plan to attack Cyprus and that he, as the leader best informed about the fortifications of the island, must "slubber the gloss of your new fortunes" (228) (delay any shining anticipations of a honeymoon) and turn his full attention upon the enterprise against the Turks—that is, these two lovers, just newly married, are to be separated because of a national crisis. And, as another example of his high character, Othello promptly acknowledges that public duty takes precedence over private desires.

Then a dramatic element of surprise occurs. When Othello asks that his wife be properly looked after in his absence and the duke suggests that she stay in her father's household, Brabantio forbids it. Othello, likewise, forbids it. And Desdemona herself rejects any such solution. She married the Moor because she did "love . . . to live with him" (249). Othello himself voices the same sentiments. His is a rational love, he says; thus he suggests that Desdemona come with him. He asks the council not to think that he will neglect duty "to comply with [the] heat" (264) of sexual desire or that he will ignore their "serious and great business scant / When she is with me" (268-69). Above all, at no time will he allow her presence to interfere with his duty to defend Venice against the Turks.

The duke tells Othello that he can make what arrangements he likes. The important thing is that he must leave this very night because "th' affair calls [for] haste" (277). Desdemona is somewhat taken aback by this order. But notice the Moor's reply: He loves her "with all [his] heart" (279). Truly, as the duke notes to Brabantio, Othello "is far more fair than black" (291). Immediately, there remains only for the Moor to leave some trusted officer behind, one who will see to it that Desdemona is brought to Cyprus safely. Tragically, Othello chooses the very man whom he can trust least in all the world—"honest Iago" (295).

Brabantio's last words to Othello in Scene 3 are important. As we shall find, they are packed with irony and provide, in part, an example of dramatic presaging. "Look to her, Moor" (293), the senator says. "She has deceiv'd her father, and may thee" (294). (Desdemona does not deceive Othello, but before long Othello will be so convinced that she has deceived him that he will murder her.) Othello's reply to Brabantio is likewise ironic: He vows, "my life upon her faith!" (295). Shortly, he will take his own life because of his lack of faith in her faith—in her innocent, chaste fidelity.

The Moor and Desdemona then leave for a last hour together, and Iago and Roderigo are left alone on the stage. Roderigo is overcome; in marked contrast to the noble, rational lover, Othello, he is the tormented, rejected lover who can find relief from his misery only by drowning himself. Iago mocks Roderigo's excessive, posturing despair over Desdemona's words. Before Iago would drown himself "for the love of a guinea-hen," he would exchange his "humanity with a baboon" (317-18). To Roderigo's confession that passion controls his will, Iago states that "our bodies are our gardens" and "our wills are gardeners" (323-24). Men, he says, have "reason to cool [their] raging motions" (333). Certainly Iago believes that he himself is a man of controlled will, whose reason is paramount in all his dealings. Hypnotically, he drones commands to Roderigo to "put money in thy purse" (345), all the while assuring him that Desdemona cannot long "continue her love to the Moor" (338). Her love for the Moor had a too "violent commencement" (350); soon she will be "sated with his body" (356), and Moors themselves "are changeable" (352). He so completely dupes his patron, emphasizing that Desdemona will yet be his, that Roderigo agrees to "sell all [his] land" (388).

Throughout his long speech, Iago reveals foremost that he is passion's slave, evidenced by his hatred for Othello, his envy of Othello's power, and his lust for Roderigo's wealth. Cynically, as Roderigo leaves, Iago condemns himself with the well-known line, "Thus do I ever make my fool my purse" (389).

In his last soliloquy in the act, Iago introduces a second motive for his hatred of Othello; he says that it is common gossip that the Moor "'twixt my sheets . . . [has] done my office" (393–94) and, for Iago, "mere suspicion . . . will do . . . for surety" (395–96). It need hardly be pointed out here that we are listening to a man whose mind is poisoned. There is not the slightest bit of evidence anywhere in this play to indicate that Othello has had an affair with Emilia.

As the act closes, Iago reveals his next malicious plan of action. Aware that Othello trusts him, he will convince the Moor that Cassio is "too familiar" (402) with Desdemona. Othello, he says, "is of a free and open nature" (405); precisely, in Iago's words, Othello is an "ass"—naive, in other words, and we recall that Othello himself has already admitted that he knows "little of this great world . . . [except that which] pertains to feats of broils and battle" (86–87). In the final couplet, which contains the reference to "hell and night" (409) and to "monstrous birth" (410), we sense Iago rubbing his hands in glee; we see all too clearly the unnaturalness and the diabolical elements of his plans to destroy the union of Othello and Desdemona.

ACT II

Summary

The time advances several weeks, and the curtains open upon the harbor of Cyprus. A fierce storm at sea has crippled the Turkish fleet and has also delayed the course of Othello's voyage. At Cyprus, Governor Montano greets Cassio, whose ship is the first to arrive; shortly afterward, Iago's ship arrives, with Desdemona on board. To assuage Desdemona's anxiety for Othello's safety, Iago jokes and composes verses, and Cassio also distracts her attention in amiable conversation. Iago privately notes Cassio's behavior toward Desdemona and plans to entrap him later by spreading gossip about him and Desdemona.

Finally Othello strides onstage; he is joyously reunited with Desdemona and embraces her. When the others have left the stage, Iago convinces Roderigo that Desdemona actually loves Cassio and urges Roderigo to pick a fight with the lieutenant that night. When he is alone, Iago discloses in a soliloquy that he has vague suspicions about both Othello's and Cassio's affairs with Emilia.

Othello's herald proclaims a night of feasting and festivity to celebrate the destruction of the Turkish fleet and also to celebrate the wedding of Othello to Desdemona.

Othello retires for the night with Desdemona, leaving Cassio in charge of the night watch. In a hall of the castle, against the background of the night's merrymaking, Iago succeeds with wine and song in making Cassio drunk and quarrelsome. Urged by Iago to start an altercation, Roderigo follows Cassio offstage; quickly the two men reappear, fighting. Governor Montano interferes in an attempt to stop them and accuses Cassio of being drunk. Enraged, Cassio turns on him and wounds the governor as Roderigo hurries to sound the general alarm. Disturbed by the alarm bell, Othello comes onstage and halts the fighting, demanding to know what caused it. After Iago's seemingly reluctant description of the disturbance, Othello finds Cassio at fault and immediately relieves him of his rank. Iago and Cassio remain behind as the wounded Montano is led off and the others follow. Cassio, sobered, regrets the loss of his military status and reputation, but Iago persuades him that perhaps he can regain Othello's favor again—with Desdemona's "help." After Cassio leaves, Iago gloats over his successful, although seemingly innocent, scheming.

Roderigo returns, sore and full of complaints after his beating. Iago soothes his patron's impatience with platitudes and points out that their success has caused Cassio's discharge. Dawn is coming and it promises good things for them; the two men part as day breaks.

Commentary

Now that the major characters have been introduced and we are aware that a national crisis threatens the city-state of Venice and that Othello's union with Desdemona is also threatened, the action of the play in Scene 1 moves from Venice to the island of Cyprus. Montano, the governor of the island, is anxiously awaiting word of Othello's ship. Othello will replace Montano as governor, but the Moor's ship is somewhere at sea, battling a great storm: "A fuller blast ne'er shook our battlements" (6), Montano says; it is unusually severe and has become a "high-wrought flood" (2), a "wind-shak'd surge" (13), and a "high and monstrous mane" (13). Were it not for its threat to Othello, we realize, this hurricane-like storm would be welcomed because it would probably mean the destruction of the Turkish fleet.

The safe arrival of Cassio is suddenly announced, but before the newly appointed lieutenant makes his actual appearance onstage, Montano and another gentleman again express their concern for the Moor. Again we have public testimony of Othello's unusual superiority as a man and as a martial commander. He will make "a worthy governor" (30), Montano comments, one who will be brave because he "commands / Like a full soldier" (35–36). Cassio's entrance is accompanied by more praise for the Moor, and he evidences added concern for Othello and his crew on this "dangerous sea" (46). He finds comfort in the knowledge that Othello's ship is "stoutly timber'd" (48) and that Othello's pilot is an expert. Suspense is the central emotion here. Within moments, Cassio and Montano's men are alerted that a sail has been sighted by the townspeople gathered on the coast. Cassio fervently expresses his hopes that it is Othello's ship, for it is upon Othello that he bases all his hopes. Guns are fired, and Cassio then reveals to Montano the good news of Othello's marriage. Desdemona, he says, is a woman who surpasses "description and wild fame" (62). To Cassio, she is "divine Desdemona" (73) and the "great captain's captain" (74). Cassio then voices a prayer to "Great Jove" (77) that Othello might be well guarded, might presently "bless this bay with his tall ship" (79), and might be reunited with Desdemona. What is significant in Scene 1 is the emphasis on Cassio's utter devotion to his general. While he is certainly in awe of the lovely Desdemona, it is clear that he is an honorable man, one who would not and could not betray the Moor (as

Iago will try to prove later). Cassio's character is clearly antithetical to that of Iago, a man who passionately covets the lieutenant's position.

Dramatically, just after we have heard extravagant claims about her, Desdemona enters, accompanied by Iago, Emilia, and several attendants. Cassio's appreciation of his general's lady becomes even more venerated here. He is so overcome that he enjoins all present to bow to her and to hail to her as if she were the Virgin herself, coming with "the grace of heaven, / Before, behind thee, and on every hand" (85–86). Cassio's effusiveness here can be explained, in part, by the fact that he is a Florentine. This same courtly manner, in fact, encourages him to kiss Emilia moments later.

After a brief word of thanks to Cassio, Desdemona's first words are inquiries after her husband, and it should be pointed out here that throughout the subsequent action leading up to the arrival of Othello, the Moor's well-being remains her foremost concern.

Iago's comments in Scene 1 about his wife, Emilia, are unnecessarily tart, and Desdemona is quick to defend her friend. For the most part, Iago is posturing here; instead of ridiculing the faults of Emilia, he is actually trying to assume a brusque, "manly" pose by deriding his wife. He fools no one. By the nature of the play, we are certain that Emilia cannot be a shrew. She must be young and attractive enough to attract the harmless (and this should be emphasized) gallantry of Cassio, and she must also be attractive enough that Iago can convince himself (if indeed he is capable of truly caring about her) that there may be an excuse for believing that she is unfaithful. Iago's anti-female bombast here adds one of the few touches of comedy in this play, but it is often too coarse. Already we are aware that his attitude toward love between men and women is completely cynical.

At this point, Desdemona's discourse with Iago might perhaps seem awkward. Because we have seen so little of Desdemona and witnessed only one example of her spirited nature (when she proclaimed her love for Othello and vowed not to be housed in her father's house while Othello was sent to Cyprus), we are not wholly prepared for her to be so witty nor so sharply able to parry Iago's salty banter. When the two cease their verbal duel, Iago emerges in this scene as a "most profane and liberal [licentious] counsellor" (165), according to Desdemona. Her label is accurate and well-spoken by a woman who, we must remember, is a well-born and well-educated daughter of a Venetian senator. It is conceivable that she has been trained to adapt herself easily to any social situation. She was certainly headstrong in her choice of a husband and equally cool in her defense of him. She will demonstrate this adaptable talent later in the play; it seems to be behavior that is not particularly difficult. She recognizes that Iago is a showoff who prides himself in being impertinent, and thus she never loses her poise nor her overriding concern for her husband. As for Iago, he knows exactly how far he can approach the obscene without offending those present. And, of course, he has the good-mannered Cassio to explain and apologize that his jesting is merely that of a "soldier"—in contrast to Cassio's own background, which we recall has already been damned by Iago as being scholarly instead of practical and military.

Iago despises this well-mannered Florentine, yet he is abnormally interested in Cassio's Renaissance gallantry—his taking Desdemona by the palm, his "smile upon her" (170), and his kissing her three fingers. He tells us here how he will capitalize on Cassio's good manners: "With as little a web as this [gallant manner] will I ensnare as great a fly as Cassio" (169–70). All this is consistent with what we have seen before. Iago will stop at nothing to ruin the reputation of the man who superseded him and, at the same time, extinguish the love between Othello and Desdemona.

The Moor and his attendants arrive, and the mood of Scene 1 changes as Othello exchanges affectionate greetings with Desdemona, his "fair warrior" (184). Lines 185–95 are the words of a great poet as the Moor speaks of his soul's joy that he has survived the storm at sea and that he is now gazing on his wife. He has triumphed over a terrifying tempest, and he describes it in lines whose cadence conveys the very turbulence of that great storm, with its "hills of seas / Olympus-high" (189–90). He has suffered "hell" and is now in "heaven" and would be content to die. He has his Desdemona, his "soul's joy" (186). In a sense, he is in a "paradise" of sorts. He has just passed through one kind of hell, one that tried every fiber of his body; shortly, he will pass through another kind of hell, one that will challenge his soul. Othello's happy reunion with Desdemona is accompanied by her prayer that their loves and comforts "increase" and also by Othello's fervent "amen" to that prayer.

Iago's immediate aside lends itself to any actor who yearns to play a master villain. The situation is "well tun'd" (202), he says, but shortly he will see that a different tune will be played in this game of life. He fancies himself to be a sort of musical puppeteer, toying with the emotions and fate of all those around him—with one end: He will destroy the Moor, and soon the beautiful harmonies of natural love will be replaced by the unnatural discords of jealousy and pain.

All this is followed by Othello's next speech, which declares good news: "the Turks are drown'd" (204). Again he stresses the natural harmony of his and Desdemona's love for one another, almost as a counterpoint to Iago's evil words and certainly as an ironic omen of an ideal that is about to be shattered. Here Othello seems almost too noble, for his exit is accompanied by an order to "good Iago" (209) to go "to the bay and disembark my coffers" (210). Plainly, he believes Iago to be completely trustworthy.

The conversation between Iago and Roderigo, after all the others are gone, is manipulated by Iago so that the gullible Roderigo is given a thorough brainwashing. Iago convinces him that Desdemona is in love with Lieutenant Cassio, and he cites "with what violence she first lov'd the Moor" (225). This infatuation, he says, has been transferred to Cassio; already she finds no delight in looking on the devil—that is, Othello. "Sport" (230) has made her blood "dull" (229), and it desires now to be enflamed. Iago alludes to the Moor as being a man who won her with his "bragging" (225) and "fantastical lies" (226); now she tires of this older man and will soon "heave the gorge, disrelish and abhor the Moor" (235-36). This is some of the most offensive language in the entire play. The imagery, however, with its stress on the physical, the unnatural appetite, and vomiting, is typical of Iago.

Iago then damns Cassio's charms as being those of a "slipper[y] and subtle knave" (245). The lieutenant's eye, he says, can "stamp and counterfeit advantages" (246), and, what's more, he is "handsome, young, and hath all those requisites in him that folly and green minds look after" (250-51). Contemptuously, Iago says that one such "green mind" is Desdemona's and that she "hath found him already" (252).

The simple Roderigo is unbelieving. He has heard Desdemona praised to the heavens; he cannot believe that she—a woman of such "blessed" character—would be attracted to the "knavish" Cassio. Yet Iago prods Roderigo's disbelief by recalling how she did "paddle with the palm of [Cassio's] hand" (259). To Iago, this was lechery, warmly offered from the hand of a "vital" woman—certainly no "blessed" woman, indeed! Such "paddling" of palms, says Iago, is the prologue to the whole "history of lust and foul thoughts" (263). Cassio and Desdemona are animals, he says, and she is no better than any woman—ever on the watch for a handsome man—and, who knows? It might as well be Roderigo, now that she's bored with the Moor.

Iago then explains his plan. Roderigo must find some excuse to anger Cassio; he suggests "speaking too loud" (275) or "discrediting" Cassio—anything that will make Cassio lose control of himself. Cassio's cheerful, courteous demeanor is only veneer, Iago lies; he says that Cassio is "rash and very sudden in choler" (278). If Roderigo can provoke Cassio into fighting, Iago can convince the Cyprians to mutiny when they see what an undisciplined officer commands them. Cassio will then be dismissed, and Desdemona will lose interest in him and be ripe for Roderigo's amorous attentions.

Roderigo takes the bait, and Iago is left alone onstage. In a long soliloquy, he assures himself (and tries to assure us) that Cassio loves Desdemona; "I do well believe 't" (295). This is a measure of how thoroughly he can convince himself of what was earlier an embroidered lie in his web to ensnarl Roderigo. Clearly, Iago believes that Desdemona loves Cassio. And, then, in one of the most surprising statements of the entire play, Iago gives Othello full credit for being such a "constant, loving, noble nature . . . [that] he'll prove to Desdemona / A most dear husband" (298-300). This stated, he next admits that he loves Desdemona but with a love that has no sexual basis; instead, he loves her as an object which affords him the opportunity to revenge himself on Othello. For the second time, he voices his conviction that the Moor has had a love affair with Emilia, concluding that he will get even—"wife for [wife]" (308). He is confident that he can poison Othello with a jealousy "so strong / That judgement cannot cure" (310-11). Ending his soliloquy, he confesses that he is not really concerned with Roderigo's fate—"this poor trash of Venice" (312) (Iago even suspects Roderigo of having had an affair with Emilia). His master plan, he sighs, is almost complete; just the details need working out: "'Tis here, but yet confus'd" (320). Chiefly, it will depend on his corrupting Othello's "peace and quiet / Even to madness" (319-20).

Scene 2 is occasionally combined with the scene that follows. Chiefly, it functions in approximately the same way that a curtain is pulled in a modern theater to indicate the passing of time. We know that the Turkish fleet has suffered "perdition," largely due to the "noble" and "valiant" efforts of Othello, and that the rejoicing celebrates the military victory and also the general's recent marriage. In short, the Moor has proclaimed a holiday to be held from five o'clock until eleven, during which the soldiers and citizens can dance, make bonfires, or make "revels [however] his [addiction] leads him" (6). Dramatically, this mood of merrymaking and celebration is a strong contrast to the tragedy that is about to follow, and, in addition, the chaos will give Iago sufficient time and opportunity to set his traps for the unsuspecting Othello. Also, this feasting and dancing will take place at night, and earlier Iago proclaimed that "hell and night / Must bring this monstrous birth [of his evil design] to the world's light" (I. ii. 409–10). This scene preludes that horror.

In Scene 3, Othello, Desdemona, Cassio, and several attendants enter a hall of the castle. The celebration has lasted for several hours, and the Moor instructs "good Michael" (Cassio) to stand guard during the night. His brief speech deserves attention in view of the subsequent change later in both Cassio and Othello. He cautions himself—and also Cassio—not to "outsport discretion" (3)— that is, they should not allow the partying to get out of hand nor last too long. He, for example, has acknowledged but has not shared in the abundant toasts, for he must not neglect his duties. His men and this island must be supervised, above all. Speaking to Desdemona, he says that only now does he look forward to some peaceful intimacy "to come 'tween me and you" (10). He counsels prudence for all, and Cassio answers that Iago has given "direction" (4). To this, Othello answers that he is satisfied: "Iago is most honest" (6).

When Iago enters, we hear that the reveling has lasted not quite five hours. Insinuatingly, he remarks that Othello left watch duty early to "wanton the night" (16) with Desdemona. But to all of Iago's carnal remarks, Cassio is deaf. To Cassio, Desdemona is "most exquisite" (18), "fresh and delicate" (20), "modest" (26), and "indeed perfection" (28). Iago scoffs at Cassio's platonic platitudes ["Well, happiness to their sheets!" (29)] and invites Cassio to have "a stoup of wine" (30). But not even Cassio's courteous excuses can stop Iago's determination. Iago insists on the two men sharing a drink;

their friendship and the nature of the occasion demand it. Repeatedly, Cassio refuses. He's already had a drink—and even that drink he diluted; very simply, he feels that he shouldn't drink any more. He already feels the "innovation" (40) of that one drink, and he "dare not task my weakness with any more" (45). Iago then tries to detain him by asking him, at least, to call in some of the other men for a drink or two. Alone, Iago reveals his next schemings: Already he has seen to it that Roderigo and the guardsmen have imbibed freely— "carous'd / Potations pottle-deep" (55–56), he calls it, meaning that they've tipped the bottoms of their tankards in toasts most of the night. "Now," he says, "'mongst this flock of drunkards / Am I to put our Cassio in some action / That may offend the isle" (61–63).

The drinking episode that follows is a lively one. Governor Montano joins the group, and Iago sets the tone with his drinking song, playing to perfection the role of the hail-fellow-well-met. Cassio does indeed become drunk, his tongue becomes thick, and his movements wavering. Yet he insists that he is not drunk—and all the others agree with him as he staggers from the stage.

Iago's plan is proceeding with perfection; his depravity is shocking. He calculated carefully on the mannerly Florentine's over-indulging simply because good manners called for him to celebrate the victory and to pacify the pleadings of Othello's ensign; it was out of courtesy that he began drinking, despite his self-admitted weakness. And note that almost immediately after Cassio leaves, Iago begins to complain excessively about the young lieutenant's "vice," making it seem that Cassio would be a model soldier were it not for his vice of alcoholism, which is sadly condoned by Othello. This is a blatant lie. Then with equal oiliness, Iago expresses concern and anxiety about the fate of Cyprus, sighing that he does "love Cassio well; and would do much / To cure him of this evil [drinking]" (148–49).

The next episode of Scene 3 focuses on the drunken Cassio in pursuit of the hapless Roderigo, whom he denounces as a rogue and as a rascal. The governor endeavors to intercede, and Cassio turns on him, giving Iago the chance to instruct Roderigo what to do. The "dupe" is told to raise a general alarm while Iago assumes the role of "peacemaker." Othello, accompanied by armed men, arrives to find that the governor has been wounded by Cassio. Iago's plans have succeeded far beyond any of his expectations.

Another opportunity for tour-de-force acting occurs when

Othello makes inquiries about the reason for "this barbarous brawl" (172), and Iago must answer. The villainous ensign holds back, seemingly, appearing to be reluctant to inform against a friend. Nor can the drunken lieutenant nor the wounded governor provide many of the details. The Moor is appalled to find that such a "private and domestic quarrel" (215) should take place when the safety of Cyprus should be the concern of all. Iago answers, hypocritically, that he would rather have his tongue cut out than "do offense to Cassio" (222). He then prattles sufficiently until Othello determines that Cassio must be punished. In fact, he believes that Iago's words against Cassio are probably too soft and that he "doth mince this matter" (247). Therefore, despite the fact that Othello loves Cassio well, he strips him of his rank.

After everybody but Iago and Cassio have exited, the ex-lieutenant mourns the reputation that he has lost, and he curses the power of alcohol: "To be now a sensible man, by and by a fool, and presently a beast" (309–10). Iago is ready with facile words of consolation. He assures Cassio that he has only to wait until the Moor is in a better mood. And, better yet, he reminds Cassio, the Moor is not really a general—that position, in truth, belongs to Desdemona, for Othello "hath devoted and given up himself" (321–22) to her. Both Othello and Desdemona are such simple people, Iago implies sarcastically; moreover, he is quite sure that Desdemona deems it a "vice in her goodness not to do more than she is requested" (326–27). Therefore, Cassio should speak to her. Cassio understands instantly: If he asks her to intercede with the Moor, all will be set to rights again. Naively, Cassio concedes that Iago does "advise me well" (332), to which Iago protests "in the sincerity of love and honest kindness" (334). Shakespeare's layering of villainy upon Iago becomes, at times, almost too heavy, but occasionally it is briefly lightened by Iago's amoral wit, as evidenced here, when Iago assesses the situation.

Alone, Iago asks how it is possible that anyone could term him a villain. Surely Desdemona's generous nature will try to heal the breach between Cassio and her husband; Iago strives for no more than what would seem true and possible. Yet he interrupts his soliloquy with a cynical cry: "Divinity of hell!" (356). In effect, he is celebrating his god: evil itself, colored in all its corruptions with ironical words of purity. Using Desdemona and her natural goodness, Iago will "turn her virtue into pitch, / And . . . make the net / That shall enmesh them all" (366–68).

As the act ends, Roderigo, the simple gull, reenters and complains of having little money left and that he has been "well cudgell'd" (372). He's ready to go back to Venice, but Iago's thoughts are ever on Roderigo's bountiful pocketbook, and so he promises him that morning will bring better things. Alone again, he reveals two more of his machinations: Emilia must ask Desdemona to speak to the Moor about Cassio, and Iago will try to position the Moor so that he sees his wife and the young, courtly ex-lieutenant in close conversation.

ACT III

Summary

Cassio brings in some musicians to "serenade" the newly wedded couple, and Othello's clown, or jester, comes in to entertain the group. This done, the musicians are paid and they exit. At this point, Iago arrives and helps Cassio arrange a private meeting with Desdemona. After Iago leaves, Emilia enters and, at Cassio's request, takes him to talk with Desdemona.

Othello gives some letters to Iago to be posted and tells him that he will be walking around the grounds of the castle with some gentlemen and requests that Iago meet him later.

In the castle garden, Desdemona promises Cassio that she will do all that she can to persuade Othello to reinstate the ex-lieutenant. As Othello and Iago enter, Cassio leaves hurriedly. As Othello is approaching his wife, Iago quickly takes the opportunity to draw Othello's attention to Cassio's "guilty" leave-taking. Desdemona launches at once into a petition for Cassio, continuing good-humoredly, yet insistently, until Othello grants her plea.

As Desdemona and Emilia withdraw, Iago begins sinister and bitter insinuations about Cassio, forcing Othello to recall that Cassio was often instrumental in Othello's courtship of Desdemona. Considering deeply what he hears, Iago pretends to be astonished. He "ponders" and Othello asks him to make plain what he is thinking, but Iago adroitly evades answering until he has fully aroused Othello's curiosity. Then he cunningly warns Othello against jealousy, the "green-ey'd monster" (166). Othello answers confidently that he will harbor no suspicions unless they can be proved. Iago then boldly suggests a hypothetical affair between Cassio and Desdemona, and in several ways, he begins to undermine Othello's faith in Desdemona's innocence. After Iago has left, Othello is somewhat reassured when Desdemona returns. She tries to soothe his aching head with her handkerchief, but he says irritably that it is too small and pushes it from him; it falls to the floor unnoticed. As they depart, it is left behind.

Emilia picks up the strawberry-embroidered handkerchief, Othello's first intimate gift to Desdemona, gives it to Iago, and exits. Othello reenters then, his mind fermenting with the doubts planted by Iago. He demands proof, immediate and positive, that his wife is guilty of infidelity. Iago claims that while spending a night with Cassio, he himself overheard Cassio talking in a dream about making love to Desdemona. He also says that he has seen Cassio wipe his beard with a handkerchief embroidered in a strawberry pattern. Enraged, Othello sinks to his knees. He is joined by Iago, and together they vow sacred revenge. On rising, Othello announces that Iago will be his new lieutenant.

Outside the castle, Desdemona sends Othello's clown to bring Cassio to her. When Othello enters, she again pleads with him to reinstate Cassio as his lieutenant, but Othello's only concern is with the lost handkerchief. Desdemona tries to console him, saying that she is certain that it is not lost. Othello warns her that the handkerchief possesses magical powers and that its loss would be a misfortune. Angrily, he leaves when she cannot produce it. Iago and Cassio enter; they too are at a loss to explain Othello's moodiness. When the others have gone, Cassio meets Bianca, his current mistress, who chides him for neglecting her for a week. Cassio changes the subject and gives her a handkerchief that he found in his room, asking her to make a copy of the embroidery. Bianca is disturbed at his neglecting her, but she nevertheless agrees to do what he asks.

Commentary

Scene 1 serves as a kind of comic relief—that is, it gives the audience's emotions a brief pause from the tension of the preceding acts and offers the audience some respite before it is plunged into the highly emotional scenes that follow very swiftly. The setting is next morning, outside the castle, where Cassio has arranged for a group of musicians to entertain Othello and Desdemona. In addition to the musicians, there is a clown, or jester, a figure that appears in many Renaissance plays and could be counted on to entertain the audience with his physical nimbleness and his witty double entendres. Here the clown makes humorous reference to "wind" instruments and purposely confuses "tails" and "tales" in several coarse puns before he pokes fun at the musicians' performance. Othello does not care for the music, and so the clown dismisses them with money and bids them to "vanish into the air, away!" (21).

Cassio then gives the clown a gold piece and instructs him to tell Emilia, "the gentlewoman that attends the [General's wife]" (26–27), that he (Cassio) wishes to talk with her.

Iago enters as the clown exits and notes that Cassio has not been to bed yet. Cassio confirms it; he has decided to follow Iago's suggestion and talk with Emilia and see if she can convince Desdemona to speak with him. Iago is obviously pleased and offers to keep the Moor busy so that the "converse and business" (40) of Cassio and Desdemona "may be more free" (41). The dramatic irony here is that Iago hopes to keep Othello "busy" while Cassio and Desdemona are talking together, meaning that the Moor will be "busy" observing his wife and his courtly ex-lieutenant exchanging serious conversation. Upon Iago's exit, Cassio remarks that he "never knew / A Florentine more kind and honest" (42–43). The irony here is self-evident. Hopefully, many Florentines are more honest than Iago, and, hopefully, most Florentines are not as naive as young Cassio.

Emilia enters and greets the Moor's ex-lieutenant and expresses her disappointment and sorrow at his misfortunes. From her, Cassio happily learns that already Desdemona "speaks . . . stoutly" (47) to her husband in Cassio's defense, but because Cassio wounded Cyprus' governor, a man of "great fame . . . and great affinity" (48–49), Othello cannot yet reinstate Cassio as his lieutenant. Yet, Desdemona thinks that there may be some hope, for Othello "protests he loves you, / And . . . [will] take the safest [soonest] occasion . . . to bring you in again" (50–53). The news is indeed good and should satisfy Cassio, but fate makes Cassio too impatient to resume his lieutenancy. Thus he beseeches Emilia to arrange for him to speak with Desdemona alone. Emilia agrees.

In Scene 2, Othello instructs Iago to see to it that certain letters are sent immediately to the Venetian senate and then rejoin him. He then leaves to inspect the Cyprian fortifications. This scene is extremely brief, consisting of less than ten lines, but it functions to show that Othello is very busy and that he is engaged in business of the state. Iago, therefore, realizes that the time is opportune for him to act: Desdemona is free, and if Iago can make the necessary arrangements, he can bring Cassio and Desdemona together so that Cassio can plead his case; moreover, the possibility exists that Iago can even arrange to have Othello secretly witness a meeting between his wife and his ex-lieutenant.

Scene 3, often called the "temptation scene," is the most important scene in the entire play and one of the most well-known scenes in all drama. In it, Iago speaks carefully and at length with Othello and plants the seeds of suspicion and jealousy that eventually bring about the tragic events of the play. Ironically, it is Desdemona's innocent attempt to reconcile Othello with Cassio that gives Iago the opportunity to wreak vengeance upon Othello, thereby causing the murder and suicide that bring this tragedy to its violent conclusion.

Ironically also, when the curtains for this act part, they reveal the loveliest scene in the entire play: the garden of the Cyprian castle. Desdemona, the well-meaning bride, has been talking with Cassio and tells him that she is sure that she can influence her husband in Cassio's behalf.

Emilia is present and adds her own good wishes for Cassio; she too hopes that Desdemona will be successful. But when Emilia adds that her husband, Iago, grieves "as if the cause were his" (4) that Cassio has lost his position and that his friendship with the Moor has been severed, even the most casual listener in the audience would probably gasp in disbelief. This is followed by an equally startling comment: Desdemona, speaking of Iago, says, "O, that's an honest fellow" (5). The dramatic irony is especially keen here as Desdemona tells Cassio that she is convinced that she "will have [her] lord and [him] again / As friendly as [they] were" (6–7).

Cassio expresses his gratitude, but he urges Desdemona not to delay, for if Othello waits too long to appoint a new lieutenant, he may "forget my love and service" (18). Again, Desdemona is most reassuring, stating that it is not in her character to violate a vow of friendship. (Later, Othello will believe not only that she has violated a vow of friendship but that she has violated their vows of marriage.) Comically, Desdemona jests to Cassio that she will "talk him

[Othello] out of patience; / His bed shall seem a school . . . I'll intermingle everything he does / With Cassio's suit" (23–26). (This too is ironically ominous; within an hour, Othello's notion of his marriage bed will be filled with false visions of Cassio.) Desdemona's final lines here are prophetic: As Cassio's solicitor, she would "rather die / Than give [his] cause away" (27–28).

Emilia then notes that Othello and Iago are approaching. When the Moor and Iago enter, Cassio excuses himself hurriedly, saying that he is too ill at ease to speak with the general at this time. And it is at this point that Iago, a brilliant tactician who is ready to make the most of every incident and occasion, begins to taint Othello's belief in Desdemona's fidelity. Yet he is careful to represent himself as an honest but reluctant witness. His "Ha! I like not that!" (35) is a blatant lie; this fraudulent tsk-tsking hides Iago's true delight; nothing could satisfy his perversity more. But because Othello sees nothing amiss, Iago must make a show of not wanting to speak of it or of Cassio while all the time insinuating that Cassio was not just leaving but "steal[ing] away so guilty-like" (39). Iago's words here are filled with forceful innuendo, and as he pretends to be a man who cannot believe what he sees, he reintroduces jealousy into Othello's subconscious.

Desdemona greets her husband and, without guilt, introduces Cassio's name into their conversation. Here, fate plays a major role in this tragedy; not even Iago wholly arranged this swift, coincidental confrontation of Othello, Desdemona, and Cassio, and certainly the pathos of Desdemona's position here is largely due to no other factor than fate. And Desdemona could not purposely have chosen a worse time to mention Cassio's name to her husband. In addition, she innocently refers to Cassio as a "suitor." All these coincidences will fester later in Othello's subconscious as Iago continues to fire the Moor's jealousy. But for now, Othello is without suspicion, even as his wife speaks openly of Cassio's wish to be reinstated as his lieutenant and of her own wish for their reconciliation. She sees no villainy in Cassio's face, she says; Cassio "errs in ignorance and not in cunning" (49). As another example of dramatic irony, note how clearly we see the contrast between Cassio and Iago, a man who certainly errs—at least morally—in his own "cunning."

But Othello seems to be concerned with other matters. Obviously, he will do what his wife asks, but his thoughts are on other things. He does not wish to call Cassio back at the moment, but Desdemona is insistent. Perhaps she is merely young and eager to have her requests granted, or perhaps she is too eager to prove to herself that her new husband is obedient; whatever the reason, she does seem to nag Othello about when he will reinstate Cassio as his lieutenant: " . . . to-night at supper? . . . / To-morrow dinner then? . . . / to-morrow night; on Tuesday morn; / On Tuesday noon, or night; on Wednesday morn. / I prithee, name the time, but let it not / Exceed three days . . . When shall he come? / Tell me, Othello" (57–68). Even though she did promise Cassio not to delay speaking to Othello about the matter, such annoying insistence seems unnecessary and leads to Othello's becoming mildly vexed with his wife's childish pestering: "Prithee, no more; let him come when he will, / I will deny thee nothing" (74–75).

Desdemona realizes that Othello's answer is curt, and she emphasizes that this is an important matter and not a trifle that she is asking. To this, Othello stresses again that he will deny her nothing, but, in return, he asks for a bit of time so that he can be alone; he will join her shortly.

As Desdemona leaves, Othello chides himself for being irritated by his wife. Lovingly he sighs, "Excellent wretch! Perdition catch my soul, / But I do love thee! and when I love thee not, / Chaos is come again" (90–92). There is an element of prophecy here not only in Desdemona's and Othello's farewells to one another but also in their lines and in the remainder of the Moor's first speech after Desdemona leaves. In a metaphorical sense, perdition will soon catch Othello's soul, and chaos will soon replace order in his life.

When Iago is alone with Othello, he resumes his attack on his general's soul. Out of seemingly idle curiosity, he asks if Desdemona was correct when she referred to the days when Othello was courting her; did Cassio indeed "know of your love?" (95). Here he prods Othello's memory to recall that Desdemona and Cassio have known each other for some time. Then again playing the reluctant confidant, he begs, as it were, not to be pressed about certain of his dark thoughts. One can see how skillfully he makes use of his public reputation for honesty, and it is necessary to remind oneself throughout the play and especially in this scene that Iago does have a reputation for complete honesty. It is for this reason that Othello is alarmed by Iago's hesitations and "pursed brow"; Othello knows that Iago is not a "false disloyal knave" (121) and that he is "full of love and honesty" (118). If Iago fears something, it must be a concern "working from the heart" (123). Othello is convinced that Iago is withholding something and asks for his ruminations, the "worst of thoughts / The worst of words" (132–33). What Iago is doing, of course, is making Othello believe that Iago's honor is at stake if he confesses his fears. Thus he lies to Othello again, saying that he is unwilling to speak further because he may be "vicious in [his] guess" (145).

But one should never doubt that Iago will speak the "worst of thoughts" (132), although at first he does not answer directly. First, he speaks only the word "jealousy" aloud, fixing it in Othello's imagination; then, sanctimoniously, he warns his general against this evil, this "green-ey'd monster" (166) and refers to the "wisdom" of Othello, implying that the general is not one to be trapped by his emotions. Filled with what appears to be moral fervor, Iago then proceeds to a glorification of reputation. One might profitably recall Iago's antithetical views on the same subject when he was talking with Cassio earlier. In Act II, Scene 3, Iago told Cassio that "reputation is an idle and most false imposition; oft got without merit, and lost without deserving" (268–70). Here in Act III, Scene 3, Iago seemingly holds reputation in the highest esteem; it is the "jewel of [a man's] soul" ("who steals my purse steals trash . . . / But he that filches from me my good name / Robs me of that which not enriches him, / And makes me poor indeed") (156–61).

Othello hears, and his "O misery!" (171) tells us that already he has begun to suffer aching pangs of jealousy even though he has vowed not to be of a jealous nature. He swears that he will "see before I doubt; when I doubt, prove" (190). And Iago approves of such a stance; he, of course, is in a position to let human nature run its course and "prove" what it wishes—irrationally. He knows that man, being human, is flawed and subject to fears and irrational suspicions. He then asks the Moor to use his "free and noble nature" (199) to determine for himself the truth of the behavior between Desdemona and Cassio. But he reminds Othello that Desdemona is a Venetian lady and "in Venice they [wives] do not let [even God] see the pranks / They dare not show their husbands" (202–203). In other words, the faithless wife is a well-known member of Venetian society. Here we should recall Othello's words to the Duke of Venice; he confessed that he knew very little of the world except for that pertaining to warfare. Othello is a master of games on the battlefield, but he is innocent of social games. Iago also urges Othello to recall that Desdemona deceived her own father by marrying Othello. To Brabantio, Desdemona pretended to be afraid of Othello's dark looks; she pretended to shake and tremble at Othello's exotic demeanor, yet "she lov'd them [Othello's features] most" (207). The implication is clear; Iago does not have to state it: If Desdemona deceived her own flesh and blood, she might just as naturally deceive her husband.

The logic of these lines is forceful, and Iago is astute enough to pause now and then, begging his superior's forgiveness and, at the same time, attributing his own frankness to his devotion and regard for Othello. When we hear the Moor say, "I am bound to thee for ever" (213), we feel that indeed he has been irrevocably trapped.

Before the two men part, Iago goes to further pains to make Othello believe in his honesty and also to insure that Othello's jealousy has been sufficiently inflamed. He must also measure how well he has succeeded thus far. Iago stresses that Cassio is his "worthy friend"; in other words, one does not lie about one's friends, and, therefore, the Moor must not exaggerate in his imagination what he hears. Yet Iago is certain that Othello has already exaggerated to himself everything he has just heard. For that reason, Iago's remark to Othello that all this has "a little dash'd your spirits" (214) is a gross understatement. Othello is no longer as sure as he was of Desdemona's fidelity, for he ponders on the possibility of " . . . nature erring from itself—" (227). This thought is similar to his father-in-law's observation in Act I, Scene 2, when Brabantio spoke of "nature erring"—when Desdemona "unnaturally" chose Othello, a man not of her own race or color. Othello turns and asks that Iago's wife, Emilia, watch Desdemona closely. Then he bids Iago farewell, painfully asking himself why he married at all; it is obvious to him that "this honest creature [Iago] doubtless / Sees and knows more, much more, than he unfolds" (242-43).

Now we hear Othello in a soliloquy (258-77), and the range of the imagery that he uses underscores the appalling change in his character. There is only one thing now of which Othello is certain— the "exceeding honesty" of Iago. The Moor is obsessed with the need to prove or disprove Desdemona's fidelity. If he indeed finds her false, he'll "whistle her off and let her down the wind / To prey at fortune" (262–63)—that is, he will turn her out and make her shift for herself. And here he begins to look for reasons for her unfaithfulness. Convulsed with introspection, he curses his black skin and his lack of social graces and also the fact that he is "into the vale of years" (266) (he is much older than Desdemona)—all these things, he fears, could turn a woman from her husband's bed. This mental agony approaches the emotional climax of the play; here is the first turning point of the drama. Othello's mind and soul are torn with irrational images of Desdemona's infidelity and of his own unworthiness. Othello sees himself as an old man, an old cuckold, one who has treasured Desdemona blindly, beyond reason. Hours ago, he was filled with the spirit of a young bridegroom; now he is reduced to ignominy. Once he felt he was one of the "great ones" (273); now his pride in himself and in Desdemona's love for him is destroyed. Othello is ravaged by self-loathing, reduced to comparing himself to a dungeoned toad; he is cursed by a "destiny unshunnable" (275).

And yet, as Desdemona and Emilia enter, he is able to move from this state of abject hopelessness to a momentary appeal to heaven (278) when he declares that he will not believe that his wife is false to him. In his few words with Desdemona, he speaks faintly, pleading that he has a headache. When Desdemona offers to bind his aching head with her handkerchief, he declines because the handkerchief is too small. He pushes it from him and it falls "unnoticed" to the floor. This dropped, unnoticed handkerchief should not escape our notice. Desdemona carries it because she treasures it deeply. It was one of her first gifts from Othello, and he has asked her to keep it with her always, and she has; in fact, Emilia has seen Desdemona, on occasion, kiss the handkerchief and talk to it. Later, this handkerchief in Cassio's possession will be sufficient "proof" for Othello to abandon all faith in Desdemona.

Alone, Emilia picks up the handkerchief. She knows how deeply Desdemona treasures it, but she recalls that Iago has asked her many times to "steal" it. She is puzzled by his request, but now she has an opportunity to have the embroidery pattern copied, and she can give it to her whimsical husband. Here it is significant that twice Emilia uses the verb steal and also the verb filch when she refers to Iago's request (293, 309, and 315).

Iago enters and, after a brief exchange with his wife, learns that she has the very handkerchief that he has longed for. He snatches it from her and refuses to tell her why he wants it. After Emilia leaves, he reveals the next step in his plan: He will go to Cassio's lodgings, leave the handkerchief there, and let Cassio find it. Cassio will keep it and then Othello will see it in the ex-lieutenant's possession. By this time, Othello's suspicions will be ripe with Iago's "poison" (325), for "trifles light as air / Are to the jealous confirmations strong / As proofs of holy writ" (322–24). Othello will then conclude that Desdemona either gave the handkerchief to Cassio as a token of their love or left it at Cassio's lodgings after a rendezvous. In fact, a conclusion is hardly necessary; for a mind as inflamed with jealousy as Othello's, the handkerchief itself is metaphor enough. Even now Othello's blood "burn[s] like the mines of sulphur" (329). This suggestion of hellfire by Iago is a reflection of his own diabolical role in this villainy.

When Othello enters, it is evident to Iago, and to us, that he is a fallen man. Never more shall he find repose. Neither the opium of poppies nor the distillation of the mandrake root will help him find sleep. Momentarily, Othello seems to revive his senses, snarling at Iago's villainy and sending him away, then he slumps into despair. Iago's evil has "set [the Moor] on the rack" (335), and Othello wishes in vain that he had remained blind to his wife's alleged infidelity. In his imagination, he has seen "her stol'n hours of lust . . . [and tasted] Cassio's kisses on her lips" (338–41). He would have been happier, he cries, if his entire company of soldiers had "tasted her sweet body" (346) and he had remained ignorant of the entire episode. But now this mental torment of suspicion gnaws at him until he knows no peace.

The superb "farewell speech" that follows emphasizes how much Othello has lost—he, the model commander, the premier soldier—his "occupation's gone!" (357). Iago appears incredulous, and it is then that Othello turns on him with words that make Iago only too aware of the danger which faces him. At last Othello utters a true appraisal of Iago: "villain, be sure thou prove my love a whore" (359). But schemer that Iago is, he knows what must be done to protect himself; he must feign another vow of honesty and concern for Othello's welfare. The Moor, he says, has taught him a valuable lesson. "I'll love no friend, sith love breeds such offence" (380). Othello promptly concedes that Iago is honest, and the villain knows that for the time being he is safe. He turns to his general and fawns over his master's distress, noting that Othello is "eaten up with passion" (391). Then, in unusually coarse imagery, he introduces the subject of what kind of evidence would resolve Othello's doubts. The bestial images that Iago conjures up reek of base sexuality, for now Iago no longer needs to rely on innuendo. Now he tells Othello a bold lie, claiming that he himself slept beside Cassio recently; kept awake by a raging toothache that night, Iago says that Cassio moaned in his sleep for "Sweet Desdemona" (419) and cautioned her to hide their love. Then Cassio seized Iago's hand, kissed him hard on the mouth, and threw his leg over Iago's thigh, kissing him all the while, and cursing fate, which "gave [Desdemona] to the Moor!" (421–26). This is Iago's "proof" that makes it perfectly clear to him that Cassio has had illicit relations with Desdemona.

Othello is beside himself. "O monstrous! monstrous!" (427) he cries. But again the ingenious Iago is quick to remind his master that, in reality, this was no more than Cassio's dream. Othello, however, thinks otherwise—as Iago was certain he would. In his rage, the Moor declares that he will tear Desdemona to pieces. Here, compare this madman, incensed by Iago's poison, with the noble Moor who, only a few hours ago, repeatedly demonstrated such complete command of himself.

Yet Iago must be sure that Othello is sufficiently mad; therefore, he makes reference to Desdemona's handkerchief with its intricate strawberry embroidery; Othello immediately remembers it as the very one he gave to his wife. Iago tells the Moor that only today he saw Cassio "wipe his beard" (439) with it. Othello is enraged to the point where he is convinced that absolutely all of his suspicions are true. "All my fond love thus do I blow to heaven. / 'Tis gone," he exclaims (445–46), and in highly rhetorical lines, he dwells upon "black vengeance" and "tyrannous hate" (446–49).

Iago urges Othello to be patient, arguing that he may change his mind, and there follows the well-known Pontic Sea simile, in which Othello compares his "bloody thoughts" (447) to the sea's compulsive current, one that never ebbs but keeps on its course until it reaches its destination, the junction of the Propontic and the Hellespont (453–60). In this simile, Othello stresses his high status (as we might expect a tragic hero to do), identifying himself with large and mighty elements of nature. Equally important, this simile makes clear the absoluteness in Othello's character; once he has decided which course to take, he cannot turn back, and this decision does much to make plausible the almost incredible actions which follow.

Othello solemnly vows to execute "a capable and wide revenge" (459), and then he kneels. He uses such words as heaven, reverence, and sacred, and it is as though he sees himself as a rightful scourge of evil, as executing public justice and not merely doing personal revenge. Iago bids the Moor not to rise yet, and he himself kneels and dedicates himself to "wrong'd Othello's service" (467). Then as both rise, Othello "greets" Iago's love and delegates a test of Iago's loyalty: see to it that Cassio is dead within three days. One cannot imagine more welcome words to Iago. As for Desdemona's fate, Othello says that he will withdraw and find "some swift means of death" (447). Othello's soul is so hopelessly ensnared in Iago's web of treachery that he proclaims Iago as his new lieutenant and states tragically, "I am your own for ever" (449).

As a sort of prelude to Scene 4, we have a brief exchange between Desdemona and Othello's clown. These twenty or so lines of broad comedy tend to relieve the great tension of the last scene and provide a short respite before Desdemona and Othello confront one another again. Yet the comedy here is not particularly amusing; it is too brief and its humor depends on wordplay involving the verb *lie*, the key verb which Iago and Othello will discuss in Act IV, Scene 1, when Iago tells his general that not only did Cassio lie with Desdemona, but he boasted of it.

Outside the castle, Desdemona is anxious to find Cassio; she promised him that she would speak to her husband about reinstating his former lieutenant, and she would like to reassure him that she has spoken to Othello and that he has promised to reappoint Cassio. Desdemona is pleased that Othello will soon be reconciled with Cassio. Ironically, Othello has never felt more hatred for Cassio. Initially, Cassio's accidental stabbing of Montano displeased him, but this was a mere trifle compared to how he now feels about Cassio's (imagined) sexual conquest of Desdemona. Remember, also, that Othello has just pronounced a death sentence on Cassio.

When the clown leaves, Desdemona asks Emilia about the strawberry-embroidered handkerchief. Emilia answers with an outright lie: "I know not, madam" (24). She knows precisely what happened to it; she gave the handkerchief to Iago, but she says nothing. Nor does she correct herself when Desdemona, a few minutes later, tells her how much she values the handkerchief. Nor does Emilia comment when, in a touch of irony, Desdemona says that she would "rather have lost my purse" (25). It is an ironic coincidence that Desdemona would use this particular analogy, for we have just heard Iago tell Othello, in regard to one's reputation (III. iii. 156–61), that someone who would steal another's purse "steals trash." This is Desdemona's point precisely, and yet not even she knows how tragically this lost handkerchief will figure in the loss of her reputation. She finds comfort, however, in her belief that her husband is "noble" (26) and "true of mind" (27) and has not the "baseness" (27) of "jealous creatures" (28). Emilia does not have her friend's faith in Othello and asks further about his qualities. Desdemona answers and elaborates on one of many images in this play that characterizes Othello's clear-mindedness. She says that "the sun . . . / Drew all such humours [dark moods] from him" (30–31). These moods, or humours, are absent from his character. Othello may be dark of skin, but he has a strong reputation for being "clear-minded," calm, self-controlled, and, most important, for not being a suspicious man.

Desdemona's words are dramatically ironic, for they prepare us for Othello's entrance and for his reaction to his wife. He comes onstage and tries to appear normal, yet we realize immediately that he is drunk with jealousy. He speaks in conundrums, taking Desdemona's hand and commenting on its moistness, then breaking into grave, exaggerated bombast about his wife's hand being "hot, hot, and moist" (39); her hand requires "a sequester from liberty" (40), he says, then sarcastically he praises it as a "good hand, / A frank one" (43–44). He is suggesting that Desdemona is unchaste; her palm openly indicates that she has strong, sexual desires. She is "liberal" (38)—that is, she gives herself too freely to others. It is as if Iago—and not Othello—were speaking, and the irony here lies in Othello's having too "liberally" (too easily) given his soul to Iago; Othello has been too easily seduced by Iago. Understandably, Desdemona is puzzled by her husband's words: "I cannot speak of this" (48), she says and changes the subject, reminding Othello of his promise to deny her nothing. She tells him that at her bidding, Cassio is coming to speak with him. How unfortunately bad her timing is hardly needs to be pointed out. The Moor, however, is not to put aside. He complains of a cold and asks for a handkerchief to see if, in fact, Desdemona can produce the one he asked her to always carry with her. When she hands him one that is not the handkerchief he has in mind, he reproves her: "That's a fault" (55).

It is then that he tells her a fantastic story about an Egyptian gypsy giving a certain handkerchief to his mother; it is a magical handkerchief and carries the power of love, but it also carries a curse. If it is ever lost or given away, disaster will damn its owner. Othello swears the legend is true, that a sibyl herself embroidered it with silk that was spun from sacred worms and dyed with a precious liquid. This, of course, alarms the young and innocent Desdemona; remember that part of Othello's charm was his dark, Moorish looks. Here is dark, exotic lore that threatens to destroy her—all because she has misplaced the treasured heirloom that Othello entrusted to her. We can understand her anguished cry to God that she wishes she had "never seen't!" (77). The handkerchief, then, is no mere piece of cloth. It is a part of Othello's past. The handkerchief was important to his mother; she could almost read minds with it; it helped her "subdue" (59) her husband's love. It is a symbol of his parents' love, and Othello believes that it is a symbol of the purity of Desdemona's love for him. It is, therefore, no mere prop in Shakespeare's construction of this tragedy. The handkerchief is a sacred talisman, but Desdemona was ignorant of its history and of its significance to her husband.

When Othello hears his wife's outcry, he pounces on her despair and almost overwhelms her with questions, while she naively tries to stop him with pleas that he must see Cassio or, at least, talk to her about Cassio. Repeatedly, he asks for the handkerchief and repeatedly she asks him to think of Cassio. Othello's rage builds, and when he can bear no more, he exits.

One wonders what went on in Emilia's mind as she witnessed Othello's fury. She knows that she found the handkerchief and gave it to Iago. She could silence Othello's mad questioning, but she remains silent and, after Othello's headstrong exit, asks if Desdemona believes that Othello is still the noble, clear-minded husband whom she just spoke of. Desdemona is ready to acknowledge the handkerchief's magic. About her husband's display of temper, she can only answer, "I ne'er saw this before" (100). Emilia's answer to her friend reveals a cynicism that has come from years of living with Iago. She believes that no woman can be certain of her husband; to her, all men are egocentric—"They are all but stomachs, and we all but food; / They eat us hungerly, and when they are full / They belch us" (104–106). It is also quite possible that she is jealous of her friend's praise for her "perfect" husband and tired of hearing about Othello's sterling perfection. To her, a handkerchief is nothing more than a handkerchief, and the fact that Othello can berate Desdemona for losing such a trifle is only proof that he is no different than any other man.

Iago and Cassio enter, Iago still urging Cassio to plead with Desdemona to speak to Othello. But when the ex-lieutenant does so, Desdemona bewails the fact that because of her husband's strange behavior, she has had no real success. Cassio, she says, must be patient; she will do all that she can for him. Iago appears to be amazed at this report; can Othello be angry? In mock horror, he cannot believe what he hears: Othello? The even-tempered paragon of perfect control that he has seen on the battlefield? He will go find his general.

Desdemona is convinced that something relating to Othello's public responsibilities or "some unhatch'd practice" (14)—some plot—has seriously disturbed her husband. When Emilia expresses her fervent wish that Othello had not become jealous, the distressed wife states that she has not given him reason to become so. And again the worldly Emilia expresses her cynicism about jealous men, her remark subtly echoing her husband's sarcastic reference to jealousy's being a "green-ey'd monster" (III. iii. 166). When Desdemona leaves to find her troubled husband, she says that she will find him and speak further of Cassio's suit. Unhappily, fate could not direct her on a more unwise course.

After the two ladies depart, Bianca, Cassio's mistress, enters and berates her lover for neglecting her bed. Cassio asks to be forgiven and asks the girl to copy the embroidery pattern of a handkerchief he found in his chamber. This becomes a variation of the jealousy theme. The girl suspects that it is "some token from a newer friend" (181) who has replaced her in Cassio's affection. Cassio scoffs at this and mildly upbraids Bianca for becoming jealous without cause. Clearly this is meant to be a miniature mirror of Othello's raging jealousy toward Desdemona. To Bianca, Cassio's admiration of the handkerchief and its unusual embroidery pattern is proof that Cassio loves someone else.

The handkerchief, indeed, seems to have special powers:

Othello's mother was convinced it did, as is Othello; Desdemona sang to it, and Iago was so fascinated by it that he insisted that his wife steal it. Cassio too finds it irresistible, and it causes even him misfortune. This thread of the supernatural would especially interest an Elizabethan audience, which believed in magic, charms, and even witchcraft. And we should remember that if Brabantio believed that Othello used magical charms to charm Desdemona away from him, we can believe that Desdemona could be persuaded of the magic of this strawberry-embroidered handkerchief.

ACT IV

Summary

Othello rages and falls into an unconscious trance when Iago tells him that Cassio has admitted that he has lain with Desdemona. Cassio enters, but Iago asks him to withdraw and to return in a short time since Othello has just suffered an epileptic seizure. Othello recovers and agrees to hide so that he can watch Cassio as Iago draws him out in a conversation about Desdemona. After Cassio's return, Iago engages him in a joking conversation about Bianca's infatuation for him. Othello, who can hear nothing, misinterprets Cassio's laughter and bawdy gestures, believing that they refer to Desdemona. Bianca enters and angrily returns the handkerchief to Cassio, saying that she refuses to copy another woman's present. She leaves, and Cassio follows, trying to appease her. Again, Othello is enraged at this seemingly irrefutable proof of Desdemona's infidelity. At Iago's suggestion, he agrees to strangle Desdemona in her bed; Iago, in turn, promises to murder Cassio.

Lodovico, meanwhile, has arrived on a ship from Venice, bringing a letter from the Duke. He enters with Desdemona. As Othello reads the letter which orders his return to Venice and appoints Cassio as Governor of Cyprus, Desdemona tells Lodovico of the breach between Othello and Cassio. Desdemona's sympathy for Cassio again angers Othello. He strikes her and torments her until she leaves, weeping. Othello, who has not lost all self-control, also leaves. Lodovico is puzzled and saddened.

Questioned by Othello, Emilia swears that Desdemona is chaste. Othello then sends for Desdemona and asks her to swear that she has been faithful. She does so, but Othello will not believe her. He accuses her of being a whore and a strumpet. When he leaves, Desdemona sends for Iago and asks him how she can clear herself. Iago tells her to be calm and patient: The fault is not in her; perhaps an official matter has temporarily disturbed Othello. Desdemona and Emilia leave as Roderigo enters. Iago has convinced him that Cassio must be killed, and together they plot the murder.

Othello orders Desdemona to go to bed unattended; she agrees to do so, and as Emilia prepares her friend for bed, Desdemona's mind wanders, preoccupied with sad thoughts. She sings the "Willow Song," a song she learned from her mother's maid, a woman who loved a man who went mad. In contrast to Emilia and her worldly opinions, Desdemona swears that she could never dishonor her husband—for any price.

Commentary

In the first part of Scene 1, Iago ostensibly tries to comfort Othello; yet, in fact, he continues to torment him with lascivious suggestions of Desdemona's infidelity. He focuses on Othello's confused thoughts as he conjures up visions of Desdemona and Cassio lying naked in bed together; he asks Othello if one can lie thus and "not mean harm" (5). Othello's answer is weighty with irony. The devil, he says, would tempt anyone who would try; as a parallel, consider that the devil (Iago) is at this moment tempting Othello. Othello says further that such lovers "tempt heaven" (8) with damnation; likewise, Othello's irrational actions tempt heaven with the same fate. How successful Iago has been at working toward his own "peculiar end" (I. i. 60) is only too clear. Iago knows only too well how deranged his general's mind is; he proclaims that a man and a woman may lie naked together and it would be "a venial slip" (9). But, he exaggerates, if a man gives his wife a handkerchief and she . . . He does not even need to finish this illogical, damning conclusion. Othello finishes it himself. He seems to be absolutely within Iago's power. His mind is reeling, and he is easily convinced by Iago's lies that Cassio has boasted of "lying" with Desdemona. Moreover, Othello cannot speak clearly; his thoughts are fragmented as he falls into a trance at Iago's feet, and he is unconscious as Cassio enters and is told by Iago to come back later.

When Othello does revive, he is given no respite from his agony as Iago continues to poison his mind. Sardonically, this newly appointed lieutenant argues that since Othello knows that his wife is unfaithful, his lot is better than the millions of men who are victims of the same deceit and never know about it. Irrationally, Othello can only praise this wisdom of Iago, and as we follow the action in this scene, we watch this tragic hero become almost contemptible because he is so thoroughly the brainwashed dupe of Iago.

As if Othello had not been punished enough by his confused imagination, he allows himself to be hidden by Iago, and Iago promises to talk with Cassio and encourage him to "tell the tale anew, / Where, how, how oft, how long ago, and when / He hath, and is again to cope your wife" (85–87). In his soliloquy, Iago reveals the details of this scheme: He will question Cassio about his mistress, Bianca, but the name of Bianca will not be spoken loudly, and, therefore, Othello will believe that Cassio will be boasting about his liaison with Desdemona. The scheme works perfectly. Hearing Cassio's raucous laughter, Othello imagines that it is the triumphal laughter of the man who has conquered Desdemona, replaced Othello, and now exults about his latest sexual conquest—Desdemona, who "hangs, and lolls . . . [and] shakes and pulls me" (143–44).

Since Othello continues to listen and does not suddenly challenge Cassio on the spot, we can only conclude that he is transfixed by this revelation and that he is still weak from his nervous collapse. It is apparently for these reasons that he remains still hidden as Bianca enters and haughtily returns the embroidered handkerchief which Cassio gave her to copy. Othello, of course, concludes that this must be the very handkerchief which Iago claims to have seen Cassio wiping his beard with.

When Cassio and Bianca have gone and Iago is alone, Othello comes forward and his first question speaks volumes: "How shall I murder him, Iago?" (180). He is determined that neither Cassio nor Desdemona shall live. He would have his wife "rot" (191); he would "hang" her (198); he will "chop her into messes" (211); he will "poison" her (216). No punishment is too severe for one who has allegedly betrayed Othello's love, his reputation, and his pride.

Iago cannot wait for his general to decide how he will kill Desdemona; he himself means to "enmesh [ensnare] them all" (II. iii. 368), and the sooner the better. Obtaining poison, he knows, is no problem, but it might not work, and Desdemona's death must be accomplished quickly—while Othello's passion is at a high pitch. For this reason, he orders Othello to "strangle her in her bed . . . the bed she hath contaminated" (220–21). Iago, meanwhile, will kill Cassio.

Othello's fury seems almost totally unsympathetic at this point. He is so very wrong, so devoid of reason. Yet Shakespeare depicts him as a man for whom we can still feel a measure of pity. We can never forget that Othello has been corrupted by a master fiend, and we must not overlook one of Othello's key lines: "But yet the pity of it, Iago! O Iago, the pity of it, Iago!" (206–207).

When Lodovico, Desdemona, and several attendants enter, Othello's words and actions would not seem so incredible if Shakespeare had not prepared us so well. Lodovico is a kinsman of the aristocratic Brabantio and has arrived here as an emissary from the Venetian senate. His cordial welcome to Othello ("[God] Save you, worthy General") is unknowingly ominous and also ironic; only God, in fact, can save Othello now, and the "worthy General" is soon to dispel all such notions about himself and his worthiness. Yet Othello does recover himself sufficiently to take care of the immediate amenities, and while he reads the letter from the Venetian senate, Lodovico asks about Lieutenant Cassio. It is Iago who answers, and his answer is portentous; his brief statement that Cassio "lives" (286) includes an unsaid "still"—that is, Othello has ordered Iago to kill the Florentine within three hours.

Desdemona's reaction to Lodovico's question is swift; she describes the division between Othello and Cassio and expresses her hope "t'atone them, for the love I bear to Cassio" (244). Emilia's comments about jealous men and about Othello's earlier, unreasonable jealousy seem to be forgotten. Desdemona's answer to Lodovico is openly naive, as is her reaction to her husband's anger. The mere mention of Cassio's name, of course, is enough to inflame the Moor. Not only does he publicly berate Desdemona as a devil, but he strikes her and orders her out of his sight. When Lodovico asks Othello to call Desdemona back, he does so, answering Lodovico coolly that concerning the senate's letter, he acknowledges that he is called back, commanded home, and will return to Venice; at the same time, he mutters in a countertempo disgusting insults about Desdemona.

He then agrees that Cassio shall have his place; remember, in this respect, that he mistakenly believes that Cassio has already taken his place in Desdemona's bed. The Moor's official welcome to Lodovico is given an added flourish; he welcomes him "to Cyprus.

—Goats and monkeys!" (274). This is an allusion to the bestial, carnal imagery that Iago used earlier to suggest Desdemona and Cassio's copulation.

Lodovico finds Othello's conduct inexcusable; he is stunned by the actions of the "noble Moor" (III. iv. 26), the man whose character "passion cannot shake" (IV. i. 277), whose "solid virtue" (IV. i. 277) has always had a reputation for being invincible. These, remember, are the virtues that were used to describe Othello before Iago began his evil machinations. Othello has permitted passion to "shake" him; it has destroyed his "solid virtue." In a word, he has not survived the supreme test that a hero in high tragedy must undergo.

As the two men conclude the scene with a brief bit of dialogue, Iago speaks to Lodovico and seems to be much aggrieved. His comment that Othello "is much chang'd" (279) is a most effective but despicable understatement. To the emissary from Venice, as to all others, Iago seems cool, honest, concerned, fair, and trustworthy—noble, even.

In Scene 2, Emilia redeems herself somewhat; earlier, she had an opportunity to speak out in defense of Desdemona and correct Othello's jealous insinuations, but she did not do so. Now, alone with her, he questions her specifically regarding the behavior of his wife, and he insinuates that being a good friend of Desdemona's, she has surely observed Desdemona in compromising situations. Emilia's answer is firm; she has never seen anything improper nor heard anything that would make her suspect that Desdemona has been less than faithful. Yes, she has seen Desdemona and Cassio together, but she stresses that she has heard "each syllable" (5) that has been uttered between them. In addition, they have never whispered together, nor did they send her out on any unnecessary errands so that they might be alone. Emilia would "lay down [her] soul at stake" (13) on Desdemona's chastity. She curses the "wretch . . . [who] put this in your head" (15); unknowingly, she curses her own husband. Othello is not convinced. At this point, his opinion of women is less than Emilia's opinion of men; Iago, we should realize, is responsible for his wife's cynicism about men, and he is also responsible for Othello's condemnation of women and of Desdemona, in particular. Thus when Othello asks Emilia for her opinion of Desdemona's fidelity, he gives her answer little credence. He sums up Emilia as "a simple bawd" (20) and his own wife as a "subtle whore" (21), secretive and hypocritical.

Parenthetically, perhaps it should be noted that Shakespeare was not as careful about his time element in this play as he was when he created his magnificent characterizations. For example, if we are to try to fathom Othello's changes of character and pity his dissolution, we must believe that sufficient time and opportunity has elapsed for Cassio to have actually engaged in an affair with Desdemona. In actuality, however, there has been no such time available, and it is impossible for Bianca to berate Cassio for neglecting her for at least a week. But such minor flaws as these must be overlooked. Shakespeare knew what he was doing. Rapidity of movement is necessary to attain dramatic tension, and because Othello insists on establishing Desdemona's infidelity, we must concentrate on the psychology of the man who has been perverted by Iago, and we must not be unduly concerned about the actual clock time elapsed.

When Desdemona is brought to Othello in Scene 2, he puts her through a cruel ordeal of questions and accusations, concluding that she is a whore and ignoring her protestations. First, he melodramatically hurries Emilia out of the room, asking her to "stand guard" and warn them [the "procreants" (28)] if anyone comes; by using the term "procreants," Othello suggests that he and Desdemona need a few stolen minutes to have sex together. This is a travesty of how they might act if they were illicit lovers. When they are alone, Othello demands uncompromisingly that Desdemona swear to heaven that she is "honest," which she does, and after which Othello feels satisfied that when he kills her, as he certainly means to do, he will be striking down one who blasphemes against heaven. Meanwhile, Desdemona, in her innocence, cannot believe that her fidelity—or infidelity—is at the root of her husband's behavior. She grasps for reasons, believing that perhaps Othello is punishing her because her father has recalled him to Venice. Perhaps to disguise a professional disappointment to his honor, Othello is punishing her because in his anger and frustration he must punish someone.

In a word, Desdemona is stunned as her once-noble husband can no longer hold back his tears. Othello regains himself, however, and at line 47, he begins an eighteen-line soliloquy in which Shakespeare restores an aura of the tragic hero to the Moor. This is great poetry, and here once again we view the high-minded Othello, a man who is capable of uttering magnificent concepts in language that carries its own sense of majesty. Notice, for example, the tacit reference to the afflictions of Job (48–49) and the broad range of imagery that expresses so clearly and movingly the turmoil in a man whose paradise is lost. The image of "a cistern for foul toads" (61), with its emphasis on gross sensuality, is followed by the startling vision of "patience, thou young and rose-lipp'd cherubin" (63). Such poetry contains keen visual oppositions of figurative language and reveals the almost unbearable tension in Othello and the sudden change that has taken place in him.

After the Moor's exit, we see the change that has taken place in Desdemona. As Emilia endeavors to comfort her mistress, she is told in a few words that Othello is no longer Desdemona's "lord" (102) and that Desdemona is too distressed even to cry, for she is at a total and complete loss to understand the unfathomable change in her husband's character. There is a faint trace of feyness and madness in this scene, as though Desdemona were speaking with a glazed countenance. Even Emilia notes this change when her mistress asks that her wedding sheets be laid out on her bed (105–106) and asks that Iago be brought to her.

When Iago enters, Desdemona cannot bring herself to utter the actual slanderous abuses that Othello has heaped upon her; this is further proof of her bewilderment. Our focus then moves to Emilia. While Othello is raging somewhere else in the castle and Desdemona is numbed and Iago is wailing in mock horror at what has happened, Emilia stands back and expresses her conviction that "some eternal villain, / Some busy and insinuating rogue, / Some cogging, cozening slave" (130–32), ambitious "to get some office" (132), has slandered Desdemona. Her insight is remarkably on target. Ironically, it is not Desdemona who has been seduced; it is Othello, whose sanity has been victimized by "some most villainous knave, / Some base notorious knave" (139–40). Emilia curses any man who would label Desdemona a whore, reminding Iago (and us) that Desdemona is a strong woman who defied "her father and her country and her friends" (126) for the man she loved. Desdemona is an extraordinary woman who could have married any number of Venetian men, but she chose Othello and thereby gave her total, undivided allegiance to him, a man of another race and of another country.

When Desdemona pleads with Iago to tell her how she may win back the trust and love of Othello, we realize that this is a dark parallel to the incident that initiated Desdemona's plight. Earlier, Cassio asked her to speak to Othello and effect a reconciliation; now Desdemona asks Iago to speak to Othello and effect a reconciliation. In both cases, Iago is the villain who is responsible for the breach of love.

Scene 2 ends as Iago once more dupes the gullible Roderigo; this time he dupes him into killing Cassio so that he can ostensibly win Desdemona's favors more easily. We also learn what mischief Iago has been into while offstage. He has pocketed enough jewels (meant for Desdemona) to "have corrupted a votarist [a nun]" (192). Finally, Roderigo is beginning to believe that he has been swindled. He knows that his advances toward Desdemona are not right—and he is ready to cease them, but he wants his jewels back. The quick-thinking Iago, however, diverts him for the time being. Again proving that he is the tactician who can nimbly improvise as he traces his path of villainy, Iago has another plan by which he convinces Roderigo that he might yet gain Desdemona's favors. The visiting commission from Venice plans to appoint Cassio to replace Othello in Cyprus, says Iago; if that happens, Desdemona will leave with her husband. But if a man of "mettle" (207)—Roderigo—were to kill Cassio ("knocking out his brains") (236), then Othello and Desdemona would have to stay on. Cassio will be dining tonight with a harlot and will probably leave between twelve and one. Roderigo can kill him then, and Iago promises to be nearby "to second [the] attempt" (244). The plan is irresistible to Roderigo.

In Scene 3, Desdemona's superior breeding is evident in the early part of the scene. She has sufficiently recovered herself and has presided as the hostess at a dinner for Lodovico and the other members of the commission from Venice; following that, when Othello expresses the desire to walk alone with Lodovico, she submits to her husband's dismissal. She seems exhausted and does not protest his ordering her to bed or even his ordering her to dismiss Emilia.

Emilia, in contrast, is resentful of Othello's behavior and deeply concerned about her friend. Othello's commands do not intimidate her; she wishes that Desdemona had "never seen him!" (18). But Desdemona, not even in her unhappiness, has no such wish. Her love "doth so approve him / . . . even his stubbornness" (19–20).

This is the man of her choice despite his roughness and rebukes, and when her wedding sheets are laid out, as she has asked Emilia to do, she announces in words that are strongly prophetic, "If I do die before, prithee, shroud me / In one of those same sheets" (24–25); it is apparent that Desdemona has a premonition of her own death. She then tells Emilia how she came to learn the mournful "Willow Song"; it was sung by poor Barbary, her mother's maid, whose lover went mad and deserted her.

Rather oddly, it seems, Shakespeare inserts a brief reference to Lodovico here; Desdemona praises him as a man who "speaks well" (37). Emilia is no less approving in her remarks. Exactly what Shakespeare intended here is hard to imagine; perhaps, for the moment, the young wife feels abandoned and is comparing her moody, raging Moor with the Venetians she once knew.

The "Willow Song" is an old one, existing in many versions before Shakespeare incorporated it into his play. Of special interest is line 52, which echoes, as it were, Desdemona's thoughts in lines19–20—that is, in the song, it is the male lover who is false and the cause of the poor woman's sighing and weeping. Obviously the mood perfectly reflects that of Desdemona, whose love is so strong that she approves Othello's frowns, just as the "poor soul" (41) in the song approves her lover's "scorn" (52).

Othello's unfair accusations have undone Desdemona; she asks Emilia if, truthfully, there are "women [who] do abuse their husbands / In such gross kind?" (62–63). The idea is unthinkable for Desdemona; "by this heavenly light" (65), she swears that she could never make love with another man. Emilia lightens the tenseness of this moment by remarking that she would never betray Iago in "this heavenly light"—that is, she herself prefers to make love in the dark. Emilia, as noted, has no illusions about men or love or marriage vows. Illicit sex is a small vice; of course she would cheat on her husband—but not for a trifle. Emilia would make a cuckold of her husband if it would make him a monarch. In fact, she would tempt purgatory if there were sufficient cause. Unfaithful wives are many, she says, and she blames husbands for their wives' loose behavior, insisting that women should have a right to do whatever men do. Since they can't, however, they must avenge themselves upon their wayward husbands. A wife should not be judged nor treated with less respect than a man—that is Emilia's firm dictum. She spurns the double standard that justifies a man's actions—right or wrong—and condemns the same acts when done by a woman. Clearly, she speaks from her years of living as Iago's wife. Too long has she seen his hypocrisy and his faults, which she—a woman—would be censored for committing. The purpose of all this chatter, of course, is to keep before us the theme of infidelity.

The mood changes, and with Desdemona's short prayer that she should never be guilty of returning evil for evil, she says goodnight to her friend. The contrast between Desdemona's young innocence and the worldliness of Emilia intensifies our pity for the young bride as she prepares for bed and for Othello's return.

ACT V

Summary

Late that same night on a street in Cyprus, Iago and Roderigo are waiting for an opportunity to murder Cassio. As Cassio enters, Roderigo's thrust at him fails, and, instead, Roderigo is wounded. Iago then darts out from where he is hiding, wounds Cassio in the leg, then exits. Othello, passing by, hears Cassio cry out the word "Murder!" and believes that Iago's plot has been successful. Lodovico and Gratiano enter, and, after them, Iago comes onstage with a light. Both wounded men are still alive; Iago comforts Cassio and then surreptitiously stabs Roderigo in the darkness. Bianca enters, and Iago tries to implicate her since Cassio just dined with her. Cassio and Roderigo are carried off. Emilia enters, and Iago sends her to tell Othello what has occurred.

Desdemona is nearly asleep in her bed chamber as Othello enters. He extinguishes his candle and, filled with regret, gives her a last kiss. Desdemona awakens, realizes her husband's intent, and pleads for mercy. But Othello will not be stopped and smothers her. Emilia pounds at the door, trying to bring news of Cassio, but Othello does not let her in to deliver Iago's message until Desdemona is apparently dead.

Emilia enters and discovers Desdemona's body; then she hears her friend faintly moaning, trying to hide Othello's guilt. Othello, however, confesses the murder, saying that it was Iago who convinced him that Desdemona was a strumpet. Horrified, Emilia tells him that Iago has told him lies; she then rushes out to announce the crime. Montano, Gratiano, Iago, and the others enter. Othello begins to tell of his suspicions, based upon the handkerchief, and Emilia, realizing her part in all this, confesses that it was she who found the handkerchief and gave it to Iago. Infuriated, Iago kills Emilia as Othello is disarmed by Montano. Othello manages to find another sword and wounds Iago for his deception. Little by little, the full circumstances are exposed. In complete despair over Desdemona's death, Othello stabs himself with a concealed dagger as the others look on in horror. Othello dies, kissing his young wife.

Commentary

In Scene 1, which precedes the final and climactic one, Shakespeare provides exciting physical action. Iago gives Roderigo final instructions for slaying Cassio; this is the moment of crisis, he says; this "makes us, or it mars us" (4), and he urges his rich, gullible friend to be firm in his resolution. Roderigo, however, is hardly a model of determination and confidence, and Iago finds it necessary to strongly reassure him. For his part, Roderigo is not eager to commit murder and he gives some evidence of a twinge of conscience before concluding "'tis but a man gone" (10). In an aside, Iago voices his thoughts: Both Roderigo and Cassio are sources of displeasure to him. He gains if one is slain, and he gains even more if both are slain. If Roderigo survives this confrontation, Iago has not yet determined how he will explain the pawned jewels; if Roderigo is killed and Cassio lives, Iago has another problem: This Florentine is young, handsome, and well-mannered, and Iago cuts a poor figure next to him. There is also the possibility that the Moor might eventually discover how Iago arranged to have Cassio killed and could, presumably, "unfold [the plan] to him" (21).

Cassio enters and is set upon, but Roderigo's sword is stopped by the young man's coat of mail. Thereupon, Cassio draws his sword and wounds Roderigo, who cries out that he is slain. At this crucial moment, Iago darts out from behind Cassio, severely wounds him in the leg, and disappears into the night. Othello enters and hears Cassio crying "Murder! Murder!" He believes that Iago has carried out his vow: Cassio is dead.

Because of the darkness, Othello mistakes Roderigo for Iago and praises him as "honest and just" (31); Iago's prompt execution of revenge convinces Othello that his lieutenant has done his duty and, satisfied, he leaves without examining Cassio any further. He is now more anxious than ever to find his "strumpet" (34) in her "bed, lust-stain'd" (36); when he is finished, both she and Cassio "shall with lust's blood be spotted" (36). He exits quickly, just before Lodovico and Gratiano enter. Both men hear Cassio's outcries and Roderigo's anguished curse against the man who has wounded him.

Iago enters with a light, much to Lodovico's delight. He welcomes help, especially that of the "very valiant" (52) Iago. Cassio is likewise relieved and tells Iago that villains have attacked him. In the melee, Iago is able to get to Roderigo's side and fatally stab him, then cry out sanctimoniously against men who kill in the dark. This done, he calls Lodovico's attention to the wounded Cassio as he bends down, tears off his shirt, and begins to bind up Cassio's wounds.

When Bianca enters, she breaks into sobs—to which Iago reacts with scorn, casting immediate suspicion on her, a "notable strum-pet" (78). He calls for a garter to use as a tourniquet, then tells them all that he suspects "this trash / To be a party in this injury" (85–86). On seeing Roderigo's corpse, he pretends great surprise to find his "friend and . . . dear countryman" (88). He continues to busy him-self with Cassio's wound, getting him into a chair and apologizing to Gratiano for this terrible unpleasantness. To Cassio, he inquires about "these bloody accidents" (94). Cassio, of course, has no answers; he doesn't even know Roderigo or why the man would want to kill him.

Scene 1 belongs to Iago. His masterly handling of the bungled murder, his cool villainy as he stabs Roderigo, and his attending to Cassio are accomplished with superb finesse. Fate even offers Iago the frightened, silent Bianca, at whom he can contemptuously point a finger of guilt as he calls Lodovico and Gratiano's attention to "the gastness [ghastliness] of her eye" (106). "Guiltiness," Iago announces, will have a way of revealing itself, even though "tongues [are] out of use" (109–10).

Emilia arrives and learns of Cassio's wound and Roderigo's death, much to her genuine sorrow. Iago, of course, takes advantage of all this to voice more sanctimonious words and to repeat his false suspicions regarding Bianca. It will be noted that Emilia still finds no reason not to believe that her husband is basically "honest," in respect to this particular violence.

Scene 1 ends as Iago sends his wife to inform Othello and

Desdemona what has happened. Alone, he acknowledges the fact that his success or failure will be determined this very night, a clear indication that the resolution of the entire action is close at hand.

In the final scene, Desdemona is asleep in her bed as Othello enters, carrying a candle. He is no longer the angry, vengeful husband. His soliloquy is quiet, and he seems to be more an agent of justice than the jealous cuckold. He speaks repeatedly of "the cause . . . the cause" (1)—that is, Desdemona's unchastity, and he himself even hesitates to speak aloud the name of Desdemona's crime before the "chaste stars" (2). At last, Othello assumes the posture of the tragic hero, grossly wrong in his determination yet steeling himself to do what he must. Here is what remains of the Othello of earlier acts—a man admirably self-possessed, the master of the situation. In this soliloquy, there are no references to strumpets or whores, nor to coupling goats or monkeys, nor to any other images that once racked him with jealousy. No longer is he possessed with revenge for his grievously injured pride. But there remains a passionate conviction of righteousness in his words—despite his monumental error. He is convinced that he is being merciful in performing a deed that must be done. Thus he will not shed Desdemona's blood (instead, he will smother her); nor will he scar her physical beauty; nor would he, as we learn later, kill her soul. Yet he will kill her; Desdemona must die "else she'll betray more men" (6). And there is devastating irony as he says, "Put out the light, and then put out the light" (7); Desdemona was once the "light" of his life, and, also, light is often equated in Elizabethan dramas with reason, especially right reason, the aim of all men. Here, however, Othello means to act righteously, but he fails to use his sense of logic or reason; he has condemned Desdemona without proof, without reason. He is torn between his love for her (evidenced by his kiss) and his resolve to coolly execute justice. Desdemona is a "pattern of excelling nature" (11), yet she is also "cunning" (11). He compares her to a rose, which, once plucked, can bloom no more and must wither. For a moment, his love for her almost persuades "justice" (meaning Othello) "to break [his] sword" (17). He weeps, but he regains his purpose; Desdemona's beauty is deceptive, he realizes, because it masks her corruption.

When Othello's words awaken Desdemona, she begins an agonizing attempt to reason with her husband. The Moor then urges her to pray for forgiveness of any sin within her soul, and she becomes increasingly terrified. This he mistakenly concludes to be additional evidence of her guilt. He is as convinced of this as she is convinced that Othello is absolutely serious about killing her. Logically, she knows that she should have no cause for fear—she has done no wrong—yet she fears her husband. Othello is not moved in the least by her insistence that she did not give the handkerchief to Cassio. And it is notable throughout this harrowing episode that Othello's language is controlled and elevated. As Desdemona cries out, first for heaven to have mercy on her and later for the Lord Himself to have mercy on her, Othello voices a solemn "amen" to her prayers and addresses her as a "sweet soul" (50). But even now he refuses to see her as anything but a "perjur'd woman" (63) (a lying woman), one who forces him "to do / A murder" (64–65). At this moment, the motive of personal revenge surfaces again within him and replaces controlled justice. His resolve of self-control breaks when Desdemona calls out for Cassio; he is convinced that he indeed heard Cassio laughing about a sexual liaison with Desdemona. When Desdemona hears that Iago has killed Cassio, her self-control likewise vanishes. She pleads for her life, asking for banishment, asking for at least a day's stay in her execution, at least half a day, but she is overpowered by the Moor. He smothers her as she begs to say one last prayer.

It is at this moment that Emilia arrives outside the door, crying loudly for Othello. The Moor does not answer immediately. From his words, we realize that he is convinced that he is being merciful, if cruel, and that he intends to be sure that his wife is dead. The monstrosity of what he has done overwhelms him. Significant are lines 100–102, in which he says that there should be now "a huge eclipse / Of sun and moon"—that is, some evidence in the heavens that should acknowledge that Desdemona is dead.

Again, Emilia calls out to Othello and, on entering, shrieks about "foul murders" (106). Othello fears she is right and blames the moon, which "makes men mad" (111). It is then that he learns that Cassio lives, and he hears Desdemona's weak voice. Once more the young wife proclaims her innocence and insists that no one but herself is to blame. Indeed, she jeopardizes her very soul by deliberately lying in order to protect Othello, her husband, to whom she asks to be commended.

At first, Othello denies having any part in his wife's death. But then he loudly denounces her as a "liar, gone to burning hell" (129), admitting that he killed her. "She turn'd to folly, and she was a whore" (132); "she was false as water . . . Cassio did top her" (134–36). His proof is "honest, honest Iago" (154). Without hesitation, Emilia denounces Iago as a liar and Othello as a deceived "dolt" (163). She defies Othello's sword to right the injustice of this murder, vowing to "make thee known / Though I lost twenty lives" (165–66) and crying out for help, proclaiming that Othello has murdered Desdemona.

When Montano, Gratiano, and the others enter, Emilia challenges her husband to disprove what Othello has told her. In response to her pointed questions, Iago concedes that he did report that Desdemona was unfaithful but that Othello himself found the same to be true. Summoning new courage, Emilia ignores her husband's command to be quiet and go home. Imploring the others to hear her, she curses Iago and prophetically states that perhaps she will never go home (197). All this finally becomes unbearable for the Moor, and he falls upon his wife's bed, only to be mocked by Emilia for his anguish. Gratiano then speaks and tells us that he finds comfort in the fact that Desdemona's father is not alive to hear of this tragedy; already he is dead of grief because of Desdemona's marrying the Moor. This is news we are not aware of, and it makes Desdemona's innocence and her deep love for Othello even more poignant.

Othello insists here that "Iago knows" (210), and, as further proof, he speaks of the handkerchief. At the mention of this, Emilia cries out again, this time appealing to God: No one will stop her now. She pays no attention to Iago's drawn sword as she tells how she found the handkerchief and gave it to Iago; she repeats her claim even though Iago denounces her as a "villainous whore" (229) and a "liar" (231).

Thus the full truth is unfolded for Othello. He dashes toward Iago but is disarmed by Montano, and, in the confusion, Iago kills Emilia, then flees. All leave except the dying Emilia and the Moor, who can only berate himself. Emilia, aware that she is near death, recalls Desdemona's prophetic "Willow Song," a bit of which she sings. She reaffirms the innocence of her mistress just before she dies and concludes, "She lov'd thee, cruel Moor" (249).

Othello finds one of his prized weapons, a Spanish sword, and, in a soliloquy, he recalls that he used the sword boldly in the past. Now, however, he has come to his "journey's end" (267). He sees himself as a lost soul—"where should Othello go?" (271). He is a "cursed slave" (276) who deserves the worst of punishment.

Lodovico, Montano, Iago (a prisoner now) and several officers enter; Cassio, in a chair, is brought in. The final moment of revelation is at hand. Othello lunges at Iago, wounds him, and is disarmed. Death is too good for Iago, he says; "'tis happiness to die" (290). Death is a relief he would not offer to his arch enemy. When Cassio states quietly that he never gave the Moor reason to distrust him, Othello readily accepts his word and asks for his pardon. Othello is freshly aware that he has been ensnared body and soul by "that demi-devil" (301) Iago, who refuses to confess his villainy. Lodovico then produces two letters found on Roderigo's body: One tells of the plan to slay Cassio, and the other is Roderigo's denunciation of Iago. The details of how Cassio obtained the handkerchief are revealed, and Othello bewails the fact that he has been a "fool! fool! fool!" (323).

Lodovico vows to punish Iago and tells Othello that he must return with him to Venice. Othello acknowledges the sentence, but before he is led away, he speaks his final lines. Unmistakably he has recovered his basic nobility and that gift of impressive language that he commanded so well prior to Iago's temptation. He reminds his listeners of his past service to the Venetian state and pleads that his story shall be reported accurately so that all will know him not as a barbarous foreigner but as one who "lov'd not wisely but too well" (334), as one who was preyed upon and became "perplex'd in the extreme" (346) and "threw a pearl away / Richer than all his tribe" (347–48). We should not overlook this simile; Othello compares himself to the "base Judean" who threw away the most valuable pearl in the world. Relentless in his self-reproach, Othello tacitly compares himself to "a malignant and a turban'd Turk" (353); then, finished, he stabs himself in an attempt to atone for all that has happened. He himself chooses to execute the necessary justice upon himself. As he is dying, he says that he kissed Desdemona before he killed her. This suggests that perhaps his love for her flickered briefly within his dark soul before he murdered her. He reminds himself that perhaps he was not wholly corrupt, but he dies knowing that his soul is lost.

Lodovico's sad words end the tragedy. The sight of Othello, slumped against Desdemona's bed, "poisons sight" (364). He asks for the curtains to be drawn, for Gratiano to administer the Moor's estate, and for Iago to be punished. He must return to Venice and "with heavy heart" (371) relate "this heavy act" (371).

1605-06

KING LEAR

KING LEAR

LIST OF CHARACTERS

Lear, King of Britain

Ruler in pre-Christian Britain, Lear is described as "a very foolish old man, fourscore and upward" and as one who is "full of changes." Because of his monumental folly in misjudging his daughters, he endures a harrowing experience but emerges as a man "more sinned against than sinning" and as one who has attained true insight.

Goneril and Regan

Lear's self-seeking, unnatural daughters whose gross flattery of their father wins for them power and possessions. Having stripped him of authority, they indeed become "the shame of ladies," "tigers, not daughters."

Cordelia

Lear's youngest daughter, the "unpriz'd precious maid" who cannot employ "that glib and oily art" that comes so easily to her cruel sisters. Rejected by her wrathful father, she survives to comfort him and to prove her own utter selflessness.

The Earl of Gloucester

The man who, if he lacks Lear's willfulness and capacity for wrath, shares with the king fatal credulity and rashness. Like Lear, he is made to suffer greatly before he gains true insight.

Edgar

Gloucester's elder and legitimate son, who stands in relation to his father as Cordelia does to Lear. His very virtue leads him to trust his wicked half brother. Forced to flee and to disguise himself as a

Bedlam beggar, he lives to bring comfort and aid to his abused father and to execute justice on the villainous Edmund.

Edmund

The bastard son of Gloucester who is described as "a most toad-spotted traitor." Motivated by envy and criminal ambition, he capitalizes upon the credulity of others and aligns himself with other evil characters in the play.

The Earl of Kent

The "noble and true hearted" courtier whose devotion to the king never wavers, yet whose downright honesty and outspokenness lead to difficulties for himself and for others.

The Duke of Albany

Goneril's "mild husband," described contemptuously by his wife as a man of "milky gentleness." He provides ethical and religious commentary on events and ultimately emerges as a positive force for virtue.

The Duke of Cornwall

Regan's husband, whose capacity for cruelty and injustice is almost limitless.

The Fool

The "bitter, all-licensed jester," devoted to both Lear and Cordelia, but whose devastating commentary on Lear's actions and fate are "a pestilent gall" to the old king.

Oswald

Goneril's steward, whom Kent promptly recognizes as "a serviceable villain," "a knave; a rascal," one who is "base, proud, shallow."

The Duke of Burgundy and the King of France

Rival suitors for Cordelia's hand in marriage.

SUMMARIES AND COMMENTARIES

ACT I

Summary

The setting is King Lear's palace. In the dialogue between the Earl of Kent and Gloucester, it is revealed that the king plans to divide his kingdom and has been considering the respective worths of his sons-in-law, the Dukes of Albany and Cornwall. Further, one learns that Gloucester has two sons, the elder legitimate, the younger illegitimate. The earl holds both equally in his affections.

Heralded by a trumpet call, King Lear makes an impressive entry, followed by the Dukes of Albany and Cornwall, and by his three daughters, Goneril, Regan, and Cordelia. Gloucester is directed to wait on the King of France and the Duke of Burgundy, suitors for the hand of Cordelia, who have not yet made their appearance. Lear promptly makes clear his purpose and the occasion for the assembly. Determined to relieve himself of "all cares and business" in his advanced age, he will divide his kingdom into three parts, giving to each of his daughters a share, the size of which is to be determined by their testimonies of love for their royal father. Beginning with Goneril, the eldest, each daughter makes her declaration. The two elder sisters declare their love for Lear to be boundless. To Goneril, he is "Dearer than eye-sight, space, and liberty"; to Regan, he is dearer than all these. The pleased Lear rewards them with portions of his kingdom and then turns to Cordelia, asking what she can say to win a share "more opulent" than those given to her sisters. "Nothing, my lord," is her reply. Incredulous, Lear urges her to speak again, warning her that she may mar her fortunes. Cordelia does so, but only to say that she loves him according to her bond, no more. Her lines of amplification serve only to enrage him, and he completely rejects her as his daughter. The share of the kingdom that he had expected her to win in this love contest he divides between Goneril and Regan. At this point, the Earl of Kent speaks out boldly, making reference to his love for and loyalty to the king. Bluntly he argues that Lear is guilty of monumental folly. But the wrathful Lear will not be moved, and Kent is declared a banished man. The earl bids the king farewell, expressing his fervent hope that the gods will protect Cordelia and that the testaments of Goneril and Regan will be justified by their deeds.

Gloucester returns with the King of France and the Duke of Burgundy, who are told that Cordelia is now destitute and friendless. France, recalling that she had always been her father's favorite daughter, is puzzled. Cordelia is given the opportunity to state that she had offended her father only because she could not indulge in gross flattery. Burgundy wastes no time in making clear the fact that he is not interested in a dowerless bride. Lear remains adamant, and Cordelia herself states that she does not wish to marry someone who is interested only in her dowry. In contrast to Burgundy, France praises her as one whose virtues make her rich indeed and gladly accepts her as his bride-to-be. In her farewell to her sisters, Cordelia says that she knows them for what they are but expresses the hope that they will love Lear well. Both Goneril and Regan make surly replies. Left alone, they comment on their father's "infirmity" and decide to work together to forestall any demonstrations of his wrath and willfulness that may affect them adversely.

In Scene 2, Edmund, Gloucester's unnatural son, appeals to nature, identifying it as a goddess whose law he follows. With cynical wit he scoffs at the idea that mere custom and the special distinctions that nations make should hold him to be inferior because he is both a bastard and a younger son. Aware that his father holds him in esteem, he expresses his determination to dupe his brother Edgar out of the paternal inheritance, for which purpose he already has prepared a letter. "Now gods, stand up for bastards!" he concludes.

Gloucester enters, distraught over what has happened at Court. Edmund hurriedly puts away the letter, sure that his father will insist on seeing it. Ostensibly, it has been written by Edgar. The writer inveighs against the "oppression of aged tyranny" and tacitly suggests that the two brothers kill their father and divide his wealth between themselves. So effectively does Edmund dissemble that Gloucester is quickly convinced, and he speaks with acute pain of recent eclipses, which, he believes, point to impending moral decay. Left alone, Edmund scoffs at his father's credulity and superstition. Brazenly he declares that his own conduct is self-determined. But when Edgar enters, he mouths part of Gloucester's remarks about astrological portents in order to stimulate his brother's curiosity. Then he tells Edgar that their father is so enraged that Edgar had best arm himself for protection. Further, if Edgar will come with him to his lodgings, he will provide proof of Gloucester's enmity.

Once more alone, Edmund gloats over the ease with which both father and brother have been deceived.

In Scene 3, Goneril learns that Lear has struck her steward Oswald for upbraiding the king's Fool. She speaks of her father's "gross crimes," his "riotous knights," his taking offense at every trifle. She will put a stop to all this. Oswald is instructed not to wait on him with usual efficiency and to say that she is sick if he should ask for her. The sound of horns announces Lear's imminent return from hunting.

Amplifying her criticism of her father, Goneril speaks scornfully of him as an "Idle old man" who foolishly believes that he still possesses the authority he has relinquished. Old men, she declares, must be treated like babies; they require not only soothing words but sharp rebukes when they are deluded. If Lear does not like such treatment, let him go to Regan, where he will be accorded the same. Oswald is also instructed to see that he and others in Goneril's service treat Lear's knights with increasing coldness. If they object, she will have the excuse for taking action against them. She will leave promptly to see to it that Regan follows her course in handling Lear and his knights.

In Scene 4, Kent, disguised, expresses his hope that he will find a place in the service of Lear, to whom he remains devoted. The king, accompanied by his knights and attendants, enters. After brusquely demanding dinner, he questions Kent: Who is he? What does he profess? The earl's straightforward answers impress Lear, who declares that Kent will be allowed to serve him. Again the king calls for his dinner and then asks for his Fool. Next, he turns to Oswald and asks where Goneril is. The steward brazenly ignores the question and leaves. When a knight is sent with orders for him to return, he refuses to comply. The knight remarks on the fact that, for some reason, the king is not being accorded the attention and courtesy that had been his in the past. Lear concedes that he had become aware of this "abatement of kindness" but had tried to ignore it. Once more he asks for the Fool and is disturbed to learn that since Cordelia's departure for France, the Fool has been pining. Lear orders attendants to inform both Goneril and the Fool that he wishes to see them without delay.

Oswald reappears and replies insolently to the king's questions. Lear excoriates and strikes him. When Oswald protests, Kent trips him and pushes him out of the hall. The grateful Lear thanks the disguised earl and gives him money as a token of acceptance into service.

At last the Fool arrives and begins the series of bitter, often ambiguous jests and comic rhymes that provide commentary on Lear's folly, dividing his kingdom and placing himself in a position where his older daughters dominate. Goneril enters and inveighs against the king's "all-licensed fool" and unruly knights. "Are you our daughter? . . . Doth any here know me?" asks Lear ironically, the questions conveying his sense of amazement that his status as king and father should be so ignored. Goneril is adamant; she demands that he reduce the number of his followers and conduct himself in a manner befitting his advanced age. Enraged, Lear denounces her as a "Degenerate bastard" whom he will no longer trouble. Has he not another daughter? He orders his horses saddled and his followers assembled so that he can leave immediately.

Albany enters, urging Lear to be patient, but the king's wrath is not to be quelled. He defends the character of his knights and, for the first time, laments his folly in preferring Goneril to Cordelia, whose "fault" now appears small indeed to him. Lear's passion now mounts as he invokes nature, calling upon it to render his thankless daughter sterile or, if she should bear a child, to make it one that will bring only misery to her. When he leaves, Albany expresses his utter bewilderment. Goneril advises him not to worry about Lear, but to let the old man rave on.

The king returns, crying out against his daughter anew, for he has learned that Goneril has dismissed fifty of his followers. He will go to Regan, confident that she remains "kind and comfortable" and will defend her father against her heartless sister. Goneril, unmoved, quickly shuts up Albany, who had begun to protest. She sends the Fool running after his master and then calls for her steward. Oswald is instructed to deliver a letter to Regan and verbally to add to the written message in order to make her argument more convincing. Finally, she turns to her husband and, in a condescending manner, reproves him for his unreasonable softness in his attitude toward her father.

Lear instructs Kent to deliver a letter to Regan, who is in the city of Gloucester, in anticipation of the king's arrival. The earl leaves at once. The Fool, aware of the torment his master is experiencing, begins his ostensibly comic routine of jibes and rhymes. Almost mechanically Lear rewards his first remarks with a forced laugh but soon is moved to fervent expressions of self-reproach and fears for his sanity. A gentleman announces that the horses are ready for the journey.

Commentary

As a good opening scene should, Scene 1 introduces most of the principals in the main plot (Lear, the daughters, Kent, Cornwall, Albany, and France) and two in the subplot (Gloucester and Edmund). Reference is made to Gloucester's legitimate son, the third important character in the subplot. Lear first appears as the absolute ruler whose word is law and as the elderly father determined to settle the future of his daughters. In the first capacity, he has already made up his mind to divide his kingdom. It has been argued that this is his first great mistake, indeed that he already is mad, since such a division will lead to chaos and thus is a violation of the law of nature at the highest social level, that of the State. In Renaissance England, certainly, the idea of a divided kingdom was regarded as monstrous. But, for the record, let it be noted that Lear's decision has also been held to be a judicious one because he had to depend upon the loyal support of feudal lords to control the more remote regions of the kingdom. Lear does state that he seeks not only to "shake all care and business from [his] age" but also to see to it "that future strife may be prevented now" (42–46). For Cordelia he had reserved the "more opulent" central portion, and it was with her that he intended to live, retaining, be it remembered, his title as king. According to this argument, the assumption is that the Duke of Burgundy was to be Cordelia's husband, for it would never do to have a king and particularly the King of France, Britain's traditional enemy, ruling the central part of the kingdom. Admittedly this is a cogent argument, particularly in view of the fact that neither Kent nor Gloucester questions Lear's judgment regarding the idea of division in general. Nevertheless, since the primary aim of monarchical policy in Shakespeare's England was a strongly centralized government, it is hard to avoid the conclusion that Lear's action was viewed as one of utter folly. Lear himself speaks of his desire to "unburden'd crawl toward death" (42), and audiences in Jacobean England, remembering the dire concern relating to the succession of Queen Elizabeth, who died in 1603, would hardly believe that the king had made a wise decision; rather they would see him as a perverse ruler who was destroying order.

If there remains some dispute as regards the division of the kingdom, there is none as regards Lear's folly in deciding upon and carrying out the love test. Love, which at its highest level involves the giving of oneself without thought of reward, is equated with material possessions, or is defined as a way of competing for such possessions. The test has been described as improbable; and basically so it is. One should recall that the Lear story in all its versions included such a test and conclude that here Shakespeare was limited by his sources. But surely it is enough to say that Shakespeare, faced with the problem of having the protagonist err grievously as early in the play as possible, accepted the love test as a structural element without essential modifications. He used this fairy-story episode as a means of probing the nature of love and to introduce the theme of appearances versus reality. Lear's lack of insight is only too apparent; in his arrogance and willfulness he sees only what he chooses to see. Goneril and Regan, practical and rational as they are in a completely self-centered way, willingly play his little game and provide for him the pat answers he expects, and each wins a coveted prize.

Cordelia's testimonial in Scene 1 provides a startling contrast to that of her sisters, and it has been subjected to much critical dispute. Shakespeare does provide some help in interpretation by means of Cordelia's aside. After listening to Goneril, she knows that she can only "love and be silent" (63). And when Regan has spoken her piece, the youngest sister can find comfort only in the awareness that her love is "more ponderous than her tongue" (79-80). The obvious point is that sincerity—absolute honesty—is a way of life with her; she cannot bring herself to gild the lily of truth. Yet her answer to Lear's question (" . . . what can you say to draw / A third more opulent than your sisters?") has disturbed commentators early and late. When the offended king asks, "So young, and so untender?" Cordelia replies, "So young, my lord, and true" (108-109). Some critics have concluded that what has been called Cordelia's "proud integrity" is a fault of excess, a manifestation of folly, for which she must pay later. If this be true, one can only say that the price is unprecedented in its exorbitance. Perhaps the best answer remains that relating to structure. Had Cordelia manifested that tenderness and tact that characterizes her conduct later, except when she is dealing with her sisters, there would have been no play. The rejecting of Cordelia is the incident that starts the action in the main plot rising. But there is much that can be said on the side of probability here. Cordelia is not merely expressing irritation over the gross flattery used by her sisters. She has been called upon not to express her selfless regard for her father but to make a bid for a prize "more opulent than her sisters" and to reform her utterance unless she wants her fortunes to be marred. The very depth and sincerity of her love prevent her from saying more than she does.

However restrained her words may seem, she speaks volumes when she tells Lear that she loves him "according to her bond." To be sure, it can be argued that love should not be bonded, but what is intended here is that Cordelia's love for her father is based upon the law of nature and involves the clearest recognition of filial obligation. According to the idealistic theory inherited from the Middle Ages, this higher law, which is divine in origin and which recognizes a hierarchical relationship among all beings and things, makes possible harmony throughout the universe. It is the very law that Lear himself depends on when he expects to be revered and obeyed both as a king and as a father. This theme of nature is of great importance in *King Lear* and appropriately Cordelia introduces it into the main plot. In his egotistic willfulness, Lear now has destroyed family ties and thus violated the natural law at this level.

One might argue that Kent could have served his king better if he had avoided bluntness, but he is depicted as a man who, in his way, is quite as strong-willed and downright as his master. "Come not between the dragon [ancient British symbol of royalty] and his wrath," exclaims Lear in Scene 1 (124), and the fierce dispute between these two, one representing absolute wrong, the other absolute right, commences. The question of whether Kent too is guilty of folly need not be raised. He emerges as courageous, honest, loyal. Surely it is too much to expect him to indulge in political maneuvering when facing a Lear who says to Cordelia:

> The barbarous Scythian,
> Or he that makes his generation messes
> To gorge his appetite, shall to my bosom
> Be as well neighbour'd, piti'd, and reliev'd
> As thou my sometime daughter.
>
> (118–22)

In the violent exchange between ruler and courtier, Kent uses some especially significant phrases. "When majesty falls to folly" (151) emphasizes the fact that Lear's action involves the rejection of reason on a scale of appalling proportions. In reply to the king's explosive "Out of my sight!" Kent replies with equal vehemence: "See better, Lear." What is stressed here is the fact that Lear suffers from a fatal lack of *insight*. In the course of the play, he must learn at great price to "see better."

The dialogue between the triumphant Goneril and Regan at the end of Scene 1 (291 ff.) is quite revealing. Regan speaks of the "infirmity of age," making understandable why some have interpreted *King Lear* primarily as a study of wrath in old age. But she adds that "he hath ever but slenderly known himself," and Goneril speaks of "the imperfections of long-engrafted conditions." Clearly, the rejection of Cordelia and the banishment of Kent represent the great climax to a long series of willful and wrathful acts.

Yet something needs to be said on Lear's behalf despite his monumental folly. The instinct for good has been present in his character. Kent's first speech at the beginning of this scene tells us that initially the king had preferred Albany to Cornwall. And it is made abundantly clear that among his three daughters, Cordelia had been the one he had cherished most; with her he had hoped to spend his last years. Finally, Lear had won the love and loyalty of the forthright Kent, who, like Cordelia, will prove his enduring affection for the king. At the end of this stirring scene, then, Lear emerges as a man who, like all others, has within himself the potential for good or evil. As a result of uncontrolled passion, it is the latter that dominates.

However disturbed some may be by her laconic honesty, Cordelia is intended to represent absolute virtue. "Fairest Cordelia, thou art rich being poor," says France (253), echoing II Corinthians 6:10. If one cannot go so far as to describe Goneril and Regan as the embodiments of unmitigated evil at this early stage in the action, it may be concluded nevertheless that they are the self-seeking, earth-bound, "rational" types who may be depended upon to consider only their own interests. Their last two lines, which relate to practical considerations, point to further consequences. Finally, it should be recognized that of the two, Goneril has the greater initiative. She will not waste any time in thinking: "We must do something, and i' the heat."

What place does divinity have in this opening scene? Lear swears by Apollo and by Jupiter, not inappropriately, since the action takes place in pre-Christian Britain, and Kent replies, "Thou swear'st thy gods in vain" (62). A bit later Kent prays that the gods will take Cordelia "to their dear shelter" (185). All that can be concluded, however, is that both Lear and Kent (and, we may presume, Cordelia) acknowledge a higher power or powers concerned with man's fate on earth.

Left to the last for commentary in Scene 1 are remarks on the Earl of Gloucester. In the informal prose dialogue between him and Kent, one learns not only that Lear is about to divide the kingdom according to the mere whim of his affections. One learns that Gloucester has a bastard son named Edmund, whom he cherishes quite as much as he does his older legitimate son. Kent takes a worldly attitude toward all this; he does not "smell a fault," to use Gloucester's words, particularly since Edmund is so handsome. One may agree with Kent and especially approve of the fact that the earl acknowledges and provides for his natural son, but the historical point of view should not be ignored. Bastardy and legitimacy were not to be accorded the status of equality. Moreover, there is a devil-may-care attitude in Gloucester's remarks ("there was great sport in the getting . . . ") that points to a flaw in the earl's character. At his own level, he too has been guilty of folly; he can discern no difference between the legitimate son and "the whoreson who must be acknowledged." Whether or not Edmund overheard these remarks is a matter of conjecture. It has been argued that Gloucester's jaunty reference to him motivates his revolt against his father. But it is enough to say that all this serves to provide the prologue to Act I, Scene 2, in which the subplot gets underway.

In Scene 2, Edmund's self-revealing soliloquy, spoken with winning vigor and replete with wit, appeals to the modern mind. If one is not perceptive, he may find himself agreeing with him, just as some find themselves admiring the Satan of Milton's *Paradise Lost*, with his eloquent declaration of personal liberty. Morality, it has been said, is largely a matter of time and geography. Today, many would agree with Edmund that custom, or tradition, should be ignored. Certainly any fair-minded person would like to see all individuals, legitimate or illegitimate by birth, judged in terms of their own abilities and performances. What must be recognized is that

Edmund's words reveal his flat rejection of moral law and an endorsement of the law of the jungle. The nature that he invokes is not the traditional nature, whose law informs much of the action in Act I, Scene 1. That law, it will be recalled, made possible a beneficent, reasonable, harmonious order throughout the universe. The phrases "plague of custom" and "curiosity of nations" very well sum up natural law as he sees it: These are no more than artificial constraints imposed upon society rather than the recognition of a sacred bond of human relations. His nature is not immoral; it is amoral. For Edmund, it is animal vitality alone that determines superiority or inferiority. From this point of view indeed "the lusty stealth of nature" may create adulterously a more worthy issue than can the "dull, tired bed of marriage." Edmund takes his place, along with Shakespeare's Richard III and Iago, as one of the Machiavellian villains who elevates will above reason in determining his course of action and thus is guilty of a great perversion of the idealistic Renaissance moral theory. His words "I grow, I prosper" reveal his real character and intentions.

Critics have pointed out that in his renunciation of the laws of religion and society, Edmund emerges as an Epicurean atheist whose ideas reflect the growing controversy that was changing the pattern of all Renaissance thinking at the time when Shakespeare was writing and that was to culminate later in the century in the Hobbesian pessimistic view of a nature anything but benign, one that was hostile, one that involved a perpetual war of appetites.

"What papers were you reading?" asks Gloucester in Scene 2 (30). "Nothing, my lord," replies Edmund. He thus picks up the words used by Cordelia (I. i. 89). The word *nothing* already is becoming something of a refrain in this play, and it is not without interest that Gloucester's tragedy, like Lear's, begins with that word. The earl's next speech is no less significant: "Let's see. Come, if it be nothing, I shall not need spectacles." A bit later he says, "Let's see, let's see" (45). The repetition of the main verb is anything but accidental. Gloucester, who as Lear would see, proves himself tragically lacking in insight. He needs the spectacles of wisdom to save himself from error. But in his own way, he is no less confident than Lear that he is right, and his denunciation of the blameless Edgar (80–83) matches Lear's denunciation of Cordelia. To be noticed also is the fact that in the forged letter, Edgar is made to inveigh against "This policy and reverence of age" (47). Respect, or reverence (the usual Renaissance term), for age had its place in the idealistic concept of universal order; disrespect for age was held to be contrary to natural law.

Gloucester's remarks about the "late eclipses of the sun and moon" may appear to be mere superstition or as a bit of rationalization, the means of avoiding the recognition of human responsibility. Despite his cynicism, Edmund presents his argument in a convincing manner, once more demonstrating his wit. But there is another point of view to be taken. First, it should be stated that Gloucester is not alone in his apparently naive belief in planetary influences. In Scene 1, Lear had sworn "By all the operations of the orb / From whom we do exist and cease to be" (113-14). Later in the play, he will refer to "all the plagues that in the pendulous air / Hang fated o'er men's faults" (II. iv. 69-70). The noble and true-hearted Kent also recognizes such a belief in causality, as when he speaks of Albany and Cornwall, whose "great stars" have "Thron'd and set high" (III. i. 21-23). Before one concludes that here the reference is no more than rhetorical, one should recall these lines spoken by Kent with reference to Lear's three daughters:

> It is the stars,
> The stars above us, govern our conditions;
> Else one self mate and make could not beget
> Such different issues.
>
> (IV. iii. 34-37)

All three—Lear, Gloucester, and Kent—acknowledge a causal connection between the celestial and the terrestrial. It is not without significance that Gloucester himself is aware of the "wisdom of nature," that is, of natural philosophy or scientific theory, which finds no such causal relationship between eclipses and events in the world of man. If he does embrace astrological determinism, more significant is the fact that he acknowledges a higher power or powers.

But even if one accepts Gloucester's view rather than Edmund's, the nature of nature is not clearly explained. Astrological determinism here seems to keep things in a realm where nature makes things evil as well as good. In refutation of this conclusion, many commentators see the late eclipses as one of the familiar trappings of tragedy introduced to indicate that Lear's rash actions represent a great violation of the law of nature that is now leading to disorder and disaster throughout the realm, as is immediately evidenced by Edmund's villainy and Gloucester's credulity.

When Edmund sees Edgar reenter in 'Scene 2, he promptly begins to sigh "like Tom o' Bedlam" (147–48), that is, like a lunatic discharged from Bethlehem Hospital, the London madhouse. The relevant point here is that this suggests the disguise that Edgar soon will adopt. Edmund's skill at dissembling is sufficiently apparent and calls for no special comment, but the reader will not ignore the fact that when Edgar asks how long Edmund has been "a sectary astronomical" (a follower of those who believe in astrology), he is quick to change the subject. Gloucester had indeed proved to be credulous, naively so; but it is primarily Edgar's nobility of character that leads him to believe that his half-brother has no ulterior motive:

> A credulous father, and a brother noble,
> Whose nature is so far from doing harms
> That he suspects none, on whose foolish honesty
> My practices ride easily.

> (195–98)

Perhaps it is not too much to say that Edgar's honesty in the subplot counterbalances that of Cordelia in the main plot. In both instances, the principals find themselves rejected, while the pragmatic, self-seeking individuals flourish.

In Scene 3, Oswald is introduced. He is no ordinary servant; properly he is referred to by Goneril as her "gentleman." In Shakespeare's day, as earlier in England, every castle or great house had its own staff directed by a gentleman who was assisted by a yeoman. The steward was usually the younger son in a good family. His employment was accepted as a worthy occupation involving no sense of social inferiority. If Oswald were a mere servant, it would be utterly unthinkable that he should reprove Lear's Fool or treat the king's knights coldly as his mistress instructs him to do.

It is Goneril the doer who, of course, dominates Scene 3 as she makes good the plan of action upon which she had determined earlier. In order to gain the possessions and authority that are now hers, flattery was necessary; now she has no need to humor her father; stern rebukes and denial of privileges will serve for a Lear who is to her an "Idle old man" and one of the infantile "Old fools." All this provides increasing evidence of her heartlessness, her flat rejection of the Order principle, according to which fathers are held in high esteem and age is respected. Yet, like other villainous characters in Shakespeare's plays, Goneril provides some realistic commentary. Lear erred grievously in assuming that he could retain the privileges of kingship while relieving himself of its responsibilities. This is just one of the several assumptions held by leading characters in the play that are soon shown to be false as the action progresses. George Orwell believed that renunciation is the real subject of *King Lear* and that the willfully blind Lear's great mistake was to assume that he could attain happiness by giving away his lands—that is, that he could, as it were, purchase happiness. But happiness is achieved when one lives for others, something that Lear is not prepared to do. Although Gloucester, whose story runs parallel to Lear's, renounces nothing, Orwell's argument remains a provocative one.

One last point relates to Lear's age. He indeed is far advanced in years, but obviously he is anything but a doddering old man. This has been apparent from his vocal outbursts in Act I, Scene 1; it is clearly established in Scene 3 when one learns that he has been leading his band of knights and squires in the hunt, a most demanding physical activity.

In Scene 4, when Kent states that he seeks to serve where he does "stand condemned" and that he will be found "full of labours" (5–7), he reveals himself as one who is completely selfless in his devotion that he will prove through hard service if given the chance to do so. Thus he is firmly established as a type of absolute honesty and love. Of some interest is his use of the words *man* and *profess* in the initial exchange with Lear. He answers the king's first question laconically, identifying himself simply as a man. At the literal level, he means no more than that he is an adult male, but at another level much more is implied. He is human, a *humane* being, one who has not and could not descend on the hierarchical scale to the bestial level where individual will and desire dominate over reason. "What dost thou profess?" asks Lear (13). The verb, of course, has two meanings: "to affirm or to avow," and "to make a pretense of." Kent is quick to state that he is one who does not make use of pretense. The phrase "to fear judgement" (17) has biblical echoes (Psalms 6:6; Jeremiah 8:7). Kent is saying that he is one who acknowledges a higher power to whom he is accountable for his conduct. That he will eat no fish (18) is to be explained historically: The loyal Englishman in a militantly Protestant England acknowledged the king as spiritual as well as temporal leader. This is Kent's way of saying that he remains loyal to Lear, who never relinquished his title as King of Britain. Appropriately, then, he is quick to reprove Oswald, who recognizes Lear only as his "lady's father" (88). Kent, who had not been deceived by Goneril and Regan and who had recognized Cordelia's virtue, again gives proof of his insight, for he recognizes wisdom in the apparent nonsense of the Fool's discourse. "This is not altogether fool, my lord," he remarks (165).

The Lear of Scene 4 remains the victim of extreme wrath. "Pray, sir, be patient," says Albany (282); but, long accustomed to having his own way, Lear cannot make use of that remedy, the only one available for one in his present condition. One properly may question the absolute truth of Goneril's indictment of Lear's train, who, she says, make her court more "like a riotous inn" or "like a tavern or brothel / Than a grac'd palace" (264–66). But if she exaggerates, it is difficult to avoid the conclusion that the king's knights and squires are a difficult group whose boisterous, unruly behavior may well reflect Lear's own willfulness and lack of control. The old king, unable to face the realities of renunciation, is filled with splenetic vindictiveness:

> I have another daughter,
> Who, I am sure, is kind and comfortable.
> When she shall hear of thee, with her nails
> She'll flay thy wolfish visage.
>
> (296–99)

Later in the play, Goneril indeed proves to be a "marble-hearted fiend," the personification of ingratitude, and a "detested kite"; but at this early point in the action, Lear's outbursts primarily reveal him to be passion's slave. Yet the king, who declares that he would "pluck out" his "old fond eyes" (323–24), is beginning—just beginning—to gain insight, for now he can distinguish between Cordelia and Goneril and is aware that he himself has fallen from the bias of nature, the very nature to whom he appeals in his denunciation of Goneril:

> O most small fault,
> How ugly didst thou in Cordelia show!

Which, like an engine, wrench'd my frame of
    nature
From the fix'd place.

(288-91)

Having given away the "wide-skirted meads," his entire kingdom, he can now ponder ironically his own identity and thus move
the nearer to truth: "Who is it that can tell me who I am?" "Lear's
shadow," replies the Fool (251), the metaphor implying that King
Lear no longer exists. His subsequent lines are no less weighty with
import: "I would learn that; for, by the marks of sovereignty, knowledge, and reason, I should be persuaded I had daughters." The three
marks by which he swears should have been his guides. Now,
having ignored them, he finds all that he conceived to be natural
becoming unnatural; specifically, daughters no longer acknowledge
filial duty and respect; kings no longer receive prompt obedience.

If Goneril's indictment of Lear's "insolent retinue" invites some
sympathy for her, Shakespeare does not weight the scale in her
favor to any great extent. The letter and her instructions to Oswald
point to the wiliness in her character. Her judgment of Lear and of
his train betrays unbecoming rancor, and her objections to Albany's
"harmful mildness" inform against her.

In Scene 4, the Fool is immediately established as a sympathetic
character when one learns that he had "much pined away" since
Cordelia had gone to France. Moreover, Lear greets him affectionately: "How now, my pretty knave! how dost thou?" (106). Yet he is a
"bitter Fool" and, often, "a pestilent gall" to his master. Superficially,
it might be concluded that he is one who seems to take pleasure in
pouring salt in open wounds, so devastating are his comments on
Lear's folly. Even after Tate's version began to lose its hold on audiences, Shakespeare's *King Lear* was presented without the Fool, an
indication that his role was not understood or that it was held to be
too painful. Long since, however, the consensus is that it is especially through the Fool that Lear's original nature is understood.
Although the king does threaten to whip him for his impertinences,
he remains "all-licensed," as Goneril describes him (220)—that is, the
privileged jester, who, unlike Kent, need not face banishment
because the king can bear to hear the truth from him. Ironically,
Lear becomes his pupil, striving to learn a hard lesson.

The Fool enters asking that he be permitted to hire Kent as Lear has done and offering his coxcomb to the loyal earl. The implication is clear: Kent is so foolish that he chooses to seek his fortune by following one who is dispossessed. For Kent, then, motley's the only wear; rational individuals would seek the favor of the Gonerils and Regans of this world. In his role as teacher, the Fool recites a bit of verse (131–40) in which types of cautious individuals are identified: the man who knows better than to develop a free and open disposition in a world that has no place for honesty; the cautious capitalist, the straight-laced puritan who is motivated not by Christian ethics but by his interest in worldly possessions. Kent dismisses all this as "nothing," leading the Fool to ask Lear whether he can make use of nothing. "Why, no, boy," replies the king; "nothing can be made of nothing" (145–46). He thus echoes his words to Cordelia: "Nothing will come of nothing" (I. i. 92). Further along in Scene 4, the Fool indicts his master:

> Thou wast a pretty fellow when thou hadst no
>   need to
> Care for her [Goneril's] frowning; now thou art an
> O without a figure. I am better than thou art now; I
>   am
> A Fool, thou art nothing.
>
> (210–13)

In just this way, it is made clear that much has grown tragically from nothing, and the divested Lear must face this crushing truth. Repeatedly, the Fool's remarks point to a topsy-turvy world, one in which traditional values no longer obtain: "May not an ass know when the cart draws the horse?" asks the Fool (144), who does not let one forget that it was his master whose stupendous folly made this possible. Yet his sincere devotion to Lear comes through. It is not merely Goneril's stern command that makes him hurry after the king; he is not one to seek favor in a society dominated by the opportunists. His final lines in Scene 4 (340–44), daring ones in context, reveal where his loyalty and interest lie. The Fool remains an individual, but one can understand why many have seen him as a kind of chorus, commenting on and interpreting what has happened and is happening, and as the voice of Lear's conscience.

Albany appears in Scene 4 as one who stands for morality but who is powerless, dominated as he is by his self-serving wife, to whom mildness and gentleness are harmful. His words directed to Goneril—"How far your eyes may pierce I cannot tell" (368)—invite attention, especially since the sight pattern of functional imagery has already been introduced with reference to the erring Lear and Gloucester. The verb *pierce* here connotes a kind of ferocity. It would seem that Albany poses the question of whether or not those who reject the virtues of mildness and gentleness will prove to be the clear-sighted ones ultimately.

Scene 5, a brief transitional scene, has been praised as one of the finest in dramatic literature. It presents a Lear attended only by Kent, who departs immediately, the Fool, and apparently just one gentleman: a Lear beset with deep regrets and fears that, having lost so much, he may now lose his mind. "I did her wrong—" (25); "To take again, perforce! Monster Ingratitude!" (43–44); "O, let me not be mad, not mad, sweet Heaven!" (49–50)—these are lines that make crystal-clear his agony. In the first, he is reminded for the second time of the grave injustice he had done Cordelia, whom, though she will not reappear until much later in the play, one is never allowed to forget; in the next two, the king contemplates forcibly taking back that part of the kingdom he had given to Goneril; and, finally, he utters a prayer that his mind will not fail. His invocation of heaven places him again among those in this play who acknowledge a higher power over man's destiny.

Perhaps the Fool is intolerably irritating here in Scene 5, particularly when he concludes, "Thou shouldst not have been old till thou hadst been wise" (47), a line that makes one recall Regan's statement that Lear had "ever slenderly known himself" and Goneril's "Old fools will be babes again." But, however bitter, there is no malice in the Fool's remarks; it is as if he were voicing words that represent Lear's full awareness of his older daughter's view of him. Lear's prayer that he remain sane seems to be motivated by the apparent madness of the Fool, who refers to Lear's attendants as asses (37) and who assures his master that he would make a good fool (41–42). Like the Kent of Act I, Scene 1, the Fool is a realistic commentator who reveals the true state of affairs—and the truth can be a most painful thing on occasion. He anticipates what will happen when Lear goes to Regan. His use of the word *kindly* (15) is ironic, for it has a two-level meaning: "affectionately" and "after her kind or nature."

ACT II

Summary

From Curan, a courtier, Edmund learns of a probable outbreak of civil dissension between the Dukes of Cornwall and Albany, and that Cornwall and Regan will arrive at Gloucester's castle that night. Left to himself, he expresses his elation. It will take delicate handling on his part, but Edmund knows that all this can be made to work to his advantage. He calls Edgar from a chamber in which the legitimate son had been hiding and urges him to flee for his life because their father has learned of his presence and the Duke of Cornwall suspects him of treasonous dealings with Albany. First he must draw his sword and make a pretense of trying to stop Edgar from escaping. Edmund plays his role expertly, even going to the extent of wounding himself in the arm after Edgar leaves. In response to his outcries, Gloucester enters with servants and is once more easily convinced that Edgar is a ferocious villain. He proclaims Edgar to be an outlaw who, with Cornwall's approval, will be hunted down. Gloucester renounces Edgar as his son and praises Edmund as his "loyal and natural boy" whom he will arrange to have recognized as his heir.

Cornwall and Regan enter and, accepting the testimony of the deluded Gloucester and the malicious Edmund, join in condemning Edgar. Cornwall has the highest praise for Edmund, who is given a place as one of the duke's trusted followers. Regan then explains that she and the duke have come to seek Gloucester's counsel relating to Goneril's quarrel with Lear. She and her husband consider it advisable to avoid a face-to-face encounter with the king when he arrives to complain of the treatment he had received.

Kent and Oswald make their appearance at Gloucester's castle. Incensed at the sight of the steward who had behaved so disrespectfully to the king, Kent first harshly berates Oswald, then draws his rapier and beats him. In response to the steward's outcries, Edmund enters with rapier drawn; he is followed by Cornwall, Regan, Gloucester, and servants. Kent is ready to engage Edmund, but Cornwall orders the two to keep the peace. Regan identifies both Oswald and Kent as couriers—the one from Goneril, the other from the king. Cornwall calls for an explanation of the quarrel between the two. With characteristic bluntness, Kent provides a devastating character sketch of Oswald as an unmanly, servile fellow "who wears no honesty." When the duke upbraids him, he fearlessly refutes the charge that he is no more than a brash ruffian. Cornwall sides with Oswald; unmoved by Kent's identification of himself as one who serves the king, he orders the earl placed in the stocks, much to Regan's satisfaction. Gloucester, deeply troubled, endeavors to intercede in Kent's behalf, but the sentence is not revoked. Trussed up in the stocks, Kent stoically accepts his fate. Before he falls to sleep, he finds solace in reading a letter from Cordelia, who has been informed of Kent's actions on Lear's behalf and who is deeply concerned about her father.

In soliloquy, Edgar explains that he had heard himself proclaimed an outlaw and had escaped capture by hiding himself in a hollow tree. To save his life, he will begrime his face and body, cloth himself only in a blanket, and thus disguised as a Bedlam beggar "outface / The winds and persecutions of the sky."

Lear, the Fool, and the gentleman arrive at Gloucester's castle. As the king expresses bewilderment over the fact that Regan and Goneril have left, Kent hails him. Lear at first cannot believe that anyone had dared to place his emissary in the stocks. When he learns the facts, he protests vehemently against "such violent outrage." The Fool continues to provide appropriate commentary in prose and verse. Striving to control his swelling rage, Lear demands to know where Regan is. Told that she is within the castle, he enters alone, returning shortly with Gloucester. When the earl speaks lamely of his efforts to restrain the "fiery Duke," Lear's rage mounts and he commands that Cornwall and Regan be brought to him at once. He begins to add to his instructions words of denunciation of the "hot duke" but manages to restrain himself with the thought that perhaps Cornwall is not well.

Gloucester returns with Cornwall and Regan. The exchange of greetings would seem to indicate that there was no break in the relationship of the king to his daughter and her husband. Kent is set free. Then, speaking at first ironically, Lear addresses Regan. As he begins to indict Goneril for her "Sharp-tooth'd unkindness," Regan urges him to have patience and expresses her conviction that Goneril cannot be at fault. Adopting a tone of apparent reasonableness and solicitation, she advises Lear to return and apologize to Goneril. But the king mocks her by playing ironically the kneeling supplicant to his own daughter. Abruptly, Regan reproves him. Stating that Goneril had taken away half of his followers and had subjected him to great verbal abuse, the king again calls down a curse upon her. Cornwall adds his expression of disapproval to that of Regan: "Fie, sir, fie!" But Lear amplifies his curse of Goneril and assures Regan that she will never deserve so to be cursed by him. He then asks who had put Kent in the stocks. Before an answer can be given, Goneril arrives, preceded by Oswald, and is greeted by her sister. Lear's pain at this evidence of collusion is increased when Cornwall states that he had ordered Kent to be placed in the stocks. Now Regan attempts to induce her father to return with a reduced train to Goneril's castle, where he will remain for a month and then can sojourn with her. She explains that she needs to make the necessary preparations to entertain him as her guest. But Lear cannot bear the thought of having any of his followers dismissed; he would rather fend for himself in the open country, or bend a servile knee to the King of France, or—worse yet—be a "slave and sumpter [pack-horse]" to the "detested groom" Oswald. Let him suit himself, says Goneril, in effect. Turning to her, the king pleads that she do not drive him mad. He will see no more of her; but now, striving as he is to achieve patience, he will not curse her again. He concludes that he and his hundred knights can stay with Regan.

"Not altogether so," says Regan, and there follows a colloquy at the conclusion of which Lear is asked why he needs even one follower since his daughters' servants can look after him. "O reason not the need!" exclaims Lear, and he points out that Regan herself is arrayed gorgeously. It is the possession of that which is in excess of bare necessity, he argues, that man is distinguished from the beast. So impassioned does he become that he cannot complete his argument. Once more he prays for patience, addressing the gods as "a poor old man" weighted down with grief and age. His mood changes, and he now calls upon the gods to grant him "noble anger," not womanish tears, as a resource in his misery. The king then denounces both daughters as "unnatural hags" and declares that he will find revenges that will be "terrors of the earth." As he insists that he will not give way to tears, the sound of the storm and tempest is heard, and Lear exclaims: "O, Fool! I shall go mad!" He leaves, accompanied by Gloucester, Kent, and the Fool. Regan remarks that she would accept her father as a guest but has no place for any of his followers; Goneril states that he himself is to blame for his present state.

Just as Goneril asks for Gloucester, the earl returns and reports that the king is in a high rage and that, as night approaches, he wanders unprotected in an increasingly violent storm. Goneril, Regan, and Cornwall are unmoved by this report. The duke bids all present to come out of the storm.

Commentary

In Scene 1, Curan's report of impending strife supports the idea that Lear's first mistake was his decision to divide the kingdom and thus make possible civil dissension. Some time will elapse, however, before this rift becomes of prime importance. Immediately, it provides material that Edmund finds useful for his purpose.

Edmund again demonstrates his utter depravity but also his superior cunning, although there is no place in this scene for jaunty wit. Carefully, he maintains his outward pose of innocence and respect for the traditional values. He greets Curan most courteously; he appears to be deeply offended morally and "loathly opposite" to the "unnatural purposes" he ascribes to Edgar. He sounds like the very voice of honesty and humility when he replies to the Duke of Cornwall: "I shall serve you, sir, / Truly, however else" (119-20). Like other accomplished Shakespearean villains, he is an opportunist. Without any delay, he makes use of the news he receives from Curan. He knows that the credulous Gloucester will be especially moved by the report that Edgar had been "Mumbling of wicked charms" (41). His masterly dissembling is demonstrated when he quotes Edgar as calling him an "unpossessing bastard" whose word would never be accepted as true when opposed by that of the legitimate son (68 ff.).

In view of Edmund's superior cunning, Gloucester is not to be dismissed as a simpleton, although he is simple enough in his credulity. A bit more can be said in his behalf. When he cries out to Regan in Scene 1, "Oh, madam, my old heart is cracked, is cracked!" (92), he invites sympathy, however aware one is that he lacks insight. There is nothing illogical in the fact that he should speak of Cornwall as "The noble Duke my master / My worthy arch and patron" (60-61); he had no reason to believe that Regan's husband would be anything other than the chief support and protector of loyal subjects. Yet how ironic it is that Gloucester should see Edmund as his "natural boy" (86) in view of Edmund's concept of nature of which the audience has been apprised. As in Lear's case, one grave mistake leads to another. And, let it be noted, Gloucester is convinced by the report of perfidy, not by the words of the principal involved.

Regan and Cornwall appear on the surface to be righteous individuals determined to forestall civil dissension and to punish evildoers. Regan seems appalled to learn that Edgar, her father's godson, had sought to kill Gloucester, but she is quick to find a causal connection between Edgar's alleged perfidy and Lear's "riotous knights." Moreover, both she and Cornwall are anxious to indoctrinate Gloucester before Lear can tell his story. In downright meanness, her decision to be away when her father arrives is at one with Goneril's instructing Oswald to snub the king.

It is too early to make any sweeping judgment of Cornwall. The chief thing against him is that he is Regan's husband. Moreover, his praise of Edmund's "virtue and obedience" and his welcoming Edmund into his service have special significance, for we see Shakespeare bringing his villains together. There is an unconscious feeling of kinship between one already proved to be a villain and the other, who will emerge as no less villainous. As a result of all this, one can well predict how Cornwall will behave as the action advances.

In Scene 2, it is easy to misjudge both Oswald and Kent and to conclude that the former is a dutiful servant who is grossly abused and that the latter is an irascible fault-finder whose scurrility is inexcusable. Oswald greets Kent civilly ("Good dawning to thee, friend") and immediately is subjected to an unmerciful tongue-lashing. But in the very beginning of this play, Kent was established as a man of unshakable honesty and true insight, just as the steward was represented as the willing instrument of Goneril's machinations. Kent knows that Oswald comes "with letters against the King" (39), taking what Kent calls "vanity the puppet's part"—an allusion to the old morality plays, in which Vanity, among other vices, was personified. That the steward is a contemptible figure is made clear by his cowardice when he fails to defend himself (40–46), by his dishonesty when he brazenly tells Cornwall that he has spared Kent's life only in deference to his age (67–68), and by his rather obvious effeminacy. Most telling is Kent's denunciation of all such creatures who minister to the base passions and desires of others:

> Such smiling rogues as these,
> Like rats, oft bite the holy cords a-twain
> Which are too intrinse t' unloose; smooth [help to
>   gratify] every passion
> That in the natures of their lords rebel.
>
> (79–82)

What Kent achieves is a prose "character"—that is, a sketch of a particular type: descriptive, analytical, and satiric in form—that anticipates the prose character writers of the seventeenth century, many of whom were influenced by Theophrastus (373–284 B.C.), who wrote studies of thirty ethical types of humanity. Interestingly enough, Cornwall provides another such "character" in his speech (101–10) beginning

> This is some fellow
> Who, having been praised for bluntness, doth
>   affect
> A saucy roughness, and constrains the garb
> Quite from his nature.

This is a sound indictment of the would-be plain dealer who is no more than the buffoonish railer like Thersites in Shakespeare's *Troilus and Cressida*. But, quite obviously, Cornwall's harsh appraisal is not applicable to Kent, who, in his own words, is too old to learn to qualify truth or to restrain himself in voicing it. Cornwall's prompt taking sides with Oswald explains why Kent immediately shows a dislike for the duke and Regan (99–101).

It may be difficult for a modern reader fully to understand why the placing of Kent in the stocks in Scene 2 was such a monstrous act, one that takes Kent by surprise and appalls Gloucester. But note the disguised earl's words:

> I serve the King,
> On whose employment I was sent to you.
> You shall do small respect, show too bold malice
> Against the grace and person of my master,
> Stocking his messenger.
>
> (135–39)

And Gloucester has this to say: "The King must take it ill / That he, so slightly valued in his messenger, / Should have him thus restrained" (152–54).

Placing Kent in the stocks is an act of rebellion against the king himself; it symbolizes the dethronement of Lear. Loyal Englishmen in Shakespeare's day would view this as an unforgivable sin. Regan has less concern for her father's emissary than she would have for his dog (143–44), and Cornwall is of the same mind. When he makes reference to Kent as "a fellow of the self-same color of whom Goneril had spoken" (145–46), it is clear that the three—Goneril, Regan, and Cornwall—are an evil triumvirate who are now dominating in a world that rejects traditional values. The repeated references to Kent as being advanced in years ("This ancient ruffian"; "old fellow"; "I am too old to learn") underscore the fact that Lear, in a sense, appears in the person of his emissary Kent. In placing him in the stocks, Cornwall and Regan reject the time-honored belief that the subject is to the king as the child is to the father and that age itself should be accorded reverence.

That Kent should have received a letter from Cordelia in which she expresses concern for the well-being of her father has posed something of a problem since not enough time has elapsed for her to have learned of Lear's difficulties or of Kent's efforts to protect the king. But here Shakespeare compresses time, as he had done in earlier plays, to serve his dramatic purpose.

In Scene 3, Edgar's stripping of himself and determination to outface the elements anticipate Lear's actions subsequently. When he describes Bedlam beggars as sticking "in their numb'd and mortified arms / Pins, wooden pricks, nails, sprigs of rosemary" (15–16), the reference is to the absence of pain believed to be due to demonical possession, but this includes a tacit reference to the greater blows that one like him must suffer in a world where innocence and honesty have no place. "Edgar I am nothing," he concludes, and the words reveal that at his level he has become the victim of usurpation and now is no more than a shadow of his former self.

The range of emotions exhibited by King Lear in Scene 4 is remarkable. At first he expresses bewilderment that Regan and Cornwall have departed without sending a word of explanation; royalty is not treated in such a casual manner. Then, when he learns that the two are responsible for placing Kent in the stocks, wrath dominates once more. Granted, he has been depicted as an inordinately willful ruler. Nevertheless, Lear's seeing all this as a "violent outrage" that is "worse than murder" is not entirely unwarranted in view of all that has been said above regarding kingship. When Lear exclaims, "They durst not do't" (22), he is trying frantically to hang on to the vestiges of royal authority. After listening to Kent's explanation, he makes another, still unaccustomed effort to control himself: "*Hysterica passio*, down, thou climbing sorrow, / Thy element's below" (57–58). But these lines provide more evidence that only adversity awaits the old ruler. Now it is Regan to whom he refers as "this daughter," not as "my daughter" or "our daughter," although he is yet to learn that she too has abandoned him. Still endeavoring to exercise the prerogatives of royalty, Lear orders that Regan and Cornwall be found and made to explain their conduct.

There is irony in Gloucester's reference to "the fiery quality of the Duke," who is described as being "unremovable and fix'd . . . in his own course" (93–95), for these words accurately describe the Lear of Act I, Scene 1. The universe of King Lear, wherein rulers and fathers receive prompt obedience, is crumbling before his eyes. The climax of this episode in Scene 4 is reached when Gloucester reports that he had "inform'd" Cornwall and Regan that the king would speak to them. It is as if Lear had humbly requested an audience! Kings command; they do not request. Again, with great effort Lear restrains himself, indulging perhaps in wishful thinking: It may be that the duke is not well. When he goes on to say that "we are not ourselves / When nature, being oppress'd, commands the mind / to suffer with the body" (108–10), he provides a diagnosis that is applicable primarily to himself. "I'll forbear," he continues; and, making reference to his own "more headier will" (110–11), he shows that the man who ever but slenderly had known himself has made progress toward self-knowledge.

Although both Regan and Cornwall greet him in the proper manner, using the titles "your Grace" and "your Highness," their real attitude toward the king is soon revealed. Lear himself cannot conceive of a second daughter behaving as unnaturally as Goneril had behaved: "If thou shouldst not be glad, / I would divorce me from thy mother's tomb, / Sepulchring an adult'ress" (132–34). The image employed here implies a violation of the law of nature. Lear, who himself had violated that very law, takes no other view of nature at this point in the action. Thus he expresses his conviction that Regan, unlike Goneril, knows better "The offices of nature, bond of childhood" (181). It is, of course, ironic that he should use the word *bond* in the exact sense in which it had been used by Cordelia, who had said that she loved her father according to her bond. Too late he is beginning to understand the full import of her words.

Lear's inability to master the passion of wrath is indicated by his calling down once more a curse upon Goneril (164–67). When she appears and promptly upbraids him for indiscretion, he exclaims, "O sides, you are too tough!" (200). He has reached a point where even an explosion, perhaps even the madness he has been fighting against, would provide a relief. Lear's impassioned declaration that he would rather "abjure all roofs" and endure "Necessity's sharp pinch" in the wilderness than return to Goneril with only fifty knights (210 ff.) is another example of lines that anticipate what is to happen later in the play. As has been true from the beginning, Lear himself makes the decisions which determine his fate. Here it would seem that he practically suggests to his evil daughters the easiest way in which they can get rid of him.

If Lear remains willfully blind to the whole truth, he nevertheless begins increasingly to win the audience's sympathy. There is pathos, certainly, in the spectacle of this old ruler, once so powerful, striving to convince himself that his is still the voice of authority, and in his repeated efforts to attain a stoical calm, to retain his sanity. He reaches a point in Scene 4 where he can tell Goneril that they will never again see each other. Yet, he is aware that this heartless woman is his own flesh and blood:

> But yet thou art my flesh, my blood, my daughter;
> Or rather a disease that's in my flesh,
> Which I must needs call mine; thou art a boil,
> A plague-sore, an embossed carbuncle,
> In my corrupted blood.
>
> (224–28)

Two significant points are to be made here. First, there is a strong suggestion that Lear, in a moment of lucidity, recognizes that the source of his daughter's evil lies in himself. The "theme of identity" is the phrase that has been used in the development of this idea. That two of Lear's daughters soon prove to be evil, in contrast to the one virtuous daughter, is held to symbolize the fact that the king has permitted the potential evil in his nature to become active and to overwhelm the good. Second, the disease image sustains the same idea of evil within Lear and recalls Kent's words in Act I, Scene 1: "Kill the physician, and the fee bestow upon the foul disease" (165–66). Perhaps Lear's acknowledgment of blame explains why his great anger subsides and he can state that he will no longer berate Goneril.

"I can be patient," says Lear (233). But if he has indicated a willingness to compromise, he has not yet learned the lesson of patience. Note that he still measures love in terms of calculation, involving, in this instance, his hundred knights. But when Lear finds to his consternation that he is to be denied even one follower, he provides an answer that reveals that his daughters are committing an offense against humanity:

> O reason not the need! Our basest beggars
> Are in the poorest thing superfluous.
> Allow not nature more than nature needs,
> Man's life is cheap as beast's.
>
> (268–71)

It is not just so many knights that Lear needs; it is sincere love, understanding, tolerance, and mercy, which his daughters, in their fine array, deny him. So great has been the provocation that he returns to the mood of Act I, Scene 1, as he denounces these daughters as "unnatural hags." The sound of the storm and tempest symbolizes at once the great perturbation in Lear's own mind and the violence of his daughters' action against him.

Kent's explanation to Lear in Scene 4 (27–45) fills in the details of antecedent action that make fully understandable his harsh treatment of Oswald in Act II, Scene 2. When he states that he had "more man than wit" (42), Kent provides refutation of the argument that he was guilty of sheer folly: He is not one of those practical individuals whose sagacity manifests itself only in looking out for himself. Once more his use of the simple word *man* reveals his humanity.

Little needs to be added to what has already been said of the Fool and his function in this play. His speech beginning "We'll set thee to school to teach thee there's no labouring in the winter" (68 ff.), which echoes verses six through eight in Proverbs 6, is typical. He appears to be indicting Kent for behaving foolishly, ironically advising him to follow the course of self-interest. Some commentators believe that he is putting Kent's loyalty to test, but clearly he does not want the earl to follow his counsel: "When a wise man gives thee better counsel, give me mine again; I would have none but knaves follow it, since a fool gives it" (75–78). The bit of doggerel that follows supports this interpretation. Neither Kent nor the Fool is a moral coward in the face of adversity (winter). The Fool's last speech in Scene 4 (123–28) satirizes Lear's practice of giving commands incessantly despite the fact that he has lost the power to win obedience; further, it provides evidence that the Fool deeply sympathizes with his master.

Gloucester appears in Scene 4 as a well-meaning but ineffectual character. The best he can do is to express his wish that Lear were not at odds with Regan and Cornwall and to lament the fact that the enraged king has left the castle to brave the storm as night approaches. That Albany is absent from this scene is quite understandable. His "milky gentleness," as Goneril called it, has no place here and must be saved for a later time when he can exercise it effectively.

If Goneril and Regan remain two of a kind in their cruelty, they are individualized to some extent. Regan makes a greater effort to keep up the appearances of propriety and reasonableness. Thus she greets her father in these words: "I am glad to see your Highness" (130). And she knows how to use truth itself to further basic dishonesty, as when she counsels Lear in the lines beginning "O, sir, you are old; / Nature in you stand in the very verge / Of her confine" (148 ff.). But in her last speech (305–10), she shows herself to be as adamant as Goneril, who minces no words when talking either to her father or about him. Cornwall's words, "My Regan counsels well" (312), sum up the role in Scene 4 of a man utterly lacking in compassion.

ACT III

Summary

After the two meet in the storm, Kent learns from a gentleman that Lear wanders about, accompanied only by the jesting Fool, "contending with the fretful elements." Kent recognizes the gentleman as one upon whom he can depend. He divulges to him the fact that there is growing enmity between the Dukes of Albany and Cornwall, and that the King of France, apprised of this and of Lear's plight, is about to lead an invasion of England. The gentleman is instructed to go to Dover and inform loyal subjects how Lear has been made to suffer. If he meets Cordelia, he is to identify himself by means of a ring that Kent gives him. She will then reveal to him Kent's identity.

Wind, rain, thunder, and lightning provide Lear with another occasion passionately to denounce ingratitude. He pronounces these elements to be the "servile ministers" (servants) of his "two pernicious daughters" engaged in battle against him. The Fool remains at his side, first urging his master to find shelter and warmth even if he must "court holy water" (flatter those in power), then providing another commentary on Lear's original error. Once more Lear expresses his determination to be patient. Kent arrives and hears the old king inveigh against secret corruption and describe himself as "a man more sinned against than sinning." Kent persuades him to seek shelter in a nearby hovel, and the disguised earl himself returns to the castle in the hope that he can make its inmates open the doors. The Fool remains behind only long enough to recite a paradoxical prophecy.

At his castle, Gloucester complains to Edmund about the treatment he has received at the hands of his guests, Regan and Cornwall. They have ordered him to abstain from seeking to help King Lear in any way. Edmund expresses his horror at such savage and unnatural conduct. Gloucester then takes Edmund completely into his confidence: He has in his possession a letter the contents of which are a source of danger to Cornwall; further, there is a power on foot that will come to the king's aid. Gloucester instructs his son to make excuse for him, for at the risk of his life he will find Lear and try to help him. Left to himself, Edmund resolves to tell Cornwall all that he has just learned.

Kent solicitously urges the king to enter the hovel and thus to protect himself from the cruelty of the storm, but Lear replies that so great is the tempest in his mind, he scarce feels the storm itself. Although he expresses his determination to endure, he cannot get out of his mind the memory of his daughters' ingratitude, which he fears will drive him mad. With his newfound gentleness, he first urges Kent to seek shelter; then he bids the Fool to go in, while he remains outside to pray before he sleeps. Next, Lear voices his deep sympathy for the "Poor naked wretches" of the world, who, ragged and hungry, must endure such foul weather. With remorse he acknowledges the fact that, as king, he had ignored them and only through personal suffering has come to realize their plight.

The Fool runs from the hovel in fear, crying that a spirit calling itself Poor Tom haunts the place. At Kent's command, the disguised Edgar emerges, raving about the "foul fiend" that pursues him. Lear, his mind now beginning to fail at the sight of such utter destitution, declares that the pitiful Tom o' Bedlam must have been victimized by cruel and ungrateful daughters. Playing his role of a religious maniac, Edgar describes himself as a depraved one-time gentleman servingman. "Is man no more than this?" asks Lear (iv. 106), and he identifies Edgar as "the thing itself"—man in his "natural" state, stripped of all that differentiates him from the beast. In his madness, he tears off his clothes to join Edgar in essential nakedness. Gloucester enters with a torch. He had defied the "hard commands" of Goneril and Regan and found refuge in a farmhouse adjoining his castle where Lear can be sheltered. The king insists upon talking further with Edgar, whom he refers to as a learned philosopher. Gloucester, appalled at the sight of the once-powerful Lear reduced to this sad state, says that he himself has been driven to the brink of madness by an ungrateful child who had sought his life. Lear agrees to go to the shelter only on the condition that Edgar, his philosopher, comes with him.

Having testified against his father, Edmund is rewarded by Cornwall with his father's title and estate. He is instructed to find out where Gloucester is hiding, and he hopes to discover his father in the act of helping the king and thus to incriminate him further.

Gloucester conducts Lear, Kent, the Fool, and Edgar to a chamber in a farmhouse near the castle and then leaves to find provisions for them. Edgar continues his babbling about wicked fiends and urges the Fool to pray. And the Fool still tries in his way to divert his master. Now Lear's madness impels him to seek retribution for his daughters' offenses. "I will arraign them straight" (vi. 22), he declares, and he appoints both Edgar and the Fool judges. Two joint-stools identified as Goneril and Regan are placed on trial. The Fool readily accepts his role, but Edgar is so moved by pity for the king that he can hardly keep up the pretense. Kent, no less distressed, urges Lear to exercise the patience of which he had boasted. Finally he succeeds in inducing the king to lie down and rest. Gloucester enters with the news that there is a plot to kill Lear, who immediately must be placed on a litter and carried to Dover, where he will find both welcome and protection. All leave except Edgar, who remains long enough to speak of his own sufferings, which now seem light in comparison to those of the king. He concludes with a prayer for Lear's safety.

Cornwall sends Goneril with a letter to Albany informing him that the army of France has landed. He then orders servants to "Seek out the traitor Gloucester." Regan urges that the earl be hanged, Goneril that his eyes be plucked out. Cornwall instructs Edmund to leave with Goneril since he should not be present to witness the punishment of his father. He is to advise Albany to waste no time, for both dukes must join forces against France. Significantly, Edmund is addressed as "my Lord of Gloucester." Oswald reports that the old Earl of Gloucester has seen to it that King Lear, accompanied by several of his knights and other followers, has been conveyed to Dover, where he expects to find "well-armed friends." Cornwall sends servants to capture Gloucester, and almost immediately the old earl is brought in. As Cornwall questions him, Regan rails at Gloucester and plucks his beard. At first Gloucester protests against this gross insult, and then he courageously declares that he had sent Lear to Dover in order to save him from their cruelty. Cornwall gouges out one of his eyes and crushes it with his foot; Regan urges her husband to gouge out the other. At this point, one of Cornwall's own servants cries out for his master to stop, and he draws his sword in Gloucester's defense. He does wound the duke but is slain by Regan. Promptly Cornwall gouges out Gloucester's other eye. The earl, now dark and comfortless, cries out for Edmund. Regan tells him that it was Edmund who had informed against him, and the tormented earl finally learns that he had cruelly misjudged his legitimate son. He prays for forgiveness and for Edgar's welfare. Regan orders that he be thrust out of the castle gates to "smell" his way to Dover. Cornwall orders that the body of the servant who had dared to oppose him be thrown upon a dunghill. Bleeding profusely, he leaves, assisted by Regan. The servants who remain express their horror of what they have witnessed. They agree to follow after Gloucester, poultice his bleeding eyes, and get Tom o'Bedlam to take him wherever he wants to go.

Commentary

At the end of Act I, Scene 1, Cordelia had expressed her distrust of her sisters and her concern for her father's welfare; in Act II,

Scene 2, Kent had found comfort in reading her letter in which she had indicated her concern for her father. Now in Act III, Scene 1, one learns the source of her information; her royal husband had secret agents who reported on the conduct of the Dukes of Albany and Cornwall and their wives. The news that an invasion from France is imminent and that Cordelia herself may have returned to England raises the hope that Lear may soon be rescued and the forces of great evil destroyed.

The gentleman's vivid description of Lear on the heath defying the elements prepares the audience for the actual sight of the oppressed king in the next scene and thus reinforces the effect. That this is a storm of unparalleled fury is conveyed especially by such phrases as "impetuous blasts" and "eyeless rage" (8). Lear's defiance underscores at once the extent of his own wrath, his stamina and courage so worthy of a tragic hero, and the threat to his sanity as he "Strives in his little world of man to outscorn / The to-and-fro conflicting wind and rain" (10–11).

Although the Fool's bitter quips have often been a "pestilent gall" to Lear, the reference to the jester in Scene 1 makes clear his status as one who is devoted to his master and who seeks to alleviate the pain that Lear is suffering by laboring "to outjest / His heart-struck injuries" (16–17).

Understandably, Kent has yet no reason to believe that Albany, husband to Goneril, is any different from Cornwall, husband to Regan; thus he speaks of their "mutual cunning" in their endeavor to conceal evidence of dissension.

Although Lear describes himself in Scene 2 as "a poor, infirm, weak, and despised old man" (20), he appears as much more than a pathetic figure. His defiance of the warring elements and the very higher powers by whom he had sworn earlier in the play (1–9, 15–24), and his denunciation of hypocrisy (49–59) have an unmistakable grandeur. He inspires a sense of awe. In his indictment of those who have within them "undivulged crimes, / Unwhipped of justice," he is a Lear whose concern extends far beyond himself. When he concludes that he is "a man more sinned against then sinning" (59–60), he acknowledges his own fault before passing judgment on others. But he is also a very human being in great distress, still trying to control his passion when the Fool, reciting another snatch of verse (27–34), reminds him of his folly in surrendering power; aware of his frailty as he admits that his "wits begin to turn" (67); capable of great tenderness, as he says to the Fool: "Come on, my boy. How dost, my boy? Art cold?" (68).

In Scene 3, Gloucester, a man who is fundamentally decent, begins to act positively. It is significant that the world being what it now is, such decent people must resort to secrecy and deception in their effort to do the right thing and cannot trust even their own flesh and blood. Edmund remains the amoral opportunist who will capitalize promptly on his father's faith in him: "The younger rises when the old doth fall."

In Scene 4, King Lear's reference to the "tempest in [his] mind" leaves no doubt of the storm's symbolic import, and the lines "In such a night / To shut me out! Pour on, I will endure" (17–18) underscore the fact that the storm's fury is equated with the unnatural treatment he had received from Goneril and Regan. Along with his continued effort to master his passion and thus preserve his sanity, there is his newborn compassion for others. This is shown first by his concern for the Fool ["In, boy, go first . . . Nay, get thee in" (26–27)] and then by his lament for all "Poor naked wretches." In his *Elegiac Stanzas*, Wordsworth wrote, "A deep distress hath humanized my soul," and he bade farewell to "the heart that lives alone." The experience to which the Romantic poet referred is far different from that of the king, but his words are applicable here, for the old ruler, who in his egocentricity had in a sense "lived alone," has learned through misery. His sympathy now extends to all suffering humanity. The lines that immediately follow are especially significant:

> Oh, I have ta'en
> Too little care of this! Take physic, pomp.
> Expose thyself to feel what wretches feel,
> That thou mayst shake the superflux to them
> And show the heavens more just.
>
> (32–36)

This incorporates at once an acknowledgement of his own fault and an indictment of those now in power who heartlessly ignore the plight of defenseless humanity. The great irony lies in the fact that only in a state of wretchedness does he come to a realization of kinship with all humanity. In the last line, it would seem, Lear implies that the heavens have not been just. But surely the intent is that heaven's justice must be revealed through the good works of men.

Lear, having given away his kingdom, having been deprived of his band of knights and squires, and having been denied shelter from the storm, sees the nearly naked Edgar as man completely divested of all that distinguished him from animal. For the old king, he is a symbol of the ultimate in injustice. There is, then, a logic in Lear's unshakable conviction that Edgar must also be the victim of thankless daughters, although it is at this point that the madness he had fought against begins to envelop him. "Reason in madness" is the phrase used to describe his discourse, for the tormented Lear is indefatigable in his quest for truth now. Once more he acknowledges his own fault as he revives the theme of identity:

> Is it the fashion that discarded fathers
> Should have thus little mercy on their flesh?
> Judicious punishment! 'Twas this flesh begot
> Those pelican daughters.
>
> (74–77)

But at this point most are willing to concede that however much to blame Lear may be, his punishment is hardly judicious; he is a man more sinned against than sinning.

Although it is several lines later that Kent says, "His wits begin to unsettle" (166), Lear's mental collapse is complete when he declares that Edgar is "the thing itself," unaccommodated man (110 ff.). Having divested himself of his power and having been divested of his train, he sees no reason why he should remain one of the "sophisticated" (clothed). "Unbutton here," he says, and joins Edgar in near-nakedness—man in his natural state. Parenthetically, it may be noted that here especially Shakespeare shows the influence of Montaigne's *Apology for Raymond Sebonde*, available in John Florio's translation dated 1603. In his attack upon human pride, Montaigne repeatedly dwells upon the helplessness of man without the trappings of civilization. For Lear, Edgar is indeed a "learned philosopher," one who can even provide an answer for that much-discussed question, what is the cause of thunder? Edgar symbolizes the true nature of man; he is the image of truth.

Edgar's description of himself as "A servingman, proud in heart and mind" (87–97) is intended to show the extent to which evil flourishes in the world. It is, of course, ironic that he should take upon himself human iniquity since he is an exemplar of virtue in this play. The bestial images, so prominent throughout the play, are particularly notable in Scene 4. Long since it has been observed that the Seven Deadly Sins were often represented by the names of animals. The implication is that man is not the paragon of animals, like unto the angels, as he was held to be in idealistic Renaissance moral philosophy (Cf. *Hamlet*, II. ii. 315–20), but a predatory creature ruled not by reason but by desire.

Kent is given few lines in Scene 4; it is enough that virtue should manifest itself in deeds, not in mere words. Gloucester, however, is accorded considerable attention once he makes his appearance. His entrance is anticipated by the Fool's words addressed to Lear: "Now a little fire in a wild field were like an old lecher's heart; a small spark, all the rest on 's body cold. Look, here comes a walking fire" (115–19). Here one is made to recall Gloucester's initial error from which his misfortunes stemmed. Lear's self-indictment is applicable to Gloucester as well. The close connection between main plot and subplot is especially emphasized here as the distraught Gloucester says, "Thou say'st the King grows mad. I tell thee, friend, / I am almost mad myself. / . . . / The grief hath crazed my wits" (170–75). Most ironic is the fact that Gloucester unknowingly speaks to the disguised Kent ("Poor banished man"), and his words are heard by Edgar, who he still believes sought to kill him ("I loved him, friend"). For the son whom he does not recognize, he shows compassion as Lear does ("In, fellow, there into the hovel. Keep thee warm").

There has been considerable conjecture regarding the closing bit of verse recited by Edgar, beginning "Child Roland to the dark tower came," which obviously derives from folklore and which requires no detailed discussion here. But it is not without relevance to recall that Robert Browning made use of this first line as the title of his well-known poem in which he depicts Roland's invincible courage as he comes at long last to the Dark Tower, wherein Death lurks—Death, which must be faced by everyone, the good as well as the bad. Once when asked if the basic meaning of the poem was "He that endureth to the end shall be saved," Browning replied, "Yes, just that." Since Edgar pre-eminently is one who has been established as stoical, his lines are quite in character. The Dark Tower metaphor also suggests that the fortunes of Lear and Gloucester, no less than those of Edgar, are at least near their lowest ebb. But whether enduring to the end will lead to salvation remains to be seen.

In the previous scenes, the betrayal of Lear and the results of that betrayal were depicted. In Scene 5, one witnesses the same process with reference to Gloucester. The action in the subplot adds to the terror of the main plot. In both one witnesses the rejection of traditional virtues. Yet both Edmund and Cornwall use the language of the virtuous. Edmund deplores the fact that his natural affection for his father must give way to loyalty since Gloucester's conduct is "treasonous"; and sanctimoniously he appeals to the heavens, although he acknowledges only a rapacious goddess of nature. Similarly, the vengeful Cornwall uses the terms *trust* and *love* as if he were a champion of order and decency.

The grotesque comedy that began when Edgar, disguised as Tom o' Bedlam, first joined Lear and his group continues and reaches its climax in Scene 6. Now it serves to develop the theme of justice. One recalls that it was in the role of "justicer" that Lear first appeared in this play. He called for and listened to the testimony of his daughters, following which he rendered his decisions relating to what each daughter deserved. Punishment, not rewards, is what he would now mete out to Goneril and Regan, the "she foxes." The emphasis is placed upon the utterly absurd. In Lear's universe now, a madman is neither a gentleman nor a yeoman; he is a king. Tom o' Bedlam, plagued by foul fiends, is the sapient one who properly should wear the robes of a judge; and the Fool is his "yokefellow of equity"—his partner in law. Edgar also deserves a place as one of the king's hundred followers (of whom he has been deprived), but his present attire (no more than a blanket) is far too luxurious and he must exchange it for simpler apparel. Goneril's crime is that she "kicked her poor father," under which understatement her gross cruelty is figured.

But in the course of this absurd farce, Lear continues his quest for truth: Let the learned judges anatomize (dissect) Regan to "see what breeds in her heart," for he must learn whether or not "there is any cause in nature that makes these hard hearts" (80–83). The extent of the king's desolation is emphasized not only by his having been "kicked" by his own daughter but by the barking of the little pet house dogs, Tray, Blanch, and Sweetheart. Even they have turned against him.

Scene 6 is the last scene in which the Fool appears, and his disappearance has been the subject of much discussion. In the very last scene in the play, Lear says, "My poor fool is hanged" (V. iii. 305), but his reference is to Cordelia, "fool" being one of the Elizabethan and Jacobean terms of endearment when used colloquially in proper context. The Fool disappears because he has served his purpose. When he first took his place in the action, one learned that he had pined for Cordelia; his attachment to Lear served to identify him as a link between the king and his virtuous daughter. Further, as has been stated earlier, the Fool's jingles and prattle provided a commentary on his master's folly and made possible the conclusion that, at one level, he often represented Lear's conscience. Finally, since Shakespeare was not at all averse to introducing the comic into tragedy, thereby heightening the tragic effect through contrast, the Fool provided unadulterated broad comedy. In this scene, for example, consider the following bit of dialogue:

Fool:	Come hither, mistress. Is your name Goneril?
Lear:	She cannot deny it.
Fool:	Cry you mercy, I took you for a joint stool.

(51–53)

The audience would greet this last line with laughter, just as they would laugh at the words of the drunken Porter in *Macbeth*, but this would not take away from their deep sympathy for Lear.

Edgar's scene-ending soliloquy, hardly notable as poetry, does serve to mark an end to this phase of the larger action. "Mark the high noises," he says (118), and one is aware that Lear no longer is just an old man, a former ruler, thrust out into the storm. The "high noises" are the hue and cry of those who now seek his life.

Scene 7 has long been recognized as the most appalling one to be found in dramatic literature. Cornwall's brutal exclamation "Out, vile jelly!'" epitomizes the extreme cruelty depicted. If Shakespeare had not prepared his audience so well for what it now witnesses, one would have to conclude that he outreached himself in sensationalism and that he was guilty of pandering to popular taste for violence. But so well had he developed the characters of those who oppose Lear that now he could depict the extremity of wickedness in all its ferocity. Increasingly one has been made aware of the fact that the "practical," self-seeking characters have attained power through a rejection of the traditional virtues—love of parents, respect for age, basic sympathy for another human being. In the last analysis, Gloucester's own son Edmund is responsible for what has happened to his father. Earlier in the play, it was Gloucester himself who, deeply distressed by the plight of Lear, had said, "Our flesh and blood is grown so vile, my lord, / That it hates what gets [begets] it" (III. iv. 150–51). In Scene 7, he learns that it is Edmund, not Edgar, who proves so vile. In the world now dominated by the evil characters, acts of loyalty and kindness represent treason. The references to Gloucester's "corky [withered] arms" and white beard make one aware that age as well as parenthood is attacked. Ironically, it is Gloucester himself who seems to have suggested the act of violence that he must endure. When Regan asks him why he had sent the king to Dover, he replies, "Because I would not see thy cruel nails / Pluck out his poor eyes; nor thy fierce sister / In his anointed flesh stick boarish fangs" (56–58). But what is significant here is that in a definite sense, the loyal Gloucester represents the king, just as Kent did when, after upbraiding Oswald, he was placed in the stocks. Although it is the earl who suffers from such inhuman treatment, the greater offense is against Lear, the old ruler and father. There is logic in the fact that it is Goneril who urges that Gloucester's eyes be plucked out and that it is Cornwall, abetted by Regan ("One side will mock another; th' other too"), who performs the almost incredible deed.

Gloucester's moral blindness had been dramatized by his according Edmund equal status with the legitimate and noble Edgar and then by his prompt acceptance of Edmund's report against his brother. But to conclude that the blinding of Gloucester represents the working out of justice is to misread the play. Gloucester, like Lear, is a man far more sinned against than sinning. In his efforts to help Lear, he had already emerged as a sympathetic character; now he invites one's unqualified admiration in his manifestation of courage, his honest acknowledgement that he had misjudged Edgar, and his prayer for his legitimate son's well being. "I am tied to the stake, I must stand the course," he says as he endures the brutal attack (54); and with unflagging courage he tells Regan exactly why he had sent the king to Dover. All dark and comfortless, he can ask his gods to forgive him and to help his abused son. Just before his eyes were plucked out, Gloucester had expressed his conviction that the "winged vengeance" would overtake the evil characters. Thus he endorsed the idea that although wickedness may be dominant, it will be destroyed ultimately—the universe is moral. The fact that one of Cornwall's own servants heroically turns upon his master provides proof that virtue still can be active. But although he wounds Cornwall, the servant himself is slain, so the basic question of Shakespeare's answer to the problem of evil in this play remains unanswered.

ACT IV

Summary

Edgar finds comfort in the thought that since fortune has inflicted the worst upon him, change can mean only improvement in his status. Immediately the blinded Gloucester, led by an old man, enters. The earl urges his guide, identified as one of his tenants, to abandon him since such an act of compassion may prove dangerous. He adds that he has no way to go and that he had stumbled when he had eyes to see. Then Gloucester expresses concern for Edgar and prays that he may live to see his worthy son by means of touch. Now Edgar realizes that no one can confidently say that he has experienced the worst.

Gloucester learns that it is a "madman and beggar" who is at hand. He recalls that he had seen such a fellow in the storm during the previous night and had been led to conceive man to be no more than a worm. At that very moment, thoughts of Edgar had come to his mind, although he then still believed that his son was a faithless villain. Now that he has learned that Edgar is guiltless, he has lost all faith in divine justice. Painfully Edgar listens to his father and laments the fact that he must continue to play the role of Tom o'Bedlam.

This meeting leads to a solution of Gloucester's immediate problem. At his request, the peasant is to supply clothing to cover the near-naked Edgar, who will then guide the earl to Dover. He explains that he wishes to be led only to the cliffs; thereafter he will require no more assistance. "Give me thy arm," says Edgar. "Poor Tom shall lead thee."

Having arrived at the Duke of Albany's palace, Goneril bids welcome to Edmund and asks Oswald where her husband is. The steward reports that Albany is a much changed man, that he smiled when told that the army of France had landed in Britain, expressed his displeasure when informed that his wife and Edmund were coming, and called Oswald himself a sot when the steward spoke of Gloucester's "treachery" and Edmund's informing against his father. Goneril speaks contemptuously of her husband's "cowish [cowardly] terror of . . . spirit," declares that she will take command, and instructs Edmund to return to Cornwall and assist him in raising and directing an armed force to oppose France. She adds that Edmund may find that it is a mistress who issues such orders, and she kisses him in token of their new relationship. Edmund expresses his complete loyalty to her and leaves.

Albany enters and upbraids Goneril for her inhuman treatment of Lear. He tells her that she and Regan are "Tigers, not daughters." Goneril refers to her husband as a "moral fool" and so arouses him by her heartlessness that he can hardly restrain himself from striking her.

A messenger arrives with the news that the Duke of Cornwall has died from the wound inflicted by his servant. Learning that Cornwall had been stabbed when he sought to pluck out Gloucester's remaining eye, Albany declares that the duke's death proves there are higher powers concerned with terrestrial events and quick to punish malefactors. In an aside, with mixed feelings, Goneril remarks that with Cornwall out of the way, perhaps she and Edmund can gain complete control of Britain; on the other hand, she is aware that Regan, now a widow, may become her rival for Edmund's love.

From a gentleman, Kent learns that the King of France has been forced to return to his own country and that his marshal commands the French troops in Britain. The gentleman then describes Cordelia's reaction to the letters Kent had written concerning the fortunes of her royal father. Deep as had been her sorrow and concern for Lear, she had controlled herself, making no violent display of her emotions, although she was appalled at the behavior of her sisters. Kent declares that it is the influence of the stars that must explain the difference between Cordelia and her cruel sisters. He tells the gentleman that Lear is nearby in Dover, but that although from time to time aware of the new turn in events, the king cannot bring himself to meet Cordelia, so filled with shame is he for having mistreated her and given her "dear rights" to his "dog-hearted daughters." The gentleman also reports that the forces of Albany and Cornwall are afoot. Kent says that he will bring the gentleman to Lear and, at the proper time, reveal his own identity.

Cordelia, now leader of the army seeking to rescue King Lear, learns that her father is nearby, grotesquely decked with weeds and flowers. At her command, the troops set forth to find him and bring him to her. In reply to her question regarding the possible restoration of Lear's sanity, a doctor assures her that efficacious herbs will induce the repose that should lead to his recovery. Cordelia prays that her father will be cured and again urges that he be found before his passion costs him his life.

A messenger reports that the British forces are approaching. Cordelia remains calm, for this news is not unexpected and her army stands ready, but she makes clear the fact that the French troops that she commands serve only to help her restore her "ag'd father's right."

Regan learns from Oswald that Albany had been persuaded with difficulty to lead his forces against the army of France. She is particularly concerned about her sister's letter to Edmund. She believes that he has gone to find and slay his father, an act of which she approves, knowing that all subjects who see the blinded Gloucester will be moved to turn against his oppressors. Oswald states that he must leave at once to deliver Goneril's letter. Pointing out that he faces danger, Regan urges him to wait until the next day when her troops will set forth. But the steward replies that in view of Goneril's firmly expressed orders, he cannot delay. Regan then asks why her sister should have written Edmund and urges Oswald to let her open the letter. As he starts to protest, Regan says that she is well aware that Goneril does not love Albany and that she has given Edmund amorous glances. She instructs Oswald to give "this" (either a token or a letter) to Edmund and to tell Goneril what she had said about her and advise her to come to her senses. Finally, Regan urges the steward to kill Gloucester if he should meet him and thus win preferment. Oswald assures her that he will do so if the opportunity presents itself.

Edgar, now dressed as a peasant, leads his father in the fields near Dover and convinces him that they are climbing to the top of the cliff and are near the sea. Gloucester says that Edgar's voice seems altered, that his speech is now clear and rational, but the son assures him that he is changed only in dress. Edgar describes a great chasm, or abyss, pretending that he and Gloucester now stand at the edge of the Dover cliff. The old earl rewards him with a precious jewel and a benediction. In an aside, spoken after he says goodbye, the son explains that he has deceived his father only to effect a cure for despair. Kneeling, Gloucester prays to the "mighty gods," renouncing a life that he can no longer endure and blessing Edgar, who he hopes still lives. He then falls down and loses consciousness. When he revives, Edgar succeeds in making him believe that he now lies at the foot of the cliff and, miraculously, has survived. Further, the earl is convinced that his guide was some fiend that sought to bring him to destruction. His son urges him to believe that the purest gods have saved him, and Gloucester resolves to endure henceforth all afflictions patiently.

At this very moment, Lear enters, fantastically dressed as Cordelia had described him at the beginning of Act IV, Scene 2—"a side-piercing sight," in the words of Edgar. His wild discourse culminates in a defense of adultery and incorporates his utter loathing of the gross inequities and evils that abound. Recognizing Lear's voice, Gloucester expresses his heartfelt sympathy for his king and his own despair for humanity at the sight of this "ruin'd piece of nature." In a colloquy with Gloucester, Lear develops the theme of justice, depicting the world as a place where, in one way or another, all offend. He concludes with a short sermon on life in this vale of tears, to which all "come crying thither."

A search party lead by a gentleman and sent out by Cordelia attempt to detain Lear, but he escapes from them. The gentleman, who remains, tells Edgar that the battle between Cordelia's army and the British forces is about to be fought. Gloucester prays to the "ever-gentle gods," imploring them to grant him death lest he be driven to attempt suicide once more.

As Edgar starts to lead his father away, Oswald enters, denounces Gloucester as an "old unhappy traitor," and declares that he will kill him. The earl offers no protest, but Edgar is quick to come to his defense. To the steward, he is a peasant who is brash enough to defend a traitor and oppose a gentleman; he must desist or be killed also. Adopting a rural dialect, Edgar courteously asks that he and Gloucester be permitted to go their way. But when Oswald moves to seize the old man, Edgar warns him to stop or suffer the consequences. They fight, and Oswald is mortally wounded. Before he dies, he asks Edgar to deliver a letter to Edmund, whom he identifies as the Earl of Gloucester. Edgar reads the letter, which contains Goneril's instructions to Edmund: He is to win her as his wife by murdering Albany. From afar the sound of a drum is heard, and the loyal son leads his father away.

Cordelia expresses her profound gratitude to Kent, who has disclosed his identity to her. He explains that he cannot yet dispense with his disguise. Cordelia learns from the doctor that her father has slept long and that he may be awakened by healing music. After he is borne in on a chair, Cordelia kisses him and speaks feelingly about all that he has suffered, marveling that he had been able to survive. He awakens, and his first words show that he believes Cordelia to be an angel and himself a soul in purgatory. Slowly he regains full consciousness and recognizes his loving daughter. He starts to kneel before her, but it is she who kneels and asks for his blessing. Lear humbly asks her to forgive him and seems to find it incredible that Cordelia should be so lovingly kind to him, knowing that she, unlike her sisters, had great cause to be offended. But Cordelia insists that she has no such cause. In reply to Lear's question, Kent informs him that he is not in France but in his own kingdom. When he remains incredulous, the doctor assures Cordelia that her father's mind has been restored but that he should not be reminded of his harsh experiences.

After Lear has been escorted away, the gentleman tells Kent that Edmund is now general of Cornwall's army and that, according to rumor, Edgar and Kent himself are exiles in Germany. Kent states that no time must be lost, for battle is imminent. It will be a bloody one, the gentleman replies. Kent recognizes that he is about to reach the climax of his career as Lear's faithful subject.

Commentary

In Shakespeare's source for the subplot, the son did not hide his identity from his blinded father. Yet, although Edgar hears his father speak of him in terms of affection and make acknowledgment of great fault, he chooses to keep Gloucester in ignorance. In Act V,

Scene 3, he will admit that he should not have done so. The most convincing explanation is that which relates to structure. Edgar is not allowed to express openly his love and forgiveness at this crucial point because it is not the dramatist's intentions to provide a discovery that would lead to the sudden and complete regeneration of Gloucester, for the earl, like Lear, is shown to be pushed not to the limits of human endurance but beyond them.

Scene 1 provides one of the major examples of ironic reversal. In his soliloquy, Edgar again shows himself to be one of the patterns of patience. His last two lines provide a summary of the Stoic position in the face of adversity. He says that the blasts of nature have done their worst upon him and that he is absolved from all obligations of gratitude. No sooner has he spoken these words than the appearance of his father, blinded and "poorly led" (led as if he were an aged beggar), provides the refutation and leaves him without the spare comfort of his philosophy. Gloucester's declaration "I stumbled when I saw" is the key line in the subplot's counter-discovery—that is, of his full realization of his folly. He now has reached the depths comparable to those reached by Lear in the main plot when the king, facing the terrors of the great storm, confronted Tom o' Bedlam and recognized him as "the thing itself" and had proceeded to tear off his clothes. Gloucester, to be sure, does not lose his mind. But, recalling having seen Poor Tom, he concluded that "a man is a worm." His words echo those of Bildad the Shuhite in reply to Job: "How much less man, that is a worm? And the son of man, which is a worm?" (Job 25:6). But Bildad's words are usually taken to be a justification of divine justice. Gloucester finds no such justification; his conclusion is a devastating one: "As flies to wanton boys, are we to th' gods, / They kill us for their sport" (38–39). These lines have been held by some commentators to summarize Shakespeare's outlook in *King Lear*. But at this time, it is most reasonable to accept them as no more than Gloucester's exclamation of despair. His subsequent lines are filled with compassion—with "ancient love," to use his own phrase. He requests that his old retainer bring "some covering" for Poor Tom, for in his humanity he would have this beggar and madman set apart from the lowly worm, from animal in general. And in handing his purse to Edgar, he shows, as Lear had done, his newfound sense of distributive justice. Finally, Gloucester's lines beginning "Let the superfluous and lust-dieted man" (70) repeat in effect Lear's prayer for all "Poor naked wretches."

All this may very well be interpreted as an advanced stage in the regenerative process that should lead to Gloucester's salvation. But it is perhaps best to say, in Albany's words, "Well, well; th' event" (I. iv. 37)—that is, we shall see the outcome.

In Scene 2, Albany, who has reappeared only after the great evil has been accomplished, emerges as a vitalized champion of right, one no longer unaware of where he should stand, one ethically strong. Since Cornwall has died, he is actually the ruler of Britain, although the formalities preliminary to actual leadership cannot be observed as yet. His status now will require him to oppose France despite the fact that, as Oswald had reported, he had smiled when he learned of the invasion. The very first line in this scene, in which Goneril speaks with contempt of her "mild husband," identifies him as humane and moral. To her, of course, humanity and morality are signs of weakness; thus she describes him as being "milk-liver'd" (50), the liver then thought to be the seat of courage. Since her concept of courage and manhood is based on brute force and self-interest, her words serve to emphasize Albany's moral superiority, which no longer is cloistered. To him, Oswald, whose loyalty to Goneril has already been well established, is a sot—that is, one who willfully rejects reason and turns "the wrong side out." In his abject servility, the steward is completely baffled by Albany, who does not look forward to meeting his wife again, does not approve of Edmund's "loyalty," and rejects the view that Gloucester was guilty of treason when he sought to aid Lear.

Albany is firm in his attitude toward Goneril. "I have been worth the whistle," she says confidently, tacitly referring to the dowry of half a kingdom that she had brought to him. But he replies, "O Goneril! / You are not worth the dust which the rude wind / Blows in your face" (29-31). In the lines that follow, he sets forth a view of nature that is at one with that expressed by Cordelia, who loved her father according to her bond. He describes an organic universe in which all beings are linked sympathetically to each other as are the twigs and the branches of a tree. One's family and indeed all society are joined by this invisible bond in accordance with natural law, the abrogation of which is a monstrous act of perversion leading to sterility and death. Goneril's scornful rejection of this doctrine does not stop him; he identifies her and Regan as the vile ones whose bestial treatment of "A father, and a gracious aged man . . . a prince [king]" is unforgivable. "Could my brother suffer you to do it?" he asks (44), thus reminding one of the great moral distinction between Albany himself and Cornwall, who was not the initiator of evil but the willing accomplice.

Albany's concluding lines, beginning "If that the heavens do not their spirits" (46 ff.), are no less significant. He is saying that if there is no divine justice, the law of nature as Edmund had defined it at the beginning of Act I, Scene 2, becomes the only law. Then "Humanity must perforce prey on itself, / Like monsters of the deep." The force of the conditional clause is not to be ignored; it remains to be seen whether or not virtue will triumph in the universe of King Lear. But unlike the abused Gloucester, who in utter despair had spoken of malicious gods, ones that enjoyed the spectacle of human suffering, Albany does not lose faith in benevolent higher powers. Nor can he be charged with mere wishful thinking at this point in the action. News of Cornwall's death does suggest that the forces of evil are, at least partially, tamed: "This shows you are above, / You justicers, that these our nether crimes / So speedily can venge" (78–80). When one comes to the end of Scene 2 and hears Albany express his debt to Gloucester for the love shown the king, one may well believe that after so much agony, wisdom and goodness are in the ascendant.

Goneril's lust for Edmund does not place the slightest strain on probability in view of her concept of manliness and his amoral, pragmatic philosophy. In the mature Shakespeare of the great tragedies, lust is consistently a symbol of general moral degradation. One should not underestimate Edmund. He remains the handsome, vibrant young man whom Kent had found to appear so "proper." And he plays his role very well indeed. "Yours in the ranks of death," he replies, speaking as if he were the gentle, perfect knight rather than partner in a brutally lustful relationship. It may be well to keep this expression of bogus chivalry in mind as one follows the fortunes of these two.

The First Folio (1623) omits Scene 3, perhaps, as Samuel Johnson believed, "only to shorten the play." It has been argued that there is no need for a preparatory scene before the reunion of Lear and his virtuous daughter, nor for the gentleman's overwrought description of Cordelia, whose moral superiority is well taken care of later in Act IV. The details about the departure of the King of France are important, to be sure, but hardly require the writing of a separate scene.

The King of France must be removed from the play—and from Britain. Shakespeare simply could not have a foreign power invade the realm. Although the Marshal of France is said to remain in command of the French troops, Cordelia will use them in defense of her father. It may be added that in the final act, France's presence, along with that of Albany, would unduly complicate the resolution of the play.

As for the gentleman's description of Cordelia in Scene 3, it does emphasize the fact that she, like Edgar, is a pattern of patience, "a queen / Over her passion, who, most rebel-like / Sought to be king o'er her" (15–17). Whether such a reminder of her spiritual beauty in contrast to the ugliness of Goneril and Regan, the "dog-hearted daughters," is needed may be questioned.

Kent's expression of astrological determinism has been held to be no more than rhetorical. But it may be, like Albany's expression of belief in heavenly justice, one of the possible answers to the problem of good and evil. Considered as the latter, it points to a nature which is responsible for evil as well as good.

In Scene 4, when Cordelia describes Lear as appearing "As mad as the vex'd sea" (2), she employs a figure of speech that is consistent with his high status as a tragic hero, for once more he is identified with one of the larger elements in nature. Like all tragic heroes, he is being depicted larger than life; thus his is no ordinary madness but madness of heroic proportions that evokes not merely pity but awe and fear.

The weeds and flowers with which Lear has decked himself have been subject to much discussion. All are native to England. Four of them (rank fumiter, hardocks, nettles, and darnel) are notable for bitter taste, biting pungency, or an irritating, burning quality. Obviously each of these may be accepted as symbolic of Lear's torment. Elsewhere in Shakespeare (*Richard II* and *Hamlet* notably), weeds symbolize disease and evil. As functional images they have the same force in *King Lear*.

At least one critic who embraces the Christian salvation interpretation of the play sees Lear in Scene 4 wearing a crown of thorns, like

Christ on Calvary. This suggests that Lear represents all humanity in his suffering and that he is bearing the weight of all transgression in order to save humanity. On the other hand, it has been argued that Cordelia is the one who, in a sense, functions as the divinely sent savior. At one point, she exclaims, "O dear father! / It is thy business that I go about" (23–24). For most members of the audience and commentators, it is enough to know that Lear has come close to the extreme in his suffering and that Cordelia is the embodiment of spiritual beauty, compassion, and selflessness in her concern for the pressed old father and king. And, let it be kept in mind, she makes it clear that she may lead the army of France but contemplates no conquest of Britain. Her whole instinct is to assuage, to heal—all for "love, dear love, and [her] ag'd father's right" (28). She does not despair but keeps her faith in "man's wisdom" (8). Specifically, her reference is to medical lore, but in a larger sense she is expressing a belief that right reason can operate. Her prayer is to a nature that is benevolent and remedial if it is understood aright, in contrast to Edmund's nature and that of the evil daughters, which is red in tooth and claw. Thus she speaks of the "unpublish'd virtues of the earth" (16).

Scene 5 focuses on Albany, who, one finds, has faced a moral dilemma. He will fight Cordelia's army but has agreed to do so only with great reluctance; thus Oswald uses the phrase "with much ado" (3) and adds that Goneril is the better soldier. Perhaps the exigencies of the plot and the dramatist's awareness of his audience's attitude toward invasion of Britain for any reason explain all this. But one may assume that Albany hopes not only to repel the foreign troops but to rescue Lear and protect Cordelia.

"I grow; I prosper," Edmund had said at the end of Act I, Scene 2. How well he has grown and prospered is stressed in Scene 5 when Regan refers to him as "Lord Edmund" and as the "noble Edmund" and now competes with Goneril for his love.

Beginning at line 11, Regan says, "Edmund, I think, is gone, / In pity of his [Gloucester's] misery, to dispatch / His nighted life." In advancing the reason for Edmund's departure, she may be indulging in irony. But according to her standards, Edmund had behaved most honorably in testifying against his father; consistently then she may very well be crediting him with a worthy motive. Moreover, earlier it had been shown that these evil characters can use the language of righteousness for their own purposes.

Most important in Scene 5, however, is the evidence that evil is beginning to prey upon itself. Goneril and Regan, who had worked so efficiently together, are now established as bitter rivals for the affections of opportunistic Edmund. And even Oswald, heretofore Goneril's most willing servingman, is willing to take orders from Regan, although he is aware that the two sisters are competing with each other for Edmund's love.

In Scene 6, Edgar, now dressed, if only as a peasant, is no longer "unaccommodated man," no longer a "poor, bare, forked animal." United with his father, he can manifest his humanity. And so he does, bearing not the slightest trace of grievance against a father who had misjudged him and asking only to show his love in selfless service. From this point of view, he is, as Gloucester insists, much changed—but only in his garments since his experience as Tom o'Bedlam has not altered his original character.

Edgar's vivid description of the view from the cliffs may have been influenced by the fact that Shakespeare's company, the King's Men, visited Dover in September 1606. This has relevance not in interpreting the play but perhaps in arriving at a date of composition. Far more important are Edgar's lines: "How fearful / And dizzy 'tis to cast one's eyes so low!" (11–12). All things below seem minute, and a man appears to be no bigger than a mouse. He will look no more "Lest my brain turn, and the deficient sight / Topple down headlong" (23–24). His aim, as later lines reveal, is to save his father from despair. But his words seem to have wider applicability. Because of "deficient sight," Gloucester had erred grievously and had been led to believe that his legitimate son was bestial. He has now reached a point where his entire faith in man as the paragon of animals has been shaken.

Before he falls, Gloucester addresses the "mighty gods," belief in whom he has never lost; he acknowledges their "opposeless will" and states that he no longer can bear to suffer. This is not the Gloucester who, shortly before (IV. i. 38–39), had inveighed against malicious gods who take pleasure in tormenting humanity. When he revives, he is ready to believe that his survival is due to divine intervention, and he declares himself ready to bear all affliction patiently. In other words, he now embraces stoicism.

"Bear free and patient thoughts," counsels Edgar (80), and one is ready to believe that his father will do so. Then occurs another supremely ironic reversal, in this instance of what appeared to be a resolution to the tragic action in the subplot: enter Lear, fantastic in dress, wild in discourse. "O ruin'd piece of nature!" exclaims Edgar (137), words that sum up the view of the king as representative of all humanity, the fall of whom means that the universe itself will come to nothing. This is close to nihilism. Gloucester, who was ready to endure anything, now finds himself facing the ultimate test. His meeting with Lear brings together subplot and main plot and provides the opportunity for simultaneous comment on both.

Lear's first words in Scene 6 are a declaration that a born king can never lose his natural rights. "I am the King himself," he declares (83–84), although in appearance and speech he now is a devastating caricature of royalty. As he goes on to provide supporting details and then to include irrelevancies, there is a certain logical coherence in what he says. As a king, he alone can authorize and guarantee coinage; next, he visualizes himself giving press money, the sum paid to recruits who enter his service. This leads him to an imagined inspection of his recruits at archery practice. His mind is distracted by the sight of a mouse (which may be as imaginary as the house dogs in Act III, Scene 4) and then turns to the enmity of his sons-in-law, whom he challenges to combat and commands that his pike-carrying foot soldiers (brown bills) be brought up.

"Ha! Goneril with a white beard!" he exclaims when he hears Gloucester speak (97). And his description of his vicious daughter seems to point up the ironic reversal in their relationship. He recalls how they had agreed with everything he had said before he had divided his kingdom. Now he is aware that "'ay' and 'no' was no good divinity"—that is, a violation of biblical doctrine (Cf. James 5:12 and particularly II Corinthians 18). Through gross flattery, Goneril and Regan had taken over the prerogatives that belong to royalty, parenthood, and age in their revolt against traditional moral and religious principles. The grotesque image of a white-bearded daughter is not an inappropriate one to convey the idea of the unnatural. But Lear recalls what he once was, thus his reply to Gloucester: "Ay, every inch a King!" (109). More especially, he dwells upon what he has since learned: "When the rain came to wet me once, and the wind to make me chatter; when the thunder would not peace at my bidding; there I found 'em, there I smelt 'em out" (102–105). It is not solely that he has learned the obvious about Goneril and Regan. He has learned that he shares in the guilt of humanity. Thus he concludes, "Go to, they are not men o' their words; they told me I was everything; 'tis a lie, I am not ague-proof" (105–107). His use of the word *men*, which in this context should refer to his daughters' husbands, is not illogical since Goneril and Regan have seized the powers that belong to man. The ironic defense of adultery that follows incorporates most of what he has learned. Primarily he has learned not to be fooled by appearances; he has learned that in all societies, those who are most ostentatious in their claim to virtue may be the greatest offenders. He is, of course, wrong in believing that "Gloucester's bastard son / Was kinder to his father" than were his own daughters, but this detail points up the fact that Lear's bitter tirade does not mean that he is unaware of the common frailty of humanity.

In his colloquy with Gloucester that follows, Lear dwells upon justice. No longer are his words directed to Goneril and Regan, for he has come to the conclusion that in a society where inequality is so great, real justice is not possible. Power, as well as appetite, corrupts humanity as even a blind man can learn:

> A man may see how this world goes with no eyes.
> Look with thine eyes; see how yond justice rails
> upon yond simple thief. Hark, in thine ear: change
> places, and handy-dandy, which is the justice,
> which is the thief?
>
> (153–58)

Vices are not concealed by tattered clothes, but the robes and furred gowns hide all. And this is the society, morally bankrupt, of which Lear had been the leader. Edgar recognizes basic wisdom in the king's words: "O, matter and impertinency mix'd! / Reason in madness!" (178–79).

But most important is Lear's new conviction that man must accept his condition and know that he inevitably is subject to tragic experiences. Lear, who before his madness had implored the gods to give him patience, now assumes the role of preacher on that subject. He paraphrases biblical text (" . . . we came crying hither"—Wisdom 7:3, 5). On this "great stage of fools," existence itself means suffering, not existence modified by an act or acts of man, be they deliberate or inadvertent. Finally, his mood shifts as his thoughts return to the sons-in-law who lead troops against those of Cordelia. Now he becomes the crafty, remorseless killer.

When the gentleman attempts to bring the king to Cordelia, Lear can refer to himself as the "natural fool of fortune" (195) and even indulge in an erotic pun: "I will die bravely, like a smug bridegroom" (202). Yet even here there is reason in madness. His eroticism is not wholly irrelevant in view of his reference to physical sex earlier in the scene; more important is his tacit declaration that knowing himself to be the toy of fortune, he can accept his lot, however painful.

The gentleman remains to remind all present that Cordelia, tender and faithful to her bond, redeems nature—and therefore Lear himself—from the "general curse," that is, from Original Sin. This may be interpreted to mean no more than that all are not evil. But it helps one understand why Cordelia, pattern of virtue, has been described by some as the one whose death makes possible Lear's salvation.

The appearance of the mad Lear and his short sermon have had their effect upon Gloucester, who now prays to "the ever gentle gods" to save him from suicide, that ultimate act of despair (221–23).

At the end of Scene 6, a climactic one as far as terror is concerned, virtue is given the opportunity to assert itself actively. Edgar, truly noble, has no difficulty in dispatching that worsted-stocking knave, Oswald. Of more than passing interest is Edgar's recognition of Albany's virtue despite the fact that the duke leads the forces opposed to Cordelia's.

Lear, the "child-changed father," had been driven away by Goneril and Regan to the sound of "deep dread-bolted thunder" (33) and suffered "untun'd and jarring senses" (16). In Scene 7, harmonious music marks his restoration in the care and protection of Cordelia. The metaphor from music is quite apposite. It suggests that order has replaced chaos. In developing the idea of a higher law of nature, one that pervades the universe and makes harmony possible in all its parts, this was a familiar figure of speech during the Renaissance. Its use with reference to Lear may well indicate that he represents not just another human being, however exalted in rank he may have been, but suffering humanity in general.

Memory of the incredible cruelty that has been dramatized in the earlier portions of this play serves only to illuminate the tender, warm, selfless love that dominates here in the person of Cordelia. One can understand why some commentators have insisted upon the morality pattern as being basic to *The Tragedy of King Lear*. Cordelia's virtues shine with a heavenly radiance, just as her sister's extreme cruelty appears as a blackness that is (to borrow a phrase from the earlier Shakespeare) the badge of hell. Cordelia's one great concern is for her father. Her sense of reverence, her full awareness of the bond between father and daughter, leads her to ask for Lear's blessing. Of course it is the old king himself who stands in need of benediction. Bound on a wheel of fire, the unforgettable sense of guilt, aware of his own ignorance and imperfection, he is truly penitent and ready to make full renunciation. The wrathful, all-powerful King Lear of Act I, Scene 1, the ruler who would relieve himself of the burdens of kingship yet retain the privileges, the man who had not learned that true love is the giving of oneself, is now the soul of humility: "You must bear with me. / Pray you now, forget and forgive; I am old and foolish" (84–85). And this was the Lear who had exclaimed, "Come not between the dragon and his wrath." Surely, if ever a person were ready for salvation, it is Lear in this last scene of Act IV.

A word more about Cordelia: Her assurance that Lear has "No cause, no cause" (76) is heartfelt; it is anything but the rather smug reassurance of a person self-conscious in expression of charity. And consistently, as her prayer to the "kind gods" indicates (14–15), she is steadfast in her belief in providence and divine justice. Inevitably, most would think that such flawless virtue must triumph.

ACT V

Summary

With drum and colors, Edmund and Regan and their troops enter. Edmund sends a gentleman to ascertain whether or not Albany is resolute in his intentions to oppose Cordelia's army. Regan expresses her conviction that Oswald has met disaster. She then avows her love for Edmund and subjects him to jealous questioning regarding his relations with Goneril. Edmund swears by his honor that he has not sought or enjoyed Goneril's favors. "I shall never endure her," says Regan, admonishing Edmund not to be familiar with her sister.

Goneril and Albany enter with their soldiers. It is the former who is first heard but in an aside: She would rather lose the battle than have Regan win Edmund from her. Albany makes it clear that he fights not against Lear and those British subjects who support him but against the foreign invaders. Edmund, Regan, and Goneril are quick to endorse his stated purpose. In Goneril's words, "domestic and particular broils / Are not the question here" (30–31). Edmund agrees to join Albany in his tent for a council of war with their seasoned officers. Regan sees to it that Goneril, who is quite aware of her sister's motives, goes with her.

Albany has remained behind. Edgar, still dressed like a peasant, appears and gives the duke the letter that reveals Goneril's murderous proposal to Edmund. He urges Albany to read it before the battle and promises to return if summoned by a herald if Albany's forces defeat the French.

Edmund reappears, reports that Cordelia's army is nearby, gives Albany the estimate of its strength, and concludes that no time is to be lost. Alone, Edmund reveals his personal plans. Perhaps he may take Goneril, perhaps Regan. Once Albany has helped to defeat the French, the duke will be put to death; Cordelia and Lear will be shown no mercy.

At the sound of an alarum, Cordelia, with Lear in her care, leads French troops across a field between the two hostile camps. Edgar takes Gloucester to the shelter of a tree, asks him to pray that right will prevail, and leaves with his father's blessing. He returns with the news that King Lear has been defeated and that both the king and Cordelia are prisoners. At first Gloucester refuses to move. "A man may rot even here," he says. But Edgar again rouses him out of his fit of despair and leads him away.

Victorious in battle, Edmund enters with Lear and Cordelia, who are now his prisoners. Cordelia's sole concern is for her father, but Lear finds no cause to lament. He is completely happy in his reconciliation with his virtuous daughter. At Edmund's command, they are taken away to prison, and a captain is sent with written instructions, which, if he follows the ruthless course of action outlined therein, will bring him "noble fortunes" from a grateful Edmund.

Albany, Goneril, and Regan enter. The duke demands that Edmund turn over the prisoners to him immediately. The latter demurs, arguing that he has sent both Lear and Cordelia to a place of detention so that their presence will not influence the conscripted soldiers to waver in their loyalty to their present commanders. The aroused Albany denounces Edmund for presuming to believe that he is the duke's equal as has been evidenced by command decisions made without consultation. Regan promptly speaks up in Edmund's behalf. A bitter exchange between the two wicked sisters ensues. Regan speaks of being afflicted with an illness that makes it impossible for her to give full vent to her wrath, but she does state her intentions regarding Edmund, whom she would have as her "lord and master." Insolently, Edmund informs Albany that he can do nothing to change matters any more than Goneril can. The duke then declares both Edmund and Goneril under arrest for treason. Bitterly ironical, he tells Regan that since Edmund is betrothed to Goneril (his own wife), she must consider him as a possible husband. He then calls upon the armed Edmund to let the trumpet be sounded—the call for a champion to prove in single combat Edmund's "heinous, manifest, and many treasons." As he throws down his glove, the duke declares himself ready to fight should no champion appear. Edmund does not hesitate to accept this challenge, stating that he is ready to maintain his "truth and honor firmly." All this while, Regan, poisoned by Goneril, sickens. Albany directs that she be conveyed to his tent.

A trumpet sounds and a herald reads the formal proclamation calling for the appearance of "any man of quality or degree" whose name is on the martial lists and who seeks to maintain the charge that Edmund is a traitor. In accordance with the ritual for such a trial by combat, the trumpet sounds three times, and Edgar dramatically enters. In reply to Albany, he declares himself to be as noble as Edmund, although he does not reveal his identity. The fight begins after the two adversaries express their defiance of each other. Edmund is mortally wounded. Goneril cries out that he is the victim of treachery, but Albany sternly rebukes her and produces the letter that incriminates her and the dying Edmund. She denies nothing; rather, she brazenly states that she, not Albany, determines what is lawful. Yet so apparent is her fury that after she leaves, the duke instructs one of his men to look after her.

Edmund, aware that death is near, freely admits that he has been guilty of all charges made against him. Moreover, if his adversary is noble, he bears him no grudge. So at last Edgar reveals his identity and moralizes on much that has happened. His half brother joins him in exchanging charity for charity and conceding that the ends of justice have been served so far as he and their father are concerned.

Albany pays tribute to Edgar's "royal nobleness," which could not be disguised; further, the duke assures Edgar that at no time had he borne enmity against Gloucester and him. Edgar then tells how he had assumed the disguise of a madman and, after meeting his blinded father, had become Gloucester's guide and mentor, saving him from despair. But, he continues, after he had revealed his identity to his father and asked his blessing, the emotional strain proved too much for the old earl, whose heart, "'Twixt two extremes of passion, joy and grief, / Burst smilingly" (iii. 198–99).

Edmund is moved by his brother's story and urges him to speak further. Edgar then tells how Kent, heartbroken, had recognized him and told him what had happened to King Lear. The sound of the trumpet calling Edgar to battle with Edmund had made it impossible for him to help the grief-stricken Kent.

A gentleman enters with a bloody knife and reports how Goneril killed herself after admitting that she had poisoned Regan. Edmund appreciates the grim irony of the situation: He and the sisters who competed for his love will be married in death. Albany orders the bodies of Goneril and Regan brought in.

Kent now appears, explaining that he has come to take final leave of his king and master. "Great thing forgot!" exclaims Albany, who only now remembers that he has not received the custody of Lear and Cordelia. Then Edmund confesses that he had given orders for the hanging of Cordelia, whose death would be reported as suicide. Repentant, he hands over his sword, which will serve as a token and will be recognized by the captain as proof that the order of execution has been countermanded. An officer hurries to fulfill this mission, but before he returns, Lear enters bearing the dead Cordelia in his arms and crying out in anguish. Although he knows that she is dead, he tries to find some sign of life in her. Kent, Edgar, Albany—all three can do no more than express their sense of utter horror. The first two attempt to comfort the old king, who now turns upon all present and wildly accuses them of murder. He next speaks movingly of Cordelia's gentleness and of how he had killed the "slave" who was hanging her. Understandably in a state of confusion, he does recognize Kent but is unaware that it was Kent who had served him so faithfully after Goneril and Regan had rejected him. His discourse lacks coherence even when he is told that the two wicked daughters are dead.

A messenger reports the death of Edmund, which Albany describes as a mere trifle. The duke acknowledges Lear as ruler of Britain and states that he will seek to provide the king with whatever comfort is possible. Further, Edgar and Kent, those noble friends of Lear, will be rewarded. Words then fail him as he sees the agonized Lear bending over the body of Cordelia, still trying to find some evidence of life in her. The strain is far too much for the old king and he dies, broken hearted.

Albany designates Kent and Edgar as the ones who must now restore order and rule Britain, but Kent replies that his master calls him and that he cannot remain in this world. Edgar speaks the last lines, emphasizing all the suffering that has been depicted in *The Tragedy of King Lear*.

Commentary

Scene 1 requires little comment. Details relating to Goneril, Regan, and Edmund amplify that which has been learned earlier. Sister viciously turns against sister; Edmund, it would seem, will benefit whatever may be the outcome of their rivalry. Characteristically, he uses the language of chivalry, which is so ironic in context: His has not been an adulterous relationship with Goneril but råther "honour'd love" (8), by which is meant respectful regard; to all this he swears "by [his] honour" (14). He remains the opportunist and improviser, for he knows that his fortune is in such a state that action, not contemplation, is necessary.

Albany's dilemma, responsible for his irresolution to which Edmund makes reference, has been solved: He will defend Britain against the foreign invader, but he will see to it that Lear and Cordelia are rescued and protected.

Effective plotting makes it necessary that Edgar depart, preparing the way for his reappearance as champion of righteousness in the last scene of the play.

In Scene 2, Edgar's reminder that "Men must endure / Their going hence even as their coming hither" and his conclusion that "Ripeness is all" (9–11) take one back to Lear's preaching to Gloucester (IV. vi. 182 ff.). When Edgar concludes that "Ripeness is all," he means (as Hamlet did when he assured Horatio that "Readiness is all") that perfect readiness resulting from the master of one's passions is the only rational way for man to face life's tribulations and death itself. This, of course, is stoicism and has been considered by some to be basic to Shakespeare's interpretation of life in *The Tragedy of King Lear*. Therefore, it is time to discuss it briefly. What is to be said may be as applicable to the main plot as it is to the subplot—inevitably, since the one complements the other.

Classical stoicism held that suffering does not result from external happening but only from one's allowing such happenings to affect him adversely. It therefore inculcates the lesson of absolute control of the passions under all circumstances. The true stoic may have erred grievously or may have been the victim of adverse fortune over which he had no control; he will, then, suffer and perhaps fall to his death. But his superior control over his passions calls forth admiration and leads to a reaffirmation of the dignity of man. Classical stoicism allowed and justified suicide (Cf. Brutus in Shakespeare's *Julius Caesar*). But clearly this is not the type of stoicism that informs *King Lear*. Gloucester is not allowed to take his life; in the latter scenes of the subplot, Edgar's chief effort is to dissuade his father from self-slaughter—and this despite the fact that Gloucester has had his eyes plucked out, has been deprived of title and possessions, has been proclaimed as a traitor, and has found the king he revered subjected to madness, abject poverty, ultimate defeat, and imprisonment.

But Hebraic-Christian teaching also inculcates patience in the face of adversity, and it does not authorize suicide under any circumstances. The Book of Job, passages from which are echoed in this play, is the great source of this doctrine. It will be recalled that Job rejected the retributive theory of suffering that his friends propounded and that he called upon God Himself for the explanation of his trials and torments. Interpretations of all this vary, but the consensus is that the Book of Job teaches that man should not expect rewards for good deeds or punishment for wickedness. Job found justification only in the knowledge that he was right. Having learned this, he accepted his ordeal with firm faith: "Even though he slay me, yet will I trust him." Earlier, Gloucester had acknowledged the "opposeless will" of the gods; now he knows that he must not rail against them or rebel by taking his own life.

But it is not argued here that Shakespeare asks the audience to interpret the play in terms of stoicism alone, be it classical or Hebraic-Christian. Rather, the reader is encouraged to see how both related concepts seem to fit into the action at crucial points in this most challenging play.

In Scene 3, packed with related lines of action, Shakespeare achieves a resolution, one subject to much dispute but universally recognized as unsurpassed in magnitude. Catastrophe is the term used for the ending of tragedy; and in Renaissance tragedy this always means the death of the tragic hero. Appropriately, the subplot is brought to conclusion first. And since this subplot is so closely related to the main plot, the leading figure therein, the Earl of Gloucester, meets death. He dies "smilingly," so Edgar reports, a fact that admits to an optimistic interpretation of the entire action. Edgar reproves himself for not having made known his identity earlier and then credits himself with having taught his father to conquer despair. Well and good. But one is left with the feeling that had Edgar not delayed, Gloucester might well have survived. And if indeed the earl had rejected despair, he hardly can be credited with having achieved mastery of passion, for he died "Twixt two extremes of passion, joy and grief." Moreover, it may be argued that his conversion to the belief that "Ripeness is all" (V. ii. 11) is negated by the death of Cordelia. Perhaps there is comfort enough, at least for some, in the knowledge that Gloucester, the man who stumbled when he saw, lived long enough to attain clear vision and to prove through his devotion to Lear that life can be noble and distinctive even if rewards and punishments are distributed indiscriminately to good and bad alike.

Cordelia's first speech in the play's last scene deserves close attention:

> We are not the first
> Who with the best meaning have incurr'd the
>   worst.
> For thee, oppressed King, I am cast down.
> Myself could else out-frown false Fortune's frown.
>
>   (3–6)

The lines reveal her mastery of passion, just as they do her selflessness. But they may suggest that one's fortune is often as not independent of conduct, good or bad. But at this point in the action, the main thing is that Lear and Cordelia are united in love even if they are prisoners. "Shall we not see these daughters and these sisters?" asks Cordelia. And Lear exclaims, "No, no, no, no!" (7–8). For both, Goneril and Regan represent the world of rapacity, hypocrisy, calculation from which they are happy to escape. The fact that Cordelia does not say "your daughter" and "my sisters" points to such a conclusion. Especially for Lear, who earlier had acknowledged that Goneril and Regan were his own flesh and blood and therefore were the embodiment of his own capacity for evil, this represents a rejection of identity with the two. It is as if he were pushing the very thought of them from his mind. For those who accept the salvation theory and see Lear as the representation of humanity, he now emerges as one completely purged of error and ready for heaven. But purgation is one thing, salvation another—others have argued.

Lear's speech beginning "Come, let's away to prison" (8 ff.) has been subject to different interpretations. For some it is just tragically ironic, revealing a tragic hero who is pathetically blind to his real condition, for he and Cordelia have more than imprisonment to fear. Others, reading ideal Christian stoicism into these lines, are impressed especially by Lear's fervent declaration, "Upon such sacrifices, my Cordelia, / The gods themselves throw incense" (20–21). Here they find complete evidence of Lear's redemption, his attainment of true insight and his mastery of passion. Nor is this an unreasonable conclusion so far. Lear's words do seem to mark the culmination of his experiences—those of a ruler who had "ever but slenderly known himself"; of one who had been spiritually blind, wrathful, self-centered; of one who, forced to endure almost incredible hardships, finally learned the lessons of compassion and humility and discovered the true nature of love. Now happy in his reunion with Cordelia, he no longer needs to cry out for patience: " . . . we'll wear out / In a wall'd prison, packs and sects of great ones, / That ebb and flow by th' moon" (17–19). These two alone "will sing like birds i' th' cage" (9); they will manifest sympathy for all suffering humanity. Nor will Lear himself lose his relatively newfound interest in searching for truths, for he and Cordelia will "take upon [themselves] the mystery of things / As if [they] were God's spies" (16–17).

If Albany had succeeded in removing Lear and Cordelia from

Edmund's custody, one would not have to go beyond the limits of the play or depend upon an allegorical interpretation to see all this as evidence that virtue triumphs and man's dignity is affirmed.

Edmund's instructions to the captain are consistent with all that has been learned about him: "Know thou this, that men / Are as the time is" (30–31). The time is that of a corrupt society, and to Edmund opportunism is all. But it is Albany who now realizes fully his potentialities for the exercise of positive virtue. In moral stature he now is a towering figure. Promptly he puts Edmund in his place: "Sir, by your patience, / I hold you but a subject of this war, / Not as a brother" (59–61). After denouncing Gloucester's illegitimate son and Goneril as traitors and arranging for the trial by arms, he now acts as ruler of Britain: "Trust to thy single virtue; for thy soldiers, / All levied in my name, have in my name / Took their discharge" (103–105).

The bitter exchange between the two wicked sisters, the poisoning of Regan, and the suicide of Goneril—all this requires little comment. The two, like monsters of the deep, to recall Albany's phrase, prey upon themselves; evil destroys itself. Again it would seem that at long last, virtue will triumph, particularly so when the truly noble Edgar mortally wounds the pretender to nobility, Edmund. Indeed, the latter endorses Edgar's assertion of divine justice. Edgar says,

> The gods are just, and of our pleasant vices,
> Make instruments to plague us.
> The dark and vicious place where thee he got
> Cost him his eyes.

And Edmund replies, "Thou'st spoken right, 'tis true. / The wheel has come full circle; I am here" (170–74).

One may question Edgar's faith in such justice, which seems not to be concerned with any proper balance between crime and punishment, but the immediate point is that Edmund is about to follow in death those other incarnations of evil, Cornwall, Regan, and Goneril. Unlike his fellow criminals, he now is forthright and honest. Why? Is Shakespeare to be charged with inconsistency in character portrayal like the writer of melodrama, concerning himself only with what happens next? Certainly not. From the first, Edmund has been depicted as the opportunist who, as his asides and soliloquies made clear, did not attempt to delude himself. He knows that he has gambled and lost; he is not vindictive for the simple reason that he no longer has anything to gain. Illegitimate though he is, he nevertheless is the son of the Earl of Gloucester and, however unscrupulously, had attained the position of general of Goneril's forces. To have been bested by a commoner—worse, to have been bested by a peasant—would have been intolerable. Thus he says to Edgar, "If thou 'rt noble, I do forgive thee" (165–66).

After the intolerable delay, Edmund strives to save Cordelia before he himself dies: "Some good I mean to do, / Despite my own nature," he says (243–44). This is a new Edmund, surely. It has been reasoned that his exclamation "Yet Edmund was beloved!" (239) goes far to explain his effort to undo his last and vilest work of evil. The "love" of Goneril and Regan is the only thing he can look back on with at least a degree of satisfaction, for it may have proved to him that he was not isolated from human ties, human affection. But, of course, the irony is profound here. Both Goneril and Regan had sacrificed any claim to humanity, and Edmund himself confuses lust with love.

"The gods defend her!" exclaims Albany once it is learned that Edmund had given the order for the hanging of Cordelia. He is answered. Reenter Lear with the dead Cordelia in his arms—the last, and the most shocking reversal in this play, one that seems to point to an unmistakable denial that there are beneficent gods concerned with justice in human affairs. Unless one takes the extreme position of finding Cordelia's reticence during the love-test in Act I, Scene 1, an act of great folly for which she now has paid the price, or of assuming that she is the sacrificial victim making possible the salvation of Lear, it is difficult to believe that Shakespeare's universe is a moral one in this play. Lear lapses into madness again, as Albany's words indicate: "He knows not what he says; and vain it is / That we present us to him" (294–95). Yet it is a Lear of agonized sanity who says a few lines later, "And my poor fool is hang'd! No, no, no life! / Why should a dog, a horse, a rat, have life, / And thou no breath at all?" (305–307). These lines pose the basic problem regarding the morality of the universe. The phrase "my poor fool" has been the subject of much debate. Most modern editors are convinced that the reference is unmistakably to Cordelia. Since the term *fool* was often used in Shakespeare's day as a term of endearment, and since in the rest of the speech Lear is obviously talking about Cordelia, this interpretation recommends itself to very many readers of the play.

But there are those who are no less convinced that here Shakespeare took the opportunity to explain the sudden disappearance of Lear's court jester earlier in the play. They find some support at least in the fact that the initial *f* is capitalized in the First Folio (1623), which may be an indication that the original editors—or at least the printer—assumed that Lear's Fool, not his daughter, was referred to in this speech.

It would be comforting to believe that the old king dies convinced that his beloved daughter lives and that this conviction represents a higher truth and points to his redemption and reunion with Cordelia in a better world. But the best that can be said, perhaps, is that Lear dies a man ennobled by great suffering. Further, all the vicious characters have died violently; Albany, Edgar, and Kent—truly virtuous men—survive to sustain the "gor'd state." But Albany designates the last two as joint rulers of Britain, whereupon Kent, as it were, abdicates, forsaking this world of tribulation to follow his master in death. Edgar is left. He has survived all trials; and, especially for those who lean heavily upon the stoic interpretation, his elevation to kingship is a fitting ending to this play, one that points to the clearing of the moral atmosphere and the restoration of order. But his last two lines are rather ambiguous: "The oldest hath borne most; we that are young / Shall never see so much, nor live so long." Is it possible that he is prophesying his own death? *The Tragedy of King Lear* remains a most challenging play, one that admits to no easy solution.

1606

macbeth

MACBETH

LIST OF CHARACTERS

Duncan

A good and honest but politically naive King of Scotland; he is murdered by Macbeth, his cousin and one of his most trusted generals.

Macbeth

One of Duncan's most courageous generals, his driving ambition to become King of Scotland corrupts him and causes him to murder Duncan and order the slaying of anyone who threatens his kingship.

Lady Macbeth

As ambitious as her husband, she taunts Macbeth's courage to insure that he will murder Duncan and become king. Fear and remorse eventually cause her to go mad.

Banquo

A general in Duncan's army, he is Macbeth's closest friend. When Macbeth fears that Banquo suspects him of murdering Duncan, he arranges to have Banquo murdered. Banquo's son is Fleance.

Macduff

A Scottish general who strongly suspects Macbeth of murdering Duncan. After Macbeth has Macduff's family murdered, Macduff swears vengeance and kills Macbeth.

Malcolm

Duncan's eldest son, named as heir to the throne of Scotland; he flees to England after his father's assassination.

Donalbain

Duncan's youngest son; he flees to Ireland after his father is murdered.

Lennox

One of Duncan's nobles, he functions largely as an observer in the play. He accompanies Macbeth to the dead king's chamber and, suspicious of what he sees, grows increasingly sarcastic and fearful for the fate of Scotland.

Ross

A cousin of Macduff, he acts as a messenger in the play, bringing good news of Macbeth's military victory and bad news of Macduff's family.

Old Siward

Earl of Northumberland; ally of Malcolm and Macduff.

Young Siward

Siward's son; slain by Macbeth in hand-to-hand combat.

Seyton

Macbeth's lieutenant.

Hecate

Sometimes referred to as the queen of the witches, she presides over all nocturnal horrors; it is she who directs the supernatural happenings and appearances of the mystical apparitions.

The Three Witches

Supernatural agents of fate who prophesy that Macbeth will become King of Scotland; they also predict his fall.

Porter

The keeper of Macbeth's castle who drunkenly imagines that he is the keeper of Hell's Gate.

Menteith, Angus, and Caithness

Noblemen of Duncan.

SUMMARIES AND COMMENTARIES

Summary

The play begins near a battlefield in Scotland during a thunderstorm. Three witches meet and agree to meet again, the next time on a heath, after the storm, and there they will greet the warrior Macbeth before sunset, "when the battle's lost and won" (i. 4). In unison they wail, "fair is foul, and foul is fair" (i. 11) and depart.

A sergeant, bleeding from wounds he has received in battle, stumbles into the camp of King Duncan. He relates how Macbeth killed the rebellious Macdonwald, then joined with Banquo and gallantly withstood a fierce attack by the Norwegian king.

No sooner has the sergeant delivered his message and gone for treatment than the loyal Thane (Lord) of Ross arrives and supplements the soldier's report with news of Macbeth and Banquo's suppression of the combined efforts of the traitorous Thane of Cawdor and the King of Norway, forcing the Norwegian to sue for a truce and to pay an indemnity.

Duncan directs Ross to announce the execution of Cawdor and to proclaim the conferring of the Thane of Cawdor's title upon Macbeth.

On a heath, with thunder still rumbling, the three witches meet as agreed upon earlier. They chatter as they prepare their magic spells, one vowing to punish a sailor because his wife cursed her and refused to give her some chestnuts. A drum announces the arrival of Macbeth, and the witches complete their spell-making, dancing hand-in-hand nine times in a ring.

Returning from battle, Macbeth and Banquo see the weird sisters and engage them in conversation. The witches greet Macbeth with triple honors—"Thane of Glamis" (his present title), "Thane of Cawdor" (his soon-to-be announced title), and the prophetic "King hereafter." Macbeth cannot conceal his surprise from Banquo, who begs the witches to prophesy his future, too. They hail Banquo as "lesser than Macbeth, and greater" (iii. 66), and as "not so happy, yet much happier" (iii. 67), and they tell him "thou shalt get kings, though thou be none"(iii. 68)—that is, he will not be a king himself but will be the father of kings. Ignorant of the fact that he has already succeeded to Cawdor's title, Macbeth commands the witches to explain their greetings, but they vanish without answering him.

As Macbeth and Banquo discuss the strange predictions they have heard, the Scottish noblemen Ross and Angus bring King Duncan's greetings to his two commanders and confirm Macbeth's accession to the title, Thane of Cawdor. Banquo is amazed that the Devil (represented by the witches) can "speak true" (iii. 108).

Fascinated by the speedy proof of the witches' foreknowledge and that the first two parts of their greetings are now true, Macbeth hides his private thoughts and ambitions by asking Banquo if he hopes that his (Banquo's) descendants do indeed become kings. Banquo replies that such speculations might be tempting but that evil forces (the witches) often do reveal some minor truths, but that, more often, they cause trouble.

In his first soliloquy, Macbeth muses on what the future may hold, and he trembles when he thinks of murdering the king. Such "horrible imaginings," (iii. 139) he says, frighten him even more than "present fears" (iii. 138). But he notes the possibility that he may become king without having to kill Duncan—that is, he may become king by chance. Deciding to allow fate to direct his destiny, he then rejoins his companions.

In the royal palace at Forres, Malcolm describes to Duncan how Cawdor, despite his treachery, confessed to treason and, after gallant repentance, died with dignity. Duncan soberly comments that no one can detect a man's character by looking at his face. As he makes this statement, Macbeth and Banquo arrive. Duncan thanks his two officers for their services and promises Banquo that he will reward him as generously as he has already rewarded Macbeth.

The king then proclaims his son Malcolm to be Prince of Cumberland, in effect designating him as his successor to the throne of Scotland. When Duncan adds that he will visit Macbeth at Inverness, Macbeth realizes that the time and opportunity are ready for him to take matters into his own hands if he is to implement the witches' prophecy.

At Inverness, Lady Macbeth is heard reading a letter from her husband that describes his meeting with the witches. She immediately senses that she must encourage Macbeth "to catch the nearest way"(v. 17)—that is, she must help him murder the king at the soonest opportunity. When a messenger tells her of Duncan's proposed visit to Inverness, she invokes supernatural aid in her bloody resolutions. Macbeth's arrival gives them a chance for a brief conversation, during which they confirm their mutual understanding of what they must do that night.

Duncan, his two sons, Banquo, and other lords enter Inverness and receive a gracious and cordial welcome from Lady Macbeth. The king finds the castle very pleasant, and Banquo agrees, saying that the place is like heaven, perhaps because nearby he sees a martlet, a bird that nests in church steeples. Duncan greets Lady Macbeth as his "fair and noble hostess" (vi. 24), unaware, of course, of what his hostess has in mind for him.

In a room in his castle, Macbeth is debating with himself whether he will kill Duncan or not. There are many arguments against the murder, but his "vaulting ambition" urges him to do it. He decides that he cannot kill the king, who is his kinsman and his guest, and when Lady Macbeth comes in, he tells her that they will proceed no further.

With a series of strong appeals and reproaches, Lady Macbeth stiffens her husband's courage and determination; at last he agrees to carry through their plan to slay Duncan in a way that will make the king's grooms appear guilty of the murder.

Commentary

The opening scene establishes a brooding sense of doom. Shakespeare uses a frightening spectacle to grip his audience. There is nothing perfunctory or boring about this short scene that sets the mood of the play. We see a trio of howling, shrieking ugly hags gathered in a thunderstorm, cackling greedily over their evil plans. It is worthwhile to remember that the audience in Shakespeare's time did believe in witches, and many "witches" were tried and executed. Even the skeptics, and there were some, were unsure in their disbelief. Thus these witches, while only a part of Shakespeare's spectacular opening scene, are used by him primarily to show that for the duration of this play, ugliness, evil, and power will be united to achieve chaos and murder.

A central question is addressed by one of the hags to her sisters: "When shall we three meet again / In thunder, lightning or in rain?" (1–2). The question concerns the concept of time. Shakespeare questions all that exists in this world and possible other worlds. The question of time is a key theme of the play, from the introductory question, quoted above, to Macbeth's despairing "to-morrow, and to-morrow, and to-morrow" dirge (V. v. 19), to Macduff's triumphant entry with Macbeth's severed head clutched firmly in his hand and his cry, "The time is free" (V. viii. 55).

There is something conspiratorial about the opening of the play: We discover these hags as they end a cabal and plan their next meeting, one that will include Macbeth. With the atmospheric excitement provided by thunder and lightning and the spectacle of what is possibly a hideous parody of humans in the form of witches, the play can be said to begin in the middle of chaos. One imagines the witches to be in motion, perhaps swirling, like their whirlpool of doggerel verse, and we are not sure of the ground we stand on. The hurly-burly of insurrection combines with the "fog and filthy air" (12) of the atmosphere; the impression is one of dark mystery.

In the text of the play, the language of paradox and the quickness of the question-and-answer format carry the sense of confusion: A battle will be "lost and won" (4) before the "set of sun" (5) on a day when the sun apparently doesn't shine. The antithesis suggests a metaphysical game that is about to be played with good and evil. Events are about to transpire at a rate faster than the mind can conceive.

Scene 2 is bright and martial and its spirit is one of heroism. The regal costumes of Duncan, his sons, and the attendants would be colorful and magnificent. There is a mood of immediacy in this scene. Both the loud alarm that we hear and the sergeant's still-bleeding wounds indicate how close we are to the actual battle site. This is a vivid contrast to the preceding scene at the witches' haunt, with its atmosphere of chaos and thick, hot dust. And here again we have a contrast between the fair and foul values mentioned in Scene 1. There are fair reports about the suppression of several foul deeds, including Macdonwald's rebellion; the King of Norway's invasion; and Cawdor's treason. In addition, the sergeant's speech carries information about the fortunes of Macbeth and Banquo, which seem to change as rapidly as a spinning wheel, and the sergeant characterizes the men as being "two spent swimmers" (8), a remark that is echoed later when Macbeth is "in blood / Stepp'd in so far that, should I wade no more" (III. v. 136). This scene prepares the way for Macbeth and Banquo's meeting with the witches in Scene 3 by relating their victories and the king's reward for Macbeth. Note that the second bearer of news is Ross, a Scottish nobleman; he will bring good news to Macbeth in the next scene and bad news to Malcolm and Macduff near the end of the play. Note, too, that the man whom King Duncan considers the hero of this bloody battle will be his murderer later in the play.

Shakespeare is specific about Scene 3's being set on a heath, symbolically suggesting a formless waste, unproductive and deserted. Once again, we return to the witches. As they chant, one of them gloats over the fate she plans for an innocent sailor: She will drain him dry, she says, and he will sleep neither night nor day. In addition, she says that "though his bark cannot be lost" (24), it shall be "tempest-tost" (25). These are parallel portents of Macbeth's own future torments, particularly the insomniac image. As another parallel to the nautical prophecy, consider the two wives: The sailor's wife is responsible for his misfortunes, and, to a great extent, Macbeth's wife is responsible for his plight. As for the "bark" being not lost, a "bark" was a commonly used metaphor for a person's soul, and here in this prophecy, if we extend its meaning to involve Macbeth, the witches alone could not cause Macbeth's soul to be damned; this would need his complicity—which he will, in time, provide.

King James I, for whom it is thought that Shakespeare wrote *Macbeth*, and before whom it had one of its earliest performances, would himself write at length on the supernatural, and a sentence quoted in the Arden edition of the play displays Shakespeare's sensitive translation of the thought and spirit of his age into this drama. "The devil," King James I writes in 1616, can "thicken and obscure so the aire, that it is next about them [witches] by contracting it strait together, that the beames of any other mans eyes cannot pearce through the same, to see them."

Into this "obscure aire" of the heath, then, step Macbeth and Banquo. Macbeth's first line in Scene 3, "so foul and fair a day I have not seen," while having the literal meaning of a battle lost and won on a stormy day, also immediately echoes the witches' "fair is foul, and foul is fair" (I. i. 11–12) and places him squarely in the rhetorical pattern of antithesis: lost and won, fair and foul, sun and storm, king and crone.

When Macbeth is greeted by the witches, note how startled he is to hear his name, complete with three titles, including that of future king. This event marks the culmination of the play so far. Macbeth has reached a plateau in his life. The war is over and he has risen as far as he can reasonably expect to go. Now he hears these prophecies. He is naturally confused and understandably thrilled. When he would question the witches further, they disappear. Here and throughout the rest of the act, the rapidity in which events culminate have the dual effect of crowding and clouding Macbeth's judgment.

Both Macbeth and Banquo take the witches' prophecies seriously, but notice that Banquo's judgment is from a religious viewpoint: If the witches are indeed to be believed, they represent the Devil and may intend more harm than good. In contrast to Banquo, Macbeth is immensely pleased by the sudden reality of "the two truths" (128). He sees them as "happy prologues" (129) to his prophesied investiture. The importance of Macbeth's aside cannot be overstated. It shows us the nature of Macbeth's ambition for imperial power and that his vivid imagination controls his thoughts so completely that it seems to be reality itself. Note also his statement, "present fears are less than horrible imaginings" (139); he is foretelling his own fate: No battle, not even the one he has just fought, will be as frightening as the fear he suffers after he decides to murder the king. In his subsequent, frantic struggles to regain peace of mind, he will be plagued by the torment of his mind as it conjures up what he must do next and wracks him with an ever-present punishment of conscience.

Macbeth never commits a single, isolated rash act. His "single" or "whole" state, he implies, is about to be broken or destroyed in some way, an act that interestingly parallels the state of Scotland, torn by civil and military strife. When Macbeth causes a further cleft in the nation and simultaneously in himself, everything seems reduced to chaos. Ironically, the nation can be made whole again only by his being totally annihilated.

Banquo notices that Macbeth is "rapt" in thought, and he offers Angus and Ross the explanation that Macbeth's "strange garments" (146), his new honors, are not yet resting easily on his shoulders. The obvious irony, of course, is that it is probably not the Thane of

Cawdor's mantle but the king's itself that in his imagination is ill-fitting and causing him apparent distress. When prodded out of his hypnotic state, Macbeth responds in a curious manner. The lines "My dull brain was wrought / With things forgotten" (150–51) can be taken as either a casual, evasive lie meaning that he was trying to remember something or as an insignificant remark that reveals an unconscious truth—that is, Macbeth is saying that his mind was wracked with thoughts of being king, an ambition that he thought he had put behind him years ago. The second interpretation is by no means far-fetched given Macbeth's fertile imagination and given Shakespeare's fondness for using ironic understatement.

In Scene 4, in Duncan's palace at Forres, the prevailing mood is fair and harmonious. Even Cawdor's execution has a healing quality. The evil that seduced the once-loyal thane has been renounced; Cawdor has repented with heartfelt emotion, and the description of his confession breathes a sense of virtue triumphant into the scene. This is a highly effective framework for Duncan's reflection before he greets Macbeth. The observation that it is no easy task to detect a hypocrite and a traitor is heavily ironic, made doubly dramatic by Macbeth's sudden arrival and Duncan's hailing him as "worthiest cousin" (15).

The welcome that the king extends to Macbeth and Banquo reflects his kindness and generosity. The imagery of planting and sowing and the promises of increased honors emphasize the extent of Macbeth's later treachery, for his treason will prove far greater than Cawdor's. The scene's impression of harmony continues when Duncan, overcome with happiness, says that he will provide for the future of his kingdom by appointing Malcolm to be Prince of Cumberland, a dramatic announcement of his chosen successor. But the dark reality of Macbeth's machinations ironically accompanies every positive act of this scene, particularly when Duncan remarks to Banquo that Macbeth is going ahead of them to make certain that Duncan will be well cared for during his visit to Inverness. The audience is fully aware that Macbeth has already considered murdering the king. The scene ends with contemporary cliff-hanging suspense—Macbeth commanding the stars to hide their fires (their lights) so that darkness will hide his dark desires, and Duncan blindly trusting his fate to one whom he considers his "peerless kinsman" (58).

In his letter to his wife in Scene 5, Macbeth relates his joy at being appointed Thane of Cawdor and recounts how he "burned with desire" (3) to ask the witches more about their prophecies. He addresses his wife as his "dearest partner of greatness," (11) a revelation of his deep satisfaction with his new title and his gratitude for his wife's part in his accomplishments. Lady Macbeth immediately launches into a soliloquy on her husband's ambition to be great and reveals her concern about certain weaknesses in his character that she thinks might impede his climb to further greatness.

What kind of woman does Lady Macbeth seem to be? Her first thoughts are of her ambition for her husband and of her husband's weaknesses—his being "too full of the milk of human kindness" (16). She uses a metaphor suggesting poison when she offers to pour her spirits into Macbeth's ear. She also unknowingly associates herself with the weird sisters when she begs the "spirits / That tend on mortal thoughts [to] unsex me here" (38–39). Remember Banquo's description of the witches, who "should be women / And yet your beards forbid me to interpret / That you are so" (45–47). She further solicits the powers of darkness to take milk from her breasts as gall and to thicken her blood, thereby preventing any interfering pangs of conscience. Lady Macbeth's mention of "thick blood" recalls the "fog and filthy air" (I. i. 11) and the bleeding sergeant of a previous scene: The incantational effect of the repeated phrase of invitation to the powers of evil reinforces the overall ominous tone of her soliloquy as she begs for spirits to come to her breasts and, at the same time, asks for night to be darker than hell itself.

All this, before the entrance of her husband, seems to make the character of Lady Macbeth somewhat predetermined to assist in the fulfillment of the third part of the witches' prophecy. Note that her first response to Macbeth's letter is her absolute certainty that Macbeth shall be king: "Glamis thou art, and Cawdor; and shalt be / What thou art promised" (14–15). She will not leave her husband's future greatness in the hands of witches or chance. She herself will decide what must be done for Macbeth to be king of Scotland.

Lady Macbeth later reacts with the same excitement to the messenger's announcement that "the king comes here to-night" (29). Her line "Thou'rt mad to say it" (30) reveals her own worst desires. She is so intoxicated with her imaginings of Macbeth's being king that she is momentarily undone. Her famous speech in the form of a prayer asking evil spirits to make her monstrous is horrifying in its imagery, especially the reference to her "keen knife" (50); she speaks as if she holds the murder weapon herself. Her dreams of securing Macbeth's future are offered to her; she must act, and, if need be, she must be more decisive and more merciless than her husband.

Note that when Macbeth enters in Scene 5, Lady Macbeth still does not use the fateful word "king" but enthusiastically welcomes him as "the all-hail thereafter" (52). When she asks Macbeth when Duncan is leaving, she elicits a definite "to-morrow," (57) which she challenges with ferocious passion: "O never, / Shall sun that morrow see" (58). She then notices the expression on her husband's face and warns him to hide his feelings more effectively, to be like his predecessor, whose "mind's construction" (12), Duncan has said, did not show in his face. One wonders whether Lady Macbeth is noticing this for the first time here or whether it has been a characteristic of the great warrior—that he is not very good at "dissembling." The latter seems more likely, for Macbeth, in time to come, must gradually learn the art of the complete tyrant, including the banal, everyday hypocrisy of covering his feelings with a mask.

The seemingly light and socially gracious Scene 6 continues the ironic and symbolic intensity of Scene 5. There, Lady Macbeth referred to Inverness as "my battlements" (38); thus, we view this castle as a literal mantrap, baited for the unsuspecting Duncan. Among the other symbols in Scene 6, note that since the castle is controlled by Lady Macbeth, it can be viewed as a place of evil: She will stop at nothing—not even murder—to satisfy her driving ambition. To further emphasize the evil nature of Inverness, Shakespeare places the good king outside the castle walls, where the air is sweet and where Banquo sees a martlet on its nest. Even the bird is a symbolic counterpart to the black raven in the last scene, which, according to Lady Macbeth, metaphorically announced to her the "fatal entrance of Duncan / Under my battlements" (37–38). Thus, the castle walls become symbolic boundaries between good and evil.

In Lady Macbeth's first speech, notice the excessive graciousness that masks her premeditated hypocrisy. She appears to be innocence incarnate, for she is referred to three times as a hostess—honour'd, fair, and noble. Even Macbeth is referred to as Duncan's host, emphasizing the ironic content of this brief scene. And it is no accident that the word "love" is used twice by Banquo and three times by Duncan but never by their charming hostess.

Scene 6 occurs at night. We are leaving the natural world, and the king, often associated symbolically with the sun, will not see another day. We are at the turning point of the plot: The stars will "hide their fires" (I. iv. 50), and "thick night" (I. v. 48) will be darker than "the dunnest smoke of Hell" (I. v. 49). The fulfillment of these portent metaphors begins as Duncan enters the castle gates.

It is especially in the last scene of Act I that we see Macbeth's measure of goodness and loyalty as he struggles against the foulness of his ambition. He knows that Duncan has been a good ruler, and he is greatly concerned about the consequences of killing him. He reveals this in his first true soliloquy, the second of a series of crucial speeches (the long aside in Scene 3 was the first) in which he must choose a decisive course of action. Much of Macbeth's tragic stature will hinge on these speeches.

The seeming incoherence of this soliloquy reflects Macbeth's inability to sort through his values and feelings, and one of the reasons (though minor) that he finally decides to murder Duncan is that he does not have time enough to assess his priorities. The sense we have in the play of an inevitable rush of events adds special poignancy to Macbeth's desire to have the present deed done quickly and to have its finite consequences skirted over, ignoring any subsequent punishment. Time, as was noted at the beginning of this commentary, is a key theme.

Macbeth hesitates to murder Duncan for several reasons. First, he wishes to be sure of several factors. He wishes that the murder could be committed without any aftereffects or results; if that were possible, he would be glad to have it over with—that is, if he could be absolutely sure of success and of the end results, then he would have no qualms. But he has to consider aftereffects and consequences, one of which is a possible afterlife. "This bank and shoal of time" (6), he says, is a mere sandbank and will soon be covered by the sea of eternity—and murder is a mortal sin. But this latter threat does not frighten him terribly. He is willing to risk the possibility of damnation, for it is just that—only a possibility. It is the earthly consequences that frighten Macbeth most. The terrors of the here-and-now weigh heavily on him. How would Macbeth's new subjects react? Duncan is a much-loved king, and his assassination would be risky. Would the kingdom disrupt in chaos? Furthermore, Macbeth cannot escape present punishment if he fails, and if he succeeds, he knows that his double offense of murdering a king and kinsman, as well as a guest, will somehow "return to plague" him (9). Therefore, he has no reasons for murdering Duncan except for his "vaulting ambition," his lust for power (27).

There is something cowardly in Macbeth's arguing with himself, a petty sort of bargaining with his own fear and conscience, a situation altogether beneath a great warrior. In the third part of the soliloquy, in which Duncan's virtues so awe Macbeth that he can no longer contemplate the murder, Macbeth's character rises in our estimation. He realizes that it is ambition that drives him on, or so he tries to convince himself:

> Besides, this Duncan
> Hath borne his faculties so meek, hath been
> So clear in his great office, that his virtues
> Will plead like angels, trumpet-tongued, against
> The deep damnation of this taking-off;
> And pity, like a naked new-born babe,
> Striding the blast, or heaven's cherubim, horsed
> Upon the sightless couriers of the air,
> Shall blow the horrid deed in every eye,
> That tears shall drown the wind.
>
> (16–25)

The poetry is powerful; it embodies an agony of decision in which all the forces of nature and the supernatural seem to partake. Everything at stake in the play comes together here: Evil is pitted against Good; the witches' world of "deep damnation" (20) is pitted against the heavenly "trumpet-tongued angels" (19); the ambiguous cry of new, bleeding life in the "naked new-born babe" (21) is in stark contrast to the implied shriek of the king's "taking-off" (20) (his life being severed) and the protesting trumpet blasts.

One can reflect on the multiple associations in this section of Scene 7. Looking back, we recall the bleeding sergeant, the ominous weird sisters, the victorious trumpet flourishes, and Duncan's tears when he sees Macbeth after the battle; and looking forward, there are children, imagined with brains smashed out, or perceived in a vision, or quite real and murdered, and cries of horror, unceasing it seems, until the end of the play.

Lady Macbeth enters, apparently disturbed that Macbeth has left the king's table. She will have none of his procrastinations and excuses, and she will not accept his wishing to enjoy his new honors awhile longer before he murders the man who bestowed them on him. Thus she strikes him where he is most vulnerable. She insults Macbeth's courage and his manhood and applies the necessary "spur" that Macbeth himself lacks. The images of innocent slaughter in Macbeth's soliloquy are paralleled even in this brief, sharp exchange between husband and wife. Lady Macbeth swiftly shifts from an ultimatum ("From this time / Such I account thy love,") to a grotesque pledge of her own deep commitment to the crime:

> I have given suck, and know
> How tender 'tis to love the babe that milks me:
> I would, while it was smiling in my face,
> Have pluck'd my nipple from his boneless gums,
> And dash'd the brains out, and I so sworn as you
> Have done to this.
>
> (54–59)

Whether or not the depravity of the imagery here is explained as a bluff calculated to shock Macbeth into action, the mind that could conceive such graphic infanticide is awesome and frightful. Macbeth is so awed by the woman that he overcomes his fear and, by implication, ironically takes his own pledge to, as it were, "unsex himself": "I dare do all that may become a man" (46). He says, "who dares do more is none" (47); he does dare to do more—to prove that he is a man—and, as a result, becomes "none." He pronounces the words: "I am settled" (79). Lady Macbeth's persuasiveness has produced new courage in her husband, and that courage, he says, is manly enough to perform murder. He agrees to his wife's plan: They will offer wine to Duncan's bodyguards, and when the men have passed out, Macbeth and his wife will approach the unguarded Duncan, deeply asleep from his day's hard journey, and after they have performed their black deed, they will mark "with blood those sleepy two / Of his own chamber" (74–75). Matters are settled. Macbeth's looks, his bearing and his appearance, will "mock the time," and his "false face" will hide what his "false heart doth know" (81–82).

ACT II

Summary

It is past midnight and Banquo and his son Fleance are talking in the courtyard of Macbeth's castle before they retire for the night. Banquo confesses that he fears to sleep; he is struggling to suppress "cursed thoughts" (i. 8) about the witches' predictions for him and his heirs. When Macbeth joins them, Banquo tells him that he dreamed about the weird sisters the night before and that he is troubled about the "truth" of their prophecies for Macbeth. Macbeth shrugs off Banquo's worries, saying that he thinks "not of them" (i. 21).

After Banquo and Fleance leave, Macbeth is alone. Before him he imagines that he sees a vision of a bloody dagger; he recoils, momentarily, from his intended crime. Then, remembering his purpose and the present opportunity, he steels himself to assassinate the king. The ringing of a bell breaks his thoughts, and he starts for Duncan's chambers.

Lady Macbeth is visibly excited; she has been drinking, and stimulated by the wine, she enters the courtyard and confides that she has drugged the two grooms who are supposedly guarding Duncan. Hearing Macbeth's voice, she fears their plans have miscarried, but her husband joins her and tells her that he has killed the king: Duncan is dead.

Both are tense and nervous. Macbeth laments the blood on his hands and asks why he was unable to say "Amen" when he overheard a guest in an adjoining room say "God bless us!" (ii. 30). He also imagined that a voice cried, "Macbeth does murder sleep . . . Macbeth shall sleep no more!" (ii. 43).

Partly to steady her husband and partly to destroy evidence of guilt, Lady Macbeth advises him to wash his hands. In dismay, she then sees that he has brought the grooms' daggers with him. She tells him to return, leave the weapons with the sleeping grooms, and smear the men with blood, but Macbeth refuses to go back to the scene of the murder.

Mocking his fears, Lady Macbeth herself undertakes the task. As she goes, a loud knocking resounds through the castle. Macbeth ruefully reflects that not all the water in the ocean can wash the blood from his hands. Lady Macbeth then rejoins him and tries to calm him while the repeated knocking drives him near the point of panic.

The knocking that Macbeth heard with such agitation grows more insistent, until a drunken porter rouses himself to open the castle gate. He imagines that he is at "hell-gate" and that various sinners are knocking for admission, but the disturbers of his sleep are only Macduff and Lennox, two of Duncan's noblemen, who have come to waken the king.

While Macbeth and Lennox converse, Macduff goes to Duncan's chamber. In a few moments, Macduff returns, horrified at the assassination of the king. In mounting confusion, the king's sons, Malcolm and Donalbain, and the loyal lords learn of Duncan's fate.

Macbeth assumes an air of grief and indignation. In the excitement, he manages to kill the two grooms to "cover up" his crime, saying that rage impelled him to slay them. Lady Macbeth faints. Malcolm and Donalbain take warning and flee, Malcolm to England and his younger brother to Ireland. Banquo appears onstage and expresses indignant suspicion of treason.

Outside Inverness, Ross and an old man talk about the events that have happened and about the unnatural phenomena that have accompanied the murder of Duncan. Macduff joins them and expresses what seems to be the popular solution of the murder—that is, the two grooms slew their master. But Macduff also says that there is much gossip about the hasty flight of Malcolm and Donalbain; many people believe that they might have paid the servants to kill the king. Ross refuses to accept this theory, stating that such an act by the sons would be unnatural and senseless, for it would only deprive them of the father upon whom they depended. Macduff remarks that Macbeth's coronation has already been scheduled to take place at Scone, the ancient capital of Scotland.

Commentary

We are reminded at the beginning of Scene 1 that it is past midnight ("the moon is down"), theatrically a fitting time for murder to occur. Banquo even notes that "o'er the one-half world / Nature seems dead" (5). He observes further that there are no stars, "their candles are out" (5), and we realize that Macbeth has been granted his wish: "Stars hide your fires" (I. iv. 50) and "Come thick night" (I. v. 49). There is no doubt in the audience that there is something ominous in the air.

Again Shakespeare places Banquo and Macbeth side by side so

that their contrasting natures are evident, and yet in Scene 1 we see that even the noble Banquo is tempted by thoughts of what the witches have prophesied. His "cursed thoughts" (8) are like Macbeth's "horrible imaginings" (I. iii. 38); he rejects them when he is rational and awake, but he despairs that when he falls asleep, he is a victim of them. He cries out for "merciful powers" (7) to give him the strength to overcome the temptations of such thoughts, and his remarks heighten the tension and suspense, alerting the audience to the fact that important events are about to occur.

Macbeth's short speeches in Scene 1, prior to his soliloquy, are models of hypocrisy. When Banquo compliments him on how pleased the king is with Macbeth's hospitality, Macbeth says, in effect, that he and his wife would have done more for him had they been sufficiently prepared for his visit. His irony is arrogant: They would certainly have plotted a foolproof murder had circumstances been different, but because Lady Macbeth realized that she and her husband would have "to catch the nearest way" (I. v. 17), they have had to devise a spur-of-the-moment solution to their dreams of greatness. A few lines later, responding to Banquo's clear agony of conscience concerning his thoughts about the witches, Macbeth says that he "thinks not of them" (21). This is an outright lie. Before they part, Macbeth asks for reassurance—if ever he needs it—that he will have Banquo's support, but Banquo answers his friend cautiously; he promises his support, but only if no compromise of integrity is involved.

Movement seems to be the key to Macbeth's soliloquy in Scene 1, both in gesture and imagery. Macbeth clutches at his vision of a dagger, then halts: "I have thee not" (35). Yet his eyes fasten hypnotically on the vision: "I see thee still" (35), and ten lines later, he says again, "I see thee still" (45); this time there is blood on the dagger. He is terrorized momentarily until he turns away in rejection with a sweep of his hand and the words "there's no such thing" (47). In this famous speech, he suppresses his imagination and seizes his resolve. He casts himself into the role of a "withered murder[er]" (52), in league with the forces of night. The dagger is only a hallucination, produced by his imagination and intensified by his emotional exhaustion and strain, but for a while its vision certainly seems real enough to Macbeth.

The hallucinatory effect of his dagger vision is central to the shifting vision in the play as a whole, as indeed it is in numerous other plays in the period: Things are not what they seem, and here specifically; although the crown remains in sight, it will never truly be attained.

In the first part of this soliloquy, we see a troubled Macbeth engaged in a grotesque dance with an elusive vision suggested to him by his own frightened imagination; in the second part, its imagery suggests the pacing of a ravenous wolf; later in his speech, he speaks of setting out for Duncan's chamber and bids the "firm-set earth" (56) not to hear his steps. When he utters this, we know that he has regained his sense of purpose. He does not need Lady Macbeth's commanding encouragement any longer; he needs only to hear her bell, a signal that all is in readiness. The bell, incidentally, is an interesting metaphor: Ostensibly, it will be a reminder for Macbeth that a bedtime drink awaits him—a convenient explanation for the servant—but the audience realizes when they hear it that it is Lady Macbeth's signal that they must act. Like the symbolic raven that "croaked" to Lady Macbeth of King Duncan's entrance into Inverness (I. v. 37), this bell also announces; it is like a bell at mass, evoking blood; here are the contents of Macbeth's "poisoned chalice" (I. vii. 11), a reversal of the religious mystery, for his chalice contains not the wine of life but that of death.

In Scene 2, Lady Macbeth's nerves are on edge. Anxious for Macbeth to return, she is startled by an owl shrieking—"a fatal Bell-man" (4), she calls it, Shakespeare's reference to a bell near Newgate Prison that tolled before a prisoner was executed. She hears yet another noise, a cry from within Duncan's chamber, where Macbeth's bloody work has been briefly interrupted. But she is more concerned lest Macbeth fail to kill the king than the possibility that they have exposed their plan. An unsuccessful attempt would be ruinous.

Macbeth's entry, fresh from butchering the king, and his first quick exchange with his wife are classics in dramatic conciseness. The fast-paced dialogue sets an irregular pace, like a racing heartbeat, connoting anxiety and confusion, and is strikingly dramatic during these first moments following the murder. Momentarily, Shakespeare elevates the central characters into two satanic figures who pledge themselves to wickedness in monumental poetry, then he shrinks them into two frightened and bickering conspirators. Colossal and awe-inspiring though they may be, Shakespeare seems to be saying that evil is also banal and petty. Note the way that Lady Macbeth, always more practical than her husband, attempts to calm him almost as a mother would calm a frightened child; she reassures him that it is merely the dwelling on the deed that so disturbs him: "Consider it not so deeply" (30), she says.

But Macbeth is overwhelmed with fear, guilt, and remorse: "I am afraid to think what I have done; / Look on 't again I dare not" (50–51), he says. He knows that he will no longer enjoy peaceful nights of "innocent sleep, / Sleep that knits up the ravell'd sleave of care" (36–37)—that is, calm, uninterrupted sleep that straightens out (the Elizabethan definition of "knits up") the tangled threads of worry and care. Once he asked for darkness; now he must live in it. Sleep is denied him, as is the light of heavenly grace; his inability to pray marks the finality of his separation from God. In contrast, throughout most of Scene 2, Lady Macbeth exhibits full self-control and immediate practicality. "A little water clears us of this deed" (67), she reassures her husband, comparing her bloody hands with his after having herself smeared the grooms with blood. Her advice to the "worthy thane," her husband, is to wash his hands, as if that could help a man who has "murder'd sleep" (36). But the washing of their hands, a practical necessity as Lady Macbeth insists, is a symbolic impossibility, as Macbeth sees.

Lady Macbeth tells her husband that everything is simple: There is no reason to lose his firmness. Control yourself, she urges, and do not lose yourself in thoughts about the crime, to which Macbeth replies that it would be better to lose himself in thought and lose all sense of who he is rather than realize and brood about what he has done. Macbeth's reward for killing his kinsman is remorse and self-loathing; he seems more afraid of himself than of discovery. The nervous tension of the scene is remarkable, stretched between fear of discovery and failure, Macbeth's horror of the deed, the flickering evidence of supernatural presences, and Lady Macbeth's bloodless resolve. It is a study in masterly construction.

It is perhaps because Lady Macbeth is a person less prone to wild imaginings that she seems relatively dispassionate in these circumstances and, for this very reason, even more horrifying than her husband. Remember at the beginning of the scene that the stimulus for her being startled was not internal anxiety—that is, an owl shrieked; it was no hallucination suggested to her imagination as was the dagger to her husband. And when she was confronted with the sleeping king, she says that she could not kill him "only because he resembled / My father as he slept" (13–14). But she can coolly and clinically take up the daggers and, if need be, further butcher Duncan's corpse and smear his blood on the grooms' faces. Her own hands drenched in blood, she reiterates her advice to Macbeth not to be "lost / So poorly in your thoughts" (71–72). Against Macbeth's shaken state, his wife imposes her hard-boiled intelligence with its rejection of the imagination as illusion. But even as she speaks, there is a clamorous knocking from the south gate, disturbing any chance of peace and signaling the torment of the rest of their days. She charges Macbeth with some sound precaution: Someone is at the gates; get on your nightgown lest we are called on, she says; after all, we are hosts.

In most of Shakespeare's plays, subplots and comic episodes interrupt to relieve or diversify the main action. In *Macbeth*, the speech of the porter in Scene 3 is the single example in a play that is otherwise austerely to the point. Shakespeare borrows the porter from the medieval "Harrowing of Hell" plays, and like the porters in those plays, this one is drunk, and the imaginary dead sinners whom he invites in all have key aspects of their characters that parallel flaws within Macbeth. The greedy farmer, for example, suggests Macbeth's greed for greatness—and to both, their reward will be despair; the equivocator refers to one to whom "foul is fair," and Macbeth is certainly a master of "double talk"; and last, the tailor who enriched himself by stealing is an obvious reference to Macbeth's plottings. Of all the three sinners, however, it is probably the equivocator who most closely resembles Macbeth. The ultimate equivocation with oneself and its final end result would be a sort of living damnation. This is Macbeth's predicament in a nutshell. Particularly in the latter part of Scene 3, we see Macbeth doomed, divided against himself in such a way that every word he speaks emanates from him, and yet not from him, strangling him and condemning him in the articulation that he is compelled to perform; it is a kind of swearing "in both the scales against either scale" (9–10), the metaphorical scales resting within Macbeth himself. One thinks here specifically of Macbeth's speech after the murder has been discovered:

> Had I but died an hour before this chance,
> I had lived a blessed time; for, from this instant,

There's nothing serious in mortality:
All is but toys: renown and grace is dead;
The wine of life is drawn, and the mere lees
Is left this vault to brag of.

(96-101)

On the surface, he is playing the hypocrite, expressing sudden and urgent grief for the king he has murdered; unconsciously, however, he is damning that hypocrite and pronouncing a true and ironical verdict on himself. He did die an hour before—when he plunged the blade in; and for him, from now on, nothing is serious in mortality; there's nothing worthwhile in life for him any longer.

Leading up to this speech and to the discovery of the murder is the brief exchange between Macbeth, Lennox, and Macduff. Note the way in which Macbeth addresses himself to them. Following the merry and entertaining porter, Macbeth's speech and manner are noticeably abrupt and cold. He is numbed by what he has done and in such a state of extreme nervous tension that he can utter hardly more than two words at a time: To Lennox's extended evocation of the tempestuous night that has just passed, which ends with the words, "some say, the earth / Was feverous and did shake" (65-66), all Macbeth can say is "'Twas a rough night" (66); the murder keeps his lips sealed in the first part of this scene, but with the announcement of the assassination and the ensuing general alarm, he turns suddenly, absurdly, eloquent. It would not be farfetched to say there is something almost schizophrenic in his behavior. That his new eloquence is madness and dangerously close to self-condemning truth is shown by the fact that Lady Macbeth resorts to a less ambiguous type of playacting to prevent him from speaking too wildly: She faints at the point in Macbeth's speech describing the murdered king, perhaps because he is showing something akin to guilty panic rather than deep-felt loss and concern. In the forthcoming banquet scene, she will again try to distract attention from her "mad" husband.

An analysis of the tone of Macbeth's speech and the phrases he uses leading up to the point where she faints reveals how serious his distraction and his inner conflict really are. The "hideous trumpet" (87) of words and sounds, with bells ringing, forms a continuity with the ominous knocking at the gates from the end of Scene 2 into Scene 3 and echoes Macbeth's expressed fear in Act I that angels would plead "trumpet-tongued, against / The deep damnation of his [the king's] taking-off" (I. vii. 19–20). When Duncan's sons, Malcolm and Donalbain, enter the scene and ask, "What is amiss?" (102), Macbeth answers them, but he does not answer with plain words that would state the facts; instead, he answers the king's sons with a nimble play on words: "What's amiss? You are" (102)—that is, the sons are amiss, missing a father. Malcolm and Donalbain are incomplete without their father, the source of their life. The phrase, metaphorically, also applies to the entire nation, which is now without a leader and, obliquely, to Macbeth, who is "amiss" within himself, cut off from the moral source of his own life.

In dramatic contrast to Macbeth and Lady Macbeth in the latter part of Scene 3, then, are Duncan's two sons and, most importantly, Banquo. While Macbeth loudly displays his feelings, however ambiguously and ironically, they remain muted in their expression of sorrow. Banquo is abrupt, even reproachful in his answer to Lady Macbeth when she reacts to the murder:

Macduff:	O Banquo, Banquo,
	Our royal master's murder'd!
Lady	
Macbeth:	Woe, alas!
	What, in our house?
Banquo:	Too cruel any where.

(91–95)

To Macbeth, Banquo says nothing here; instead, he pledges "In the great hand of God I stand; and thence / Against the undivulged pretence I fight / Of treasonous malice" (136–38). And Macbeth concurs, along with the rest, with another ironical invocation of his manhood: "Let's briefly put on manly readiness, / And meet i' the hall together" (139–40). Malcolm and Donalbain, who should be moved, cannot even show the resolve that Macbeth broadly exhibits. Their exit at the end of the scene, the first in a series of departures from Scotland, represents the beginning of the end of normal life in the country. Not until their return in Act V can the storm in Scotland be quieted and order be restored to the kingdom.

The final scene of Act II rounds off the act by dealing with the immediate results of Duncan's death. It is sort of an interlude that precedes the coronation and the tragic events still to come. The old man whom Ross talks to is probably meant to represent the people of Scotland, those who are affected by the action of the play, although they are not part of it. It is an important enlargement of the scope of the action if we are aware of these people whose lives and fortunes are determined by their rulers. In addition, the old man, because of his age and his Christian character, represents an orderly and godly civilization—that is, he speaks from the point of view of balance and moderation. In talking with Ross, he comments on the unnatural deed that occurred, and although he describes a troubled, natural world (the dead king's favorite horses have suddenly gone wild and devoured each other, and mousing owls have attacked and destroyed a falcon), he himself seems to embody a calm, almost tranquil wisdom after the savage hysteria of the previous scene. His opening words, "Threescore and ten I can remember well" (1), offer a new perspective, a sense of continuity with the past in contrast to the "hurly-burly" rush of events in the play so far. The audience needs this scene to catch its emotional breath and reflect on the events just passed.

The second half of Scene 4 begins with Macduff's entrance. He remarks that it's most likely that Macbeth will be named the new sovereign and is surprised to learn that Macbeth has already been named successor; Ross himself will soon leave for Scone, the site of the coronation. Macduff says that he leaves for his home in Fife and, before leaving, observes that they may not be as happy under the new regime as they were under the old. One suspects some sort of antagonism between Macduff and Macbeth; perhaps this is the reason for his remark and for his hasty departure. There is also a possible ambiguity in the old man's concluding line; he has silently observed the guarded exchange between Macduff and Ross and responds to the latter's "Farewell, father" (39): "God's benison go with you; and with those / That would make good of bad, and friends of foes!" (40–41). Although this could be taken as a straight-forward blessing, the atmosphere of mistrust and conspiracy in the play, evident even in apparently innocuous exchanges, would make it not inconceivable that the old man might direct his lines to Ross as a petty time-server and toady of the royal court: "make good of bad, and friends of foes!" (41).

Macbeth has achieved his desire but now must enjoy it in the company of his outraged imagination, his country's disturbance,

Banquo's unblemished virtue and integrity, and the suspicious enmity of Macduff.

ACT III

Summary

In the palace at Forres, Banquo reflects on the fact that Macbeth has acquired all the titles with which the witches hailed him, and he is rather inclined to suspect his old comrade of foul play. He also recalls the witches' prophecy about his own descendants, but he gives no indication of taking steps to promote his ambitions for them.

Macbeth and Lady Macbeth, now arrayed as king and queen, enter with a procession of attendants. Through a series of clever questions, Macbeth finds out Banquo's plans for the day and who will be with him.

In a soliloquy, Macbeth expresses his fear of Banquo, whose integrity and principles he recognizes as nobler than his own; he also hates Banquo because the witches have declared that Banquo's heirs will someday gain the throne that Macbeth has seized. For these reasons, he is determined to get rid of both Banquo and Fleance.

When a servant enters with two murderers for whom Macbeth has sent, Macbeth poisons their minds against Banquo, wins their promise to kill both father and son, and insists that they must carry out the crime in such a way as to keep him free of blame.

In another room, Lady Macbeth, aware of her husband's growing fears and oppressing guilt of conscience, attempts to strengthen his resolution and to renew his courage.

Outside Forres, a third, unidentified murderer joins the first two as they ambush Banquo and Fleance. They succeed in killing Banquo, but in spite of their elaborate preparations, Fleance escapes.

In the banquet hall, Macbeth and Lady Macbeth are welcoming their guests. One of the murderers comes to the door and reports to Macbeth what has occurred; Macbeth is delighted to hear of Banquo's death, but he is dismayed to learn of Fleance's escape.

Lady Macbeth urges her husband to welcome his guests, and Lennox asks him to take his seat at the table. But when Macbeth looks for the empty place, he sees a vision: Banquo's ghost glares at him. Terrified, Macbeth addresses the ghost in words that make his part in Banquo's death increasingly more evident to all who are present. Thinking that her husband is prey to his overactive imagination and realizing the damage that he is doing to his reputation, Lady Macbeth declares that he often suffers from such seizures and orders the guests to depart immediately.

As soon as they are alone, Macbeth calls Lady Macbeth's attention to Macduff's absence and tells her that he keeps paid spies in the households of all of Scotland's lords. He also states his intention of consulting the weird sisters again, for he now places great faith in their powers to reveal the future.

In bitter self-recrimination, he tells Lady Macbeth that he has been responsible for spilling so much blood that there is no turning back. "Returning were as tedious as go o'er" (iv. 138), he says. She insists that he is merely tired and needs sleep. Macbeth agrees but says that he will sleep more to strengthen himself for future deeds of violence than to revive from those he has already committed.

In Scene 5, Hecate rebukes the three witches for dealing with Macbeth without consulting her and gives them instructions for their next meeting with Macbeth.

Back at Forres, Lennox, talking with another lord, makes the point that all who have consorted closely with Macbeth have suffered for it. He believes that Malcolm, Donalbain, and Fleance would pay dearly if Macbeth could get his hands on them.

Lennox's companion tells him that Macduff has gone to England to assist Malcolm in enlisting aid from King Edward against Macbeth.

Commentary

In Scene 1, the conversation between Macbeth and Banquo is double-edged; although it seems pleasant enough on the surface, there is an undercurrent of evasiveness and suspicion on Banquo's part and an intention to manipulate on Macbeth's. The "indissoluble tie" (17) that binds them together, one imagines, is probably a sense of evil, first encountered jointly in the presence of the witches and subsequently felt inwardly. Perhaps, however, Banquo might unknowingly be referring to something as basic as temptation, for prior to Macbeth's entry, Banquo seemed to be toying with temptation in a speech that reminds us of the witches and of Macbeth's lines, "This supernatural soliciting / Cannot be ill . . . Why hath it given me earnest of success, / Commencing in a truth?" (I. iii. 131–33). Recall, too, that in Act II, Scene 1, Banquo revealed that he, like Macbeth, was tempted by the witches' prophecy. He does reject them, but it is clear that temptation is so strong that he fears to fall asleep. Banquo is a good man, basically, but because of present circumstances and because he is human, he is subject to temptation. Of particular significance, then, in this scene is the revelation that Banquo's lines here do not contain the sterling resoluteness and integrity that he declared after the discovery of Duncan's murder.

In Macbeth's soliloquy, the atmosphere of envy and distrust is extended and intensified. He says that compared to Banquo, his own "genius is rebuked" (55)—that is, the controlling genius or spirit that directs his acting is abashed, or put to shame. In Macbeth's words about Banquo's "royalty of nature" (49), one recalls a previous soliloquy in which he wrestled with the temptation to murder Duncan (I. vii. 16 ff.). Furthermore, he recognizes Banquo's valor and wisdom:

> . . . in his royalty of nature
> Reigns that which would be fear'd! 'Tis much he
> dares;
> And, to that dauntless temper of his mind,
> He hath a wisdom that doth guide his valour
> To act in safety.
>
> (49–53)

There is, however, a considerable distance between the two sentiments, for whereas the first speech had at least some basis in conscience, the second is motivated by fear and envy, both debasing emotions.

Notice the progression of tone in the speech. As Macbeth convinces himself, or, rather, reaffirms to himself, that Banquo's sons are prophesied to inherit the throne, he grows steadily more agitated and impassioned. The line "no son of mine succeeding" (163) is anguished, coming from a man without sons himself—thus far—and from one apparently who is sensitive about his "manliness." Macbeth continues further, stressing "Banquo's issue" and the "seed of Banquo." Macbeth has virtually sold his soul, given it to the Devil, the "common enemy of man" (68), and his fighting spirit is showing; he will do whatever he must to prevent anyone, even after his death, taking what he has received in exchange for that soul: "Rather than so, come fate into the list, / And champion me to the utterance!" (70-71). Macbeth once vowed to submit his destiny to fate, but he has changed his mind. He killed Duncan deliberately and with premeditation. Chance did not crown him; he committed the murder himself, and the thanes elected him king because he was the natural successor after Malcolm's flight to England. If the witches represent fate and declare that Banquo's descendants should reign, Macbeth denies the possibility of that prophecy. In the same spirit of defiance that Romeo utters when he defies the stars after Juliet's death, Macbeth too defies fate. The throne he has gained is not enough; it is "fruitless" and "barren." Thinking about the brevity of his sway, he desires to extend it into the future—by means of the descendants he expects: "Bring forth men children only" (I. vii. 72); thus will Macbeth triumph over time and fate.

Macbeth then abruptly changes his tone on the entrance of the two murderers he has sent for: The progression of his temper has been mercurial—from a seething, controlled anger when thinking of Banquo, then a startling and harsh command, and now, quite surprisingly, a beguiling and smooth manner with his hired killers. Why does Shakespeare dedicate so much stage time, in his shortest play, to what seems to be a purely "plot" scene? What do we learn about Macbeth in Scene 1? Macbeth enters into a deceitful persuasion of the two murderers with considerable relish, marshaling rhetoric, insinuation, and a veiled promise of favor until he sees he has won them; then he cuts them short, dismissing them with a great air of self-satisfaction.

Macbeth's character is undergoing a change in Scene 1; or, rather, we are shown the results of a change he has undergone. He is exercising his powers of manipulation over people, a necessary skill for a tyrannical ruler. We listen to Macbeth rehearsing his own previous arguments (and those of his wife) on the murderers, arguments that significantly focus on "manhood," and we hear the murderers reply in words not unlike Macbeth's—for example, "I am reckless what / I do to spite the world" (109-10). The effect is a kind of capsule recapitulation of Macbeth's metamorphosis, superimposed upon his present self.

The special fascination in Scene 2's short domestic interlude lies in the fact that it shows an almost tender moment between Macbeth and his queen. At the same time, it shows the inevitable decay of any relationship that there might have been between them. Disorder and division still follow the royal couple. As soon as Macbeth is no longer engaged in his intrigues and tries to relax, he finds that he cannot live with himself. Lady Macbeth, too, is gnawed by discontent ["Nought's had, all's spent / Where our desire is got without content" (4-5)]. Furthermore, she is lonely. She sends a servant for Macbeth in order to have a few words with him, for she no longer knows what is happening, especially now that Macbeth seems to be brooding excessively over the murder of Duncan. But she still asserts her resolute common sense, although in the face of her undefined discontent, it is beginning to sound a little hollow.

Then we learn what the new spur is that drives Macbeth into new action: fear of suspicion by day, terrible dreams by night [not true sleep "that knits up the ravelled sleave of care" (II. ii. 37)]. Macbeth is "tempest-tost" (I. iii. 25), and because of his fear and his wife's, they are united as they try with words to comfort one another: "Be bright and jovial among your guests tonight" (28); "So shall I, love; and so, I pray, be you" (29). But there is in all this a kind of equivocation; first, they engage jointly as a couple anxious to evade the true horror of their past actions; and second, as individuals they become more and more isolated. At one point, in language reminiscent of his wife's earlier advice, Macbeth describes to Lady Macbeth the sort of performance they will have to give. They will have to "make our faces vizards to our hearts, / Disguising what they are" (33-34). In this, Macbeth echoes an image related to certain words of Lady Macbeth in Act I: "look like the innocent flower, / But be the serpent under 't" (I. v. 66-67).

Becoming angry, as he did in a previous soliloquy at the thought of Banquo, and despite the murder plot, Macbeth seems possessed and cries, "O, full of scorpions is my mind, dear wife!" (36). Then suddenly he becomes calm as his wife reminds him of Banquo's mortality and the sentence of death that "Nature" has passed on him. Could Macbeth momentarily have forgotten his pact with the killers? Can he be fearful lest they fail? Could his conscious mind have repressed the truth? Could he be trying to hide his newest treachery from her in order to protect her from further anxiety? Not one of these possibilities fully explains what Macbeth is doing here, but they do indicate the range and depth of confusion in his soul.

A perfect counterpoint to Macbeth's doubtful aspect and ominous words is his wife's surprised awe and admiration for Macbeth's affirmation of her former sentiments. In Act I, she prayed that her blood would be thick and that night would be even darker than hell. Here at the end of Act III, Scene 2, Macbeth bids, "Come, seeling Night, / Scarf up the tender eye of pitiful day; / And, with thy bloody and invisible hand / Cancel and tear to pieces that great bond / Which keeps me pale! Light thickens" (46–50). We see Macbeth hurling himself toward chaos ("Let the frame of this disjoint") as if by tearing the universe apart he could root out the source of his afflictions. The tone of his voice and the true horror of his meaning affect his wife visibly, he notes—so much so that he is moved to say to her, "Thou marvell'st at my words" (55).

Particularly in his last two speeches of this act, Macbeth expresses his new fascination with evil, and his speeches gather poetic echoes of the play's symbols: the creatures of night, Hecate, and beasts of prey. And yet another sinister invocation of darkness, in addition to his former "Stars hide your fires" (I. iv. 50) and "Come thick night" (I. v. 49), affirms Macbeth's resolution. Macbeth seems now to be in full control of his and Lady Macbeth's dark future, and, like other Shakespearean villains, he is willing to take the rest of the universe with him.

Scenes like Scene 3 of Act III are not dramatic literature; they are merely a part of plot progression or narrative continuity. The scene, which contains a hastily performed murder, begins in the midst of a conversation between the two murderers. A third murderer has appeared to join the two conspirators, and he utters the name "Macbeth" when asked who sent him. By doing so, he evokes for us the presence of the newly crowned tyrant. The conversation continues briefly and serves the dramatic function of giving the audience time to focus on what is about to happen: Suspense, in however brief a scene, has to be built on anticipation.

The murderers do not have to wait long. They see Banquo approaching and hear him cry out to a servant to light his and Fleance's way. They note that Fleance takes the torch and that the servant leads the horses to the rear of the castle. Macbeth, it would seem, has suggested that the murder take place after Banquo and Fleance have dismounted, which allows the use of fewer assailants—and also avoids bringing horses onstage. Banquo's casual remark about "rain to-night" (16) shows that he is off-guard and informs the audience of the cloudy sky—in harmony with murder. Furthermore, it is dusk when the murder is committed, and the waning light continues the mood and metaphor of Macbeth's last words in Scene 2: "Light thickens, and the crow / Makes wing to the rooky wood; / Good things of day begin to droop and drowse, / Whiles night's black agents to their preys do rouse" (50–53).

Ironically, it is because Fleance's torch is extinguished that he manages to escape. The murder of Banquo, thus, is accomplished in blackness, under the cover of chaos, a force that has been steadily building since we heard the noise of a storm and the cackling cries of the witches at the beginning of Act I.

The stage direction "Banquet prepared" opens Scene 4. This miming show of activity by the attendants preparing and setting tables, combined with the ordered entrance of lords and ladies, as Macbeth instructs, "You know your own degrees" (1), establishes a harmonious mood and provides a dominant visual image of peace and good order. What we have in reality, however, is an elaborate picture of false order that will soon collapse into disorder and chaos, for hardly before the banquet gets underway, a man with "blood upon [his] face" (12) calls the king aside. Before long, the gathering will break up in chaos, with Lady Macbeth hurrying her guests away and urging them to "stand not upon the order of your going" (119), an obvious metaphor for things to come.

The style of conversation in the opening of Scene 4 is conventional, with royalty receiving compliments and, in turn, making gracious and clever remarks, duly applauded by the assembled company. Lady Macbeth, in particular, is adroit in her hypocrisy as she gently and punningly chides her husband for standing apart (with the returned murderer):

> You do not give the cheer. The feast is sold
> That is not often vouch'd, while 'tis a-making,
> 'Tis given with welcome. To feed were best
>   at home;
> From thence, the sauce to meat is ceremony;
> Meeting were bare without it.
>
> (34–38)

In other words, Macbeth should make the guest (the murderer) feel at home; unless he does, the guest will feel like he is paying for the feast; as for more eating, one could do it better at home. All of this sparkling wit is a prelude to notable disaster for Macbeth and will mark the end of his dream of security.

Like his wife, who is playacting the role of gracious queen and hostess, Macbeth is also playacting during the banquet, trying out another of his roles; now he is a generous host to his loyal subjects, just as he had previously tried to be a calculating diplomat while wooing the disgruntled murderers. From other preceding actions, we know that King Macbeth's crown sits uneasily on his brow, so his "performance" at the banquet might naturally seem strained; his real interest, we know, is his security—hence the eagerness with which he questions the murderer, and therefore also the reason, as we soon learn, for his keeping a servant "fee'd" in every house.

Of riveting interest in this "public" scene is the mental state of Macbeth himself—the contradiction between what he is playing and what he is—between "anon we'll drink a measure / The table round" to the company, and his next line, spoken to the murderer: "There's blood upon thy face." It was suggested in Scene 2 of this act that he may unconsciously have been repressing thoughts about his machinations to kill Banquo; here in Scene 4, the counterpart may be true: His unconscious sense may be forcing him to acknowledge his murdered friend—that is, there may be a deeply ironic sense in which Macbeth means exactly what he says, despite himself, when he invokes Banquo the first time: "Here had we now our country's honour roof'd, / Were the graced person of our Banquo present" (39–40). Although on the surface he is being patently hypocritical, as he was when he "acted out" his grief at Duncan's death, he is also inviting the instrument of his own punishment.

The man who populated his country with spies first reacts to the apparition by accusing his guests: "Which of you have done this?" (49). Next, in a rather cowardly fashion, he disclaims responsibility for the murder: "Thou canst not say I did it" (51). One can imagine the reaction of Lady Macbeth and the guests as Macbeth loses control of himself here, for they see nothing whereas Macbeth sees the apparition. His breakdown disturbs his wife, for she imagines that Macbeth is still being haunted by Duncan. She quickly reverts to her earlier, chiding role ["Are you a man?" (58)] and accuses him of being over-imaginative and weak.

Macbeth seems to steel himself slightly to the presence of the ghost when he challenges it: "If thou canst nod, speak too" (70). Following this, once he has regained his composure, Macbeth defies fate once more. His invitation to Banquo to return is more direct this time: "Would he were here!" (91). His disorder and his challenge to any foe except an "unreal mockery" end with the words "Why, so; being gone, / I am a man again" (108).

In his marginal notes to Macbeth, Coleridge makes an interesting observation about Macbeth's state of "manhood" in this scene. He comments, particularly about lines 122–26, that he "who by guilt tears himself live-asunder from nature is himself in a preternatural state; no wonder, therefore, if [he is] inclined to all superstition and faith in the preternatural."

Macbeth concludes Scene 4 with two things in mind: Macduff and a determination to return to the weird sisters, to the supernatural. Macduff's absence means that he will now succeed Banquo as Macbeth's prime foe. And to cope with this new threat, Macbeth must seek out the witches. His is a grim determination, coupled with a dark realization that he is beyond hope: "I am in blood / Stepp'd in so far that, should I wade no more, / Returning were as tedious as go o'er" (136–38). He has indeed eaten his "meal in fear," and he goes off to bed still condemned to sleeplessness. In images of things as basic to everyday life as food and sleep, Shakespeare conveys the gradual but total disintegration of Macbeth.

Some critics believe that Scene 5 was probably inserted by some other writer than Shakespeare—perhaps Thomas Middleton, whose play *The Witch* makes similar references to loving and bribing witches, points that Shakespeare most likely would never have made. Also, Hecate (the goddess of witchcraft) speaks in iambics, accenting the second syllable of each two-syllable foot, whereas Shakespeare's supernatural characters usually use trochaic speech, with the accent on the first syllable of the foot.

Whoever the author, Scene 5 is largely spurious, as its language seems below Shakespeare's standards and its music and dancing seem awkward at this point in the tragedy. Yet, an interesting, incidental fact is that when this play was presented to a Restoration audience, it was precisely this scene that Dr. Johnson labeled "enchantment."

As the authenticity of this scene cannot be proven or disproven, it is finally up to each reader to decide whether or not it fits Shakespeare's tragedy. In all fairness, it must be said that Shakespeare was capable of writing poor verse on occasion, that he does indicate something like dance elsewhere in the play, and that sententious statements like the one on human presumption (30–33) are commonplace in the drama of the period.

The final scene of Act III is devoted to the state of affairs in Scotland, as seen by observers rather than by participants, and in this it resembles Scene 4 of Act II, the scene with Ross and the old man, outside Inverness. As Lennox speaks with an unidentified lord, we are conscious of a most eloquent irony in his opening speech. Clearly he has talked with this particular man before and expects the man to draw his own conclusions about Duncan's and Banquo's murders from the abundant hints available. Lennox is concerned that Macbeth's sole proof of Duncan's sons' guilt lies in their flight. He strongly hints in line 16 that Macbeth's real motive in killing the grooms ("the two delinquents") was to keep them from talking, and he further insinuates that the grooms could not have killed Duncan, for they were in a drunken stupor. Even Macduff hides "in disgrace" (23) because he failed to appear "at the tyrant's feast" (22). The word "tyrant" is noteworthy here, for it replaces "king" and further separates Macbeth from his Scottish subjects.

From here until the end of the play, there is a high proportion of these public scenes, ones in which the state of Scotland—"our suffering country"—is discussed and in which plans are laid for the overthrow of Macbeth. The individual tragedy is brought into balance with the larger issue of the state of the country.

Lennox's review in Scene 6 of the fathers killed and sons fled and of the dubious behavior of Macbeth serves to bring the tyrant's acts under a kind of public scrutiny. It presents a consideration of the tyrant's heinous deeds followed by a reference to Macduff, the possible instrument of his nation's vengeance and of his own terrible personal revenge:

> But, peace! for from broad words and 'cause he
> fail'd
> His presence at the tyrant's feast, I hear
> Macduff lies in disgrace. Sir, can you tell
> Where he bestows himself?
>
> (21–24)

The lord has hopes that Macduff may rally sufficient forces in

England to challenge Macbeth, and in his answer to Lennox, he places the struggle on a religious footing, between the evil Macbeth and "the most pious Edward . . . the holy king" (27–30). He also refers us back in time to the false communal banquet scene, when he invokes "Him above" (32) "To ratify the work we may again / Give to our tables meat, sleep to our nights, / Free from our feasts and banquets bloody knives" (33–35).

In addition, an interesting shift occurs in the characteristic imagery of speed, which so dominated the first part of the play when prophecies were being fulfilled as fast as they were made, and now Macbeth's "vaulting ambition" is hurling itself forward. The lord invokes speed on the opposite side of the cosmic battle when he prays that

> Some holy angel
> Fly to the court of England and unfold
> His message ere he come, that a swift blessing
> May soon return to our suffering country
> Under a hand accursed!
>
> (45–49)

There is something prophetic in the lord's words about the messenger—that he should "hold what distance / His wisdom can provide" (44–45). Before long, Macbeth's isolation will be complete, when no one will willingly fight for him. The conversation between the lord and Lennox is representative of conversations all through the country, which is perhaps a reason for the lord's being anonymous, emphasizing his representative function.

ACT IV

Summary

Around a cauldron, the three witches are preparing their "hell-broth" and "winding up" their spell. Macbeth joins them and asks them to answer his questions. The witches are eager to do so and, to please him, produce a series of apparitions. Before Macbeth can speak to the spirits, the first apparition, an Armed Head, anticipates his questions and warns him to "beware Macduff." The second apparition, a Bloody Child, tells him that "none of woman born shall harm Macbeth." The new king hopefully interprets this statement as a contradiction of the first. Although he now sees no need to fear

Macduff, he nevertheless resolves to kill him and be doubly certain of his own safety. The third apparition, a Child Crowned, holds a tree in his hand and promises Macbeth that none shall vanquish him until Birnam Wood moves to Dunsinane Hill.

Taking courage from the second and third apparitions, which seem to nullify the warning of the first, Macbeth inquires whether "Banquo's issue" will ever reign in Scotland. Advising Macbeth that he will find grief in their answer, the witches reluctantly produce a procession of eight kings (some of whom carry double and triple scepters), after which Banquo's ghost appears. Macbeth realizes that this display is an omen: Banquo's descendants will rule, and they will rule more kingdoms than merely Scotland.

As soon as the apparitions and witches vanish, Lennox enters and tells Macbeth that Macduff has fled to England. Macbeth instantly resolves to attack Macduff's castle of Fife and put his family and household to the sword.

At Fife, Lady Macduff is indignant at her husband's apparent desertion. Ross tries to explain to her the reasons for her husband's sudden departure but finds it impossible and leaves. Lady Macduff turns to her young son, and while she is attempting to explain that his father is no doubt dead by now, a messenger enters and warns her to flee. Before she can act, however, Macbeth's agents arrive, slay her son, and pursue her until they kill her also.

In England, Malcolm and Macduff discuss the unhappy condition of Scotland under Macbeth's despotic rule. Malcolm would like, were it manly, to weep for his country's fate. Macduff has no time for weeping; he would wreak his vengeance against Macbeth's bloody rule. Thus he offers his services to Malcolm if the latter has need of them. Malcolm, however, is uncertain of Macduff's sincerity. To test Macduff's loyalty and love for his country, Malcolm tells Macduff that if he recovers the throne of Scotland, he intends to be far more tyrannical and bloodthirsty than Macbeth has ever been or could ever be. Macduff, pessimistic and discouraged, finds Malcolm neither fit to govern nor to live and prepares to leave him. Now convinced of Macduff's integrity and patriotism, Malcolm praises him and pledges himself to restore peace and prosperity to their native land.

Before Macduff can find an explanation for Malcolm's contradictory statements about himself, Ross arrives with news of the massacre of Macduff's wife, children, and servants. Seeing Macduff overcome with grief, Malcolm urges him to avenge himself like a man. This Macduff swears to do, although he declares that no revenge can be adequate since Macbeth has no children of his own. Malcolm and Macduff vow to join forces and overthrow Macbeth.

Commentary

Thunder and hypnotic witches' chants and dancing around their "hell-broth" create an overall effect of a storm brewing and nature being ill-at-ease in Scene 1. Macbeth even produces an imaginary verbal "hurricane" when he pleads with the "secret, black, and midnight hags" to answer his questions; he will have answers even if the witches have to

> untie the winds and let them fight
> Against the churches; though the yesty waves
> Confound and swallow navigation up;
> Though bladed corn be lodged and trees blown
>   down;
> Though castles topple on their warders' heads;
> Though palaces and pyramids do slope
> Their heads to their foundations; though the
>   treasure
> Of nature's germens tumble all together,
> Even till destruction sicken; answer me
> To what I ask you.
>
> (52–61)

His insistence on answers from the witches, even if that means that destruction itself will be sickened by the chaos that Macbeth imagines within the universe, is powerfully effective in this passage. The urgency of Macbeth's need to know what is in store is expressed in the strongest of his expressions of disregard for order. Possessed by a mad will to know the worst, Macbeth demands to see phantoms; he wants no more prophecies from the witches. A thunderclap announces the first apparition, an Armed Head. The apparition seems to be uneasy and even fearful of being conjured before Macbeth. Unlike the next two apparitions, this one is anxious to be freed. There even seems to be pain in his cry, "Dismiss me. Enough."

It is this very cry that Macbeth will utter when he begins "to be aweary of the sun, / And wish the estate o' the world were now undone" (V. v. 49–50).

The second apparition, a Bloody Child, speaks longer than the first apparition, just as the third will speak longer than this one. The tone of the second is confident and reassuring. On the surface, the pattern of the three apparitions appears to be that of Macbeth's later soliloquies—from a spirit of hesitation and fear, to resolution, and at last to a bold statement.

Macbeth bristles at hearing his name repeated thrice more. He is impatient, certainly, and annoyed at the monotony of the repetition. But it is also possible in his state of alienation that the objective pronouncement of his name is loathsome and even frightening to him because of its identification with his threatened kingship.

The blood that drips from the second apparition, a child, is sickening to the sight and to the imagination, but this image has been threaded throughout the play and is strikingly visual here and an appropriate image for the prophecy. "None of woman born" (80), it announces, shall harm Macbeth, and in the final scenes we learn that Macduff was "untimely ripped" from his mother's womb. Of course, the Bloody Child as an image of birth could also be an ironic affront to Macbeth in another way: While the child is symbolic of Macduff's murdered children, it is also symbolic of birth and regeneration, specifically of Banquo's successors. Macbeth's first response to the Bloody Child is one of scorn. Then he grows skeptical and decides to kill Macduff anyway in order to force the hand of fate. The very last lines of his response are "Thou shalt not live; / That I may tell pale-hearted fear it lies, / And sleep in spite of thunder" (84–86). These lines reveal an undertone of weariness at a moment of apparent strength. Thunder cracks in the background as Macbeth refers to his lack of sleep and to his dominating emotion—fear.

The third apparition, a Child Crowned, triumphantly holding a sapling as a scepter, extends the metaphor of the Bloody Child. This is a once-dead child, now risen against its murderer. The sapling is regenerate Nature itself, risen up against Macbeth, who would have "trees blown down" to suit his wishes. This figure is an emblem of a central theme in this play: Nature versus the Unnatural. Macbeth accepts the comforting words of the apparition as "sweet bodements! good!" (96). They are assurances that the "rebellious dead"—

Banquo, for example—will never rise up against him. Parallel to his response to the second apparition, there is an undertone here that belies the spoken confidence. Macbeth yearns for the more normal existence he has renounced, one free from struggle and anxiety. He would like to live to a ripe age ["live with the lease of nature" (99)], but his "heart throbs" (100) obsessively with the fear that Banquo will reap his fruits by having his issue "reign in this kingdom" (103).

By conjuring visions to parade before Macbeth, the witches are doubly torturing him: He threatens them with an "eternal curse" unless they satisfy him, and they present him with images of apparent stateliness. The number of shades was possibly meant to flatter King James I at the first performance of this play because he was a direct descendant of Banquo, but the scene also serves to redouble Macbeth's pain by means of a seemingly endless procession of figures: "Horrible sight! Now, I see 'tis true; / For the blood-bolter'd Banquo smiles upon me, / And points at them for his. What, is this so?" (122–24). He sees it is so yet would not have it so.

Damning himself in an obvious irony when he damns "all those that trust them [the witches]" (139), Macbeth turns to Lennox and receives the news of Macduff's escape. The news has come fast, giving credence to the witches' words. With Lennox silently looking on from a distance, Macbeth deliberates on his next act of murder. He will kill Macduff's wife and children, an apparently gratuitous act of destruction. Why should he commit the crime unless, following the torment of seeing "Banquo's issue" steal his throne, he is unconsciously so inflamed at the idea of anyone producing offspring that he wants to murder impulsively, in a broad swath. Barren himself, he wants to depopulate the earth; Macduff's "wife, his babes, and all unfortunate souls / That trace him in his line" (152–53) bear the brunt of his insane lust for power.

Some of Macbeth's last lines in Scene 1 boldly express his intent to carry out the worst of his evil intentions: "From this moment / The very firstlings of my heart shall be / The firstlings of my hand" (146–48). Thus the scene ends on a curious note. While filled with confidence of his impregnability, there seems to be something within Macbeth that cannot escape guilt and that suspects the witches of duplicity: He cannot escape his deepest fears and utters another exasperated cry, "But no more sights!" (155). And it is of value to note the reintroduction of the "time" theme at this point in the play. The time that will elapse between thought and deed will be negligible, muses Macbeth, and the "damnation" he wishes on all those who trust the witches will ironically be meted out on him very soon. In the next scene, he "give[s] the edge o' the sword" (151) to Macduff's family, as promised, and from now to the end of the play, with only the Malcolm-Macduff scene intervening, the action is at a speed not experienced since the first act of the play.

In the presence of Lennox, Macbeth speaks his mind now without caution, indicating the irrational security he has taken from the latest prophecies. He has seen his attempt to secure himself through crafty villainy fail as a result of both supernatural interference and the swift march of events. He decides, therefore, to act on impulse and outrace time.

Scene 2 of Act IV is often omitted from performances of the play because, according to several commentators, it adds nothing absolutely necessary to the story. One could quarrel with that viewpoint on several counts, however. The scene is certainly relevant to the theme in that it offers a picture of the brutal disorder of the country: division of families, anxiety, dismay, and slaughter. It is also worthwhile for Ross' moving description of life in a "police state."

The scene also recalls an earlier scene that contained a parent and a child set against a backdrop of impending doom. In Act III, Scene 3, Banquo cried out to his son, "Fly, good Fleance, fly, fly, fly!" (17); here, it is the son who begs his mother, "Run away, I pray you!" (81). Earlier the son escaped; now the son is killed onstage, and the mother soon after is killed offstage.

This gratuitous slaughter is one of the most unspeakable horrors in the play. Shakespeare shows onstage, in terms that can be felt by anyone, the experience of destruction for its own sake. But it is not merely the deep pathos of Scene 2 that makes it so keenly felt. There is also the heavy ambiguity and uncertainty of motivation behind the murders.

There is a faint ray of hope as the messenger risks his life to warn Lady Macduff of danger. He is anonymous; he is a quite ordinary person, and his deed is one of gratuitous goodwill, as Macbeth's gratuitous evil is just the opposite. There is faith and hope implied in this act, along with Macduff's son's bravery and his faith in his father—all this coming just before Lady Macduff's cynical indictment of a person's trying to do good in this world:

> I have done no harm. But I remember now
> I am in this earthly world; where to do harm
> Is often laudable, to do good sometimes
> Accounted dangerous folly: Why then, alas,
> To say I have done no harm?
>
> (73–77)

On reflection, these lines of Lady Macduff attenuate the overall gruesomeness of the scene's mood.

Of all the scenes in the play, Scene 3 of Act IV is one of the longest and one of the most static. Its action is all in the minds of the characters, agonizing over the past and preparing for the future. It is the only scene in the play not set in Scotland, and thus we should look for details to point up the symbolic contrast between orderly England and disordered Scotland, particularly in Shakespeare's light and dark imagery. Structurally, this scene may be divided into three sections: first, the overcoming of division between Malcolm and Macduff; second, the idea of England being a peaceful restorative; third, the news from Scotland.

Macduff's first words in the scene, coming as they do just after we have heard his wife's anguished cries of death, are painfully ironic: "Each new morn / New widows howl, new orphans cry, new sorrows / Strike heaven on the face" (4–6). Soon Macduff, too, will howl, but for the present, Shakespeare is conjuring up these sorrows to describe widespread murders and applying them to the nation as a whole; in fact, all nature laments "like a syllable of dolour" (8), Malcolm says, despairing that his country "sinks beneath the yoke; / It weeps, it bleeds; and each new day a gash / Is added to her wounds" (39–41). He is the orphaned future king and also a father-figure for his nation. Seemingly Macduff is one father who has survived with his family in this mutilated kingdom. Symbolically, however, it is as if no family unit has remained intact under Macbeth's bloody reign.

Considering their roles, the behavior of Malcolm and Macduff in Scene 3 is interesting in the way it shifts and changes. Malcolm's first words are ones of despair; he would like them both to "weep our sad bosoms empty" (2). But Macduff's mood is darker and more fierce; he advises Malcolm, instead, that they "hold fast the mortal sword, and like good men / Bestride [defend] our down-fall'n birthdom" (3–4). There is clearly a tension between them, founded in mutual suspicion. Distrust is epidemic in Scotland. When Malcolm remarks that he is young, it may mean that he hasn't the experience to judge what really needs to be done in Scotland; but, more to the point, he could also be inferring that he hasn't the cunning to tell friend from foe now that his father has been murdered by unknown assassins. And one recalls his late father's words in Act I: "there's no art / To find the mind's construction in the face" (11-12).

Several of Malcolm's remarks, uttered to test Macduff's allegiance, incense the older man understandably, for Macduff will not allow himself to be considered a man who would "offer up a weak poor innocent lamb / To appease an angry god" (15-16). Here, Macduff's innocence blinds him as to Malcolm's motivations. The playacting in this scene is elaborate. Malcolm follows his provocations with a self-accusation, one in which he paints himself as a mock-Macbeth, so black that Macbeth "will seem as pure as snow, and the poor state / Esteem him as a lamb" (53-54). Such lines as

> Nay, had I power, I should
> Pour the sweet milk of concord into hell,
> Uproar the universal peace, confound
> All unity on earth
>
> (97-100)

are calculated directly to call Macbeth to mind and to emphasize the distance that Malcolm has traveled from the time when he was "too full o' the milk of human kindness" even to commit a single crime.

Malcolm must be absolutely sure of Macduff's allegiance, and of all his ploys to test Macduff, none is as potent as his promising to indulge in every variation of every crime imaginable, for this elicits from Macduff absolute, empty despair over the fate of his beloved Scotland. Malcolm says,

> But I have none. The king-becoming graces,
> As justice, verity, temperance, stableness,
> Bounty, perserverance, mercy, lowliness,
> Devotion, patience, courage, fortitude,
> I have no relish of them, but abound
> In the division of each several crime,
> Acting it many ways,
>
> (90-96)

and Macduff cries out in exasperation as he hears these false confessions, enraged by Malcolm's promise of such tyranny which "goodness dare not check" (33). Of course, however, there is also the possibility that the force of Macduff's outburst owes something to his own latent guilt, to the feeling that he may imprudently have left his family. Surely his late wife accused him of such villainous behavior.

The effect, then, is like an exorcism chanted by a priest, rhetorically "dressed up," as it were, as he fights a demon. Macduff reinforces this idea when he accuses Malcolm of "blaspheming" the kingly heritage and adds,

> Thy royal father
> Was a most sainted king; the queen that bore thee,
> Oftener upon her knees than on her feet,
> Died every day she lived.
>
> (108-11)

What Macduff does not realize is that when Malcolm says that if he were king he would be so greedy for land that he would slay most of the nobles of Scotland by "surmised accusations," Malcolm is only playing the "tyrant-king" as part of a ritual to expose the present king, in solemn preparation for becoming the ideal king himself.

Only when Macduff despairs, "O my breast / Thy hope ends here!" (112-13), does Malcolm finally reveal his true self, which is such a startling revelation that Macduff finds it difficult to fathom. Their conversation is another echo of Macbeth's and the witches' words but in a different key and with a meaning the reverse of theirs. The tide, it seems, is at last turning against the tyrant.

The religious theme, combined with the idea of healing the wounded kingdom, continues with the chance arrival of a doctor. He describes the "holy king" Edward as a savior who can effect cures miraculously with nothing more than his royal blood; furthermore, this English king's powers, described by Malcolm as "a heavenly gift of prophecy" (157), make him an obvious antithesis to the weird sisters, who use their magic to destroy life.

Malcolm's reaction to Ross when he approaches suggests some change in Ross' appearance. The passage of time might account for the change, but the reason could also be to the inner ravages caused by his experiences in Macbeth's inferno and by the knowledge of his complicity in it. Whether or not Ross is guilty of acquiescing his honor to Macbeth, the fact of Lady Macduff's savage murder seems to have momentarily undone him; certainly the first seconds of the encounter are tense. Uncertainty and suspicion are like a fog in the air, separating the men from one another.

If Scene 2 showed naked crime at its most horrible, the last moments of Scene 3 show the deep grief that follows a personal tragedy. The audience knows of the murder, and Macduff probably suspects disaster. The "poor country" that cannot be "called our mother, but our grave" (166) has poignant meaning for Macduff as he questions Ross about the welfare of his family. And Ross' answer ["They were well at peace when I did leave them" (79)] is equally poignant; in fact, it is so disturbing to Ross that he changes the subject, leaving Macduff still brooding over his possible "rawness" in leaving his wife and child. Dramatically, the interlude succeeds in holding the audience gripped in empathy with Macduff until Ross finally reveals that Macduff's family has been slaughtered.

Macduff is struck dumb. Malcolm awkwardly cries out for Macduff to "give sorrow words" (209); to brood, he says, would be deadly. But words fail, and Macduff at first seems able only to babble and repeat his questions, incredulous at the horror. "He has no children," he moans, meaning that only a man who has no children could perpetrate such a crime and that there can be no fitting revenge for such a monster.

Ross is silent until the end of the scene, but Malcolm, as befits a prince, tries to comfort his kinsman. That he cannot adequately do so is not his fault; such is the severity of Macduff's pain, for Macduff represents an older generation. The last of his lineage has been extinguished, and before he can fully recover his composure and resolve his will to pursue Macbeth as a soldier must, Macduff must give full vent to his emotions. He feels that he has been "unmanned"; he has been robbed of the family that he headed, and he must find his own way to "dispute it like a man":

> I shall do so;
> But I must also feel it as a man.
> I cannot but remember such things were,
> That were most precious to me. Did heaven look
>   on,
> And would not take their part? Sinful Macduff!
> They were all struck for thee! Naught that I am,

> Not for their own demerits, but for mine,
> Fell slaughter on their souls.

(220-27)

His pain is intensified by his guilt, but he turns his guilt and pain to good use as he concludes his solitary meditation. He resolves no longer to weep, no longer to "play the woman with mine eyes" (230). Malcolm's last words, "This tune goes manly" (235), fittingly concludes the scene in a double resolution of individual and national consequence.

ACT V

Summary

In Dunsinane castle, Lady Macbeth's physician and her waiting-gentlewoman are discussing their mistress' sleepwalking. The doctor would like to know more, but the gentlewoman absolutely refuses to tell him what she has heard Lady Macbeth say on these occasions. While they converse, Lady Macbeth appears, carrying a candle. Her eyes are open, and she constantly rubs her hands together as if washing them. Unaware of what she is saying, she refers to the bloody murder of Duncan, the slaying of Macduff's wife, and Banquo's burial. "What's done cannot be undone" (i. 59), she says as if she were addressing her husband.

Appalled by what he has seen and heard, the doctor comments that Lady Macbeth needs divine aid more than she does the services of a mere physician. He advises the gentlewoman to watch her mistress carefully lest she harm herself.

In the countryside near Dunsinane, English and Scottish forces are grouping for their attack against Macbeth. The Scottish lords are filled with hope and entertain their English allies with the rumor that no one any longer serves Macbeth from either a sense of love or loyalty.

Macbeth, deserted by his former supporters, takes desperate courage from the prophecies of the witches and their apparitions. A servant, attempting to report the proximity and size of the attacking armies, earns only reproaches and curses from his master.

Calling for Seyton, his one remaining officer, Macbeth confesses that his life "is fall'n into the sere, the yellow leaf" (iii. 23), and that he cannot hope to have "honour, love, obedience, troops of friends" (iii. 25). Macbeth commands Seyton to bring him his armor and then orders him to scout the countryside and to hang all who talk of fear or desertion.

When Macbeth asks the doctor how Lady Macbeth is faring, the physician says her trouble is more mental than physical. To Macbeth's demand that he cure her, the doctor replies, "Therein the patient must minister to himself." "Throw physic [medicine] to the dogs" (iii. 47), Macbeth cries. He then expresses the wish that the doctor could diagnose and cure Scotland's illness. The physician remarks to himself that if he could escape from Dunsinane, he would not return for any fee.

Outside, Malcolm orders his advancing troops to cut boughs from the trees of Birnam Wood to use as camouflage. He assures Old Siward that those who remain with Macbeth are "but constrained things" (iv. 12), acting under duress and having no heart for their business.

In Dunsinane, as Macbeth prepares to meet the attack, Seyton brings him news that Lady Macbeth is dead. Stricken with grief and depressed by the emptiness of his achievements, Macbeth declares that life "is a tale told by an idiot, full of sound and fury, / Signifying nothing" (v. 27–28).

Another messenger brings news that Birnam Wood is moving toward Dunsinane. Disheartened by this report of what he supposed to be impossible, Macbeth senses that his end is near, but with desperate fury he determines to die with his armor on.

In the field, Malcolm, Siward, and Macduff plan their attack, station their forces, and advance.

With his retreat cut off, Macbeth seeks some small cause for hope in the apparition's assurance that "no one of woman born" can harm him. At this moment, Young Siward, the son of the English general, faces and defies Macbeth. Macbeth quickly kills the youth in hand-to-hand combat.

Finding comfort in the thought that his assailant must have been born of woman, Macbeth departs just before Macduff storms upon the scene looking for his mortal enemy.

Malcolm and Old Siward announce the surrender of Dunsinane and predict an early conclusion of the battle.

On the battlefield, Macbeth, scorning suicide as a means of escaping the fate slowly overtaking him, meets Macduff. At first,

Macbeth says that he has avoided Macduff and urges him to withdraw, but Macduff presses for a fight. When Macbeth boasts that he is immune to blows from any man born of woman, Macduff reveals the startling fact that he "was from his mother's womb / Untimely ripp'd" (viii. 15–16).

Dismayed, Macbeth curses the misleading statements of the witches and declares that he will not fight with Macduff. At this, Macduff orders Macbeth to surrender and prepare for the humiliation that his victors will heap upon him. Disdaining to yield, Macbeth renews the struggle and calls, "Lay on Macduff and dam'd be him that first cries, 'Hold, enough!'" (viii. 33). Raining blows on each other, they disappear as Malcolm and his allies come on the scene.

Old Siward, moved with sorrow at the news of Young Siward's death, finds comfort in the knowledge that his son was brave, "parted well, and paid his score."

Macduff now enters with Macbeth's head and hails Malcolm as King of Scotland. Malcolm, promising rewards to his supporters and further restoration and relief to his people, invites everyone to his coronation at Scone.

Commentary

Scene 1 is composed largely of Lady Macbeth's confused memories, reviewing for us the tragic action of earlier acts and employing symbols that reawaken the themes and oppositions that give meaning to the story. For example, the candle crystallizes all of Shakespeare's previous light/darkness symbolism. Lady Macbeth once desired darkness ("Come thick night"), but she now finds it horrible. Her candle is a pathetic attempt to dispel real darkness with artificial light. Among the references to the washing of her hands, "all the perfumes of Arabia" (44) balances and recalls Macbeth's "all great Neptune's ocean" (II. ii. 60–63) and makes ironic contrast with "a little water clears us of this deed; / How easy it is then!" (II. ii. 68–69).

Dramatically, this quiet and touching sleepwalking episode prevents the last act of this drama from degenerating into merely a headlong clash of blood and thunder. Shakespeare is creating a new pattern here for Macbeth and his wife: Macbeth will deteriorate from a complex, inward suffering villain into a madman, and at the same time, Lady Macbeth will rise above her role as the hysterical, ambition-obsessed wife; now she will drop her villainous robes and be exposed as a woman confused by what is happening around her. Her inner confusion and disharmony engulf her in madness. Here we see the prophesied injunction to "sleep no more" (II. ii. 37) fulfilled. Sleep no longer has meaning for her: Such natural divisions as night and day no longer apply. The experience of guilt and suffering and the torturous external repetition of her actions from a horrid past—these events so dominate her soul that the ordinary texture of her life crumbles. It is this experience of total alienation and "disconnectedness" that overwhelms us as we relive, in her imagination, the dreadful past: notes written and delivered; fear of lights being extinguished; gushing fountains of blood ["Yet who would have thought the old man to have had so much blood in him" (35)]; Lady Macduff being killed; and Banquo's burial. In an obvious and important sense, Scene 1 shows "the wages of sin" to be a living death, entombed in heavy guilt: Murder and madness return to plague their creator. But Lady Macbeth's total madness, evident in her piteous mindless jingle, "The Thane of Fife had a wife" (37), transcends mere madness. Here, indeed, is a woman damned by her unnatural deeds; one should note that this is the same Lady Macbeth who seemed, more than her husband, to be made of steely resolution in the first acts of the play.

Scene 2 is among several that rapidly alternate, one with the other, drawing the play to its final conclusion; here we are visually shown the solidarity of those who struggle against the tyrant Macbeth, and verbally we listen as Shakespeare brings together several thematic threads before the climax. It is, for example, symbolically fitting that soldiers in their "first of manhood" should rise to "un-man" the tyrant. And their cause is of such grandeur that not only are they spurred on, but likewise even "mortified men" (dead men) will rise up, like Banquo, and even the "rebellious dead," which Macbeth fears, will oppose him. Macbeth's murders, says Angus, stick "on his hands," and we are reminded of the blood that Macbeth's wife imagines to be on her own hands. Macbeth is cornered and doomed, and his situation is made even more bizarre, and perhaps pathetic, in Shakespeare's imagery of his ill-fitting clothing: "Now does he feel his title / Hang loose about him, like a giant's robe / Upon a dwarfish thief" (20-22). Macbeth is indeed "dressed in borrowed robes" (I. iii. 109-10), as well as in "strange garments" (I. iii.

145–46), "golden opinions worn" (I. vii. 33–34), and "old robes [that] sit easier than new" (II. iv. 38).

Although Scene 2 is short, it is masterfully constructed and rich with meaning, as we have come to expect; yet what is most interesting here is the sympathy that Shakespeare inserts for Macbeth. Remember, we have not seen Macbeth since the first scene of Act IV. We have seen and heard about his kingdom disintegrating, and even that of his own household. The ominous name of Birnam Wood has been uttered, and we are readied for a prophecy of the witches to be fulfilled. When we hear that Macbeth is defended by only those who are commanded to do so, that he has no loyal supporters for his cause, knowing Macbeth as we do, we anticipate the further collapse of his mind; thus it is a brief but humane touch that Shakespeare gives to the tyrant when he reveals the enemies' understanding of his madness. Menteith, in particular, asks, "who . . . shall blame [him when] his pester'd senses [begin] to recoil and start . . . ?" (21–22). Macbeth's crimes are loathsome, yet Shakespeare never lets us forget that the man himself is human.

Scene 3 presents a stunning portrait of a man who has lost his wager with fate and who will soon be faced with his own damnation. Here and in Scene 5, Macbeth alternates wildly between furious ranting and quiet, weary melancholy. His soldierly common sense causes him to fear while, at the same time, he clings irrationally to the false security of the witches' prophecy. He knows that the witches were right in foreseeing his three titles; after all, he is king, and they have said that he will not be vanquished until Birnam Wood comes to Dunsinane.

Each line of Macbeth's speeches is two-edged and two-layered—contemptuous and braggartly, yet lined with deeply felt fear. He kicks his servant verbally and physically in a petty show of authority. Likewise, when he insists on having his armor and ill-fitting clothes, he would like to reassure himself of his own reality and importance. Sadly, he is at odds with himself, just as Scotland tears itself apart by civil war. The medicine which he calls for, the medicine that will purge him and Scotland, will be young Malcolm; not only will Macbeth be purged of his sickness, but Scotland will soon be purged of Macbeth.

Scene 4 is functional and spectacular rather than intense or poetic. It shows us a meeting of Malcolm's supporters, and we note the impatience of the old soldier, Siward, and see again the revenger, Macduff, and hear their plans to advance the war and the means whereby this part of the witches' prophecy will come true.

Significantly, it is Malcolm who gives the order to cut down the Birnam boughs so that Macbeth's scouts will be in doubt (or error) about the size of the combined forces; recall that in Act IV, the third apparition assured Macbeth that he could never be vanquished unless the woods moved against him.

Thus the prophecy is fulfilled. Whereas in Scene 3 of this act, a cranky and disturbed tyrant compelled his servant to arm him and prepare him for war, threatening to "hang those that talk of fear" (36), in Scene 4 a harmonious group, including a man and his youthful son, make calm preparations for battle. The give-and-take of their dialogue, with Macduff and Old Siward gently moderating Malcolm's strident confidence that Macbeth has no allies left, contrasts markedly with the ranting and cowering witnessed in Macbeth's camp.

Old Siward's words echo and re-echo the course of temptation, hesitation, and crime run by Macbeth since his first meeting with the witches: "Thoughts speculative, their unsure hopes relate, / But certain issue strokes must arbitrate" (19–20). Once Macbeth's speculative thoughts were decided by "strokes"; now, however, his game is over. In other words, others are now hoping, and calculations state reasonable but not entirely certain hopes about Macbeth's being defeated. Only battle, however, will produce results; only the "strokes" of war. In broadly symbolic terms, note that nature itself, in the collective figure of the green boughs marching, is preparing for the purge.

In Scene 5, we witness Macbeth's gathering awareness of what is culminating for him. When he utters a wish for death, it is a last, unlikely desperate recourse considering the chaos around him, but it is a wish that he has hinted at earlier. In Act III, Scene 2, for example, Macbeth said that it would "better be with the dead / Whom we, to gain our peace, have sent to peace" (19–20) than to be tortured by the mind. Later, Macbeth noted that "Duncan is in his grave; / After life's fitful fever, he sleeps well" (III. iii. 22–26). These speeches and several speeches of Lady Macbeth's equate death ("sleep's counterfeit") with peace; thus are we somewhat prepared for Macbeth's final death wish here. Reflecting on his wife's death, he would also be rid of time if it were as easily extinguished as a candle's flicker.

The "cry of women" startles Seyton and others onstage and is followed by Macbeth's question, "What is that noise?" He seems matter-of-fact, commenting "I have supp'd full with horrors; / Direness, familiar to my slaughterous thoughts, / Cannot once start me" (13–15). This prelude to the announcement of Lady Macbeth's death is most unheroic. When Macbeth finally hears the announcement, "The queen, my lord, is dead" (16), it would normally be a time for intense feeling, as it was when Lady Macduff's death was announced, for instance, but here it fails to provoke a normal response. One feels only a horrible emptiness within Macbeth; his line "She should have died hereafter" (17) (she would have died anyway) denotes a colossal and painful indifference. In his famous denunciation of life, Macbeth seems to realize anew that the vanity of human ambition is in sharp contrast to the "bank and shoal of time" that he mentioned in Act I when he saw clearly that a person's lifetime was merely a sandbank, soon to be covered by the sea of eternity.

At present, Macbeth is devoid of normal feeling; certainly there was a time when his life with Lady Macbeth was a tender one. But this confusion of feelings is part of his torture. His profound emptiness at this moment is verbalized in the famous lines "To-morrow, and to-morrow, and to-morrow" (19). These lines ache with the rhythm of a slowly beating heart and the monotony of a futureless future, one that is pointless.

Macbeth's dark ruminations are abruptly interrupted, ironically, by a messenger with a "story" to tell: The woods do move. In the last lines of Scene 5, the "sound and fury" which Macbeth lamented about are translated into the "alarum-bells" of war, and his redoubled anger at the "equivocation of the fiend" (43) expresses itself in violent gestures of despair. Now that he is faced with his final challenge, he will not die easily; if necessary, he will take the entire universe with him. Only violent action will give him solace now.

In Scene 6, Malcolm is in command and assumes for the first time in the play the royal "we." He orders the soldiers to discard their camouflage: It is at last time to drop all disguises and to boldly confront King Macbeth.

It is a mistake to think of Scene 7 as being one that evokes all the noise and confusion of battle and pursuit. Although some men are indeed killed, it is interesting to note the conclusion of the scene itself. Old Siward says, "The day almost itself professes yours, / And little is to do." Malcolm then responds, "We have met with foes / That strike beside us," to which Old Siward proudly says, "Enter, sir, the castle" (27–29). The battle, in one sense, is equivocal and can hardly be called a battle; it is neither lost nor won because there were no real antagonists on a large scale. The phrase "foes / That strike beside us" (28)—that is, that purposely miss us, or even join us—means that there were no real foes.

The first opponent Macbeth comes face-to-face with in the scene is Siward's young son; Macbeth, of course, expects him to quake and recoil at the words "My name is Macbeth," which he delivers with great force. But the young lad does nothing of the kind. He simply enters into combat, identifying Macbeth not as a fearsome warrior but merely as the epitome of the forces of evil, "Macbeth" being only a label so hateful that nothing in hell can equal it.

The identification of Macbeth with hell-hounds in this scene reintroduces the theme of cosmic conflict. Macduff's "Make all our trumpets speak" recalls the "angels trumpet-tongued" of Act I, which Macbeth likened to Duncan's virtues that defended him from Macbeth's murder-blow.

In the end, Macbeth is alone with nothing more than his obsessive memory of the apparitions and their promises, which the witches presented for him. He paraphrases their words again and again, reducing his utterances to the bawling of an idiot. When Macduff enters, just as his enemy has spoken of women and birth, we realize that he himself is haunted by ambiguous thoughts of "wife and children's ghosts." He crosses the stage in quick pursuit and begs Fortune let him find Macbeth. The themes of death and regeneration, guilt and a sense of the "mysterious" in men's affairs, in the form of prophecies fulfilled and reliance on Fortune, are thus coalesced and reiterated.

As the last prophecy of the apparitions is fulfilled, Macbeth can recognize how completely he has been misled; he now knows what we know. Thus stripped to the very bed-rock of existence, his will comes to a dead stop. There is no desire now, only bitterness. It requires Macduff's taunt to arouse the last of his warlike pride before he will "fight the course" (vii. 2) and "die with harness on his back" (v. 52).

In a sense, it is not just a single death but two deaths that share the focus in Scene 8: The first, that of Old Siward's son, is reported in Ross' careful tone of regret, and the other is, of course, glaringly evident as Macbeth's trunkless bleeding head is brought onstage. The deaths balance one another, as the scene divides and balances between the chaos of Macbeth's last moments and the unifying, pacifying statements of Malcolm's concluding speech.

Siward's reaction to his son's death is quite different from Macduff's grief in Act IV, Scene 3, but remember that Macduff reacted as a man to the senseless decimation of his family; Siward reacts as a man to his son dying while carrying out his duty: "Then he is dead? . . . Had he his hurts before? / Why then, God's soldier be he!" (46–47). The last scene of the tragedy, among other things, is a meditation on death, and Macbeth's death elicits the most complex response.

In what sense can Macbeth be called a tragic hero? Certainly one cannot identify with him as one can with Hamlet or Othello; his crimes are too hideous and his willfulness too great to elicit normal sympathy. Yet it isn't with the simple satisfaction of justice being done that we receive his death. His last "hour upon the stage" is one of confusion and of fear, pride, contradictory impulses and thoughts, and, above all, there hovers another reality, that of the "juggling fiends" (18), who may in some way have shaped his end. Their words are still on his lips. Perhaps it is because he is tethered and baited like a bear and because he vacillates so wildly in facing death at the last that he strikes a chord within us: From his will to obliterate all creation rather than destroy himself, as Lady Macbeth has done, he encompasses regret, tired old fears, and a measure of hopeless energy and fury. There is only a last, single, pathetic death spasm in his challenge to Macduff. The imagery of Macbeth's adversary, once painfully birthed, confronting Macbeth, only moments from a harrowing death, is a dramatic juxtaposition for the imagination, and thus does this drama end. A cycle of life is complete. Macbeth's time is over. Now nature will create anew and things will be "planted newly" (65). With reinstated order, the age will regenerate itself.

1607

timon of
athens

TIMON OF ATHENS

LIST OF CHARACTERS

Timon

An Athenian lord and a former military leader. He is very generous to his friends while he is wealthy, but those same friends refuse
to assist him when he becomes bankrupt as a result of his irresponsible generosity. Disillusioned with humanity, Timon leaves Athens
to live in a cave in the woods, where he discovers a large cache of
gold. He gives gold to Alcibiades to help finance the army threatening Athens, and he gives gold to all whom he meets in the belief that
it will further corrupt their already-degenerate natures. He dies in
the woods, and he is buried (by whom, we never know) in a grave
by the sea.

Lucius

An Athenian lord and a "friend" of Timon's. He sends Timon a
gift of four richly harnessed horses when Timon is still supposedly
wealthy, but Lucius pretends to be without funds when Timon
requests a loan from him.

Lucullus

An Athenian lord and a "friend" of Timon's who sends a gift
of four greyhounds when Timon is still believed to be rich, but,
like Lucius, he refuses to loan Timon some money when Timon is
in need.

Sempronius

Another Athenian lord who refuses to loan Timon money
because he is "affronted" that Timon has insulted him by requesting
loans from other lords before approaching him.

Ventidius

An Athenian lord and another "friend" of Timon's. When Ventidius is imprisoned because of debts, Timon gives him enough money to pay off his creditors and thereby gain his freedom. During Timon's theoretically solvent period, Ventidius offers to repay his old friend with money he has inherited. Timon refuses to accept the money; later, when Timon is greatly in need off funds, he asks Ventidius for some money, but Ventidius refuses the request, proving that he is the most ungrateful of all the men whom Timon has befriended.

Alcibiades

The commander of the Athenian army and a friend of Timon's. When the Senate rejects his plea to spare the life of a friend of his who has been condemned to death for murder, Alcibiades decides to use his army to conquer Athens in revenge. He meets Timon in the woods, and Timon gives him some gold, hoping that Alcibiades will decimate the city. Alcibiades, however, enters the city (at the conclusion of the play) with plans to establish a government built on honorable principles.

Apemantus

An extremely cynical misanthrope. He is the only person who does not flatter or lie to Timon while it is believed that Timon is a very prosperous man. Timon, at first, rejects Apemantus' vile opinion of human nature, but after his monetary reversal, Timon adopts a similar attitude himself and goes to live alone in the woods. Significantly, Timon gains a measure of satisfaction by believing that despite his poverty, he is still superior to Apemantus as a human being.

A Poet and a Painter

These two men call on Timon when he is still thought to be prosperous and present him with their works, of which he is the chief subject. They hope to please him so much that he will feel obligated to become their patron. After learning that Timon is again rich, they visit him in the woods. He curses them for being villains, but he gives them gold and beats them as they leave.

Flavius

Timon's honest steward. He tries to tell Timon that his resources are rapidly being depleted and that Timon should cease his reckless spending, but Timon refuses to listen to him. Flavius shares his meager supply of money with Timon's other servants after their master has left Athens. Later, he visits Timon in the woods and offers to be his servant in adversity; it is then that Timon becomes convinced that Flavius is the only honest man alive.

Flaminius

Another of Timon's servants; he calls on Lord Lucullus to request a loan for his master, Timon. Lucullus attempts to bribe Flaminius to tell Timon he could not be located, but Flaminius refuses and continues to be faithful as long as he remains in Timon's service.

Lucilius

Another servant of Timon's. Timon befriends him by giving him enough money to make him an acceptable son-in-law to the rich father of the young woman whom he loves.

Servilius

Another servant of Timon's; he unsuccessfully solicits Lord Lucius for a loan but remains faithful to Timon until the servants disperse, following Timon's departure from Athens.

Caphis

A servant of an Athenian senator who realizes that Timon is financially irresponsible. The senator sends Caphis to Timon's house to plead with Timon to pay his debts, but by then all of Timon's fortune is exhausted.

Philotus, Titus, and Hortensius

Servants of Timon's creditors; they call on Timon with requests for money for their masters.

Phrynia and Timandra

Two harlots accompanying Alcibiades when he finds Timon in the woods. Timon gives them gold and encourages them to remain prostitutes so that they will continue to corrupt youth and spread diseases.

SUMMARIES AND COMMENTARIES

ACT I

Timon of Athens, for reasons that remain unknown, is an unfinished play. It was probably not acted in Shakespeare's lifetime, and it appeared first in print in the collected edition of Shakespeare's plays, which was published in 1623, over seven years following his death.

The play opens in a hall in Timon's house in Athens. A poet, a painter, a jeweler, a merchant, and others enter and wait for an audience with Timon, a noble Athenian famed for his generosity. The poet and the painter strike up a conversation in which they agree that the matters of the world are growing worse, and the poet comments on the power of Timon's generosity to draw an audience. Attention shifts momentarily to the jeweler, who tells the merchant that he has a fine jewel that he hopes to sell to Timon. The poet then recites some of his verses, and the painter asks if he is currently absorbed in creative concentration on a poem intended for Timon. The poet contends that his poems grow out of an inspiration that feeds upon itself, not from a conscious effort to create. He adds that he will publish his book shortly after Timon sees it, indicating that he is here to seek Timon as a patron. The painter then shows the poet a portrait of Timon that he is carrying with him, and the poet praises it lavishly for being even more realistic than life. The painter, feigning modesty, agrees that it is a good representation.

Some Athenian senators pass through the hall as they leave Timon's chambers, and the poet remarks that they are "happy men" because they have access to Timon. He then describes his poem briefly. It is an allegory in which the goddess Fortune once favored Timon above all other men but, without warning or reason, abandoned him to a friendless misfortune; as such, it presents in miniature the main dramatic theme of the play. The poet asserts that the moral to be drawn from his "rough work" is applicable to a wide range of people and is not intended to injure any specific person. The painter asks for a more complete explanation. The poet replies that because Timon is acknowledged to be a good and generous man, he is fawned upon by people of all social stations and temperaments, from deceitful commoners to solemn noblemen, from false flatterers to the cynic Apemantus, who rants about self-hatred, but who nevertheless enjoys the attention that Timon bestows on him.

In his fable, the poet has placed the goddess Fortune on the top of a hill, and at the base of the hill is a group of men of all types and social ranks, all seeking financial gain. Fortune looks with the most approval upon Timon, whose grace and nobility are so apparent that all who are with him appear to be servants and slaves by comparison, and she motions for him to climb the hill.

The painter interrupts to say that the poet's conception has a parallel in their own endeavor to gain Timon's patronage. The poet listens to the comment, then continues: When Timon begins to mount the hill, the other people, including some of even higher social status than he, begin to follow him with flattering compliments, referring to him in godlike terms, even blessing him for the air that they breath. However, when Fortune casts Timon backward down the hill, none of the people return with him nor offer him assistance. The painter says that the poet's story is consistent with human nature, but he argues that he could create a thousand paintings depicting the reverses of Fortune even better. He does, however, compliment the poet for presenting Timon as a man who, like everyone, is subject to the caprices of Fortune.

Accompanied by a messenger from Lord Ventidius, his own servant Lucilius, and other servants, Lord Timon enters and speaks courteously to everyone present. The messenger reports that Ventidius has been imprisoned for a large debt and that he deeply hopes that Timon can pay off his creditors. Timon declares that he is not a man to abandon a friend in need, and he agrees to pay Ventidius' debts. He instructs the messenger to have Ventidius come to him after being freed to receive more money if he needs it.

The messenger exits, and an old Athenian enters and entreats Timon to forbid Timon's servant Lucilius from courting the old man's daughter. The old man argues that Lucilius is too poor to be either an acceptable husband for his expensively educated daughter or a deserving inheritor of his great estate. Timon argues that Lucilius is honest, but the old man maintains that honesty alone is not enough to gain his consent for a marriage. Timon asks whether or not the old man's daughter loves Lucilius; the old man answers that the girl is too inexperienced to understand her own passions. Timon then asks Lucilius if he loves the girl, and Lucilius replies that he loves her with her approval. The old man insists that he will dispossess his daughter should she marry against his will, but he answers Timon that he is prepared to give his daughter an immediate dowry and make her sole inheritor of his wealth and property if she marries a man of wealth equal to her own. At that point, Timon promises to match the father's dowry and legacy with equal gifts to Lucilius, and the father then agrees that the young people may marry with his consent. Lucilius thanks Timon profusely and swears that he will be in his debt for all that he may ever possess. Timon's dealings with Ventidius and Lucilius demonstrate that he is simultaneously both genuinely generous and extravagantly irresponsible in dispensing his wealth.

After Lucilius and the old man leave, the poet gives his manuscript and the painter his portrait to Timon. Timon praises the painting for its representation of the ideal inner nature of man, which he finds more pleasing than the actual outward countenances that experience in the corrupt, real world has forced men to adopt. He promises to reward the painter for the gift. He then accepts a jewel from the jeweler for approval, but he says that it has been appraised so highly that he cannot afford to buy it. The jeweler insists that the advertised value is correct, but he adds that objects gain or lose true value according to their owners, and he contends that Timon will enhance the value of the jewel by wearing it. Timon compliments the jeweler on his ability to flatter, but the merchant assures Timon that the jeweler is only repeating what everyone says about him.

Apemantus enters, and Timon asks those soliciting him if they are ready to be chided. The jeweler and the merchant reply that they are willing to endure Apemantus' churlishness if Timon can endure it. Timon ironically greets "gentle" Apemantus, and Apemantus snarls that he will become "gentle" only when Timon becomes a dog and the "knaves" present become honest. (There are many references to dogs in the play, and one reason for this is that Apemantus is a cynic, and Timon, after his rejection by his false friends, becomes a cynic; significantly, the word "cynic" is derived from the Greek "kynikos" meaning "doglike.") Apemantus declares that those presently soliciting Timon, and in fact all Athenians, are dishonest scoundrels.

Timon asks Apemantus if he is not proud, and Apemantus retorts in terms that will be reflected later by Timon: "Of nothing so much as that I am not like Timon." Apemantus then ridicules both the painting and the painter, and he answers Timon's request to join him for a meal with this biting comment: "No; I eat not lords," implying that all the others present are parasites, gathered here to gain at Timon's expense. Timon jokingly says that eating lords would anger the ladies, and Apemantus returns the banter by referring to ladies who get pregnant by eating lords. The two men continue to exchange wordplay with sexual connotations, and then Apemantus turns and dismisses the jewel as worthless and chides the poet for answering to his salutation of "poet" and for claiming to be that which he is not. Apemantus claims that Timon is worthy of the poem, however, because those who accept flattery deserve to be misled by flatterers. He then exclaims, "Heavens, that I were a lord!" And he answers Timon's inquiry as to what he would do—if he were a lord—by asserting that he would hate himself for having no more sense than to desire to be a lord. Then, discovering that he has neglected to insult the merchant, Apemantus curses the fellow for being a slave to trade.

A trumpet sounds, and a messenger enters to announce the arrival of Alcibiades and a company of twenty soldiers. Timon tells the messenger to escort them in, and he entreats the solicitors to remain to dine with him. Apemantus prays that their joints will be wracked with pain, and he ridicules the excessive courtesy customarily expressed by scoundrels who detest each other. He ends with the observation that humanity has degenerated into a race of baboons and monkeys. Timon and Alcibiades greet each other, and all but Apemantus leave the hall.

Two lords enter, and Apemantus accuses them of being dishonest, but he agrees to go to Timon's feast so that he can "see meat fill knaves and wine heat fools." The Second Lord says farewell to Apemantus twice, and Apemantus calls him a fool to "waste" a farewell since he, Apemantus, will not give one in return. Apemantus then leaves, trading curses with the lords. The First Lord suggests that they attend Timon's feast, and the Second Lord observes that Timon is more extravagant than Plutus, the god of gold, never accepting a gift without rewarding the giver seven times over—an insight into Timon's behavior that a senator will elaborate on further at the beginning of Act II. Agreeing that Timon is the most noble-minded man who has ever lived, they leave to join the feast.

Scene 2 is set in a banqueting room, where Timon, Alcibiades, Ventidius, several nobles, and Apemantus enter to enjoy a lavish meal. Ventidius, newly released from prison, informs them that his father has died, leaving him a very large inheritance. He offers to repay his debt to Timon, but Timon refuses, insisting that he intended for the money to be considered a gift, not a loan. Ventidius thanks him, and Timon postulates that courtesy was invented to accompany insincere acts of generosity; true acts of friendship need no accompaniment. He declares that he would rather share his wealth with those present than keep it to himself. A lord "confesses" that they have long known and spoken of Timon's liberality, eliciting a curse from Apemantus because of the word "confess." Timon tells Apemantus that he is welcome, but Apemantus says that Timon will have to throw him out for what he will say later.

Timon accuses Apemantus of having an especially rude manner and of belying the old saying "anger is a brief madness" because Apemantus is always angry. Timon then calls for a separate table to be set for Apemantus, but Apemantus asks to remain at Timon's table where he can comment more pointedly on the activity. Timon again tries to soothe Apemantus by welcoming him as an Athenian, and he hopes that the food will silence him.

Apemantus rejects the food, asserting that he will never flatter Timon and lamenting that Timon encourages so many men to take advantage of his generosity. He questions why wealthy men dare to dine with men holding knives since the wealthy are always in danger from false friends. He ends his brief tirade by advising the wealthy to wear more armor on their throats when dining in company. Timon proposes a toast to health, and a lord asks to second it, again eliciting a curse from Apemantus; he criticizes the lord for using flattery and chides Timon for letting his estate be eaten up by irresponsible extravagance. Apemantus then raises a toast of water and offers a grace, in which he prays for nothing nor for no man but himself. He prays that he will trust no man, even a supposed friend, and he concludes with the observation that he will avoid the rich man's gluttony and will, instead, eat roots.

Timon shifts attention away from Apemantus by turning to Alcibiades and asking him if battle is not preferable to the banquet table. Alcibiades answers in the affirmative, and Apemantus interjects a wish that the flatterers around Timon were Alcibiades' enemies in the field so that he could kill them. A lord requests that Timon give his friends an opportunity to express their great friendship for him, a speech that will prove to be ironic in light of later events.

Timon answers with a short speech on friendship, and he assures these men present, his particularly close friends, that the gods will provide means for them to express their friendship. He believes friends are like unused musical instruments if others do not call on them when in need, and he believes that people should consider their friends' property their own. He then falls to joyous weeping because he is blessed by being among so many worthy friends who are willing to share each other's fortunes. A lord proclaims that the same joy has brought the guests to tears, and Apemantus derides Timon for weeping only to solicit more flattery and mocks the lord for lying.

A trumpet sounds, and a servant enters to inform Timon that a group of ladies and their "forerunner" have arrived and their desire is to enter (they turn out to be entertainers provided by the guests). Timon bids them enter. The forerunner, an actor dressed as Cupid, salutes Timon and his guests. He announces that the five human senses, in recognition of Timon as their chief benefactor, have come to entertain him. Timon welcomes them and calls for music, as a lord tells him that the provision of the masque demonstrates how much his friends love him.

Cupid returns with a group of women dressed as Amazon warriors, playing stringed instruments and dancing before the diners. Apemantus is overjoyed by the vain extravagance of the display and enters into a diatribe comparing the "insane" dance to the insanity of life in general and especially to the insanity of Timon's feast. He maintains that men make fools of themselves in order to prosper by flattery, but in the end, men become only spiteful and envious. He asks if there is anyone alive who is not depraved, or if there is anyone who has died who truly appreciated a gift from a friend.

The lords rise, display an exaggerated affection for Timon, and dance with the Amazons. At the end of the dance, Timon thanks the ladies for their performance and thanks his guests for providing the entertainment. Apemantus suspects that exacting discourse would label the ladies for what they are—harlots. Timon ignores the comment and tells the women to partake of the banquet. They thank him and, along with Cupid, exit.

Timon asks his steward, Flavius, to bring in his jewel case. In an aside, Flavius regrets that he cannot stop Timon from giving away all he owns, and he speculates that before long, Timon's irresponsible generosity will lead him into debt. While Flavius is gone, the lords put on a show of pretending that they are in a great bustle to leave. Timon takes his jewels and pleads with one of the lords to accept a jewel, and in unison the lords acknowledge their indebtedness to Timon for earlier gifts.

A servant enters to announce the arrival of several senators, and Timon sends his welcome. Flavius tries to draw Timon aside to explain that his master's wealth is rapidly running out, but Timon puts him off until after he has received and entertained his new guests. Another servant enters to report that Lord Lucius has sent four horses harnessed in silver as a gift for Timon. Timon accepts the gift and commands that gifts be bestowed on his guests. A third servant enters to bring word that Lord Lucullus has sent Timon four greyhounds and an invitation to go hunting on the following day. Timon accepts and orders that the servant be generously rewarded.

In an aside, Flavius anguishes over Timon's continuous spending and his refusal to acknowledge his impending ruin. Flavius knows that Timon has no money left and that his present expenses are driving him deeper into debt and into the necessity of mortgaging his lands to those who are even now benefiting from his bounty. He states proverbially that a man is better off with no friends than with friends who do more harm to him than his enemies do. With a deepening sadness, he exits.

Timon accuses the lords of unjustly undervaluing their merits, and he continues to pass out gifts, to which the lords respond with flowery thanks. Timon gives one of his horses to a lord who praised it a few days earlier. The lord acts as though he will decline it, but Timon insists, promising that he will ask the lord for assistance one day. In unison, the lords assert that they would welcome a request from Timon. Timon wishes that he had kingdoms to reward the lords who please him so much with their visits. He tells Alcibiades that since he is a soldier of little means, he must interpret Timon's gift as having been motivated solely by friendship. Timon and the lords thank each other for their mutual generosity, of which Timon's has been significantly greater. Timon then calls for lights, and after the lords exit, Timon and Apemantus are left alone.

Apemantus mocks the exaggerated gestures of courtesy made by the departing lords. He curses them for being dishonest and comments that "honest fools," of which Timon is one, will willingly exchange money for such courtesies. Timon says that he would be good to Apemantus if he were not so obstinate, but Apemantus insists that he alone—of Timon's friends—refuses to be bribed. One man, says Apemantus, must be left to point out Timon's error and to curb his wasteful spending. Otherwise, Timon will soon give away all he has on useless ostentation. Timon refuses to listen any longer and leaves. Alone, Apemantus threatens not to advise Timon later if he will not listen now, but he laments that Timon, who is so susceptible to flattery, steadfastly refuses to listen to sound advice.

ACT II

The first scene of this act puts into dramatic motion the events that Flavius foresaw at the banquet. In Athens, a senator is at home, examining records of Timon's debts to him, and he affirms for us that Timon is still carelessly giving his money away even though he is deeply in debt. The senator says that if he himself should need money, he would only have to steal a beggar's dog and give it to Timon to get gold, or give a horse to Timon to get enough money in return to buy twenty better horses. He can see nothing but disaster for Timon in the future. He calls his servant Caphis and instructs him to go to Timon and to insist that he be paid what is due the senator, taking care not to be put off by pleasantries but to demand the money and say that the senator's credit is being damaged because Timon's repayment is past due. He realizes that when all demands have been met, Timon will be completely broke. The senator's final instructions to Caphis include a command to collect all interest due on the loans as well, demonstrating that Timon's creditors will be relentless toward Timon now that they have no more to gain from his generosity.

In the next scene, Timon finally realizes the full extent of his financial problems, and he begins to suspect the true nature of man. In a hall in Timon's house, Flavius is studying a large number of bills from Timon's creditors, all demanding payment. He is frustrated because Timon will neither cease his exorbitant giving nor take the time to understand the reality of his situation. Flavius resolves to force Timon to listen as soon as he returns from hunting. Caphis, a servant of Isidore, and a servant of Varro enter, and they learn from each other that all have been sent by their masters to collect from Timon. However, none of them actually expects to receive payment.

Timon, several lords who have accompanied him on the hunt, and Alcibiades enter, and Timon announces that they will resume the hunt after they have eaten. Caphis approaches Timon, but Timon refers him to his steward. Caphis retorts that Flavius has put him off repeatedly before and that his master is now in desperate need of money and expects Timon to follow his noble precepts and to pay immediately. Timon asks Caphis to return the next morning. The servants of Varro and Isidore rush to present their bills to Timon, and Caphis joins them in pleading for payment. Timon asks them all to excuse him for a moment, and he asks Flavius why so many people are accosting him for money. Flavius begs the departing servants to hold off their demands until after dinner and after he has talked to Timon; he and Timon then exit.

Apemantus and a jester, on an errand for a harlot, enter. Caphis thinks that it would be great sport to tease them, and the other servants agree, although apprehensively. Apemantus and the jester exchange insults immediately with the servants, each calling the others fools. The jester claims that the servants will soon become infected with venereal disease, and he derides them for not being able to afford his mistress' prices. A page of the jester's mistress enters and greets the jester and Apemantus, who remarks that a whipping is the only appropriate answer for the page. The illiterate page asks Apemantus to read the addresses for two letters that he has been sent to deliver, and Apemantus tells him that they are for Timon and Alcibiades; after a further exchange of banter, the page exits, and Apemantus offers to accompany the jester to see Timon.

The two men joke about serving usurers, with overt sexual connotations involving the jester's mistress' use of her body to make money. The jester wonders why men who visit usurers leave happy while men who visit their mistresses leave sad. Varro's servant offers an answer, then asks what a "whoremaster" is—that is, what is someone who frequents prostitutes? The jester answers that a whoremaster can be someone like Varro's servant or someone like a lord, a lawyer, a philosopher, a knight—any male from fourteen to eighty. Varro's servant compliments the jester for not being a complete fool, and the jester compliments the servant for not being completely wise. Apemantus, in turn, compliments the jester for answering with wit that could have been uttered by Apemantus himself.

Timon and Flavius enter, and Apemantus, the jester, and the servants exit. Timon is astounded to realize the seriousness of his financial plight, and he asks why Flavius did not inform him earlier so that he could have lived within his means. Flavius refers to his many attempts, but Timon argues that his steward deliberately approached him at times when he was preoccupied. Flavius points out that Timon has continually escaped studying his accounts by insisting that he trusts his steward. He states further that he has seen Timon returning expensive presents for trifling gifts, and he believes that he overstepped his bounds in the past as steward when he advised Timon emphatically to spend less freely, advice for which Timon reproved him severely.

He then tells Timon that there is not enough money and property left to pay half the debts. Timon orders him to sell land, but Flavius reports that some land has already been sold, some mortgaged, and what remains will not go far toward satisfying Timon's current debts. He questions how the estate can be run and how Timon's affairs can be settled permanently with debts continuing to mount. Timon refers to the vast extent of his former lands, but Flavius reminds his master that had he owned the entire world he would have given it away, and Timon finally accepts his predicament for what it is.

Flavius requests that auditors be called in if Timon suspects mismanagement, swearing that for a long time he has wept to see such excessive waste of food, drink, and entertainment. Timon asks him to say no more, but Flavius calls on the heavens to witness the waste of this very night, and he predicts that those who fawn so effusively upon Timon will abandon him totally when all his wealth is gone. Timon beseeches Flavius to preach no more because he has been unwise, not dishonest, in his spending. He tells the steward to dry his tears; Timon is sure that his friends will freely open their coffers to him if he asks them for loans. Flavius can only hope that Timon's faith will be confirmed.

Timon envisions a blessing in his need since it gives him reason to test his friends, and he calls his servants and sends them to the Lords Lucius, Lucullus, and Sempronius to borrow large sums of money from each. After the servants leave, Flavius questions whether the Lords Lucius and Lucullus, in particular, will respond. Timon tells him to go to the senators of Athens and to ask for an immediate loan. Flavius says that he has already contacted the senators, to no avail, and Timon is astounded. Flavius reports that the senators have refused unanimously, some claiming to be low in funds, others wishing that they could help an honorable friend, still others alleging that Timon's dealings may have been dishonest. But all gave short, ungracious answers and went on with what they said were more important things to be considered. Timon urges Flavius to cheer up since it is only natural for old men to lack generosity. He sends another servant to Ventidius to ask for the return of the money that Timon paid to have him released from jail. Timon instructs Flavius to use the money from Ventidius to pay the most demanding bills and to rest assured that his friends will assist him. Flavius hopes they will repay Timon's generosity with their own; otherwise, people will cease to be generous.

ACT III

Timon's servant Flaminius enters the house of Lord Lucullus, and Lucullus, in an aside, expresses joy at seeing him because he is sure that Flaminius has come to deliver an expensive gift from Timon. He sends for wine and asks about Timon's health. Flaminius reports his master is well, and Lucullus asks with exaggerated politeness what he is carrying beneath his cloak. Flaminius answers that it is an empty box—which Timon is sure that Lucullus will fill with money. Lucullus immediately insults Timon for expecting money from him after spending so lavishly on entertainments. Lucullus ironically recounts his dining with Timon for the express purpose of counseling his friend to spend less, but Timon would not heed his warning.

A servant brings wine, and Lucullus hands Flaminius a cup, offering a toast and flattering him for the wisdom that he has displayed so often. Leading up to an attempt to bribe Flaminius, Lucullus continues to praise him for his intelligence and industry. He sends his servant out and privately tells Flaminius that he is wise enough to know that this is no time to loan money secured only by friendship even though Timon has been generous. Lucullus then offers money to Flaminius to say he could not be located. Flaminius damns Lucullus for being thoroughly unprincipled and hurls the money back at him. Lucullus responds that Flaminius is obviously as great a fool as his master. Angered, Flaminius "prays" that Lucullus will be scalded with molten money and that he will grow sick from the food he has eaten at Timon's and die a lingering death.

In Scene 2, set in a street in Athens, Lord Lucius is speaking of Timon's nobility with three strangers. One of them says that he has heard rumors that Timon is nearing bankruptcy, but Lucius denies such a possibility. Another of them relates the urgent request that Timon sent to Lord Lucullus and Lucullus' subsequent refusal. Lucius protests that he is shamed by Lucullus' action, and, referring to the many gifts that he himself has received, he swears that *he* would not deny a similar request from Timon even though his own gifts were less expensive than those given to Lucullus. Timon's servant Servilius enters, seeking Lucius, and Lucius greets him with commendations for his "very exquisite" friend Timon. He then interrupts Servilius' statement to inquire eagerly what Timon has sent, expecting another gift. When Servilius answers that Timon has sent a request for a loan, Lucius declares that such a request is not possible since Timon possesses a fortune. Servilius says that Timon's need could not be considered a fortune but that it is a need so great and so honest that Servilius must insist on Lucius' honoring the request. Lucius asks if he is serious, and when Servilius answers in the affirmative, Lucius pretends to curse himself for having made an excessive, recent expenditure that left him short of funds. He tells Servilius that these fellows to whom he was talking can attest that he was just about to send for a loan from Timon. He sends his best wishes to Timon, and he also sends his regret that he cannot send the money requested, but he hopes that Timon will continue to think well of him anyway. Servilius leaves, and Lucius tells the strangers that Timon is indeed broke but that he will probably not make another request from someone (meaning himself) who has denied him once.

After Lucius leaves, one of the strangers states that all flatterers are like Lucius. He says that Timon has been like a father to Lucius, providing money to sustain his credit, to run his estate, and to pay his servants' wages. Yet Lucius has refused to give Timon a sum of money no larger than most charitable men willingly give beggars. The last stranger holds Lucius' behavior to be an offense against religion. Although he himself has received no gifts from Timon, the first man declares that had he been asked, he would have gladly given Timon over half his wealth out of respect for his honor, nobility, and generosity. He quickly demonstrates the falsity of his generous sentiment, however, by saying that experience has taught him that self-interest is more to be valued than conscience.

Scene 3 is set in Sempronius' home in Athens, and Sempronius is telling a servant of Timon's that his master should have first asked for loans from the Lords Lucius, Lucullus, and Ventidius, all of whom owe their estates to Timon. The servant answers that all have been approached and all have denied Timon. Sempronius seems incredulous that all three lords have refused, but he suddenly realizes how he can refuse as well. He acts as though he is offended that Timon did not come to him first, he who was the first man ever befriended by Timon. He contends that people will think him a fool if he sends money now after being insulted so grievously, and he vows never to loan money to any man who has so dishonored him. Left alone, the servant calls Sempronius a villain, and he theorizes that the devil made an error when he made man deviously cunning because it gave man a capacity for villainy that will eventually make the devil appear good by comparison. Noting that Sempronius has acted with the zeal of a religious fanatic, the servant reveals that Sempronius was Timon's best hope; now all that Timon can do is trust in the gods. All the doors in Athens have been shut against Timon, and thus he must remain a prisoner in his own house to avoid arrest for nonpayment of his debts.

In Scene 4, in a hall in Timon's house, shortly before nine o'clock in the morning, a group of Timon's creditors' servants have gathered, and they discuss the fact that their missions are all the same—money. Philotus, another servant of a creditor, enters and wonders why Timon has not yet appeared since he customarily arises at seven. Lucius' servant speculates that Timon's days are shorter now because his extravagance has brought him to bankruptcy. Another usurer's servant, Titus, comments on the "strangeness" of Hortensius' master's having sent for money while he still wears jewels given him by Timon. Hortensius admits that he does not like what he is doing since he personally considers ingratitude to be worse than stealing.

The servants are adding up the total amount that they have come to collect when Flaminius enters, and they ask if Timon is ready to meet them. Flaminius answers that Timon is not ready, and he tells them sarcastically that he "knows [they] are too diligent" to leave. Flaminius leaves then, and Flavius walks in with his cloak pulled over his head. The servants recognize him and call to him. He asks what they want, and they answer that they have come for money. Flavius asks why they did not demand money when their "false masters" were enjoying Timon's bounty; he tells them that they are wasting their time now because Timon is broke. The servants refuse to accept this answer, and Flavius agrees that it is inappropriate since it is not undignified enough for the servants of scoundrels. He goes on his way, and two servants of Varro remark about their satisfaction in knowing that Flavius is as poor as Timon. Servilius enters, and Titus asks if Timon will answer them. Servilius asks them to come later because ill health is keeping Timon in his room. Lucius' servant observes that many choose seclusion who are not sick, and he suggests that if Timon is ill, he should prepare himself for heaven by paying his debts. Servilius is revolted by the servants' insensitivity.

Flaminius calls from within for Servilius to help him with Timon, who now enters in a rage, questioning why his house has become a prison for him. The creditors' servants rush to present their bills, and Timon angrily encourages them to keep up their assaults on him. He leaves, and Hortensius expresses doubt that the creditors will ever regain their money now that Timon has become insane. All the servants leave, and Timon returns with Flavius. Timon blames the servants for making him so angry that he cannot speak; then he conceives a plan to gain revenge upon his creditors, but he keeps the details to himself. He instructs Flavius to invite Lucius, Lucullus, Sempronius, and his other friends to a feast. When Flavius protests that they cannot afford to provide even a modest meal, Timon says that he and his cook will make adequate provisions.

In Scene 5, Alcibiades appears before the Athenian Senate to plead for a pardon for a friend who killed a man in self-defense and who is now condemned to die. In many ways, his situation parallels Timon's in several ways. Alcibiades is being generous with what he has most of—renown and honor—to benefit a friend. His pleas, however, will be rejected by the elderly senators just as Timon's requests were refused by elderly lords and senators. The "friends" of Timon practice usury; here Alcibiades accuses the senators of having grown rich on usury while he has remained poor in service to Athens. The Senate will finally be ungracious to a man who has benefited them enormously, just as Timon's "friends" have been ungracious to him. However, Alcibiades readjusts quickly when the Senate banishes him, gaining fortitude from the knowledge that he has the means to right the wrongs done him.

In the Senate House, arguing that mercy encourages crime, a senator adds his approval to a decision that an unnamed man be executed for murder. Alcibiades greets the Senate and speaks on behalf of his friend, the condemned man, one who remains anonymous. He proposes that the greatest virtue of law is pity and that only tyrants use law in a cruel manner. He admits that his friend is guilty of a crime of passion, but he argues that the man is essentially virtuous. He did not kill in a cowardly manner but fairly and honorably to defend his reputation. He fought his enemy not in a fury of passion but in a detached anger to defend his honor.

A senator claims Alcibiades' defense is merely a rationalization intended to make a bloody crime appear noble, proper, and valorous. Manslaughter, says the senator, is, in fact, valor misdirected, and it has always been accompanied by arguments involving "sects and factions." The senator then argues that the truly valiant man is one who can endure wrongs dispassionately without becoming angry or seeking revenge. Alcibiades tries to interject a response, but the senator cuts him short, saying that Alcibiades cannot justify heinous crimes by making "gross sins look clear."

Alcibiades then asks permission to speak like a soldier. If the greatest honor and wisdom lie in suffering, he asks, why do men engage in battle rather than allow their enemies to cut their throats while they sleep, and why are women not considered more valiant than soldiers, and, finally, why are bound convicts not considered wiser than their judges? He agrees that cold-blooded murder is abhorrent, but he is defending murder in self-defense since all men are subject to anger. When a senator tells him that he argues in vain, Alcibiades tries a new tactic and refers to the battles in which his friend distinguished himself. A senator responds that the man is well known for his past recklessness and drunkenness in which he allowed his passion to overcome his valor, leading him into violence, outrageous behavior, and membership in factions. Another senator declares that the death sentence is final.

Alcibiades appeals for the Senate to combine his own service to Athens with that of his friend. He pledges his military reputation and his honor as surety, and he asks that the sentence be commuted to combat duty against the enemies of Athens. A senator warns Alcibiades not to risk angering the Senate by arguing further because the man has committed murder and thus must be executed. Alcibiades again pleads that the Senate owes him a debt for the protection he has given it on the battlefield, and he suggests that it is poor memory, brought on by old age, that has caused the senators to be so ungracious to him. In anger, a senator banishes Alcibiades, who responds, "Banish me! / Banish your dotage! Banish usury. / That makes the Senate ugly!" One of the senators gives Alcibiades two days to leave Athens, and he orders the immediate execution of Alcibiades' friend.

The senators then file out of the Senate House, and Alcibiades delivers a soliloquy. He prays that the already aged senators be damned to an even longer life of misery, and he repeats his conviction that he has remained a poor soldier protecting Athens while the senators have grown rich on usury. However, he becomes heartened when he realizes that his command of the army gives him the power to gain revenge. He ends with a declaration that soldiers, like the gods, should endure no wrong.

Scene 6 takes place in the banquet room of Timon's house, where a group of unnamed lords have arrived for a feast. They discuss the requests for money that Timon has made of them lately, and the First Lord says that he hopes Timon's finances are not as bad as his messengers have implied. The Second Lord points out that the present preparations for a feast belie the idea that Timon is broke. Both lords claim to have put off other important engagements in order to attend Timon's banquet, and all the lords express regret for recent events. Timon enters with his attendants and greets the lords with feigned enthusiasm. The lords return the greeting, and the Second Lord compares their devotion to Timon with the swallows that follow summer. In an aside, Timon notes that they also abandon him as quickly in the winter of his adversity. Aloud, he tells the lords to enjoy the music in anticipation of a splendid dinner. The lords apologize for not sending money when he requested it, but Timon acts as though he has dismissed their refusals without a second thought. He calls for food to be brought in, and the lords exclaim that the covered dishes promise a fine, expensive meal indeed. They begin to discuss Alcibiades' banishment, but they agree to delay the subject when Timon invites them to the table.

The lords gather around the table and comment that Timon is still as extravagant as ever. Timon bids them to find their places as quickly as they would rush to kiss their mistresses, and he invites them not to stand on protocol but to begin eating as soon as they wish. However, he radically changes his tone when he begins to say the grace. He asks the gods to be plentiful, but he reminds them to be careful that they save something to give in the future or men will come to despise even them. He also asks the gods to give every man enough so that he will not have to borrow because men will forsake even the gods should the gods become indebted to men. He prays that men will love food more than the hosts who provide it, that all men will become villains, that all women will become harlots, and that the gods will make preparations to destroy the senators along with the remaining citizens of Athens.

After stating that the worthless guests deserve nothing, he ends his bitter grace by shouting "Uncover, dogs, and lap!" as his attendants uncover the serving dishes, which are filled with lukewarm water. The lords are amazed. Timon is sure that they will never enjoy a better meal because "smoke and lukewarm water" are precisely what he thinks they deserve. Promising that this is his final feast, he throws water on the lords and curses them all with long, unpleasant lives. He calls them parasites, fair-weather friends, and obsequious slaves to the well-to-do. Proclaiming that he will lend them money but borrow none, he pelts them with the dishes. He prays that his house will burn and that Athens will sink into the ground, and he leaves, announcing that from this time forward he will hate all humanity. Another group of lords and senators enter and ask the cause of the disturbance. Looking for articles of clothing that they have lost in the melee, the confused guests declare that Timon has gone mad.

ACT IV

As he leaves Athens, determined to become a hermit, Timon looks back on the walls of the city and vents his anger in a lengthy soliloquy. He prays that the walls will sink into the earth and leave the city defenseless. He hopes for social order and government to break down, for innocent youth to become morally corrupt, for bankruptcy to ruin all creditors, for servants to steal from their masters, and for young men to murder their fathers. He hopes that piety, peace, justice, honesty, domestic peace, sleep, human fellowship, education, manners, crafts, trades, social distinctions, customs, laws, and all other civilized ceremonies will decline into destructive chaos. He hopes that diseases and sicknesses will poison the entire population. He prays for crop failures and cries out proudly that he takes nothing away from the city but his nakedness; he will live in the woods, and there he expects the most ferocious beast to be more kind to him than men have been. He calls on the gods to damn all Athenians, both inside and outside the city, and he beseeches the gods to increase his hatred for all classes of men. Timon has become a misanthrope.

Scene 2 returns us to Timon's house, where a servant asks Flavius where Timon has gone and what, if anything, has been left to pay the servants; Flavius answers sympathetically that he is as poor as the rest. The servant laments the fall of Timon, who has been left without a single friend to accompany him. Another servant criticizes Timon's former friends for having dismissed him as completely as men customarily bid farewell to the dead. A third servant says that they are still comrades and still wear Timon's livery, but now their strongest bond is their mutual sorrow. He compares himself and the others to sailors abandoning a sinking ship; they must go their separate ways "into this sea of air." Flavius, however, offers to share what money he has, and he proposes that they continue the bond they established by being fellow servants of Timon. The servants at first refuse his money, but when he insists, they partake, embrace, and go their separate ways.

Alone, Flavius reveals his decision to follow Timon. He declares that the misery brought on by wealth should lead all to avoid riches.

He sees the irony in Timon's having destroyed himself through acts of goodness, and he wonders if Timon's example will prevent everyone from doing good deeds in the future. He knows that Timon has gone into the woods without food or the means to purchase necessities, but he plans to continue in his service as long as he has any money remaining.

The third scene begins near a cave in a woods, next to the seashore; it is here that Timon has come to live as a misanthrope. He asks the sun to draw infectious vapors from the earth with which to infect humanity. He notes that even an identical twin will scorn a brother who is less fortunate financially; this, he says, is a trait common to human nature. If a beggar becomes wealthy and a senator becomes poor, Timon maintains that the beggar will reap honor, but the senator will reap only contempt. He believes that society is permeated with flattery, causing scholars to be forced to cater to rich fools and forcing all social intercourse (excepting villainy itself) to accept all sorts of false practices. He swears that he will never again live in the accursed society of humanity, which he hopes will be destroyed. Incensed at the injustice he has suffered, he begins furiously digging for roots and—to his amazement—discovers a large hoard of gold. He tells the gods that he wants only roots, not gold, which can alter every concept and condition of humanity, which can cause murder, inspire widows to remarry, restore the most grievously ill to full health, create and destroy religions, make the accursed blessed, the leper adored, and make thieves into senators. However, he does keep the gold and promises to put it to its proper use. Distant drums announce the approach of an army, and Timon buries the gold, keeping a bit, however, for present use.

Alcibiades and two prostitutes, Phrynia and Timandra, enter. Alcibiades sees Timon and asks him to identify himself. Timon declares he is a "beast," similar to Alcibiades, and he hopes that Alcibiades will become afflicted with cankers for bringing humanity into Timon's presence again. Timon then says that his name is Misanthropos, meaning one who hates humanity, and he wishes Alcibiades were a dog so that he could have at least a little affection for him. They admit that they recognize one another, and Timon urges Alcibiades to continue his military profession, but, becoming sarcastic, he says that he has full confidence that Phrynia can cause more destruction as a prostitute than Alcibiades can as a soldier.

Phrynia is furious, and she and Timon curse one another, and Alcibiades asks, with concern, what has caused Timon to change so drastically. Timon answers metaphorically that unlike the renewing moon, he now lacks "light to give." Alcibiades inquires what he can do to aid Timon, and Timon answers that Alcibiades can follow nature and falsely promise to be a friend. Alcibiades admits to having heard rumors of Timon's condition, and Timon counters that Alcibiades was familiar with his miseries when he was prosperous. Alcibiades refers to that as "a blessed time," and Timon states that it was a time very much like what Alcibiades is experiencing now, accompanied as he is by two harlots; Timon is equating the harlots following Alcibiades to the parasites who once flattered him.

Timon encourages Timandra to continue her profession so that she may infect the young with wealth-destroying diseases, and Alcibiades entreats her to forgive the offensive statements of a madman. He regrets that the financial demands of his campaign against Athens will not allow him to be as generous with his resources as he would like, but he assures Timon that he, himself, is very aware of the fact that Athens has forgotten her indebtedness to Timon for his successful leadership in war and his generosity in peace. Timon interrupts to beg Alcibiades to continue on his march, and Alcibiades expresses renewed friendship and pity for Timon. He even offers Timon some gold, but Timon rejects everything. However, when Alcibiades again alludes to Timon's hatred toward Athens, Timon excitedly calls for confusion to fall first on the Athenians and, second, on Alcibiades. Alcibiades asks why Timon has cursed him, and Timon replies that he does so because Alcibiades will conquer his country by killing villains. He then tells Alcibiades to keep his gold, and he gives him more, hoping that it will assist him to visit Athens like a plague, sparing neither the elderly, mothers, virgins, babes, nor priests because all are inwardly evil. Alcibiades takes the gold but rejects the advice; Timon states that he does not care what Alcibiades does and curses him in any event.

Phrynia and Timandra, greedy at the sight of Alcibiades' gift, also ask for gold. Timon brags that he has enough to make a whore either give up her trade or become the madam of her own brothel, and he orders them to hold up their aprons to receive the gold. He is confident that the two whores will continue to spread diseases even though they themselves may have to resort to wearing wigs to disguise venereal disease-induced baldness. He concludes by shouting for them to remain whores until the time when they must use so much makeup that a horse will mire down in it. The women respond only by asking for more gold, admitting that they will do anything for it. Timon continues to curse the harlots, telling them to spread corruption, to destroy the lawyer's false-pleading voice, to give leprosy to the false priests, to rot the noses of those who abandon duty for personal gain, to make pimps bald, and to infect cowardly soldiers. In summation, he charges them to infect the whole of Athens, giving them even more gold as he damns them. The women ask for more advice—so long as he accompanies it with money—and Timon promises to give them even more after they have done their "mischief."

Alcibiades calls for his drummer to signal the resumption of the march to Athens, and he promises to visit Timon again if he is successful. Timon hopes never to see Alcibiades again. Alcibiades insists he has never harmed Timon, but Timon disagrees, maintaining that Alcibiades has spoken well of him, a thing that men daily find to be harmful. Alcibiades, his army, and the two women leave, and Timon resumes his digging for roots. He prays that mother earth, who provides for all and who is responsible for the creation of all animal life, will yield one poor "root" who is universally hated. He beseeches the earth to cease producing ungrateful men and to produce only fierce animals and "new monsters." After suddenly coming upon a root and giving thanks to the earth, he asks nature to dry up the fruit, vines, and pasturelands, which provide the produce that ungrateful men use for their own corruption.

Apemantus enters, causing Timon to curse the presence of another man. Apemantus has come to confirm a rumor that states that Timon has started to act like Apemantus. Timon attributes his behavior to Apemantus' not having a dog he can imitate. Apemantus blames Timon's alteration on depression, caused by his change of fortune, and he asks Timon why he lives as he does while the flatterers who have forgotten him live in splendor. He tells Timon not to shame the woods by pretending to be a cynic but, instead, to thrive by becoming a dedicated flatterer, deeming it to be only just that a man who once believed flatterers should now become one himself. However, he admits that Timon would only give any wealth he might again possess to flatterers, and he suddenly demands that

Timon quit acting like him. Timon cuttingly responds, "Were I like thee, I'd throw away myself."

Apemantus counters with the assertion that Timon has degenerated from being a longtime madman into now being a fool. He questions if Timon believes that wild nature will take care of him and assume the duties once performed by servants, and he sarcastically asks him to solicit flattery from the animals of the woods. Timon interrupts; he orders Apemantus to leave, but Apemantus vows that he now cares for Timon more than ever. Timon declares that he hates Apemantus more than ever for flattering misery. In answer, Apemantus says that he has searched out Timon only to chide him. He argues that it would be fine if Timon had assumed his own personal role of a cynic in order to repent having once been proud, but he contends that Timon plays his own role reluctantly, really wanting to live again in luxury. He alleges that people who genuinely accept misery as the lot of humanity are happier than those who prefer the pomp of high station, which consistently promises but never delivers contentment. He thinks that Timon should desire to die since he is so miserable.

Timon asserts that he will not listen to someone who is even more miserable than himself, someone who has been so shunned by Fortune that he has been a "dog" since birth. He speculates that if Apemantus had ever enjoyed Timon's one-time good fortune and authority, he would have succumbed totally to lascivious living and would have ignored reason altogether. Timon reminisces about his former position of wealth, respect, and power, and he compares the many who once attended him in numbers to the leaves on a tree. Citing his own experience, he can attest that it is indeed a severe burden for one to endure severe want, especially one who has known only plenty previously. He avers that Apemantus has become hardened to suffering because that is all he has ever known; it is not surprising that Apemantus cannot curse men for not flattering him—he has never given anyone anything. Apemantus can logically curse only his father for begetting him a beggar's life and condemning him to a life of depravity. Apemantus wonders whether Timon can still be proud, and Timon answers, "Ay, that I am not thee," which echoes Apemantus' insult in the first scene of the play. Apemantus then responds sharply that he is proud that *he* is not a spendthrift, and Timon again asks him to leave; he says that if Apemantus could contain all the "wealth" that Timon has now, Timon would tell the cynic to hang himself. Timon then eats a root, and Apemantus offers him another, but Timon says that he only wants Apemantus to leave. He shows Apemantus some gold and asks him to hurry to Athens with the news that he is again wealthy.

Apemantus can see no use for gold in the woods, but Timon argues that it is put to its best use there, for it can do no harm in the woods. Apemantus asks where Timon sleeps; Timon answers that he sleeps in the open, and he asks where Apemantus eats. Apemantus answers that he eats wherever he finds food; Timon says that he wishes Apemantus' food were poisoned. Apemantus tells Timon, "The middle of humanity thou never knewest, but [that he has known] the extremity of both ends," emphasizing that the once sophisticated Timon now associates with only the most base. He asks Timon if he likes sour medlars (apple-like, decaying fruit), but Timon says he "hates" medlars—even though they look similar to Apemantus. Apemantus then asks if Timon has ever known a spendthrift who was genuinely loved; Timon answers by asking if Apemantus has ever loved anyone who was not a spendthrift. Apemantus answers, "Myself," and he asks what is most comparable to the men who once flattered Timon. Timon answers that women are similar but that "men are the things themselves." He asks what Apemantus would do if he had the power to change the world; Apemantus says that he would rid it of men and give it to the beasts. Timon asks Apemantus if he would like to remain as one of the beasts after the destruction of men. Apemantus answers, "Ay," and Timon hopes that Apemantus' "beastly ambition" will be fulfilled because all animals have natural enemies, possess evil traits, and live in danger. Timon cites a long list of animals, combining each with an enemy or an obnoxious trait, and he asks Apemantus to name an animal that is not prey to another, declaring that Apemantus is already a beast without realizing it. Apemantus admits that this cynicism would be pleasing, were it possible for Timon to please him with any conversation, because all the citizens of Athens have become beasts. Timon wonders if a donkey has broken the wall of Athens to let Apemantus escape. Apemantus announces the approach of a poet and a painter and offers to leave (they do not, in fact, appear until the next act). Timon contends that he could welcome Apemantus' presence only if nothing else were left alive, and Apemantus accuses Timon of being the "cap of all the fools alive" (the greatest fool living). They continue to hurl increasingly insulting invectives at each other, provoking Timon to finally throw a stone at Apemantus.

Timon reaffirms that he is "sick of this false world," and he decides that it is time to prepare a grave by the sea and to write an epitaph expressing his belief that death is preferable to life. He sings a sarcastic paean to his gold, praising it for defiling human nature, disrupting human order, and uniting things that should remain apart. He prays that gold will finally set men at odds and bring about the destruction of humanity. Apemantus agrees with Timon's curse, vowing to spread the word that Timon is again rich so that people will throng to see him. Timon once more asks Apemantus to leave; Apemantus wishes Timon a long life in which to enjoy his misery. Timon returns the wish for long life, but he judges his own life to be nearly finished. Announcing that more men are approaching for Timon to be disgusted with, Apemantus leaves.

Three bandits enter, discussing Timon and his rumored gold. The First Bandit thinks that perhaps Timon has retained only a small portion of his former wealth, but the Second Bandit says that reports indicate that the amount is large. The Third Bandit suggests that if they ask Timon for it he will give it to them willingly if he does not value it or else he will lead them to its hiding place if he does. They greet Timon, who salutes them as thieves. They claim to be soldiers, however, but this makes no difference to Timon, who equates soldiers and thieves. The bandits state that they are men who desire a great deal. Timon claims that their greatest desire is meat, and he questions why they are not content with the fresh water and fruit that nature abundantly provides in the woods. The First Bandit answers that they cannot live like beasts. Timon notes they cannot live by eating beasts either; they should eat men, he says, although he admits that there is at least some honesty in their being professed thieves. He gives them some gold and tells them to use it to drink themselves into a stupor. He advises them not to trust doctors since doctors kill more people with poisonous antidotes than the thieves rob, and he urges them always to kill their holdup victims. Timon philosophizes on everything's being in a sense a thief, including the sea, the earth, and human law. Hoping that his gift will spur them to even greater thievery, he gives them more gold and advises them to continue their profession in Athens, where they will be stealing only from other thieves. Commenting on Timon's extreme hatred of humanity and on his speech encouraging thievery, the bandits depart for Athens.

Unnoticed by Timon, Flavius enters; he is clearly saddened by the sight of his former master ruined in wealth and declining in health, and he construes Timon's plight to be a good example of the folly of bestowing good deeds on those who do not deserve them. He questions if anything on earth can be more evil than the "friends" who have brought Timon to his present condition, and he hopes that he will never allow himself to be deceived by people who pretend to be friends. At this point, Flavius vows to continue to serve Timon faithfully and steps forward. Timon asks who he is and orders him to go away. Flavius asks if Timon has forgotten him; Timon replies that he has forgotten all men. When Flavius identifies himself as an honest servant, Timon answers that he has always been served by dishonest scoundrels. Flavius swears that he genuinely grieves for Timon, and Timon confesses that he can love Flavius after all because Flavius' tears prove that he is a woman and not a hardhearted male, inherently incapable of weeping. Flavius dismisses the sarcasm and begs Timon to accept him again as a steward and allow him to share his modest supply of money. Timon is moved by Flavius' offers, and he asks the gods to forgive him for not realizing that there were exceptions when he damned all humanity for being ungracious and evil, but he insists that Flavius—a lowly steward—is the only honest man alive. He believes Flavius to be foolish not to realize that he could get a better position by taking advantage of his wretched master, for such is customary, and he asks if Flavius has any ulterior motives for being kind. Flavius answers that he does not and that he wishes Timon had developed a suspicious nature earlier, when he was spending extravagantly. He swears that his only concern is for Timon's well-being and for his becoming prosperous again.

Timon realizes that Flavius is sincere, and he gives him a large amount of gold, advising him to live richly and happily but to hate all men, to live apart from them, and to give charity to no one—no matter how terrible his plight might appear. He hopes that all men will eventually be imprisoned, consumed by debt, and infected by disease. He commands Flavius to leave, and when Flavius expresses a desire to stay, Timon confesses that he would only curse him if he stayed. He repeats his wish for Flavius to live a free and happy life, but a life apart from men in general and from himself in particular.

ACT V

The first scene of this act is set in the woods, outside Timon's cave. The poet and the painter who presented their works to Timon in Act I have heard of his new wealth, and they are now seeking him in the woods. Unknown to them, however, he observes them from within his cave. They are sure that he is rich again because of the gold that he has reportedly given Alcibiades, Phrynia, Timandra, and Flavius. The poet postulates that Timon has feigned bankruptcy to test his friends. The painter agrees, adding that Timon will surely be a great man once again in Athens. He theorizes that it will look honorable on their part if they befriend him in his need, and he speculates that Timon will no doubt reward them with gold.

The poet asks what the painter has brought to present to Timon, and the painter replies he has brought only the promise of an excellent future work. The poet says that he also will have to rely on a promise, evoking a comment on current trends from the painter. He explains that mere promises are fashionable, arouse expectations in the patron, and are far more interesting than the dull work of actual production. He concludes by observing that only foolish artists actually deliver their creations since the more sophisticated patrons do not expect anything beyond promises.

Unseen, Timon leaves his cave and muses on the villainy of the two men. The poet plans to promise Timon a satire on flattery, but he contends that they would do well to find Timon before he gives all his gold away. Speaking to himself, Timon says that he is confident that he can match their deviousness. He contemplates the power of gold and prays that all who worship it will become diseased. He steps forward, and the poet and the painter greet him respectfully. Timon asks if he has lived long enough "to see two honest men." The poet informs him that they have heard of the "monstrous" ingratitude with which his noble and generous nature has been repaid, an ingratitude beyond their powers to express adequately. Timon flatters them again for being honest.

The painter acknowledges that he and the poet profited from Timon's generosity, and he offers their services to Timon, who continues to flatter them for being honest men and asks casually if they can live on roots and water. Both say that they can, and Timon again flatteringly refers to their honesty and asks pointedly if they are truthful and honest. The painter affirms that they are, but in an unintentional irony he adds, "but therefore / Came not my friend nor I." With intentional irony, Timon flatters the painter for being able to "counterfeit"—that is, to paint portraits *and* to deceive—better than any other Athenian, and he praises the poet for succeeding so well in his composition that his verse reflects his true nature.

Timon seemingly interrupts his praise to suggest that both of them suffer from a minor fault that he wishes that they would try to correct. They beg him to tell them what it is, promising not to become upset by his reply. Timon tells them that they trust a rascal who greatly deceives them, and they are eager to learn who it is. He tells them that they listen to a knave's lies, see his pretenses, and realize his clear dishonesty, yet they hold him in dearest friendship even though they know him to be an archvillain. They deny knowing such a person, but Timon promises them gold now—and more later—if they will rid themselves of their villainous acquaintance with this man by stabbing, drowning, or by any other deadly means—and then return to him. They cry for him to name the villain. Cryptically but pointedly referring to their individual and collective dishonesty, Timon tells them that each of them always carries an "archvillain" with him wherever he goes, no matter how alone he may be. He then gives them gold, curses them, and beats them away from his cave, calling them "rascal dogs."

Timon returns to his cave, and Flavius enters, escorting two senators from Athens. Flavius tells the senators that their mission to seek Timon's assistance in the defense of Athens is hopeless because Timon has become a misanthrope. The First Senator wants to see Timon anyway to fulfill his promise to the Senate; the Second Senator believes that Timon may revert to his former self when he learns that they bring word that he will have his former fortune and position restored in return for his assistance. Flavius accompanies them to the cave and announces them to Timon. Timon curses them, hoping that the sun will burn them and that each word will raise a blister on their tongues.

When they tell him that they have been sent by the Senate, he says that he wishes he could send the plague back to Athens with them without endangering himself. The First Senator says that the

Senate, in unanimous resolution, decreed that "special dignities" be bestowed on Timon when he returns. The Second Senator reports that the Senate's current need of Timon has made it aware of its past ungracious treatment of him and that the Senate has sent them to make amends and to offer recompense even greater than its acknowledged great offense warrants. He hopes that his offer will erase the Senate's wrongs and reconcile Timon to Athens.

Timon tells them that they have bewitched him "to the very brink of tears," and he sarcastically concedes that he would weep over the Senate's offer if they could give him "a fool's heart and a woman's eyes." The First Senator invites Timon to return to Athens as commander of the army with absolute power and with his reputation and wealth restored. Then, he asserts, they will defeat Alcibiades. Timon answers that it matters not to him if Alcibiades sacks Athens totally. He insists that nothing can arouse his pity for his former country. However, he values his own life even less than that of any Athenian, and he bids them farewell with a sarcastic prayer calling on the gods to protect them.

Flavius calls for him to stay, but Timon says that he must finish the epitaph that will be needed tomorrow, and he hopes again that Alcibiades will destroy them. The First Senator realizes that all entreaties are in vain, but Timon suddenly decides to feign that he has relented. He declares a love for his country and a desire to prevent its destruction. He sends his greetings to his "loving countrymen," and the senators rejoice in their success. Timon says he will show them how to oppose Alcibiades. The First Senator naturally interprets this to mean that Timon will return to lead the defense, but Timon has led them into a rhetorical, philosophical trap that he now prepares to spring. He says that he has a tree outside his cave that he must shortly cut down (to use for his coffin), and he tells the senators to tell everyone in Athens that if anyone wished to put a stop to his misery, then he should come and hang himself from the tree. Flavius tells the senators to leave ("all's in vain") because Timon is always in this humor. Timon then asks the senators to report that he is in a grave, washed daily by the tides. He wants his gravestone to become an oracle who will proclaim the evil and the futility of life. Telling the sun to hide its beams, he leaves. The First Senator suggests that because their mission has failed, they should hurry to Athens to prepare alternate defenses.

Scene 2 opens outside the walls of Athens. A messenger reports to two senators that Alcibiades is ready to attack Athens in full force. One of the senators expresses fear that a successful defense of the city will be lost if the emissaries fail to bring Timon back. The messenger tells of meeting another messenger carrying letters from Alcibiades seeking Timon's help in his attack on Athens. The senators return from their mission to Timon to announce their failure. One of them also reports that Alcibiades and an eager army are near, and he expects the worst to befall.

The third scene takes place in the woods near Timon's cave. A soldier comes across a crudely constructed tomb. He knows that this is the place where Timon has been living, and therefore he suspects that the tomb is Timon's. He cannot read, so he takes a wax impression of the inscription to deliver to Alcibiades.

Scene 4 begins as a trumpet heralds the approach of Alcibiades and his army before the walls of Athens. Alcibiades orders the trumpeter to announce their arrival "to this coward and lascivious town." Some senators appear atop the walls, and Alcibiades shouts that the days of their unrestrained power and their arbitrary disposal of justice are over. Those who have endured Athenian tyranny have finally cried "No more"; they now intend to overthrow the Senate. The First Senator informs Alcibiades that the Senate has long ago sent messages to him offering to compensate for its act of ingratitude. The Second Senator adds that they have also tried to reach a reconciliation with Timon, demonstrating that they are neither without kindness nor deserve war. The First Senator argues that it will not be proper for Alcibiades to revenge himself by destroying walls, monuments, and schools built by a different generation of Athenians than those who offended him. The Second Senator relates that those who offended Alcibiades are all now dead; they have died from shameful remorse over their shameful treatment of Alcibiades. He invites Alcibiades and his army to enter the defenseless city and to satisfy his revenge by slaughtering one-tenth of the population. The First Senator argues that it would be unjust to kill those not responsible. The Second Senator tells Alcibiades that no matter what course he decides to follow, they hope he will do it peacefully, and the First Senator tells him that if he will come in friendship, the gates to the city will be opened readily. The Second Senator asks him to give them a sign that he intends peace, and

Alcibiades throws down his glove and asks for the gates to be opened, agreeing to punish only those who have been unjust to Timon and himself. He promises that if any of his soldiers violate established law, they will be punished by that law.

As Alcibiades prepares to enter the gates, the soldier who visited Timon's grave enters and reports Timon's death. He gives to Alcibiades the wax impression that he made from the inscription on the tomb. Timon left two epitaphs, both of which are distinctly different. One states that the tomb holds an unnamed corpse; it asks passersby not to seek the name of the occupant, and it hopes that all who are left alive will contract diseases. The second epitaph states that the "hated Timon" lies within the grave; it asks all observers to "curse thy fill" but to be sure not to linger. Alcibiades says that the inscriptions express Timon's opinions well. He speaks imaginatively to Timon, telling him that even though in life he hated his friends' expressions of grief, he has taught those friends to weep forever on his humble grave. Alcibiades turns to enter the city, promising to use his military power to ensure peaceful ends and promising that he will heal the civic wounds of Athens: "I will use the olive with my sword."

1607

antony and
cleopatra

ANTONY AND CLEOPATRA

LIST OF CHARACTERS

Mark Antony

A middle-aged Roman general who rules the Roman Empire along with Lepidus and Octavius Caesar. He is torn between his desire for Cleopatra and the demands of his position as a world ruler.

Octavius Caesar

The adopted son of Julius Caesar, his grand-uncle, he is only in his early twenties, but he is determined to ultimately be the sole ruler of the Roman Empire.

Lepidus

As a member of the Triumvirate, he serves as a mediator between Antony and Caesar, the two rivals; he has no real power of his own.

Cleopatra

She is aware of her duties as Queen of Egypt, but she is deeply infatuated with Antony; her heroic courage is revealed when she and Antony are defeated and she chooses to die in Egypt rather than return to Rome as a captive.

Octavia

She becomes engaged to Antony in order to cement a political and military truce between Antony and her brother, Caesar.

Sextus Pompeius (Pompey)

Formerly a Roman, Pompey left Rome with a faction that included several pirates and some of Julius Caesar's navy. He attempted to form his own kingdom, and he is able to cause the Triumvirate trouble by plundering their ships.

Enobarbus

Antony's trusted lieutenant and close friend; eventually he deserts the man he both admires and pokes fun at, yet he later commits suicide in remorse.

Ventidius

Another of Antony's officers, he is sent to fight the Parthians. He is a brave and capable general and is absolutely loyal to Antony.

Scarus

Another of Antony's officers; he serves as Antony's aide after Enobarbus deserts his general.

Dercetas

He is one of the first to find Antony after Antony has tried to kill himself. Dercetas deserts to Caesar's faction, taking Antony's sword as a sign that the enemy is almost defeated.

Demetrius and Philo

These friends of Antony's are among those who go with him to Egypt. They long to see their general as he was before he fell in love and forgot about his political and military duties.

Canidius

He is a lieutenant general to Antony, but he deserts Antony's camp for Caesar's faction after Antony's first major defeat.

Euphronius

He serves as an ambassador from Antony to Caesar.

Fulvia

She does not appear in the play, but she is Antony's first wife.

Taurus

As lieutenant general to Caesar, his strategies help Caesar to win the war against the forces of Antony and Cleopatra.

Maecenas

An officer and a friend of Caesar; when the triumvirs meet at the house of Lepidus in Rome to effect a truce, Maecenas is present.

Agrippa

Another friend of Caesar; along with Maecenas, he never judges Antony quite as lightly as does his general.

Proculeius

This friend of Caesar acts as a messenger and tells Cleopatra on behalf of Caesar that she need not be afraid for her welfare.

Dolabella

Unlike Proculeius, Dolabella feels pity for Cleopatra and warns her that Caesar's promises to her may be empty ones.

Thyreus

He also acts as a messenger, telling Cleopatra of Antony's defeat and Octavius' victory.

Charmian

She is one of Cleopatra's closest friends and court confidantes.

Iras

Another of Cleopatra's attendants.

Alexas

A servant of Cleopatra who acts as a messenger between her and Antony.

Mardian

This member of Cleopatra's entourage is a eunuch, a fact which Cleopatra enjoys teasing him about.

Menas

A pirate; he advises Pompey to take the triumvirs captive and have them murdered while they are attending a banquet aboard his ship.

Menecrates

As a chief officer of Pompey, he helps his general plan strategies.

Varrius

He is warlike and ambitious, like Pompey, but he is less unscrupulous than Menas.

Eros and Gallus

Eros is a friend of Antony's; Gallus is a friend of Caesar's.

Silius

An officer in Ventidius' army.

Seleucus and Diomedes

Attendants to Cleopatra.

A Soothsayer

A fortuneteller who tells Charmian that she will outlive Cleopatra.

SUMMARIES AND COMMENTARIES

ACT I

Summary

The play opens in Alexandria, in one of the rooms of Cleopatra's palace. Two of Antony's friends, Demetrius and Philo, are discussing Antony's increasing fondness for Cleopatra. Philo, in particular, is worried about "this dotage" that his general has for the Egyptian queen; to him, Antony's passion "o'erflows the measure." He feels that a general's passion is best spent on the battlefield "in the scuffles of great fights." As they ponder their general's unreasonable behavior, there is a fanfare of trumpets, and Antony and Cleopatra enter, accompanied by the queen's ladies-in-waiting and her attendant eunuchs. Philo is fearful that all this pomp and beauty has turned his general from a fierce warrior into an addled lover. Significantly he worries that Antony, "The triple pillar of the world," has bean translated into "a strumpet's fool."

Cleopatra's first words to Antony are teasing. She wants to know how much Antony loves her, and he boasts that if any love can be measured, then it is poor love indeed ("There's beggary in the love that can be reckoned"). But Cleopatra tantalizes him for still more compliments—more verbal proof of his love. Foolishly he tries to appease her.

They are interrupted by a messenger who has brought news from Rome, but Antony clearly is in no mood to hear or discuss military matters. All of his thoughts are on his beloved Cleopatra, who mocks the messenger's urgency; she sarcastically jests that Caesar is probably sending yet another order to "do this, or this; / Take in that kingdom . . . " Games of war bore her; she delights in equating the taking of whole kingdoms to being no more than a mere daily errand, ordered by the "scarce-bearded Caesar."

The queen's strategy works; Antony is furious that *anyone* would interrupt his thoughts and his time with his beloved Cleopatra. "Let Rome in [the] Tiber melt," he roars. The only "messenger" he will see is Cleopatra; his devotion to the worthy Cleopatra comprises "The nobleness of life." They exit with the queen's attendants, and Demetrius and Philo are left alone to ponder their general's transformation. Rumor has already reached Rome of Antony's romantic waywardness. Demetrius hopes that tomorrow he will once again see proof that his general is still "that great property."

In Cleopatra's palace in Alexandria, Cleopatra's servants are talking to a fortuneteller (a soothsayer) and are trying to get him to predict how they will all fare in love. Charmian and Iras, two of Cleopatra's attendants, and Alexas, one of her male attendants, are trying to get the soothsayer to specify their futures. He avoids direct answers, however, and instead predicts that Charmian will outlive her mistress, Cleopatra. Enobarbus, a friend to Antony and an officer in his army (and also something of a cynic), is also present, and he interrupts the chatter of the servants when he hears someone coming. It is Cleopatra, looking for Antony. She says that Antony was mirthful until a "Roman thought" struck him and destroyed his happy mood.

Antony enters then, accompanied by a messenger, but Cleopatra and her attendants leave before he sees them. The messenger describes to Antony the outcome of a battle involving Antony's brother, Lucius, and Antony's wife, Fulvia, against Caesar. Lucius and Fulvia, formerly enemies, united forces in order to defeat Caesar but failed.

The messenger has more to say, but he hesitates to speak plainly. Antony assures him that he need not mince words and bids him to give his message, even to the point of describing Cleopatra as she is talked about in Rome (for this is why Antony thinks that the messenger is hesitant): " . . . mince not the general tongue / Name Cleopatra as she is call'd in Rome."

Another messenger enters and gives Antony a letter telling him that his wife, Fulvia, is dead and explaining what has happened. For a moment, Antony is overcome with remorse.

Enobarbus, Antony's lieutenant, enters then, and Antony tells him that they must prepare to leave for Rome. Enobarbus quips that if they leave, all the women will suffer and perhaps die from their absence. Antony, however, appears determined to forsake all of the enchantments of Egypt and return home. Enobarbus at first cannot imagine why Antony has had such a sudden change of heart, but then Antony reveals to him that Fulvia is dead.

Still, however, Enobarbus looks upon the whole matter rather cynically and tells Antony not to feel so bad; after all, Antony lost a wife he didn't want, and he now has a lover whom he does want: "This grief is crowned with consolation; your old smock brings forth a new petticoat." Enobarbus' comments, however, are ill-timed, for Antony is no longer in his usual devil-may-care mood, and he does not take Fulvia's death as lightly as his earlier behavior had led Enobarbus to expect: "No more light answers," Antony says, as he refuses to let his friend treat Fulvia's death flippantly. Furthermore, these events serve to remind Antony not to neglect his duties entirely. He resolves to return to Rome and see to business. For the time being, he must give up the pleasures of Egypt.

Scene 3 opens with Cleopatra instructing her attendants, Charmian, Alexas, and Iras, to aid her in a plan. They are to find Antony and observe what sort of mood he is in. If he seems to be happy, they are to tell him that Cleopatra is ill. But if he seems sad or moody, they are to tell him that she is "dancing." Presumably, her purpose is to make Antony feel guilty about being away from her; she wants to make him think about her—anything to draw his attention to her. It is a transparent and childish device, more typical of an adolescent than of a woman deeply in love.

Antony enters and wants to tell Cleopatra the sad news of Fulvia's death. However, Cleopatra is so involved in the game that she is playing that she doesn't notice that Antony is trying to tell her something important. He keeps trying to interrupt her egotistical monologue, but he cannot manage to communicate his sorrow. First Cleopatra feigns illness, but when she sees that Antony doesn't notice, she begins berating him for his faithlessness. After a good deal of melodramatic emoting from Cleopatra, Antony is finally able to tell her that he must leave immediately. She is caught off-guard and is so distraught that he plans to leave so quickly that she accuses him of playacting. She accuses him further of being as false to her as he is false to Fulvia. At this point, Antony is finally able to tell her that Fulvia is dead.

This announcement, however, does not have the expected effect on Cleopatra. She merely retorts, selfishly, "Now I see, I see / In Fulvia's death, how mine receiv'd shall be." But Antony is not moved by her childish histrionics, and he repeats that he must return to Rome.

Cleopatra continues to goad Antony but to no effect. She repeats the charge that he is an excellent actor and that he plays well the role of an irritated, angry man. He answers Cleopatra that her own show of grief at his leaving might also be merely an act. She vows that her love for him is real and that her pain is as real as the pain of a woman in labor. Finally, it seems, she realizes that Antony's emotions may be genuine, and she also seems to realize that the quality of love is something that a person must take on faith. When the scene ends, Cleopatra is reconciled to the fact that Antony must leave, and thus they separate and swear vows of fidelity.

The scene now shifts to Rome and focuses on a discussion

between Antony's co-triumvirs as they discuss the problems facing the empire. Here we have our first glimpse of Octavius Caesar and Lepidus. Although the subject of their discussion is Antony, their criticisms of him reveal a good deal about their own characters, not all of it praiseworthy.

Caesar enters reading a letter and is followed by Lepidus and their attendants. The two Romans catalogue Antony's faults ("he fishes, drinks, and wastes / The lamps of night in revel"), and there is heavy irony in their apparent concession that Antony's activities might be acceptable under other circumstances. That is, Caesar says, "let's grant it is not / Amiss to tumble on the bed of Ptolemy" (Cleopatra's former husband); of course, Julius Caesar, Octavius' uncle, enjoyed engaging in such sexual activities.

A messenger enters then with news from abroad: Pompey and two infamous pirates, Menecrates and Menas, are making "the sea serve them"; they have made "many hot inroads" into Italy, as well as creating havoc in the Mediterranean. Caesar uses this bad news as one more excuse to disparage Antony, who is conveniently absent and cannot defend himself. As an example of Antony's character, or lack of it, Caesar recalls an incident when Antony was "beaten from Modena," and not only was Antony defeated, but "famine did follow." Caesar also recalls that Antony escaped with his forces to the Alps, where he "didst drink / The stale of horses and the gilded puddle / Which beasts would cough at." Caesar is saddened: "It wounds thine honor," he says, that Antony can now act so immaturely.

Again we return to Alexandria; Cleopatra is in her palace with her attendants, Charmian and Iras, and Mardian, a eunuch. Now that Antony has departed, Cleopatra is at a loss for something to occupy her time. Primarily she spends most of her time thinking of him and worrying about what he is doing; she seems to be more like a lovesick adolescent in this scene than the ruler of a great country. She asks for mandragora, a sleeping potion, so that she can "sleep out this great gap of time [that] Antony is away."

She asks Mardian, perhaps only half-jokingly, if he has any "affections" or passionate feelings at all. He tells her that he does, although he can "do nothing"; yet, there are acts that he thinks about "fiercely." This is a play on words to some extent, for Cleopatra may be referring to any strong emotional feeling. Although Mardian's answer is ambiguous, one gets the impression that he is conscious of both meanings, and his answer seems to hint that although his sexual role in life is limited, he is as capable of passion and feeling as his mistress, Cleopatra, is.

Cleopatra then turns to Charmian and asks her to imagine what Antony is doing at this moment, how he looks, and what he is thinking. She can think of nothing that is not concerned with her love for Antony. She is about to swallow the "delicious poison" (her melodramatic term for the sleeping potion) when one of her servants, Alexas, enters with news of Antony. Cleopatra is delighted, and she tells Alexas that the mere fact that he has been near Antony makes him more precious in her eyes.

Alexas gives the queen a pearl, a gift from Antony. It is a particularly valuable pearl, for Alexas says that Antony kissed it; in fact, Antony bestowed upon it "many doubled kisses." In addition, Alexas says that Antony will "piece / [Cleopatra's] throne with kingdoms. All the East . . . shall call her mistress." Cleopatra then eagerly questions Alexas about Antony: how he appeared and what sort of mood he was in. She also asks Alexas whether Antony seemed sad or merry, but Alexas quickly perceives that both potential responses could be wrong answers at this point; therefore, he diplomatically states that Antony seemed neither very sad nor very happy. This seems to satisfy Cleopatra, who would have been disturbed if Antony were distressed, but she would have been furious if he seemed too happy—without her. She then gives Alexas a message to deliver to Antony.

Cleopatra asks Charmian, as proof of Cleopatra's love for Antony, if she ever saw Cleopatra love Caesar (Julius Caesar, Octavius' adoptive father) so well. Charmian, not as clever nor as astute as Alexas in gauging Cleopatra's moods, gives an answer that praises Caesar. That is a mistake; Cleopatra wants unqualified assurance that she never loved *anyone* as much as she loves Antony; she wants to hear it confirmed that every lover she had before Antony was a mere trifle, a flirtation. Only now has Cleopatra discovered true love. In response to Charmian's comment, Cleopatra orders Charmian *never* to compare Antony with Caesar again, nor even to suggest that they are equal in any way.

Commentary

Shakespeare does not dally with theatrical conventions of

lengthy exposition. Almost immediately we are introduced to the two lovers, who are clearly passionate lovers. There is only a modicum of introduction as the play opens. Briefly, two of Antony's friends discuss their general's infatuation with Cleopatra. They describe Antony as if he had undergone some strange sort of metamorphosis; it seems to them that his eyes, which once looked upon battlefields, "now bend, now turn / The office and devotion of their view / Upon a tawny front." His soldier's heart is no longer courageous; instead, it "reneges all temper / And is become the bellows and the fan / To cool a gypsy's lust."

After Antony and Cleopatra have made their entrance in Scene 1, it is clear that Antony has indeed let himself be seduced—body and soul—by Cleopatra's sensuality and charm. It is also clear that the Romans in general dislike Cleopatra in spite of her legendary ability to enchant males—or perhaps because of it. This prejudiced view toward Cleopatra is developed throughout the play, but as we will see, Shakespeare was not content to present her as only a one-dimensional character; she is more than merely a sensual woman who happens to rule an entire country.

As Antony and Cleopatra talk, both of them use exaggerated language to swear that their love is greater than any other love in the world; their love, they believe, is more than this world can hold. This is not idle overstatement, for their intense love for one another will be the cause of their deaths. Time and again in the play this key idea will be emphasized: Love and the worlds of politics and war belong in separate spheres and can never coalesce or merge. The central theme of this play is exactly that—love versus war—and Shakespeare will weave this theme in and out of the action as the play progresses. By the end of the tragedy, it will seem as if the concept of war has won, but we should not be too hasty to come to that decision. Upon reflection, we will see that the final act of this play is ambiguous. It is possible that love may finally be the victor after all.

In Act I, however, Shakespeare's emphasis is clearly on Antony's current displeasure with political matters. The messenger who has come with a letter from Rome gives Cleopatra a chance to tease Antony that he is dominated by Octavius Caesar, a much younger man. Her motive is to goad Antony into declaring his independence of Rome, and she succeeds, for Antony retorts that "kingdoms are clay; our dungy earth alike / Feeds beast as man." Impetuously, he denies that Rome and the concerns of the political arena have any hold on him. Here, we should note his choice of words: Antony says that the earth is "dungy" and that kingdoms "melt" like mud into the rivers of the world. This comparison is ironically striking when we consider the "earthy" (sensual) interest for which he is forsaking Rome.

Antony thus reveals in Scene 1 how malleable he really is, for Cleopatra clearly delights in toying with his vacillating passions. She teases him that since he has been unfaithful to his wife by becoming involved with her, it is quite likely that he will be unfaithful to her one day. Antony, of course, vehemently denies such a speculation. Here he is willful and self-indulgent, and he is cetainly fickle. We initially see him perhaps at his worst. Later, Shakespeare's dramatic portrait of him will be enlarged and will be developed in detail, stature, and complexity.

As for portraying Cleopatra, the Egyptian queen, Shakespeare remains faithful to the popular image of Cleopatra as the strumpet queen, so to speak, but he suggests that she, like Antony, is more complex than one might initially suppose. On one hand, she is a coquette who manipulates Antony so skillfully that he does what she wants. On the other, she emotionally needs to have Antony tell her how much he loves her; she needs to have him affirm for her that nothing else matters as much as their love. This clearly reveals a certain amount of insecurity on her part, and in that sense, it is quite possible that she has a genuine, if momentary, feeling of sympathy for Antony's wife; she can see herself in the same position— that is, Antony loves her now, but she can envision losing him later to another woman.

Scene 2 introduces us to some of the minor characters, and it also includes a conversation about the nature of love. Thus, the main theme of the play remains in the foreground. The servants' witty, if somewhat cynical, treatment of the subject of love contrasts considerably with the exalted declarations of love that were made in the opening scene. An additional touch of dramatic irony is added when Charmian is exceedingly pleased at the idea that she will live longer than her mistress; little does she realize that her mistress will soon be dead.

Cleopatra's troubled comments about Antony's change of mood are characterized by her reference to Antony's "Roman thought." In

Elizabethan times, the term "Roman" was often used because it was believed that the Romans as a nation were typically serious and devoted to duty (the theme of Virgil's *Aeneid*); thus, here Cleopatra may be suggesting that Antony's thought was consistent with that sort of character; another possibility is that Antony was reminded of business that had to do with Rome—that is, his thoughts were about Rome; he literally had a "Roman thought."

Antony's demeanor is changed upon learning of the death of his wife, Fulvia. Immediately, he regrets that he once wished for her death. He sorrowfully remarks, "There's a great spirit gone!" Antony's guilt, to some extent, appears to spur his resolve to leave Egypt and return to Rome. When Enobarbus cynically comments upon the effect that their departure will have upon the women, Antony is not amused, and in contrast with his earlier speeches, where he seemed to be prepared to give up everything for the sake of love, he now seems quite willing to do just the opposite. Antony does not fear that Cleopatra will "die"; she is cunning, he says, echoing Enobarbus' comment that he has seen "her die twenty times upon far poorer moment" (for Shakespeare's audience, this allusion to dying possibly refers to the ecstasies of love, the moment of sexual climax which the Elizabethans often poetically likened to death).

In conclusion, Scene 2 basically shows the conflicting desires that struggle for dominance within Antony. He feels torn between his duties at home and his love for the Egyptian queen, and worse, he believes that he will never be able to reconcile these two passions. Yet he knows that, ultimately, he must choose one or the other. We also see contrasted in this scene the frivolity and the sensuality of life in Egypt, as typified by the games played by the servants with the soothsayer, and, in addition, we glimpse the troubled and serious world of the Romans, dominated by politics, not by love. Antony, too, senses the contrast, making plausible his sudden resolve to return to Rome and to more important matters.

In Scene 3, several themes are developed. Once again we see Cleopatra in a rather unfavorable light. She still seems to be more of a scheming coquette than a woman who loves Antony sincerely. Yet Cleopatra's insecurity, her constant comparing of her own situation with that of Fulvia, could also be interpreted to mean that she does love Antony a great deal and fears to lose him.

If Scene 3 could be said to have one basic focus, it probably centers on acting and the theater—illusion as opposed to the real world. The second half of the scene, in particular, with its many references to acting, echoes the actual "staged scene" that we saw in the first half—that is, when Cleopatra instructed her servants to encourage Antony to worry about her and thus attract his attention. It is ironic that it is Cleopatra who accuses Antony of only acting as if he loves her; significantly, it was she, not he, who planned the earlier scenario with her servants. She herself "acts" according to plan when Antony enters, but her scheme fails when Antony refuses to humor her. As a result, they argue about whether or not their love is genuine.

The familiar Shakespearean theme of reality versus illusion is paramount here. Egypt is a dream world, a world of romance and sensual delight, compared to Rome, a world of harsh reality, a world of politics and war. As a parallel, the relationship between Antony and Cleopatra exhibits dreamlike features, as well as serious sparring. Their love vacillates between a tawdry, superficial romance, a sort of romp in the garden of earthly delights, and a love that is sadder, a deeper kind of love that is more than sensual and may possibly survive the burdens placed on it by time and the world.

At this point, Shakespeare is still developing his theme of love and intrigue according to the popular ideas of his time concerning Antony and Cleopatra. Traditionally, these lovers have been presented as being entirely devoted to sensuality and self-gratification. Now, however, we see that while the faults of Shakespeare's hero and heroine are not entirely dispelled, the characters gain considerably in depth and humanity as the play progresses.

In Scene 4, Caesar admonishes Antony, the absent triumvir, to leave his "lascivious wassails" (revels) and to return to duty. He dwells on Antony's sensuality and his love of food and drink, and he hints further that Antony lacks character, for it is well known that in the difficult journey across the Alps, Antony would eat virtually anything rather than starve. Caesar cites the fact that Antony drank "gilded puddle" (animal urine) and "browsed on" (ate) tree bark rather than die in defeat. These acts of desperation, he says, suggest that Antony is a man of ignoble tastes, preferring as he does now the base pleasures of Egypt. Yet while it is true that Antony is a far more sensual and even a more self-indulgent man (in theory) than Caesar, that Antony could and did survive the rigors of an Alpine winter attests to the fact that Antony has the prime virtues of strength and courage, regardless of whatever flaws of character which Caesar might accuse him of. Caesar, it should be noted, interprets Antony's character in the worst possible way. As a result, his attempt to turn these incidents into an indictment against Antony tells us, in reality, more about young Caesar's insecurities than it does about Antony. In the course of this play, we shall find that although Caesar is probably the more clever of the two men, Antony has a generosity of spirit that seldom permits him to level such abuses on Caesar and his excesses.

Scene 4 ends as Caesar tells Lepidus that he is eager for the two of them to "show ourselves on the field"; he and Lepidus then pledge their loyalty to each other, echoing an earlier, similar pledge between Antony and Cleopatra in the previous scene.

In Scene 5, the portrait of Cleopatra is, to a great extent, very much like her legendary reputation—that is, Cleopatra is a beautiful seductress, whose power to charm men is derived, in part, from her beauty and, in part, from her beguiling craftiness. Shakespeare doesn't deviate far from this characterization, one that was well known in his day. But beneath Cleopatra's whims and her girlish melodramatics over her absent lover, there is a hint that the very strength of her feeling portends a deeper affection than her behavior would indicate. It is as if adversity and tragedy must work their magic on this all-too-earthly pair before they and we, the audience, realize that the love that they profess may, in fact, be almost a supernatural love, a force ultimately more powerful to Antony than the fate of the Roman Empire itself.

ACT II

Summary

In Scene 1, set in the insurrectionists' camp, Pompey (Sextus Pompeius), a rival general of the Triumvirate, plans his strategy with two of his officers, the sea pirates Menas and Menecrates. Pompey brags that he shall do well. Menas, however, is cautious and tells Pompey not to be overconfident, for Caesar and Lepidus are in the field and are prepared to fight and defend the empire. Pompey, however, rejects this news; he says, "I know they are in Rome together, / Looking for Antony." Furthermore, he says that Cleopatra's wiles and her "Epicurean cooks [will so] sauce [Antony's] appetite" that

Antony will be completely seduced by luxury and will either forget about politics altogether or else be unable to defeat his enemies—if he finally does remember where his duty lies.

Varrius, an officer, enters bearing a message: Antony is expected to arrive in Rome momentarily, and, in fact, he has probably already arrived. This news disturbs Pompey, who now realizes that Antony may indeed be a threat. However, Pompey is not easily discouraged, and so he makes new plans. Menas suggests to Pompey that there is a weak link in the chain that forms the Triumvirate; a rumor persists that there is an enmity between Antony and Caesar. He also tells Pompey that Lucius Antony (Antony's brother) and Fulvia (Antony's late wife) joined forces against Caesar not long ago. Although it is doubted that Antony had anything to do with the attack, as he apparently didn't, perhaps there is some truth to the rumor that there are hard feelings within the Triumvirate. Pompey, of course, hopes that these alleged quarrels between Antony and Caesar will cause a sufficient rift and that the Triumvirate will be weakened as a fighting force. Pompey can thus easily overwhelm them. However, Pompey is also aware of the possibility that the threat of an invasion from the outside will cause the Triumvirate to set aside their personal differences for the time being in order to meet with and oppose a common enemy. This is, in fact, what happens, at least for a while.

At the beginning of Scene 2, in Rome, Lepidus meets briefly with Antony's friend Enobarbus. He asks Enobarbus to suggest to Antony that he exercise some tact and gentleness when he meets with Caesar. But Enobarbus, who is aware that Antony will not accept any suggestion that would make him appear weak to his rival, retorts that Antony will answer Caesar's questions in a manner worthy of himself. Antony will not demean himself to Caesar; if necessary, he will "speak as loud as Mars."

Caesar and Antony and their attendants enter, and Lepidus urges them to reaffirm their alliance before the security of the empire is destroyed. To emphasize the gravity of the situation, he uses the image of a surgeon who kills his patient by treating him too roughly; he hopes that this metaphor will vividly reveal what might happen to Rome if the two men don't mend their differences. He further compares the petty quarrels of Caesar and Antony to a minor wound; it would be a pity, he says, to lose the patient as a result.

The two rivals greet each other politely and proceed to discuss their problems. Antony asks Caesar directly if his (Antony's) living in Egypt has bothered Caesar. Caesar hesitates; he denies that he cares where Antony lives unless Antony's purpose in living far from Rome was to "practice on my state"—that is, to plot against Caesar. This is a far different statement that Caesar makes in Antony's presence compared to the bold words he used earlier when he was damning Antony's actions to Lepidus.

At this point, Antony asks Caesar what he meant when he used the word "practice." Caesar replies that he was referring to the attack made on him by Fulvia and Lucius Antony. Antony denies that he himself had any part in that plot, and he accuses Caesar of attempting to find a ground for a quarrel where none exists.

Having gotten nowhere with his arguments, Caesar says that he felt personally slighted when Antony refused to receive his ambassadors, an incident that we ourselves witnessed in the opening scene of the play. Since this accusation is true, Antony doesn't dispute it. On the contrary, he attempts to be conciliatory without conceding any more than he has to.

Maecenas, an officer of Caesar's, suggests a change of subject, and Enobarbus adds that they should save their petty disagreements for a time when Pompey is no longer a threat. Antony tells Enobarbus to "speak no more." Since Enobarbus is only a soldier and not a statesman, he should not attempt to give advice to his superiors. Enobarbus responds by saying that he had forgotten that "truth should be silent" and that out of consideration for Antony he will be a "considerate stone," or, more colloquially, as "dumb as a stone."

Now that the generals' differences have been aired, Agrippa, a friend of Caesar's, suggests that their differences could be healed by a marriage that would cement their alliance, a marriage that would stand as a pledge of loyalty between them. He proposes that a marriage should be arranged between Antony (now a widower and, therefore, free to marry) and Caesar's sister, Octavia. Such a marriage would show the world the solidarity of the Triumvirate and would increase public confidence in their rule. Caesar watches to see how Antony reacts to the idea, and when he sees that Antony agrees to it immediately, he too gives his approval. Thus the two men shake hands to seal the agreement.

The discussion then turns to the subject of their common

enemy, Pompey. Pompey's main strength is derived from his sea power because of his great naval fleet. At last Antony is fully aware of the imminence of Pompey's threat, and he urges them all to make plans to face Pompey as soon as possible and defeat him before his power increases even more.

With their differences settled for the time being, the three triumvirs exit, leaving behind their officers, Enobarbus, Maecenas, and Agrippa. At this point, Enobarbus tells the others about Egypt, describing the luxury in which he and Antony lived. He describes Cleopatra, recalling one incident in particular, when she was sailing on the Nile in an elegant barge. From this description, it is possible to see how Antony could be so entranced by Cleopatra.

Enobarbus also describes one of the first times that the lovers met. Antony had invited Cleopatra to dine with him, but she insisted that she provide a dinner for him. Of course, he accepted. Comparing this meal to a dinner bought in a tavern, Enobarbus comments, without exaggeration, that Antony paid the bill with his heart.

Maecenas comments that it will be a sad thing indeed if Antony must now give up Cleopatra since he is about to marry Octavia, but Enobarbus replies that Antony will *never* be able to leave Cleopatra, for no other woman can match her charm and beauty. Maecenas is not so sure; he says that if any woman can compare with Cleopatra, the beautiful and equally charming Octavia can. The scene ends with Enobarbus' accepting Agrippa's invitation to stay at his house while he and Antony are in Rome.

As Scene 3 opens, still in Rome, Antony and Octavia, the betrothed couple, bid each other good night, and Antony admonishes Octavia not to believe all that she hears of him. Seemingly, he hopes to reassure his future wife that he will be a good husband in spite of his past reputation for sexual excesses. His words, however, ring hollow at this point.

As Octavia and her brother Caesar leave, the soothsayer from Egypt enters, and Antony is reminded of Egypt and all his pleasures there. Antony asks the soothsayer, "whose fortunes shall rise higher, Caesar's or mine?" The soothsayer warns Antony that he can never achieve any great success so long as he remains "by [Caesar's] side," for Caesar will always overshadow him. This answer disturbs Antony, and he abruptly tells the Egyptian not to speak of such things. Instead, he turns his attention to tactical matters. He speaks of a plan to send his officer Ventidius to Parthia to suppress some trouble in the East.

Antony is troubled; he cannot forget what he has just been told by the soothsayer. He is also troubled by his memories of how he has always fared the worse in any competition with Caesar, even in mere games. He wonders if the soothsayer has indeed spoken truthfully. But again he resolves to put such matters out of his mind, and he decides impulsively to go to Egypt ("In the East my pleasure lies"). Although he will soon marry Octavia, he cannot forget his strong passion for Cleopatra, and although he tried to reassure Octavia that he would be a good husband, and despite the fact that he wants to maintain harmony between himself and Caesar, Antony decides that he must go to Cleopatra. He is not an evil man; he does not purposely want to hurt Octavia, but he cannot calm his passions. Politics are one matter, but love is another, and thus we see his duplicity in the fact that he can pledge his loyalty to Octavia one minute while planning all the while to return to his real love, Cleopatra, as soon as possible. While such marriages of convenience were no doubt common and quite acceptable, Antony's sudden shifts of thought, and especially his surges of desire, again illustrate how Antony is caught between the pressing duties of Rome and the urgent demands of love. In one moment, Antony seems to be all business—planning military strategy like a militaristic Roman general—and in the next minute, he can think of nothing but Cleopatra and the pleasure that awaits him in Egypt. Significantly at this point, Antony cannot face the challenge of facing up to Caesar and testing his valor, so, for the moment, he puts all thoughts of that problem out of his mind and decides to hurry back to Cleopatra.

As Scene 4 opens in Rome, Lepidus is being escorted by two officers, Maecenas and Agrippa, and after they have walked with him for a while, he tells them that they may return to their business, which at this point is to prepare for possible battle with Pompey.

In Scene 5, Cleopatra is bored and pensive in Alexandria. She turns to her servants and asks them to amuse her. She wants Charmian to play billiards with her, but Charmian begs off and suggests that Cleopatra play billiards instead with Mardian, the eunuch. The idea of thrusting balls into pockets with a long billiard stick gives Cleopatra plenty of opportunity to tease the eunuch about his physical disability; the many double entendres of the dialogue in this scene no doubt amused Shakespeare's audience and provided a short and rather bawdy comic interlude.

As Charmian and her mistress talk together, Cleopatra reminisces about the things that she and Antony did together; she recalls their going fishing together and how she tricked Antony into catching an old salt fish. She also tells about another time, when they pretended to be Hercules and Omphale, who enslaved Hercules with her charms and made him wear her clothes as a joke while she strutted around wearing his sword.

A messenger enters then with news of Antony, and Cleopatra is so excited that she hardly gives him a chance to speak. She interrupts him, she rambles, she threatens him with punishment if the news is bad, and then she promises him wealth if the news is good. The messenger is understandably anxious. He rightly suspects that his queen will not be pleased to learn that Antony has made friends with Caesar and that he has married Octavia.

Upon hearing the news, Cleopatra strikes the messenger and threatens to stab him. She later regrets her impulsiveness, however, for she realizes that it is ignoble for one in power to hit someone who has done no wrong and who is powerless to defend himself. She asks that the messenger be brought back to her, and she asks him to tell her more about what has happened. Again she hears the incredible news, and again she orders the messenger from her sight. Cleopatra is grief-stricken; she can think of nothing but her need to get away and hide. She wants to be alone with her distress, but she wants to know more. Since the messenger is too frightened to speak further in her presence, she sends her servant Alexas after him. She wants Alexas to find out what he can and to report back to her what Octavia is like. Although Cleopatra is deeply hurt, she has not been defeated yet. If she can find out what kind of woman Octavia is, she can make plans to win Antony back.

The focus of Scene 6, set near Misenum, centers on the meeting of Caesar, Antony, Lepidus, and Pompey; earlier the triumvirs sent a letter to Pompey in which they said that they were prepared to allow Pompey to rule Sicily and Sardinia if he would agree to "rid all the sea of pirates" and send an annual tribute of wheat to Rome. Pompey is prepared to accept the offer, but he says that Mark Antony has put him to "some impatience." Pompey reminds Antony of past debts—for example, Lucius, Antony's brother, and Fulvia,

Antony's late wife, joined with Caesar and attacked Pompey. Antony acknowledges this fact. Antony and Pompey then exchange pleasantries about the good life in the East while Caesar remains silent; negotiations are concluded for the time being. Pompey then invites them all to celebrate the treaty by dining aboard his galley.

Pompey comments on the fine cuisine of Egypt, and he also mentions how (Julius) Caesar enjoyed life there, relating how "a certain queen" was smuggled in to Caesar. He presses for more details, and Enobarbus explains that the queen was carried secretly to Caesar "in a mattress." Pompey suddenly recognizes Enobarbus; he remembers him as being a good soldier. Honest as always, Enobarbus returns the greeting by admitting that although he has never much cared for Pompey, he has always admired Pompey's skill and ability as a general.

All exit then, except Enobarbus and Pompey's officer, the pirate Menas. The two men discuss the treaty that has just been made. Menas claims that Pompey placated too easily; Pompey's father, Pompey the Great, would never have settled on terms so favorable to the Romans. Enobarbus agrees; he says that Pompey may have seriously reduced his chance of becoming a powerful force in the empire. Menas then asks why Antony has come to Rome; it was thought by many, he says, that Antony had married Cleopatra and ruled in Egypt. Enobarbus tells him, however, that Antony is now married to Octavia, an arrangement that they both realize was a political match. Enobarbus cynically predicts that Antony will betray Octavia by returning to Cleopatra. Caesar, they know, will be enraged.

As Scene 7 opens on Pompey's galley, the servants are getting ready for the feast; they gossip among themselves, joking that the three Romans are already well on the way to becoming drunk. They have been taking turns pouring part of their wine into Lepidus' glass, and he is getting even more intoxicated than the others and doesn't even realize that they are amusing themselves with jokes at his expense.

Caesar and Antony lose no opportunity to taunt each other, a situation that the drunken Lepidus ineptly tries to reconcile. Here again, the servants comment shrewdly that it is a sorry fact that although Lepidus is one of the triumvirs (and theoretically one of the most powerful men in the world), he is really only a figurehead.

The other two triumvirs have no respect for his opinions nor for his ability as a leader; rather, they see his role as no more than that of a bit player in a major drama; he balances their power, and he serves as a buffer to prevent the worst effects of their rivalry.

Commentary

Pompey, an enemy of the Triumvirate that currently rules Rome, believes that his hold over that portion of the Mediterranean that he controls is increasing. He believes, moreover, that he is now in a position to challenge the empire with little threat from Antony, who appears to have forsaken politics for love. Pompey is convinced that Antony, an experienced soldier, is the only real obstacle in his quest for power, and now with Antony diverted by Cleopatra, Pompey can accomplish a decisive victory. To Pompey, young Caesar is not much more than a whelp, an upstart who has little support from the masses. As for Lepidus, Pompey simply discounts him as being no more than an ineffectual figurehead. Scene 1, then, gives us a view of the unstable political arena which such men as Pompey and Caesar move in. It is not a particularly attractive place. We also see how the struggles between Antony and Caesar are viewed by an outsider, a somewhat more objective viewer than either of the two triumvirs themselves. Unlike Caesar, though, Pompey does not underestimate Antony's ability. However, like Caesar, Pompey feels that Antony has gone to extremes in his total absorption in sensual pleasure to the exclusion of the real world. But if Antony has been lured so completely by love that he has forgotten his place as ruler of one-third of the empire, then perhaps he may be discounted, after all, as an enemy worth worrying about. At this point, Pompey seems fairly confident that he could win a war against the other two-thirds of the world—against Caesar and Lepidus—and thus place himself in a position to rule all of the empire.

Scene 2 focuses on power, its psychology and its strategies. The language concerns politics and negotiation, with the key emphasis here on vantage status. Shakespeare's description of the dispute between the triumvirs as being similar to "murder [committed] in healing wounds" reflects the playwright's concern with the way in which nations are governed, and also the wit with which he can draw back and describe the situation so that we can see the dangers and the emotions involved.

The bickering in Scene 2, coupled with the astronomical illusions of the preceding scene with Pompey, suggests the precariousness of men's fortunes and the extent to which they are guided, often wrongly, by a lust for power.

Lepidus acts as a go-between to some extent—that is, he hopes that this meeting will enable Antony and Caesar to resolve their differences. Realistically, of course, he fears that the pride and the quick tempers of both men might interfere with any lasting reconciliation. In particular, he knows that Antony can only manipulate with great tact, and he does not think that the young Caesar, who at the moment feels as if he has been slighted, realizes this.

Although both generals pride themselves on their skill at high-level political negotiating, their egos, rather than their reason, appear to dominate this debate. The audience is left with an impression of totally useless and petty bickering. Caesar is obviously a testy and suspicious young man; he trusts no one, and while this is not an endearing quality, it will ultimately help him succeed in the world of politics and in his struggle for power.

The proposed marriage between Octavia and Antony involves yet another sharp difference in the two worlds of love and politics: In the scenes set in Egypt, we clearly saw that Antony and Cleopatra were genuinely attracted to each other. However, this Roman marriage between Octavia and Antony is a purely political alliance. Antony and Octavia hardly know each other. Love has no part in this union, and here Shakespeare is emphasizing the political views of the powerful, practical Romans. This was no imaginative plot complication; power is a strong aphrodisiac.

Scene 3 illustrates very briefly and very succinctly Antony's greatest weakness: his inability to face facts. He is not wholly honest with himself, and so he fares poorly when he is matched with those who are more self-confident than he is. Antony's weakest flaw of all, however, is his overpowering passion for Cleopatra—especially its illegitimacy. This fact was not lost on Shakespeare's audience; great love stories were often told and much admired, but the ideal love story centered on a love that was climaxed by marriage. Here, this is impossible; despite Antony's love for Cleopatra, it has led him to duplicity, and eventually it will cause his death. The question that Shakespeare is already posing for us is whether or not Antony's means of achieving his love's desires are justified.

Scene 4, a transition scene, seems to serve no critical purpose except to remind the audience of the counterforce to love in this drama—that is, the forces of politics and power, twin forces that are forever struggling for Antony's loyalty. We are also reminded again that intrigue abounds and that events will soon begin to move rapidly toward a crisis.

Scene 5 illustrates yet another facet of the complex personality of Cleopatra. Although at times she can be giddy and superficial, the depth of her feeling for Antony is not shallow. In this scene, for example, we also see evidence of her emotional fury, caused by the most terrible thing she could imagine in her relationship with Antony: Antony is involved with another woman, and not only is he involved with her, but he has *married* her. Yet Cleopatra recovers sufficiently to take some tentative steps to find out if she can regain Antony's love, which in itself is proof of her inner strength and resourcefulness.

Cleopatra is a person of extremes—that is, she is dramatic and emotional, to excess, but she is also a warm and vulnerable woman, and she is mature enough to be rightly suspicious of Antony. In fact, her passion for Antony frightens her; we see evidence of this when she realizes that she was wrong when she blamed the messenger for telling her that Antony had married Octavia. Even though she is an absolute ruler, she does not have the right to punish a messenger by threatening him with a knife for the content of a distressing message.

In Scene 6, it seems as if the threat to the Triumvirate from without—that is, from Pompey—will be defused, and the struggle will again focus on the real issue at stake: the conflict between Caesar and Antony.

Act II ends on a rather light note, but once again the theme of excess is repeated. It might also be noted that excess and indulgence are not inherent vices of the Egyptians, as the Romans would like to think. They are states of mind, attitudes, and choices that can exist anywhere, as the party aboard Pompey's barge illustrates.

ACT III

Summary

The act opens on a plain in Syria. Ventidius, a Roman officer, was sent to fight the Parthians by Antony at the end of Act II, Scene

3. It is not clear how much time has passed, but Ventidius has returned to Rome, and he describes his victory over the Parthians to Silius, one of his officers. Ventidius relates how he killed Pacorus, the Parthian king's son, in revenge for the death of Marcus Crassus, a noble Roman, killed by the Parthians in another battle in which Crassus' entire force was annihilated. Silius encourages Ventidius to make the most of his victory by returning home in triumph, but Ventidius refuses, noting that it is better not to appear too successful lest he shame his commander, Antony, by comparison. He tells about another officer of Antony's, Sossius, who served well in Syria but fell out of favor; it is implied that his great success as a warrior may have had something to do with it.

Silius praises Ventidius' discretion, and Ventidius says that he will write to tell Antony about the victory, although he will be careful not to boast.

As Scene 2 opens, in Rome, Agrippa and Enobarbus enter and discuss recent events. Octavia is to leave Rome with her new husband, Antony. Caesar is sad to see her go, and, for the moment, Lepidus is the butt of everyone's joking. For example, they discuss Lepidus' excessive devotion to both Caesar and Antony and his futile attempts to act as a mediator between them. This is a fittingly ironic foreshadowing of what is soon to happen, for Caesar, Antony, Lepidus, and Octavia enter, and they begin to discuss Octavia's imminent departure with Antony. Like Lepidus, she too is a mediator who loves both her brother and her husband, but she senses a conflict that she feels is somehow tragic.

Caesar admonishes Antony to take good care of his sister, and Antony says he must not seek fault where none exists. He promises that Caesar will find no "cause . . . for what [he seems] to fear"; Antony will be kind to Octavia. Enobarbus and Agrippa, meanwhile, make asides concerning Caesar, comparing his appearance to that of an ill-tempered horse. They wonder if Caesar will cry (he is apparently trying not to), yet even Antony has wept before, they note, and he is certainly no less masculine for having done so. The two men make their farewells, and Antony and Caesar embrace briefly.

Scene 3 returns us to Alexandria and provides us with some light comic relief as Cleopatra questions a messenger about Octavia. This is the same messenger whom she terrorized earlier when he told her about Antony's marriage. Now she is pleasant and ingratiating as she tries to find out what her new rival is like. After she questions the messenger about Octavia's manner and appearance, she is satisfied with the answers he gives her, and she pays him well for the good news.

Scene 4 opens in Athens, in the middle of a conversation between Antony and Octavia. Apparently they have been discussing the recent activities of Caesar, and Octavia defends Caesar; she urges Antony not to take offense at what Caesar might have said about him. Caesar is preparing for war, and Antony tells Octavia that he too must prepare and that his preparations will overshadow those of her brother. He encourages his wife to return to Rome, presumably to act as a mediator and reduce the growing hostility between Caesar and Antony.

In Scene 5, while Antony and Octavia, in Athens, discuss matters in one part of the house, Enobarbus and Eros (a friend of Antony) talk about recent events. Eros tells Enobarbus that as soon as Caesar and Lepidus defeated Pompey, Caesar turned on Lepidus and accused him of treachery. Lepidus now awaits death in a prison cell.

Enobarbus asks where Antony is, and Eros replies that he is in the garden and that he is angry about what has happened. Antony cries out in vain that Lepidus was a fool for submitting to Caesar; in addition, he mutters threats to kill the officer who murdered Pompey. At this point, Enobarbus is summoned by Antony, and the two men exit.

Scene 6 opens in Rome. Antony has now returned to Egypt, and Caesar tells two of his officers, Maecenas and Agrippa, about Antony's recent activities there. Antony has formally appointed Cleopatra to be Queen of Egypt, lower Syria, Cyprus, and Lydia, and he has also made his two small sons titular kings of various lands that he has conquered. Caesar interprets Antony's actions as being political ploys to usurp the authority of Rome; thus, they are an insult to both the empire and to Caesar personally.

As a further insult to himself, Caesar says, Antony (in a letter, apparently) has accused Caesar of not giving him his due portion of Pompey's realm in Sicily and has also suggested that Caesar's detention of Lepidus was solely for the purpose of acquiring his property. Caesar says that he has sent a messenger to explain why Lepidus was arrested. He also agrees to grant Antony part of the kingdom that he, Caesar, has conquered but only if Antony reciprocates by granting him land from his own conquests. He suspects, however, that Antony will never agree to this.

Octavia arrives with her attendants, and Caesar chides her for giving him no warning that she was coming; he had no time to welcome her with proper ceremony. She tells him that she heard that Caesar was making preparations for war, and when she begged to return, Antony allowed her to do so.

Caesar tells his sister that Antony's real reason for permitting her to return to Rome was for one reason only—so that Antony could return to Cleopatra. Octavia is agonized that her brother, Caesar, and her new husband, Antony, "do afflict each other."

Shakespeare next focuses on several battle scenes. The first opens at Antony's camp, where Antony, Cleopatra, and Enobarbus are planning their strategy. The main issue concerns whether or not they will fight Caesar on land or on sea. Against his better judgment, Antony chooses to fight Caesar on the sea.

Scene 8 reveals the exchange between Caesar and his trusted lieutenant Taurus and establishes the fact that Caesar's army will indeed attack by sea and that Caesar believes that this move will prove advantageous to his side: "Our fortune lies upon this jump," he boasts.

Antony and Enobarbus meet in an equally brief scene and plan to position their men so that they can see how many ships Caesar has sent and act accordingly.

Canidius with his armies and Taurus with his troops are seen briefly on the stage in Scene 10. They exit, and the audience hears offstage the noise of the battle at sea. Enobarbus and Scarus, another soldier, enter, and we learn that Antony's fleet has retreated. Scarus exclaims that because of Antony's ignorance, they have lost their chance to be rulers of a segment (a cantle) of the empire. Scarus, in describing the battle, blames the defeat on the presence of Cleopatra. She retreated first ("like a cow in June"), and Antony followed her rather than staying to fight.

Canidius says that Antony has not lived up to his reputation; Canidius has decided to surrender to Caesar. While Enobarbus agrees with Canidius that Caesar will undoubtedly win, he vows to stay on with Antony although the decision is against his better judgment.

Instead of staying to battle Caesar's forces, Antony is defeated in battle, in Scene 11, when he follows Cleopatra's sudden retreat. He is despondent and is not comforted even when Cleopatra enters and tries to soothe him. On the contrary, he is so ashamed of his cowardice that to some extent he places the blame upon her. Cleopatra apologizes, but there is, in fact, nothing to apologize for; obviously Antony cares for her above all else. For this, no apology is possible. He changes the subject and tells her that he has sent Euphronius, their children's tutor, as an ambassador to request the terms of a peace treaty.

In Scene 12, in his camp in Egypt, Caesar is meeting with some of his officers and also with Antony's ambassador, Euphronius. Euphronius presents Antony's requests to Caesar: Antony requests to be allowed to remain in Egypt, but if that is impossible, he asks that he at least be allowed to live as a private citizen in Athens. Euphronius also tells Caesar that Cleopatra acknowledges that Caesar is the victor and the supreme ruler of them all, but she requests that she be permitted to remain as Queen of Egypt and to retain the crown of the Ptolemies, the Egyptian royal family, for her heirs.

Caesar ignores Antony's request and makes an offer to Cleopatra: If she will betray Antony and drive him from Egypt, or kill him there, then he might consider her requests. Caesar then orders his servant Thyreus to return to Cleopatra with Caesar's answer. He comments that women are no stronger than their own interests and that Cleopatra, being a woman, can probably be bribed with the promise of her own safety in exchange for Antony's life.

In Scene 13, in Alexandria, Cleopatra and her servants (including Antony's cynical officer Enobarbus) discuss their plight. Cleopatra asks Enobarbus if the defeat was truly Antony's fault or if it was the fault of the Egyptians. Enobarbus answers that Antony was solely at fault but not only for his retreat. He also erred when he made "his will [the] Lord of his reason." Enobarbus adds that Antony's love and/or lust for Cleopatra affected his judgment; this, in his soldier's opinion, "Twas a shame no less / Than was his loss."

At this point, Antony and Euphronius enter. Apparently, Euphronius has told Antony what Caesar said, and Antony instructs Euphronius to relate the news to Cleopatra so that she may decide what action she wishes to take. Antony then scornfully tells her that the "boy Caesar" wishes her to send "this grizzled head" (Antony's) to him in exchange for her freedom. He is insulted by Caesar's treatment, and he is piqued that the "boy" general would flatter or attempt to persuade Cleopatra in such a way. Antony tells Cleopatra that he dares Caesar to meet him in a one-to-one match ("ourselves alone"). He is confident that he, Antony, will prove to be the victor.

Antony and Euphronius leave. Enobarbus remarks to himself that it is possible that Caesar might agree to such a match, but in his opinion, it would be foolish. He believes that Antony's judgment is "a parcel of [his] fortunes" and that his bad luck is reflected in his bad judgment.

A servant enters to tell Cleopatra that a messenger from Caesar has arrived. The queen is offended by the brusqueness of his entrance, and Enobarbus again comments cynically on their fate, yet finally he concludes that there is a certain amount of honor even in following a fallen lord.

The messenger is Thyreus, and he states to Cleopatra that he would like to speak with her privately. She says, however, that there are only friends present; they all may hear what he has to say. Thyreus begins and attempts to gain Cleopatra's confidence while actually promising nothing. He urges her to trust Caesar and insinuates that it is well known that she did not stay with Antony freely but rather because she was forced to, perhaps to placate him in order to protect her realm.

Cleopatra appears to agree with what Thyreus says, and thus Enobarbus stalks off, convinced that all of Antony's friends, even Cleopatra, are now deserting him. She concedes that Caesar *is* the victor, then says little else except to acknowledge that single fact. Thyreus kneels to kiss her hand in reply just as Antony and Enobarbus enter. The gesture is courteous but could not have been timed worse. Antony enters, and he is outraged. He orders Thyreus to be punished for his impertinence, and then he turns on Cleopatra and rages at her faithlessness. He is quite explicit about her faults, using words similar to those that she used against him when she accused him of faithlessness in the past. The servants reenter with the beaten Thyreus, and Antony sends him back to Caesar, telling him to tell his general that if he doesn't like the treatment that the messenger received from Antony, then he can do as he likes with *his* hostage (Hipparchus, who, according to Plutarch, hoped to save his life and apparently deserted Antony and joined Caesar).

When Antony returns, he begins to berate Cleopatra again, and she asks him, "Not know me yet?" This stops him, and she affirms that it is he whom she loves and no one else; all else was a charade. Antony, as quickly as he was enraged, is apparently satisfied with her explanation, and they are reconciled. He vows to fight Caesar to the end. Then, as Antony and Cleopatra leave to spend her birthday night together, he brags that not even death itself will frighten him in what will probably be the final battle; he will "contend even with [Death's] pestilent scythe."

Only Enobarbus is left onstage, and he continues to comment on Antony's loss of judgment. More valor, he suggests, will not compensate now: "When valor preys on reason, it eats the sword it fights with." Utterly disgusted and disappointed in his doomed master, the once-loyal Enobarbus finally decides that he must desert Antony if it is possible to do so.

Commentary

The subject matter of the entirety of Act III is war, and Scene 1 serves to introduce this facet of the play to the audience while also continuing the theme of the on-going foreign battles, a theme that has been woven into the plot by events in earlier scenes, such as Antony's command to Ventidius in Act II.

Scene 1 focuses primarily on the relationship between war and power. Not only are the rival generals, Caesar and Antony, vying against each other for ultimate power, but the lesser officers are also continually seeking their own advancement. Ventidius is wise here to avoid seeking excessive military glory. He does not want Antony to think he is trying to rival him in military achievements.

The language used by Shakespeare in this brief scene suggests the power, the action, and the cruelty of war. The Parthians, a fierce nation of horsemen, are described as being "darting" Parthians. It has been suggested by several critics that this word was meant to refer to the Parthian practice of turning around to shoot arrows at their enemy while riding away from them. Whatever their military strategy, however, they have been defeated.

Perhaps it should be noted that Shakespeare was paralleling history when he made Ventidius cautious about boasting too much of his success. Ventidius is wary of Antony's thinking that he might perhaps be trying to become "his captain's captain"; a soldier should not be so successful that he overshadows his commander. This concern with ambition and the consequences of seeming too ambitious are understandable when we consider the means used at that time to acquire power. Soldier-emperors like Antony or Caesar would inevitably be suspicious of any officer who might remind them too much of themselves during their earlier careers when they were filled with bravery and unbridled ambition.

Silius praises Ventidius for having that "distinction" (discretion) without which a skilled soldier grants no "distinction" (honor) at all. This play on words suggests the dual qualities that are the key ingredients for the best officers: valor and the discretion to know when to act and when not to.

There is some irony in the contrast between the cautious and soldierly Ventidius and the more impulsive Antony. As we shall see later in this act, Antony actually *lacks* that very discretion talked about here when he plans his battles. Tragically, it leads to his own destruction.

The gossipy tone in the first part of Scene 2, where Agrippa and Enobarbus make fun of the futile efforts of Lepidus to be loyal to both Antony and Caesar, foreshadows the fact that Octavia's role as a mediator will also prove ultimately unsuccessful. Yet for now, the key focus is on Lepidus; he is described by Enobarbus as suffering from the "green-sickness" ever since Pompey's feast, described earlier. "Green-sickness" was an ailment supposedly suffered by adolescent girls when they fell in love; they became wan and weak from worry about their lovers. In this context, it probably refers to the painful hangover that Lepidus probably suffered the day after he was encouraged to drink too much at the banquet.

Lepidus is said to love both Caesar and Antony and to be totally devoted to both men. Of course, this is impossible. The two men are rivals. Yet it is true that Lepidus is very much unable to decide to whom he should give his loyalty. And in comparison to both Antony and Caesar, Lepidus has so little power that all he can do is fret and worry. Agrippa says bluntly, "both he loves," to which Enobarbus retorts, "They are his shards, and he their beetle." This figure of speech refers to the shiny wing-cases of beetles, which were called "shards" because of their resemblance to fragments of shiny pottery or glass. Figuratively, Lepidus is like a beetle in that he is helpless without his bright wings—Antony and Caesar. In addition, Lepidus can be compared to the dull-colored insect whose bright wings are far more noticeable than the small little body to which the wings are attached.

Agrippa and Enobarbus leave as the others enter, and Caesar tells Antony,

> Let not the piece of virtue which is set
> Betwixt us as the cement of our love,
> To keep it builded, be the ram to batter
> The fortress of it; for better might we
> Have loved without this mean, if on both parts
> This be not cherish'd.
>
> (29–34)

The image here that Caesar evokes is of a building, and the love of the two men for the virtuous Octavia is the cement. (She is the "piece" or masterpiece of virtue referred to here). But were Octavia to be ill-treated, or were she to be considered as a hostage, she would be the battering ram that would cause the whole structure of their precarious alliance to crumble. Thus, Caesar says that he would hate Antony more if Octavia were to be misused than he would hate Antony if Octavia had never been given to him to "cement" their peace.

Antony warns Caesar not to pursue this mistrust any further lest he (Antony) take offense at it. Caesar then says goodbye to Octavia, who is weeping; her tears Antony gallantly describes as being like "April's [showers] in her eyes; it is love's spring." He suggests that like the spring rains that water the ground, her tears commemorate the beginning of the growth of their love for one another.

When Octavia says that she wishes to whisper in Caesar's ear, perhaps to give some private message or ask that he not forget her, he is touched by her grief. Antony too is affected, and again he tries to be gallant. He suggests that she is too filled with emotion to speak clearly, and like "the swan's down-feather / That stands upon the swell at full of tide," she cannot clearly express her loyalty and love to either Caesar or Antony—that she is torn by her devotion to both, and thus she turns first one way and then another, like a feather fluttering on the water. This image aptly sums up her helplessness as an object who will be used later by both men in their competing for power.

Enobarbus and Agrippa observe Caesar and Antony, and they

comment that Caesar "has a cloud in his face," meaning that he is either frowning or attempting to suppress tears. Agrippa notes that Antony, in contrast, was not too proud to weep when Julius Caesar was killed nor later when Brutus was slain; in neither case was he considered less manly for having wept. Enobarbus quips that Antony did indeed have a lot of "rheumy colds" that year, meaning that he wept a lot, and he suggests that Antony perhaps wept because of what he had destroyed—meaning Brutus.

The soldiers' comments are not very complimentary to either of the triumvirs. It is hinted that Caesar refrains from crying because he is too insecure to permit himself to show any weakness, while Antony almost too willingly expresses emotions that perhaps he doesn't actually feel. Thus, his gallantry towards Octavia may rest on a questionable basis—that is, his devotion to her is likely to be short-lived.

In Scene 3, because of Cleopatra's earlier fury, it is quite understandable that this messenger would be wary of arousing the queen's ire. He is very careful to describe Octavia in such vague and neutral terms that Cleopatra can infer what she likes from them. And this she does: Cleopatra wants to be reassured, and so she interprets the messenger's words to suit herself. He says that Octavia is not tall; accordingly, Cleopatra assumes that Octavia is dwarfish, or dumpy. The messenger says that Octavia is "low-voiced," and Cleopatra interprets this as meaning that she is "dull of tongue." She then asks the messenger if there is "majesty in her gait," and he replies, "She creeps." Cleopatra is pleased by this description, and she compliments his "good judgment."

The brief Scene 4 highlights the fact that Octavia is trying to be a peacemaker between her brother and Antony. She will not succeed, and the urgency with which Antony insists that she should go to Rome makes one question his motives. It is almost certain that he is anxious to rendezvous in Alexandria with Cleopatra.

Basically, Scene 5 gives us an important piece of information about Lepidus, and, equally important, it shows us Antony's reaction to Lepidus' imprisonment. We are almost certain that the recent bond between Antony and Caesar has begun to crack. Clearly Antony will not allow himself to be manipulated as easily by Caesar as Lepidus was. In addition, it seems as if Caesar is rapidly trying to consolidate his power. The outcome of the rivalry between these two fiery, ambitious triumvirs will ultimately depend on whether or not Antony can counter Caesar's strategies. It seems unlikely that he can; as we shall see, he does not. The singleness of purpose that is characteristic of Caesar (to the point of being a fault) is not a trait that Antony shares. Torn by his desire to spend his time with Cleopatra and his equally potent desire for power in Rome, Antony unfortunately hesitates too frequently and too long about what he will do.

The two lieutenants comment that Caesar and Antony are a couple of "chaps" (a pun meaning "fellows" and also "jaws") who will grind up men like food, themselves included. The truth of this observation will soon be revealed as Caesar, Antony, and Cleopatra become increasingly embroiled in their individual wars and intrigues.

In Scene 6, we see Caesar finally deciding to take overt action against Antony. He would not have dared to do so earlier, but because of Antony's return to Egypt, because of Antony's assertion of military and political authority there, and because of Antony's adulterous insults to Octavia, Caesar now has sufficient reasons to do what he has wanted to do all the time—that is, he can now attack Antony, defeat him, and become sole ruler of the world.

If Antony were more farsighted and if he had realized what an ambitious foe Caesar was, perhaps he would have been more careful in giving Caesar an excuse to attack him. But one suspects that even if Antony had not given Caesar sufficient reasons to provoke him, Caesar would have created them. Very simply, Caesar is overly ambitious and pathologically power-hungry.

When we hear Caesar say in Scene 6 that he explained to Antony in a letter that Lepidus was deposed because he was "too cruel; / That he his high authority abus'd," one should not miss the irony here. Of all people, the ineffectual and powerless Lepidus is most unlikely to have abused his authority. It is Caesar *himself* who would be most likely to abuse "high authority." But such duplicity is as typical of Caesar in achieving his goals as it is of Antony and Cleopatra. Caesar deceives himself; he rationalizes acts that further his ambition, and Antony likewise deceives himself when he believes that what he is doing will have no consequences; naively, Antony sees no danger in spending time with Cleopatra. As another example of self-deception, we have just witnessed how Cleopatra deceives herself; she interpreted the messenger's description of Octavia as being wholly negative in order to satisfy her need to believe that it is she alone whom Antony really cares for.

Caesar's duplicity here is evident even in the way he scolds Octavia for not giving him a chance to welcome her properly. In fact, he is really less concerned about *her* than he is about his last opportunity to show the world how badly Antony has treated his sister. This motive is unstated, but it is clearly consistent with the self-serving way in which he has explained other events—for example, Lepidus' fall from favor.

As Scene 7 opens, Enobarbus bitterly chides Cleopatra for being present on the battlefield. She retorts that since Rome has declared war on her and Antony, she has the right to be present.

Antony and Canidius enter, and Antony reports on Caesar's past victories at sea. Cleopatra chides her lover for not taking swifter action against Caesar, and Antony agrees: If Caesar chooses to fight "by the sea," Antony will do likewise; Antony's valor is at stake. Caesar "dares us to it," he says. Enobarbus objects that this is poor planning, that Antony's forces are not as well-equipped to take to the sea as Caesar's are. Caesar's men, he says, are experienced, and his ships are light and swift. By comparison, Antony's forces have been hastily drawn together, and many of them are inexperienced in battle. But Antony impulsively insists on a sea battle. He will not retreat from Caesar's challenge.

Enobarbus, Antony's loyal advisor and friend, again patiently tries to explain that if Antony pursues this course of action, he will "throw away the absolute soldiership [he has] by land." But Antony replies again, "I'll fight at sea." The length and patience of Enobarbus' speeches and the repetition and brevity of Antony's replies all illustrate Antony's impulsiveness. He doesn't offer a reason why he feels that a battle on the sea is a good choice; he simply insists upon it. At this point, Cleopatra offers him the use of sixty ships, and he accepts.

A soldier enters and begs Antony not to fight Caesar at sea. But Antony rejects this advice. Antony, Cleopatra, and Enobarbus leave then, and the unnamed soldier and Canidius remain. The two men blame Antony's foolish and headstrong decisions on Cleopatra's influence. There is, of course, reason enough to accept their evaluation of the situation, but we should be careful to assess these characters' opinions. Shakespeare does not allow any single character in this play to speak as an all-knowing mouthpiece. Rather, he gives us a variety of viewpoints and lets the audience discern where the truth of the drama lies and what the decisive motivations are for the action.

In Scene 8, after Shakespeare has focused on Antony for several scenes, he now turns his attention to Caesar. Confident and proud, Caesar is convinced that victory awaits him.

In Scene 9, it seems as though Antony is planning a defensive campaign because he decides to leave part of the land forces under Enobarbus' command.

In one sense, Antony is at his weakest and most pitiful in Scene 11. He is utterly defeated because of his own poor judgment (or perhaps his cowardice), yet he cannot resist making excuses; in particular, he thinks that it is possible that he was so bewitched by "Egypt" that his judgment was affected. Yet at the same time, he is aware that this is only partly true: His defeat was also the result of his own choice—that is, he placed Cleopatra above all else in his life. And in the end, he says he is not sorry that he made this choice. Of course, ideally he would have liked to have won the battle and spent as much time as possible with Cleopatra, but he failed. He tried, however, and one can easily suspect that a part of Antony's shame comes from the knowledge that he was defeated by a young upstart for whom he had little respect. Underestimating Caesar was an error that he, an experienced soldier, should have foreseen and avoided.

Antony's unfortunately underrated estimate of his enemy focuses at times on imaginative fantasy. Caesar, he says, behaved in battle unlike a soldier. He says that Caesar held his sword "like a dancer," meaning that he wore it more as an ornament than used it as a warrior. Still rationalizing, Antony also accuses Caesar of having depended on his lieutenants rather than getting involved in the actual fighting himself. These are scenes of frustration, confusion, and self-pity. Antony prided himself in being a rational general. His love for Cleopatra has changed that, and in the next few scenes, at times he will seem to be petty, over-critical, and often too eager to make excuses for himself. That this is probably the result of his defeat and not a part of his normal personality is shown by Iras' comment that Antony is "unqualitied with very shame"—that is, he is not acting like himself because of the great shame that he suffers.

Caesar's own insecurity is revealed in Scene 12 by the harshness of his settlement. Certainly he has the right to demand Antony's life, but most Romans were known for being relatively generous to those whom they conquered. In this case, however, Caesar may be a more accurate judge of Antony's character than Antony was of Caesar's. Caesar knows, and rightly so, that he can never really feel safe as long as Antony is alive or free. Note, however, that Caesar is a very poor judge of Cleopatra's character. Since he can't see beyond the popular stereotype of her as being little more than a prostitute, he believes that she can easily be bought. This is not an unusual mistake for someone like Caesar to make; as far as we know, he does not really know what it is like to fall in love. Here, Caesar shows himself to be the complete soldier or strategist, not only in his ignorance about aspects of life not connected with war or politics but also in the care he takes in his negotiations. He instructs Thyreus to be "cunning." Interestingly, Caesar is at *his* most "cunning" here, for he makes no *firm* promises to do anything at all for Cleopatra.

In Scene 13, Cleopatra's character begins to reveal a more complex nature than we have heretofore seen. Although her methods are devious, her purpose seems more mature and noble, in the sense that she never wavers from her loyalty to Antony. Likewise, Antony appears brave and generous. But, as always, he is also impulsive and stubborn. He rapidly jumps to the conclusion that Cleopatra is altering her loyalties when in fact she is not. Yet even Enobarbus thinks that Cleopatra may be making a truce with Thyreus. Throughout the play, we see that the men generally give Cleopatra less credit than she deserves, and we shall see that even Antony, though temporarily reassured, will doubt her again.

ACT IV

Summary

At Caesar's camp outside Alexandria, Agrippa and Maecenas attend their general. He is reading an insulting letter from Antony, and after he finishes, he considers its contents. "He calls me boy," Caesar says, and he adds that Antony challenges him to "personal combat." Prudently, Caesar refuses to accept the challenge.

Maecenas advises Caesar to press forward in the battle while Antony is so obviously at a disadvantage. Caesar agrees, for not only ış his army strong, but he has gained additional men who have deserted Antony's army.

The scene now shifts to Cleopatra's palace and focuses on Antony's reaction to Caesar's refusal to fight in "personal combat." Antony is surprised at Caesar's refusal, but he vows that he will beat him in battle. He then calls for a meal to be served, and he compliments his servants for their loyalty. He speaks as if this is the last night they will serve him, and before long they are all weeping. Even the hardened old Enobarbus is "onion-eyed" and begs Antony not to give them such discomfort, and Antony responds by laughing. He did not mean to be taken seriously, he says, and he assures those present that he expects victory—not defeat.

Antony's soldiers stand guard before Cleopatra's palace; all of them are aware that this is the night before the final battle that shall determine Antony's fate. Suddenly they hear strange noises and eerie music, and one soldier claims that this is an ill omen from the god Hercules, from whom Antony is believed to be descended. The soldier fears that these events are a sign that the god no longer favors Antony. The soldiers attempt to follow the source of the music but cannot discover it.

It is early morning on the day of the great battle, and Cleopatra and some servants are helping Antony prepare for battle. Cleopatra urges him to sleep a bit longer, but Antony refuses; he calls for Eros, a servant, to bring him his armor. In a brief comic scene, Cleopatra says that *she* will help Antony put his armor on; she knows nothing about donning armor, of course, and so what she does is very clumsy. She picks up the wrong pieces, she buckles badly, but she eventually manages to get Antony dressed.

Trumpets sound offstage, soldiers enter, and Antony turns to Cleopatra and tenderly kisses her. He tells his men that the morning looks good, "like the spirit of a youth." He bids Cleopatra farewell, and he and his men exit. Cleopatra goes to her room to await the outcome.

At Antony's camp near Alexandria, a soldier brings word that Enobarbus, Antony's most trusted aide, has deserted and pledged his allegiance to Caesar's side. Moreover, Enobarbus fled in such haste that he left all his money and belongings behind. Antony is dismayed at Enobarbus' departure, but he honorably orders his former friend's belongings to be sent to him as a final gesture of friendship. Antony then tells Eros to write a letter to Enobarbus, saying in effect that Antony understands his actions and does not condemn him.

We now see Enobarbus at Caesar's camp as Caesar, Agrippa, and Dolabella plan for the coming battle. Caesar instructs his soldiers to place Antony's deserters on the front lines, presumably to demoralize Antony and his remaining men, for they will be unprepared for the psychological shock when they discover that they are fighting against their former comrades.

They all exit then except Enobarbus, who contemplates his fate. He describes the fates of other deserters, especially Alexas, Cleopatra's confidential secretary. Alexas was followed, seized, and hanged. Obviously Caesar is not welcoming Antony's deserters; they can expect little honor or trust at the hands of their new sovereign, but Enobarbus appears to be an exception.

A soldier enters to tell Enobarbus that Antony has sent "all thy treasure." Enobarbus doesn't believe him at first, and he is heartbroken when he realizes that the soldier has told the truth. He swears to himself that he cannot fight against such a noble-hearted general; his disgust with himself is so great that he vows to "go seek some ditch wherein to die."

Scene 7 describes Antony's reaction to the battle that has begun. Apparently Antony's forces are winning, although the odds were initially against it. Scarus, one of Antony's men, is badly wounded, but he bravely urges the rest of his men to continue the fight, "snatching them [the enemy] up like hares." Antony praises the soldier's valor, and he and his men leave to rejoin the battle.

The battle continues. Antony is next to the walls of Alexandria, and he tells his men to report to Cleopatra how well the battle is going. At that point, Cleopatra enters and greets them all. Antony takes Scarus' hand and presents him to Cleopatra. She congratulates him for his valor, and Antony embraces her. They are delighted with the battle's progress thus far, and they predict a complete victory by the next day. They leave then, preparing to celebrate that evening in anticipation of their victory.

The scene shifts briefly back to Caesar's camp. Sentries are keeping watch throughout the night, and they hear Enobarbus, still distraught, speaking to the moon. In a moving soliloquy, Enobarbus makes his final speech; he is a symbol of melancholy and madness, and he despairs that he deserted Antony. As he falls and dies, probably of self-inflicted wounds, the sentries go to him, thinking that he has merely fainted. When they discover that he is dead, they carry his body back to the camp.

On the battlefield, between the two camps, Antony and Scarus are conversing. Caesar was defeated on land yesterday, and they observe that he is now preparing for an attack on Antony by sea. Antony fearlessly states that wherever Caesar chooses to fight, he will fight him—whether on land, sea, fire, or air (the four elements of which the Elizabethans believed everything in the world to be made).

We now return briefly to Caesar and his army, also on the battlefield. He instructs his men that unless they are attacked, they should keep their strongest forces on land to hold the positions they have.

Antony and Scarus watch the battle from a hill near Alexandria. Things are not going as well as Antony had hoped. From their position, they can see that the sea battle is lost and that Caesar has retained enough forces on land to continue the fight.

Antony leaves to find out how "'tis like to go." He returns almost immediately and tells Scarus that they have lost. He believes that Cleopatra has betrayed him, and he curses her. She enters shortly thereafter, and he calls her a traitor and orders her away. Then he continues to rage, and he predicts that Cleopatra will die for her treachery.

At the palace with her attendants, Cleopatra is confused by Antony's wrath; she does not understand his anger, and she tries one last scheme to see if she can win him back. Charmian has suggested that she go to her monument (the tomb that she has had built in the event of her death). There, she is to send word to Antony that she is dead; she instructs Mardian, the eunuch, to report to her how Antony reacts to this news.

Antony and Eros have returned to the palace, and Antony asks Eros if he can still *see* him. Eros doesn't understand the question, and so Antony explains; he describes himself as being like a shadow or a cloud, insubstantial yet taking on various shapes. He seems to be only a mere shadow of his former self because of his defeat by Caesar and because of what he assumes to be Cleopatra's treachery.

Mardian enters and tells Antony that Cleopatra ("My mistress [who] loved thee") is dead and that the last words that she spoke were "Antony! most noble Antony!" Antony is horribly shocked and instantly regrets his mistrust of her. He vows that he too will end his life. He calls Eros and commands him to kill him. Eros hesitates, and Antony pleads with him, saying that surely Eros would not wish to see him a captive of Caesar, defeated and shamed. Eros agrees, and he asks Antony to turn the other way so that he will not see Eros' sword. Antony does so, and Eros kills himself instead after saying farewell to Antony.

Antony, both abashed and impressed by Eros' courage and loyalty, follows his example and attempts to kill himself by falling upon his sword. Antony's sword, however, does not pierce him fatally. Hearing his cries, Dercetas and other soldiers enter, and although Antony begs them to kill him, no one will do so. Diomedes enters and finds Antony still alive. He tells Antony that Cleopatra has sent him word that she is, in fact, not dead—that she lives. He explains that Cleopatra had hoped to defuse his rage by sending him word of her death, but then she feared that he might take his life. Thus she has sent Diomedes to tell Antony the truth. Antony calls for his guards and tells them to take him to Cleopatra.

Scene 15 opens at Cleopatra's monument, or tomb. Cleopatra is being comforted by her attendants when Diomedes enters to tell them what has happened to Antony. Shortly thereafter, Antony is carried in on a stretcher by his soldiers and is raised up to the balcony. There, he makes a farewell speech and bids Cleopatra to seek safety from Caesar. But Cleopatra refuses, and as Antony dies, she faints, mourning the loss of the only person who made her life worth living. She vows to bury him in Roman fashion, and, in addition, she vows to follow his example. As the scene ends, she and her women carry Antony's body away.

Commentary

At this point, Shakespeare's vision of Caesar does not change; he will remain throughout the rest of the drama as a cool, calculating strategist. While Antony's defeat is a loss of honor to Antony, a matter to be resolved on the dueling field, to Caesar it is nothing more or less than the result of a battle. Caesar is irritated at Antony's slighting remarks in Scene 1, but unlike his foe, he does not let his emotions affect his judgment. There remains for him one single goal: total victory. In order to achieve this goal, he needs his army;

wisely, he is not willing to gamble on his own prowess when he is convinced that his army can destroy Antony and his forces. It is far wiser strategy, he believes, to "laugh at [the] challenge . . . [of] the old ruffian."

Antony reveals two interesting character traits in Scene 2: bravado and sentimentality. At their best, these qualities give Antony great courage and a generous and forgiving nature, but at their worst they become sentimental pap, which Enobarbus is quick to point out.

In Scene 3, both classical and Elizabethan accounts of the Battle of Actium mention the occurrence of supernatural omens before the battle. Plutarch's version of these events varies considerably from Shakespeare's, but Shakespeare was establishing a sense of foreboding. It is also probable that Shakespeare inserted Scene 3 to establish the importance of the final battle, which is, of course, the climax of the play; he often made use of supernatural omens to foretell a tragic death—for example, in *Julius Caesar*, *Macbeth*, and *Hamlet*. Historians writing before and after Shakespeare's time often referred to such events, so it is difficult to know whether they did so because they believed that these events really occurred or because they were ingredients for a good story. At any rate, Scene 3 creates a tense feeling of suspense. Our attention is focused wholly on this final battle, the one that will determine the fates of Caesar, Antony, and Cleopatra.

Scene 4, a fairly straightforward scene, adds a momentary bit of lightness to the gloom of the preceding scene. The tender affection between Antony and Cleopatra is touching, for there is a sense of tragic irony here; we are familiar with the story, as were probably most of the theatergoers in Shakespeare's day. We know what the outcome will be. Still, however, there is a great deal of interest in seeing how the lovers' fates develop and how the dramatist will decide to create the tragedy's climax.

In Scene 5, many of Antony's actions display not only a generous spirit but at times almost a prescient awareness that he will be a victim of fate. Rationally, he knows that his love for Cleopatra has changed his destiny. In Act I, Scene 2, he reflected that his dalliance with her caused him "ten thousand harms, I know." Yet love defies reason, and so, of course, it is additionally deeply demoralizing when Antony's "voice of reason," his trusted advisor, Enobarbus, loses faith and deserts him. Yet it is to Antony's credit that he does not suddenly become incensed and hate his old friend for this act.

Antony's gesture of friendship to his old friend in Scene 6 has tragic repercussions. Enobarbus is not grateful for his treasure; instead he is remorseful about his decision to desert his former general. Because of Antony's trust in him and because of Enobarbus' reputation for honesty and integrity, Enobarbus is very respected by Caesar. But regardless of his treatment at Caesar's hands, Enobarbus has lost all sense of his own honor and integrity. It seems that there is nothing that can return these intangible qualities to him unless he takes his life.

One should note here that in ancient Rome and in other countries of the ancient world, suicide did not bear the stigma that it does now; then it was often considered to be an honorable solution to many a problem. In particular, those whose lives might well be forfeited because they were conquered or taken captive often sought to end their lives rather than submit to the decrees of an enemy. Enobarbus' situation, however, is a bit different in that his resolve results from despair rather than from a fear of captivity or execution.

In Scene 7, we have another brief glimpse of Antony's impulsiveness and bravery. We also meet Scarus, a brave soldier who replaces Enobarbus, to some extent, as Antony's closest comrade. Unlike Enobarbus, however, whose intelligence and insight were useful to Antony precisely because he was calmer and more rational than his general, Scarus is very much like Antony. He is much more like a brave and faithful baying dog; he can be of great help to his master, but he cannot see beyond the immediate goal nor look beyond the decisions of his master and predict consequences.

Scene 8 has ironic overtones; Antony's preparations for his victory celebration are premature. In addition, his adoration for Cleopatra seems as changeable and unpredictable as the weather. Based on the earlier behavior of both lovers, we wonder when the next lapse in trust and the resulting quarrel between them will occur.

It is theatrically fitting that Enobarbus' final irrational despair and delirium should occur in a scene bathed in moonlight. Many people in Shakespeare's time believed that night air and moonlight could cause illness, depression, and even madness. Even now we have words based on such notions—"moonstruck," "lunatic," and "looney," for example. It is not clear from the stage instructions whether Enobarbus falls on his sword or whether he simply dies of self-inflicted wounds. Perhaps he has already stabbed himself, and we are hearing his last words. It is possible, however, that "the flint and hardness" of his fault is figurative only and that he dies of grief and of a broken heart.

In Scene 10, Antony's bravery is somewhat emotionally exaggerated, but it is exactly right for his character and for his military strategy, for we have seen that for whatever reason, his forces do fare better on land than on sea. Thus his victory on land is not altogether a surprise. The battle at sea, however, is another matter. Antony is courageous, but he is not the careful tactician that Caesar is.

Caesar's apparent sea preparations in Scene 11 are a ruse. He hopes, by this maneuver, to draw off Antony's best men to sea and take advantage of this strategy on land, where, thus far, Antony has been the victor.

Antony's rage overpowers Scene 12. His accusations against Cleopatra seem especially unfair. We should remember, however, that in the past, Cleopatra has advised against (without luck) the use of sea power against Caesar. It is likely here that Antony is remembering Caesar's earlier overtures to Cleopatra; it is also highly likely that bitter doubts arise again in his mind regarding Cleopatra's loyalty and love.

Scene 13 contains a dangerous ploy on Cleopatra's part, but she is desperate to dispel Antony's persistent doubts about her. Here we see the nature of the conflicts that have continually arisen between these two lovers. Cleopatra has always responded to adversity with a subtle scheme to circumvent its worst effects if she can. This has made her seem more devious than perhaps she is; in fact, her response may be more of a cultural trait, part and parcel of life in an Egyptian court, than it is a personal character trait. Antony, on the other hand, responds directly and impulsively to negative events; as a result, he frequently falls into the error of acting rashly and embroiling himself in unnecessary complications. Now both Cleopatra and Antony misjudge the other's motives—with tragic results.

In Scene 14, we see the results of Antony's poor judgment and mistrust. Having believed that he had lost everything, he attempted to kill himself, learning too late that he acted too rashly. Cleopatra, not fully understanding the agony of her Roman lover, precipitated his death by her melodramatic, manipulative playacting. (If this play is the first Shakespearean play you have read, it may seem unreal that Antony takes so long to die; most people who stab themselves do not make long speeches about it. However, in opera and in Shakespeare's dramas, this is very often the case.)

In Scene 15, we have proof that Cleopatra truly loved Antony. Yet we shall still see one last bit of her wily scheming as she deceives her Roman captors long enough to end her own life and follow Antony.

ACT V

Summary

The final act opens at Caesar's camp in Alexandria. Dercetas enters with Antony's bloodied sword. Caesar is startled by the sight, and then Dercetas explains that this is the sword with which Antony killed himself. Caesar is affected by the irony of this moment, for while he fought hard for Antony's defeat or death, he is saddened by the fact that his rival is now dead, by his own hand. As he considers the tragedy of all that has happened, he speaks of Antony as being like his "brother," his "competitor," and his "mate in empire." Like many of Shakespeare's great characters, Caesar speaks of men's fates as being determined by the stars. His and Antony's fates, he says, were ultimately "reconcilable."

An Egyptian enters with a message from Cleopatra, asking for instructions from Caesar, the conqueror. Caesar promises kindness, and he sends Gallus and Proculeius to her with a message.

Back at her monument in Alexandria, Cleopatra and her attendants plan their immediate future. She does *not* intend to be taken alive by Caesar, however seemingly kind his intentions. Proculeius enters, and she remembers that Antony told her earlier that this man could be trusted. He asks what she would request from Caesar, and Cleopatra responds that she would like "conquered Egypt" for her son. Proculeius tells her not to worry but to submit herself to Caesar and that she will be taken care of. Suddenly, however, soldiers enter and seize Cleopatra. She attempts to stab herself with a dagger but is disarmed. She vows, however, that she will die, somehow, before she will permit herself to be taken alive to Rome. She asks what Caesar plans to do with her and is told that she will be led as a captive into Rome.

Caesar and his party enter, and Caesar tells Cleopatra that if she does not resist him, she will be treated well; otherwise he will have to use the same degree of force that he used against Antony. Cleopatra then gives Caesar a list of all her property, and she asks Seleucus, her treasurer, to affirm that the list is complete. He cannot swear to it, however, and states that it is not complete. Cleopatra admits to Caesar that she kept back a few "trifles," then turns on Seleucus, virtually accusing him of deception. He flees, and Caesar generously ignores this incident and tells Cleopatra to keep whatever she would like. He asks her not to consider herself a prisoner (although, in fact, she is one), and he leaves.

Cleopatra tells her ladies Iras and Charmian that Caesar's promises of friendship are empty; she whispers to Charmian to make preparations for her death according to their plan. An officer of Caesar, Dolabella, enters and tells Cleopatra that Caesar intends to send her and her children to Rome. He then takes his leave, and Cleopatra comments to Iras what their reception in Rome is likely to be like. There, she predicts, they will be dragged through town like whores, and amateur actors will put on cheap plays portraying Antony as a drunk and portraying her as a harlot.

When Charmian enters, Cleopatra tells her attendants to fetch her best clothing so that she may be properly dressed to meet Antony. A guard enters and tells Cleopatra that some "rural fellow" has arrived with a basket of figs for her; she tells him to permit the man to enter. The peasant enters, carrying a covered basket that contains poisonous asps. Cleopatra asks him about the nature of the "worm of Nilus," meaning the asp, and he tells her how dangerous it is. He warns her to be careful in handling it. It is not clear whether or not he realizes how she intends to use it, but as he leaves, he says, "I wish you all joy of the worm," a heavily ironic statement.

Iras enters with Cleopatra's robe and crown, and Cleopatra puts them on and makes her farewells. She kisses Iras and Charmian, and Iras falls dead, unexplainably, at her feet.

Cleopatra and Charmian are both grieved at Iras' death, but Cleopatra resolutely places an asp upon her breast. Charmian protests, but it is too late. The Egyptian queen lets another asp bite her arm, and she dies, saying that soon she will be with Antony.

A guard enters, and Charmian tells him not to wake Cleopatra. He says that Caesar has sent a message, but she interrupts and says

that Caesar sent "too slow a messenger." Charmian then kills herself
with an asp.

By this time, the guards call for Dolabella. He enters and confirms that what Caesar feared has happened. Caesar enters then and
discovers that Cleopatra and her women are dead. While it frus-
trates his purposes, he respects her integrity, perhaps for the first
time in the play: "Bravest at the last! / She levell'd at our purposes,
and, being royal, / Took her own way" (ii. 339–41). They are all puzzled as to the cause of her death until they discover the asp bites.
Caesar again is impressed with her devotion and integrity, and he
vows to see her buried in a fitting manner:

> Take up her bed,
> And bear her women from the monument.
> She shall be buried by her Antony.
> No grave upon earth shall clip in it
> A pair so famous.
>
> (ii. 359–63)

Commentary

Caesar's response to Antony's death evokes a reassessment and
a new recognition of Antony's good qualities, his courage and sense
of honor, which perhaps finally outweigh his faults. In Scene 1, we
also note the unusual tenor of Cleopatra's letter since the previous
scene informed us that she intended to follow Antony into death.
Obviously, she is planning something. Shakespeare's heroine
remains a schemer to the end.

In the final scene, Cleopatra meets with Caesar's representatives and cleverly feigns that she is interested in continuing her life;
she attempts to negotiate with the Romans and even offers Caesar a
list of her property (with the exception of certain secret items that
she would need; it is possible, of course, that Seleucus was privy to
this plan in order to make Cleopatra's act all the more convincing).
Realistically, of course, if we can believe Cleopatra, she has no need
to retain any of her property, for ostensibly she plans to commit suicide like Antony. What we see in her final actions, then, is her characteristic manner of facing difficult situations. Of necessity,
Cleopatra schemes and playacts one last time; thus, by her very coy-
ness, her childish quality becomes, ironically, the means by which
she maintains her loyalty to Antony. What was once a game for her

now becomes a weapon and enables her to prolong her life long enough to defy Caesar himself.

Caesar is the military victor, but the final scene suggests that he is ultimately no victor. He lacks something of the larger-than-life humanity of Antony and Cleopatra. Yet Shakespeare does not falsely idealize the lovers either. Their faults are visible to the end, but they do not overshadow the lovers' honor. If there is any ultimate character flaw in this play, it is one that all three of the main figures possess: lack of proportion. Caesar single-mindedly pursues power and, as a result, seems too often to be merely a cold and calculating person. Antony and Cleopatra exalt love above their responsibilities; their respective realms, as a result, suffer. Cleopatra is particularly self-indulgent, preferring to play games with Antony while war develops almost at her doorstep. Antony, in contrast to both Cleopatra and Caesar, is never consistently a Roman *nor* an Egyptian. His vacillation about his duty and about his love ultimately results in his downfall.

1608~09

CORIOLANUS

CORIOLANUS

LIST OF CHARACTERS

Caius Marcius (Coriolanus)

He receives the honorary name of "Coriolanus" following his exploits in the battle at Corioli. His pride and his supremely conservative political views in support of patrician rule are products of his early training by a military-oriented and class-conscious mother. He has little control over his behavior if he is angered, and he cannot compromise on matters concerning politics or honor. After Coriolanus leads the Roman army to victory over the Volscians, the plebeians enthusiastically support his bid to become consul, but after the tribunes use their "brain-washing" tactics, the plebeians reverse their initial endorsement of Coriolanus and banish him. As a result, Coriolanus joins the Volscian army and marches on Rome, but he ultimately yields to the pleas of his mother and calls off the attack. Driven by envy and jealousy, the Volscians' chief commander, Aufidius, has Coriolanus murdered.

Cominius

A senator and the chief general of the Roman army that opposes the Volscians. After the battle at Corioli, he rewards Marcius with the appellation "Coriolanus" and later supports him for consul; significantly, Cominius is more willing than Coriolanus to compromise with the plebeians and their representatives. Later in the play, even he fails to persuade Coriolanus to call off his attack on Rome.

Titus Lartius

Along with Cominius and Coriolanus, he is a general in charge of the Roman army fighting the Volscians. He is junior in rank to Cominius, and although he is a constant admirer of Coriolanus' bravery and nobility during the early battle scenes, he ceases to be a factor in the climactic action of the play.

Menenius Agrippa

A conservative senator of Rome who serves as a patrician ambassador to the plebeians. The plebeians like him and, to a degree, trust him, and he is willing to offer compromises to calm the rioting citizens. However, he is firmly convinced that the patrician class *alone* should possess political power. He is unsuccessful in his early attempts to have Coriolanus moderate his anti-plebeian expression and also in his later efforts to convince Coriolanus to spare Rome. Throughout the play, however, Menenius remains a devoted friend and admirer of Coriolanus.

Sicinius Velutus and Junius Brutus

Two newly elected tribunes responsible for protecting the rights of the plebeian class. They oppose Coriolanus because they think that he is the epitome of elitist, patrician social bigotry. They are convinced that Coriolanus genuinely hates the lower-class citizens of Rome. These two tribunes are, ironically, strongly politically ambitious themselves and, moreover, are cleverly manipulative; in a sense, they are able to turn the people against Coriolanus almost too easily. Later, of course, they regret their role in banishing Coriolanus when he joins Aufidius. When Coriolanus threatens to besiege Rome with the Volscian army, the citizens hold the tribunes responsible, and they turn on Brutus and threaten to torture him to death.

Young Marcius

The son of Coriolanus and Virgilia. He has only a small role in the drama, but Valeria's (a family friend) description of his tearing a butterfly to pieces with his teeth indicates that Marcius is very much like his father; this is evidence that Volumnia, his grandmother, has had more influence on his upbringing than Virgilia, and here, in miniature, we have a sense of what Coriolanus' own childhood may have been like.

Tullus Aufidius

The military leader of the Volscians and also the opponent whom Coriolanus respects most of all those whom he has met in battle. Defeated by Coriolanus several times in combat, Aufidius likewise respects Coriolanus as a noble enemy in the first portion of the play; not really surprisingly, he welcomes the exiled Coriolanus as an ally. Nevertheless, his envy becomes compounded with jealousy when Coriolanus easily wins the broad admiration of the Volscian army. As a consequence, Aufidius has Coriolanus murdered after the armistice with Rome.

Volumnia

The mother of Coriolanus. She is responsible for her son's military-oriented upbringing and for instilling in him his concepts of honor, nobility, and class superiority. When she asks Coriolanus to compromise his political and social principles in order to appease the plebeians—while seeking election as consul—Coriolanus becomes frustrated; his mother's early training taught him that victory alone is honorable and that compromise is ignoble. Volumnia finally convinces her son to spare Rome, but it is a decision that leads directly to his death at the hands of the Volscians.

Virgilia

The devoted wife of Coriolanus. She does not share Volumnia's love of honor, nobility, and valor. Instead, she fears for Coriolanus' safety whenever he is involved in battle, and she would prefer a life with him that is family-oriented rather than one that focuses on his duty to the state. Virgilia is characterized primarily by her silent presence.

Valeria

A friend of Volumnia and Virgilia; she admires Coriolanus for his achievements and for his ideals. She attempts to prompt Virgilia to take more satisfaction in her husband's accomplishments and to suffer less in fearing for his well-being. She accompanies Volumnia, Virgilia, and young Marcius to the Volscian camp outside Rome when Volumnia finally convinces Coriolanus to call off his proposed attack against Rome.

Nicanor

A Roman who spies for the Volscians. He meets Adrian and reports the plebeian uprising, Coriolanus' banishment, and the susceptibility of Rome to an attack by Aufidius.

Adrian

A Volscian agent who is sent to contact Nicanor.

SUMMARIES AND COMMENTARIES

ACT I

Summary

The first scene opens in Rome, where a hungry, unruly mob has gathered to protest the Senate's injustice. Armed with clubs and spears, the citizens demand that action must finally be taken: They are starving, and the corn that is due them will not be released at a fair price from the city's warehouses. The First Citizen names the man who is most responsible for their problems: a patrician, Caius Marcius (later known as Coriolanus). The First Citizen says that the mob must unite and kill Coriolanus even though they may die in the attempt. Death, he says, is not to be feared; he himself would rather "die than famish." The mob is ready to rush to the Capitol when Menenius Agrippa, a patrician, enters.

As one of the city's elders, he asks the meaning of this riot, and the Second Citizen tells him that the unrest among the citizens is not new. On the contrary, the discontent among the populace is common knowledge to the Senate. Furthermore, Coriolanus is determined not to be dissuaded from acting on their common resolve now that the moment is climactic. He is convinced that the patrician class cares only for itself and that it makes rules that profit only itself and Rome's usurers. Menenius urges the Citizen to reconsider his plan; he tells him that revolt against the Roman state is futile.

At this point, the object of the mob's fury, Caius Marcius—Coriolanus—enters. His tone is haughty as he addresses the mob. Asking for the meaning of these "dissentious rogues," he arrogantly asserts that by "rubbing the poor itch of [their] opinion," they make themselves no more than "scabs." He calls them all "curs," and sardonically he declares that while some of the mob may fancy themselves as "lions," in reality they are merely "hares"; moreover, they are ignorant and fickle, changing their loyalties in a moment. He reminds them that they defy "the noble Senate," and thus they defy "the gods [who] keep [them] in awe" lest they devour one another. When he is told that they demand "corn at their own rates," his fury increases. "Hang 'em!" he cries; if he had *his* way, he would "make a quarry / With thousands of these quartered slaves as high / As I could pick my lance." He tells Menenius that revolt has already erupted in the city, with the citizens demanding the same thing—corn at a fair price. He says that he quelled that dissension by granting the "dogs" five tribunes to defend their "vulgar wisdoms." This action, however, was done against his better judgment; were he in absolute command of the situation, "the rabble" could have "unroofed the city," and he would not have yielded; he would have resisted unto the death. He says that no good can come from placating such mobs; they will ultimately only demand more, and eventually they will become even more rebellious. Turning to the crowd of citizens, he orders them to go home: "Go . . . you fragments!"

A messenger suddenly rushes onstage with news: The Volscians have gathered arms and now threaten Rome. Coriolanus is jubilant: Now that there is a threat to Rome from without, this rabble can be dispersed, and more important matters can be attended to. Moments later, a deputation of senators arrives and confirms the news of the Volscians' preparations for war. Coriolanus comments on the enemy's leader, Tullus Aufidius. He says that he envies the man's "nobility": " . . . were I anything but what I am, / I would wish me only he." He compares his opponent to a lion, one whom he is "proud to hunt." The prospect of battle pleases him, especially a battle against an enemy who is so daring and courageous.

The First Senator then asks a favor from Coriolanus: Titus Lartius is not well and cannot fully assist Cominius during battle; would Coriolanus aid or replace him? Coriolanus is grateful for the chance to do so. The Volscians, he says, have much corn; "take these rats [the mob] thither / To gnaw their garners." He exits with the senators, and the mob disperses.

The two tribunes, Sicinius and Brutus, are left onstage, and Sicinius asks his comrade if there was ever a man as proud as Coriolanus. Brutus answers that he knows of no one to match Coriolanus. In Sicinius' opinion, Coriolanus is filled with such excessive pride that he was surprised that Coriolanus agreed "to be commanded / Under Cominius." To this, Brutus answers that Coriolanus' actions are only further proof of his proud craftiness: If the battle miscarries, the fault will be Cominius', not Coriolanus'; if "things go well," Coriolanus will see that he himself reaps many honors "though indeed . . . he merit not." To this, Sicinius says that it is time that they should leave and learn what Coriolanus is doing— how "he goes / Upon this present action."

Scene 2 opens a few days later in the Senate House of the Volscians. Tullus Aufidius, the man singled out by Coriolanus as an enviable "lion," is speaking with several Volscian senators. He acknowledges that the Romans already know of the Volscian preparations for war and, despite the fact that the Roman citizens are mutinous, have begun to march forward toward Corioli, the Volscian capital, led by Cominius, Titus Lartius, and Coriolanus, Aufidius' "old enemy." Aufidius is angered at being foiled in his military strategy, and he accuses the First Senator of indiscretion in keeping their "great pretences veiled"; Aufidius had hoped to subdue the towns between their own capital and Rome. Then he could have conquered Rome before she could mount a defense. Such a maneuver is now impossible. The Second Senator speaks up and asks Aufidius if he, the senator himself, and the First Senator might guard Corioli; meanwhile, Aufidius could make war where he might choose to. If the Romans attacked Corioli, the Volscian army could surprise them and surround them. "I think," he says reassuringly, "you'll find / They've not prepared for us." Aufidius knows better; the Romans are wise in matters of warfare. He leaves, announcing that if he and Coriolanus meet in battle, they have sworn to fight "till one can do no more," and his followers wish him well: "The gods assist you!"

The setting for Scene 3 is Coriolanus' house, where Volumnia (Coriolanus' mother) and Virgilia (Coriolanus' wife) are sewing and talking. Volumnia chides her daughter-in-law for her low spirits. If *she* were married to Coriolanus, she would rejoice in his exploits on the battlefield rather than mourn for his absence in their empty marriage bed. To her, military honor excels love. She recalls when Coriolanus was a boy; she loved him so dearly that not even "kings' entreaties" could have taken him from her. She has wanted only one thing for her beloved son: honor and glory. Therefore, she decided long ago "to let him seek danger where he was like to find fame"— that is, in warfare. She remembers when Coriolanus returned from his first battle; he wore the oak wreath of a hero around his brow. She saw him being honored as a *man*, and she was more overjoyed than when she first heard the news that she had given birth to a "man-child."

Virgilia is unimpressed. She asks her mother-in-law how she would have felt if Coriolanus had been killed in battle. Volumnia's answer is quick: If she had twelve sons, she would rather see eleven of them die bravely in battle than be mother to a son who preferred a life of idle, sensual pleasure.

Valeria, one of Virgilia's friends, is announced, and Virgilia asks permission to leave; she is depressed and wants to be alone. Volumnia refuses her daughter-in-law's request; she tells Virgilia that perhaps Valeria brings news from the battlefield. She envisions her son's "bloody brow" and his armored hand mowing down his enemies in a harvest of destruction. The image sickens Virgilia: "O Jupiter, no blood!"

Volumnia loses her patience; angrily she tells the servant to bring Valeria to them. Blood, she tells her daughter-in-law, becomes a real man; not even Hecuba's breasts, as Hector suckled them, were as beautiful as Hector's forehead "when it spit forth blood." She vows that Coriolanus will "beat Aufidius' head below his knee / And tread upon his neck."

Valeria enters, compliments the ladies on their superb housekeeping, and asks about Virgilia's young son, Marcius. Volumnia answers that her grandson is splendid: "He had rather see the swords and hear a drum than look upon his schoolmaster." Valeria is delighted at the news. "The father's son," she comments, adding that she recently saw the young boy running after a "gilded butterfly." He teased it so unmercifully, she says, that he finally fell upon it and tore it to pieces with his teeth. Valeria recalls the scene with awe; the boy is truly "a noble child," she declares. Then she tries to coax Virgilia to go with her to see an ailing neighbor, but Virgilia declines; she will not go "over the threshold till [her] lord return from the wars." Valeria scoffs at her friend's melodramatics; she tells Virgilia that she is another silly Penelope who accomplished nothing—except that she filled "Ithaca full of moths."

Valeria pleads again with Virgilia to accompany her, but Virgilia is resolute. Thus, Valeria teases her with news of Coriolanus; according to one of the senators, she says, Cominius is soon to meet Aufidius in battle, and Coriolanus and Titus Lartius are besieging the city of Corioli. Virgilia repeats her decision: She will not leave the house. Volumnia is exasperated with her son's wife; she puts her sewing aside and tells Valeria that they will leave: "As [Virgilia] is now, she will but disease our better mirth." Valeria asks Virgilia one final time if Virgilia will go with them, but Virgilia says she cannot leave; she is too troubled to indulge in gaiety and gossip.

Scene 4 is set outside the city of Corioli; Coriolanus sees a messenger approaching, and because he is anxious for good news, he turns to Lartius and bets his prized horse against Lartius' horse that they will soon learn that Cominius has already engaged the enemy in battle. The messenger arrives and says, however, that Cominius has sighted the enemy but that he has not yet attacked them. Lartius is overjoyed: "The good horse is mine," he cries. Coriolanus is not anxious to loose his steed: "I'll buy him of you," he says, but Lartius refuses. He will lend his friend the horse, but he will neither return Coriolanus' horse nor resell it to him. Then he changes the subject to matters of warfare. "Summon the town," he says, for he wants to parley with those still remaining inside the besieged city.

Two Senators, along with others, appear on the walls, and Coriolanus asks them if Aufidius is still inside the city. The answer is curt: Aufidius is not in the city, nor is there "a man [within] that fears you less than he."

From far off, the sounds of a battle can be heard. The citizens of Corioli rally; they believe that their men have been victorious. Lartius thinks otherwise; the noise, he says, is his "instructions," and he calls for ladders to be placed against the city walls. At that moment, however, the Volscian army rushes through the city gates and forces the Romans to retreat to their trenches.

Coriolanus reenters a moment later, cursing his cowardly comrades—"boils and plagues / Plaster you o'er." He despairs at the lack of courage in his men, and he tells them that they have the "souls of geese." Then he orders them forward and says that if they refuse to advance on the Volscians, he will "leave the foe / And make [his] wars on [his own men]." Another alarum is heard, and the Volscians flee into the city. Coriolanus follows behind them, and the city gates close.

Lartius enters and asks for Coriolanus. One of the soldiers tells him that Coriolanus is doubtlessly slain "following the fliers at the very heels . . . He is himself alone, / To answer all the city." Lartius wails aloud: "O noble fellow," he cries, recounting his comrade's daring. Yet hardly has he finished his oration than Coriolanus enters, bleeding and wounded. The Roman forces cheer: Their leader lives.

Within moments, they mass together and besiege the city in one last victorious battle. When they are finished, Corioli is theirs.

In Scene 5, the Romans are exulting over the victory and relishing in the spoils when Coriolanus enters. He reprimands his men for their vulgar greediness, and then, hearing the sounds of battle in the distance, he orders them to pack up. Corioli may be taken, but Aufidius is still alive and "piercing our Romans." He means to finally destroy "the man of my soul's hate." He tells Lartius to take the necessary men whom he needs to hold the city, and he himself will take the rest and relieve Cominius. Lartius reminds his friend of his wounds, but Coriolanus is unconcerned; not even this last battle has "yet . . . warmed [him]"; the blood that he loses is only "physical"—that is, his spirit has not been injured, nor is it sated: "To Aufidius . . . I will appear, and fight." He exits and Lartius wishes him well.

In Scene 6, Cominius enters camp and speaks with his men. They are in retreat, but he assures them all that they have fought well. They have fought like Romans—"neither foolish . . . nor cowardly." He expects the enemy to attack again, but he is not afraid; he has heard the sounds of Coriolanus doing battle against the soldiers defending Corioli, and he expects reinforcements from his comrade to arrive shortly. A messenger enters, but his news is not good. He says that Coriolanus was forced to retreat. This is so; initially Coriolanus' forces *were* driven back, but later they were able to regroup and were successful in claiming the city. When Coriolanus' men fell back, the messenger says, he himself fled with a number of Volscian soldiers behind him.

Unexpectedly, Coriolanus enters. Cominius is aghast. His comrade is so bloody that he scarcely recognizes him. Coriolanus, however, is absolutely unconcerned with his wounds. His only concern is whether or not he has arrived too late: "Where is the enemy? Are you lords o' the field?"

Cominius tells him that they have retreated momentarily but that he believes Aufidius to be among the vanguard that may presently attack. This is good news to Coriolanus. He begs Cominius "by the blood we have shed together [and] by the vows / We have made . . . to set [him] against Aufidius." Cominius would prefer to see Coriolanus bathed and bandaged, but he cannot deny this request. Thus he offers his comrade whatever men are necessary to quell the next attack. Coriolanus states that he will choose only those soldiers who "love this painting [his blood] / Wherein you see me smeared"; he wants only those soldiers who value their country more than their lives. The soldiers shout, wave their swords, and hoist Coriolanus on their shoulders, and he acknowledges that he alone is fit to be the "sword" that will be used against the Volscians. He also recognizes that only a small number of these soldiers are bold and daring enough to accompany him. He will take those men and leave the rest to fight wherever Cominius thinks best. Cominius orders his men to do as Coriolanus commands; all spoils will be equally divided later.

Scene 7 is set outside the gates of Corioli; Lartius has assigned guards and is now ready to leave and join Cominius and Coriolanus. He speaks briefly with one of his lieutenants and reminds him to guard the city well. It is possible that Lartius and his fellow commanders may need more soldiers; if so, the lieutenant is to send reinforcements as soon as possible.

Scene 8 opens on the battlefield. Coriolanus and Aufidius meet one another at last. They restate their fierce hatred for one another and vow to fight until one of them is dead. Coriolanus taunts Aufidius that the blood that covers his body is not his own; it is Volscian blood, shed only three hours earlier during the conquest of Corioli. Then swords are drawn and the battle begins. Several Volscians rush to Aufidius' side, but Coriolanus finally manages to drive back Aufidius until the latter flees, crying out in shame as he realizes that Coriolanus has "shamed [him in what he hoped would be Coriolanus' last] condemned seconds."

As Scene 9 opens, an alarum is sounded in one of the Roman camps, and Cominius enters. Speaking with Coriolanus, he praises his comrade's exploits and says that the Roman senators will soon hear of Coriolanus' deeds. Cominius himself will tell them, and Romans everywhere will praise Coriolanus and will "thank the gods [that] Rome hath such a soldier." Lartius enters then and also begins to praise Coriolanus, but Coriolanus interrupts him. He says that he acted only as any Roman soldier would; he did only what was necessary; thus, he will hear no more praise. It is excessive and it is unhealthy; it reminds him of his mother's excessive praise for his military deeds. He asks to be excused so that he can attend to his wounds, but Cominius insists that Coriolanus stay and help divide the spoils. Coriolanus refuses, calling the booty "bribe."

At that moment, there is a loud flourish of trumpets, and all the soldiers hail their hero. When the camp is quiet again, Coriolanus reiterates his earlier statement. His deeds were only those of a Roman soldier, and a Roman soldier should not be seduced by the flattery of drums and trumpets. Cominius chides his friend for such modesty and offers him all glory of the battle—"this war's garland." From now on, he says, his comrade will no longer be known as Caius Marcius; he will now bear a new name: Coriolanus, named in honor of his conquest of Corioli. Trumpets and drums again sound a tribute, and Cominius issues orders to be sent to Rome, announcing this day's military success. Coriolanus then asks one favor: There is a man who is still imprisoned in Corioli, one who helped him and whom he could not rescue because of his vow to defeat Aufidius; he asks Cominius to ensure this man's safety. Cominius agrees to see that Coriolanus' wish is granted, and the two men exit to attend to Coriolanus' wounds.

Back in camp, in Scene 10, Aufidius discusses the capture of Corioli with one of his soldiers. He cannot fathom the soldier's naive concern about whether or not the city is in "good condition" following its defeat. To him, the defeat of Corioli has been a devastating blow. He knows the Roman mind; they will exercise no mercy to their enemies. Coriolanus has already defeated him five times in battle; there is sure to be another encounter, and once more, they will battle until one of them is dead—or until Aufidius has fled. He vows anew to kill his enemy once and for all, whether it be by "true sword to sword" or by "wrath or craft." Then he turns to one of his soldiers and instructs him to find out how many hostages have been taken to Rome and what the terms of surrender are. Then he will decide how he must "spur on my journey"—that is, what he must do next to regain his pride and his nation.

Commentary

Coriolanus is a play that deals with class warfare in Rome. In the first act, Shakespeare dramatizes this social conflict by focusing on the confrontation between the plebeian-citizen faction and an elitist patrician, Caius Marcius (later honored with the name "Coriolanus"). Coriolanus is the symbol of the mob's fury and wrath; they believe that his death will solve the problem of high grain prices. Significantly, Coriolanus' first words reveal his attitude toward the people. He shows utter contempt for them; he calls them "dissentious rogues" and tells them, "With every minute you do change a mind"; to him, the mob's chief trait is fickleness, both in war and peace, and he welcomes the news of impending war as a means of ridding Rome of this surplus plebeian "rabble," for whom he has no compassion. Coriolanus believes that patricians alone should rule because of the plebeians' inferior powers of reason. He is convinced that civic order can be maintained only by a strong Senate that will control the people. He passionately disapproves of the concessions now being made by the Senate because they will lead only to other demands that will cause further insurrection if not met and will lead to political chaos if the decision-making process is extended any further to the irrational lower class. At the end of Scene 1, two tribunes, Brutus and Sicinius, acknowledge that they are also aware of the plebeians' "giddy censure" and fickle opinion. In contrast to this attitude throughout the play is the steadfastness of Coriolanus' ethics. The common citizens are depicted as being men of very little character; Coriolanus, although certainly not a model hero, remains remarkably consistent to his views.

On the surface, the old and sage patrician Menenius seems like a good man; the citizens respect him and listen to his reasoned fable, but they do not genuinely comprehend the true opinions of this man whom they consider to be their greatest friend within the ruling class. Actually, however, Menenius believes that the patricians are so superior to the plebeians that the possibility of a successful citizen revolt does not exist. He tells them, "You may as well / Strike at the heaven with your staves as lift them / Against the Roman state." Nevertheless, he does realize that the plebeians have the power to create chaos, and he urges Coriolanus not to provoke them further.

Many of Coriolanus' values are due to the influence of his mother, Volumnia. She educated him to commit his life to a set of heroic and noble principles, and she sent him to war as a teenager so that he would learn to value the honor and fame that would result from valiant combat; she deeply wanted him to always seek danger and glory in war. As a result, Coriolanus developed a sense of honor based more on egoism and social station than on patriotism. Consequently, later in the play, he will see no treason in his joining Aufidius because righting a personal wrong will mean more to him than abstract loyalty to a country from which he is estranged. In addition, Volumnia has succeeded so well in training her son that he believes absolutely in adhering to her concepts of honor. Honor is more valuable to him, ultimately, than life. For that reason, Coriolanus will later feel that his mother has betrayed him when she asks him to compromise and appease the plebeians.

During the battle scenes in Act I, note how Coriolanus acts when the Volscian army proves momentarily to be braver and more eager to fight than the Romans. Coriolanus reacts in a rage, cursing his soldiers with an even greater intensity than he had cursed the plebeians who were rioting in Rome. However, it is Coriolanus' *anger* that is one of his greatest martial assets, causing him to attack the enemy with a ferocity that even his own men and Lartius consider foolhardy but that ultimately inspires the Romans to victory. He refuses to consider the possibility that his brave soldiers can be beaten, and his immediate response is a counterattack, spurring his men onward not only with exhortations of honor and patriotism but with deadly threats. He seems obsessed, and so by devoutly following the principles that he has learned from Volumnia and his previous experiences in war, this is the moment of glory which he has lived for. His lack of control in moments of high passion characterizes him; it makes him the exemplary warrior he is; but, ironically, it is this quality that will destroy him eventually in the political arena into which his victories will thrust him.

Unlike Coriolanus, who can accept nothing less than immediate and total victory, Cominius commends his soldiers for having fought honorably—even if they have retreated. When Coriolanus enters, however, his first words are, "Come I too late?" He assumes command of the Roman offensive, and the Roman soldiers are inspired to new boldness by this consummate man of action who is eager for battle. Characteristically, Coriolanus shuns recounting his own bravery and success, desiring, instead, to be apprised of the present situation and to lead the attack against Aufidius' strongest position. His enthusiasm infects the entire army, causing all of them to volunteer to follow him into the most dangerous part of the battlefield.

After the battle is over and Cominius suggests that Coriolanus' feats may go unrecognized unless public acknowledgment is made of them, Coriolanus confesses that he finds praise uncomfortable. He does not like to receive public acclaims. He has satisfied his and his mother's desires by simply living up to the standards that they revere. He even commends his soldiers for having surpassed him in bravery. Of particular significance here is Coriolanus' consistency of character in his rejection of his share of the spoils of Corioli. To accept them would make him a mercenary, and war is far too important to him to be equated in any way with financial gain.

As the act ends, Aufidius laments having been beaten by Coriolanus for the fifth time in single combat. Defeat and shame have altered him. He is no longer proud to be a Volscian; he admits to Coriolanus' superiority as a soldier, but he is determined to destroy the man who has humiliated him. Ironically, he wishes he were a Roman, just as Coriolanus will soon desire to become a Volscian. Aufidius thoroughly understands Coriolanus, whom he assesses as being "bolder, though not so subtle" as the devil. And of equal importance here is Aufidius' realization that "craft" may be the most promising approach to use against a man who lacks the cunning to use deceit either to gain his own ends or to detect it when it is used against him.

ACT II

Summary

In Rome, Menenius and the tribunes Sicinius and Brutus argue about the excessive pride of Coriolanus. Menenius says that the tribunes themselves are ambitious and foolishly proud; he admits that he himself is intemperate in drink, argument, and the free expression of his opinion, but he criticizes them for being excessively ambitious and exceptionally poor magistrates who fail to recognize their own pride while attacking Coriolanus for his pride.

Volumnia, Virgilia, and Valeria enter, and Volumnia greatly pleases Menenius with the news that Coriolanus has written letters to him, to her, to Virgilia, and to the state informing them that he will presently return, acclaimed as a hero. Volumnia and Menenius discuss Coriolanus' wounds, his bravery, his fight with Aufidius, and Volumnia is sure that his fresh wounds, combined with his earlier battle scars, will be advantageous when he shows them to the populace and asks to be a candidate for consul. Cominius, Lartius, and their army enter, escorting Coriolanus, who wears the oaken garland of victory. A herald announces Coriolanus' single fight within the gates of Corioli and the honorable addition to his name. Coriolanus asks for the adulation to cease; he kneels before his mother, then leaves for the Capitol to visit the Senate. Volumnia confesses her long desire for him to finally become consul, but Coriolanus expresses reluctance to enter politics.

Left alone, Brutus and Sicinius note that all classes of Romans are equally enthusiastic over Coriolanus, and they fear that they and the other tribunes will lose power if a worshipful populace accepts Coriolanus as consul. They agree, however, that it shouldn't be too difficult to remind everyone of Coriolanus' excessive pride; thus, it should be equally easy to provoke him into revealing his true contempt for the lower classes. A messenger enters and tells them that the Senate awaits them and that the people will likely choose Coriolanus to be consul. The tribunes leave, agreeing that they will pretend to honor Coriolanus while, in fact, they will be trying to conjure up some means whereby Coriolanus' temper and pride will destroy him.

At the Capitol, a group of officials and senators enter, and Menenius asks Cominius to delineate the deeds of Coriolanus. A senator implores him to be thorough and asks the tribunes to listen carefully and to inform the people. The tribunes agree but ask for Coriolanus to change his behavior.

Coriolanus leaves, not wishing to hear his heroism proclaimed, and Menenius reminds the tribunes that Coriolanus' modesty will also prevent his flattering the people. Cominius then speaks of Coriolanus' valor, his many battles, his bravery at Corioli, his responsibility for the recent victory, and his lack of greed while the spoils of Corioli were being meted out. The Senate calls Coriolanus back, and Menenius tells him that the Senate has chosen him as a candidate for consul. Coriolanus promises always to follow the will of the Senate, but he asks if he might waive the custom of wearing the coarse garment of humility; likewise, he does not want to display his wounds and plead, as it were, for plebeian votes. Menenius urges him to follow tradition, and finally Coriolanus agrees. The tribunes, confident that Coriolanus cannot but help conceal his true contempt for the people, leave to inform the populace.

At the Forum, a group of citizens who await Coriolanus discuss his ingratitude, as well as the patricians' contempt for the plebeian class. Then, accompanied by Menenius, and cursing the common people, Coriolanus enters, wearing the traditional gown of humility. Menenius urges his friend to moderate his speech, then exits. Three citizens approach Coriolanus and ask why he is in the Forum, and he answers that he is there because he deserves to be, not because he desires to "beg" for their votes. Two more citizens approach and accuse him of abusing them; he maintains that his honest elitism is a virtue, but he says that he will act as he is supposed to act and that he will "plead" for their votes. They consent—even though he refuses to show them his wounds.

Coriolanus is deeply troubled; he laments having to humble himself for an office that he has already earned and the Senate has already granted him. However, he decides to forbear since his ordeal is half over. Three more citizens approach, and he "begs" for their votes. They give them to him, then exit as Menenius returns with the news that the tribunes have verified the election.

After Menenius and Coriolanus have left so that Coriolanus can change out of his gown of humility and have his election made official, Brutus and Sicinius comment on the proud bearing of Coriolanus; similarly, several citizens recount his mocking behavior and his refusal to show them his wounds. The tribunes secretly rejoice and chide the citizens for approving Coriolanus too willingly. The citizens proclaim that they can still reverse the unofficial election, and the tribunes urge them to do so and to act swiftly. Craftily, the tribunes take care to hide their instigation of the people from the Senate; they want to make it appear that they have argued for Coriolanus. Brutus contends that a preventative mutiny now will forestall a greater rebellion later, and the tribunes thus make plans to take advantage of Coriolanus' reaction to the news of his rejection.

Commentary

Before word of the Roman victory has had time to reach Rome, it is clear that peace will bring about an even greater polarization between the plebeian and the patrician classes. The tribunes have become the chief spokesmen for the plebeian faction, and Coriolanus has become both representative for and emblem of the extreme, conservative element within the patrician ranks. However, with Coriolanus absent, Menenius has taken over the role of protector of patrician interests.

The tribunes Sicinius and Brutus are the first popularly elected officials of the young Roman democracy, and in Menenius' estimation the new system has already produced representatives who are inefficient and incompetent; to him, they attempt to compensate for their inabilities and to protect their positions by using demagoguery. Although the tribunes' suspicion of Coriolanus' class arrogance has been shown to be well-founded because of his many slurs against the plebeians, the private conversation between the tribunes at the end of the first scene of this act reveals Menenius' assessment to be at least partially correct. Sicinius and Brutus resent the adoration that the people are giving to Coriolanus, and they clearly reveal to us their plan to take advantage of their newly gained power. They plan to deceive the Senate by feigning support for Coriolanus while scheming to publicly provoke Coriolanus' haughtiness. Significantly, the patricians grossly underestimate the capacity of the tribunes to undermine their authority. Menenius, for example, looks on the tribunes and their function as subjects of ridicule. He dismisses them as "herdsmen of the beastly plebeians."

Coriolanus has returned to Rome at the zenith of his exceptional military career. He has achieved all that a soldier could imagine: The Roman nobility and populace have given him sole credit for having inspired and led a resounding victory. But he is not the only one to have succeeded to the utmost; Coriolanus' mother, Volumnia, has fulfilled her mission to mold her son into the ideal warrior, and Coriolanus acknowledges her contribution by kneeling respectfully before her even before he greets his wife and son. Note here that Volumnia welcomes her son *not* with warmth and relief that he has returned home safely but rather with pride and satisfaction that he has returned from war for the third time wearing the garland of victory and bearing the title of his nation's hero. Likewise, Menenius, Cominius, and Lartius worship and respect Coriolanus for embodying abstract qualities honored by Roman soldiers and patricians, but they do not relate to him as a mutual friend. Only Coriolanus' wife, Virgilia, loves him in purely human and emotional terms, but in his presence she remains always in the background; she is never assertive and she seldom speaks.

Volumnia's role in Coriolanus' life and in this drama is a key factor. She trained Coriolanus to adhere to a strict code of conduct applicable only to the military and to patrician society, and Coriolanus has consistently followed the principles of the code devoutly;

those principles have dictated his attitudes and his reactions, and consequently he has not had to develop an ability to apply reason to circumstances and situations. He has always relied on his mother's code for concepts and on his mother for guidance. Therefore, when Volumnia decides that the next step in her son's career should be his election as consul, she thrusts him into a situation where the assets that have made his success possible will quickly become detriments that will doom him to utter failure. Initially Coriolanus rejects her suggestions about role-playing in order to please the masses, but he has grown too used to following her principles to deny her now.

Although the government of Rome has convened specifically to honor Coriolanus for his latest military deeds and to nominate him to run for consul, the tribunes have already initiated their plan to destroy Coriolanus. They begin with Brutus' sarcastic suggestion that it is *not* modesty that compels Coriolanus to leave the highly formalized ceremony; Brutus implies that Coriolanus is incapable of following tradition and humbly pleading for votes. Menenius quickly comes to Coriolanus' defense, and he tells the tribunes that Coriolanus "loves your people, / But tie him not to be their bedfellow," contending that Coriolanus can serve the interest of the people without attempting to meet them as social equals. The debate continues, but by the end of Scene 2, we see that the tribunes are satisfied that their plan to provoke Coriolanus will work. They have cunningly enfolded themselves in the mantle of righteousness by arguing that *custom* must be upheld—for the rights of the people—while in actuality they are using subterfuge to establish a condition in which they will be able to take advantage of Coriolanus' "flaw"—that is, his dislike of "begging" for approval and, also, publicly showing his wounds to the masses.

When the citizens have gathered in the Forum, they agree that Coriolanus' military accomplishments have indeed qualified him to be a worthy candidate for consul. *If* he follows the prescribed practices of displaying his wounds, proclaiming his services to the people, and requesting their votes, they in turn will be bound by the dictates of the "law of gratitude" to approve him. The citizens also resolve to ignore Coriolanus' earlier attitude towards them.

Suspense is keen at this point—approval seems certain—because the populace is caught up in the emotion of the victory celebration and seems willing to approve Coriolanus as consul. Yet we see in the final scene of Act II that Coriolanus' pride and the code of conduct that he learned from Volumnia will prevent him from playing the role of humble supplicant. In fact, nowhere in the play thus far is Coriolanus' pride more evident than here. He disregards Menenius' entreaties to moderate his speech, and he proceeds to ridicule the ritual that he is trying to follow. With biting sarcasm and mockery, he scorns the people as being cowards and simple-minded creatures worthy only of hanging. He believes that he should already be consul because of his record in war, his position within the patrician class, and his selection by the Senate. He does not think that the people should have the power to approve or reject the Senate's selection, and he remains firm in his conviction that the Senate made a grave mistake by conceding such power to the people. He considers himself to be an innovator who should be exempt from all traditional rules. In his opinion, it is men such as he who correct existing wrongs, and the current wrong that he would immediately correct is the growing power of the common people.

He refuses to display his wounds, and he sheds his traditional gown of humility as quickly as possible. He says that he should be honored by the people and respected for expressing his attitudes honestly and for not offending the populace by condescending to flatter them with unfelt affection. He sarcastically proclaims that, if he must, he *will* become a false-speaking flatterer, but what Coriolanus does not comprehend is that he *must* at this moment choose either to abandon his candidacy or become, in actuality, a demagogue and pretend to speak to the people as an equal. As a consequence of his conduct in the Forum, he will become easy prey for the tribunes when they set about attempting to reverse the decision of the people. It will be then that the masses will quickly recall Coriolanus' proud behavior. Moreover, the tribunes will easily use the citizens' inconstancy, a trait that Shakespeare has emphasized several times already. Thus, they can manipulate them into changing their minds and rejecting Coriolanus.

The tribunes' plan succeeds, of course. The citizens not only remember Coriolanus' behavior, but they remember it in detail; therefore, we see that the tribunes are easily appealing to the people's fickle natures and manipulating them into nullifying the election. Clearly, the "villains" of this play are the tribunes.

Coriolanus hates the common people and objects to sharing

power with the plebeian class, and the tribunes are fulfilling their duty to protect the rights of the people when they oppose him. However, the tribunes have also become demagogues obsessed with protecting and extending their own power, and they have no reluctance to gain their ends by taking advantage of both Coriolanus' proud nature and the people's fickleness. They have instructed the people to follow a procedure during the election designed to provoke Coriolanus into offensive acts of pride and contempt. The citizens approach him in groups of two or three rather than *en masse* in order to prolong his ordeal and to try his patience. Nevertheless, they fail to follow the tribunes' explicit instructions to shower the candidate with provocative questions that will force him either to commit himself to enforcing plebeian rights or to expose himself as an enemy of the people—an enemy not deserving to be consul. However, note that the tribunes refuse to concede defeat and that they patiently instruct the people again. They are determined to revoke the people's initial vote by inflaming them against Coriolanus with accounts of his behavior in the Forum and by insisting to the Senate that they were too blinded by their admiration of Coriolanus' service to detect his true nature. The tribunes justify their devious maneuverings to themselves with the argument that a provoked rebellion by the populace now will prevent greater bloodshed in the future. At the center of their plan is Coriolanus, who cannot lie nor flatter; he is locked in combat for which he is poorly prepared with men who have no scruples against using any weapons that promise expediency.

ACT III

Summary

Coriolanus, along with several members of the Roman Senate and a number of patricians, is on his way to the marketplace to receive confirmation of his election. Lartius reports that Aufidius has raised a new army, and Coriolanus says that he is eager to fight him again. A few moments later, the patricians meet the tribunes Sicinius and Brutus, who command them to halt. They announce the revocation of the election and predict that the people will riot if the procession continues to the marketplace. Coriolanus angrily accuses the tribunes of plotting to usurp political power, and, of course, Brutus denies instigating any such plot; he lays all blame on Coriolanus. As the debate grows more heated, Sicinius warns Coriolanus to moderate his speech if he hopes to become consul. Cominius, like Coriolanus, agrees that the people have been deliberately deceived.

Menenius and a senator try to restore calm, and Coriolanus curses the common people and advises against sharing power with them. Brutus accuses Coriolanus of speaking like a wrathful god, and Sicinius tells him that his mind is like a poison that "shall remain" out of government. Coriolanus takes issue with the word "shall," with its connotation that the tribunes have the authority to command him; he warns them that the word "shall" is indicative of a political movement that if not halted will lead to absolute plebeian rule. Cominius suggests that they continue on their way.

Menenius attempts to restrain Coriolanus, but Coriolanus continues to scorn the common people: They are undeserving cowards whose claim to authority is based solely on their numbers, and they do not have the ability to rule responsibly. He suggests that the Senate suppress the plebeians before they gain the power to destroy both themselves and the state. The tribunes label Coriolanus as a traitor, and he answers that they should be removed from office. Incensed, they cry out for the aediles (officers attached to the Tribune) and instruct them to arrest Coriolanus. The gentry try to defend Coriolanus, more aediles enter, and a "rabble of citizens" enter. Chaos ensues, and while Menenius again asks for calm, Sicinius warns the people that Coriolanus deserves to die. They tell the aediles to apprehend him and to execute him. Menenius pleads with Brutus, but Brutus answers that violence is the only way to curb Coriolanus. Another scuffle ensues, and after the gentry finally prevail, they urge Coriolanus to go home. Coriolanus calls the plebeians "barbarians" and says that he could beat forty of them, but Cominius notes the odds and again urges him to leave. Most of the gentry leave, but Menenius and two patricians remain behind.

Menenius says that Coriolanus is "too noble for the world," that Coriolanus is a man who will not flatter, one who always speaks his mind. The tribunes, however, insist that Coriolanus must be executed. Menenius reminds the tribunes and the people of Coriolanus' service to Rome, and he begs them to follow due process of law; otherwise, Rome will become divided and destroyed by civil strife.

He reminds them that Coriolanus is a warrior who is unversed in polite speech, and he promises to bring him before a court of law in order to answer all their charges. The tribunes accept Menenius' offer while maintaining that they retain the authority to proceed as they please against Coriolanus if Menenius should fail.

Attended by a group of patricians at his home, Coriolanus insists that he will continue to act according to his principles in defiance of the tribunes; then he questions why his mother has not been more supportive of his stand. Volumnia enters and reproaches him for not being more reserved until his appointment as consul has been actually confirmed. Menenius and some senators enter, and he and Volumnia agree that Coriolanus *must* make some concessions in order to maintain civic order. Volumnia argues that since deceit is an honorable strategy in war, it can now be considered an honorable policy to maintain the stability of the government.

Coriolanus asks his mother why she is being so persistent. Admitting that her suggestions are indeed repugnant, she advises her son to feign a role and to speak kindly to the people in order to safeguard the fortunes of Rome, as well as his own. She contends that the people are more emotional than reasonable, and she urges him to kneel before them, to apologize to them, and to promise them that he will change. Cominius enters and also advises Coriolanus to calm the mob with conciliatory words; Volumnia continues to plead, and finally Coriolanus yields. Momentarily he changes his mind. Then Volumnia tells him to do as he likes, noting that it is as dishonorable for her to plead with him as it is for him to humble himself before the plebeians. He tells her to have patience; he will act a false role and return home as consul. Cominius warns him against further provocation by the tribunes, and the two men leave for the marketplace.

At the Forum, Brutus tells Sicinius to provoke Coriolanus with accusations of tyrannical ambition and, if that fails, to charge him with harboring malice toward the people and hoarding the spoils of war. An aedile then brings news that Coriolanus is on his way, and Sicinius orders the aedile to assemble the people and to instruct them to shout either "Fine" or "Death" for Coriolanus when they hear the tribune say "It shall be so / I' the right and strength o' the commons." Coriolanus and his party arrive, and he assures Menenius that he will remain calm. The aedile returns with a group of citizens, and Coriolanus asks if any further charges will be brought against him. Sicinius answers Coriolanus by asking him if he will submit to questioning by the people and their representatives. Coriolanus agrees and asks why he has been deprived of the consulship. Sicinius charges him with tyrannical ambition and with being a traitor. Coriolanus heatedly calls Sicinius a liar. Sicinius asks the people to note Coriolanus' service to Rome. Rashly Coriolanus objects to Brutus' mentioning his service, and Menenius quickly reminds him of his promise to his mother; Coriolanus, however, says he *cannot* beg. Sicinius then decrees that Coriolanus must be banished from Rome forever; if he returns, he will be executed. Sicinius then signals to the aedile and the people. On cue, the citizens shout for banishment. Cominius attempts to defend Coriolanus, but Brutus says that the sentence is final. Coriolanus predicts that after he is exiled, Rome will become an easy target for invaders, and he leaves, stating, "There is a world elsewhere." The citizens shout in triumphant joy, and Sicinius goads them to follow and torment Coriolanus as he leaves the gates of the city.

Commentary

Coriolanus' attitude toward the state, the people, and the tribunes does not change with his election. Even before he learns that the people have reversed their vote, he scorns the tribunes when he sees them because he is offended by their acting like figures of authority. The revocation of his position by the people only reinforces his belief that they are too irresponsible to be trusted with political power, and he warns the patricians again that anarchy will result if the people are not curbed immediately because once the masses have been given power, they will never again submit to patrician rule. He acknowledges that granting the people's demand to select tribunes may have been good policy as a means of halting a rebellion, but he fervently believes that the nobles must resume their traditional power and must remove the tribunes from office now that order has been restored.

Coriolanus sees no loss of honor by the patricians' reversing their promises to the plebeians, for the plebeians are not a class that deserves fair treatment. For Coriolanus, the only acceptable government for Rome is a benevolent patrician dictatorship, and thus he refers to the Senate's gift of grain as an instance when the patricians demonstrated their *care* for the working class. In reality, however, Coriolanus views the distribution of food as a courtesy to a populace that had to be conscripted to defend their homeland when the Volscians threatened invasion; in contrast, the people and the tribunes view it as a concession to their demands, a concession that has encouraged them to seek more freedom and more authority. Coriolanus is a wary man; he warns the nobles what might happen if they continue to submit to the people, and he points to Sicinius' use of the imperative "shall," with its connotation that a tribune has authority to command a noble; this is also an example of what the future holds if the tribunes are not removed. Coriolanus' theory is that when two factions contend for political power, one will inevitably dominate the other, and the people have numbers on their side. Only a commitment to compromise by both parties can reconcile their differences, and neither is willing to compromise. Indeed, Coriolanus cannot.

In their class struggle, the two parties have decidedly different concepts of what constitutes "Rome." The patricians define Rome in terms of its established social order and its buildings, both of which they desire to preserve. Coriolanus, as the most extreme conservative among the patricians, thinks of Rome as consisting preeminently of its *nobility*, and all else is worth risking to protect noble rule. The tribunes and the plebeians, on the other hand, consider the people as the essence of "Rome." Thus, Act III dramatically embodies class warfare; here Shakespeare focuses on the clash between the tribunes (supported by the citizens) and Coriolanus (supported by the patricians).

In his efforts to restore calm, Menenius appeals to the tribunes to act as good citizens, but he fails to see that a wide difference of opinion exists between what he considers to be good citizenship and what the tribunes consider to be good citizenship. Menenius wants patrician-dominated order restored; the tribunes believe that they are acting as good citizens by inciting the people as a means of eliminating Coriolanus from the government while simultaneously increasing their own power. They believe that Coriolanus considers himself to be above the law, and it is essential to their success to show that he is *subject* to the law and that they have the authority to apply the law in his case.

In their political battle against Coriolanus and the patricians, the tribunes consistently display a superior ability to understand their opponents, to plan thoroughly, and to rally the people to their support. After they succeed in stopping the patricians from continuing to the Forum, the tribunes know that they can provoke Coriolanus into a rage by referring to his demand for their removal from office as being "manifest treason"; as a result, they can label him a traitor, a rebel, and an enemy to Rome. When Coriolanus does return to the Forum to face questions, he immediately reveals his incapacity to be a political leader in a democracy. He turns to the people whom he promised to placate and accuses them of being dishonorable in reversing their votes. Sicinius seizes on this flare of temper and calls Coriolanus a "traitor to the people." He knows that the word "traitor" will outrage Coriolanus; as expected, Coriolanus damns the tribunes *and* the people, fulfilling the tribunes' hope that he would offend the people and force them into even further support of their "representatives."

By manipulating Coriolanus' public behavior, the tribunes have established their right to try him—where it counts—in the minds of the plebeians. The tribunes are equally effective with the patricians. Because the patricians are uncertain about the outcome of a widespread plebeian revolt, the tribunes take every advantage of this fear of political chaos in order to drive a wedge between the nobles and Coriolanus. Throughout the entirety of Act III, we see them focusing wholly on the short-term goals of getting rid of their most formidable opponent and of solidifying their recent accumulation of power.

At the end of Act III, the tribunes clearly represent a dangerous challenge to the existing order. Following the armed clash, when the patricians offer to vouch for Coriolanus and Menenius pleads for due process of law, the patricians, in effect, recognize the tribunes as being the de facto authority of Rome. Volumnia, second only to Coriolanus in her hatred of the plebeians and their representatives, upbraids her son for voicing his anti-plebeian opinions prior to his confirmation. Coriolanus agrees; the tribunes *are* legal officials, and they do have the right to question him, but now they have charged him with treason and have sentenced him to banishment. They are now the men who will determine the fate of Rome. However, they do not carry their new stature flawlessly, for they reveal weaknesses in themselves that they have condemned in Coriolanus. They exhibited their excessive pride when they interrupted Cominius in midsentence without regard for his social standing in Rome, and they added unnecessary insult to Coriolanus when they ordered the plebeians to hound him to the gates of the city. Caught up in the excitement of the moment, they clearly intend to humiliate their victim.

At the end of Act III, the citizens hail them with "The gods preserve our noble tribunes!" but the phrase is potent with foreshadowing. The tribunes have, in fact, replaced the nobles in real power, and they have succeeded in preventing Coriolanus' confirmation as consul; but they have acted ignobly in using deceit to defeat him, and they have set up a condition in Rome that will jeopardize *all* classes of citizens.

ACT IV

Summary

Coriolanus bids farewell to his family, his friends, and several young nobles at the gates of Rome. He consoles his mother and his wife, and he declines an offer by Cominius to accompany him for a month. He promises that they will hear good reports of him, and he leaves. Following his departure, the tribunes disperse the people to avoid further confrontations with the patricians. Along with Menenius and Virgilia, Volumnia approaches and curses the tribunes for banishing her son, who she hopes will revenge himself upon them. Declaring Volumnia to be mad, the tribunes exit. Volumnia grows even more furious as she leaves, escorting Virgilia.

On a highway between Rome and Antium, Nicanor, a Roman spying for the Volscians, meets the Volscian Adrian, who is on his way to Rome to search for Nicanor. Nicanor describes the recent insurrection and the banishment of Coriolanus, and he suggests that Aufidius attack while civil strife is still rampant in Rome. Adrian predicts that Aufidius will probably do so since his army is prepared to move on an hour's notice.

Disguised as a poor man in Antium, Coriolanus learns from a passerby that he is standing in front of Aufidius' house. Considering whether he should use this chance to make enemies of friends and friends of enemies, he enters the house, knowing that either he will be slain by his former enemy or else invited to join him. A servingman asks Coriolanus to leave, and then more servingmen enter and join in an exchange of mild insults with Coriolanus.

A servant leaves and returns with Aufidius, who asks Coriolanus to identify himself, but Aufidius fails to recognize Coriolanus until Coriolanus mentions their battles and blames his banishment on the cowardice of the nobles of Rome. He states his desire to join the Volscians so that both of them can take revenge on Rome. He advises Aufidius either to accept his offer or to kill him since those are the only options Aufidius has of freeing himself of the shame of defeat. Aufidius welcomes him with an embrace and a promise of friendship. He professes to love Coriolanus more than he loved his wife on their wedding night, and he informs Coriolanus that the Volscian army is waiting in readiness to fight. He invites Coriolanus to speak to several senators who are making preparations to invade Roman territory, he gives him command over half of the Volscian army, and he invites him to decide whether or not they should first attack outlying territory or whether they should attack Rome itself. Coriolanus and Aufidius exit, and two servants consider which man is the more formidable, carefully and comically avoiding absolute statements. Another servant enters with a description of the senators' treatment of Coriolanus and with news that the army will move within hours. The servants talk of the advantages that war has over peace; they clearly welcome the upcoming engagement.

In Rome, Sicinius compliments himself and Brutus for the peace that has followed the banishment of Coriolanus. Menenius enters and argues that matters would be even better if Coriolanus had compromised. Several citizens pass by and pay their regards to the tribunes. An aedile enters to tell them of a "slave's" claim that the Volscians have successfully invaded Roman territory with two armies. Menenius comments that Coriolanus' absence has given Aufidius courage. A messenger reports that the slave's rumor is true but that the Senate is planning a defense and that Coriolanus is in command of one of the invading armies. The tribunes insist it can only be a rumor, and Menenius agrees that a reconciliation between Coriolanus and Aufidius is highly unlikely. Another messenger brings news of Volscian victories and of the Senate's desire for the presence of the tribunes.

Cominius enters, blaming the tribunes for all these troubles, and he reports that Coriolanus has indeed joined with Aufidius and that citizens in the invaded regions either have joined the Volscians or have been defeated by them. Menenius hopes that Coriolanus will be merciful, but Cominius does not expect mercy from one who has been treated so inconsiderately. A group of citizens enter, and Menenius curses them for bringing the wrath of Coriolanus upon Rome; they, of course, deny ever really wanting to banish him. Cominius and Menenius leave for the Capitol, followed by the tribunes after they have tried to calm the confused, frightened citizens.

In a camp near Rome, a lieutenant tells Aufidius that the Volscian soldiers have grown to worship Coriolanus. Aufidius is aware that Coriolanus has behaved proudly, but at this point, Aufidius does not wish to harm the Volscian cause by trying to restrain his new comrade. He admits that Coriolanus has managed his unit of the army well and that he has fought ferociously, but he insinuates "yet he hath left undone" something that will endanger one or the other of them. Aufidius foresees little resistance from Rome, but he is aware that some defect in character has caused Coriolanus' banishment, and he plans to deal with his old enemy—once Rome has been captured.

Commentary

After the people have derided Coriolanus on his way to the gates of the city as a way of demonstrating their complete victory over him, the tribunes are astute enough to try to heal political wounds by avoiding any further provocation of the patricians. Brutus suggests, "Let us seem humbler after it is done / Than when it was a-doing." The tribunes smugly believe that they have brought about tranquillity and that they have proven the patricians wrong who had feared that chaos would be the result of any further plebeian gains. Sicinius gleefully notes that they now receive even kinder treatment from Menenius, who admits that Coriolanus should have been more temperate.

The people credit the tribunes for bringing peace, but it is not long before they become fickle and blame the tribunes (while absolving themselves) for provoking Coriolanus and the Volscians to lay siege to the city. Sicinius tries to make the best of a bad situation by telling the people that the resulting turmoil pleases the patricians, but his efforts are futile. People in the outlying areas revolt, and it is not long before Cominius and Menenius defend Coriolanus for seeking revenge for wrongs done him by the tribunes, the people, and the nobles who betrayed him. The tribunes panic. At first they proclaim the news to be a rumor spread by the patricians to frighten the citizens into accepting Coriolanus' return, and they order the aediles to whip the bearer of bad news. Significantly, they willingly relinquish policy-making to the Senate.

Volumnia has been devastated by her son's banishment. She accuses the tribunes of inciting the people, and she prays that the working class will be utterly destroyed. When she confronts the tribunes, she commands that they "shall" stay to hear her scorn, and this command echoes Sicinius' earlier "shall," which was directed to Coriolanus. Of course, Volumnia no longer has any actual authority to command them, and her curses are empty except as an expression of her profound grief.

Coriolanus promises Volumnia that he will either exceed what is expected of him "or be caught / With cautelous baits and practices," meaning deceitful cunning and trickery. His words are prophetic because he will suffer as a result of his own questionable actions and because of Aufidius' fulfilling his earlier vow to defeat Coriolanus by any means available. Coriolanus evaluates his banishment on strictly personal terms. He can ignore the past rewards from his country, the patriotism he once felt for Rome, his friends, and even his family in his desire to revenge what remains an affront to his character, albeit a very serious one. He complains that Rome has only given him the surname "Coriolanus" in recognition of his extensive service, forgetting that his gaining renown was his and Volumnia's primary goal in life.

It was only when he entered the treacherous labyrinth of democratic politics where he would be judged by standards entirely new to him and by a class of people abhorrent to him that he established goals that could not be achieved by earning an honorable surname or other official acclaim. He now blames his predicament on the people for being envious, the tribunes for being deceitful, the nobles for being cowardly, and his country as a whole for being corrupt. He accepts none of the responsibility himself, and he admits to Aufidius that his desire for revenge is motivated by "mere spite." He philosophizes on the capacity of chance to change friends to enemies and enemies to friends, ignoring that he is creating his own circumstances with a willful decision. His alteration from a plain-speaking man to a man willing to join his country's enemies is signified by his appearing in Antium wearing a disguise and by Aufidius' inability to recognize an enemy whom he has fought face to face a dozen times.

The sense of insidiousness that has flowed from the Roman tribunes' practice of deceit and the many spies serving both Rome and the Volscians continues as a dominant theme with the exchange between Nicanor and Adrian and with Aufidius' resolve to ultimately bring down Coriolanus. Aufidius initially accepts Coriolanus enthusiastically as a fellow warrior, one whose wrongs he is eager to help revenge, but he mistakenly gives him too much authority over the Volscian army and the strategy to be used against Rome, a mistake quickly realized by Aufidius' servants. Like the Roman nobles who revere Coriolanus for embodying traditional values more than they love him as a personal friend, Aufidius addresses him as "Thou noble thing," and his attitude toward him quickly grows more distant. He realizes that he has misjudged Coriolanus, that either pride, poor judgment, or an inability to adjust from war to peace has caused the Roman people to fear and to banish him.

Following the battles at Corioli, Aufidius swore he would use even dishonorable means to defeat his enemy, and he plans to follow that resolve, but he has allowed Coriolanus to become so essential to the Volscian army and its campaign that he believes that he must wait until Rome falls before he can act. His conversation with his lieutenant at the end of Act IV counterbalances the preceding scene, and the peril threatening Rome has a parallel in Coriolanus' situation; he will lose regardless of the outcome of the Volscian war with Rome.

ACT V

Summary

In Rome, Menenius tells the tribunes that he will not go to plead with Coriolanus, and he suggests that they go instead. Cominius describes Coriolanus' earlier rejection of him on the grounds that Rome is not worth sparing for the few friends whom Coriolanus has there. Menenius, however, takes some comfort in knowing that he and a few others are still in Coriolanus' thoughts. Sicinius pleads for Menenius to intervene. At first he refuses, but he finally agrees after Sicinius promises that all Romans will appreciate his effort. Thus, he leaves to visit Coriolanus, but Cominius predicts that Menenius will fail because Rome's only real hope lies with Volumnia and Virgilia.

In the Volscian camp, two sentinels stop Menenius and tell him that he may not see Coriolanus. He argues to no avail that he is a special friend of Coriolanus. They answer that the weak pleas of elderly women, virgins, and old dotards such as he cannot be expected to have an effect on the man whom they, the Romans, have banished. They advise him to return prepared to perish with the city, and they refuse his further entreaties with insults and threats. Coriolanus and Aufidius enter then, and Menenius asks Coriolanus after an elaborate greeting to spare Rome. Coriolanus tells him to go away because he has only the power to *revenge*; the power to *pardon* lies with Aufidius and the Volscians. He acknowledges their former friendship, but he gives Menenius a prepared letter and asks him again to leave. Coriolanus and Aufidius exit, and the sentinels ridicule Menenius, who leaves for Rome totally dejected.

Inside his tent, Coriolanus tells Aufidius that they will attack Rome the next day, and he asks that his conduct of the war be reported to the Volscian lords. Aufidius compliments him for being successful and for being loyal to the Volscian cause. Volumnia, young Marcius, Virgilia, and Valeria then arrive to plead for Rome, and Coriolanus finds it very difficult to deny them. He begs forgiveness of Virgilia, but he repeats that he *cannot* forgive Rome. He kneels before his mother, who tells him to rise; then she kneels before him. Coriolanus is touched and speaks lovingly to his wife and son, asking them all not to take his refusal personally. He asks Aufidius to note that he is undertaking no private conversations.

Volumnia says the women and young Marcius are the most unfortunate of people because they will lose regardless of which side wins—should Coriolanus attack—and young Marcius pledges to run away so that he can fight when he is older. Coriolanus starts to leave, but Volumnia reminds him that peace will benefit both parties and that he will be branded a traitor if he continues. She accuses him of never having shown proper appreciation for her role as his mentor and of being dishonorable and unfilial in dismissing her. The women and young Marcius then kneel before him, and Volumnia charges him with being excessively proud; in addition, she calls him a true Volscian. The women and young Marcius then prepare to depart, and Coriolanus capitulates.

Coriolanus tells Volumnia that while she has won a victory for Rome, she has also placed his life in dire jeopardy. He promises

Aufidius that he will conclude a just and fair peace, and he asks for Aufidius' advice. Aufidius admits that he has also been moved by Volumnia, but in an aside he confesses that he is happy that Coriolanus has given him a chance to raise his own fortunes. Coriolanus invites the women to drink with him while the treaty is being written, and he suggests that a temple should be built to honor them for their victory for Rome.

In Rome, Menenius tells Sicinius that he has little hope for the women's visit because Coriolanus has devoted himself totally to living as a warrior. But at that moment, a messenger enters, informing them that a mob has captured Brutus and that Brutus will be killed if the women fail. A second messenger enters with news of the women's success, and celebration breaks out. Menenius leaves to welcome the women, and Sicinius is greatly relieved. Two senators escort the ladies through the streets of Rome and proclaim Volumnia as the savior of the city.

In Corioli, Aufidius plans to bring charges against Coriolanus. Some "conspirators" enter and encourage Aufidius to let them murder Coriolanus. Aufidius claims Coriolanus has used flattery to win the favor of the Volscian lords and thereby replace Aufidius as one of the chief military leaders. He also wants to punish Coriolanus for betraying Volscian honor by yielding to the pleas of Volumnia and Virgilia. The conspirators refer to Coriolanus' triumphant return from Rome, to the lack of welcome extended to Aufidius, and to the necessity for Aufidius to kill Coriolanus. The Lords of Corioli enter, and they also agree that Coriolanus has betrayed the Volscian cause.

Coriolanus arrives and proudly announces his success in the war, his capture of spoils, and an honorable peace. Aufidius accuses him of being a traitor and, refusing to honor him any longer with the name of "Coriolanus," calls him "boy." Enraged, Coriolanus calls Aufidius a liar and a slave, and he asks the lords to proclaim Aufidius a liar. He then challenges the Volscians to kill him, boasting of his feats of Corioli. Aufidius asks if the lords will endure Coriolanus' bragging, and the people shout for his immediate death, but one of the lords judges that Coriolanus deserves a fair hearing.

Coriolanus wishes he were free to fight Aufidius, but before he can act, the conspirators kill him, and Aufidius stands on his body. The lords reproach Aufidius for the murder and the desecration of the body, and Aufidius asks to be allowed to delineate Coriolanus' offenses in the Senate. One of the lords orders an honorable funeral for Coriolanus, and another says that Coriolanus' fiery nature somewhat justifies Aufidius' actions. Somewhat calmed, Aufidius helps carry out the body of Coriolanus in a stately procession through Corioli.

Commentary

The plebeians of Rome remain consistently inconstant in their allegiances. For example, they rashly capture Brutus and threaten to torture him to death for his role in causing Coriolanus to join the Volscians, and they welcome Volumnia's return after she has managed to stop the Volscian advance on Rome. Their joyous tumult of welcome for her is reminiscent of their welcome of Coriolanus when he returned from the victories at Corioli. The Volscian citizens, likewise, are shown to be as inconstant in their loyalties as are the Roman citizens. Seemingly, fickleness is universal among the lower classes. One of the Volscian citizens advises Aufidius that the people will remain uncommitted until either he or Coriolanus shows clear evidence as to which of them is the prevailing leader; then the people will rally behind the man who seems to be the stronger. They do exactly this. When Aufidius publicly has the endorsement and support of the Volscian lords and when he has Coriolanus on the defensive, the Volscian citizens suddenly remember that the man whom they have recently welcomed among them is the same man who slaughtered their cousins, sons, wives, and fathers in the past.

Coriolanus, in contrast, has remained constant—especially in his contempt for the plebeian class, and he still feels strongly that revenge is the best way to satisfy a personal affront, but Coriolanus has affected a regal bearing that reflects both his insecurity and his pride. He tells Volumnia, for instance, that he will never capitulate to "Rome's mechanics"; on the other hand, he is ready if necessary to sacrifice his family and friends, whom he refers to unemotionally as "one poor grain or two," in order to gain his revenge. His rejection of basic human compassion is further emphasized when he vows to be ungrateful rather than merciful and when he rebuffs Menenius, who has appealed to him as a "son." The Volscian guards believe that nothing can shake their new general's resolve to defeat Rome.

It is Volumnia who ultimately is able to change Coriolanus'

resolves; first she falls on her knees before him; the mentor has become suppliant. Volumnia then confronts her son with a subtle argument, the type that Coriolanus is least prepared to resist. She shifts the blame away from Rome and away from its nobility and places it upon him. If he rejects her arguments, she claims it will be because of his "hardness" and not because justice is on his side. Echoing Menenius' figurative rhetoric, she blames Coriolanus for desiring a war that will tear "his country's bowels out." She reminds him that his family and friends have been placed in the unenviable position of being losers—no matter which side wins; they will either see their country devastated or else they will see a loved one beaten and dishonored. Furthermore, she tells him that his past renown will be forgotten and that he will be branded a traitor forever. She ridicules him for wanting to act like a god, she accuses him again of being too proud, and she even charges him for neglecting to show proper gratitude and courtesy to her in the past—a charge obviously not consistent with previous events in the play. Ironically, she asks the son whom she has trained to be the superior warrior to become a peacemaker. Then, after she wins his consent, the irony is compounded when Coriolanus' role of peacemaker leads directly to his slaughter by Aufidius, who previously failed to defeat Coriolanus in combat. Coriolanus' last hopes are for his son; he hopes that young Marcius will follow in his footsteps but only as a warrior—not as a politician. His experiences have confirmed his belief that war and warriors are noble, but peace and politicians are ignoble.

Before Aufidius kills Coriolanus, he notes that Coriolanus is not "subtle"—that is, Coriolanus is not wily; thus Aufidius can defeat his old enemy in any way he can. Coriolanus does not have the insight to realize that Aufidius is working to turn the Volscian people and nobles against him. Aufidius' most decisive act in arousing Coriolanus' ire occurs when he provokes Coriolanus by calling him a traitor, a "boy of tears," and refusing to refer to him by his honorary title "Coriolanus." Coriolanus flares into a rage, offending the Volscian citizens and giving Aufidius a chance to claim that he had no alternative, that he was forced into having the conspirators murder Coriolanus. In fact, Aufidius carefully manipulates events so that Coriolanus will appear dangerous; then Aufidius arouses the people, and then, to satisfy his own envious and resentful drive for revenge, he defeats Coriolanus—decisively and finally. Significantly, it is Coriolanus' pride and sense of social rank that dominate his life and interfere with his ability to function effectively when he is not on the battlefield. It is dramatically fitting that these factors should contribute to his death.

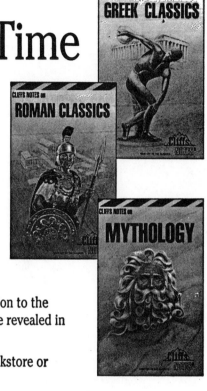